EA

FRIENDS
OF ACPL

W9-CZX-135

Critical Terms
for
Religious Studies

Critical Terms

for

Religious Studies

Edited by

Mark C. Taylor

The University of Chicago Press

Chicago & London

MARK C. TAYLOR is Cluett Professor of Humanities and director of the Center for Technology in the Arts and Humanities at Williams College. For futher details, see p. 397 below.

The University of Chicago Press, Chicago 60637
The University of Chicago Press Ltd., London

© 1998 by The University of Chicago
All rights reserved. Published 1998
Printed in the United States of America

07 06 05 04 03 02 01 00 99 98   1 2 3 4 5

ISBN 0-226-79156-4 (cloth)
ISBN 0-226-79157-2 (paperback)

Library of Congress Cataloging-in-Publication Data

Critical terms for religious studies / edited by Mark C. Taylor.
        p.   cm.
    Includes bibliographical references and index.
    ISBN 0-226-79156-4 (alk. paper). — ISBN 0-226-79157-2
(pbk. : alk. paper)
    1. Religion—Terminology.   I. Taylor, Mark C., 1945–   .
BL31.C75   1998
210′.1′4—dc21   97-52257
                                                  CIP

Contents

Introduction

Mark C. Taylor

A century that began with modernism sweeping across Europe is ending with a remarkable resurgence of religious beliefs and practices throughout the world. From Protestant and Catholic churches in America to Orthodox churches in Russia, from temples in Israel and mosques in Iran to temples in India and mosques in Indonesia, religion is flourishing. As the millennium approaches, spiritual concerns pervade the personal lives of a growing number of individuals and are ever more significant in the political affairs of nations. Neither the private nor the public sphere can be understood today without an adequate appreciation for the role religious beliefs and practices play in shaping subjects, societies, and cultures.

For many students of modernity and postmodernity, this widespread revival of religious activity has been unexpected and remains puzzling. In the eyes of some of its most influential prophets and analysts, the progressive advance toward modernity is supposed to be inseparable from a gradual movement away from religion. As Gustavo Benavides points out, "a condition of modernity presupposes an act of self-conscious distancing from a past or a situation regarded as naive." While modernity and modernism are not the same, they are closely related and mutually constitutive. "If we understand modernity," Benavides continues, "as involving a kind of perpetual critique, the parallels with the distancing techniques and polemical intent of aesthetic modernism become apparent; indeed, literary modernism, and aesthetic modernism in general, can help us grasp the oppositional, distancing, and self-referential nature of modernity" (chap. 10).

Modernity, according to this analysis, defines itself in and through the constitution of and contrast with its own other. Throughout the course of the so-called modern era, this other has assumed a variety of guises, ranging from the "primitive" and "aboriginal" to the "ancient" and "traditional." The constitutive contrast between the modern, on the one hand, and the primitive, aboriginal, ancient, or traditional, on the other, implies a related set of oppositions, which includes, inter alia, emotion/reason, intuition/thought, superstition/science, undifferentiation/individuation, and simplicity/complexity. For many who celebrate modernity and its expression in modernism, these contrasts are not equivalent but, rather, are ordered in such a way that the latter term is privileged over the former. When understood diachronically—that is, as it occurs over time—this hierarchical structure leads to an interpretation of history according to which the movement from primitivism to modernism involves a progression from emotion to reason, undifferentiation to individuation, simplicity to complexity,

1

and superstition to science. Following the maxim "Ontogeny recapitulates phylogeny," proponents of this evolutionary vision of history tend to associate religion with infantile and primitive behavior, which either is or should be overcome by mature individuals who live in the modern world.

The decline in religious belief and practice in many modern societies has not, however, been merely a matter of growing intellectual sophistication and psychological maturation but has also been the result of important political and economic factors. It is undeniable that the fate of religion has been decisively influenced by the rise of the secular nation-state and concurrent spread of a market economy. The modern nation-state emerged from the ashes of religious conflicts that ravaged Europe in the wake of the Protestant Reformation. As Bruce Lincoln notes in his essay on the term "Conflict," with Hobbes's formulation of

> a social contract theory that derived legitimacy from the people who constitute the nation, rather than from God, the early modern state was freed of its ideological dependence on the church, and increased its power at the latter's expense, assuming an ever larger share of functions that had previously fallen under religious purview: education, moral discipline and surveillance, social relief, record keeping, guarantee of contracts, and so on. Conversely, the scope and influence of religious institutions (now in the plural rather than the singular) were greatly attenuated, as religion—disarticulated from its symbiotic relation with the state—was reconceived as an element of a rapidly expanding civil society in which competing institutions and forms of discourse (arts, sciences, philosophy, secular ideologies, journalism, popular opinion, folk wisdom, etc.) also had their place. (Chap. 3)

As recently as the 1960s, historians and social theorists insisted that modernization and secularization were inseparable. In addition to the shift of social, political, and economic power from church to state, advances in modern science and technology led to the gradual disenchantment of the world and experience in it. In the mechanistic universe defined by Descartes and described in encyclopedic detail by Enlightenment philosophers, there seemed to be little room for either divinity or things divine. With the supernatural in full retreat, God first withdrew to a deistic heaven to watch his creation from afar and then seemed to disappear from the lives of his erstwhile followers. From this point of view, as modernity waxes, religion seems to wane.

But matters are considerably more complex than this unidirectional line of historical development suggests. To identify modernization merely with the eclipse of religion is to fail to discern the religious dimensions of modernity itself. Religious devotion and belief do not simply disappear but initially are turned inward in a way that renders them as invisible as the transcendent God who is present as an abiding absence. This interiorization of religion began with Luther's turn to the individual self and reached closure with Kierkegaard's singular individual for whom "the paradox of faith is an interiority that is incommensurable with exteriority." Imagining an encounter with the knight of faith, Kierkegaard's pseudonymous author Johannes de Silentio marvels:

> The instant I first lay eyes on him, I set him apart at once; I jump back, clap my hands, and say half aloud, "Good Lord, is this the man, is this really the one—he looks just like a tax collector!" But this is indeed the one. I move a little closer to him, watch his slightest movement to see if it reveals a bit of heterogeneous optical telegraphy from the infinite, a glance, a facial expression, a gesture, a sadness, a smile that would betray the infinite in its heterogeneity with the finite. No! He is solid all the way through. (Kierkegaard 1983, 38–9)

If, as Kierkegaard finally admits, the knight of faith is indistinguishable from the philistine, opposites collapse into each other in such a way that it becomes impossible to distinguish religious from nonreligious conduct.

Such a dialectical reversal of the religious into the secular and vice versa lies at the heart of the philosophy of Kierkegaard's lifelong foe: Hegel. While Kierkegaard insists that the private interior of individual subjectivity provides refuge for religious life in a world that is increasingly secular, Hegel maintains that processes of modernization do not result in the disenchantment of the world but actually involve what is, in effect, a sacralization of nature and history and a naturalization and historicization of religious realities. Within Hegel's speculative philosophy, the natural world and human life are nothing less than the self-embodiment of God. According to this theological scheme, the incarnation is not a unique event limited to the lifetime of a single individual but, instead, is a universal process that reaches completion in the modern West. Hegel summarizes his conclusion in the closing lines of the *Phenomenology of Spirit*:

> The *goal*, Absolute Knowledge, or Spirit that knows itself as Spirit, has for its path the recollection of the Spirits as they are in themselves and as they accomplish the organization of their return. Their preservation regarded from the side of their free existence appearing in the form of contingency is history; but regarded from their comprehended organization, it is the science of knowledge in the sphere of appearance; the two together comprehend history; they form the recollection and the Calvary of Absolute Spirit, the actuality, truth, and certainty of his throne, without which he would be lifeless and alone. Only
>
> > from the chalice of this realm of spirits
> > foams forth for Him his own infinitude. (Hegel 1977, 493)

As "Absolute Spirit" is embodied in nature and history, truth is gradually revealed first in religious symbols and artistic images and then is translated into philosophical concepts. Speculative philosophy brings this incarnational process to closure by comprehending the modern secular world as the realization of divine life.

While the theological and metaphysical presuppositions of Hegel's philosophical project might seem dated, the complexity of his dialectical vision enables us to discern religious dimensions of modernity that less-sophisticated interpreters overlook. Even when appearing resolutely secular, twentieth-century culture is haunted by religion. From Mondrian's theosophical painting to Le Corbusier's purist architecture, from Kafka's kabalistic parables to Derrida's deconstructive criticism, from Joyce's eucharistic vision to Madonna's pop music and videos, and from Alexander Graham Bell's telepathic spiritualism to cyberculture's telematic mysticism, religion often is most effective where it is least obvious. When analysis is historically and critically informed, it becomes clear that the continuing significance of religion for contemporary culture extends far beyond its established institutions and manifest forms.

*   *   *

Though religion does not disappear even when it seems to be absent, there has nonetheless been an extraordinary revival of traditional religious belief and practice in recent years. How is this unexpected development to be interpreted? There is, of course, no simple answer to this difficult question. While the revival of religious institutions always depends upon complex local conditions with long and tortuous histories, several general factors shed light on the growing significance of religious belief and practice.

The first noteworthy consideration is the close association between the processes of secularization and modernization, on the one hand, and Westernization, on the other. The modern nation-state and market economy are, as I have noted, Western inventions. The relationship between modernization and Westernization has meant that for many societies, the price of modernity is the repression of local customs and traditional institutions. Political reform and economic development combine to promote the spread of Western hegemony, whose protean forms range from the machinations of military power to the fascination with consumer culture. When confronted by the growing power of institutions that seem alien, many individuals and groups turn to traditional forms of religion to legitimize strategies of resistance designed to secure a measure of independence and autonomy. Once again, Bruce Lincoln's keen observation is helpful:

> In recent years, contradictions between nation and state have also manifested themselves in a particularly debilitating fashion. Where this is so, it has proven relatively easy for militant factions of the population to wage aggressive campaigns in which they seek to redefine the principles on which nation and state are constituted and the ways in which they relate to each other. Of the instruments they

have used for mobilization, religious discourse and practice have often been among the most effective, just as their appeals to a sense of religious community have been among the most powerful bases for a novel sense of collective identity. (Chap. 3)

The Westernization that this tactical revival of religion is fashioned to resist is inseparably bound to accelerating processes of globalization. While the growth of a global economy has been the focus of much attention lately, global culture is not a new phenomenon. From the emergence of the earliest trade routes, through the spread of imperialism and colonialism, to the appearance of a post-industrial information society, globalization has been a function of advances in transportation and communications technologies. As people and information travel greater distances at faster speeds, different cultures are brought into closer contact, thereby creating the possibility both for mutual understanding and for violent conflict. In the late twentieth century, speed, which has become an end in itself, produces a sense of vertigo that many people find utterly disorienting. When culture is commodified and currencies are telecast, the line separating cultural suprastructure from economic infrastructure becomes obscure. Global capitalism promotes global consumerism, which, in turn, fuels global capitalism to create a circle that is as vicious as it is efficient. While analysts frequently stress the importance of the globalization of capital, they usually overlook the no less significant globalization of labor. The deterritorialization of capital is inseparable from the nomadization of labor. Multinational corporations cannot operate without a multinational workforce. From the managerial and technocratic elite to an uneducated and unskilled underclass, workers circulate throughout the world along networks of exchange that form material shadows of the immaterial currencies pulsating at the speed of light through fiber-optic webs.

This nomadization sometimes promotes a cosmopolitanism in which the differences separating people and societies seem less important than their shared outlooks and values. But deterritorialization and nomadization can also lead to a sense of alienation created by the necessity of living and laboring in a strange society and a foreign culture. For people uprooted physically, psychologically, and politically, traditional religions once again become attractive. Summarizing the complex interplay between modernization and religion in his controversial book *The Clash of Civilizations and the Remaking of World Order*, Samuel Huntington argues:

> Initially, Westernization and modernization are closely linked, with the non-Western society absorbing substantial elements of Western culture and making slow progress towards modernization. As the pace of modernization increases, however, the rate of Westernization declines and the indigenous culture goes through a revival. Further modernization then alters the civilization balance of power between the West and the non-Western society, bolsters the power and self-

confidence of that society, and strengthens commitment to the indigenous culture.

In the early phases of change, Westernization thus promotes modernization. In the later phases, modernization promotes de-Westernization and the resurgence of indigenous culture in two ways. At the societal level, modernization enhances the economic, military and political power of the society as a whole and encourages the people of that society to have confidence in their culture and to become culturally assertive. At the individual level, modernization generates feelings of alienation and anomie as traditional bonds and social relations are broken and this leads to crises of identity to which religion provides an answer. (Huntington 1996, 75–6)

One does not need to share Huntington's political perspective or policy agenda to appreciate the force of his insight about the growing significance of religion in the world today.

*   *   *

Just at the moment when it seems urgent to develop a more sophisticated understanding of religion, there appears to be little consensus about precisely what religion is and how it can best be studied. In many ways, the situation in religious studies is no different from the state of other disciplines. Literary and art critics are no more certain about their objects and methods of investigation than philosophers are about what constitutes philosophy and how one should philosophize. Indeed, the very way in which the question of a particular discipline—or anything else, for that matter—should be asked has itself become controversial. For interpreters schooled in postmodernism and poststructuralism, the seemingly innocent question "What is . . . ?" is fraught with ontological and epistemological presuppositions that are deeply problematic. To ask, for example, "What is religion?" assumes that religion has something like a general or even universal essence that can be discovered through disciplined investigation. From this point of view, the object of inquiry is antecedent to and a condition of the possibility of any study whatsoever. Furthermore, the insistence that religion as such can be defined presumes that religion, though obviously related to other phenomena, cannot be completely reduced to psychological, social, economic, or political factors. Religion, in other words, is not epiphenomenal but is, in an important sense, sui generis.

But what if religion has no such essential identity? What if religion is not a universal phenomenon? What if religion has not always existed or has never existed? Recent investigators working in a variety of fields have argued that religion is a historical phenomenon that emerges only in particular intellectual and cultural circumstances. Far from existing prior to and independent of any inquiry, the very phenomenon of religion is constituted by local discursive practices. In-

vestigators create—sometimes unknowingly—the objects and truths they profess to discover. Some critics claim that appearances to the contrary notwithstanding, religion is a *modern Western invention.*

Surveying the notion of religion, Winston King maintains that "the very attempt to define *religion,* to find some distinctive or possibly unique essence or
set of qualities that distinguish the 'religious' from the remainder of human life,
is primarily a Western concern." While King's attempt to explain the preoccupation with religion as "a natural consequence of Western speculative, intellec-
tualistic, and scientific disposition" might not be convincing, his most telling
observation about the genealogy of religion is persuasive: "What the West calls
religion is [in many societies] such an integral part of the total ongoing way of
life that it is never experienced or thought of as something separable or narrowly
distinguishable from the rest of the pattern. . . . Indeed, in a real sense everything
that is is divine; existence *per se* appears to be sacred" (King 1987, 282). However, if everything is divine, then, in a certain sense, nothing is sacred. If structuralism and poststructuralism have taught us anything, it is that identity is
inescapably differential: there can be no religion apart from its opposite. Thus,
when religion is everywhere, it is nowhere.

The emergence of religion as an identifiable phenomenon is inseparable from
processes of differentiation that are simultaneously generated by and generative of
modernization. The very concept of religion entails a level of self-consciousness
that is distinctively modern. Jonathan Z. Smith concludes his highly informative
and deliberately provocative essay "Religion, Religions, Religious" with the following:

> "Religion" is not a native term; it is a term created by scholars for
> their intellectual purposes and therefore is theirs to define. It is a
> second-order, generic concept that plays the same role in establishing
> a disciplinary horizon that a concept such as "language" plays in
> linguistics or "culture" plays in anthropology. There can be no dis-
> ciplined study of religion without such a horizon. (Chap. 15)

Elsewhere, Smith elaborates this insight by underscoring the modernity of
"religion":

> If we have understood the archeological and textual record correctly,
> man has had his entire history in which to imagine deities and modes
> of interaction with them. But man, more precisely western man, has
> had only the last few centuries in which to imagine religion. It is this
> act of second order, reflective imagination which must be the central
> preoccupation of any student of religion. That is to say, while there
> is a staggering amount of data, of phenomena, of human experiences
> and expressions that might be characterized in one culture or an-
> other, by one criterion or another as religious—*there is no data for*

religion. Religion is solely the creation of the scholar's study. It is created for the scholar's analytic purposes by his imaginative acts of comparison and generalization. Religion has no independent existence apart from the academy. For this reason, the student of religion, and most particularly the historian of religion, must be relentlessly self-conscious. Indeed, this self-consciousness constitutes his primary expertise, his foremost object of study. (Smith 1982, xi)

To many people, Smith's insistence that religion is a modern invention "created for the scholar's analytic purposes" doubtlessly will seem both counterintuitive and historically mistaken. Even if one were to admit that religion is not "a ubiquitous human phenomenon" but a recently constructed analytic category, surely it would seem that the experiences this second-order term designates are as old as humanity itself. But this conclusion is also problematic. The relation between term and experience is no less complex than the relation between category and object or phenomenon. Indirectly extending Smith's analysis of "religion" to "religious experience," Robert Sharf argues that "religious experience is relatively late and a distinctively Western invention" (chap. 5). Experience, in other words, is no more prior to the terms designated to represent it than objects are antecedent to the concepts fabricated to grasp them. Historically and culturally specific practices constitute both the experiences of subjects and the objects of analysis.

Of course, the term "religion" appears before the modern era. Though its etymology is uncertain, "religion" appears to be derived from the Latin stem *leig,* which means "to bind." The Latin word *religio* designates the bond between human beings and the gods. As early as the fifth century, Augustine defines *vera religio* in terms of the bond between the worshipper and God.

> Let our religion bind us to the one omnipotent God, because no creature comes between our minds and him whom we know to be the Father and the Truth, i.e., the inward light whereby we know him. In him and with him we venerate the Truth, who is in all respects like him, and who is the form of all things that have been made by the One, and that endeavor after unity. (Augustine 1964, 106–7)

In contrast to Augustine's preoccupation with "Truth," many influential modern theorists have been more interested in the origin and, by extension, the function of religion. The urgency of the question of religion's origin and function was partly the result of an explosion of information about different religions. Throughout the eighteenth century, travelers, explorers, missionaries, and merchants brought back to Europe reports of extraordinary religious beliefs and practices. In addition to these firsthand accounts, many non-Western sacred texts were translated during the Enlightenment. This ever expanding body of material was compiled in massive encyclopedias, which appeared in English, German,

French, and Italian. Confronted with this vast array of new data, interpreters sought to devise taxonomic schemes and explanatory theories to account for religion.

With the shift from the question of Truth to the questions of origin and function came a corresponding shift from explanations based on supernatural agency to accounts based on natural or, more precisely, human causality. To avoid censure by religious and political authorities, many early students of religion directed their arguments toward so-called primitive or pagan religions, thereby appearing to protect Christianity from conclusions that might be construed as detrimental to faith. By the middle of the eighteenth century, however, Hume dared to develop an analysis of religion as such. In his exemplary *Natural History of Religion*, he attempts to determine the "origin [of religion] in human nature." While speculation about the origin of religion can be traced to pre-Socratic philosophers, the rigor with which Hume developed his analysis lent his argument particular force. Far from being the creation of a supernatural agent, Hume argues, religion grows out of "ordinary affections in human life." Drawing on the principles of his empirical epistemology, he traces religion to the experiences of hope and fear. In an effort to account for and cope with these psychological states, human beings create gods in their own image and then proceed to attribute causal agency to them.

> It must necessarily, indeed, be allowed, that, in order to carry men's attention beyond the visible course of things, or lead them into any inference concerning invisible intelligent power, they must be actuated by some passion, which prompts their thought and reflection; some motive, which urges their first enquiry. But what passion shall we here have recourse to, for explaining an effect of such mighty consequence? Not speculative curiosity surely, or the pure love of truth. That motive is too refined for such gross apprehensions. . . . No passions, therefore, can be supposed to work upon such barbarians, but the ordinary affections of human life; the anxious concern for happiness, the dread of future misery, the terror of death, the thirst of revenge, the appetite for food and other necessaries. Agitated by hopes and fears of this nature, especially the latter, men scrutinize, with a trembling curiosity, the course of future causes, and examine the various and contrary events of human life. And in this disordered scene, with eyes still more disordered and astonished, they see the first obscure traces of divinity. (Hume 1976, 33)

As this argument makes clear, Hume's purpose is not merely to understand religious beliefs and practices but to explain them in terms of the experiences in which they appear to be grounded.

Explanation, however, is never innocent. When religion is explained in terms of nonreligious factors and the supernatural is attributed to natural forces, the veracity of religion is called into question. Analysis, in other words, is not disinterested but involves covert criticism. "Put conversely," James S. Preus avers,

> so long as a supernatural (or some objective, transcendent) ground
> of religion was assumed as the really existent referent and generative
> source of religious language, the study and criticism of religion was
> limited to some, but not all, of its aspects, and no decisive line of
> demarcation could be drawn between theology and the study of re-
> ligion. One could (and can) investigate the functions of religion,
> engage in historical-critical studies, and argue about hermeneutical
> approaches to myths and behavior without any essential contradic-
> tion arising between theology and the study of religion. But with the
> question of origins and causes it is a different story. (Preus 1987, xvi)

For many individuals who remain personally committed to religious belief and practice, the insistence that the origins and causes of religion are nonreligious involves a pernicious reductionism that must be steadfastly resisted.

Throughout the course of the nineteenth century, historical and comparative analyses of different religious traditions both proliferated and became more sophisticated. The critical issue of the origin of religions was vigorously pursued by thinkers as different as Feuerbach, Strauss, Marx, Nietzsche, and Freud. By the end of the second decade of the twentieth century, the major psychological, sociological, and anthropological approaches, which still inform the study of religion, had been articulated. This is not to imply, of course, that there have been no noteworthy advances in the past seventy-five years. We only need recall the contributions of structuralism and poststructuralism to appreciate the increasing refinement of our understanding of religion. With the advantage of hindsight, however, it is possible to understand these recent developments as expansions or revisions of earlier interpretive paradigms, which include Hegel's speculative logic as well as Saussure's structural linguistics.

While profoundly influenced by developments dating back to the Enlightenment, the distinctive contours of the contemporary study of religion have emerged since the Second World War. In order to understand the significance of recent discussions of religion, it is necessary to appreciate the institutional contexts in which they have unfolded. Prior to the 1960s, most graduate study of religion in the United States was conducted in divinity schools, which often were Protestant. When religious traditions other than Christianity and Judaism were considered, they were usually summarily classified as non-Western. The strategies for privileging Western religions ranged from overt hierarchical and evolutionary schema to covert methodological discriminations in which contrasting interpretive frameworks were applied to different religious traditions. On the undergraduate level, departments and programs in religion tended to be either extensions of the chaplain's office, which was almost always Christian and usually Protestant, or affiliated with philosophy departments, which were primarily if not exclusively concerned with Western intellectual history. Over the course of the 1960s, two developments beyond the academy had a significant impact on the way religion was studied in America.

First, U.S. Supreme Court decisions in the cases of *Engel v. Vitale* (1962) and *Abington School District v. Schempp* (1963) cleared the way for teaching religion in public schools and universities. Prior to this decision, the constitutional separation of church and state had limited the study of religion to private institutions, which often had a religious affiliation. As Sam Gill points out, these Supreme Court decisions "distinguished between teaching religion and teaching *about* religion" (chap. 17). While religious instruction was outlawed, instruction about religion was permitted. Though the difference between teaching religion and teaching about religion is not always as clear as this legalistic distinction suggests, the Court's landmark decisions prepared the way for a significant expansion of the study of religion. As the institutional context shifted, the approach to religion changed. When they were no longer constrained by implicit or explicit religious authority or confined by prescribed theological commitments, investigators were free to explore all religious traditions in whatever ways seemed most illuminating and effective.

The second factor that contributed to changing approaches to the study of religion is less obvious but no less important. During the 1960s, the Civil Rights and antiwar movements gave rise to multicultural sensibilities, which are still socially significant and politically influential. As minorities within and cultures beyond our borders found their distinctive voices, the Eurocentrism that had characterized the study of religion as well as the arts and humanities was increasingly called into question. Though the connection is rarely recognized, the emergence of the study of religion in its current form is inseparable from the flowering of the 1960s counterculture. As disillusion with the abuses of American power at home and abroad grew, many students who were convinced of the integrity and viability of other cultural traditions were drawn to the exploration of different religions. Nowhere was the impact of these developments more keenly felt than in divinity schools. Many students and faculty committed to the exploration of religious and ethical issues were persuaded that any intellectual orientation that does not respect cultural differences is misguided and repressive. Political resistance led to educational reform, which opened the curriculum to new approaches to religion as well as a vastly expanded range of cultures. Surveying the current intellectual landscape, William Scott Green testifies to the abiding significance of these changes:

> American colleges and universities now offer an educational context of concentrated pluralism, in which students, faculty, and administrators encounter and assess divergent and often conflicting theories, methods, experiences, points of view, and intellectual loyalties. The contemporary educated American is marked no less by possession of

an erudite and analytical intellect than by the capacities to engage in
and negotiate with argued conviction. To be educated is to know how
to understand, experience, and respect difference. (1994, 1191)

A responsible understanding of difference is, however, far from easy.

The recent obsession with difference in the arts, humanities, and social sciences has obscured the fact that much of the pioneering work in "non-Western"
cultural traditions was done in the field of religious studies. As attention shifted
from a more or less exclusive focus on Western religions to a broader range of
religious beliefs and practices, it quickly became apparent that it was imperative
to rethink not only *which* religions were to be investigated but *how* they were to
be studied. This critical reevaluation resulted in the two most important characteristics of contemporary religious studies. The responsible study of religion today is multidisciplinary and multicultural.

With the range of religions open to investigation continually expanding, the
problem of how best to approach religious diversity has become unavoidable. The
question of method is, of course, a distinctively modern concern. One could go so
far as to argue that in philosophy, modernity actually began with Descartes's
search for a method to "direct the mind toward the enunciation of sound and
correct judgments on all matters that come before it" (Descartes 1955, 38). By
formulating the proper method for rational reflection, Descartes insists, one can
overcome the doubt that is characteristic of modern experience. But Descartes's
optimism has not been universally shared. As others took up the search for
a method, they discovered that critical reflection can exacerbate doubt rather
than yield certainty. By the end of the nineteenth century, thinkers like Marx,
Nietzsche, and Freud had developed what Paul Ricoeur aptly labels a "hermeneutics of suspicion," which extends Cartesian doubt by turning it back on consciousness itself. Rather than being foundational, consciousness, these "masters
of suspicion" argue, is an epiphenomenon that simultaneously reflects and de-
flects economic, biological, and psychological forces. If, however, consciousness
is not what it appears to be, then subjective awareness itself becomes unavoidably
doubtful. Since consciousness can never fully comprehend itself, certainty and
security seem to be forever inaccessible.

When doubt becomes profound, questions of method in religious studies become more pressing. It is no longer sufficient to think about different religions;
now it is necessary to consider *how* one thinks about these religions. As students
of religion search for methods to aid them in their inquiries, they frequently turn
to the social sciences for guidance. In many cases, this strategy is as much a reaction against theology as it is an argument for the social sciences. Within a
remarkably short time, the conditions governing the study of religion underwent
a revolution that began in the 1960s. No longer granted a place of privilege,
theology was displaced by religious studies. Ray L. Hart describes the result of
this shift in his comprehensive survey of the field published in 1991:

A sharp distinction between Religious Studies and Theological Studies, with Theological Studies the *bête noire* within Religious Studies: this appears to be the passion of public institutions, and is especially strong in those with graduate programs (as it is in private universities with graduate programs). The graduate programs in such institutions see their *raison d'être* as the reorientation of Religious Studies as a whole: they aspire to diverge from and offer an alternative to what is regularly if not uniformly (in such institutions) called "the seminary model." Negatively, the majority are clear that they are *not* doing Theological Studies. . . . They are more agreed on what is "wrong" with the study of religion than with what should be "right" about it. What is wrong is that it still "includes theology." (Hart 1991, 732)

Like all such contrasts, the opposition between theological studies and religious studies is oversimplified and subverts itself in and through its own development. Insofar as religious studies defines itself as essentially antitheological, theology continues to set the terms for debate. Furthermore, in many cases ostensibly nontheological approaches to religion tend to become as theological as the positions they are designed to overturn. Critics of theology often embrace the methods of social sciences ranging from history and psychology to sociology and anthropology with an enthusiasm bordering on the religious. As it assumes ever greater importance, methodology approaches the status of "queen of the sciences" once reserved for theology. The Cartesian promise of a proper method is, in fact, a secularized version of theology's dream of an unconditional principle of principles. For those with eyes to see, theology casts a long—perhaps inescapable—shadow.

As this shadow becomes obvious, thought once again bends back on itself to expose undeniable faults in every foundational inquiry. Methodological preoccupation gradually gives way to critical theory in which the possibilities as well as the limitations of alternative approaches to the study of religion are precisely delineated and analytically assessed. When critically conceived, theory calls into question every method that claims to be exhaustive. In the absence of any foundational method or comprehensive explanatory theory, no single approach to religion is adequate. In order to appreciate the richness and complexity of religious life, it is necessary to deploy a variety of interpretive strategies. As the partiality of every particular perspective is exposed, a multidisciplinary approach to the study of religion becomes unavoidable.

* * *

The contemporary study of religion is, as I have noted, not only multidisciplinary but also multicultural. The growing recognition of the importance of different religious traditions not only has raised difficult methodological and theoretical issues but also has led to complex comparative questions. The comparative study of religion as a formal discipline began in the late nineteenth century with the work of F. Max Müller. Trained as a philologist, Müller extended the comparative methods he had devised in his work on Indo-European languages to the study of religion. While his claim that myths are nothing more than "a disease of language" has been widely criticized, his insistence on the centrality of language and the necessity of comparative analysis of cultural phenomena has been very influential.

The motivations for comparative analysis, however, vary widely. While always involving an interplay between sameness and difference, the activity of comparison can have as its goal either the reduction of differences to identity or the establishment of differences that have little or nothing in common. When carried to extremes, the former approach leads to a monistic perennial philosophy according to which all religions are purported to express the same truth differently, while the latter issues in a dualistic heresiological model in which true religion is privileged over and set against false religions. The challenge of effective comparison is to find a mean between these extremes that allows interpreters to understand differences without erasing them.

But even when they are committed to staking out such a middle ground, some analysts find similarities more intriguing than differences, while others are convinced that differences are more instructive than similarities. In an effort to counterbalance what she regards as the current infatuation with difference in much critical theory, Wendy Doniger argues:

> The tension between sameness and difference has become a crucial issue for the self-definition of postmodernism. Now the mere addition of *accent aigu* transforms the modest English word into the magic buzzword for everything that right-thinking (or, as the case may be, left-thinking) men and women care about: *différence* (or, even buzzier yet, *différance*). For postmodernism, sameness is the devil, difference the angel. . . .
>
> [T]he academic world . . . now suffers from a post-post-colonial backlash: in this age of multinationalism, to assume that two texts from different cultures are 'the same' in any significant way is regarded as demeaning to the individualism of each, a reflection of the old racist attitude that 'all wogs look alike'—in the dark, all cats are gray. And in the climate of anti-Orientalism, it is regarded as imperialist of a scholar to stand outside (presumably above) two different cultures and to equate them.
>
> I am unwilling to close the comparativist shop just because it is being picketed by people with whose views I happen, by and large, to agree. I want to salvage the broad comparative agenda, even if I acquiesce, or even participate, in the savaging of certain of its elements. In particular, I want to make peace between premodern ty-

pologies and postmodern *différance* in comparativism, to bring into a single (if not necessarily harmonious) conversation the genuinely different approaches that several cultures have made to similar (if not the same) human problems. (Doniger 1996, 532–3)

"To make peace between premodern typologies and postmodern *différance*," it is necessary to develop comparative analyses that do not presuppose universal principles or reinscribe ahistorical essences. Whether or not it is possible to realize such a comparativist program, many critics schooled in poststructuralism insist that the very effort to establish similarities where there appear to be differences is, in the final analysis, intellectually misleading and politically misguided. When reason is obsessed with unity, they argue, it tends to become as hegemonic as political and economic orders constructed to regulate whatever does not fit into or agree with governing structures. In this situation, critical theory becomes a strategy for resisting dominant power by soliciting the return of the repressed.

Though not committed to the agenda of poststructuralists, Jonathan Z. Smith shares their concern for cultural differences. In contrast to Doniger's search for the same, Smith persistently tracks differences. "It is axiomatic," he argues,

> that comparison is never a matter of identity. Comparison requires the acceptance of difference as the grounds of its being interesting, and a methodical manipulation of that difference to achieve some stated cognitive end. The questions of comparison are questions of judgment with respect to difference: What differences are to be maintained in the interests of comparative inquiry? What differences can be defensibly relaxed and relativized in light of tasks at hand? (Smith 1987, 13–4)

The task of the student of religion is, in the words of the French poet Francis Ponge, "to name the differential quality" of the phenomena under investigation. But, of course, the preoccupation with difference can become as problematic as the fixation on similarity and unity. Not only is difference as such incomprehensible but differences that share nothing in common can fragment selves and divide peoples. If the multiple cultures in the midst of which we live are to be understood and the conflicts they engender negotiated, it is necessary both to search for commonality in the midst of differences and to respect differences that sometimes cannot be mediated.

* * *

Though the contemporary study of religion is the product of developments dating back to the Enlightenment, its distinctive multidisciplinary orientation and multicultural focus reflect a world that is undeniably postmodern. The variety of approaches and plurality of traditions not only enrich the investigation of religion but also create considerable confusion. *Critical Terms for Religious Studies* is intended as a guide for people who are seeking a more adequate understanding of the history as well as the contemporary significance of religion.

Having examined the complexities entailed in the notion of religion as well as the range of methodological alternatives available for its investigation, we must consider what is involved in the effort to identify critical terms for religious studies. The word "term" derives from the Latin *terminus,* which means boundary or limit. The Roman deity Terminus was the god of boundaries whose statue marked limits that were not to be transgressed. Whether conceived spatially or temporally, terms function as enabling constraints that simultaneously create possibilities and circumscribe the limits of exploration. But even when lines of definition seem to be clearly drawn, terms remain irreducibly complex. As Deleuze and Guattari observe in their discussion of concepts, "There are no simple concepts. Every concept has components and is defined by them. It therefore has a combination. It is a multiplicity, although not every multiplicity is a concept" (Deleuze and Guattari 1994, 15). Constituted by the intricate interplay of sameness and difference, the distinctive contours of any term are a function of both its multiple components and its relation to other terms. Boundaries that join and separate terms are necessarily permeable, and thus terms are never simple. This complexity renders terms polysemous and multivocal. Consider, for example, one of the terms included in this volume: liberation. Within the context of religious studies, liberation is associated with salvation, redemption, and renewal, and may be understood in terms of emancipation, purification, absolution, illumination, enlightenment, and, perhaps most important, freedom. But, of course, what one is liberated from and what one is liberated for vary considerably from time to time and place to place. Consequently, any discussion of liberation will lead to far-reaching questions of theology, anthropology, and cosmology. This range of associations points to related themes like conflict, transgression, value, personhood, ritual, and sacrifice. Rather than a limitation or shortcoming, such rich equivocity lends terms an openness and flexibility. The terms included in this volume harbor a multiplicity and complexity that extend their analytic range and enhance their interpretive potential.

If terms are to be useful for the contemporary study of religion, they must not only be strategically selected but must also be critically assessed. "Critical" means, inter alia, crucial, decisive, important, momentous, pivotal. The terms included in this book are in this sense critical for the study of religion. From the perspective of modernity and postmodernity, however, the word "critical" carries further connotations. Ever since the publication of Kant's three critiques, the notion of criticism has been inseparable from the self-reflexivity of self-consciousness. Indeed, as we have already discovered, the second-order reflection inherent in self-reflexive awareness is tacit in the very term "religion." In Kant's critical philosophy, consciousness turns back on itself to examine how knowledge arises. Transcendental inquiry is the investigation of the conditions of the possibility and limitation of knowledge. Kant concludes that the mind is, in effect, hardwired: consciousness and self-consciousness presuppose forms of intuition (space and time) and twelve categories of understanding. Since these structures of cognition are not supposed to originate in experience, Kant regards them as universal. The forms of intuition and categories of understanding function as something like a grid that filters experience and organizes knowledge. In a more contemporary idiom, the mind operates according to a program that processes data. The a priori grid or program is what makes knowledge possible by defining its boundaries.

Though the dream of a universal program lives on in the conscious and unconscious codes of structuralism, many of Kant's successors, who agree that the mind is not a tabula rasa, disagree with his contention that mental patterns are universal and unchanging. As Hegel was quick to realize, the mind, like everything else, has a history. The particular categories through which we structure experience and organize knowledge are historically specific and culturally relative. But Hegel's critique of Kant extends beyond the historicization and relativization of the categories to a recognition of the intricate interplay of cognitive forms. While Kant simply appropriates Aristotle's categories of judgment, Hegel attempts to demonstrate the necessary relationships among forms, which he insists are both epistemological and ontological. In place of Kant's universal grid, Hegel postulates a metastructure that is analogous to a living organism in which thought and being gradually evolve. Though it is continuously developing, this organic structure is nonetheless essentially closed. When fully comprehended in Hegelian philosophy, everything that appears to be arbitrary or aleatory assumes its proper place within an all-inclusive synchronic and diachronic structure.

Hegel's insistence that categories, which make knowledge possible, are historical and not universal represents a significant corrective to Kant's critical philosophy. But the claim that the forms of knowledge constitute an organic totality, which reaches closure in Hegel's speculative philosophy, is historically indefensible and analytically problematic. If one is not committed to the principles of philosophical idealism, it is possible to identify alternative structures of knowledge. Rather than positing a universal grid or seamless organism, critical reflection articulates an incomplete web of open and flexible terms. This seamy network of constraint, which is riddled with gaps that can be neither bridged nor closed, constitutes a constantly shifting cultural a priori that renders critical knowledge possible while circumscribing its unavoidable limits.

The terms selected for *Critical Terms for Religious Studies* constitute such an enabling network of constraint. The essays devoted to these terms provide something like a map for exploring the territory of religion. In choosing the terms for this volume, we have tried to create a balance between the expected and the unexpected. While the use of terms like "belief," "God," "sacrifice," "time," and "value" have long histories, terms like "culture," "gender," "image," "performance," "relic," "transgression," and "writing" have not always been central to the study of religion. The tactic of establishing an interplay between the familiar and the strange represents an effort to raise old questions in new ways and to promote a dialogue between religious studies and important work going on in other areas of the arts, humanities, and social sciences. Any such assemblage of terms is undeniably arbitrary and unavoidably incomplete. Moreover, the historical specificity and cultural relativity of cognitive structures means that terms are not universally translatable. In some traditions, even the seemingly critical terms "religion" and "God" are missing. The list of terms in this book makes no claim to be exhaustive. To the contrary, we insist that every cultural a priori that renders knowledge possible and interpretation necessary is always incomplete.

The following essays all reflect the multidisciplinary and multicultural character of contemporary religious studies. Contributors have presented neither comprehensive surveys of terms nor global overviews of traditions. Each author has first analyzed the theoretical importance of a specific term and then examined this term in a particular religious tradition. In working through this volume, readers will discover that methods, cultures, and terms cross and crisscross in constantly changing ways. As lines of affiliation and association unravel and rewind, a shared analytic vocabulary that enables interpreters to discern commonalities without erasing differences begins to emerge. These essays only mark a beginning, for the work of analysis is interminable. Far from a definitive work or indeed even a finished book, *Critical Terms for Religious Studies* is an open— even interactive—text that challenges the reader to take up and extend the critical study of religion.

SUGGESTED READINGS

De George, Richard T., and Fernande M. De George. 1972. *The Structuralists: From Marx to Lévi-Strauss.*

Despland, Michel. 1979. *La Religion en Occident: Evolution des Idées et du Vécu.*

Eliade, Mircea. 1959. *The Sacred and the Profane: The Nature of Religion.*

Feyerabend, Paul K. 1983. *Against Method: An Outline of an Anarchistic Theory of Knowledge.*

Gordon, R. L. 1981. *Myth, Religion, and Society.*

Jastrow, Morris. 1981. *The Study of Religion.*

Kittagawa, Joseph M. 1967. *The History of Religions: Essays on the Problem of Understanding.*

Manuel, Frank E. 1967. *The Eighteenth Century Confronts the Gods.*

Preus, J. Samuel. 1987. *Explaining Religion: Criticism and Theory from Bodin to Freud.*

Proudfoot, Wayne. 1985. *Religious Experience.*

Sharpe, Eric J. 1975. *Comparative Religion: A History.*

Smart, Ninian. 1973. *The Science of Religion and the Sociology of Knowledge: Some Methodological Questions.*

Smith, Jonathan Z. 1982. *Imagining Religion: From Babylon to Jonestown.*

Smith, Wilfred Cantwell. 1963. *The Meaning and End of Religion.*

Waardenburg, Jacques. 1973–1974. *Classical Approaches to the Study of Religion.*

Wach, Joachim. 1958. *The Comparative Study of Religions.*

Welch, Claude. 1972. *Religion in the Undergraduate Curriculum: An Analysis and Interpretation.*

References

Augustine. 1964. *Of True Religion,* translated by H. S. Burleigh. Chicago: Henry Regnery.

Deleuze, Gilles, and Félix Guattari. 1994. *What is Philosophy?* translated by Hugh Tomlinson and Graham Burchell. New York: Columbia University Press.

Descartes, René. 1955. *Descartes Selections,* edited by Ralph M. Eaton. New York: Scribner's.

Doniger, Wendy. 1996. "Myths and Methods in the Dark." *Journal of Religion* 76 (4).

Green, William Scott. 1994. "The Difference Religion Makes." *Journal of the American Academy of Religion* 62 (4).

Hart, Ray L. 1991. "Religious and Theological Studies in American Higher Education: A Pilot Study." *Journal of the American Academy of Religion* 59 (4).

Hegel, G. W. F. 1977. *Phenomenology of Spirit,* translated by A. V. Miller. New York: Oxford University Press.

Hume, David. 1976. *The Natural History of Religion,* edited by A. Wayne Clover. New York: Oxford University Press.

Huntington, Samuel P. 1996. *The Clash of Civilizations and the Remaking of World Order.* New York: Simon and Schuster.

Kierkegaard, Søren. 1983. *Fear and Trembling,* translated by Howard and Edna Hong. Princeton: Princeton University Press.

King, Winston. 1987. "Religion." *The Encyclopedia of Religion,* Vol. 12, edited by Mircea Eliade. New York: Macmillan.

Preus, James S. 1987. *Explaining Religion: Criticism and Theory from Bodin to Freud.* New Haven: Yale University Press.

Smith, Jonathan Z. 1982. *Imagining Religion: From Babylon to Jonestown.* Chicago: University of Chicago Press.

———. 1987. *To Take Place: Toward Theory in Ritual.* Chicago: University of Chicago Press.

ONE

Belief

Donald S. Lopez, Jr.

I n the Castello Sforzesco in Milan, there is a painting by Giovanni Battista
Moroni (1529/30–78) entitled "Martirio di San Pietro da Verona." It depicts a key moment in the martyrdom of Peter of Verona, better known as
Peter Martyr, the Dominican saint sometimes depicted in Italian Renaissance
painting with a bloody wound in the crown of his shaven monk's pate, sometimes with the cleaver that made the wound still embedded in his skull. In the
painting, one blow has already been delivered by Peter's persecutor, for he has
been felled to his knees. His head bears the wound of the first blow and the
executioner stands poised with raised cleaver, ready to deliver the fatal blow—
the blow that will deliver Peter into sanctity, for above the scene fly two cherubs,
one bearing a crown, the other a lily. The viewer's eye is drawn from the wound
in Peter's head to his finger, with which he has just performed his final act. On
the ground he has written in his own blood (and in perfect block letters) a single
word, CREDO, "I believe."

This statement, so simple and so familiar, has a long and complicated history
in Christian theology, in philosophy, and in writing about religion. The accumulated weight of this discourse has resulted in the generally unquestioned assumption that adherents of a given religion, any religion, understand that adherence in terms of belief. Indeed, belief (rather than ritual, for example) seems to
have been the pivot around which Christians have told their own history. And
with the dominance of Christian Europe in the nineteenth century, Christians
have also described what came to be known as the "world religions" from the
perspective of belief. Scholars of religion and anthropologists have almost invariably defined religion in terms of *belief* or perhaps *beliefs and practices,* those
deeds motivated by belief. And through complicated patterns of influence, the
representatives of non-Christian religions have come to speak of themselves in
terms of belief. "Belief" is, or has become, perhaps the most common term we
use to describe religion to one another, despite Max Müller's observation of a
century ago, "[T]hat the idea of believing, as different from seeing, knowing,
denying, or doubting, was not so easily elaborated, is best shown by the fact that
we look for it in vain in the dictionaries of many uncivilized races" (Müller 1897,
2:448).

After a very brief survey of some of the philosophical questions surrounding
the term, this essay will focus on two historical cases, one in medieval Europe,
one in colonial Sri Lanka, in which the term "belief" has figured prominently.
In the first case, belief served as a substitute, an elusive interior state that masked
a host of far more material circumstances. In the second case, belief served as

a concave mirror placed rather forcibly before an Asian subject, enlarging the periphery and shrinking the center.

The English word "belief" can be traced back to the Old High German *gilouben*, meaning to hold dear, cherish, trust in. The Germanic *laub* is related to the Indo-European *leubh-*, meaning love or desire: hence, the English "libidinous," "love," "believe"; the Latin *lubet* (he is pleased by); the Italian *libito* (will, desire); the German *lieb* (dear), *lieben* (to love), *loben* (to praise), *glauben* (to believe) (see Needham 1972, 41–3). The multivalence of the root is perhaps exceeded only by the multivalence of the term derived from it, belief. It seems possible, for example, to believe what one knows to be untrue ("I believe for every drop of rain that falls, a flower grows.") and not to believe what one knows to be true ("I can't believe I ate the whole thing.").

In the discussions that preceded the choice of terms for this volume, one of the editors argued for the inclusion of the small words that nonetheless prove the most problematic: the "and" of "Religion and Nature" or "Religion and Literature"; the "of" of "Philosophy of Religion" or "Psychology of Religion." To that list one might add the "in" that occurs in such disparate statements as "I believe in you," spoken as encouragement; "I do believe in spooks," spoken by the Cowardly Lion in the film version of *The Wizard of Oz;* and "I believe in one God the Father almighty, maker of heaven and earth, of all things visible and invisible," spoken at the beginning of the Nicene Creed.

In the philosophical and religious European traditions, belief has rarely been discussed alone but is most often paired with another term to which it stands in a relationship of weakness or strength. When one looks up belief in the *Encyclopedia of Philosophy,* one is directed to "Knowledge and Belief." When one looks up belief in the *Encyclopedia of Religion,* one finds the instruction: "See Doubt." In other resources, belief is regarded merely as a weak synonym for a more potent term; for example, under "Belief" in *The New Catholic Encyclopedia,* one is advised to "see Faith."

Hume, who pondered belief perhaps more than any philosopher prior to the present century, described it in 1739 as "one of the greatest mysteries of philosophy: tho' no one has so much as suspected, that there is any difficulty in explaining it" (1967, 628). In philosophical literature, belief has often been portrayed as a mental state of assent to a proposition already contained in the mind, although the nature of this assent has been much debated. For Hume, belief is "nothing but a more vivid and intense conception of any idea" (119–20). Belief is often portrayed as weaker than knowledge, since one may believe something that is either factually true or false, whereas knowledge only knows what is true. In Kant's terms in the *Critique of Pure Reason,* belief is a judgment that is subjectively sufficient but objectively insufficient (1968, 648–50). Thus, knowledge has sometimes been defined as "justified true belief," a view challenged by Plato in the *Theaetetus.* Philosophers have also considered the relation, if any, between belief and action.

In Christian theology, belief has generally been discussed in relation to questions of the existence of God and of miracles, notably the Resurrection. There have, of course, been many attempts to demonstrate that the existence of God can be philosophically proven, or if not proven, that belief in God is at least reasonable. The most famous instance of the latter is Pascal's "wager" (1962, 200–205), in which he argues that if God exists, his existence is incomprehensible; it is impossible to know with certainty whether or not God exists. If God does exist, the consequences of belief and disbelief are profound, both for the present and for eternity. To believe that God exists, therefore, is the prudent and reasonable course, in which nothing is lost and everything may be gained.

Accepting Pascal's premise that God is ultimately unknowable, some philosophers and theologians have argued that religious belief is qualitatively different from other forms of belief because it is an assent to that which can never be justified by conventional means. Religious belief is, furthermore, often resistant to contrary evidence and oblivious to negative consequences. Tertullian's paradox is *Credo quia absurdum,* "I believe because it is absurd." Aquinas argued that belief (or faith) is superior to reason because it is an assent to a transcendent truth, and that by definition, to believe *(credere)* is to believe in what is true; if its object is not true, it cannot be faith *(fides)* (see Smith 63).

Scholars of religion have also considered the causal relation, if any, between belief and knowledge of the truth. Some see belief as a preliminary stage of knowledge that under the proper circumstances can evolve into knowledge. Others, such as William James, ascribe more autonomy to belief: proof is not essential for belief but is rather something derived from belief for the consumption of others. In *The Varieties of Religious Experience,* James asserts:

> The truth is that in the metaphysical and religious sphere, articulate reasons are cogent for us only when our inarticulate feelings of reality have already been impressed in favor of the same conclusion. Then, indeed, our intuitions and our reason work together, and great world-ruling systems, like that of the Buddhist or of the Christian philosophy, may grow up. Our impulsive belief is here always what sets up the original body of truth, and our articulately verbalized philosophy is but its shadowy translation into formulas. The unreasoned and immediate assurance is the deep thing in us, the reasoned argument is but the surface exhibition. (1961, 74–5)

Belief, then, is the primary state for James, intuitive and fundamental, upon which the secondary structures of theology are built. Without the foundation of belief already in place, reasoned arguments have little persuasive power. This was also the view of Wittgenstein, whose comments on belief are found throughout the published records of his lectures and conversations. In his *Remarks on the Philosophy of Psychology* (1980, vol. 1, pars. 62–64), for example, he asks, "How does such an expression as 'I believe . . .' ever come to be used? Did a phenomenon, that of belief, suddenly get noticed? Did we observe ourselves and discover this phenomenon in that way? Did we observe ourselves and other men and so discover the phenomenon of belief?" For Wittgenstein as well, religious belief seems unlike other forms of belief because it cannot be supported by ordinary forms of evidence: "The point is that if there were evidence, this would in fact destroy the whole business" (1966, 56). Thus, statements of belief are not to be judged by the criteria used for other types of utterances but by a different kind of meaning as use, the use provided not in semantics but in the practice of one's life.

Near the end of his study of the term "belief" in philosophy and social anthropology, Rodney Needham (1972) concludes:

> The concept of belief certainly seemed, by the great reliance placed upon it in the western tradition, to have an essential and irrefragable significance, formulated over centuries of theological exegesis, philosophical analysis, and its numerous applications in common discourse. Yet the deeper and more minutely we go into the meaning of 'belief', the harder it is to concede it any discrete character or any empirical value as an index to the inner life of men. (234)

This is not to say, however, that the notion of belief is not without its historical effects, that belief is not an index of the outer life. To consider the more outward expressions of belief, let us return to the painting of Peter Martyr. When we read the martyrologies, we learn that the artist seems to have captured him not after having written the last word of his testament but the first. We learn that the man poised with the cleaver, dressed so stylishly in Italian velvets, is a Cathar, a Manichean, an advocate of the famous dualist school which held that there are two gods, a good god of spirit and an evil god of matter. And we learn that the Cathar may not have been depicted by the artist in the last instant before the fatal blow but that he might have paused, perhaps out of curiosity about what else Peter would write. According to some accounts, Peter did not simply write *Credo*, "I believe," but *Credo in deum*, "I believe in God." More rarely, it is reported that he wrote *Credo in unum deum*, "I believe in one God." It may have been this adjective that incited the Cathar, a dualist, to strike the fatal blow.

The account of Peter's life in the martyrologies tells us that he was born in Verona circa 1206, the son of Cathar parents, but was sent to a Christian school where he learned to say the Apostles' Creed, which, of course, begins, "I believe in God, the father almighty, creator of heaven and earth." This apparently caused his family consternation, for the Cathars believed that an evil god had made the world. At the urging of St. Dominic, Peter joined the Order of Friars Preachers (the Dominicans) in 1221 and devoted himself to the purpose for which the order had been founded, the battle against heresy: opinions that had been rejected by the church. The most prominent heresy in the thirteenth century was that of the Cathari ("the pure," also known as the Albigensians). Perhaps in-

24

fluenced by doctrines brought from Eastern Europe by traders and returning crusaders, the Cathars held that the material world, including the body, is the creation of the evil god. They thus rejected involvement with the world, abstaining from marriage and food that resulted from procreation (meat, eggs, dairy products). Although they considered themselves Christians, the Cathars rejected the doctrines of the virgin birth, physical resurrection, and sacraments. The practice of severe asceticism, which was entailed in their doctrine, was not demanded of all but was limited to a select group of virtuosi known as "the perfecti." They lived their lives in sharp contrast to the opulence and wealth characteristic of the Roman Catholic clergy, to whom the Cathars responded with scorn. In 1218, the Catholic monk Pierre des Vaux de Cernay described the Cathars' challenges to the beliefs of Roman Catholics:

> They said that almost all the Church of Rome was a den of thieves, and that it was the harlot of which we read in the Apocalypse. They so far annulled the sacraments of the Church, as publicly to teach that the water of baptism was just the same as river water, and that the Host of the most holy body of Christ did not differ from common bread, instilling into the ears of the simple this blasphemy, that the body of Christ, even though it had been as great as the Alps, would have long ago been consumed by those who have eaten of it. (Peters 1980, 124)

By the end of the twelfth century, the Cathars were regarded as the most dangerous of heretics, those who held a doctrine in defiance of papally defined orthodoxy.

A manual for inquisitors from 1248 names the heretic's crime in terms of belief: "We, the inquisitors . . . adjudge (so and so), named above, to be a heretic, because he believed in the errors of heretics and is proved still to believe them and because, when examined or when convicted and confessing, he flatly refused to be recalled and to give full obedience to the mandates of the Church" (Peters 1980, 205). The penalty, however, was something much more material:

> We cause the goods of heretics, the condemned and the imprisoned as well, to be confiscated, and we insist that this be done, as we are duty bound to do. . . . And if justice is well done in respect of the condemned and those who relapse, if their property is surely confiscated, and if prisoners are adequately provided with necessities, the Lord will gloriously and wonderfully be made manifest in the fruit of the Inquisition. (206)

Peter of Verona had already made a name for himself as a fiery preacher against the Cathars, and had been one of the first called to the new profession of inquisitor by Pope Gregory IX. He had led the holy work of combating heresy in Milan, where a number of heretics were burned in 1231. In 1244, his impassioned preaching in Florence inspired the formation of a military order dedicated to the protection of the Dominicans and the inquisition. Peter played a leading role in the inquisition in northern Italy, zealously attacking the faith of his family and persecuting those who professed it. His mission led to the imprisonment and confiscation of the property of many Cathars. Two of his victims, Venetian nobles, are said to have hired assassins to avenge their losses. They attacked Peter and his attendant in a lonely forest on 6 April 1252. As the story is told, the assassin Carino first struck Peter in the head before pursuing his attendant. He returned to find Peter still alive. According to one version, he was reciting the Apostles' Creed. (The *Oxford English Dictionary* lists the Apostles' Creed as one of the archaic meanings of "belief." Thus, from 1377, "I . . . sat softly adown and seide my belieue.") According to another version, he was writing its first words on the ground in his blood. Carino dispatched him by plunging a dagger into his chest. Peter was canonized by Innocent IV in the following year ("the most speedy creation of a saint on record" [Lea 1888, 216]) shortly after the pope issued his famous bull *Ad extirpanda,* which ordered that heretics be executed five days after arrest and which permitted the use of torture in the courts of the inquisition. Peter Martyr became the first martyr of the Dominicans and the patron saint of the inquisition.

The death of Peter Martyr is depicted both in painting and in hagiography as an enactment of belief. Peter, who believes in one God, is martyred by Cathars, who believe in two. But, as we have seen, his CREDO is written in blood, on the ground, in a specific time, and in a specific place; the words "I believe" seem to obscure the historical circumstances of his death. Indeed, the available evidence suggests that he was not a martyr and that he did not die for his beliefs. According to Roman Catholic doctrine, martyrs are those who die witnessing their faith in Christ at the hands of persecutors of the church. But Peter's death, as others have noted, was an assassination rather than a martyrdom, with the witness to his faith provided only by the addendum in blood, a tradition doubted in *Butler's Lives of the Saints.* Peter was murdered not for his beliefs but for his deeds, specifically for the confiscation of the property of two Cathar noblemen. Yet so powerful is the ideology of belief that "martyr" has virtually become his surname. Furthermore, the conflict that led to the inquisition in northern Italy seems not to have been so much about belief as about who would control the Lombard League, the pope or the Holy Roman Emperor. That the inquisition only succeeded after the death of Frederic II suggests the conflict was certainly between two gods, but that these gods were not the two gods of the absolutist Cathars. If the motivations were finally political, so were the effects, with the contents of men's and women's minds serving as the pretext to justify the taking of property and the taking of lives. Of one who had died before being condemned, the manual for inquisitors declared that "his bones be exhumed from the cemetery, if they can be distinguished from others, and burned in detestation of so heinous an offense" (Peters 1980, 206).

In this case of belief, then, one is distinguished from others not by sounds produced by the tongue and actions performed by the body but by the invisible content of the mind. Once the presence of error is inferred in the other's mind, his or her body is subject to punishment, even if the person's deeds remain unobjectionable. When a bishop asked a knight why the Waldensian schismatics had not been expelled and shunned, he answered, "We cannot do that, for we were raised with them, and we have relatives among them, and we see that they lead honest and decent lives." The Catholic chronicler of this exchange observed, "Thus does falsity in the appearance of a good life lead people away from the truth" (Peters 1980, 107). The lesson of Peter's martyrdom, then, may be that the safer course is to allow belief to remain the nebulous mental phenomenon Hume found it to be, left unmanifest in word or deed. The more famous painting of Peter Martyr is that by Fra Angelico, which shows him standing upright and facing the viewer, with an ax in his head, a dagger in his chest, and his finger to his lips.

Three centuries after Peter's death, Catholic monks had again set out to preach the gospel, not to combat heresy but to convert the infidel, the unbelievers. The accounts of the Christian missions, both Catholic and Protestant, suggest, however, that belief, portrayed as an inner state, was again employed as a surrogate for more visible concerns. In 1596, a Spanish merchant vessel foundered off the coast of Japan and its cargo was seized by the shogun. Both Jesuit and Franciscan missionaries demanded the confiscated cargo, and a bitter dispute developed ending in the execution (by crucifixion) of six Franciscans, three Jesuits, and seventeen laymen. That group is known as The Twenty-six Martyrs.

Such cases suggest that when Pascal placed his wager some decades later, the concerns of this life were as much at stake in the wager of belief as were the concerns of the life everlasting. Still, in the seventeenth century the options for the European remained either belief or unbelief in the Christian God; other religions lacked the full revelation of God's truth. By the end of the nineteenth century, the situation was rather different. William James wrote in 1896:

> It is evident that unless there be some pre-existing tendency to believe in masses and holy water, the option offered by Pascal is not a living option. Certainly no Turk ever took to masses and holy water on its account; and even to us Protestants these means of salvation seem such foregone impossibilities that Pascal's logic, invoked for them specifically, leaves us unmoved. As well might the Mahdi write to us, saying, "I am the Expected One whom God has created in his effulgence. You shall be infinitely happy if you confess me; otherwise you shall be cut off from the light of the sun. Weigh, then, your infinite gain if I am genuine against your finite sacrifice if I am not!" (James 1956, 6)

For James, then, belief, at least for the modern man, has little to do with logic. A Turk (the quintessential infidel) would not be persuaded to convert to Christianity by Pascal's argument, just as an American Protestant would not be persuaded to convert to Islam based on claims by the Mahdi (for late nineteenth-century America, the equivalent of the Ayatollah Khomeni). James's point is, in part, a point about history and culture, that what may be compelling in one time and place may not be in a different era or in a different part of the world. It is also an acknowledgment that the question no longer involves simply belief or unbelief in the one true faith; it is a recognition of other traditions called "religions" or even "world religions." His assumption remains, nonetheless, that each of these religions is above all a set of truth claims, a system of belief.

But before dispensing with Pascal's wager altogether, we may wish to pause to explore the notion of belief as wager. Roman emperors are said to have wagered with God for victory in battle, and Venetian doges built cathedrals in return for salvation from the plague. The contractual nature of belief has been explored by a more recent Catholic thinker, Michel de Certeau. The believer, in a position of inferiority in relation to the object of belief (we speak of belief being owed and credence being given), gives something away in the hope of getting something back, not now, but sometime in the future. "The 'believer' abandons a present advantage, or some of its claims, to give credit to the receiver" (de Certeau 1985, 193). It is this element of time, this deferral into the future, that characterizes the relation between subject and object in belief, and differentiates believing from the simultaneity of subject and object characteristic of knowing or seeing. In belief, the benefit accrues to the believer only with the passage of time; belief, in other words, is an "expectational practice" (195). In order for the contractual relation to be maintained, there must be the expectation of some return on the initial investment, a surety of some salvation, and this in turn depends on the presumption of the ability of the object of belief to guarantee the loan. The object of belief is thus present in its promise but absent in the fact that the debt is not yet repaid (201). In the case of the painting of Peter Martyr, the artist offers an image of Peter Martyr representing his belief, inscribed on the ground in his blood. The contract between Peter and his God is a familiar one: by dying for his belief, he will be delivered into the eternal presence of God. The angels are already hovering above; the return on his investment will not be deferred much longer. But as we have seen, other economies of exchange are also at work. Peter has invested notions of belief and heresy in the purposes of the church against the Cathars, who have repaid the debt of their heresy, their deficit of right belief, with their property and their lives. But each contract has produced another contract: Peter's disposition of the property of the Cathars produced their contract with the assassins, and Peter paid for the property with his life.

But de Certeau seems to assume that the believer's entry into the contract is somehow free, and is never compelled by the foreign. The notion of belief, however, is neither natural nor universal. It might be described as an ideology, not so much in the sense of false consciousness but as an idea that arises from a specific set of material interests. In the case of Peter Martyr, the interests were those of the Roman Catholic Church in northern Italy. But belief can also be introduced into domains where it was not previously present, and for reasons that appear less material than those of medieval Europe.

We turn, then, to Sri Lanka in the late nineteenth century (when it was called Ceylon). Our concern is not to compare Buddhist and Christian beliefs or theories of belief, nor to consider how Christian beliefs may have influenced Buddhists. Instead, we shall examine a case in which the ideology of belief, the idea that a religion must have beliefs in order to be a religion, was introduced to Ceylon by an American Civil War veteran, Colonel Henry Steel Olcott (1832–1907), who in 1881 published *The Buddhist Catechism*.

Colonel Olcott was the founder, with Helena Petrovna Blavatsky, of the Theosophical Society. By 1878 Blavatsky and Olcott had shifted their emphasis away from the investigation of psychic phenomena toward the broader promotion of a universal brotherhood of humanity, claiming affinities between Theosophy and the wisdom of the East, specifically Hinduism and Buddhism. With the aim of establishing links with Asian teachers, they traveled to India, arriving in Bombay in 1879 and proceeding to Ceylon the next year. Although they both took the vows of lay Buddhists, Blavatsky's interest in Buddhism remained peripheral to her Theosophy. Olcott, however, enthusiastically embraced his new faith, being careful to note that he was a "regular Buddhist" rather than a "debased modern" Buddhist; he described "the shocking ignorance of the Sinhalese about Buddhism" (Prothero 1996, 100). "Our Buddhism was that of the Master-Adept Gautama Buddha, which was identically the Wisdom Religion of the Aryan Upanishads, and the soul of the ancient world-faiths" (96). Olcott took it as his task to restore true Buddhism to Ceylon and to counter the efforts of the Christian missionaries on the island. In order to accomplish this aim, he adopted many of their techniques, founding the Buddhist Theosophical Society to disseminate Buddhist knowledge (and later assisting in the founding of the Young Men's Buddhist Association) and publishing in 1881 *The Buddhist Catechism* "on the lines of the similar elementary hand-books so effectively used among the Western Christian sects" (101). Olcott, who had earlier professed his ignorance of Buddhism, took on the task of writing the catechism himself. In the preface to the thirty-sixth edition he wrote, "It has always seemed incongruous that an American making no claims at all to scholarship, should be looked to by the Sinhalese [Ceylonese] nation to help them teach the Dharma to their children, and as I believe I have said in an earlier edition, I only consented to write the *Buddhist Catechism* after I found that no Bhikku [monk] would undertake it" (1947, xii). That no such monk was forthcoming suggests more about Olcott's assumptions about Buddhism than it does about any deficiencies in the Sinhalese clergy.

It is a remarkable work, opening with a certificate from H. Sumangala, a prominent Sinhalese monk and a leading figure in the Buddhist revival of the late nineteenth century who declares, "I hereby certify that I have carefully examined the Sinhalese version of the catechism prepared by Colonel H. S. Olcott, and that the same is in agreement with the Canon of the Southern Buddhist Church.

I recommend the work to teachers in Buddhist schools, and to all others who may wish to impart to beginners about the essential features of our religion." It should be noted that there is no such thing as the "Southern Buddhist Church" and that many scholars reject the notion of a "canon" in the case of Buddhism. The catechism comprises 384 questions and answers, organized under five headings: The Life of the Buddha, The Dharma or Doctrine, The Sangha, The Rise and Spread of Buddhism, and Buddhism and Science. Here is a typical passage:

> 118. Q. *Why does ignorance cause suffering?*
> A. Because it makes us prize what is not worth prizing, grieve for what we should not grieve, consider real what is not real but only illusionary, and pass our lives in pursuit of worthless objects, neglecting what is in reality most valuable.
> 119. Q. *And what is that which is most valuable?*
> A. To know the whole secret of man's existence and destiny, so that we may estimate at no more than their actual value this life and its relations; and so that we may live in a way to ensure the greatest happiness and the least suffering for our fellow-men and ourselves.
> 120. Q. *What is the light that can dispel this ignorance of ours and remove our sorrows?*
> A. The knowledge of the "Four Noble Truths", as BUDDHA called them. (Olcott 1947, 27)

Despite the evocation of the preamble to the United States Constitution in passages like this, much of the content of the *Catechism* seems quite accurate, even natural, to those who have studied Buddhism in the West and who remember from "Introduction to World Religions" that the Buddha taught the four noble truths (and the eightfold path). The ease with which we read without pause through passages like this is testimony to the success of this work, and those upon which it relies, to represent Buddhism as above all a system of beliefs. Few Buddhists over the course of Asian history would have been able to recite the four noble truths and the eightfold path, yet this is precisely what the *Catechism* trains the children of Ceylon to do.

Olcott did not learn to read Buddhist texts in Pali, relying instead on translations available to him in English. He claimed to have read "15,000 pages of Buddhist teaching" in preparing for his task. The translators from whom he drew, notably Thomas W. Rhys Davids, are never far away. ("165. Q. *In the whole text of the three Pitakas how many words are there? A.* Dr. Rhys Davids estimates them at 1,752,800" [p. 39]). In addition to relying on the translators' information, he also assumed their view of Buddhism as a moral philosophy ("170. Q. *If we were to try to represent the whole spirit of the Buddha's doctrine in one word, which word should we choose? A.* Justice" [pp. 40–41]) that had been corrupted over the centuries by the introduction of popular superstitions ("186. Q. *Are charms, incantations, the observance of lucky hours, and devil dancing a part of*

Buddhism? A. They are positively repugnant to its fundamental principles. They are surviving relics of fetishism and pantheistic and other foreign religions" [pp. 44–45]. . . . 191. Q. *When such perversions are discovered, what should be the true Buddhist's earnest desire?* A. The true Buddhist should be ever ready and anxious to see the false purged away from the true, and to assist, if he can" [p. 47]).

In the *Catechism,* then, Olcott seems determined to restore to Ceylon the spirit of true Buddhism, which appears to be largely defined as a set of beliefs best expounded in negative terms or, more specifically, as that which is non-Roman Catholic:

> 187. Q. *What striking contrasts are there between Buddhism and what may properly be called "religions"?*
> A. Among others, these: It teaches the highest goodness without creating a God; a continuity of life without adhering to the superstitious and selfish doctrine of an eternal, metaphysical soul-substance that goes out of the body; a happiness without an objective heaven; a method of salvation without a vicarious Savior; redemption by oneself as the Redeemer, and without rites, prayers, penances, priests or intercessory saints; and a *summum bonum, i.e.,* Nirvana, attainable in this life and in this world by leading a pure, unselfish life of wisdom and compassion to all beings. (p. 45)

Even with his deference to Sinhalese chauvinism ("318. Q. *In which country have we reason to believe the sacred books of primitive Buddhism have been best preserved and least corrupted?* A. Ceylon" [p. 82]), it seems ludicrous to imagine Sinhalese school children learning to answer the question ("305. Q. *Through what Western religious brotherhoods did the Buddha Dharma mingle itself with Western thought?* A. Through the sects of the Therapeuts of Egypt and the Essenes of Palestine" [p. 79]). Indeed, a much shorter version was produced for children by another Theosophist, C. W. Leadbeater in 1902. Still, Olcott's version was printed in some forty editions in twenty languages, and is still in use in schools in Sri Lanka.

Olcott's activities in Ceylon appear not so much as attempts to beat the Christian missionaries at their own game but as the inevitable consequences of an ideology of belief, that is, an assumption deriving from the history of Christianity that religion is above all an interior state of assent to certain truths. In Victorian Europe and America, the Buddha was seen as the greatest philosopher of India's Aryan past, and his teachings were regarded as a complete philosophical and psychological system based on reason and restraint; opposed to ritual, superstition, and sacerdotalism; and demonstrating how the individual could live a moral life without the trappings of institutional religion. This Buddhism was to be found in texts, rather than in the lives of modern Buddhists of Ceylon, who in Olcott's view had deviated from the original teachings. Olcott (and his Western infor-

31

mants) therefore could portray Buddhism as a set of propositions, propositions that Olcott himself (unlike most of his informants) assented to, that is, "believed in." It was then necessary that there be strategies for the propagation of that belief. Thus, he composed *The Buddhist Catechism,* he founded the Buddhist Theosophical Society, and through it he established Buddhist secondary schools and Sunday schools.

But his fundraising efforts for the Buddhist Theosophical Society initially proved unsuccessful, endangering his propagation of Buddhist belief. In response, he briefly shifted his focus from belief to practice. When he learned that Catholic missionaries were making claims about the healing powers of a shrine, he implored Buddhist monks to perform faith healings in order to demonstrate the truth of the Buddha's teachings. None volunteered. Olcott himself then decided to employ his knowledge of mesmerism (while publicly crediting the Buddha) to effect cures. Through word of mouth and public testimonials, Olcott gained a reputation as a healer, and his efforts at fundraising began to meet with success (Prothero 1996, 107–8).

Returning to his vision of Buddhism as belief, Olcott set out on the grander mission of healing the schism he perceived between "the Northern and Southern Churches," that is, between the Buddhists of Ceylon and Burma (Southern) and those of China and Japan (Northern). Such a division has been rejected by scholars for its simplification of the already problematic (although at least Buddhist) categories of Hinayana and Mahayana. But Olcott believed that a great rift had occurred in Buddhism 2,300 years earlier and that if he could simply have representatives of the Buddhist nations agree to a list of "fourteen items of belief" (he also referred to them as "Fundamental Buddhistic Beliefs"), then it might be possible to create a "United Buddhist World." He participated in the design of a Buddhist flag that could "serve the same purpose as that of the cross does for Christianity" (Prothero 1996, 116). Olcott traveled to Burma and Japan, where he negotiated with Buddhist leaders until he could find language to which they could assent. He also implored them to send missionaries to spread the Dharma. In the end, however, Olcott's beliefs led to another schism. He incurred the wrath of Sinhalese Buddhist leaders when he mocked their belief in the authenticity of the precious tooth relic of the Buddha at Kandy by stating that it was in fact a piece of deer horn. Shortly thereafter, H. Sumangala, the monk who had certified the authenticity of the *Catechism,* found seventeen answers that were "opposed to orthodox views of the Southern Church" and withdrew his certification (Sumangala 1906, 57).

Concerning the *Catechism* Olcott's biographer writes, "[B]efore Olcott, no Sinhalese Buddhist had thought to reduce Buddhism to its belief and then to compress those beliefs into a simple question-and-answer format, as Olcott did, in his celebrated *The Buddhist Catechism*" (Prothero 1996, 10). This brief survey of belief has suggested that it may be better not to seek to imagine what a person had or had not thought but rather to examine what he or she did. The fact that no Sinhalese Buddhist had produced a text that reduced Buddhism to its belief suggests that the category of belief is not so easily transferred from one society to another, and that those who seek to do so are subject to the consequences of their deed. Sumangala stated that Olcott's attack on the tooth relic was something "we could only expect from an enemy of our religion" (1906, 58).

Colonel Olcott, acting as the uninvited agent of Sinhalese Buddhists at the end of the nineteenth century, entered into a contract on their behalf, not with God but with the ideology of belief itself. He invested his efforts in belief, hoping that in the end his investment would be repaid with the restoration of true Buddhism to Ceylon. The enemy, for Colonel Olcott, were the European and American missionaries who wanted to convert the Sinhalese to Christianity, causing them no longer to believe in Buddhism. By entering into a contract with belief, the Sinhalese were promised a certain salvation, the salvation of not losing the beliefs that they never knew they had. The result, however, was that Olcott was rejected by many of those he had sought to save. In the meantime, the movement that he founded, Theosophy, which he regarded as the true science, has come to be regarded as a quaint remnant of a bygone age. It has, in short, become a belief, in de Certeau's sense of mental occurrences in the mind of someone else, "known as 'beliefs' precisely because we do not believe them any longer" (de Certeau 1985, 196). That is, the view of belief as an inner state, as an assent to a proposition, can only occur with a loss, when the believer has terminated the contract with the believed, leaving the object of belief as a lonely component of someone else's religion, either of another time or of another place.

Belief appears as a universal category because of the universalist claims of the tradition in which it has become most central, Christianity. Other religions have made universalist claims, but Christianity was allied with political power, which made it possible to transport its belief to all corners of the globe (if not the universe), making belief the measure of what religion is understood to be. Belief, then, or perhaps the demand that there be belief, is implicated both in the activities of Christian missionaries and in the "native" efforts (and those of their invited and uninvited surrogates) to counter them. The question that remains, however, is what the Sinhalese gave up by giving credit to belief. What are the costs of seeing oneself in that mirror?

All of this leads to the conclusion that the statement, "I believe in . . . ," is sensible only when there are others who "do not"; it is an agonistic affirmation of something that cannot be submitted to ordinary rules of verification. The very impossibility of verification has historically functioned as a means of establishing a community against "the world," hinting at a counterfactual reality to which only the believers have access. When the world has threatened to destroy that community, as in the case of Jews and Shi'a Muslims at certain moments in their histories, dissimulation has been permitted. Thus, a statement of belief is a convention appropriate to a specific situation, sanctioned by a history and a community. As Wittgenstein notes, "the expression of belief . . . is just a sentence;—

and the sentence has sense only as a member of a system of language; as one expression within a calculus" (1958, 42). It is only when we extend that language, that calculus, to include the historical circumstances of the statement that the multiple meanings of the statement become clear, even when it is written in blood.

The problem, then, is not whether belief exists—this is difficult to determine—but whether religion must be represented as something that derives from belief, as something with external manifestations that can ultimately be traced back to an inner assent to a cognitive proposition, as a state of mind that produces practice. As we have seen, in thirteenth-century Italy the inquisition hunted and punished heretics in the name of belief. There, even when it appears with such priority, belief is the afterthought, belatedly depicted as having existed inside someone else's head. In the nineteenth century, Colonel Olcott and other foreigners created a world religion called Buddhism in the name of belief. Its role in turning other traditions, including the Christian, into world religions remains to be investigated. A century after Colonel Olcott, we continue to speak of the "world view" of this or that religion, demonstrating that, even though we may no longer believe in God, we still believe in belief.

SUGGESTED READINGS

Certeau, Michel de. 1985. "What We Do When We Believe." In *On Signs*, edited by Marshall Blonsky.
Hume, David. 1967. *A Treatise of Human Nature*, edited by L. A. Selby-Bigge.
Lambert, Malcolm. 1992. *Medieval Heresy: Popular Movements from the Gregorian Reform to the Reformation.*
Needham, Rodney. 1972. *Belief, Language, and Experience.*
Peters, Edward, ed. 1980. *Heresy and Authority in Medieval Europe: Documents in Translation.*
Quine, W. V., and J. S. Julian. 1970. *The Web of Belief.*
Smith, Barbara Herrnstein. 1997. *Belief and Resistance: Dynamics of Contemporary Intellectual Controversy.*
Smith, Wilfred Cantwell. 1977. *Belief and History.*
Wittgenstein, Ludwig. 1966. *Lectures and Conversations on Aesthetics, Psychology, and Religious Belief*, compiled by Yorick Smythies, Rush Rhees, and James Taylor; edited by Cyril Barrett.

REFERENCES

Certeau, Michel de. 1985. "What We Do When We Believe." In *On Signs*, edited by Marshall Blonsky. Baltimore: Johns Hopkins University Press.
Hume, David. 1967. *A Treatise of Human Nature*, edited by L. A. Selby-Bigge. London: Oxford University Press.

James, William. 1956. *"The Will to Believe" and Other Essays in Popular Philosophy*. New York: Dover Publications.

———. 1961. *The Varieties of Religious Experience*. New York: Collier Books.

Kant, Immanuel. 1968. *Critique of Pure Reason*, translated by Norman Kemp Smith. New York: Macmillan.

Lambert, Malcolm. 1992. *Medieval Heresy: Popular Movements from the Gregorian Reform to the Reformation*. 2nd ed. Oxford: Blackwell.

Lea, Henry Charles. 1888. *A History of the Inquisition of the Middle Ages*. 3 vols. New York: Harper and Brothers.

Müller, Friedrich Max. 1897. *Contributions to the Science of Mythology*. 2 vols. London: Longmans Green.

Needham, Rodney. 1972. *Belief, Language, and Experience*. Oxford: Blackwell.

Olcott, Henry Steel. 1947. *The Buddhist Catechism*. 44th ed. Adyar, Madras: Theosophical Publishing House.

Pascal, Blaise. 1962. *Pensées*, translated by Martin Turnell. London: Harvill Press.

Peters, Edward, ed. 1980. *Heresy and Authority in Medieval Europe: Documents in Translation*. Philadelphia: University of Pennsylvania Press.

Prothero, Stephen. 1996. *The White Buddhist: The Asian Odyssey of Henry Steel Olcott*. Bloomington: Indiana University Press.

Quine, W. V., and J. S. Julian. 1970. *The Web of Belief*. New York: Random House.

Smith, Wilfred Cantwell. 1977. *Belief and History*. Charlottesville, Va.: University of Virginia Press.

Sumangala, H. 1906. "High Priest Sumangala and the Theosophical Society." *The Maha Bodhi* [Calcutta] 14 (April).

Wittgenstein, Ludwig. 1958. *The Blue and Brown Books*. New York: Harper and Row.

———. 1966. *Lectures and Conversations on Aesthetics, Psychology, and Religious Belief*, edited by Cyril Barrett. Berkeley and Los Angeles: University of California Press.

———. 1980. *Remarks on the Philosophy of Psychology*, translated by G. E. M. Anscombe; edited by G. E. M. Anscombe and G. H. von Wright. Vol. 1. Oxford: Blackwell.

TWO

Body

William R. LaFleur

The fact that "body" has become a critical term for religious studies, whereas "mysticism," for instance, has largely dropped out, can itself signal significant change in how we study religion. Twenty or thirty years ago the situation would have been reversed: Mysticism would have been a core term and bodies, although mentioned in discussion of the theology of resurrection, would not have deserved a separate entry. Certainly one reason for this change has been the degree to which ethnographic materials—and the ethnographer's capacity to show that bodies speak loudly about mentalities—now have an important role in how we go about describing religions. Even the history of the major religions of the "West" has been dramatically altered by this; nowhere has this been more clear than in studies of how sexuality and gender were historically represented and contested in both Christianity and Judaism, religions now recognized as having always been far more ensconced in the semiotics of the body than the theologians of either faith had realized or admitted. The acknowledgment of chemistry's role too has altered how we view religion. Reaching out from the suggestion of William James (1902) that anesthetics could induce religious experience, more recent research into psychedelics, the brain, and the chemical components of health and happiness has been impressive. Even when experiences tagged as religious are *not* induced by outside agents, it appears that chemicals such as endorphins, natural to the body, are involved. The leverage on our minds exerted by our DNA and what has been called the "selfish" gene cannot be denied. Studies that reject or ignore such data now seem out-of-date; we have moved from recognizing that religion involves the body to acknowledging, sometimes begrudgingly, that the body is conditioned very powerfully by its own chemistry and biological prehistory.

Nevertheless, almost as impressive has been the accumulated evidence for a human readiness or eagerness to manipulate, redesign, and even maim the human body—not infrequently for reasons linked to religion. Persons who considered themselves "modern" thought that the physically redesigned body was a sign of the "primitive" and felt disgust vis-à-vis the sadism or masochism recorded on such bodies. Is it, then, a sign of postmodernity when that ethos of disgust is itself rejected by persons in today's Berlin or Boston who take delight in being whole-body tattooed or having their skin pierced by nose, nipple, and genital rings? And is it not possible that such intentional modification of the body registers a move away from the Judeo-Christian body code ("You shall not make cuttings on your flesh" [Lev. 19:28]) and is itself a religion-based choice to identify with the practice, more nearly universal in its scope, of taking the body as something to be creatively redesigned?

If the human being's body is its own ready-made canvas, it is also its most readily accessible altar or temple. The yogi and Zen practitioner insist that the whole of religious practice can be carried out within the domain of the epidermis. Many people, for reasons of religion, will make use of some kind of tool—knives, rings, paints, and the like—to alter their bodies. And the fact that they insist on doing so suggests why religion cannot be explained *entirely* through chemistry and biology.

We humans cannot exist without representation, including that of the body itself. The number and variety of such representations are immense. A history of the human body would be virtually coextensive with a history of human beings. To write it up would be impossible, a fact recognized when such a project reached 1,500 pages and ended by being titled "fragments for" such a history (Feyer, Naddaff, Tazi 1989). And even that enterprise was less a history of the body itself than of how bodies have been represented by the mind.

This essay will focus primarily on such representation. It will begin by further specifying the gap between conceptualizing religious duty as acceptance of the received body and what we have here called the practice of religious redesign of the body. Secondly, it explores how the medicine we call "modern" upset the tidiness of that distinction by developing technologies for the most radical cutting and most drastic refashioning of the body. Ethical and religious questions brought into play by the astounding medical technologies of the present and probable future are at the center of the third section, one that also suggests reasons why some in the West have expressed concern about the way in which such technologies seem to "play God." Religious reasons for Japanese resistance to organ transplants, however, are very different from the "playing God" rationales. The fourth section, describing what studies of religion have learned from Foucault about power, vulnerability, and institutions, goes on to indicate why this has made for deepened ambivalence about modernity. Fifthly, what was noted about Japanese opposition to organ transplantation becomes a focused aperture for seeing how a non-Western society can conclude that the supposedly "secularized" treatment of the body in Western medicine is, in fact, itself an unconscious embodiment of a Western religious tradition. The focus of the sixth section is on why, nevertheless, anthropologists and students of religion now have deep reservations about the older posture of ethical neutrality vis-à-vis instances of what must be called bodily mutilation and gender repression. Finally, an argument is advanced in favor of giving the "no cruelty" criterion an edge over the usual "ideological" objections when deciding what is morally objectionable. Moreover, because we need to recognize that notions such as what is "natural" or what amounts to playing God are no longer viable in deciding on the morality of the biotechnological modification of bodies or potential bodies, the no cruelty criterion, it is argued, should preferably be applied in this area as well.

I. Bodies—As Given and as Malleable

Religious ideas and functions have usually tended to come strongly to the fore when it was thought that a rationale was needed for accepting certain bodily conditions as necessary and "given" or, alternatively, when it was assumed that an existing body might be altered. Cultures, subcultures, and religious institutions position themselves somewhere on a spectrum between one pole, where the body is considered a given, and its opposite, where somatic plasticity is regarded as not only allowed but even desirable, an index to religious identification and involvement.

The appeal of the "acceptance" mode cannot be denied. Within it the transformation is entirely *mental*, because in this way even severe bodily deformity or damage can be changed into something with *meaning*. Such bodily conditions would have been interpreted, for instance, as the product of sin, as the evidence of a negative karmic account, or as part of a plan set by a god or gods to test and refine the "spirit" of the person so afflicted. Greek notions of *moira* or fate, Indian views on karma, and Judeo-Christian-Islamic ideas about the inscrutibility of the deity's doings are examples of humans explaining to themselves certain bodily conditions deemed unalterable. Our own society's readiness to attribute disability and deformity at birth to genetics or to interpret subsequent limb loss or maiming as due to an accident is a relatively recent development; accustomed to such views, we neglect to see how unusual such a view is in the context of human history. *Accident,* a meaning-deprived and comfortless concept, is still often resisted in societies and religious communities clinging to more traditional theodicies.

If religion can rationalize acceptance, it can in other cases justify the opposite—namely, intentional bodily modification. The spectrum here is broad, but two types may be differentiated: one that does not cut or violate the body's surface and another that clearly does. The former includes the variety of yogic asanas found primarily in Hindu and Buddhist contexts; baptismal washings; the removal of all clothing to recapture a sense of primal nudity; and the temporary addition to the body of paint, masks, or clothing that are assumed to transform either the person's status or role. In work that had a wide-ranging impact on theorizing about religion, Mircea Eliade (1958) brought yoga to the forefront as a traditional context in which humans used their bodies as virtual laboratories, experimenting with various experiential states and often assuming that the resultant euphoria conferred some kind of immortality. Because ecstasy is frequently viewed as an opening onto a higher spiritual or ontological level, sex has been seen either as an unusually apt route of access or, alternatively, as a dangerous obstacle to religious realization. Oscillations between the extremes of sexual austerity and promiscuous orgies occurred in Europe, especially in the fringe Christian sect of the Khlysty in Russia. India appears to have first decoupled sex from procreation and to have done so by transmuting intercourse into a yogic or meditational regimen, with the retention of semen being crucially important to the *religious* objective of this mode of sexual intercourse.

Bodily modifications that involve a violation of the body's surface or a removal of its parts are more drastic. The range of impact can be considerable—all the way from tonsuring, which can occur without inducing pain, to "mortifications," which in some instances literalize that term by resulting in death. At various points within this wide spectrum fall circumcision, tattooing, fasting, flagellation, the gradual reshaping of body parts such as lips and feet, and eunuchization. In what follows, the term "malleation" will be used to denote this spectrum.

Any notion that the so-called Western religions embraced the "natural" body and refrained from modification is belied by the facts. Jews and Muslims put a rite of malleation, circumcision, at the center of their religious identities. However it was defined theologically, foreskin removal was also thought to "perfect" nature and make for unambiguous maleness by removing what some saw as a vestigial vagina. (Those within Muslim and other religious communities who surgically remove the clitoris will sometimes argue that such an excision of a penis-like part will "perfect" the female.)

Peter Brown documents the variety of concrete ways in which Christians in late antiquity problematized sexuality, often holding that the distinctiveness of their faith gained articulation in that way, thus providing a new model for the body politic. The cult of virginity became extensive and a thinker such as Origen (c. 185–254) "was prepared to look at sexuality in the human person as if it were a mere passing phase" (Brown 1988, 168). By turning themselves into eunuchs, some early Christians (possibly including Origen) saw themselves as adhering to Matt. 19:12*c* (". . . there are eunuchs who have made themselves eunuchs for the sake of the kingdom of heaven."). Others found this repulsive, the removal of a boundary between the sexes. In that sense self-eunuchization was the polar opposite of circumcision: one type of cutting removed gender difference and the other was interpreted as accentuating it. Each mode could be valorized by religion. Neither was satisfied with the given, natural body.

Eunuchism in traditional China provides an instructive case of how significant bodily modification may occur within a society that insists upon the religious import of its opposite, that is, on strict acceptance and nonalteration of the body. Confucianism disclosed its religious dimension in its insistence that dead ancestors were de facto deities and that their descendants' filial piety was expressed in a total acceptance of their own bodies, which were given them as somatic inheritances. This entailed that any intentional alteration of it—tatooing, piercing, and so on—constituted a violation of religious duty and placed the all-important beneficence of a dead but still involved ancestor's favor in jeopardy. Conversely, the bodily mutilation of criminals was not just a secular marking but also a religiously charged punishment; it turned the malefactor's body into one that disgraced his or her ancestors. When men in China, therefore, became eunuchs simply in order to advance themselves in terms of employment and receive positions in the palace, their newly defective bodies put their postmortem lives in jeopardy. Many eunuchs faced and tried to overcome this crisis by insisting that their genitalia, removed earlier, be bottled and stored throughout their lives so that the atrophied organs could at least be interred with the rest of the corpse. Thus there would be "wholeness" in the afterlife, even if not in this one (Mitamura 1970).

II. Shamans and Medics

Part of Europe's self-identity was rooted in the supposition that Christians, unlike peoples referred to as pagans, did not disfigure or even redesign the body given by God. Medieval Europeans saw somatic alteration as a desecration of bodies thought to possess the *imago dei* or "image of god." In medieval Europe, this became the stated objection, for instance, to the circumcision of Christian males, although it seems clear that this nuance of bodily difference served additionally as a way of differentiating Christian males from Jewish and Muslim ones.

There is, then, some irony in the fact that it was within Europe—that is, within the civilization holding the notion of body as *imago dei*—that, through processes of deep cutting, severing, extracting, and observing, a progressively exact knowledge of the body's inner parts and functions was gained. The Renaissance saw a frenzy of interest in experimentation, sometimes of the cruel sort. Camporesi (1988) documents how powerful persons used hallucinogens, even poisons, to induce temporary lunacy or "bestial" behavior in their servants—to provide themselves with spectacles. Here cynicism mixed with curiosity. Many showed an "irresistible urge to penetrate the barriers of the unknown, dark territories, on the frontiers of reason" (215).

Once sanctioned as providing enhanced knowledge that could result in healing, bodily investigations became increasingly invasive. This necessitated social and religious toleration of anatomical exploration, especially that performed on the bodies of the deceased. To define the corpse as a "cadaver" and to treat it routinely as a "thing" that might be dismembered, anatomically explored, and then disposed of required elimination of a taboo. Most traditional societies, including those of Europe, had strictures in place against violating the bodies of the dead. Although it is clear that the principal trajectory of anatomical exploration had a temporary phase during the epoch of the early Greeks, it is important to note that Galen (c. 129–199) would dissect pigs and apes but would scrupulously refrain from doing so to human corpses. Arabs preserved part of Galen's *On Anatomical Procedures*, but an Islamic objection to the dissection of human corpses prevented them from pushing further. It is significant that in Renaissance Italy, when human corpses were cut up for study, the subjects of study were criminals who had been hanged or beheaded. The bodies of such persons were not considered sacrosanct (Roberts and Tomlinson 1992, 2–6).

Yet for the most part the taboo against dissecting humans was liquidated with

comparative ease in Europe, perhaps because there a streak of popularized, Christianized Platonism as well as a longing for purification of the soul had often already described the body as latrine, dung heap, and bag of food for worms. Why, then, not cut it up and learn from it? In contrast to the strenuous Christian objections to the new cosmological knowledge in the Renaissance and to Darwinism in the nineteenth century, invasive technology applied to the dead human body became quickly acceptable. (Some orthodox Jews, it needs noting, still have reservations.)

This in itself hints at the strength of a dualism established within Christian theology and praxis: in spite of doctrines of incarnation, resurrection, and *imago dei*, and theories about the ingestion of the very body of Christ in the mass, both the Catholic and Protestant Churches, perhaps especially during some of the modern centuries, have conceived their principal domain as that of the soul and its salvation. This emphasis left an opening for modern medicine to treat human bodies, both living and dead, with considerable latitude and without protest from the clergy. The kind of scientific experiment memorably portrayed by Rembrandt in his *Anatomy Lesson* did not, importantly, stir up religious protest within Christendom, whereas it might very well have done so in many other societies, especially those informed by Confucianism.

In some ways the flip side of Christianity's tendency to prioritize the soul was a secularization of the body, especially when the growth of medical knowledge during the Renaissance was greatly benefited by the supposition that the body and soul were radically different entities. In the dualism of René Descartes (1596–1650) philosophy extended and deepened the theologians' judgment about the body. Thus in Europe medicine and religion rapidly became increasingly divided domains—to a degree that was not the case in indigenous, shamanic religions, in Indian Ayurvedic practices, in Islam, or in Taoist and Confucian East Asia.

This growing difference between what was happening in the "West" and those parts of the world more resistant both to modernization and a secularization of the body became, paradoxically, a point of pride within Christendom, especially during the nineteenth century. Trust in the use of modern medicine came to be seen as an index to the difference between a civilization with "enlightened" religion, Christianity, and the rest of the world now interpreted as "benighted" and locked in the grip of the demonic "witch doctor" or "medicine man." A major difference in paradigms of the body and in healing modes became itself an index to what was seen as the uniqueness and superiority of Christianity. The connections between this view of religious difference, the empirical successes of modern medicine, and Western colonializing moves were intimate.

In a spectacular turn of language, this newer form of medical praxis (and one totally dependent upon the secularization of the body) succeeded in getting itself nominated as the "modern miracle." Yet this dramatic reinterpretation becomes more comprehensible when viewed as connected to Enlightenment-spawned studies of the "historical Jesus," studies suggesting that he had been much more of a thaumaturge—that is, in fact, a shaman or witch doctor—than had been recognized before. With modern scientists denying the possibility of contemporaneous miracles (and hinting that such would have been equally problematic in the ancient world), the interpretation of modern medicine as *the real* miracle and of Christian medics as the dispensers of such miracles did much to cover over the epistemic anomalies in such a construction. The actual successes of such medics were linked to their Christian faith and were interpreted as proof of the superiority and viability of Christianity. No one embodied this better than the medical missionary, the person who penetrated "dark" continents and cultures. His or her successes in healing illness and in preventing disease, although accomplished through wholly naturalistic means, were valorized as Christlike acts. This was thought to be demonstrated by the dispensing of pharmaceuticals and the amputation of gangrenous limbs in Africa, India, and China.

Perhaps the most significant exemplar of this was Albert Schweitzer (1875–1965), a world-renowned figure who, before becoming a doctor in Africa, had in his biblical research concluded that Jesus had mistaken views and was self-deceived in his apocalyptic vision. Schweitzer rejected these views and redescribed Jesus as principally an "ethical ruler." And such redescription allowed Schweitzer to try to reembody that same ethical concern by serving as medical missionary for decades in Africa. Awarded the Nobel Peace Prize in 1952 and hailed as a "modern saint," he represented the high point in the West's confidence that historic Christianity could be successfully repristinated in a modern medicine dispensed with moral concern. The shamanic dimension of Jesus had become an embarrassment but could be translated into something more comfortably modern.

Essentially this kind of reinterpretation of the tradition was in keeping with the kind of hermeneutic enterprise that Rudolf Bultmann (1884–1976) would hail as "demythologization." But what now seems fairly clear about all such efforts to translate traditional Christianity into terms that are unambiguously "modern" and "existential" is that they involved the removal not only of what was seen as dispensable myth in Christianity but also the pervasive, often embarrassing, *somaticity* of everything—including a bloody crucifixion—that had been important in the New Testament. Bultmann was probably the apex of a Christianity completely accommodated to the dynamics of modernization and secularization, but there was something ethereal, Platonic, and body negating in such a vision of what religion is all about.

III. Bodies on the Horizon

The easy confidence of an earlier generation that medical or scientific advances constitute signs of moral progress is one we do not now share. The "break-throughs" in medical technology remain impressive and have even been accelerating. Medics now do what was once thought impossible in the domains of plastic surgery, bodily reconstruction, transplantation of organs, in vitro fertilization, gender alteration, and genetic engineering.

Yet, although the technology is more spectacular than ever, we are today more cautious about indulging the old, heady rhetoric suggesting a wondrous uniqueness in ourselves and our era. Science at the end of a century that has seen the bodies produced at Hiroshima and Chernobyl, as well as those formed by thalidomide and Minamata disease, is a science forced to acknowledge the mixed, sometimes horrific, impact it can have upon human life. The specter of manmade monstrosities hovers closely.

Bioethics as a field of inquiry arose because of the discovery of this worrisome ambiguity and because the human body, especially in those molecular and embryonic states anterior to birth, has become malleable and manageable in ways and with results never before imagined. The body is now becoming intentionally *designable* in ways and at times unimagined by the tribal shaman. Moreover, just when and where the redesign of individuals will become an alteration of our species is less than clear. In *individual* cases the prospect of medical intervention or biotechnological manipulation will almost always be set forth as a clear desideratum—to enhance bodily functioning or appearance, to facilitate pregnancy, to extend the span of a life, or to alter a given genetic inheritance. Bioethicists, however, articulate a more general anxiety about the panhuman implications of some of these procedures, especially when they become routine. Plastic surgery may be little more than the modern aesthetic equivalent of the religion-dictated somatic deformations common in earlier and traditional societies; the individual who undergoes it does not pass the given modification on to his or her descendants. The ethical questions about malleation become qualitatively different, however, when what we can genetically craft might turn out to be strangely both like and unlike what we had until then called "human." And what if such not-quite-like-us forms of life are ones with which we can mate and reproduce?

This was a central question posed initially by Paul Ramsey (1913–88), whose own approach was to counsel extreme caution and to insist that these questions about genetic manipulation and the bodies of the future were at their core *religious* ones (Ramsey 1970). Ramsey's own response was articulated in unambiguously theological terms; his critique of efforts to fabricate various kinds of enhanced or protracted corporeal life was based on what he saw as violations of a clear distinction between Creator and creation, something he claimed to be sacrosanct in the religious history of the West. He saw this violation articulated down into a range of specific forms: sperm donation and in vitro conception as changing the fundamental structure of parenthood, radical and repeated spare parts surgery as holding out the illusion of human immortality, and genetic or mechanical engineering of the body as producing mutants or cyborgs. All such God-playing enterprises must, he held, be rejected.

43

The explicitly theological part of Ramsey's analysis did not itself become part of the basic language of subsequent bioethical discussions. His hearty confidence about being able to delineate the shape and implications of the Judeo-Christian tradition has not been widely shared; for the most part, bioethicists have found it far easier to articulate their own concerns in terms of dangerous risks, astronomical costs, legal complexities, and the need for egalitarian distribution. To follow Ramsey in postulating ontological boundaries would strike most bioethicists as too problematic a dive into what is metaphysical, nonempirical. Nevertheless, it is striking that in public and political discourse terms like "playing God" often come into play to express public anxieties vis-à-vis biomedical technology. Criticisms of some research agendas as "Promethean"—with the implication of overstepped boundaries—frequently surface. For instance, in explaining the reasons for their experience of "burnout" in studying organ transplant practices, two social scientists wrote of their growing discomfort with the medical community's "bellicose, 'death-is-the-enemy' perspective" and "hubris-ridden refusal to accept limits" (Fox and Swazey 1992, 199). Is it the case that in the West some sense of a religion-related *boundary* perdures, even though the important theorists necessarily are unable to state exactly where such a border might lie?

Interestingly, some of the most vehement protests against what is deemed to be improper malleation of the human body by science and medicine come from outside the civilization shaped by the Judeo-Christian traditions. Contemporary Japan provides an instructive instance of this, perhaps especially because the reservations expressed by many Japanese have been explicitly articulated in the terms of religion. The focus there has been on the morality and propriety of extracting usable (what we call "harvestable") organs from freshly dead corpses and transplanting them into the bodies of needy recipients. Objections to this have been grounded in the terms of Buddhism, Shinto, and Confucianism, *none* of which, curiously, has traditionally had any clear sense of an ontological demarcation between a creating deity on the one side and something called the creation on the other. These traditions, polytheistic in the case of Shinto and largely agnostic in the case of Buddhism and Confucianism, would not be inclined to find fault with persons and institutions for playing God.

If, therefore, religious objections to some forms of body modification have arisen from within Japan, we rightly would expect that the reasons behind them would differ significantly from those advanced, for instance, by Ramsey. That is, what is argued on religious bases need not be grounded in what we ordinarily think of as theology proper. Analysis of the Japanese resistance to transplanting organs from corpses supports this. Materials from the spirited public debate in Japan on this issue focus on what many claim to be the organ transplanter's impious dishonoring of the bodies of the deceased. The Confucian component in Japanese religious life awakens concern that the surgical opening of a corpse for organ harvesting is an impious way to deal with the body of someone who has just become a veneration-worthy ancestor. Shintoist arguments, often phrased as meaningful returns to an "animism" discredited by Western theorists of religion, express anxiety about the difficulty of knowing that *all* vestiges of life have, in fact, departed from a body that is declared dead only on the basis of a technology that measures the activity of the brain. Japanese Buddhist objections to transplantation typically focus on the tradition of maintaining that death is a natural and necessary part of life, not some kind of enemy to be resisted and fought against at all cost and with all available technologies. Of course, arguments on behalf of transplants are also shaped in religious and moral terms, most especially the need to show compassion—itself a virtue within Buddhism—to persons whose lives might be saved through such radical surgery. Japanese Christians have, significantly, been more ready to sanction such transplants. The vigor of the public debate in Japan on this issue is worthy of note, perhaps because of implicit concern that the fabric of the body politic (or cultural) is under threat when the bodies of the freshly dead can be readily invaded to procure salvageable organs.

IV. Power and Vulnerability

Japan's public debate on organ transplants leads naturally to consideration of what has been one of the most impressive developments in our thinking about bodies, namely, how our physical selves and the representation of such selves are intimately linked to regimes of social and political power. If questions of how the body is to be represented have become critically important during the second half of the twentieth century, this is due in large part to the influence of Michel Foucault (1926–84).

With unconventional tools and insights, Foucault tore away at the assumptions of a self-confident, rational modernity. His analyses of the historical development of institutions—especially the clinic, the hospital, the prison, and the asylum for the insane—were intended to show that, although such institutions had been established with rhetoric about their being "modern," "humane," and "enlightened," they usually were, in fact, arenas in which powerful persons manipulated, constrained, maimed, and sometimes even destroyed the bodies of the powerless (Foucault 1973). This indictment of moral pretentiousness was carried on also by Scarry's study (1985) of physical pain as an anomalous, expression-defying experience that renders its subject socially vulnerable.

Foucault implicitly and Scarry more explicitly opened up the intellectual space for recognizing that religious institutions such as the church, monastery, temple, and mosque deserve close scrutiny on the issue of how and why the bodies of the powerless might be manipulated. Medieval religious institutions too have begun to receive the scrutiny that Foucault gave to modern ones. The claim by some religious authorities that their operations require secrecy has occasioned even more suspicion; sadism, we recognize, can sometimes cloak itself in esotericism. Within hierarchically structured religious institutions, assumptions about spiritual benefits resulting from being "humbled" have often resulted in violations of the bodies of initiates. Sexual violation, sometimes of children and adolescents, has come to be recognized as having been far more common in monastic institutions—including Roman Catholic and Buddhist ones—than had ever been acknowledged before.

Some studies, even more striking and controversial, have begun to suggest that the language of agonic, muscular competition for power lies at the *center* of religious traditions, not merely in some later corruption or deformation. Perhaps most revolutionary in this domain have been exegetical studies that analyze the anatomical details of the crucifixion, dismemberment, and resurrection of Jesus to suggest the extent of the New Testament's dependence upon themes of submission, torture, penetration, and erection—often with only lightly disguised sexual referents. Recent studies, departing radically from the demythologizers, undercut the notion that the biblical writers slighted bodies. Foucault here too has induced a perspectival revolution: some studies offer evidence that the biblical writers were *obsessed* with bodies, especially "perfect" ones. Both Jahweh and the resurrected Christ are depicted as having physically impressive, "glorious," bodies—so much so that only special persons have eyes that can accommodate the sight of them. Much of the biblical story is of a kind of taunting, and then a wrestling match, between the deity (sometimes in angelic form) and human beings, many of whom wish to match him in developing a perfect body. Even before Jews and Muslims struggled over who owns Abraham, Abraham himself struggled with Jahweh over who really owned the body of Isaac. The rivalries seem to have been sexuo-religious in all instances and homoerotic at times. And the partner/contenders were multiple. That contention, not surprisingly, extends to the present—especially with feminist claims that the *maleness* of Jahweh or any other preeminent deity is merely the idolatrous projection of their own gender by the human males who controlled the writing of the scriptures.

In all of this attention to the body of the god or gods, the debt to Foucault is deep. Bultmann's modern demythologizing is shown to have involved a decorporealizing. His clear distaste for the classical Anselmian view of the bloody atonement had taken the physicality out of the crucifixion, turning it instead into something that merely demonstrates a potential for *reform* and change from "within" (Moore 1996). The surprising result of new research, then, is a sardonic return to the physically raw, blood- and torture-drenched corporeality of older theology—even if it now suggests that what God the Father did to his son smacks of an unconscionable degree of child abuse. The internal life not only of the so-called Holy Family but even of the Trinity, it turns out, has its own very dark corners.

Still needing to be more candidly acknowledged and studied is the extent to which other traditions, the Hindu and Buddhist especially, also envisioned religious affiliation as a means to link up with allies depicted as having especially powerful bodies. For Hindus and Buddhists too, life was often envisioned as a struggle. Epidemics and illnesses were customarily seen as caused by demons who, although invisible, were still *physical*. "Worship" often involved invoking suprahuman figures who could suppress such demons. What differentiates the South, Southeast, and East Asian religious traditions from those originating in the Near East, however, is that the representation of larger-than-life allies in iconic form was not problematic. Lying outside the Near East's iconophobic tradition, Hindus and Buddhists made worship-worthy figures of swarthy, muscled deities, Buddhas, and Bodhisattvas. These kept demons literally underfoot. Sometimes this kind of ally came equipped with beady eyes, knives, and garments drenched in the blood of already defeated foes and sexually penetrated consorts.

The raw physicality of these figures as well as their adherents' interest in gaining corporeally impressive allies has often been misconstrued by Western art historians. Their eagerness to make these figures more presentable to modern viewers often resulted in a translation of even the horrific aspects of such images into *symbols*—usually a set of uplifting, unthreatening, moral and spiritual "virtues." When flooded with electric light in the modern museum, such muscled deities have been not only bereft of their original, essential "darkness" but also given labels that misrepresent them. Originally they were not symbols but their devotees' means for gaining physically strong allies. In this the modern museum has, it may be said, carried out its own version of demythologization—and decorporealization. Here too a distinctively modern and Western paradigm of what religion is or ought to be has exerted itself to change—by way of a forced misrepresentation—the reality of what lies outside its own religious ambit. Our museums, we now see, are also contexts within which one paradigm, that of the modern West, subtly attempts to muscle away those of other times and cultures. A Foucauldian sensitivity forces recognition of this as a power play; it also suggests the need to give alternative scenarios adequate time and occasion to make their own cases.

V. Resisting the Western Body

One instance of a scenario different from the ones to which we are accustomed is the above-mentioned Japanese resistance to organ transplants. In order to make this instructive, it needs contextualization here. Even though the "brain death" definition of death at last became legal in 1997 and the transplantation of inner organs may become routinized in Japan, the irruption there of a passionate debate on questions of how traditional religious concepts interface with advanced medical technologies warrants our attention. Some in Japan have pointed to the push to transplant organs as a largely Western *religious* colonialism implicit in the agendas of modern, scientific medicine. If so, this would suggest that something referred to above as a process of secularization—namely, modern medicine's success in getting the dismembering of corpses released from traditional religious taboos regarding such acts—is *itself* a subtle way in which a Western and primarily Christian view of the body is being perpetuated. This implies that the struggle between the sacred and the secular is not a zero-sum game. Modern medicine constitutes, then, a set of practices in which the *religious* biases and predilections of Europe have been made merely more subterranean, more difficult to detect.

A questioning of the West's assumptions comes strongly to the fore in the writings of Yasuo Yuasa, a Japanese philosopher with an extensive knowledge of Western thought and religion. In his view Descartes's dualism is largely a reformulation of the Christian insistence on dividing flesh and spirit, a view that is pronounced in a thinker such as Augustine of Hippo (Yuasa 1987, 42 ff.). Descartes sharpened this divide and from that point on modern medicine's readiness to conceptualize the body as a machine comprised of separable "parts" was a logical and predictable consequence. The medical community's language about organs of the dead that have not been properly "harvested" and, therefore, constitute "waste" is revealing. It indicates that the body is already considered to be a *thing*. Perhaps this is why the specific issue of organ transplantation was selected as ground on which Japanese religionists could marshall their own arguments in an effort to resist what they saw as medical practices that go on missionizing, even if unconsciously and unintentionally, for a largely Western religious perspective.

In any case it now seems true that there is in the modern West's paradigm of the body and its medical modality a *contingency* that would not have been recognized even a few decades ago. It is no longer the only model within view. Traditional Chinese medicine has led a small pack of systems and practices that have opened up awareness of optional medicine. The Western scientist's capacity to laugh off the acupuncturist as conceptually flawed has greatly diminished due to demonstrable practical results, perhaps most spectacularly when open-brain surgery has been performed on fully conscious subjects anesthetized by acupuncture. Although on one level the proven healing techniques of "Western" medicine are being universally employed, there is today much less rhetoric about the need to jettison traditional technologies and pharmacologies as worthless. The societies of East Asia, at least, seem determined to retain those practical technologies that can complement the ones borrowed from the West. Sivin demonstrates, furthermore, that *ch'i,* the vital energy central to traditional Chinese medicine, continues to be widely regarded as both real and capable of conceptualization, in spite of not having been, at least to date, located by the usual scientific tools (Sivin 1987). The degree to which such research—increasingly done jointly by East Asian and Western scholars—is likely to give renewed credence to theories of the body found in Taoist texts and practices is now shaping up as one of the most fascinating of ongoing agendas. Studies of the "Taoist body" incorporate a tradition of praxis in which the distinction between medicine and religion is difficult, if not impossible, to draw.

VI. Restraining Orders

It would be inaccurate, however, to suppose that greater acceptance of traditional ways of viewing the body has led us to accept a pluralism of body paradigms and the coexistence of radically different societal ways of treating others' bodies. Even among anthropologists and historians of the non-Western religions, once champions of the parity of cultures, there is a new nervousness about the ramifications of being "value-free," that is, of holding that all worldviews need to be *equally* respected. The new skittishness results, in large part, from heightened awareness that bodies are affected deeply by cultural concepts, and that there may be limits to the extent to which the outside observer can wink at some practices. Researchers today worry more about whether what they say (or do not say) runs the risk of being in implicit collusion with real, sometimes rather horrible, oppression. Scholars with feminist concerns have, of course, been most acutely aware of this problem. If it is true that the women and children of a studied society, relatively powerless therein, are having their bodies forcibly, even painfully, malleated, how far may the toleration of divergent beliefs and practices go?

An openness to each and any form of "malleation" could, then, easily muffle what may be screams of protest from persons being constrained, pierced, and even cut when they do not wish to be. Then what we have is more properly called "maltreatment" or "abuse." And here is where the Western scholar's eagerness to show open-mindedness and toleration runs into a moral wall. The most salient instance of this dilemma is the debate that has centered around what should be said and done about societies that routinely submit females to infibulation or clitorectomy. Religious functionaries in some cultures and subcultures, primarily in Africa, insist that such cuttings are the female counterpart of male circumcision and, in any case, are a part of traditional religion that the Westerner ought not bring under censure. Indignation at what look to be forced violations of the bodies of women and girls is, such apologists insist, merely an instance of Western ideologues pushing their own religious and ethical worldview onto cultures, Islamic and indigenous for the most part, with variant beliefs and practices. Nevertheless, the fact that voices, usually those of women, from *within* those cultures also rail against such practices indicates that the sensitivity to injustice and cruelty is not limited to Westerners or even to feminists.

The religious institutions of the West have hardly been immune from such scrutiny and critique. Finely nuanced accounts of religion and changing sexual moralities in the West, of creative coping strategies devised by medieval women (Bynum 1991), and of the treatment of gay persons within Christendom (Boswell 1980) have been augmented by more scathing indictments of oppression. Right

49

down to the present the obvious power imbalance between, on the one hand, a male-dominated religious institution such as the Roman Catholic Church speaking in the name of its deity to condemn abortion and, on the other hand, women who see abortion as a painful but necessary choice in their lives has made this an agonizingly and deeply contested issue. Questions about bodies and who makes decisions regarding them are central here. Duden (1993) shows how what she calls "ideological gynecology," often spurred on by pronouncements from Christians, has prioritized the fetus as the *only* life deemed inviolable. In all this it is clear that cultural practices and assumptions about metaphysics feature strongly. Japanese society, at least to the extent that Buddhist ideas are influential, shows interesting points of contrast; when it is assumed that an aborted fetus will have other opportunities to reenter the world, abortion appears to be more easily tolerated by religious authorities than when it is assumed, as is most common in Christianity, that an abortee is forever dead (LaFleur 1992).

VII. Metaphors, Cruelty, and Crossed Lines

Instances of religions sanctioning and even abetting corporeal and social abuse are so numerous and so pervasive that persons made aware of these abuses have often tried to envision a society or world that has been liberated from religion itself, and thereby rendered much more moral than any society we have known to date. Marx, of course, provided the classic instance of such an act of envisioning. In the mind of Marx, religion was a narcotic and humanity, through the cold turkey process called "revolution," has the potential to become drug free.

Whether or not that metaphor is apt or adequate is problematic. Therefore, although now we dare not—if we wish to be ethical—ignore how religion will function as ideology, that same ethical imperative compels us to see that the Marxist version of reality may itself have been an eschatological dream. How that account itself was used in practice during the twentieth century to justify the extensive manipulation of minds and unspeakable torturing of bodies suggests an ideology imploding in on itself.

Others, not necessarily Marxist, have been so keenly aware that metaphors can facilitate bodily cruelty that they have wanted to free our social language from it. Susan Sontag (1977) has articulated what others more dimly sensed: illnesses such as tuberculosis, cancer, and AIDS have, largely through the metaphors used by society to depict them, been made more tortuous to their subjects than would otherwise have been the case. Why not free illness of *all* its metaphors? The impulse, most often showing up in the writings of philosophers, to rid ourselves completely of metaphor has been strong. It thrusts forward the question: Would we not all be much better off if we could live our lives no longer socially constrained and even maimed by the society's metaphors? The projection of metaphor-free concepts and discourse, however, has itself more recently come under criticism, through a trajectory of analyses running from Ludwig Wittgenstein to Richard Rorty. Johnson (1987) suggests that the fact that we *are* bodies will make it impossible for us to ever be "free" from metaphor. One implication of this could be that as long as we have bodies, we will have metaphors, and as long as we have metaphors, we will have religion.

To prevent such an insight from serving as an imprimatur on old or new injustices, however, is a moral imperative. Shklar (1984) addresses that problem. She suggests that intellectuals, too often prone to prioritize what they themselves do best—namely, the unmasking of concealed ideologies—should instead "put cruelty first" within the list of practices to be monitored and censured. While not ignoring the need to expose how ideas, including those of religion, frequently put a happy face on grossly immoral structures and actions, Shklar's point, it could be argued, reorders the focus of our ongoing surveillance of ourselves and others. Through this reordering we are urged to monitor first—but not exclusively—what is being done to *bodies*. To "put cruelty first" on the list of objectionable things is also to allow that some ideas, including ones put forward in the name of religion, might be harmless even though patently untrue. Our task should be that of exposing the *specific* metaphor, representation, or religious idea that causes or sanctions cruelty, not the more generalized—and ultimately impossible—task of trying to make a world in which metaphor, narrative, and religion cease to exist. Wittgenstein showed that we cannot live without pictures. We can and must, however, constantly monitor our pictures to see what they are doing or neglecting to do.

Something similar might be said for the attitudes we may need to take with respect to advancing forms of medical technology and biological engineering. Demands that we limit ourselves to what is "natural" fall flat. We have not been natural for a very long time: spectacles, dentures, pacemakers, and condoms—even clothing—moved us over that imaginary line long ago. "Unnatural" will not even work as a rebuke to persons in our society—those with whole-body tattoos, nipple rings, and the like—who malleate their bodies in ways to which the West has not been accustomed.

It is too early to say whether or not these modes of body redesign are a passing fad. Yet, it is perhaps not coincidental that this popular, street public experimentation with modified bodies appears in our own culture precisely at a time when many people are captivated—and probably made anxious—by the development of the cyborg. The human being who will live with infinitely replaceable parts—although, of course, more fully a machine than is now possible—will also have transcended our tendency until now to wear out, malfunction, and die. Metals and synthetic materials will show more durability than flesh. And if immortality is a constituent of deity, it is conceivable that in the future there may be persons who literally, corporeally, become gods *in that sense*.

One after another the things used to erect barriers between traditionally separate categories—"life" to differentiate the organic from the inorganic, language or tool-making to separate humans from putatively lower creatures, "rationality" to distinguish mind from brain, and the like—have been either dismantled or made precarious by new research. Projects to alter our DNA presuppose that information is not just "stored" in brains and libraries but is also in a far more living and mutatible form in our genes.

Natural and artificial interweave. Dagognet (1992), who holds that nature's own malleability is an open invitation to the "artificial," would have us relinquish our fondness even for that distinction. Taylor (1997, 337), who deftly charts how we have gotten where we are today, argues that "virtual reality" is not a limited technology but something "neither real nor nonreal . . . , something other, something that remains fraught with opportunity as well as danger." He sees it as a trope for the current condition of our culture.

Our dilemma arises from our awareness that the whole range of distinctions, long cherished, are false. They are concepts projected onto the world by our anxieties about not being unique or, at least, inherently different from mere "things." In an earlier era the notion of a creator god as having once and for all put such a structure into the creation was the ultimate consolation. That now is gone.

And anxiety seems to result. Recent popular culture is full of it; science and animation cyborg films thrive on it. Moreover, with considerable intelligence films such as those by David Cronenberg—*Scanners, Videodrome, Dead Ringers, The Fly*—express our fascination and our deep fears vis-à-vis our growing potential as a race to change how we look and what we might become (Shaviro 1993). Genetically inheritable malleation has become, for the first time, a real possibility.

Here is an area in which we should be monitoring instances of cruelty rather than becoming preoccupied with some idea of the natural. That is, our sense of what is ethical should be more constrained by what we already know of ourselves than by some supposed, always elusive demarcation line between categories of beings. Actual episodes in the history of our behavior can be instructive here— much more so than some conceptualized zone of divine prerogatives into which we dare not deliberately or inadvertently intrude. The point is that we *already* have knowledge of the kinds of cases in which our technology has carried out agendas rendered impermissible by their cruelty: for instance, Nazi eugenics; the woefully deficient prior testing of chemicals that resulted in thalidomide babies; the virtual hells of Hiroshima and Chernobyl; the bacteriological warfare experiments carried out by Japanese unit 731 in Manchuria; and the deformed bodies that result from industrial pollution.

What is objectionable in these is the resultant intrahuman cruelty, not the passage over some imagined ontological line. Humans, we here have insisted, have been malleating their own bodies, often for religious reasons, for all of known time. And because much of medicine (and surgery most obviously) has itself always involved malleation, the rationale for new levels of bodily and genetic engineering will, we can predict, be articulated in terms that appeal to our habit of assuming that advances in medical technology are altruistically intended and will benefit the needy.

Contemporary religious authorities, especially in Europe and America, have become loath to do anything other than sanction what is promoted as patently beneficial to humankind; medical technology has its own ethical aura. Circumspection here should probably be based on history rather than theology. Instances of science resulting in catastrophic levels of cruelty are numerous. Collectively they tell us that there is something unearned in the *ethical* aura in which much scientific technology has long been basking. The results of technology, including the medical and biological varieties, are often anything but unambiguously positive. Our need to be circumspect arises from what we already know about our own past.

SUGGESTED READINGS

Brown, Peter. 1988. *The Body and Society: Men, Women, and Sexual Renunciation in Early Christianity.*

Bynum, Caroline Walker. 1991. *Fragmentation and Redemption: Essays on Gender and the Human Body in Medieval Religion.*

Camporesi, Piero. 1988. *The Incorruptible Flesh: Bodily Mutilation and Mortification in Religion and Folklore,* translated by Tania Croft-Murray.

Duden, Barbara. 1993. *Disembodying Women: Perspectives on Pregnancy and the Unborn,* translated by Lee Hoinacki.

Feyer, Michel, with Ramona Naddaff and Nadia Tazi. 1989. *Fragments for a History of the Human Body.* 3 vols.

Eliade, Mircea. 1958. *Yoga: Immortality and Freedom,* translated by Willard R. Trask.

Foucault, Michel. 1973. *The Birth of the Clinic: An Archaeology of Medical Perception,* translated by A. M. Sheridan Smith.

Johnson, Mark. 1987. *The Body in the Mind: The Bodily Basis of Meaning, Imagination, and Reason.*

Kasulis, Thomas P., Roger T. Ames, and Wimal Dissanayake. 1993. *Self as Body in Asian Theory and Practice.*

LaFleur, William R. 1992. *Liquid Life: Abortion and Buddhism in Japan.*

Moore, Stephen. 1996. *God's Gym: Divine Male Bodies of the Bible.*

Scarry, Elaine. 1985. *The Body in Pain: The Making and Unmaking of the World.*

Sivin, Nathan. 1987. *Traditional Medicine in Contemporary China.*

Sontag, Susan. 1977. *Illness as Metaphor.*

Taylor, Mark C. 1997. *Hiding.*

Yuasa, Yasuo. 1987. *The Body: Toward an Eastern Mind-Body Theory.*

REFERENCES

Boswell, John. 1980. *Christianity, Social Tolerance, and Homosexuality: Gay People in Western Europe from the Beginning of the Christian Era to the Fourteenth Century.* Chicago: University of Chicago Press.

Brown, Peter. 1988. *The Body and Society: Men, Women, and Sexual Renunciation in Early Christianity*. New York: Columbia University Press.

Bynum, Caroline Walker. 1991. *Fragmentation and Redemption: Essays on Gender and the Human Body in Medieval Religion*. New York: Zone Books.

Camporesi, Piero. 1988. *The Incorruptible Flesh: Bodily Mutilation and Mortification in Religion and Folklore,* translated by Tania Croft-Murray. Cambridge: Cambridge University Press.

Dagognet, François. 1992. "Toward a Biopsychiatry," translated by Donald M. Leslie. In *Incorporations,* edited by Jonathan Crary and Sanford Kwinter. New York: Zone Books.

Duden, Barbara. 1993. *Disembodying Women: Perspectives on Pregnancy and the Unborn,* translated by Lee Hoinacki. Cambridge: Harvard University Press.

Eliade, Mircea. 1958. *Yoga: Immortality and Freedom,* translated by Willard R. Trask. Princeton: Princeton University Press.

Feyer, Michel, with Ramona Naddaff and Nadia Tazi. 1989. *Fragments for a History of the Human Body.* 3 vols. New York: Zone Books.

Foucault, Michel. 1973. *The Birth of the Clinic: An Archaeology of Medical Perception,* translated by A. M. Sheridan Smith. New York: Random House.

Fox, Renée C., and Judith P. Swazey. 1992. *Spare Parts: Organ Replacement in American Society.* New York: Oxford University Press.

James, William. 1902. *The Varieties of Religious Experience: A Study in Human Nature.* New York: Longmans.

Johnson, Mark. 1987. *The Body in the Mind: The Bodily Basis of Meaning, Imagination, and Reason.* Chicago: University of Chicago Press.

LaFleur, William R. 1992. *Liquid Life: Abortion and Buddhism in Japan.* Princeton: Princeton University Press.

Mitamura, Taisuke. 1970. *Chinese Eunuchs: The Structure of Intimate Politics,* translated by Charles A. Pomerov. Rutland, Vt.: Charles E. Tuttle.

Moore, Stephen. 1996. *God's Gym: Divine Male Bodies of the Bible.* New York: Routledge.

Ramsey, Paul. 1970. *Fabricated Man: The Ethics of Genetic Control.* New Haven: Yale University Press.

Roberts, K. B., and J. D. W. Tomlinson. 1992. *The Fabric of the Body: European Traditions of Anatomical Illustration.* Oxford: Clarendon Press.

Scarry, Elaine. 1985. *The Body in Pain: The Making and Unmaking of the World.* New York: Oxford University Press.

Shaviro, Steven. 1993. *The Cinematic Body.* Minneapolis: University of Minnesota Press.

Shklar, Judith N. 1984. *Ordinary Vices.* Cambridge: Harvard University Press.

Sivin, Nathan. 1987. *Traditional Medicine in Contemporary China.* Ann Arbor: Center for Chinese Studies, University of Michigan.

Sontag, Susan. 1977. *Illness as Metaphor.* New York: Farrar Strauss and Giroux.

Taylor, Mark C. 1997. *Hiding.* Chicago: University of Chicago Press.

Yuasa, Yasuo. 1987. *The Body: Toward an Eastern Mind-Body Theory.* Albany: State University of New York Press.

THREE

Conflict

Bruce Lincoln

There are many fine studies of individual conflicts in which religious groups and issues have figured prominently (Mooney 1896; Hodgson 1955; Cohn 1970; Boyer and Nissebaum 1974; Naquin 1976; Appadurai 1981; Fields 1985; Powell 1986; Peires 1989; Diefendorf 1991; Nirenberg 1996). Similarly abundant are discussions of what might constitute a "just war" under various interpretations of Christian doctrine, given the propensity of theologians and ethicists to rehearse that topic whenever the troops ship out (most recently, Johnson and Kelsay 1991; Walzer 1992; Elshtain 1992). Beyond these bodies of literature and those that chart the conflict between religion and science or other sorts of discourse (Neusner 1989; Drees 1996; cf. Draper 1875), several major schools of social analysis and criticism also offer clear, if unidimensional, understandings of the relations they take to obtain between religion and conflict.

Functionalism, for instance, understands religion as something almost antithetical to conflict, construing it either as a sanctification of the well-integrated social totality and its collective representations (Durkheim 1915) or, alternatively, as one of the primary instruments through which otherwise threatening conflicts can be contained and rendered socially productive (Hubert and Mauss 1964; Girard 1977). In contrast, those of more critical orientation theorize religion as a misguided response to the types of conflict they take to be salient, and for which they claim to offer more effective and realistic remedies. Thus, for example, orthodox psychoanalysts treat religion as a displacement of oedipal turmoil (Freud 1918, 1939; Reik 1975), while Marxists of equal orthodoxy regard it as a mystificatory response to processes of exploitation and class struggle (Marx and Engels 1964; Bloch 1989).

Mythic materials also frequently thematize conflict and have received much scholarly attention. Vedic hymns, for example, provide divine prototypes for cattle raids and invest this relatively squalid activity with nothing less than cosmogonic significance (Srinivasan 1979; Lincoln 1981). Babylonian and Greek myth treat creation as involving the victory of one set of deities over another, while Irish, Iranian, and Germanic narratives describe similar conflicts that are resolved by compromise but hold the promise of breaking out again with catastrophic consequences (Oosten 1985; Wilson 1979). At times, the distinctions among myth, scholarship, and ideology become seriously blurred, as in the master narrative of European racism, which made categories of nineteenth century research into language and myth the basis for a pointed contrast of "Aryan" and "Semite," and narrated their largely imaginary conflict from primordial beginnings to the all-too-real attempts at a "final solution" (Rosenberg 1935; Poliakov 1974; von See 1994).

For the most part, however, serious students of conflict in the twentieth century have concerned themselves rather little with questions of religion, and students of religion have been only too happy to return the favor (a regrettably simplistic and occasionally hysterical exception is Huntington 1996). Although other factors have contributed to this unfortunate distribution of intellectual labor, it reflects the relatively minor role religion has played in the wars fought by European and American powers since the struggles associated with the Protestant Reformation. In truth, the form these powers have characteristically taken— that of the secular nation-state (the nation being a self-consciously cohesive population and the state a governmental apparatus that manages their relations) —was shaped in response to those same wars of religion, which are best understood not just as the struggle of Protestants against Catholics but as a tripartite affair. Thus, the ideological, political, and military challenge mounted by Protestants in the sixteenth and seventeenth centuries effectively ended the medieval church's position as the dominant and defining institution of society, without that role passing to the Protestant camp. Rather, the long-term beneficiary of this brutal conflict was the modern nation-state, which emerged in England, France, and later elsewhere following lines of theory initiated by Hobbes in the wake of the Thirty Years' War and the English Revolution, which were pursued thereafter by Enlightenment philosophes up through Kant.

Equipped by the philosophes with a social contract theory that derived legitimacy from the people who constitute the nation, rather than from God, the early modern state was freed of its ideological dependence on the church, and increased its power at the latter's expense, assuming an ever larger share of functions that had previously fallen under religious purview: education, moral discipline and surveillance, social relief, record keeping, guarantee of contracts, and so on. Conversely, the scope and influence of religious institutions (now in the plural rather than the singular) were greatly attenuated, as religion—disarticulated from its symbiotic relation with the state—was reconceived as an element of a rapidly expanding civil society in which competing institutions and forms of discourse (arts, sciences, philosophy, secular ideologies, journalism, popular opinion, folk wisdom, etc.) also had their place.

The world of the eighteenth, nineteenth, and twentieth centuries is, in large measure, the product of the processes just described. As Europe imposed its model of the nation-state on the rest of the globe, political institutions detached themselves from religious ones and eclipsed their former partners almost everywhere. One result of this was that international conflicts came to be fought primarily on the basis of state allegiances and material interests rather than religious commitments. Or so it seemed until recent years, when a large number of conflicts have arisen in which religious issues and identities once again play a major and, in many cases, a defining part. It is particularly significant, moreover, that most of these are fought in contexts where structural problems inherent to the nation-state have become manifest: specifically, the potential contradiction between nation and state.

Briefly, and at the risk of overly schematic generalization, I would like to sketch out in Weberian manner four ideal types of conflict that have become common in recent decades. In order that their differences may become clear, I will cite several examples of each type, and offer a summary diagram that calls attention to three separate moments. Thus, prior to the outbreak of conflict proper, the tensions, contradictions, and lines of cleavage are still contained within the nation-state of the status quo ante. Then, as a result of precipitating factors, which are so varied and locally contingent as to defy generalization, specific fractions of the preexisting nation commit themselves to a struggle against others and also, quite often, against the state. Finally, it is possible to identify a moment when the outcome of that struggle—actual or desired—becomes apparent.

Religious Reconstruction of the State

Even in nations where the population is relatively homogeneous with regard to its religious affiliation, states designed along the Enlightenment model still tend to define themselves as secular: that is, officially neutral and benevolently disinterested in questions pertaining to religion. The initial appearance of homogeneity may be deceptive, however, since broad variation often exists regarding the nature and intensity of the religious commitments held by different fractions of the nation. Some of these accept and are pleased by state neutrality, while others are deeply offended, particularly as they find themselves and their specifically religious concerns excluded from state support and consideration.

In this situation, certain clergy and laypersons may come to understand and portray themselves as the most—or indeed the only—faithful adherents of the nation's traditional religion. Such actors find they can make effective use of religious language, symbols, and signs of identity to authorize mass struggles against the secularity of the state. Initially, their goal may be limited to forcing revision of specific policies: abortion laws in the United States, Sabbath closings in Israel, the sexual content of movies or standards for women's dress in Pahlavi Iran, to cite some obvious examples. Confrontations of this sort can play out in many ways, but the Iranian example reveals the extent of their potential, even when the state in question is relatively powerful by all conventional measures (Fischer 1980; Salehi 1988; Moaddel 1993; Ram 1994).

In dealing with the demands of aggrieved groups who claim to represent the religious nation, a secular state runs clear risks. Should its responses be—or be perceived as—dismissive, insulting, indecisive, inconsistent, provocative, heavy handed, arrogant, patronizing, or unsatisfactory in countless other fashions, leaders of such groups may use this to telling advantage. Most traditions possess a large discursive repertoire that knowledgeable actors can deploy, in open or

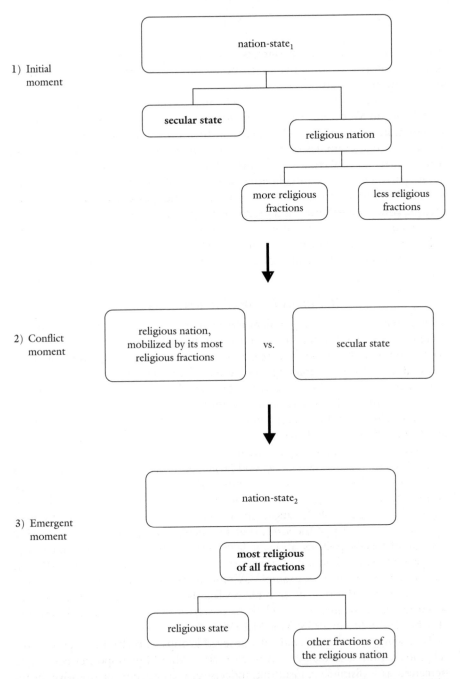

Fig. 3.1. Religious reconstruction of the state. Power relations among the various entities are marked by primacy along left-right and up-down axes. The dominant entity is also marked by boldface type.

densely coded fashion, to identify their immediate campaign with a sacred and transcendent cause, while representing themselves as heroic defenders of the faith against demonic opponents.

As such rhetoric finds and persuades its audience, the movement will grow and may ultimately gain the ability to face down repressive organs of the state, which are, after all, staffed by people who share their religious identity and convictions, at least in nominal fashion. A crucial moment may come when rank and file soldiers have to decide whether to obey orders to fire on crowds. At issue is the question of whether their ties of affinity to those who identify themselves with the (religious) nation are more compelling than the demands of loyalty and obedience to their superiors, who defend the (secular) state. Should they decide not to shoot, as happened during the Iranian Revolution, other changes will rapidly follow.

As insurgents meet with success and gain hope of winning the struggle, their goals may well expand from the desire to reform select policies to that of seizing power and reconstructing the state along explicitly, even rigorously, religious lines. Examples other than the Islamic Revolution in Iran might include the activity of the Muslim Brotherhood in Egypt and Algeria, the Welfare Party in Turkey, the Taliban militia in Afghanistan, Orthodox activists in Israel (Gush Emunim, Kach, etc.), Hamas in Palestine, the Religious Right in the United States, and—to cite a more historic example—the crusade waged by Falangists, Carlists, and Cedistas in the Spanish Civil War (see figure 3.1).

Construction of a Religious Hegemony

Somewhat different is the situation of a secular state and a religiously pluralist nation, for here an important part of the state's ideological justification is the claim that it alone is capable of maintaining peace among the religious groups within its borders while exercising evenhanded power over them. This is the model developed in Europe during the Enlightenment, and designed to preclude the internecine slaughter of the wars of religion. Beyond its local usefulness, it also had advantages when European powers extended their reach into Africa and Asia during the eighteenth and nineteenth centuries, since it permitted them to aggregate local populations of widely different languages, religions, and cultures within a single colony. Here, the new overlords could maintain control of "the natives" by playing one fraction off against another, all the while claiming that their presence was necessary to protect vulnerable minorities against their more numerous, bellicose, or "savage" neighbors.

As Europeans withdrew from their overseas empires, they bequeathed this model of the secular nation-state to their former colonial subjects, making it part of their price for departure. Whatever its benefits—and they are not negligible—it remains inconsistent with precolonial traditions, and insofar as it bestows state power on the most successfully Westernized fractions of the population, it has created numerous difficulties. Of particular interest is the situation that develops

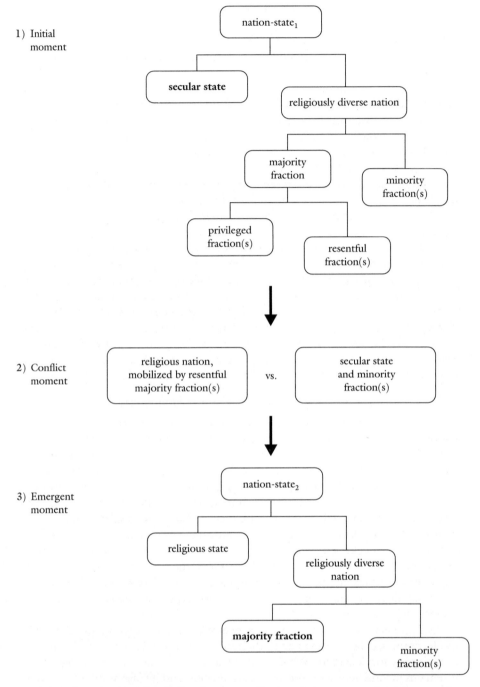

1) Initial
   moment

nation-state₁

secular state

religiously diverse nation

majority
fraction

minority
fraction(s)

privileged
fraction(s)

resentful
fraction(s)

2) Conflict
   moment

religious nation,
mobilized by resentful
majority fraction(s)

vs.

secular state
and minority
fraction(s)

3) Emergent
   moment

nation-state₂

religious state

religiously diverse
nation

majority fraction

minority
fraction(s)

Fig. 3.2. Construction of a religious hegemony. Power relations among the various entities are marked by primacy along left-right and up-down axes. The dominant entity is also marked by boldface type.

when members of the majority religion in postcolonial nations feel that the state operates to their systematic disadvantage, while benefiting members of the minority religions: people from whom they may also feel estranged on other grounds. In such circumstances, the disaffected can find powerful instruments of agitation and mobilization in narratives that recall the former grandeur of "their" nation, when it was constituted primarily, if not exclusively, by their coreligionists, whose interests were protected by a state whose power and very existence were sacralized by its mission of supporting their religion. In such narratives—as much mythic as historic—they imagine and seek to realize the future they desire.

By way of example, one could cite the situation of Sinhala Buddhists in Sri Lanka and that of Muslims in the Sudan. The best example, however, is India, where a large fraction of the Hindu population, composed of those whose caste, education, and income let them expect neither important positions within the state nor substantial largesse from it, has embraced a militant Hindu nationalism, as championed by the Bharatiya Janata Party (BJP) (Embree 1990; van der Veer 1994; McKean 1996). Among the items that figure prominently in BJP rhetoric are invocations of past Hindu glory, depictions of Muslims as eternal enemies (never members!) of the Indian nation, and the charge that Muslims and other minorities retain unfair preferences and advantages introduced by the English. Among the party's most spectacular initiatives was the campaign that led to the 1992 destruction of the Babri Masjid mosque in Ayodhya that stood on the putative site of the god Rama's birthplace. Although this act prompted weeks of communal violence throughout India, the BJP emerged with more support than ever, and electoral victories in 1996 brought it briefly to power. Although its government fell quickly for lack of parliamentary allies, it remains a force to reckon with, and one committed to a vision of the Indian state as a Hindu entity (see figure 3.2).

Schism Along Religious Lines

The third case begins more or less where the second leaves off; that is, with a situation in which the dominant religious fraction of a pluralist nation enjoys systemic advantages vis-à-vis all others, including effective if not necessarily unmediated or total control over the state. In such instances. the state may or may not be defined as religious but even when nominally secular, it is anything but evenhanded. Particularly complicated are colonial situations like that of Northern Ireland (and before 1921 of Ireland as a whole), where state power is in the hands of foreigners who favor the local fraction with which they have religious affinity (Fulton 1991; Smith and Chambers 1991; Buckley 1995).

When the unequal distribution of advantages from the state—jobs and funds, for example, but also such things as simple respect and protection under law—is chronic and grievous, or perceived to be so, those fractions that suffer (usually minorities, but not necessarily so, as the example of prepartition Ireland dem-

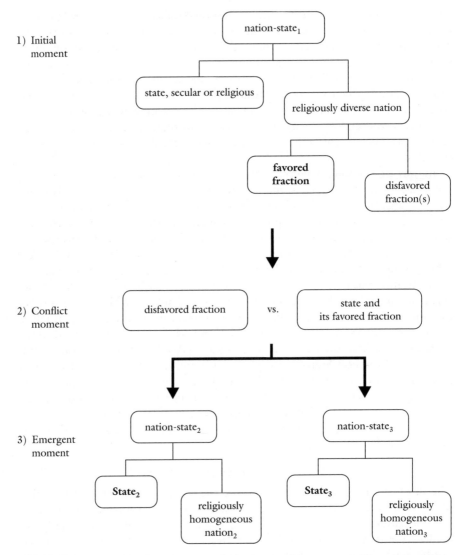

1) Initial
   moment

2) Conflict
   moment

3) Emergent
   moment

Fig. 3.3. Schism. Power relations among the various entities are marked by primacy along left-right and up-down axes. The dominant entity is also marked by boldface type.

onstrates) can mobilize around their religious identity to challenge those of other faiths and the state that prefers them. Independence is usually their goal, as in the case of the Palestinian *intifada* against Israel and the struggles of Tamil Hindus against Sinhalese Buddhists in Sri Lanka and of Tibetan Buddhists against China. Alternatively, insurgents may pursue union with a nation-state controlled by their coreligionists, a strategy that worked for the Muslim minority of Cyprus, and is favored by Catholics in Northern Ireland. In all of these cases, the issue of whether the new state is religious need not arise, so long as it can be expected to support the religious nation constituted by the insurgents (see figure 3.3).

Devolution

Finally, there is the situation in which a modern nation-state deconstructs in decidedly postmodern fashion. At such times, groups that were encompassed in the decaying formation may take advantage of the state's (temporary?) weakness to reassert other sorts of identity. Should leadership fall to their most militant fractions—as is likely to happen—they may also wage open war against once and future rivals, the state included. Sometimes the groups, causes, and communities to which people commit themselves on such occasions have little connection to issues of religion, as is the case for Somalia, Liberia, Rwanda and Burundi where lines of kinship, ethnicity, patronage, and geography define the lines of cleavage. But religion can also play a role of decisive importance, as was true in the partitions of India and Palestine at the end of colonial rule and in the Lebanese civil war of the 1970s and 1980s.

Elsewhere, religious considerations may be one of several correlated bases for the construction of communal identities, insofar as they replicate ethnic and linguistic lines of division. Thus, Bosnian Muslims, Catholic Croats, and Orthodox Serbs battle each other in the Balkans, while in the Caucasus Christian Armenians fight Muslim Azerbaijanis and Muslim Chechens fight the Russian state, which is as ethnically and religiously alien to them in its present as it was in its previous incarnations (Ramet 1989; Ramet 1992; Bringa 1995; Sells 1996). There is a chaotic turbulence to all these conflicts where contending parties struggle awkwardly toward multiple goals. These include putting an end to an old, constraining state; constructing a new one of a different sort and along different lines; constructing (or reconstructing) a coherent and more or less homogeneous nation; extricating themselves from lingering connections to other emergent nations, from whom they feel bitterly estranged but who were recently fellow subjects of the same state; winning international recognition, financial, and diplomatic support; and gaining whatever territory and booty are possible at their enemies' expense.

Such cases are not limited to postcommunist environments, and one can imagine scenarios in which Nigeria could come apart (as it almost did during the Biafran Civil War of 1967–70), or the Canadian state could give way to new nations constituted by francophone Catholics, anglophone Protestants, and indigenous peoples. Still, it is probably no accident that the most spectacularly destructive situations should have arisen in the former Yugoslavia and the former Soviet Union. Here, disparate nationalities were dominated by atheist states unconstrained by the Enlightenment model of secularity and evenhandedness in matters of religion. Rather, they undertook the more radical project of suppress-

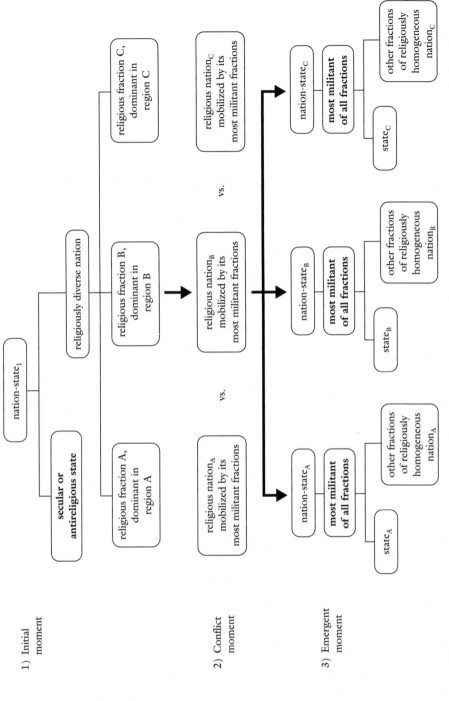

Fig. 3.4. Devolution. Power relations among the various entities are marked by primacy along left-right and up-down axes. The dominant entity is also marked by boldface type. Note that nation-state$_A$, nation-state$_B$, and nation-state$_C$ may themselves be subject to further processes of evolution, schism, and atomization.

ing religious ideology and institutions to the best of their ability. With the inevitable reassertion of the repressed, religion became a favored site of resistance to the state and a privileged instrument for rallying nationalist sentiment. Reactions of this sort are apparent in Poland, Afghanistan, and Tibet and, with less success in opposing anticlerical regimes of earlier sorts, the Cristero movement of the Mexican Revolution and the Vendée rising in France (see figure 3.4).

Beyond the State

Confronted with the disquieting reality of religious conflict, popular wisdom typically comforts itself with the ironist's refrain: "How sad to see wars in the name of religion, when all religions preach peace." However well intentioned such sentiments may be, they manage to ignore the fact that virtually all religions allow for the righteous use of violence under certain circumstances (e.g., self defense), the definitions of which have proven conveniently elastic. In similar fashion, academic commentators often regard the religious side of conflicts like those in Sri Lanka or Northern Ireland as relatively unimportant or, alternatively, they deplore it as a debasement of all that is properly religious. Although one can empathize with those who offer such views (Tambiah 1992, for example), their analyses rest on an understanding of what constitutes religion that is simultaneously idealized and impoverished: a "Protestant" view that takes beliefs and moral injunctions (such as those that normally inhibit conflict) to be the essence of the religious, while ignoring most other aspects that might be included.

Preferable, in my opinion, is a model in which "religion" involves multiple components that can relate to one another in a variety of ways, including disjuncture and contradiction. These components include (a) a discourse that claims its concerns transcend the realm of the human, temporal, and contingent, while claiming for itself a similarly transcendent status; (b) a set of practices (ethical, ritual, and sometimes also aesthetic) informed and structured by that discourse; (c) a community organized around the discourse and its attendant practices, whose members define their identity with reference to them; and (d) an institutional system that regulates discourse, practices, and community, reproducing and modifying them over time, while still asserting their eternal validity and transcendent value. Whenever any of these components plays a role of some seriousness within a given conflict, one ought to acknowledge that the conflict has a religious dimension. Considerations of community have proved particularly volatile.

For the sake of completeness, I should also indicate that I take conflict to be the situation that arises when rival interests can no longer be denied, deflected, negotiated, or contained by the structures and processes ordinarily competent to do so. As a result, after an indeterminate period of confusion and crisis, normal competition moves into phases that are more open, bitter, confrontational, costly, and violent. Like all others, communities and institutions that define themselves in terms of religion still wage their conflicts primarily around rival claims to scarce resources: people, territory, wealth, positions of power and economic advantage, as well as such nonmaterial resources as dignity, prestige, and symbolic capital. Unlike other groups, however, those with a religious cohesiveness are concerned to reconcile the gritty nature of their struggles with the precepts featured in their discourse, a task that may be sufficiently difficult as to prompt a highly selective reading of texts and tradition, along with the most ingeniously strained hermeneutics.

When relevant actors fulfill this task to their own satisfaction, they are able to define themselves and their cause as both moral and holy. Beyond that, they can define the goods they desire in similar terms: sacred land, sacred offices, sacred symbols. Similarly, they can construe their enemies as desolate populations (e.g., "infidels," "pagans," "heretics") waiting to be brought into their sacred community. Such understandings condition the morale, intensity, and commitment of those who accept them, and they have the potential to transform even the most sordid squabbles into *jihads* and crusades from which retreat, surrender, and compromise are equally inconceivable.

The modern nation-state was created, in large measure, as a check against the violence and destruction unleashed in religious conflicts of this sort. For the past three centuries it has succeeded in this task, if not in that of suppressing conflict more broadly. Rather, wars between states replaced wars between religions as the largest and most common form of conflict, as the state sought to constitute itself—as Lenin put it—as a monopoly on the legitimate use of force. Even so, the state acknowledged limitations on its ability to legitimate its own violence, as on the many occasions when it relied on docile religious institutions to obligingly consecrate its wars. And when the state launched campaigns of such horrific violence that no institution and no means could cover them with even a fig leaf version of legitimacy, the Enlightenment model of the nation-state found itself irreparably compromised. The Jewish Holocaust and other Nazi atrocities, of course, are the prime example, alongside which one could cite the genocidal actions of Turkey against its Armenian Christians or those of Australia, Guatemala, and the United States against their indigenous populations.

In recent years, contradictions between nation and state have also manifested themselves in particularly debilitating fashion. Where this is so, it has proven relatively easy for militant fractions of the population to wage aggressive campaigns in which they seek to redefine the principles on which nation and state are constituted, and the ways they relate to each other. Of the instruments they have used for mobilization, religious discourse and practice have often been among the most effective, just as their appeals to a sense of religious community have been among the most powerful bases for a novel sense of collective identity.

Inevitably, there is the question of what may be reasonably expected in the future, and here our reading of the past may permit us to advance only the most tentative speculations. For much as the first age of religious wars left the institution of the medieval church fragmented and diminished in power, so also may the current wave of conflicts leave the nation-state similarly reduced in scope and stature, with multinational corporations, multimedia communications conglomerates, and transcontinental mafias of other sorts poised to take up the slack. The sole scenario we can confidently rule out is that religion—or anything else—will put an end to conflict.

SUGGESTED READINGS

Adas, Michael. 1979. *Prophets of Rebellion: Millennarian Protest Movements against the European Colonial Order.*

Aho, James. 1982. *Religious Mythology and the Art of War: Comparative Religious Symbolisms of Military Violence.*

Allen, Douglas, ed. 1992. *Religion and Political Conflict in South Asia: India, Pakistan, and Sri Lanka.*

Arjomand, Said, ed. 1993. *The Political Dimensions of Religion.*

Dekmejian, R. Hrair. 1995. *Islam in Revolution: Fundamentalism in the Arab World.*

Hobsbawm, E. J. 1959. *Primitive Rebels: Studies in Archaic Forms of Social Movement in the Nineteenth and Twentieth Centuries.*

Juergensmeyer, Mark. 1993. *The New Cold War? Religious Nationalism Confronts the Secular State.*

Kapferer, Bruce. 1988. *Legends of People, Myths of State: Violence, Intolerance, and Political Culture in Sri Lanka and Australia.*

Lanternari, Vittorio. 1963. *Religions of the Oppressed: A Study of Modern Messianic Cults.*

Lincoln, Bruce, ed. 1985. *Religion, Rebellion, Revolution: An Interdisciplinary and Cross-cultural Collection of Essays.*

Riemer, Neal, ed. 1996. *Let Justice Roll! Prophetic Challenges in Religion, Politics, and Society.*

See, Katherine. 1986. *First World Nationalisms: Class and Ethnic Politics in Northern Ireland and Quebec.*

Tambiah, Stanley. 1996. *Leveling Crowds: Ethnonationalist Conflicts and Collective Violence in South Asia.*

Westerlund, David, ed. 1996. *Questioning the Secular State: The Worldwide Resurgence of Religion in Politics.*

REFERENCES

Appadurai, Arjun. 1981. *Worship and Conflict under Colonial Rule: A South Indian Case.* Cambridge: Cambridge University Press.

Bloch, Maurice. 1989. *Ritual, History, and Power: Selected Papers in Anthropology.* Atlantic Highlands, N.J.: Athlone Press.

Boyer, Paul, and Stephen Nissebaum. 1974. *Salem Possessed: The Social Origins of Witchcraft*. Cambridge: Harvard University Press.

Bringa, Tone. 1995. *Being Muslim the Bosnian Way: Identity and Community in a Central Bosnian Village*. Princeton: Princeton University Press.

Buckley, Anthony. 1995. *Negotiating Identity: Rhetoric, Metaphor, and Social Drama in Northern Ireland*. Washington, D.C.: Smithsonian Institution Press.

Cohn, Norman. 1970. *The Pursuit of the Millennium: Revolutionary Millenarians and Mystical Anarchists of the Middle Ages*. Rev. ed. New York: Oxford University Press.

Diefendorf, Barbara. 1991. *Beneath the Cross: Catholics and Huguenots in Sixteenth-Century Paris*. New York: Oxford University Press.

Draper, William. 1875. *A History of the Conflict between Science and Religion*. New York: Appleton.

Drees, Willem. 1996. *Religion, Science, and Naturalism*. Cambridge: Cambridge University Press.

Durkheim, Emile. 1915. *The Elementary Forms of the Religious Life*. London: Allen and Unwin.

Elshtain, Jean Bethke. 1992. *Just War Theory*. Oxford: Blackwell.

Embree, Ainslie. 1990. *Utopias in Conflict: Religion and Nationalism in Modern India*. Berkeley and Los Angeles: University of California Press.

Fields, Karen. 1985. *Revival and Rebellion in Colonial Central Africa*. Princeton: Princeton University Press.

Fischer, Michael M. J. 1980. *Iran: From Religious Dispute to Revolution*. Cambridge: Harvard University Press.

Freud, Sigmund. 1918. *Totem and Taboo: Resemblances between the Psychic Lives of Savages and Neurotics*, translated by James Strachey. New York: Moffatt, Yard.

———. 1939. *Moses and Monotheism*, translated by James Strachey. New York: Knopf.

Fulton, John. 1991. *The Tragedy of Belief: Religion, Division, and Politics in Ireland*. New York: Oxford University Press.

Girard, René. 1977. *Violence and the Sacred*, translated by Patrick Gregory. Baltimore: Johns Hopkins University Press.

Hodgson, Marshall. 1955. *The Order of Assassins: The Struggle of the Early Nizari Ismailis against the Islamic World*. The Hague: Mouton.

Hubert, Henri, and Marcel Mauss. 1964. *Sacrifice: Its Nature and Function*, translated by W. D. Halls. Chicago: University of Chicago Press.

Huntington, Samuel. 1996. *The Clash of Civilizations and the Remaking of World Order*. New York: Simon & Schuster.

Johnson, James, and John Kelsay, eds. 1991. *Just War and Jihad: Historical and Theoretical Perspectives on War and Peace in Western and Islamic Tradition*. New York: Greenwood Press.

Lincoln, Bruce. 1981. *Priests, Warriors, and Cattle: A Study in the Ecology of Religions*. Berkeley and Los Angeles: University of California Press.

———. 1986. *Discourse and the Construction of Society*. New York: Oxford University Press.

Marx, Karl, and Friedrich Engels. 1964. *On Religion*. New York: Schocken Books.

McKean, Lise. 1996. *Divine Enterprise: Gurus and the Hindu Nationalist Movement*. Chicago: University of Chicago Press.

Moaddel, Mansoor. 1993. *Class, Politics, and Ideology in the Iranian Revolution*. New York: Columbia University Press.

Mooney, James. 1896. *The Ghost Dance Religion and the Sioux Outbreak of 1890*. Washington, D.C.: Bureau of American Ethnography.

Naquin, Susan. 1976. *Millenarian Rebellion in China: The Eight Trigrams Rising of 1813*. New Haven: Yale University Press.

Neusner, Jacob, Ernest R. Frerichs, and Paul V. M. Flesher, eds. 1989. *Religion, Science, and Magic: In Concert and Conflict*. New York: Oxford University Press.

Nirenberg, Robert. 1996. *Communities of Violence: Persecution of Minorities in the Middle Ages*. Princeton: Princeton University Press.

Oosten, Jarich G. 1985. *The War of the Gods: The Social Code in Indo-European Mythology.* London: Routledge and Kegan Paul.

Peires, J. B. 1989. *The Dead Will Arise: Nonqawuse and the Great Xhosa Cattle-Killing Movement of 1856–1857.* Bloomington: Indiana University Press.

Poliakov, Leon. 1974. *The Aryan Myth: A History of Racist and Nationalist Ideas in Europe.* New York: Basic Books.

Powell, James. 1986. *Anatomy of a Crusade, 1213–1221.* Philadelphia: University of Pennsylvania Press.

Ram, Haggay. 1994. *Myth and Mobilization in Revolutionary Iran: The Use of the Friday Congregational Sermon.* Washington, D.C.: American University Press, 1994.

Ramet, Pedro, ed. 1989. *Religion and Nationalism in Soviet and East European Politics.* Durham, N.C.: Duke University Press.

Ramet, Sabrina. 1992. *Balkan Babel: Politics, Religion, and Culture in Yugoslavia.* Boulder, Colo.: Westview Press.

Reik, Theodore. 1975. *Dogma and Compulsion: Psychoanalytic Studies of Religion and Myths.* Westport, Conn.: Greenwood Press.

Rosenberg, Alfred. 1935. *Der Mythus des 20. Jahrhunderts: Eine Wertung der seelisch-geistigen Gestaltenkampfe unserer Zeit.* Munich: Hoheneichen Verlag.

Salehi, M. M. 1988. *Insurgency through Culture and Religion: The Islamic Revolution of Iran.* New York: Praeger.

See, Klaus von. 1994. *Barbar, Germane, Arier: Die Suche nach der Identität der Deutschen.* Heidelberg: Carl Winter.

Sells, Michael. 1996. *The Bridge Betrayed: Religion and Genocide in Bosnia.* Berkeley and Los Angeles: University of California Press.

Smith, David, and Gerald Chambers. 1991. *Inequality in Northern Ireland.* New York: Oxford University Press.

Srinivasan, Doris. 1979. *The Concept of Cow in the Rigveda.* Delhi: Motilal Banarsidas.

Tambiah, Stanley J. 1992. *Buddhism Betrayed? Religion, Politics, and Violence in Sri Lanka.* Chicago: University of Chicago Press.

Veer, Peter van der. 1994. *Religious Nationalism: Hindus and Muslims in India.* Berkeley and Los Angeles: University of California Press.

Walzer, Michael. 1992. *Just and Unjust Wars: A Moral Argument with Historical Illustrations.* New York: Basic Books.

Wilson, J. V. Kinnier. 1979. *The Rebel Lands: An Investigation into the Origins of Early Mesopotamian Mythology.* Cambridge: Cambridge University Press.

Culture

Tomoko Masuzawa

Few terms are more foundational to our sense of reality and more thoroughly naturalized in our everyday discourse than "culture." It is indeed difficult for us to imagine a time when the term or the concept was not available for regular use, but the notion of culture in the sense familiar to us— like "art," "race," "class," and "religion," which are intimately related to it—is of modern origin. Having its prenatal stirring in the eighteenth century, the concept of culture was ushered to life by a series of ground-shifting transformations of the nineteenth century in the ever expanding domain of the West. According to Raymond Williams, who first brought to general attention the historical emergence of these and other related concepts, "culture" is for us one of the most important reality-constituting terms, or key words; it embodies the spectrum of intellectual responses to the "general pattern of change" (Williams 1983, xvii) that we associate with modernity, such as industrialization, democratization, and, we may add in light of the more recent works by Edward Said, Eric Wolf, Michael Taussig, and others, the forceful globalization of "the West" in the form of colonial and postcolonial processes.

In the contemporary use of the terms, the relation between "culture" and "religion" appears to be multiple, complex, and contradictory to some extent. First, in a highly ordinary sense, religion is seen as one of the cultural aspects or institutions of a given society. (Many classical ethnographic accounts and many monographs on individual nations are typically organized in this way.) If at times religion is to culture as a part is to the whole, at other times the synecdochic relation amounts to a plain equation, with the result that in such cases culture is considered more or less synonymous with religion. With regard to "premodern" and "theocratic" societies especially, it is often suggested that religion is coextensive with the entire national culture. On the other hand, most notably in the language of theologians and other partisans of religion, religion is claimed to be that which always and necessarily exceeds culture, something essentially distinct from, surpassing, and sometimes standing decidedly against "mere culture." But even when religion and culture are thus viewed as separate, there is typically a presumption of an intimate relation or complicity between the two, or of a commanding and controlling influence of one over the other. Hence we often think of the mainstream culture of the United States as having been largely determined by particular strands of Protestant Christianity, whereas religion is said to undergo metamorphosis over time and take on culture-specific characteristics as presumably happened when, for example, Buddhism migrated from its native India to China and farther east. In the quintessentially "modern" societies of Western Europe and North America, culture is envisaged as a vehicle, at its best, for the most profound and essential thoughts and attitudes underlying religion. The assumption here is that, in a society such as "ours," something like the general essence of religion, which is perforce less tangible and more universal than any particular religion (and is nowadays often referred to as spirituality), *used to be* embodied in religious institutions but now has been partially liberated from those traditional institutional confinements and can find more personal, "freer" expressions through a variety of cultural venues. This deinstitutionalization takes place, supposedly, as society becomes "modernized" and "secularized."

The overwhelming sense that somehow all this is self-evident tends to mask an important reality: the categories religion and culture in these configurations are both historically specific, fairly recent formations, and our daily employment of these terms, however natural and uncontroversial it may seem, is in fact mobilizing and energizing a powerful ideology of modernity, both feeding on and feeding into a certain logic that is central to our notion of who we are and what we are. Our sense of worth and self-identity as moderns is very much vested in a particular conception of selfhood. We bank on the assumption that the self is an intrinsically free, unitary center of each person, a pure point of subjectivity; and we count on the assumption, moreover, that it is our conscious possession of this essential individuality that makes us different from nonmoderns. According to this ideology, the modern self is the quintessential self: it is the universal that makes us exceptional. Once the enormity of this ideological investment is recognized, it is not hard to understand the highly charged, often polemical air permeating our discussion about different cultures. As the debates over "multiculturalism" make clear, our uses of the term "culture" are anything but innocuous but are often overtly argumentative. One might say that culture has become one of the most loaded, least subtle, and often indiscriminately used fighting words available in current parlance.

In view of this situation, it might be useful to begin by stressing that the extraordinary facility, versatility, and utility of the idea of culture derive in part from the power of the ideology of modernity. It is significant that the efficacy of the idea does not diminish given that the term "culture" is dangerously capacious, semantically vague and confused, and finally, taken as a whole, inconsistent. The rampant and varied use of the term, as well as its remarkable serviceability in spite of (or possibly because of) this lack of conceptual unity and integrity, may be better understood by examining the historical formation and ideological constitution of the idea.

In the interest of analytic simplicity, the following discussion will be divided into four sections. The first will review the advent of the idea of culture that is inherently hierarchical and evaluative, that is, the notion of culture as the sum total of superior, morally and spiritually edifying human accomplishments (often labeled "high culture"), as well as the relation between this idea and the problem of national identity. The second will examine what is often considered to be the alternative tradition of the culture idea, a more inclusive and holistic notion or so-called anthropological concept of culture as "a whole way of life" or "a complex whole" that refers to the totality of various customary practices of a given society. This idea also implies that there are not one but many cultures, and that any given culture is ultimately a *meaningful* entity that must be *interpreted*. The third section will then focus on the formation of the position of the cultural observer/interpreter and the high value placed on the ideals of objectivity and cultural specificity and the method of participant observation. The final section will discuss briefly some of the new perspectives on culture, often associated with the emerging domain of academic discourse variously identified as cultural studies, cultural criticism, and critical theory, which are largely critical of the evaluative logic and the hermeneutical assumptions embedded in hitherto dominant concepts of culture.

I. Culture as Edification

ENGLAND

Raymond Williams's pathbreaking work, *Culture and Society, 1780–1950* (1983, pub. 1958), focuses on the most palpably value laden sense of the term "culture." Williams argues that this notion of culture, associated with the aspiration for the betterment of humanity, arose from a preeminent English literary tradition, in part in reaction to but ultimately in consonance with the emergent middle-class interests predicated on the new industrialized economy and the new social order. The concept of culture changed dramatically in the course of the nineteenth century largely in response to industrialization, the rise of democracy, and the new problems of social class. According to Williams, before that time culture

> had meant, primarily, the "tending of natural growth", and then, by analogy, a process of human training. But this latter use, which had usually been a culture *of something,* was changed, in the nineteenth century, to *culture* as such, a thing in itself. It came to mean, first, "a general state or habit of the mind", having close relations with the idea of human perfection. Second, it came to mean "the general state of intellectual development, in a society as a whole". Third, it came to mean "the general body of the arts". Fourth, later in the century, it came to mean "a whole way of life, material, intellectual and spiritual". (xvi)

This tradition of the culture idea was born of a crisis, of needs acutely felt by a number of English intellectuals beginning in the late eighteenth century: the need to shore up the defense against the threat of erosion and disintegration of the previously known mode of social integration, the need to articulate new grounds and new principles for the edification of the individual and the rectification of the community in view of the shifting order of society. This tradition of culture discourse is intentionally regulative and disciplinary, and its objectives are somewhat polemically tempered, with an eye zealously fixed on the ideal of human perfection. At the same time, this notion of culture is allied with the increasingly important sense of national identity, the presumption of the hegemony of the West over the rest, and the recognition of the West as the vanguard, if not the sole proper agent, of the civilizing process.

Although four meanings transforming the concept culture are identified by Williams as occurring in the nineteenth century, *Culture and Society* mainly follows the historical development of the first three. Concerning the fourth— culture in the sense of "a whole way of life"—Williams recognizes that this use of the term "has been most marked in twentieth-century anthropology and sociology," but he does not explore the development of the idea in relation to those various burgeoning enterprises of knowledge that seek to *represent* cultures (ethnography, philology, comparative religion, etc.). Therefore, while Williams acknowledges the significance of the anthropological and sociological studies to the formation of the idea and notes how T. S. Eliot, for example, "like the rest of us, has been at least casually influenced by these disciplines," he nevertheless concludes that this sense of culture also

> depends, in fact, on the literary tradition. The development of social anthropology has tended to inherit and substantiate the ways of looking at a society and a common life which had earlier been wrought out from general experience of industrialism. The emphasis on "a whole way of life" is continuous from Coleridge and Carlyle, but what was a personal assertion of value has become a general intellectual method. (1983, 233)

Focused exclusively on that aspect of the culture idea nurtured by a group of English literary elites, Williams's study tends to emphasize the ultimately conservative, often nostalgic, reactive, and expressly discriminating tenor of the notion as expressed in the words high culture. It is important, however, not to overlook his own decidedly critical intentions in examining the idea. Among many writers his study covers, the towering figures are all celebrated conservatives: Edmund Burke in the last decades of the eighteenth century, Samuel Coleridge at the turn of the eighteenth to the nineteenth centuries, Matthew Arnold in the middle of the nineteenth century, and T. S. Eliot in the early twentieth century.

An influential opponent to the rising tide of democracy and "aggressive individualism," according to Williams, Burke established two ideas that were to prove significant in the formation of the culture concept: the idea of the state as the necessary agent of human perfection, and the idea of what has been called an "organic society," in which the emphasis is on the interrelation and continuity of human activities (1983, 11). Before the term "culture" was ever employed in such contexts, the notion in germinal form was already operating in Burke. "Immediately after Burke," Williams adds, "this complex which he describes was to be called the 'spirit of the nation'; by the end of the nineteenth century, it was to be called a national 'culture'" (11).

This incipient idea comes into its own and is at last given a single name, culture, in Matthew Arnold's renowned essay *Culture and Anarchy* (1994, pub. 1869). Echoing Burke, Arnold conceives the state as a necessary (if ultimately temporary) agent of human perfection, on the grounds that individuals as such, or the ordinary candidates for political influence or leadership, are all too often delimited by their own class interests, and are thus unable to stand for "a general *humane* spirit, . . . the love of human perfection" (73). Only those who are in a certain sense marginal to their individuality and their class—an alien minority unfettered by those limitations—are poised to assume the agency of culture and, by implication, that of the state. Moreover, it is above all literary education in poetry and criticism, Arnold believes, that can engender and nurture such agents capable of transcending individual and class limitations. Culture, reified in this manner (and, rather ominously, the state as its proper body politic), is abstracted from any empirical body of people or institutions. As an arena of human perfection, culture has become something of a substitute for religion. Arnold's characteristic invocations of the edifying property of culture in such well-known phrases as "the best which has been thought and said in the world" and "the passion for sweetness and light" effectively transfer familiar emotions traditionally attached to religion into a new, yet unrealized ideal.

What T. S. Eliot (1968, pub. 1948) adds to this tradition is an emphasis on wholeness in the culture idea. He objects to Arnold's deposing the traditional social class in favor of a newly conceived group of educated elites as the custodians of culture. Yet Eliot's reasons for these emendations are not really different in sentiment from the tradition of culture discourse running from Burke through Arnold and beyond to cultural neoconservatives of our time. Much as Eliot's notion of culture as "a whole way of life" is influenced by the emerging disciplines of anthropology and sociology, the wholeness of culture he has in mind has little to do with the existing empirical conditions of any given society as an actual totality. In fact, expressing a sentiment similar to those cultural moralists before him—not to mention their present reincarnations among us—Eliot depicts cultural wholeness as something quintessentially embodied in (real or imagined) *traditional* society, which is supposedly in grave danger or on the verge of loss. Always rumored to have existed sometime in the past, culture in this paradigmatic sense is alleged to be naturally coherent and harmonious, if not also entirely homogeneous. In such an exemplary community that represents "culture as a whole way of life," Eliot rather dogmatically assumes, the stratification of the society would not breed conflict or oppression, because hierarchy is only a matter of natural, organic differentiation and cooperation, rather than a mechanical division and functional coordination fraught with competition and strife. Those who can be entrusted with the task of preserving this endangered cultural community are necessarily, or so Eliot and others like him assume, a certain select segment or stratum of society.

Having traced this literary tradition of the idea of culture, Williams proposes a reconceptualization of this wholeness of culture, with an eye toward a more genuinely egalitarian community and a common culture that is not predicated on the governing minority. Such a reconception of culture does not materialize simply in an attempt to include the hitherto excluded, by a mere expansion of the definition of culture, or through relaxation of the presumed standard once held normative by the present (elite) claimants of culture. Rather, what Williams calls for is a fundamental reconfiguration of the dominant logic of culture. He indicates the general directions to which a reconstituted perspective on the cultural logic points. The agenda for further study, which he carries out in his subsequent works, consists of rigorous materialist analyses of popular culture and more historically nuanced studies of technology and media. This is the principal reason Raymond Williams is considered a founding figure of a new approach to the problem of culture or cultural studies.

GERMANY

Meanwhile, the idea of culture as an entity and process intimately tied to the notion of spiritual growth and maturation affecting the formation and destiny of a whole nation had an illustrious career in the German-speaking world throughout the nineteenth century. In a sense, what for Arnold's England could have been but a matter of advocacy for the future—a mere hopeful projection of the advent of a new type of governing class consisting of intellectually superior individuals dedicated to the general enhancement of culture—was already realized and instituted to some extent in Germany, all this *before* the German nation as such existed. As early as the beginning of the nineteenth century in this region of Europe, a highly educated minority or, in the terms made famous by Fritz Ringer, "German mandarins," was already present. This powerful "aristocracy of learning" in its broad sense included the governing bureaucrats of various principalities and newly prominent and increasingly well-paid university professors, as well as their lesser colleagues in the educational profession. According to Ringer (1969), the twin concepts of culture *(Kultur)* and spiritual formation *(Bildung)* became current as key terms expressing the mandarins' ideal of learning as an antithesis to instrumental, institutional training. Thus these concepts were also inseparable from the notion of education *(Erziehung)*, though not in the narrow "mechanical" sense of instruction *(Unterricht)* but in the sense of "religious and neo-humanist conceptions of 'inner growth' and integral self-development" (87). The ideal expressed in this set of potent terms was actively implemented as the official educational policy through a systematic reform of schools and universities.

In the German usage, then, culture is even more visibly allied with the formation of a specialized social class and the identity construction of a modern nation-state, which was facilitated by means of a well-articulated ideology of *Bildung*. The characterization of culture, learning, and nurturing of the spirit *(Geist)* as specifically *German* attributes—an assumption that roughly parallels Arnold's identification of culture with the idealized notion of Englishness or T. S. Eliot's unqualified equation of culture with his idiosyncratic conception of "Christian community"—has had an intriguing history, which is also implicated in the history of related terms:

> The German word *Kultur* was adapted from Cicero's *cultura animi* by Samuel Pufendorf and by Gottfried von Herder. Until late in the eighteenth century, it remained very closely related to the concept of *Bildung*. It had the meaning of "personal culture"; it referred to the cultivation of the mind and spirit. Then gradually, it was used in German learned circles in its more general sense to epitomize all of man's civilized achievements in society. In France, this second step was not taken. *Culture* there remained principally *culture de l'esprit,* while *civilisation,* introduced by the physiocrat Marquis de Mirabeau, came to stand for the totality of man's social and intellectual creations and arrangements. (Ringer 1969, 87–8)

In a development similar to that of the English word, then, German *Kultur* acquired an expanded meaning, in the sense of something like "a whole way of life." But in the course of this development two different terms, *Kultur* and *Zivilisation,* emerged, with the result that the would-be synonyms became invested with an unexpected significance: "By the time of Napoleon at any rate, culture was German and civilization was French" (88).

This opposition between culture and civilization, of course, was not value neutral. The evaluative intentions of the dichotomy are plainly expressed, for instance, in a dictionary entry from the 1920s written by Oswald Spengler, author of the once famous *Decline of the West.* According to this source, *Kultur* was to be distinguished from civilization because the former referred to "the ennoblement *[Veredelung]* of man through the development of his ethical, artistic, and intellectual powers." "Civilization," Spengler concluded, "is to culture as the external is to the internal, the artificially constructed to the naturally developed, the mechanical to the organic, 'means' to 'ends'" (qtd. in Ringer 1969, 89).

This contrast does more than preferentially characterize Germany over France, reversing the usual ranking between the two nations. We recall that the political reality of modern Europe was such that, by the nineteenth century, France had long been a leading political power and a model of the modern nation-state, alternately emulated and feared by the rest of Europe. Germany, by contrast, was hardly a nation but a mere aggregate of relatively minor principalities long subsumed under the medieval rubric of the Holy Roman Empire, with one northern district, Prussia, in ascending preeminence. In the absence of material statehood, then, German *Kultur* was conjured up as an imaginary nation or, even better, as a spiritual *(geistige)* manifestation of a virtual totality not so much organized by a sociopolitical reality as enlivened by a natural, organic folk spirit *(Volksgeist)*. In comparison to such a sublime idea of a nation, any actually existing nation-state could be construed as merely a materially constructed, artificially contracted, mechanically maintained body politic, quite possibly lacking in any spiritual authenticity. In light of this logic, the French Republic, on the one hand, would be seen as a nation in its external form only, with its internationally conceived mission of civilization reflecting only the superficial aspect of reason and of modern scientific spirit, and its ultimate objective nothing more than a facile egalitarian universalism that would defy the distinct character of the *Volk*. On the other hand, mother nature itself would appear to authenticate and justify the German nation insofar as it was perceived as the embodiment of a distinct *Kultur*. In short, the discourse of *Kultur* helped German intellectuals represent the undeniably powerful French nation as a somewhat unnatural, inauthentic entity predicated on a one-sided development of modernity, and to proclaim in turn their own authentic—but as yet virtual—German nationhood with a heavy emphasis on the organic and the deeply spiritual.

II. Culture as "a Complex Whole"

If the nineteenth-century career of the culture/*Kultur* idea has the appearance of a veritable tradition, it is above all because the integral unity and coherence—and with it a sharply discriminating system of valuation and of the ways of institutionalizing those normative principles—has been the intent of this type of culture discourse. The *seeming* integrity of this tradition is less empirically real than polemically advocated. The impression of continuity is forged by the insistent claim on the part of some academics, journalists, politicians, and others who, for one reason or another, wish to uphold this ideology of culturedness and perhaps even to identify themselves with certain nineteenth-century upper-middle-class intellectuals. The domain of culture discourse today in reality is considerably more mixed and complicated. This situation is in large measure due to the introduction of the anthropological concept of culture.

As Williams already noted, while this newer conception of culture is by no means unrelated to previous notions, the nature of the relation has been such that the appearance of a second, ethnographically nurtured tradition of the culture idea was in deliberate distinction from, and, in a sense in protest against, the earlier, literary, socially elitist concept. In contrast to this latter, the ethnographers' view of culture is expressly holistic rather than narrowly discriminating, descriptive rather than evaluative, and fundamentally pluralistic. It presupposes the multiplicity of cultures and does not imply any obvious "standard for excellence." An important assumption implicit in this concept of culture is that the empirical totality of a given society is something that can be *represented* and that this totality can be *interpreted*. This leads to the related conclusions that to know a culture is to understand its *meaning;* and that to grasp the "essential truth" of a culture requires a *hermeneutical science.*

One of the earliest statements defining the anthropological notion of culture can be found in the opening paragraph of Edward B. Tylor's *Primitive Culture* (1873, vol. 1, p. 1): "Culture or civilization, taken in its wide ethnographic sense," says Tylor, "is that complex whole which includes knowledge, belief, art, morals, law, custom, and any other capabilities and habits acquired by man as a member of a society." This seemingly inchoate collection of diverse objects and phenomena, lofty as well as quotidian, is conceptually held together by the yoking phrase, "complex whole." No longer a matter of consciously selective, superior, or privileged activities and achievements, culture has thus become an all-inclusive category naming the totality of social facts and deeds. This shift in meaning from the exclusive to the inclusive parallels the development of the term "society" itself: from the sense of companionship or association of a certain select group of people (as in "polite society" or "musical society") to what may be called the sociological sense of the term, meaning the totality of humans in the same habitat and their mode of being together, while counting all the strata as its members.

The wholeness of culture, insofar as it means more than a mere aggregate of discrete items, is, however, anything but immediately apprehendable or readily demonstrable. It is indeed the task of ethnography, classically conceived, to produce and represent such wholeness and to render it comprehensible, or else at least to present a sense of totality indirectly as a "web of significance," in Max Weber's celebrated phrase, against the backdrop of which more particular phenomena can be shown to make sense. What is at stake in the notion of a complex whole, therefore, is not only the coherence, confluence, or consonance of the whole but, more important for the anthropologist, its intelligibility. This notion of the cultural whole renders the entire domain of human activity as *meaningful,* that is, as a *hermeneutical* reality that can be understood and communicated, even if it is not, as in the objects of natural sciences, a mechanically measurable or predictable entity. In this way, culture has come to define not only the object but also the objective of the ethnographic enterprise. As such, it is central to the new science of anthropology, which purports to lead from the cumulation of exotic particularities to a set of general truths about humankind. Hence Tylor (1873) proceeds to elaborate his programmatic agenda:

> The condition of culture among the various societies of mankind, in so far as it is capable of being investigated on general principles, is a subject apt for the study of laws of human thought and action. On the one hand, the uniformity which so largely pervades civilization may be ascribed, in great measure, to the uniform action of uniform causes; while on the other hand its various grades may be regarded as stages of development or evolution, each the outcome of previous

history, and about to do its proper part in shaping the history of the future. (Vol. 1, p. 1)

Although this was written in 1871 by no less a figure than Tylor, who is generally considered to be the most prominent anthropologist of the Victorian era, the term "culture" in the anthropological, holistic sense, according to Margaret Mead, remained "the vocabulary of a small and technical group of professional anthropologists" well into the twentieth century. By the middle of the century, however, "the world [was] on such easy terms with the concept of culture, that the words 'in our culture' slip[ped] from the lips of educated men and women." In our own day, we might add, it has become a primal category of everyday conversation whether the speaker is especially educated or not. Mead suggests with some authority that the greater currency the concept of culture now enjoys is in no small measure due to the success of Ruth Benedict's *Patterns of Culture* (1959, pub. 1934), which served as an excellent introduction to "a comparative study of different cultures, through which we can see our own socially transmitted customary behavior set beside that of other and strangely different peoples" (Mead 1959, vii).

A comparative study of cultures, perhaps somewhat counterintuitively, emphasizes the integral unity of a given society, and presupposes that a proper understanding and valuation of specific elements is possible only if those elements are considered in the context of that particular unitary whole. This culture-specific, contextualist approach—advocated by many American anthropologists including Benedict, Franz Boas, and Mead—was a deliberate departure from what they perceived to be "the old method of constructing a history of human culture based on bits of evidence, torn out of their natural contacts, and collected from all times and all parts of the world" (Boas 1959, xv). Their approach is in marked contrast to the predominantly British, Victorian "armchair" anthropology of Tylor. As Benedict puts it, anthropology up to her time "ha[d] been overwhelmingly devoted to the analysis of culture traits . . . rather than to the study of culture as articulated wholes. . . . If we are interested in cultural processes, the only way in which we can know the significance of the selected detail of behavior is against the background of the motives and emotions and values that are institutionalized in that culture" (1959, 48–9).

Thus a significant development had taken place in the anthropological concept of culture at this point, from Tylor's inclusive sense of it as a *general,* cumulative human construction (in which sense it is most appropriate to speak of human culture, of which "primitive culture" is an aspect, moment, or stage) to the more contemporary sense of *a* culture as a distinctive, autochthonous entity belonging to a particular local group, however small or large such a group may be. It is this later articulation that has endowed the Tylorian "complex whole" with a more explicitly *interpretive* significance.

Furthermore, according to Boas, the understanding of such a pattern of integration, or configuration of the elements as a whole, is tantamount to "a deep penetration into the genius of the culture" (1959, xvii). As this phrasing indicates, the conception of a culture as a meaningful whole, thus as an object *and* context of interpretation, renders the anthropological study of culture analogous to the study of a work of art or literature in its most typically hermeneutical formulation. Not only does "culture" turn out to be a relatively finite and distinctive body of work that can be "read like a text," but its essential truth is ultimately a matter of a genius, that is, a deeply spiritual, creative principle, of which the multifarious elements of a given culture are particular manifestations. Nothing short of a hermeneutical science, it would appear, is equal to the task of grasping such an essence. The deeply penetrating understanding of a culture in this fashion, of course, would also lead to aesthetic appreciation and all the moral and spiritual edification that comes from such an experience. In this connection, Mead observes, it is no accident that Benedict herself was originally a student of literature, and, on that account, she could understand better than other anthropologists of her time that "each primitive culture represented something comparable to a great work of art or literature. . . . [I]f one took these cultures whole—the religion, the mythology, the everyday ways of men and women— then the internal consistency and the intricacy was as aesthetically satisfying to the would-be explorer as any single work of art" (1959, ix).

Since the early decades of the twentieth century, the interpretive approach to culture as a meaningful whole and the accompanying hermeneutical assumptions have been enormously influential in the development of the contemporary discourses on religion. Theological appropriation of the hermeneutics of culture was effected by a number of prominent European émigré theologians who had highly influential academic careers in North America, including H. Richard Niebuhr (author of *Christ and Culture*), Paul Tillich (*Religion and Culture*), and more recently Paul Ricoeur. They have been inspirational or instrumental in spawning a whole range of academic enterprises, usually with a title that begins "Religion and," such as "Religion and Literature," "Religion and the Arts," or "Religion and Culture."

Apart from this theological tradition, if we look at the development of the notion of culture in anthropology, one of the principal figures to be noted is undoubtedly Clifford Geertz. He gave a particularly sharp articulation to the idea that a culture is "an historically transmitted pattern of meanings embodied in symbols" (1973, 89). This symbolic notion of culture is directly relevant to the subject of religion, and he expresses this view in the title of one of his most influential articles, "Religion as a Cultural System." An implicit but obvious assumption here is that the term "culture," understood as a system of meaning, is more or less interchangeable with "a tradition," "a religious tradition," or simply, "a religion," insofar as the wholeness of each of these entities can be said to represent a complex configuration of signs and symbols which, taken as a whole, furnish significance to various aspects of a people's commonwealth. As Geertz stated it in his oft-cited definition of religion (1973, 90–1), there is a cognitive/theoretical aspect as well as an emotional/practical aspect to this system, and these two aspects correspond respectively to "religion as a world view" (metaphysics) and "religion as an ethos" (ethical and aesthetic disposition) (126–41). These elaborations have further enriched the anthropological notion of culture by considerably complicating Benedict's basic thesis that no part of a cultural complex is to be understood or evaluated without reference to the whole, which is a distinct system. And the implication has become more pronounced in that, if a culture is something to be *analyzed like a text,* it also seems to have something to *say.*

The most obvious analogue in religious studies to this conception of culture as a meaningful whole is Mircea Eliade's characterization of the history of religions as a "religious hermeneutics" (1969, 1–11, 54–71). He sought to mark out a distinct territory for the scientific study of religion (*Religionswissenschaft* or, in his own parlance, the history of religions). At the same time Eliade was intent on situating this enterprise firmly in the general context of the interpretive study of culture, as opposed to the context of positivistic sciences, philosophical speculations, or theological apologia. To this end, Eliade underscores the importance of hermeneutics:

> Hermeneutics is of preponderant interest to us because, inevitably, it is the least-developed aspect of our discipline. Preoccupied, and indeed often completely taken up, by their admittedly urgent and indispensable work of collecting, publishing, and analyzing religious data, scholars have sometimes neglected to study their meaning. Now, these data represent the expression of various religious experiences. . . . [T]he scholar has not finished his work when he has reconstructed the history of a religious form or brought out its sociological, economic, or political contexts. In addition, he must understand its meaning. (2)

According to this argument, sociology, economics, political science, and other cognate disciplines can, at their best, help elucidate the context in which various "religious experiences" occur, while leaving the question of their *meaning* untouched. By the same token, if the historian of religion merely collected and analyzed data and stopped short of "understanding their meaning," it would be tantamount to studying only "the *exterior* aspects of the spiritual universe" (Eliade 1969, 60). For Eliade and other like-minded religionists, the essential nature of religious experience perforce falls outside the purview of secularist disciplines because

> The hierophanies—i.e., the manifestations of the sacred expressed in symbols, myths, supernatural beings, etc.—are grasped as structures, and constitute a prereflective language that requires a special hermeneutics. For more than a quarter of a century [Eliade wrote this in the 1960s], historians and phenomenologists of religion have at-

tempted to elaborate such a hermeneutics. . . . By means of a competent hermeneutics, history of religions ceases to be a museum of fossils, ruins, and obsolete *mirabilia* and becomes what it should have been from the beginning for any investigator: a series of "messages" waiting to be deciphered and understood. (Preface, n. p.)

A hermeneutics proper to this task is therefore "a *total hermeneutics,* which can decipher and explicate every kind of human encounter of man with the sacred, from prehistory to our day" (58). Here, Eliade to some extent resuscitates the world historical perspective of Victorian anthropology, without seeming to support the evolutionist assumptions of Tylor.

To be sure, not everyone professionally engaged in religious studies would subscribe to this particular conception of "religious hermeneutics." More broadly speaking, however, the hermeneutical paradigm has become so insidiously pervasive in the human sciences generally in the course of the twentieth century that it now seems to strike many people as perversely unnatural, if not entirely impossible, to entertain the possibility that "culture" or "religion" could be construed in any way other than as an intricately intrareferential "meaningful whole," or that an act of interpretation could be conceived in some way other than as probing of the depths, or hunting in the forest of words and images for some less-than-obvious *meaning* that is the essential truth of that whole.

In the last section of this essay, we will consider some of the challenges to this hermeneutical paradigm predominant in both cultural anthropology and the study of religion. For the moment, let it suffice to note that the overwhelming emphasis on *meaning* as the ultimate constitutive substance of a cultural wholeness has had the effect, among others, of bringing the anthropological notion of culture into closer association with the more literary, aesthetic, and moral concepts of culture discussed earlier. If a culture could be read, interpreted, and appreciated like a work of art or literature, "to read a culture" would not only yield scientific truths but would also prove just as morally edifying and spiritually enriching as reading "great books" is reputed to be. In fact, one might say that in the long run it should prove more rewarding, because what the reader of a culture will come to grasp is not merely a genius of a particular time and place embodied in an individual "great author" but the collective genius and the destiny of a whole people or nation. Thus, over and above the chastely scientific purpose of research, there is room for the student of a culture to hope that any given culture, however alien and idiosyncratic some of its constitutive elements might appear, could in the end be *saying something,* imparting a secret message, a forgotten promise, perhaps even a hidden anecdote of destiny.

III. *The Making of the Participant Observer*

If the hermeneutical notion of culture makes feasible such a providential prospect for the study of culture, the moral investment in the position of the interpreter of cultures is considerable. For what is being discovered here (or shall we say invented?) is not only a new kind of general object, that is, culture, but also a new seat of knowledge and understanding proper to this object: the position of the observer/interpreter of culture. The making of this new subjectivity, which is indispensable to the emergent science of culture, has not been seriously examined. The issue tends to be almost always confused with, or rather occluded by, what are taken to be more or less technical problems concerning the principles of scientific objectivity and the method of empathic understanding. Even the most obviously moralizing phrases often used to express the ideals of research, for example, "doing justice to the data," "not violating the integrity of the tradition as a whole," "observing facts impartially without distorting them with one's own values and interests," have not invited the critical attention that would expose the historical circumstances contributing to the development of the underlying ideology of cultural observation.

A welcome exception is Christopher Herbert's admirable study *Culture and Anomie: Ethnographic Imagination in the Nineteenth Century* (1991), which is the first sustained critical analysis of the emergence of the anthropological concept of culture. This work demonstrates that the seemingly new, seemingly neutral, pluralistic, and relativistic notion of culture, which made its first appearance around Tylor's time and gradually gained prominence in the course of the twentieth century, was in fact neither new nor neutral. Moreover, this idea was far from being merely empirical, descriptive, or value free but was as much a product of the intellectual and moral crises of eighteenth- and nineteenth-century Europe as the other, literary, normative, and more explicitly Eurocentric idea of culture. This argument, of course, is based on the observation that the particular "way of thinking" that eventually solidified into the ethnographic notion of culture had been around long before it became attached to the word itself. It is also predicated on an entirely novel but compelling hypothesis that what was truly at issue in this way of thinking was the problem of desire.

The problem of desire, and that of human volition more generally, has been primarily a theological problem in the West. In the theological context, the issues most pertinent to the question of desire are not paths to fulfillment or impediments to satisfaction but, rather more typically and ominously, transgression and sin. Accordingly, the question of desire immediately evokes the problem of regulating and controlling the natural exuberance of human acts, which are always imbued with desire, and the problem of organizing these acts positively as constitutive elements in an orderly, consecrated community. This leads to the problem of freedom. The entire complex of problems—desire, inhibition-discipline, order, freedom—was acutely felt by the educated Europeans of the eighteenth and early nineteenth centuries, when the basic assumptions about the world were reportedly undergoing a radical transformation. Change and progress, rather than permanence and constancy, became the norms instead of anomalous occurrences. Consequently, the question of freedom and autonomous will came to be framed in a new way, as new institutions of governing were replacing the old. It is against the backdrop of these transformations at the turn of the eighteenth to nineteenth century, Herbert suggests, that the question of desire—and the general dissatisfaction with the traditional theological answers to it—provided grounds for the eventual formation of the culture idea. While keeping this general argument in mind, let us attend to the issue of particular interest for us here, namely, the historical formation of the ethnographic observer.

The hypothetical state of nature, a brutish existence ruled by nothing but instinctive desire and unfettered intercourse of animal life, was imagined to be the condition of the human race prior to the onset of the civilizing process. This fantasized state of lawless desire has functioned as a template for the Europeans' representation of those they considered to be savages, namely, the native inhabitants of the Americas, Oceania, the Pacific Islands, and many parts of Africa and Asia. For most Europeans, the exotic denizens of those faraway places remained a matter of distant rumors embellished by their own imagination rather than firsthand experience of any kind. More an object of fancy than of direct social intercourse, the savage was portrayed all the more vividly as a reverse image of the domestic and familial European society (or what was construed as such), where natural instincts and desires were fastidiously checked and disciplined by the authorities of religion, state, and increasingly science.

Among the small number of Europeans who did venture out to those faraway places were Christian missionaries, and they were among the first to record in detail the life of the savages in their native habitat. By the official "scientific" standards of the twentieth century, however, these early records left by the missionary observers are generally regarded as unreliable reports of facts, and valued even less when it comes to their interpretations of these facts. Missionaries' views and opinions were informed and predetermined by dogmatic Christianity, so it is said, and such religiously biased observations are palpably at odds with the principle of scientific objectivity and impartiality. This commonplace assessment of the missionary ethnography largely ignores, though it does not necessarily deny, that there is a significant continuity between "prescientific" ethnographic writings and later, academically certified anthropologists' studies, especially with regard to the position of the observer and the style of notation.

To be sure, the missionaries' professed motives and objectives differed sharply from the scientific credo of the later anthropologists. But those soldiers and servants of God, on a mission to win the heathen souls for Christianity, found themselves surrounded by, indeed thoroughly immersed in, the actualities of the native life, not unlike the situation of the anthropologist at his/her fieldwork. However opinionated, prejudicial, or parochially skewed their views of the perditious native ways finally may have been, theirs were also veritable eyewitness accounts based on direct experience while they lived among the natives for extended periods, usually many times longer than the average length of fieldwork considered adequate for dissertation research in anthropology today. As a rule, the missionaries' observations were recorded in great empirical detail, as meticulously particular as any field notes of the modern anthropologist.

These points of commonality between the habits of the two types of ethnographers—the religious and the scientific—may seem unremarkable, but Herbert probes further into the nature of the intensity of their immersion and the high premium placed on the precise recording of details and empirical specificity common to both groups. The obsessively minute attention to what was seen, heard, and measured, and the voluminous retention of these empirical particulars, goes hand in hand with the idea, emphatically maintained by these observers, that empirical notation, generated from a specific position of observation amidst the life-world of unmediated experience (or what was taken as such), ultimately speaks for itself and possesses a self-validating power. It is as though the ethnographic writing at its best were dictation taken directly from the lived experience, as though the recorded minutiae were the fingerprints left by real events. These fundamental beliefs about the ideal transparency of ethnographic writing, however, were tantamount to a symptomatic response—or, as psychoanalysis would put it, reaction formation—against a certain ambivalence and anxiety inherent in their theory and practice of observation. What, then, was the nature of this anxiety?

As noted before, the missionaries shared with their fellow Europeans at home the theory that represented savage life as a state of unrestrained desire: an anarchic condition governed by nothing except the capricious forces of natural instincts. Sexual license, cannibalism, witchcraft, devil worship, and other diabolical customs were attributed to this state of nature. At the same time, the missionaries were among the first to confront the actual conditions of the savage life, which did not necessarily conform to this preconceived theory. They were, in effect, witness to the fact that, far from being a lawless free-for-all, the lives of the tribespeople were often highly rule bound, checked and regulated by an elaborate system of obligations, prohibitions, customs, and protocols, which initially are largely incomprehensible to outsiders and therefore tend to appear altogether irrational. We know that, by the very nature of their mission, these Europeans were not only obliged to recognize and comprehend the basic social systems of the natives but also to familiarize themselves with native ways, and even to adapt to them to a degree, in order to be able to communicate with the potential converts. To learn the native language, for instance, entailed an adaptation to an enormous system of inherited signs, rules, and shared idioms.

Hence the paradoxical situation of the missionary observers: on the one hand, their European-manufactured theory of unrestrained desire supposedly dominating the savage life; and on the other, their own increasing entanglement in the "web of significance" that was the native way of life but, in a certain sense, was not supposed to exist. Even in the face of this contradiction, however, the missionaries were not free to abandon the theory that portrayed the savage as the epitome of indomitable desire bereft of organized sociability, not only because this view was sanctioned by their ecclesiastic authority but also, and most important, because the veracity of the theory was the precondition of their very mission, which was to save the savages from the anarchy of natural desire. Seen in this way, it is evident that this paradox of the missionaries' position was essentially an epistemological problem, a logical disharmony disturbing their inherited ideology of cognition. But this dilemma is not readily recognizable as such in the missionaries' own writing because, as Herbert suggests, this incongruity was experienced or expressed "not as uncertainty about principles of research . . . but as a seemingly unresolvable moral and emotional predicament" (1991, 162).

Accordingly, it appears, the missionaries' response to this moral predicament was also akin to the traditional religious discipline of body and soul: active diminution of the observing self to the point of near invisibility, and, conversely, almost morbid heightening of the faculty of perception. It is as though they hoped and believed that the hallucinatory vividness of the extraordinarily detailed observations amassed over a sustained period could finally overwhelm and completely inundate the potentially problematic dimension of the observer, reducing his/her position to near nothing under the deluge of "facts." Whether or not this novel form of self-denial afforded any moral comfort, missionary observers of what were later to be called "primitive cultures" were engaged, unawares, in "an extravagantly risky experiment with modern modes of thought . . . in a project amounting to the invention of a new subjectivity" (Herbert 1991, 156). The total immersion in the sea of alien life, and thus to some degree participation in such a life, was a precondition of this new mode of observation, and it entailed an extraordinary crisis of perception, with an imminent danger of counterconversion. The discipline of reducing the problematic self to the minimal point of seeing eye, or invisible observer, and the concomitant amplification of vigilance resulted in the voluminous accumulation of sharply focused, high-resolution images and records of what was observed—images and records that seem to stand all on their own with their intrinsic power of self-evidence and self-authentication. In short, their notations seem to present themselves as a direct recording of incontrovertible facts, independent of the material dimension and the historical circumstances of the observing body. The minutiae of the data thus appear to silence the "unresolvable moral and emotional predicament" in which the observer was necessarily embroiled.

This hyperinvestment in the eyewitness and in the power of self-evidence attributed to the object/phenomenon described, and the concomitant erasure of the materiality of the observer, suggests Herbert, produced the prototype of the so-called *participant observer,* the uniquely valorized subject position of modern ethnographic science. But if there is a continuity between the missionaries' self-immersion in the starkness of facts and the twentieth-century anthropologists' insistence on the absolute efficacy of participant observation, what is the comparable ambivalence or anxiety underlying the position of the modern anthropologist? What, in other words, is the epistemological disharmony or contradiction inherent in the ideology of anthropological observation analogous to the missionaries' predicament at the observation of the allegedly lawless savage?

According to Herbert, the predicament of the modern anthropologists ultimately stems from the same root as the missionary observers'. In fact, the seemingly scandalous comparison between the prescientific and the scientific ethnographies is useful precisely because the case of earlier, religiously engaged ethnographic observers illumines

> the moral and epistemological predicament of the European observer in primitive society . . . with an anguish of frankness that throws strong light on the academic complacencies of a later era. It reveals the secret . . . not only that the ethnographic and relativistic doctrine of culture was not invented out of thin air by a high-minded caste of disinterested professional researchers, but such a doctrine bears from its inception the mark of almost fatal self-contradiction. (1991, 155)

For the newer generation of empirically oriented anthropologists from Malinowski to Geertz, the precise location of the intelligible pattern, order, or system of "culture as a complex whole" has been an ever present, seemingly irresoluble problem. Is this "pattern" of culture something that exists "out there," so to speak, "in the things themselves," *or* is it in the mind of the observer? No unequivocal answer to this flat-footed question is possible, however, because the ethnographer cannot relinquish either pole of this experience. While it is acknowledged that such a system or pattern is not immediately present in the things observed but ultimately made comprehensible and representable only in the work of the ethnographer after an elaborate analysis, the very principle of ethnography as an objective science demands that its truth finally reside in the things observed and not in the theoretic mind of the observer. On the heels of this admission, it is emphatically claimed that such a truth becomes discernible in the actuality of things themselves *only from a very specific, highly disciplined point of observation.* But if so, "culture as a meaningful, complex whole" must be an entity whose cognitive reality is entirely dependent on this especially constructed standpoint and, by implication, on the particular theory of perception and the ideology of empirical notation that supports the authority of such an Archimedean point. The idea of culture, therefore, turns out to be more than a mere concept; it is an argument, a theoretical object that comes with a certain discipline, persuasions, and admonitions. As Herbert puts it,

> the formalized idea of culture emerges as a gloss on the Malinowskian research method, "culture" being defined in effect as that which can only be perceived by personal immersion in an alien society and can only be represented by a notation of the seemingly insignificant so detailed as to constitute a new mode of awareness (and of prose style). From the first, the culture thesis seems to crystallize in this

fashion around the solitary figure of the ethnographer executing a program. (1991, 163)

In sum, the reality of "culture as a complex whole," its intelligibility to the disciplined observer, and, in fact, all that is vested in the so-called anthropological notion of culture is contingent on the singular point of participant observation and the vigilantly empiricist prose generated from that position. Once the staying power supposedly endemic to the seat of observation is questioned or hypothetically denied, once the heightened rhetoric of empirical reality and self-evidence of data (with all the moralizing phrases that go into this rhetoric) is relaxed, and once the position of the observer ceases to be supercharged—or, in psychoanalytic terms, hypercathected and fetishized—the gossamer reality of the "complex whole" will likely begin to appear no more substantial than the phrase itself.

IV. Beyond the Hermeneutics of Culture

It remains to consider briefly some recent perspectives on the question of culture that are largely critical of the hitherto dominant, hermeneutical assumptions. The domain of academic and intellectual practice in which these critical tendencies are most prominent may be the widely interdisciplinary field variously called "cultural studies," "cultural criticism," "critical theory," or sometimes just "theory." The following is frequently asked: Since every existing department of humanities and social sciences can be said to be an enterprise to "study culture" in one aspect or another, what could "cultural studies" possibly be other than all of these traditional disciplines combined, perhaps with a few not so traditional areas of inquiry added? This common expression of confusion may be a useful place to begin considering how these new perspectives on culture are situated in relation to the established organization of knowledge in human sciences or what might be collectively called—to the extent that these established disciplines have been influenced or dominated by hermeneutical assumptions as embodied in the idea of culture—cultural hermeneutics.

It is notable that the trajectory for much of the counterhermeneutical moves in cultural studies has been charted by theorists studying literature. For this reason above all, the discipline of literary studies has been and continues to be an important component in the development of cultural studies, some would say *despite* the preponderant focus on so-called high culture. For the last several decades, the major trends in literary criticism have dislodged the conception of literary interpretation as an enterprise geared toward the recovery of the author's life-world or penetration into its genius; instead they have focused on developing rigorous rhetorical readings. As a rule these new schools of literary studies make the point of paying meticulous attention to the material properties of the text, such as the rhetorical apparatuses of language; figures and tropes; and social technologies of production, circulation, and reception of the text—as opposed to the more ideational meaning supposedly hidden or contained in the text.

These interpretive strategies are often called by the simple name "close reading." This is a plainly descriptive phrase but not entirely informative of its counterconventional orientation. Indeed, much of the confusion about cultural studies and what is more commonly referred to in literary studies simply as "theory" seems to stem from the fact that a surprisingly large number of scholars and writers who are not themselves regular practitioners of literary analysis continue to assume that these interpretive strategies—including psychoanalysis, structuralism, and poststructuralism—are merely more advanced forms of hermeneutics in the conventional sense.

In addition to literary studies, various other types of scholarship also challenge the dominant hermeneutical paradigm for the study of culture and its objectivist ideology epitomized by cultural anthropology and history of religions, as well as orthodox historical and literary studies. A study of popular culture, for instance, does not merely add to or fill the gap left by the traditional scholarship fixated on high culture; it often has the effect of questioning, contesting, and exposing the unavowed interests inherent in the established organization of knowledge and system of valuation, which is supposed to be objective and value-free. Studies of various media—including photography, film, and other representational and reproductive technologies—eschew the hermeneutical obsession with the non-material, symbolic, or spiritual *content* of a body of work and change the nature of scholarly attention by placing a greater emphasis on the materiality of its medium (Kittler 1990). Museum studies—which examine the important modern institution whose primary function is the representation of cultures—have been effective in analyzing the intricate connections between the seemingly objective, scientific, and disinterested cultural representation on the one hand, and the elemental forms of value-laden, desire-driven transactions such as acquisition, appropriation, aestheticized exhibition, and eroticized consumption of the material bodies and objects native to foreign or colonized territories on the other (Haraway 1989; Karp and Lavine 1991; Duncan 1995).

Colonial and postcolonial studies, meanwhile, have done much to illumine the specific ways in which culture as an object of knowledge and of representation emerged inextricably intertwined with the process of colonization. Some of these works demonstrate that what we customarily take to be a defining characteristic of a certain culture—*caste* in India, for example—was not really an indigenous tradition that had existed in the non-Western society prior to contact with the West but was either invented or developed into what it is today over the course of the colonial process (Dirks 1992; Hobsbawm and Ranger 1983). Some historians have put these insights in a more general form and have argued that the very notion of a particular culture as something clearly alien and distinct from the European civilization originated precisely from the condition of Western-non-Western contact, that is, from the condition of hybridity. They argue that something like a so-called traditional culture came to be projected retrospectively as that which defines the non-West in essence, and that this projection has been broadly instrumental in the ongoing contentious "contact" that is colonization. What is posited as a "pure" alien culture, like the notion of "pure race," they suggest, is but an ideological fiction. Cultural contact and hybridity are the primary conditions from which these fictions of pristine cultures originate (Young 1995; Thomas 1994).

Two of the most important contributions made by literary scholars to the critical investigation of cultural representation are the above-mentioned works by Raymond Williams and Christopher Herbert. These studies demonstrate that culture has been posited and advocated, rather than discovered and named, as a universal category of science, a body of work, or a system of values, which in itself supposedly possesses permanent objective validity transcending individual, class, regional, or parochial interests. They also show that the emergence and further development of the idea of culture have been inextricably bound to the moral and cognitive problems keenly felt at various historical moments. The culture idea is therefore less a conceptual tool than a bundle of arguments, moral persuasions, in brief, an icon of a certain epistemological position we are persuaded to assume. As such, the idea embodies certain highly *interested* attitudes. This notwithstanding, since the ideal of objectivity and transcendence beyond the personal is paramount in the culture discourse of both literary and anthropological traditions, the interests and attitudes actually animating and energizing the idea of culture are largely disavowed; they become palpable only through the labor of critical analysis. For this reason, although the historiography of a concept is not typical of the works in cultural studies generally, investigations by Williams, Herbert, and others like them have contributed significantly to the critical objectives of cultural studies.

There are, however, some common retorts against this kind of intellectual history. One protesting argument comes in the form of a reminder that, however significant and portentous the modern transformation of the concept of culture might have been, culture in the sense of certain civic training and nurture is not completely a modern invention but most assuredly has its roots and precedents in earlier times. More seriously, it might be protested that there is something monolithic and imperious about the very notion of modernity that is supposed to denote such an overwhelming and fundamental shift in the course of history. How much objective validity should be attributed to the claim that all these transformations somehow began in the late eighteenth century? This line of protest is worthy of attention if only for its power to warn against a certain (mis)construal: we would likely run into serious problems if we were to take the thesis about the modern emergence of the culture idea as an absolute historical claim, instead of a strategic one. For, in the last analysis, the significant contribution Williams's and Herbert's works make is not a discovery concerning when, where, and under what circumstances the idea of culture originated. Rather, the value of genealogical analyses such as these resides in what they would allow us to see when a concept so thoroughly ingrained in our everyday discourse (and therefore made largely invisible) is denaturalized and suspended before our eyes as an object of scrutiny. A heuristically simplified historical thesis is sometimes effective in procuring such a strategic condition favorable for critical analysis.

Another criticism to be anticipated is the complaint that a study such as Williams's or Herbert's is nothing more than a history of an idea and is therefore not about the actual, empirical reality of culture. By overvaluing this type of analysis, a critic would say, we run the risk of reducing the historical and empirical issues to a matter of Western or Western-generated *ideas*. Although a warning against idealist tendencies is generally valuable, this particular line of protest is in this context more reactive than responsive, because it is tantamount to reasserting the reality of culture as something pregiven, as something naturally real over and above the "mere concept" of it. As we have seen from these studies, however, there is nothing mere about this concept, or about the ways in which some real consequences follow when we wield it in our daily politics at all levels.

What is barely submerged in this murmur of protests and counterarguments is the question of what it means to be *historical*. For reasons that are not altogether simple or apparent, history has become one thing that no one, it seems, wants to be accused of forgetting or ignoring. To do so in the present mores amounts to losing touch with such duty-awakening exigencies as the materiality of life itself, the real people, one's own situatedness, and so on. The moral imperative of "being historical" is so great that the student of culture of any persuasion is immediately made to feel answerable. What is not at all clear and is not even acknowledged as such is that there is a tremendous disagreement—or perhaps it is more accurate to say *confusion*—about how this demand of the real might be met, and how the order of the historical/material/real is constituted for us, not for always, but here and now.

This is to suggest that a certain theoretically inflected wing of cultural studies has contributed to the explosive situation of the current state of human sciences precisely because it has directly challenged the assumptions and strategies of traditional historiography established in the nineteenth century and still dominant today, or what might be roundly termed old and new (but perhaps not so new) historicism. What if "being historical" is not a matter of recovering and reconstructing a richly nuanced narrative truth, full of "thick descriptions," of a certain wholeness of a past, but instead is a matter of more or less outwitting such a compelling narrative truth and letting some forgotten moments and contours of the past "flare up," as Walter Benjamin would say, in order to illumine and decompose the compulsive narrativity of history that dictates the ideology of the present?

The posthermeneutical moment of cultural studies is also an antihistoricist (and antivulgar materialist) moment. And this is the principal reason Benjamin—a figure rather difficult to classify, who might arguably be called a kabalistic Marxist, dialectical materialist literary critic and philosopher, who wrote not only about high modernist art and new media but also about the streets of Paris, children's books, books written by the insane, etc.—has been an important resource for today's practice of cultural studies and continues to be a significant marker for a new direction in the study of culture.

SUGGESTED READINGS

Benjamin, Walter. 1996. *Selected Writings.* 2 vols., edited by Marcus Bullock and Michael W. Jennings.

Brantlinger, Patrick. 1990. *Crusoe's Footprints: Cultural Studies in Britain and America.*

Dirks, Nicholas B., ed. 1992. *Colonialism and Culture.*

Graff, Gerald. 1992. *Beyond the Culture Wars: How Teaching the Conflicts Can Revitalize American Education.*

Herbert, Christopher. 1991. *Culture and Anomie: Ethnographic Imagination in the Nineteenth Century.*

Smith, Barbara Herrnstein. 1988. *Contingencies of Value: Alternative Perspectives for Critical Theory.*

Hobsbawm, Eric, and Terrence Ranger, eds. 1983. *The Invention of Tradition.*

Karp, Ivan, and Steven D. Lavine, eds. 1991. *Exhibiting Cultures: The Poetics and Politics of Museum Display.*

Taussig, Michael. 1993. *Mimesis and Alterity: A Particular History of the Senses.*

Weber, Samuel. 1987. *Institution and Interpretation.*

Williams, Raymond. 1983. *Culture and Society: 1780–1950.*

———. 1983. *Keywords: A Vocabulary of Culture and Society.*

Young, Robert J. C. 1995. *Colonial Desire: Hybridity in Theory, Culture and Race.*

REFERENCES

Arnold, Matthew. [1869] 1994. *Culture and Anarchy,* edited by Samuel Lipman. New Haven: Yale University Press.

Benedict, Ruth. [1934] 1959. *Patterns of Culture.* Boston: Houghton Mifflin.

Boas, Franz. 1959. Introduction to *Patterns of Culture,* by Ruth Benedict.

Dirks, Nicholas B., ed. 1992. *Colonialism and Culture.* Ann Arbor: University of Michigan Press.

Duncan, Carol. 1995. *Civilizing Rituals: Inside Public Art Museums.* New York: Routledge.

Eliade, Mircea. 1969. *The Quest: History and Meaning in Religion.* Chicago: University of Chicago Press.

Eliot, T. S. [1948] 1968. "Notes toward the Definition of Culture." In *Christianity and Culture.* New York: Harcourt, Brace, Jovanovitch.

Geertz, Clifford. 1973. *The Interpretation of Cultures.* New York: Basic.

Haraway, Donna J. 1989. *Primate Visions: Gender, Race, and Nature in the World of Modern Science.* New York: Routledge.

Herbert, Christopher. 1991. *Culture and Anomie: Ethnographic Imagination in the Nineteenth Century.* Chicago: University of Chicago Press.

Hobsbawm, Eric, and Terrence Ranger, eds. 1983. *The Invention of Tradition.* Cambridge: Cambridge University Press.

Karp, Ivan, and Steven D. Lavine, eds. 1991. *Exhibiting Cultures: The Poetics and Politics of Museum Display*. Washington, D.C.: Smithsonian Institution.

Kittler, Friedrich A. 1990. *Discourse Networks 1800/1900,* translated by Michael Metteer with Chris Cullens. Stanford: Stanford University Press.

Mead, Margaret. 1959. Preface to *Patterns of Culture,* by Ruth Benedict.

Ringer, Fritz K. 1969. *The Decline of the German Mandarins: The German Academic Community, 1890–1933*. Cambridge: Harvard University Press.

Thomas, Nicholas. 1994. *Colonialism's Culture*. Princeton: Princeton University Press.

Tylor, Edward B. [1871] 1873. *Primitive Culture: Research into the Development of Mythology, Philosophy, Religion, Language, Art, and Custom.* 2nd ed. 2 vols. London: John Murray.

Williams, Raymond. [1958] 1983. *Culture and Society, 1780–1950*. New York: Columbia University Press.

Young, Robert J. C. 1995. *Colonial Desire: Hybridity in Theory, Culture, and Race*. New York: Routledge.

FIVE

Experience

Robert H. Sharf

The exercise of thought cannot have any other outcome than the negation of individual perspectives.

—Georges Bataille

I

One might expect an essay on the term "experience" to begin with a definition, but immediately we confront a problem. To define something entails situating it in the public sphere, assuming an objective or third-person perspective vis-à-vis the term or concept at issue. The problem with the term "experience," particularly with respect to its use in the study of religion, is that it resists definition by design; as we will see, the term is often used rhetorically to thwart the authority of the "objective" or the "empirical," and to valorize instead the subjective, the personal, the private. This is in part why the meaning of the term may appear self-evident at first yet becomes increasingly elusive as one tries to get a fix on it. (Gadamer places experience "among the least clarified concepts which we have" [1975, 310].)

In spite of (or perhaps owing to) the obscurity of the term, experience as a concept has come to play a pivotal role in the study of religion. The meaning of many religious symbols, scriptures, practices, and institutions is believed to reside in the experiences they elicit in the minds of practitioners. Moreover, a particular mode (or modes) of experience, characterized as "religious," "spiritual," "visionary," or "mystical," is thought to constitute the very essence of religion, such that the origin of a given tradition is often traced to the founder's initial transcendent encounter, moment of revelation, salvation, or enlightenment. This approach to religious phenomena is not confined to academic discourse alone; many lay adherents feel that the only *authentic* form of worship or scriptural study is one that leads to a personal experience of its "inner truth." Consequently, scholarship that does not attend to the experiential dimension of religious practice is dismissed by many as reductionistic.

Some scholars go further. Not content with limiting the range of the term "experience" to particular individuals, they go on to speak of the "collective experience" of an entire community or culture. Attention to the collective or "lived" experience of a religious community is touted as one way of overcoming cultural bias—our tendency to view the beliefs and actions of people different from ourselves as backward, foolish, or bizarre. If we can bracket our own presuppositions, temper our ingrained sense of cultural superiority, and resist the

94

temptation to evaluate the truth claims of foreign traditions, we find that their *experience* of the world possesses its own rationality, its own coherence, its own truth. This approach, sometimes known as the phenomenology of religion, enjoins the "imaginative participation in the world of the actor" in order to arrive at "value free" and "evocative" descriptions (Smart 1973, 20–1).

This use of the concept "religious experience" is exceedingly broad, encompassing a vast array of feelings, moods, perceptions, dispositions, and states of consciousness. Some prefer to focus on a distinct type of religious experience known as "mystical experience," typically construed as a transitory but potentially transformative state of consciousness in which a subject purports to come into immediate contact with the divine, the sacred, the holy. We will return to the issue of mystical experience below. Here I would only note that the academic literature does not clearly delineate the relationship between religious experience and mystical experience. The reluctance, and in the end the inability, to clearly stipulate the meaning of such terms will be a recurring theme in the discussion below.

II

It is not difficult to understand the allure of the rhetoric of experience in the modern period. Both Western theologians and secular scholars of religion found themselves facing, each in their own way, a host of challenges that, for the purposes of this essay, I will group under the two headings *empiricism* and *cultural pluralism*.

By empiricism I refer to the notion that all truth claims must be subject, in theory if not in fact, to empirical or scientific verification. This was a potential problem for modern theologians, as many essential elements of theological reflection are simply not amenable to empirical observation or testing. By emphasizing the experiential dimension of religion—a dimension inaccessible to strictly objective modes of inquiry—the theologian could forestall scientific critique. Religious truth claims were not to be understood as pertaining to the objective or material world, which was the proper domain of science, but to the inner spiritual world, for which the scientific method was deemed inappropriate.

Unlike the theologian, the secular scholar was not necessarily invested in the truth claims of any particular religious tradition. However, scholars of religion do have a vested interest in the existence of irreducibly *religious* phenomena over which they can claim special authority. That is to say, other academic disciplines—history, anthropology, sociology, or psychology, for example—could (and sometimes did) claim to possess the requisite tools for the analysis of religion, a claim that threatened to put the religion specialist out of a job. By construing religion as pertaining to a distinct mode of "experience," the scholar of religion could argue that it ultimately eludes the grasp of other more empirically oriented disciplines.

The second challenge for both theologians and secular scholars was that of cultural pluralism. By the twentieth century it had become difficult for Christian theologians to simply ignore the existence of non-Christian traditions, much less to smugly assert Christian superiority. But to take other traditions seriously entailed the risk of rendering Christianity merely one of several competing systems of belief. In privileging religious experience, theologians could argue that all religious traditions emerged from, and were attempts to give expression to, an apprehension of the divine or the ultimate. Differences in doctrine and forms of worship are to be expected due to vast differences in linguistic, social, and cultural conditions. What is key, however, is that as a response to a fundamentally human (and thus pancultural and ahistorical) sense of the transcendent, all religious traditions could lay *some* claim to truth. This allowed Christian theologians to affirm the validity of Christian revelation without necessarily impugning their non-Christian rivals.

Cultural pluralism was no less a problem for secular scholars of religion, who had to contend with the knowledge that the category "religion" was itself a cultural product. Many, if not most, non-Western traditions lacked an indigenous lexical equivalent for "religion" altogether, and attempts to define or stipulate the nature of religion were often tainted with Western presuppositions. Like the theologian, the scholar of religion found the very existence of his ostensible subject of expertise open to question. By appealing to non-tradition-specific notions such as the "sacred" or the "holy"—notions that blur the distinction between a universal human experience and the posited object of said experience—the scholar could legitimize the comparative study of religion even while acknowledging the specifically Western origins of the category itself. The scholar could then argue that if places such as India or Japan or pre-Columbian America lacked an indigenous term for religion, it was not because they lacked religious experience. On the contrary, every aspect of their life was so suffused with a sense of the divine that they simply did not distinguish between the secular and the sacred.

III

The ideological aspect of the appeal to experience—the use of the concept to legitimize vested social, institutional, and professional interests—is most evident when we turn to the study of mysticism. As mentioned above, mystical experience is generally construed as a direct encounter with the divine or the absolute, and as such some scholars claim that the "raw experience" itself is not affected by linguistic, cultural, or historical contingencies. Obviously, a given individual's understanding and articulation of such an experience will be conditioned by the tradition to which he or she belongs. Thus a Christian might talk about witnessing the Holy Spirit, a Hindu about absorption into Brahman, a Buddhist about the extinction of the self. But if one is able to see beyond the superficial, culturally determined differences between these accounts one discovers a single unvarying core. Or so goes the argument advanced by William James (1961

[1902]), Rudolf Otto (1958 [1917]), Aldous Huxley (1946), W. T. Stace (1960), and Robert Forman (1990), among others. Needless to say there are important differences in the views of these scholars, but all more or less agree that it is possible to distinguish between a core experience (or core experiences) proper, and the divergent culturally conditioned expressions of that core. Such a position led naturally to attempts to isolate the universal features of mystical experience through the analysis of "firsthand reports." William James (1961), for example, proposed four such features, namely, noetic quality, ineffability, transiency, and passivity; Rudolf Otto (1958) speaks more loosely of "creature feeling," awefulness, overpoweringness, energy, and fascination. Others reject the essential features approach altogether in favor of a looser "family resemblance" model, and several scholars argue that not one but two or more primary experiences exist, distinguishing, for example, between "introvertive" and "extrovertive" types (Stace 1960).

This understanding of mystical experience, sometimes known as the "perennial philosophy" (a term popularized by Huxley's 1946 book of that title), proved quite influential among scholars of religion. But how is one to make conceptual sense of such an experience? One popular explanation goes as follows: logically we can, and indeed must, distinguish the object of consciousness from the *knowing* of that object; otherwise, we would be indistinguishable from insentient robots or automatons that are able to respond to stimuli without being conscious of them. There is, in other words, a residue in all conscious experience that cannot be reduced to the content of consciousness alone. This knowing factor, variously referred to as pure consciousness, prereflective experience, the true self, the cogito, and so on, is the proper object of a mystic's self-knowledge. Mystical experience consists in the direct, though somewhat paradoxical, apperception of, or absorption into, the knowing subject itself. Since this experience of pure subjectivity is free of individuating ego, mystics are led to speak of being one with the world or one with the absolute. (If some theistically oriented mystics avoid explicitly monistic language, it is due to the doctrinal constraints imposed by their respective dualistic traditions.)

This is, of course, a highly simplified account of the perennialist position, and its defenders do not speak with a single voice. Be that as it may, in the past few decades this approach to mysticism has come under concerted attack from a number of scholars, notably Gershom Scholem (1969), Steven Katz (1978, 1983, 1992), Wayne Proudfoot (1985), and Grace Jantzen (1995). The objections are manifold. To begin with, critics note that we do not have access to mystical experiences per se but only to texts that purport to describe them, and the perennialists systematically misconstrue these texts due to their a priori commitment to the perennialist position. Read impartially, there is little internal evidence to indicate that these very disparate accounts are actually referring to one and the same experience.

Besides, the very notion that one can separate an unmediated experience from a culturally determined description of that experience is philosophically suspect. According to Katz, "neither mystical experience nor more ordinary forms of experience give any indication, or any grounds for believing, that they are unmediated" (1978, 26). In other words, mystical experience is wholly shaped by a mystic's cultural environment, personal history, doctrinal commitments, religious training, expectations, aspirations, and so on.

Yet another problem with the perennialist position emerged as scholars turned to the intellectual genealogy of the category "religious experience" itself. The concept turns out to be of relatively recent, and distinctively Western, provenance. Wayne Proudfoot traces the roots of the idea to the German theologian Friedrich Schleiermacher (1768–1834), who argued that religion cannot be reduced to a system of beliefs or morality. Religion proper, claimed Schleiermacher, is predicated on a feeling of the infinite—the "consciousness of absolute dependence" (see, for example, Schleiermacher 1928). According to Proudfoot, this emphasis on feeling was motivated by Schleiermacher's "interest in freeing religious doctrine and practice from dependence on metaphysical beliefs and ecclesiastical institutions" (1985, xiii; see also Jantzen 1995, 311–21). Schleiermacher's strategy proved fruitful: the notion of religious experience provided new grounds upon which to defend religion against secular and scientific critique. The "hermeneutic of experience" was soon adopted by a host of scholars interested in religion, the most influential being William James, and today many have a difficult time imagining *what else* religion might be about. Yet prior to Schleiermacher, insists Proudfoot, religion was simply not understood in such terms, and it is thus incumbent upon us to reject the perennialist hypothesis insofar as it anachronistically imposes the recent and ideologically laden notion of religious experience on our interpretations of premodern phenomena.

IV

The claim that religious experience is a relatively late and distinctively Western invention might strike the reader as dubious at best. Did not mystical experience play a central role in the religions of Asia since time immemorial? We read repeatedly that Asian mystics have charted the depths of the human psyche, explored a vast array of altered states of consciousness, and left behind detailed maps so that others may follow in their footsteps. Hinduism and Buddhism, to pick the two best-known examples, are often approached not as religions, philosophies, or social systems but rather as "spiritual technologies" intended to induce a transformative experience of the absolute in the mind of the practitioner. Thus, while the emphasis on experience might be relatively new in the West, this is clearly not the case in the East. Or so one might suppose from the plethora of writings on the subject.

But not so fast. The notion that Asian religions are more experientially rooted than their Western counterparts is one of those truisms so widely and unquestioningly held that corroboration of any kind is deemed superfluous. But when we turn to premodern Asian sources, the evidence is ambiguous at best. Take, for example, the many important Buddhist exegetical works that delineate the Buddhist *mārga* or "path to liberation"—works such as "Stages on the Bodhi-sattva Path" *(Bodhisattvabhūmi)*, "The Stages of Practice" *(Bhāvanākrama)*, "Path of Purity" *(Visuddhimagga)*, "The Great Calming and Contemplation" *(Mo-ho chih-kuan)*, "The Great Book on the Stages of the Path" *(Lam rim chen mo)*, and so on. These texts are frequently construed as descriptive accounts of meditative states based on the personal experiences of accomplished adepts. Yet rarely if ever do the authors of these compendiums claim to base their expositions on their own experience. On the contrary, the authority of exegetes such as Kamalaśīla, Buddhaghosa, and Chih-i lay not in their access to exalted spiritual states but in their mastery of, and rigorous adherence to, sacred scripture (Sharf 1995a). This situation is by no means unique to Buddhism: premodern Hindu-ism was similarly wary of claims to authority predicated on personal experience (Halbfass 1988).

The notion that meditation is central to Asian religious praxis might seem to support the thesis that Asian traditions exalt personal experience. But here too we must be cautious: contemporary accounts of Asian meditation typically *presume* that they are oriented toward meditative experience, and thus such accounts must be used with considerable caution. Besides, while meditation may have been es-teemed in theory, it did not occupy the dominant role in monastic and ascetic life that is sometimes supposed. (This point is often overlooked by scholars who fail to distinguish between prescriptive and descriptive accounts.) Even when prac-ticed, it is by no means obvious that traditional forms of meditation were ori-ented toward the attainment of extraordinary "states of consciousness." Medi-tation was first and foremost a means of eliminating defilement, accumulating merit and supernatural power, invoking apotropaic deities, and so forth. This is not to deny that religious practitioners had *experiences* in the course of their training, just that such experiences were not considered the goal of practice, were not deemed doctrinally authoritative, and did not serve as the reference points for their understanding of the path (Sharf 1995a). Indeed, as we will see below, personal experience, no matter how extraordinary, *could not* serve as such a ref-erence point precisely because of its ambiguous epistemological status and essen-tially indeterminate nature—a point appreciated by not a few medieval Buddhist exegetes.

The complementary notions that Asian religious traditions are predicated on mystical experience, and that meditation is a means to induce such experience, are so well ingrained that it might be useful to pause for a moment to consider their provenance. The valorization of experience in Asian thought can be traced to a handful of twentieth-century Asian religious leaders and apologists, all of whom were in sustained dialogue with their intellectual counterparts in the West. For example, the notion that personal experience constitutes the heart of the Hindu tradition originated with the prolific philosopher and statesman Sarvepalli

Radhakrishnan (1888–1975). Like his European and American predecessors, Radhakrishnan argued that "if philosophy of religion is to become scientific, it must become empirical and found itself on religious experience" (1937, 84), and "it is not true religion unless it ceases to be a traditional view and becomes personal experience" (88). Thus in a single stroke Radhakrishnan could associate true religion with both personal experience and the empirical method. Radhakrishnan did not stop there, however, but went on to place the rhetoric of experience in the service of Hindu nationalism. He argued that if "experience is the soul of religion," then Hinduism is closest to that soul precisely because it is not historical but based directly on the "inward life of spirit" (89, 90).

Radhakrishnan's intellectual debt to the West is no secret. Although he was educated in India, he was steeped in Western philosophical and religious thought from an early age, and his specific interest in experience can be traced directly to the works of William James, Francis Herbert Bradley, Henri Bergson, and Baron F. von Hügel, among others (Halbfass 1988, 398). Radhakrishnan held numerous academic posts in India and England, including the Spalding Professorship of Eastern Religions and Ethics at Oxford, and his writings are filled with appreciative references to a variety of American and European thinkers popular at the time, from Evelyn Underhill to Alfred North Whitehead. What is curious is not that he should have placed his synthesis of Western and Indian philosophy in the service of an overtly apologetic and nationalist project, but that given this project he is nevertheless considered by many to be a credible "native source" on the subject of traditional Hinduism.

One can, perhaps, find antecedents of Radhakrishnan's hermeneutic in the writings of Debendranāth Tagore (1817–1905), an early leader of the Western-influenced Hindu reform movement Brāhmo Samāj, who held that the teachings of the Vedas may be affirmed through one's own experience. However, Tagore, like his predecessor Rāmmohun Roy (1772–1833), was intimately acquainted with Western thought in general and Christian critiques of Hinduism in particular. His exegetical writings, and his work for the Brāhmo Samāj, were directed toward the "purification" of Hinduism so as to stay the growing influence of Christian missionaries and their converts. In the end there is simply no evidence of an indigenous Indian counterpart to the rhetoric of experience prior to the colonial period (Halbfass 1988).

Western conceptions of Asian spirituality are equally indebted to the writings of that indefatigable proselytizer of Zen Buddhism, D. T. Suzuki (1870–1966). According to Suzuki, religious experience is not merely a central feature of Zen, it is the whole of Zen. In his voluminous writings, Suzuki advanced the notion that Zen eschews all doctrine, all ritual, all institutions, and is thus in the final analysis not a religion at all. Zen is pure experience itself, the experiential essence lying behind all authentic religious teachings. Zen is associated, of course, with particular monasteries, forms of worship, and works of literature and art, but these are all mere "fingers pointing at the moon." The moon is none other than the unmediated experience of the absolute in which the dualism of subject and object, observer and observed, is transcended. This view of Zen has become so well established that many hesitate to speak of Zen at all for fear of being censured as insufficiently experienced.

Suzuki, like Radhakrishnan, places this understanding of Zen in the interests of a transparently nationalist discourse. Suzuki insisted that Zen is the wellspring of Japanese culture, and that the traditional arts of Japan—tea ceremony, monochrome painting, martial arts, landscape gardening, Noh theater, et cetera—are all ultimately expressions of Zen gnosis. Japanese culture naturally predisposes the Japanese toward Zen experience, such that they have a deeply ingrained appreciation of the unity of subject and object, human being and nature. This is in marked contradistinction to the excessively materialistic and dualistic traditions of the West.

Suzuki's musings on the "Japanese mind" must be understood in the context of Japan's sense of technological and scientific inferiority vis-à-vis the Occident in the earlier part of this century. In the final analysis, Suzuki, like Radhakrishnan, attempts nothing less than the apotheosis of an entire people. And like Radhakrishnan, Suzuki's emphasis on experience owes as much to his exposure to Western thought as it does to indigenous Asian or Zen sources. In fact, Suzuki's qualifications as an exponent of Zen are somewhat dubious. Suzuki did engage in Zen practice at Engakuji during his student days at Tokyo Imperial University, and he enjoyed a close relationship with the abbot Shaku Sōen (1859–1919). But by traditional standards, Suzuki's training was relatively modest: he was never ordained, his formal monastic education was desultory at best, and he never received institutional sanction as a Zen teacher. This is not to impugn Suzuki's academic competence; he was a gifted philologist who made a lasting contribution to the study of Buddhist texts. In the end, however, his approach to Zen, with its unrelenting emphasis on an unmediated inner experience, is not derived from Buddhist sources so much as from his broad familiarity with European and American philosophical and religious writings (Sharf 1995c).

Suzuki's early interest in things Western was wide-ranging, and included such fashionable quasi-religious movements as Theosophy, Swedenborgianism, and the "Religion of Science." The latter doctrine was the brainchild of the German-American essayist Paul Carus (1852–1919), who worked as editor at the Open Court Publishing Company in La Salle, Illinois. Carus was convinced that once the "old religions" were purified of their superstitious and irrational elements, they would work in conjunction with science to bring humankind to the realization that there is no distinction between the immaterial and the material—between mind and matter. Carus was particularly attracted to Buddhism, which he felt was close in spirit to his own philosophy.

Suzuki was initially drawn to Carus after reading *Gospel of Buddha*, a compendium of Buddhist teachings compiled by Carus and published in Open Court's "Religion of Science" series in 1894 (see Carus 1915). Carus had taken available

European translations of Buddhist scriptures and, through the use of careful selection, creative retranslation, and outright fabrication, managed to portray the
teachings of the Buddha as humanistic, rational, and scientific. Suzuki, who had
been asked to translate the *Gospel of Buddha* into Japanese, was so impressed with
Carus's work that he arranged to travel to America to study under his tutelage.
Suzuki was to remain in La Salle for some eleven years, and it was toward the end
of this period that he became familiar with the writings of William James.

Suzuki appears to have been responsible for introducing James's work to his
high school friend Nishida Kitarō (1870–1945). It was through Nishida, who
was to emerge as Japan's leading modern philosopher, that the notion of a distinctively religious mode of experience took hold in Japan. Nishida's first philosophical monograph, published in 1911 under the title *Zen no kenkyū* ("A Study
of the Good"; see Nishida 1990), was dedicated to the elucidation of *junsui
keiken,* or "pure experience," a notion culled directly from James. But the context of Nishida's "pure experience" was much removed from that of James.
James sought to overcome the substance ontology that continued to infect classical empiricism, and to this end he proposed a pragmatic account of experience
that avoided the reification of either subject or object. Nishida, on the other
hand, was interested in integrating Western philosophy with his understanding
of Zen, and consequently his notion of pure experience seems to function both
as an ontological ground that subsumes subject and object and as a psychological
state of heightened self-awareness.

Suzuki seized upon Nishida's notion of pure experience and made it the central element in his exposition of Zen. And it proved to be an effective hermeneutic strategy, for here was an approach to Zen that was both familiar and attractive
to Suzuki's Western audience. The irony of the situation is that the terms used
by the Japanese to render "experience"—*keiken* and *taiken*—are both modern
neologisms coined in the Meiji period (1868–1912) by translators of Western
philosophical works. (As far as I have been able to determine, *keiken* was first
used to render the English "experience," while *taiken* was used for the German
erleben and *Erlebnis.*) There simply is no premodern Japanese lexical equivalent
for "experience." Nor, I would add, is there a premodern Chinese equivalent.
Chinese translators borrowed the Japanese neologisms in their own renderings
of Western texts.

The interest in religious experience among twentieth-century Asian intellectuals is not difficult to fathom. Like their Western counterparts, Asian apologists
were forced to respond to empiricist and pluralist critiques of their religious heritage. But Asian intellectuals had another threat with which to contend as well,
namely, the affront of Western cultural imperialism, sustained as it was by the
West's political, technological, and military dominance. Asian intellectuals, many
of whom were educated in Christian missionary schools, were deeply aware of
the contempt with which Occidentals viewed the religious culture of Asia. Cas-
tigated as primitive, idolatrous, and intellectually benighted, Asian religion was
held responsible for the continent's social, political, and scientific failings. This

is the context in which we must understand the Asian appropriation and manipulation of the rhetoric of experience. Men like Radhakrishnan and Suzuki would not only affirm the experiential foundation of their own religious traditions, but they would turn around and present those traditions as more intuitive, more mystical, more experiential, and thus "purer" than the discursive faiths of the West. In short, if the West excelled materially, the East excelled spiritually. This strategy had the felicitous result of thwarting the Enlightenment critique of religion on the one hand and the threat of Western cultural hegemony on the other.

The polemics of Radhakrishnan, Suzuki, and their intellectual heirs has had a significant impact on the study of religion in the West. Few Western scholars were in a position to question the romanticized image of Asian mysticism proffered forth by these intelligent and articulate "representatives" of living Asian faiths. Besides, the discovery of common ground offered considerable comfort. The very notion that religious experience might function as a universal in the study of world religions evolved, in many respects, out of this cross-cultural encounter. In time the dialogue grew into a veritable academic industry, complete with its own professional societies, its own journals, and its own conferences and symposia, all devoted to the comparative study of "Western" and "Eastern" thought. The striking confluence of Western and Asian interests prevented those on both sides from noticing the tenuous ground on which the exchange had been built.

V

Seemingly oblivious to matters of historical context, arguments continue over the nature of mystical experience to the present day with no resolution in sight. The issues have not changed: scholars disagree over the extent to which mystical experiences are shaped by prior culturally mediated expectations and presuppositions, over whether one can separate a mystic's description of her experiences from her interpretations, over the existence of so-called "pure consciousness" devoid of intentional objects, over competing schemes for typologizing mystical states, and over the philosophical and ethical significance, if any, of mystical experience. (The *Journal of the American Academy of Religion* alone has, of late, seen fit to publish an article a year on the topic; see Barnard 1992; Forman 1993; Shear 1994; Short 1995; and Brainard 1996.) What is curious in these ongoing discussions is not so much the points of controversy as the areas of consensus. Virtually all parties tacitly accept the notion that terms such as "religious experience," "mystical experience," or "meditative experience" function referentially, that is, their signification lies in the signifieds to which they allegedly refer. Hence scholars of mysticism are content to focus on the distinctive characteristics and the philosophical implications, if any, of religious or mystical experiences without pausing to consider what sort of thing *experience* might be in the first place.

What exactly *do* we mean by experience? The dictionaries provide several overlapping definitions, but for our purposes we can focus on two more or less distinct usages. The first is to "participate in," or "live through," as one might say "I have combat experience" or "I have experience with diesel engines." This use of the term is relatively unproblematic; it does not elicit any particular epistemological or metaphysical conundrums since the referent of the term would seem to lie in the social or public sphere. The second more epistemological or phenomenological meaning is to "directly perceive," "observe," "be aware of," or "be conscious of." Here there is a tendency to think of experience as a subjective "mental event" or "inner process" that eludes public scrutiny. In thinking of experience along these lines it is difficult to avoid the image of mind as an immaterial substrate or psychic field, a sort of inner space in which the outer material world is reflected or re-represented. Scholars leave the category experience unexamined precisely because the meaning of experience, like the stuff of experience, would seem to be utterly transparent. Experience is simply given to us in the immediacy of each moment of perception.

This picture of mind clearly has its roots in Descartes and his notion of mind as an "immaterial substance" (although few today would subscribe to Descartes's substance ontology). And following the Cartesian perspective, we assume that insofar as experience is immediately present, experience per se is both indubitable and irrefutable. (While the *content* of experience may prove ambiguous or deceptive, the fact that I am experiencing *something* is beyond question.) The characteristics of immediacy and indubitability galvanized the "hermeneutic of experience." Experience, construed as the inviolable realm of pure presence, promised a refuge from the hermeneutic and epistemological vagaries of modern intellectual life. Just as some scholars of literature would invoke "authorial intent" as a way to overcome ambiguity in the interpretation of literary works (see esp. Hirsch 1967), the notion of experience promised to ground the meaning of religious texts and performances through an appeal to the experiences to which they refer. (The analogy is more than fortuitous: authorial intent and religious experience both occupy the same highly ambiguous but ultimately unassailable "ontological space.")

Yet the problem is unavoidable: if talk of shamanic experience, mystical experience, enlightenment experience, or what have you is to have any sort of determinate meaning, we must construe the term "experience" in referential or ostensive terms. But to do so is to objectify it, which would seem to undermine its most salient characteristic, namely, its immediacy. So we are posed with a dilemma: experience cannot be determinate without being rendered a "thing"; if it is a thing it cannot be indubitable; but if it is not a thing, then it cannot perform the hermeneutic task that religious scholars require of it—that of determining meaning. We will return to this point below.

But first I must respond to the following inevitable rebuke: that a scholar such as myself should have a difficult time *situating* the locus of religious experience merely attests to his own spiritual impoverishment. If only I had a taste of the real thing, I would quickly and humbly forgo my rueful attempt to explain away such phenomena. Indeed, I would sympathize with the difficulty mystics have in expressing themselves. Do not mystics repeatedly allude to precisely this problem, that is, the problem in conceptualizing that which transcends all concepts?

This objection would seem to rest on an appeal to ethnographic evidence, to the witness of real mystics or religious adepts with firsthand experience of nonconceptual states. Of course, the problem is exacerbated by the fact that, according to the historical critique summarized above, the category experience is itself of recent provenance, and thus the testimony of mystics of old, who talk in rather different terms (not to mention in dead languages), is going to prove ambiguous at best. So let us keep things simple and select a contemporary religious community that (1) unquestionably valorizes religious experience, and (2) possesses a sophisticated technical vocabulary with which they describe and analyze such experience.

Vipassanā or "insight" practice (also known as *satipaṭṭhāna* or "foundations of mindfulness") is a Buddhist form of meditation that is popular in Theravāda communities in Southeast Asia. (It is also influential among Buddhist enthusiasts in the West.) It must be noted that the specific techniques propagated today under the *vipassanā* rubric, with their unequivocal emphasis on exalted meditative states, cannot be traced back prior to the late nineteenth century, and thus they are an unreliable source for the reconstruction of premodern Theravāda. (The techniques were reconstructed in the modern period on the basis of scriptural accounts; see Sharf 1995a). Be that as it may, contemporary adepts believe that their experiences in meditation tally with the "descriptions" of progressive soteriological stages found in Buddhist scriptures. They thus treat the ancient scholastic terms pertaining to stages of Buddhist practice as if they designated discrete experiences accessible to contemporary practitioners. The claim that adepts in *vipassanā* can clearly recognize and reproduce the various stages mentioned in canonical sources has encouraged some scholars to treat Theravāda meditation theory as a sort of empirical phenomenology of altered states of consciousness that can be applied to non-Buddhist as well as Buddhist phenomena (Sharf 1995a, 261).

On closer inspection, however, we find that the scriptures upon which the *vipassanā* revival is based (primarily the two *Satipaṭṭhāna-suttas* and the *Visuddhimagga*) are often ambiguous or inconsistent, and contemporary *vipassanā* teachers are frequently at odds with each other over the interpretation of key terms. For example, Buddhist sources categorize the range of available meditation techniques under two broad headings, *samatha* or "concentration," and *vipassanā* or "insight." Judging from scriptural accounts, one would presume that it would be difficult to confuse the two; both the techniques and the goals to which the techniques are directed differ substantially. *Samatha* practices, which involve focusing the mind on a single object, are supposed to result in an ascending series of four "material absorptions" (or "trances," *rūpa-jhāna*) and a further series of four (or five) "immaterial absorptions" *(arūpa-jhāna)*, that bestow upon the practitioner various supernatural powers. *Vipassanā*, on the other hand, involves the disciplined contemplation of seminal Buddhist doctrines such as impermanence or nonself, and leads directly to nirvana or full liberation. Nirvana is achieved in four successive stages known as the "noble attainments" *(ariya-phala)*, the first of which is called *sotāpatti* or "entry into the stream." While *samatha* is an effective means to acquire specific spiritual powers, such as the ability to levitate or to read minds, only *vipassanā* leads to enlightenment proper. Since the soteriological ramifications of *samatha* and *vipassanā* differ so markedly, one would suppose that the experiential states with which they are associated would be easy to distinguish on phenomenological grounds.

All contemporary Theravāda meditation masters accept the canonical categories outlined above. But curiously, despite the fact that these teachers have "tasted the fruits" of practice, there is little if any consensus among them as to the application of these key terms. On the contrary, the designation of particular techniques and the identification of the meditative experiences that result from them are the subjects of continued and often acrimonious debate. More often than not the categories are used polemically to disparage the teachings of rival teachers. Since all agree that *vipassanā* leads to liberation while *samatha* does not, *samatha* is used to designate the techniques and experiences promoted by one's competitors, while *vipassanā* is reserved for one's own teachings. Other teachers may *think* they are promoting authentic *vipassanā* and realizing stages of enlightenment, but in fact they are simply mistaking *jhānic* absorption for *sotāpatti*, the first stage of enlightenment achieved through *vipassanā*.

I do not have the space to explore the *vipassanā* controversies in detail here (see the full account in Sharf 1995a). Suffice it to say that there is simply no public consensus in the contemporary Theravāda community as to the application of terms that allegedly refer to discrete experiential states. Not surprisingly, the same is found to be true in Japanese Zen. Again, it is important to remember that, *pace* much of the popular literature on Zen, premodern Zen masters rarely emphasized exotic experiential states, and terms such as *satori* ("to understand" or "to apprehend") and *kenshō* ("to see one's true nature") were not construed as singular "states of consciousness." Be that as it may, some contemporary Zen teachers, notably those associated with the upstart Sanbōkyōdan lineage, do approach Zen phenomenologically. In other words, they unapologetically present Zen practice as a means to inculcate *kenshō*, which they understand to be an unmediated and transitory apprehension of "nonduality." Some Sanbōkyōdan masters go so far as to present certificates to students who achieve *kenshō* to validate and celebrate their accomplishment.

Even if the Sanbōkyōdan understanding of *kenshō* does not accord with classical models, one might suppose that it is nevertheless an identifiable and reproducible experience. After all, it is verified and certified by the masters of the school. But once again the ethnographic evidence points in another direction.

One quickly discovers that eminent teachers from other living Zen traditions (Rinzai, Sōtō, Ōbaku) do not accord legitimacy to Sanbōkyōdan claims of *kenshō*. This might be dismissed as mere sectarian rivalry or sour grapes. But even within the Sanbōkyōdan itself there has been a long-standing controversy surrounding the verification and authentication of *kenshō* experiences that has threatened to result in schism (Sharf 1995b). In modern Zen, as in Theravāda, eminent meditation masters prove unable to agree on the identification of a "referent" of terms that supposedly refer to specific and replicable experiential states.

The lack of consensus among prominent Buddhist teachers as to the designation not only of particular states of consciousness but also of the psychotropic techniques used to produce them *(samatha* versus *vipassanā)* belies the notion that the rhetoric of meditative experience, at least in Buddhism, functions ostensively. Critical analysis shows that modern Buddhist communities judge "claims to experience" on the basis of the meditator's particular lineage, the specific ritual practice that engendered the experience, the behavior that ensued, and so on. In other words, a meditative state or liberative experience is identified not on the basis of privileged personal access to its distinctive phenomenology, but rather on the basis of eminently public criteria. Such judgments are inevitably predicated on prior ideological commitments shaped by one's vocation (monk or layperson), one's socioeconomic background (urban middle class or rural poor), one's political agenda (traditionalist or reformer), one's sectarian affiliation, one's education, and so forth. In the end, the Buddhist rhetoric of experience is both informed by, and wielded in, the interests of personal and institutional authority.

The modern Theravāda and Zen reform movements discussed here are of particular import, as both claim to possess an elaborate technical vocabulary that refers to a set of exotic but nonetheless verifiable and reproducible experiences. Clearly, if these experiential states are not determinative, then the baroque visions, ineffable reveries, and exotic trances associated with various other mystical traditions inspire even less confidence that the rhetoric of experience functions ostensively.

VI

At this point the reader may well be growing impatient. Surely, even if mystics and meditation masters cannot always agree among themselves as to the designation or soteriological import of their experiences, it is clear that *something* must be going on. Those Buddhist meditators are clearly experiencing *something* in the midst of their ascetic ordeals, even if they cannot ultimately agree on whether it should be called *jhāna, sotāpatti, kenshō,* or whatever. The vigorous and often exuberant language used by mystics the world over to describe their visions, trances, and states of cosmic union must refer to *something*.

This objection attests once again to our deep entanglement in the Cartesian paradigm, to the lingering allure of what Richard Rorty (1979) has called the "glassy essence" or "mirror of nature" view of mind. This is not the place to plunge into the hoary controversies waged under the auspices of "philosophy of mind." Rather, I will defer once again to an ethnographic case that underscores issues of immediate relevance to the study of religion.

Consider, for a moment, a distinctly contemporary form of visionary experience: reports of alien abduction. There are now hundreds if not thousands of individuals from across America who claim to have been abducted by alien beings. A number of apparently reputable investigators have found the abductees' stories compelling, in large part because of the degree of consistency across the narratives (e.g., Mack 1995; Bryan 1995). For example, many of the abductees "independently" report encountering the "small greys"—short hairless humanoid beings with large heads, big black eyes, tiny nostrils, no discernible ears, and a thin slit for a mouth that is apparently little used. (The small greys communicate telepathically.) Their torsos are slender, with long arms and fingers but no thumb, and they sport close-fitting single piece tunics and boots (Mack 1995, 22–3). After being transported to the alien craft, abductees report being subjected to various medical examinations and procedures, many of which focus on the reproductive system. The abductees are then returned, usually to the place from which they were first spirited away.

The vast majority of the abductees have no initial recall of the episode at all. They may be aware only of an unaccountable gap of a few hours or so, and a lingering sense of anxiety, confusion, and fear. They are able to fill in the blanks and reconstruct the details of their abduction only with the help of therapy and hypnosis.

The abductees, known among themselves and in the literature as "experiencers," come from a wide variety of economic and social backgrounds. According to investigators, as a population the abductees show no significant prior history of, or propensity toward, psychopathology. Many of the abductees insist that prior to their alien encounter they had no interest in, or exposure to, reports of abductions, UFOs, or other "new age" phenomena. In fact, the one thing on which both believers and skeptics agree is that the abductees are on the whole sincere; they are not consciously fabricating the narratives for personal fame or profit. On the contrary, the abductees are convinced that their memories accord with objective events, and they stand by their stories even when ridiculed or ostracized by neighbors and relatives. Investigators sympathetic to the abductees' plight report that they manifest the sort of confusion, stress, and chronic anxiety characteristic of post-traumatic stress syndrome. In fact, the psychological disorders suffered by the abductees, and their own steadfast belief in their stories, constitute the closest thing we have to empirical evidence for the abductions.

Despite the pleas of a few prominent investigators such as John Mack, most scholars are understandably skeptical. Skeptics can cite the striking absence of corroborating physical evidence, as well as the questionable methods used by investigators. As mentioned above, many abductees have no memory of the event until it is "recovered" by therapists who have made a speciality out of treating victims of alien abductions. Finally, folklorists are able to trace the origins of many central elements and motifs in the abduction narratives—the physiognomy of the aliens, the appearance of their spacecrafts, the ordeal of the medical examination, and so on—to popular science fiction comics, stories, and films of the past fifty years. The scholarly consensus would seem to be that the abductions simply did not take place; there is no *originary event* behind the memories.

The notion of originary event is crucial here. Clearly, we will not get far by denying the existence of the memories themselves. Our skepticism is rather directed at what, if anything, may lie behind them. We suspect that the abductees' reports do not stem from actual alien encounters but that some other complex historical, sociological, and psychological processes are at work. Whatever the process turns out to be (and we are a long way from an adequate explanation of the phenomenon), it is reasonable to assume that the abductees' memories do not faithfully represent actual historical occurrences.

One might argue that skepticism with regard to the existence of aliens does not imply that there is no *other* determinate historical event at the root of the memories. The memories must refer back to *some* previous incident, even if the nature of this incident is systematically misconstrued by the credulous abductees. Memory is fickle.

This has been the approach of some psychoanalytically oriented observers who treat the alien encounters as "screen memories" that cloak an early repressed trauma such as childhood sexual abuse. The problem with this hypothesis is that the epistemological problems raised by postulating repressed memories turn out to be, in many respects, of the same order as those associated with alien abductions. Childhood trauma has been the etiology du jour, and is typically only recovered in a therapeutic encounter with a specialist whose training and institutional investments predispose him to this specific diagnosis. In the end childhood trauma is as elusive a beast as the aliens themselves (see Hacking 1995).

Several scholars have drawn attention to the religious patterns and motifs running through the abduction narratives. The reports are reminiscent, for example, of tales of shamanic trance journeys, in which the subject is transported to an alien domain populated by otherworldly beings with inconceivable powers and ambiguous intentions. Many abductees are entrusted with important spiritual messages to be propagated among the human race, messages about the importance of peace, love, and universal brotherhood (Whitmore 1995). Moreover, the role of the therapists who help to elicit and shape the abduction narratives is analogous to the role played by priest or preceptor in more established religious traditions. The question is unavoidable: Is there any reason to assume that the reports of experiences by mystics, shamans, or meditation masters are any more credible as "phenomenological descriptions" than those of the abductees?

It should now be apparent that the question is not merely whether or not mystical experiences are constructed, unmediated, pure, or philosophically significant. The more fundamental question is whether we can continue to treat the texts and reports upon which such theories are based as referring, however obliquely, to determinative phenomenal events at all.

VII

> But I have felt so many strange things, so many baseless things assuredly, that they are perhaps better left unsaid. To speak for example of the times when I go liquid and become like mud, what good would that do? Or of the others when I would be lost in the eye of a needle, I am so hard and contracted? No, those are well-meaning squirms that get me nowhere.
> —Samuel Beckett, *Malone Dies*

Consider the taste of beer. Most would agree that beer is an acquired taste; few enjoy their first sip. In time many come to enjoy the flavor. But what has changed? The flavor, or merely our reaction to it? More to the point, how could one possibly decide the issue one way or the other? Something seems fishy about the question itself.

This is one of a series of illustrations and anecdotes used by the philosopher Daniel Dennett (1992) to undermine the concept of *qualia* (see also Dennett 1991). *Qualia* (the singular form is *quale*), is a term proposed by philosophers to designate those subjective or phenomenal properties of experience that resist a purely materialistic explanation. (The notion is an attempt to capture that aspect of consciousness that, say some, could never be reproduced by a "thinking machine.") In short, *qualia* refer to the way things *seem*. "Look at a glass of milk at sunset; *the way it looks to you*—the particular, personal, subjective visual quality of the glass of milk is the *quale* of your visual experience at the moment. The *way the milk tastes to you then* is another, gustatory *quale*" (Dennett 1992, 42). As it is never possible to communicate exactly how things appear to us (How could we ever know whether your experience of red is precisely the same as mine?), *qualia* are construed as essentially private, ineffable, and irreducible properties of experience.

Dennett thinks the whole notion of *qualia* is wrongheaded and employs a series of "intuition pumps," such as his musings on the flavor of beer, in order to undermine our confidence in the existence of intrinsic properties of experience. "If it is admitted that one's attitudes towards, or reactions to, experiences are in any way and in any degree constitutive of their experiential qualities, so that a change in reactivity *amounts to* or *guarantees* a change in the property, then those properties, those 'qualitative or phenomenal features,' cease to be 'intrinsic' properties and in fact become paradigmatically extrinsic, relational properties" (Dennett 1992, 61). And if these most salient aspects of experience are in fact extrinsic and relational, one must relinquish one's picture of experience as a determinate *something* that occurs someplace "inside the brain," in what Dennett calls the "Cartesian theater" (Dennett 1991). In short, one must give up what, in the Cartesian view, is a fundamental attribute of experience: its privacy.

In a somewhat similar spirit, I have suggested that it is ill conceived to construe the object of the study of religion to be the inner experience of religious practitioners. Scholars of religion are not presented with experiences that stand in need of interpretation but rather with texts, narratives, performances, and so forth. While these representations may at times assume the rhetorical stance of phenomenological description, we are not obliged to accept them as such. On the contrary, we must remain alert to the ideological implications of such a stance. Any assertion to the effect that someone else's inner experience bears some significance for *my* construal of reality is situated, by its very nature, in the public realm of contested meanings.

Before we throw out experience altogether, however, we must take stock of what is at stake. The appeal of the rhetoric of experience lay in its promise to forestall the objectification and commodification of personal life endemic to modern mass society. By objectification I refer to the projection of the "subject" or "self" into a centerless physical world of "objective facts" amenable to scientific study and technological mastery—a projection that threatened to efface subjectivity altogether (Nagel 1986). The flip side of objectification has been the rampant alienation that characterizes modernity—the sense of being rootless and adrift, cut off from tradition and history. Into this vacuum rushed the experts—sociologists, psychologists, anthropologists, and even scholars of religion—who claimed to understand *my* memories, *my* dreams, *my* desires, *my* beliefs, *my* thoughts, better than I. We are understandably reluctant to cede such authority to a guild of specialists, no matter how enlightened or well intentioned they may be. Our last line of defense has been the valorization of the "autonomous self," construed as a unique and irreducible center of experience.

This raises a host of complex political and philosophical issues concerned with the modern notion of selfhood and self-determination, issues that, for lack of space, I am unable to pursue here. As students of religion, our more immediate theoretical concerns are hermeneutic: How are we to understand people very different from ourselves without somehow effacing the very differences that separate us? Scholars have become acutely aware of the methodological problems entailed in using *our* conceptual categories and theoretical constructs to comprehend the world of others. In addition, recent postcolonial and feminist critiques have forced us to focus on the asymmetrical relationship between the investigator and his or her subjects. We are wary of the intellectual hubris and cultural chauvinism that often attend scholars as they claim insight into the self-representations of others, especially when those others are at a political and economic disadvantage. And again, the one defense against the tendency to objectify, to domesticate, to silence and eviscerate the other has been to sanction the other's singular and irreducible experience of the world.

Therein lies the rub. We believe it politically and intellectually essential to respect diverse "worldviews," but at the same time we are hesitant to abandon the hermeneutic suspicion that is the mark of critical scholarship. We want to valorize the self-representations of others, yet we balk when "respect for others" places undue demands on our own credulity. Most draw the line, for example, when it comes to acceding the existence of the small greys. And well we should; a critical investigation of the abduction phenomenon can only begin once the decision has been made to look for alternative explanations—explanations that do not involve the existence of interloping aliens.

One strategy to negotiate this impasse has been to empower experience by affirming the truth of the experience narrative, but only to the one doing the narration. This strategy, which is closely allied with the phenomenological approach to religion mentioned above, tends to fragment reality into "multiple objective worlds" (Shweder 1991)—a consequence that does not seem to trouble many scholars of religion. In her book on near-death experiences, for example, Carol Zaleski engages in a critical historical analysis of the sociological and mythological factors that have contributed to near-death narratives in both medieval and modern times. But, somewhat incongruously, she concludes her sophisticated contextual analysis by insisting on the inherent truth value of the experiences themselves. Zaleski manages this by identifying the "other world" described in the near-death accounts with the "inner psychological world" of the subjects themselves. This allows her to valorize the near-death experiences as a "legitimate imaginative means through which one can instill a religious sense of the cosmos" (1987, 203). Zaleski is thus able to countenance the experiences without subscribing to the fantastic cosmologies—the baroque views of heaven, hell, and everything between—that attend them.

Felicitas Goodman (1988), in her study of spirit possession, goes a step further, assuming a decidedly agnostic stance toward the existence of the spirits reported by her subjects. "The experience of [the] presence [of spirits] during possession is accompanied by observable physical changes. We should remember that whether these changes are internally generated or created by external agencies is not discoverable. No one can either prove or disprove that the obvious changes of the brain map in possession or in a patient with a multiple personality disorder, for that matter, are produced by psychological processes or by an invading alien being" (126). Goodman's agnosticism is but a small step away from John Mack's qualified acceptance of the existence of alien abductors.

This methodological stance is made possible by the peculiar nature of claims to experience, particularly religious experiences that are, by definition, extraordinary. Reports of mystical or visionary experiences can be likened to reports of dreams insofar as it is difficult, if not impossible, to separate the report of the experience from the experience itself. In a philosophical examination of dreams, Norman Malcolm (1959) argues that the dream report is indeed the *only* criterion for the dream, and thus to report that one has dreamed *is* to have dreamed; there is simply no other criterion for the dream's existence. Malcolm concludes that dreams are therefore not experiences, a claim that has more to do with how he stipulates the meaning of experience than with the nature of dreaming itself.

Scholars such as Zaleski and Goodman (as well as Steven Katz and other "constructivists") tacitly, if not explicitly, adopt a similar perspective toward religious experience. They acknowledge that there is no way to tease apart the representation of a religious experience from the experience itself. Malcolm would argue that if the two cannot be separated—if the only criterion for the experience is the report itself—then one cannot claim to be dealing with an experience at all. But Zaleski and Goodman move in a different direction, treating the reports as if they provided unmediated access to some originary phenomenal event. The constructivists seem to assume that since the historical, social, and linguistic processes that give rise to the narrative representation are identical with those that give rise to the experience, the former, which are amenable to scholarly analysis, provide a transparent window to the latter.

While we might laud the humanistic impulse that motivates this line of reasoning—the desire to countenance a diversity of "worldviews"—it fails to grasp the rhetorical logic of appeals to experience. The word "experience," insofar as it refers to that which is given to us in the immediacy of perception, signifies that which by definition is nonobjective, that which resists all signification. In other words, the term experience cannot make ostensible a *something that exists in the world*. The salient characteristic of private experience that distinguishes it from "objective reality" is thus its unremitting indeterminacy. At the same time, the rhetoric of experience tacitly posits a place where signification comes to an end, variously styled "mind," "consciousness," the "mirror of nature," or what have you. The category experience is, in essence, a mere placeholder that entails a substantive if indeterminate terminus for the relentless deferral of meaning. And this is precisely what makes the term experience so amenable to ideological appropriation.

Again, I am not trying to deny subjective experience. (Indeed, how would one do that?) I merely want to draw attention to the way the concept functions in religious discourse—in Wittgenstein's terms, its "language game." I have suggested that it is a mistake to approach literary, artistic, or ritual representations as if they referred back to something other than themselves, to some numinous inner realm. The fact that religious experience is often circumscribed in terms of its nondiscursive or nonconceptual character does not mitigate the problem: that nothing can be said of a particular experience—that is, its ineffability—cannot in and of itself constitute a delimiting characteristic, much less a phenomenal property. Thus, while experience—construed as that which is "immediately present"—may indeed be both irrefutable and indubitable, we must remember that whatever epistemological certainty experience may offer is gained only at the expense of any possible discursive meaning or signification. To put it another way, all attempts to signify "inner experience" are destined to remain "well-meaning squirms that get us nowhere."

SUGGESTED READINGS

Halbfass, Wilhelm. 1988. "The Concept of Experience in the Encounter between India and the West." In *India and Europe: An Essay in Understanding.*

James, William. 1961. *The Varieties of Religious Experience: A Study in Human Nature.*

Jantzen, Grace M. 1995. *Power, Gender, and Christian Mysticism.*

Katz, Steven T., ed. 1978. *Mysticism and Philosophical Analysis.*

———. 1983. *Mysticism and Religious Traditions.*

Nagel, Thomas. 1986. *The View from Nowhere.*

Proudfoot, Wayne. 1985. *Religious Experience.*

Rorty, Richard. 1979. *Philosophy and the Mirror of Nature.*

Sharf, Robert H. 1995. "Buddhist Modernism and the Rhetoric of Meditative Experience." *Numen.*

Stace, W. T. 1960. *Mysticism and Philosophy.*

Wittgenstein, Ludwig. 1958. *Philosophical Investigations,* translated by G. E. M. Anscombe.

REFERENCES

Barnard, G. William. 1992. "Explaining the Unexplainable: Wayne Proudfoot's *Religious Experience.*" *Journal of the American Academy of Religion* 60 (2).

Brainard, F. Samuel. 1996. "Defining 'Mystical Experience.'" *Journal of the American Academy of Religion* 64 (2).

Bryan, C. D. B. 1995. *Close Encounters of the Fourth Kind: A Reporter's Notebook on Alien Abduction, UFOs, and the Conference at M.I.T.* New York: Arkana.

Carus, Paul. 1915. *The Gospel of Buddha.* Chicago: Open Court.

Dennett, Daniel C. 1991. *Consciousness Explained.* Boston: Little, Brown.

———. 1992. "Quining Qualia." In *Consciousness in Contemporary Science,* edited by A. J. Marcel and E. Bisiach. Oxford: Oxford University Press.

Forman, Robert K. C. 1993. "Mystical Knowledge: Knowledge by Identity." *Journal of the American Academy of Religion* 61 (4).

———, ed. 1990. *The Problem of Pure Consciousness: Mysticism and Philosophy.* New York: Oxford University Press.

Gadamer, Hans-Georg. 1975. *Truth and Method,* translated by Joel Weinsheimer. New York: Crossroad.

Goodman, Felicitas D. 1988. *How About Demons? Possession and Exorcism in the Modern World.* Bloomington: Indiana University Press.

Hacking, Ian. 1995. *Rewriting the Soul: Multiple Personality and the Sciences of Memory.* Princeton: Princeton University Press.

Halbfass, Wilhelm. 1988. "The Concept of Experience in the Encounter between India and the West." In *India and Europe: An Essay in Understanding.* Albany: State University of New York Press.

Hirsch, E. D. 1967. *Validity in Interpretation.* New Haven: Yale University Press.

Huxley, Aldous. 1946. *The Perennial Philosophy.* London: Harper and Brothers.

James, William. 1961. *The Varieties of Religious Experience: A Study in Human Nature.* New York: Collier.

Jantzen, Grace M. 1995. *Power, Gender, and Christian Mysticism.* Cambridge: Cambridge University Press.

Katz, Steven T. 1978. "Language, Epistemology, and Mysticism." In *Mysticism and Philosophical Analysis,* edited by Steven T. Katz. New York: Oxford University Press.

———. 1983. "The 'Conservative' Character of Mystical Experience." In *Mysticism and Religious Traditions,* edited by Steven T. Katz. New York: Oxford University Press.

———. 1992. "Mystical Speech and Mystical Meaning." In *Mysticism and Language,* edited by Steven T. Katz. New York: Oxford University Press.

Mack, John E. 1995. *Abduction: Human Encounters with Aliens.* Rev. ed. New York: Ballantine Books.

Malcolm, Norman. 1959. *Dreaming.* Studies in Philosophical Psychology. London: Routledge and Kegan Paul.

Nagel, Thomas. 1986. *The View from Nowhere.* Oxford: Oxford University Press.

Nishida Kitarō. 1990. *An Inquiry into the Good,* translated by Masao Abe and Christopher Ives. New Haven: Yale University Press.

Otto, Rudolf. 1958. *The Idea of the Holy: An Inquiry into the Non-Rational Factor in the Idea of the Divine and its Relation to the Rational,* translated by John W. Harvey. London: Oxford University Press.

Proudfoot, Wayne. 1985. *Religious Experience.* Berkeley and Los Angeles: University of California Press.

Radhakrishnan, Sarvepalli. 1937. *An Idealist View of Life.* The Hibbert Lectures for 1929. Rev. 2nd ed. London: Allen and Unwin.

Rorty, Richard. 1979. *Philosophy and the Mirror of Nature.* Princeton: Princeton University Press.

Schleiermacher, Friedrich Daniel Ernst. 1928. *The Christian Faith,* translated by H. R. Mackintosh and J. S. Stewart. 2nd ed. Edinburgh: Clark.

Scholem, Gershom G. 1969. *On the Kabbalah and Its Symbolism,* translated by Ralph Manheim. New York: Schocken Books.

Sharf, Robert H. 1995a. "Buddhist Modernism and the Rhetoric of Meditative Experience." *Numen* 42 (3).

———. 1995b. "Sanbōkyōdan: Zen and the Way of the New Religions." *Japanese Journal of Religious Studies* 22 (3–4).

———. 1995c. "The Zen of Japanese Nationalism." In *Curators of the Buddha: The Study of Buddhism under Colonialism,* edited by Donald S. Lopez, Jr. Chicago: University of Chicago Press.

Shear, Jonathan. 1994. "On Mystical Experiences as Empirical Support for the Perennial Philosophy." *Journal of the American Academy of Religion* 62 (2).

Short, Larry. 1995. "Mysticism, Meditation, and the Non-Linguistic." *Journal of the American Academy of Religion* 63 (4).

Shweder, Richard A. 1991. *Thinking through Cultures.* Cambridge: Harvard University Press.

Smart, Ninian. 1973. *The Science of Religion and the Sociology of Knowledge: Some Methodological Questions.* Princeton: Princeton University Press.

Stace, W. T. 1960. *Mysticism and Philosophy.* London: Macmillan.

Whitmore, John. 1995. "Religious Dimensions of the UFO Abductee Experience." In *The Gods Have Landed: New Religions from Other Worlds,* edited by James R. Lewis. Albany: State University of New York Press.

Zaleski, Carol. 1987. *Otherworld Journeys: Accounts of Near-Death Experience in Medieval and Modern Times.* Oxford: Oxford University Press.

SIX

Gender

Daniel Boyarin

Ten years ago, an essay of this type would have begun with a confident explanation of the distinction between sex and gender as analytical concepts, something on the order of "gender is the set of social roles, symbolic functions, and so on, that are assigned to the anatomical difference between the sexes in different cultures/societies." The task of writing the entry would have been much simpler in those halcyon days, as religion is clearly for many if not most cultures one of the primary systems for the construction of gendered roles as well as for the interpellation of sexed subjects into those gendered roles. Things are not quite as simple anymore, however, and the distinction between "sex" and "gender" is no longer as clear. One important group of recent feminist theorists (materialist feminists) has argued that the set of distinctions summoned in the sex/gender opposition invokes the terms of the nature/culture opposition upon which so much of Western misogyny is based. Thus to speak of a natural sex upon which culture operates to construct gender is to reinvoke the Aristotelian myth of the female as unformed matter to which the spirit of the male gives form. "Gender" has thus been redefined by Judith Butler in a by-now classic passage:

> Gender ought not to be conceived merely as the cultural inscription of meaning upon a pregiven sex (a juridical conception); gender must also designate the very apparatus of production whereby the sexes themselves are established. As a result, gender is not to culture as sex is to nature; gender is also the discursive/cultural means by which "sexed nature" or "a natural sex" is produced and established as "prediscursive," prior to culture, a politically neutral surface *on which* culture acts. (1990, 7).

Accordingly now when we study gender within a given historical or existing culture, we understand that we are investigating the praxis and process by which people are interpellated into a two- (or for some cultures more) sex system that is made to seem as if it were nature, that is, something that has always existed.

The perception of sex as a natural, given set of binarily constructed differences between human beings, then, is now seen as the specific work of gender, and the production of sex as "natural" signifies the success of gender as a system in imposing its power. Materialist feminist Monique Wittig has perhaps articulataed this most sharply:

> The ideology of sexual difference functions as censorship in our culture by masking, on the ground of nature, the social opposition be-

tween men and women. Masculine/feminine, male/female are the categories which serve to conceal the fact that social differences always belong to an economic, political ideological order. Every system of domination establishes divisions at the material and economic level. . . . For there is no sex. There is but sex that is oppressed and sex that oppresses. It is oppression that creates sex and not the contrary. The contrary would be to say that sex creates oppression, or to say that the cause (origin) of oppression is to be found in sex itself, in a natural division of the sexes preexisting (or outside of) society. (1992a, 2)

It is the socioeconomic needs of particular groups of people that generate the necessity for reproductive sexual intercourse, and that necessity is best served by the ideology of sexual difference, of sexual dimorphism as the primary salient feature for the classification of human beings, and the charge of desire for intercourse that it is designed to produce. As Christine Delphy has observed, "The concept of class starts from the idea of social construction and specifies the implications of it. Groups are no longer *sui generis,* constituted before coming into relation with one another. On the contrary, it is their relationship which constitutes them as such. It is therefore a question of discovering the social practices, the social relations, which, in constituting the division of gender, create the groups of gender (called 'of sex')" (1984, 26). (Compulsory) heterosexuality, then, is at least one of the social practices that constitutes sexual difference and not the opposite (Butler 1990, 25). Like any ideology, the ideology of sex works best when it is invisible, precisely because it appears simply to be natural. Has there ever been in history a culture within which gender did not operate in this way to produce so-called natural sex?

I wish to put forth the suggestion that early Christianity is just such a culture. Indeed, I will propose that the most current dilemmas of feminist theory reproduce dialogues within Western culture that go back to its origins in the split between rabbinic Judaism and the hegemonic Christian tradition. Early Christianity demonstrates an awareness of precisely the ways that gender and sex (both the difference of bodies and sexual practice/desire) conspire to produce a juridical conception, which Christianity itself resists. We understand the radicalism of Christianity in this matter by observing its contrast to one of its main contemporary rivals: Early rabbinic Judaism is fully committed to a completely naturalized "sex." The division between Christianity and early Judaism is reproduced in the split between different schools of feminist theory in our time, which will be exemplified here by typical representatives Monique Wittig and Luce Irigaray, respectively. The point is precisely to show how each of these representative thinkers reproduces in large part both the promises and predicaments that some of the earliest Western thought about gender had already encountered.

The problems that plague the respective social systems of Christianity and

Judaism in their search for an ethical society can be shown to haunt the feminist systems of thought corresponding with their respective articulations of the relations between gender and sex as well. Rather than presenting religion here as an ideological system for the inculcation and mystification of the relations of sex/gender, I will treat two monotheistic religious traditions as bodies of thought about those relations that bear strikingly on our contemporary theoretical emergency.

Let us begin, then, at the beginning.

One of the foundational thinkers for the version of Judaism that was to become Christianity was Philo, a Jew of Alexandria and a slightly older contemporary of Paul of Tarsus. Although Philo's work was completely ignored by the later rabbinic Jewish tradition, it was a generative and important source for later orthodox Christian thinking, to the extent that Philo is frequently listed as one of the fathers of the church. An eye-opening legend developed in the Middle Ages that claimed he had actually converted to Christianity (which he hadn't) (Bruns 1973). Philo was preoccupied with sexual difference. In accordance with one of the characteristic features of his discourse, he articulated his concern as part of a commentary on Genesis, specifically on the dual accounts of the creation of humanity and sexual difference that we find in the first two chapters of the Bible:

Genesis 1:26–28
[27] And God created the earth-creature in His image; in the image of God, He created him; male and female He created them.
[28] And God blessed them, and God said to them: Reproduce and fill the earth.

Genesis 5:1–2
[1] This is the book of the Generations of Adam, on the day that God created Adam in the image of God He made him. [2] Male and female He created them, and He blessed them, *and called their name Adam,* on the day He created them.

Genesis 2:7ff
[7] And God formed the earth-creature of dust from the earth and breathed in its nostrils the breath of life, and the earth-creature became a living being. [20] And the earth-creature gave names to all of the animals and the fowls of the air and all of the animals of the fields, but the earth-creature could not find any helper fitting for it. [21] And God caused a deep sleep to fall on the earth-creature, and it slept, and He took one of its ribs and closed the flesh beneath it. [22] And the Lord God constructed the rib which He had taken from the earth-creature into a woman and brought her to the earth-man. [23] And the earth-man said, this time is bone of my bone and flesh of my flesh. She shall be called wo-man, for from man was she taken.

In the first story it seems clear that the original creation of the species humanity included both sexes, while the second story is seemingly a narrative of an original male creature for whom a female was created out of his flesh. The contradiction of the two texts accordingly presents a classical hermeneutic problem.

In the interpretation of Philo, the first Adam is an entirely spiritual being, the noncorporeal existence of whom can be said to be male and female, while the second chapter first introduces a carnal male Adam from whom the female is constructed. Bodily gender—structurally dependent, of course, on their being two—is thus twice displaced from the origins of "man":

> "It is not good that *any* man should be alone," For there are *two* races of men, the one made after the (Divine) Image, and the one molded out of the earth. . . . With the second man a helper is associated. To begin with, the helper is a created one, for it says "Let us make a helper for him": and in the next place, is subsequent to him who is to be helped, for He had formed the mind before and is about to form its helper. (1929, 107)

Philo here regards the two stories as referring to two entirely different creative acts on the part of God and accordingly to the production of two different races of "man." Thus both myths are encompassed in his discourse: a primal androgyne of no sex and a primary male/secondary female. Since the two texts, from Genesis 1 and from Genesis 2, refer to two entirely different species, Philo can claim that only the first one is called "in the image of God," that is, only the singular, unbodied Adam-creature is referred to as being in God's likeness and his male-femaleness must be understood spiritually. That is to say that the designation of *this* creature as male-female really means neither male nor female. We find this explicitly in another passage of Philo:

> After this he says that "God formed man by taking clay from the earth, and breathed into his face the breath of life" (Gen. ii. 7). By this also he shows very clearly that there is a vast difference between the man thus formed and the man that came into existence earlier after the image of God: for the man so formed is an object of sense-perception, partaking already of such or such quality, consisting of body and soul, man or woman, by nature mortal; *while he that was after the Image was an idea or type or seal, an object of thought, incorporeal, neither male nor female,* by nature incorruptible. (107)

Philo's interpretation is not an individual idiosyncrasy. As Thomas Tobin has shown, he is referring to a tradition known to him from before (1983, 32). The fundamental point that seems to be established is that for many Hellenistic Jews, the oneness of pure spirit is ontologically privileged in the constitution of humanity. Putting this into more secular terms, we could argue that for Philo and thence for those who follow in his wake, the essence of the human subject precedes its accidental division into sexes. The "true self"—we would say the "subject"—exists before being assigned a gender. This is symbolized within Philo's writing as though it is historically dual creation of humanity, such that the on-tological secondariness of the division into sexes is reproduced, as it were, in the actual order of creation.

Although Philo doesn't quite come out and say it, one can also detect here the presence of another foundational myth, namely, the myth of a "fall." The dual creation of the human, primarily as a subject undifferentiated by sex and then secondarily as a sexed creature, inscribes a hierarchy of value whereby the unsexed is superior to the creature marked by sexual difference. The latter al-ready implies the Fall, for it is the very twoness of sexual difference that is dis-turbing according to this ontology. Humanity as divided into male and female is corruptible, always already fallen, while humanity undivided by sex is immortal.

In his *On the Contemplative Life,* Philo describes a Jewish sect living in his time on the shores of Lake Mareotis near Alexandria (Kraemer 1989). It is clear from the tone of this entire depiction of this sect and its practice that he considers it an ideal religious community. The fellowship consisted of celibate men and women who lived in individual cells and spent their lives in prayer and contem-plative study of allegorical interpretations of Scripture (such as the ones that Philo produced). Once every seven weeks the community came together for a remarkable ritual celebration. Following a simple meal and a discourse, all of the members sang hymns together. Initially, however, the men and the women re-mained separate from each other in two choruses. The extraordinary element is that as the celebration became more ecstatic, the men and the women joined to form one chorus, "the treble of the women blending with the bass of the men." I suggest that this model of an ecstatic joining of the male and the female in a mystical ritual re-creates in social practice the image of the purely spiritual masculofeminine first human of which Philo speaks in his commentary, indeed, that this ritual of the Therapeutae is a return to the originary Adam (Macdonald 1988, 289). Although obviously the singing and dancing are performed by the body, the state of ecstasy (as its etymology implies) involves a symbolic and psy-chological condition of being disembodied and thus is similar to the condition of the primal androgyne.

The society and religious culture depicted by Philo *do* permit parity between men and women, as well as religious, cultural creativity for women as for men so long as women renounce that which makes them specifically female. Autonomy and creativity in the spiritual sphere are predicated on renunciation of both sexu-ality and maternity. Spiritual androgyny is attained only by abjuring the body and its difference. I think two factors have joined in the formation of this struc-ture, which are repeated over and over in the history of Western religion, includ-ing at least one instance within early modern Judaism (Rapoport-Alpert 1988). On the materialist level, there is the real world difference between a woman who is bound to the material conditions of marriage and childbearing/childrearing and a woman who is free of such restraints. Even more to the point, however, is the symbolic side of the issue. As the category "woman" is produced in the heterosexual relationship, so in Philo a female who escapes or avoids such relationships escapes from being a woman. In Tertullian's *On the Veiling of Virgins,* precisely the issue between Tertullian and his opponents is whether virgins are women or not! (D'Angelo, 1995) This division in Philo is also reproduced in his interpretations of the status of female figures in the Bible, who fall into two categories: women and virgins (Sly 1990, 71–90). See, for example, the characteristically Philonic usage, "When a man comes in contact with a woman, he marks [i.e., makes her marked—notice the semiotic terminology] the virgin as a woman. But when souls become divinely inspired, from being women they become virgins" (Quaestiones in Ex. 2:3). Those biblical figures defined as "virgins" by Philo are not women and thus do not partake of the base status that he accords women. By escaping from sexuality entirely, virgins thus participate in the "destruction of sex," and attain the status of the spiritual human who was neither male nor female. A passage from the Hellenistic-Jewish novel *Joseph and Aseneth,* cited by MacDonald (1988, 289), also supports this reading, for Aseneth is told, "today you are a pure virgin and your head is like that of a young man." When she is no longer a virgin, only then does she become a woman. We begin to see in this passage, however, something else, something that will be crucial a bit further on. While a virgin, Aseneth is a virtual man, notwithstanding that she is described as "a virgin hating men." The transcendent androgyne is male. This paradoxical figure of a transcendence of gender that is still, as it were, male is not a factitious by-product of male domination but is, I will suggest, crucial to the whole structure of gender transcendence itself. All theories of transcendence are already appropriated by the male.

"Some Lesbians and Nuns Escape": Monique Wittig and the "Christian" Thinking of Gender

Following in the wake of Philo and thinkers like him, much of early Christianity beginning with Paul seemed to be dedicated to seeking a transcendence of gender, for example, Paul's famous and stirring declaration in Galatians: "For you are all children of God through faith in Christ Jesus. For as many of you as were baptized into Christ have put on Christ [saying]: 'There is neither Jew nor Greek; there is neither slave nor freeman; there is no male and female. For you are all one in Christ Jesus'" (3:26–9). Putting on Christ, baptism, meant for Paul, among other things (at least ideally), an eradication of gender, becoming like Philo's Therapeutae an avatar of the first Adam for whom there was no male or female.

Wayne Meeks (1973) and more recently Dennis Ronald MacDonald (1988) have demonstrated that Gal. 3:28 encapsulates a very early Christian mythic formation and its liturgical expression in the pre-Pauline church. According to Meeks, the original baptism was a "performative" ritual utterance in which, "a factual claim is being made, about an 'objective' change in reality which fundamentally modifies social roles" (1973, 182). Pauline baptism seems more similar to the initiatory rites of the Mysteries, in which, as Meeks himself argues, "the exchange of sexual roles, by ritual transvestism for example, was an important symbol for the disruption of ordinary life's categories in the experience of initiation. This disruption, however, did not ordinarily reach beyond the boundaries of the initiatory experience—except, of course, in the case of devotees who went on to become cult functionaries" (170). Following the researches of MacDonald (1987) we can further assume that the expression "no male and female" originally referred to a complete erasure of sexual difference in some forms of earliest Christianity and is cited by Paul here from such contexts. In such groups, the declaration that there is no male or female may very well have had radical social implications in a total breakdown of hierarchy and either celibacy or libertinism. The key to my interpretation of Paul here is that he did intend a social meaning and function for baptism, namely, the creation of a new humanity in which all difference would be effaced in the new creation in Christ, but—and this is a crucial *but*—he did not think that this new creation could be entirely achieved on the social level *yet*. Some of the program was already possible; some would have to wait.

Paul could never imagine a social eradication of the hierarchical deployment of male and female bodies for married people. While it was possible for him to conceive of a total erasure of the difference between Jew and Greek, he could not imagine that male and female bodies would be in any condition other than dominant and dominated when they were in sexual relationship with each other. It is (hetero)sexuality, therefore, that produces gender, for Paul as for Philo and also, as we shall see, within crucially paradigmatic texts of the Christian cultural tradition. Marriage is a lower state than celibacy (He who marries a virgin does well and he who does not marry does better [1 Cor. 7:38].), but it is not by any means forbidden or despised. However, and this is the crux, any possibility of an eradication of male and female and its corresponding social hierarchy is only possible on the level of the spirit, either in ecstasy at baptism or perhaps permanently for the celibate.

The crucial text for strengthening this interpretation, or at least for rendering it plausible, is arguably 1 Cor. 11:1–16. In my reading of this passage, Paul makes practically explicit his theory of gender as produced in the sexual relation:

> I would have you know, however, that every man's head is Christ, but a woman's head is the man, and Christ's head is God. (1:3)

> For a man must not veil his head, since he is the image and reflection of God but a woman is the reflection of man. For man did not originate from woman, but woman from man. Neither was man created for woman's sake, but woman for man's. (1:7–9)

> Of course, in the Lord there is neither woman without man nor man with woman. For just as woman originated from man, so, too, man exists through woman. But everything comes from God. (1:11–12)

These verses have been discussed form many points of view. It is far beyond the scope of this article to analyze either the theological or hermeneutic issues involved in the text, but however we interpret them, it is clear that Paul explicitly thematizes two (partially opposed) forms of conceptualizing gender, one in which there is an explicit hierarchy and one in which there is none. Paul himself marks this difference (the gap between the hierarchy asserted in verses 7–9 and the sentiment expressed in "there is neither woman without man nor man without woman" of verse 11) as the situation of "in the Lord" *(ἐν κυρίῳ)*. I do not think it is going too far—nor is it unprecedented in Pauline interpretation—to connect this "in the Lord" with the "in Christ" of Gal. 3:28, reading them both as representations of an androgyny that exists on the level of the spirit, however much hierarchy subsists and needs to subsist on the fleshly level in the life of society even in Christian communities. These two levels may well correspond to the two myths of the origins of the sexes found in Genesis 1 and 2. The no-male-or-female that is "in the Lord," or "in Christ," would represent the androgyne of Genesis 1, understood, as in Philo, as neither male nor female. The man who "is the image and reflection of God," and the "woman [who] is the reflection of man," which Paul cites here, would be a reference to the story in Genesis 2, "For man did not originate from woman, but woman from man" (interpretation suggested by Karen King, personal communication). "In the Lord" might even be seen then as an allusion to "in the image of God," and the latter human of Genesis 2 would be "in the flesh" in contrast. According to this reading, Paul's interpretation of Genesis is virtually identical to Philo's. This perhaps speculative proposal is dramatically strengthened if Josef Kürzinger's suggestion is accepted that 1 Cor. 11:11 means, "In the Lord woman is not different from man nor man from woman" (1978). Ultimately, as Karen King suggests (personal communication), the two myths of gender "are quite compatible in that both imagine the ideal to be a unitary self, whether male or androgynous, whose nature is grounded in an ontology of transcendence and an epistemology of origins"— and thus, I would add, always masculine in its configuration.

In early Christianity, just as in Philo, virgins were not women but androgynes, representations in the appearance of flesh of the purely spiritual, nongendered, presocial essence of human beings. For these forms of Christianity, as for the Hellenistic Judaism of Philo, this dualism is the base of the anthropology: equality in the spirit, hierarchy in the flesh. As Clement of Alexandria, a second-century follower of Paul expressed it, "As then there is sameness [with men and women] with respect to the soul, she will attain to the same virtue; but as there is difference with respect to the peculiar construction of the body, she is destined for child-bearing and house-keeping" (1989a, 20). This quotation suggests, and Christian practice reveals, that this version of primal androgyny provided two elements in the gender politics of the early church. On the one hand, it provided an image or vision of a spiritual equality for all women, which did not, however, have social consequences for the married; on the other hand, it provided for real

autonomy and social parity for celibate women, for those who rejected "the peculiar construction of the body," together with its pleasures and satisfactions. As
Clement avers in another place, "For souls themselves by themselves are equal.
Souls are neither male nor female when they no longer marry nor are given in
marriage" (1989b, 100).

Much of the paradigmatic literature of early Christianity involves this representation of gender and its possibilities. Elizabeth Castelli has described the situation with regard to one of the earliest and most explicit texts of this type, the
Gospel of Thomas:

> The double insistence attributed to Jesus in the *Gospel of Thomas* say-
> ing— that Mary should remain among the disciples at the same time
> as she must be made male—points to the paradoxical ideological
> conditions that helped to shape the lives of early Christian women.
> At once they are to have access to holiness, while they also can do so
> only through the manipulation of conventional gender categories
> (1991, 33).

One of the most striking and powerful narrative representations of this "paradoxical ideological condition" is the story of Paul and Thekla from the Apocryphal Acts of the Apostles. In this account, the young woman refuses the marriage
bed, cuts her hair, dresses like a boy, and becomes Paul's close companion in his
travels and apostleship. In another text of the same genre, we find a strikingly
similar moment of erasure of gender through celibacy. In the Acts of Andrew,
the apocryphal apostle begs Maximilla to remain steadfast in her decision to cease
having sexual intercourse with her husband in the following terms, "I beg you,
then, *O wise man (ὁ φρόνιμος ἀνήρ)*, that your noble mind continue steadfast; I
beg you, O invisible mind, that you may be preserved yourself" (Elliott 1993,
257, emphasis added). Here it is absolutely and explicitly clear that through celibacy the female ceases to be a woman and becomes a man. The "manipulation
of conventional gender categories" seems to produce an androgyne who is always gendered male.

Castelli notes with regard to this and similar stories: "It is striking that in all
of these narratives, the women who perform these outward gestures of stretching
dominant cultural expectations related to gender are also embracing a form of
piety (sexual renunciation and virginity) which resists dominant cultural expectations vis-à-vis social roles" (1991, 44). If my reading of Philo and Paul and of
the general cultural situation is compelling, however, this connection is not so
much striking as absolutely necessary. Insofar as the myth of the primal, spiritual
androgyne is the vital force for all of these representations, androgynous status is
always dependent on the notion of a universal spiritual self that is above the differences of the body, and its attainment entails *necessarily* a renunciation of the
body and its sexuality. From Philo and Paul through late antiquity, gender parity
is founded on a dualist metaphysics and anthropology in which freedom and

equality are for pregendered, presocial, disembodied souls and are predicated on a devaluing and disavowing of the body, usually combined with a representation of the body itself as female. As Philo put it, "The helper is a created one, for it says 'Let us make a helper for him': and in the next place, is subsequent to him who is to be helped, *for He had formed the mind before and is about to form its helper*" (1929, 107). The "helper," then, that is the woman, is the body itself. Transcending of this "female" body is for both men and women a virilization. (This point does not deny the argument made by Verna Harrison [1991] that there were valued female characteristics and metaphors for male Christians as well.)

On my reading, then, these Christian imaginings of gender bending don't even really comprehend a "destabilization of gender identity." Rather, insofar as they are completely immured in the dualism of the flesh and the spirit, they represent no change whatsoever in the status of gender. All of these texts are mythic or ritual enactments of the "myth of the primal androgyne," and as such simply reinstate the metaphysics of substance, the split between Universal Mind and Disavowed Body, which constitutes a reinstatement of masculinism: The androgyne in question always turns out somehow to be a male androgyne. Mary is made male, Thekla becomes a virtual boy, and the celibate Maximilla is a "wise man." These are mythic representations by Christianity of its understanding that the metaphysics of substance that subtends the notion of transcendence is itself a masculinist inscription of the abstract (spirit) over the concrete (body), in other words what Jean-Joseph Goux has called "metamorphosis into the masculine-neutral," a neutrality or universality that in its drive toward that neutrality, is already masculine. The early Christians understood this well and remarked on it explicitly; therefore, I would claim that Goux is quite mistaken in seeing this as a modern phenomenon, that is, as "the immanent logic of modernity" (1994, 178).

The parallels between the mode of thinking gender that we find in these prerabbinic Jewish and early Christian texts and that of the feminist thought of Monique Wittig are stunning. Wittig takes Simone de Beauvoir's notion that "one is not born a woman" to its logical extreme. Like Philo and Paul and the traditions that they represent, she considers sexual intercourse to be what produces women. Wittig, realizing this connection, explicitly connects lesbians and nuns: "One might consider that every woman, married or not, has a period of forced sexual service. . . . Some lesbians and nuns escape" (Wittig 1992a, 7). She calls for a "destruction of sex" as the necessary condition for liberation of the class of people called "women." Butler demonstrates clearly how dependent Wittig's "destruction of sex" is on the same metaphysics that generated Philo's destruction of sex "in the beginning," and is thus finally also predicated on the same masculinist ideologies of transcendence:

> Hence, Wittig calls for the destruction of "sex" so that women can assume the status of a universal subject. . . . As a subject who can real-

ize concrete universality through freedom, Wittig's lesbian confirms rather than contests the normative promise of humanist ideals premised on the metaphysics of substance. . . . Where it seems that Wittig has subscribed to a radical project of lesbian emancipation and enforced a distinction between "lesbian" and "woman," she does this through the defense of the pregendered "person," characterized as freedom. This move not only confirms the presocial status of human freedom, but subscribes to that metaphysics of substance that is responsible for the production and naturalization of the category of sex itself. (1990, 20)

The consequence of Butler's incisive analysis is that Wittig ends up being almost entirely a reflection of the patristic ideology of freedom as pregendered and of nongender as male. Wittig's lesbian is another version of the woman of Hellenistic Judaism or early Christianity made male and thus free through celibacy, although to be sure with the enormous difference that sexual pleasure is not denied Wittig's lesbian. Metaphysically speaking, nothing has changed. Thekla and Philo's virgins are not women, and Wittig's lesbian is not a woman (Wittig 1992b, 32).

What, however, is to become of a human being born with a "vagina" who happens not to be a lesbian or a nun? Is she condemned to be a woman, and is heterosexuality always and only "forced sexual service"? In Wittig's writing, not being a lesbian, that is, "being a woman" seems finally as pejorative as it was in Philo and patristic writings. Diana Fuss makes a related point when she writes, "One implication of this ideality is that Wittig's theory is unable to account for heterosexual feminists except to see them as victims of false consciousness" (1989, 44). The problem seems to be that Wittig does not distinguish between "heterosexuality" (compulsory by definition) as a political regime and "heterosex" as the relation of desire/pleasure between sexes that would not be compelled but would exist along a continuum of genital (and nongenital) practices, including love between women and love between men. "To speak of 'compulsory heterosexuality' is," indeed, "redundant" as Louise Turcotte has argued (1992), but only if we understand hererosexuality precisely as "the production of a population of human[s] . . . who are (supposedly) incapable of being sexually excited by a person of their own sex *under any circumstances*" (Halperin 1990, 44).

According to certain thinkers, *all* sexual activity involves domination, so that it is not only the "destruction of sex" as a taxonomy of human bodies but a destruction of desire/pleasure itself that can produce parity. In this view, only nuns, and not even lesbians, would escape. Andrea Dworkin poses this plight directly (if, I suspect, inadvertently) when she cites the Gospel to the Egyptians, and writes, "it would be in keeping with the spirit of this book to take Christ as my guide and say with him: 'When ye trample upon the garment of shame; when the Two become One, and Male with Female neither male nor female'" (1974, 173). Dworkin cites this passage in support of an early vision of gender

equality, little realizing, it would seem, that the "garment of shame" to be tram-
pled on is the body, male or female, that garment of skin that Adam and Eve put
on after their Fall and shamefaced realization of their nakedness (Smith 1966).
As Meeks has put it, "'Male and female' are to be made 'one,' but they are by
no means treated as equals. Rather, if the female is to become a 'living spirit' and
thus be saved, she must become male—and that, of course, through celibacy"
(1973, 194). Fiorenza's translation of this as, "a Christian ought not to look at
other Christians as sex objects, as males or females, but as members of the same
'family of god,' as brothers and sisters" (1983, 212) exemplifies the problem.
The point of the textual complex around "the two becoming one, neither male
nor female" is the destruction of sex, not the transformation of sexual partners
into subjects, or as Marc Shell has put it rather pithily, when all are brothers and
sisters, all sex (even "lesbian" sex) is incest (Shell 1988).

The Insistence/Assertion of Sex: Luce Irigaray and the Rabbinic Thinking of Gender

In sharp contrast to Philo's and Paul's interpretations of the ratio between
Genesis 1 and 2, interpretations that initiated the Christian reading of gender,
stands the exegesis of the rabbis (the authorities of Palestinian and Babylonian
Judaism of late antiquity). The dominant rabbinic interpretation insisted that the
first male-female human was a physical hermaphrodite. According to these midrashic texts, the primordial Adam was a dual-sexed creature in one body. The
story in the second chapter is the story of the splitting of the two equal halves of
an originary body:

> *And God said let us make a human etc.* . . . . R. Samuel the son of
> Nahman said: When the Holiness (Be it blessed) created the first
> human, He made it two-faced, then He sawed it and made a back
> for this one and a back for that one. [The Rabbis] objected to
> [R. Samuel]: but it says, "He took one of his ribs *(tsela')*." He
> answered [it means], "one of his sides," similarly to that which is
> written, "And the side *(tsela')* of the tabernacle" [Exod. 26:20].
> (Theodor and Albeck 1965, 54–5)

The first Adam, the one of whom it is said that "male and female created He
them," had genitals of both sexes, and the act of creation described in Genesis 2
merely separated out the two sexes from each other and reconstructed them into
two human bodies. Far from gender (and woman) being a secondary creation,
we have in the second creation of humanity an Aristophanic separation of an
androgynous pair of joined twins, physically sexed from the very beginning.

The myth of the first human as androgyne is, of course, well known from
Greek literature as old as the pre-Socratic Empedocles, and it is mocked in Plato's
Symposium as well. The Rabbis, however, were much more likely to have en-
countered the myth in its widespread form known among both Jews and Gen-

tiles in late antiquity, the myth of the spiritual, primal androgyne. As I have already proposed, for Philo and many early Christians the return to the original and perfect state of humankind involved putting off the body and sexuality and returning to a purely spiritual androgyny (King 1988, 165). In the rabbinic culture, the human race was thus marked from the very beginning by corporeality, difference, and heterogeneity. For the Rabbis, sexuality belonged to the original created (and not fallen) state of humanity. Humanity did not fall from a metaphysical condition, nor was there any Fall into sexuality in rabbinic Judaism (Pardes 1989). The midrashic reading of the text cited above presents the originary human person as dual sexed, as two sexes joined in one body. Thus, according to the rabbis, it was the splitting of the androgynous body into two sexes that ordained (hetero)sexuality ("therefore a *man* will leave his father and mother and cleave to his woman") and not, as in Hellenistic/Christian and Jewish thought, heterosexuality that produced the two sexes.

For all its problematic aspects (which I will focus on presently), I wish to locate in this version of the creation myth a rabbinic opposition to what Goux has called "the utopia of the neutral sex": the utopia that I identified above as Philonic-Christian in its origins in that it reads sexedness as always already fallen. Actually this vision of utopia is much older than either Philo or the Christians. In Aristophanes's *Ecclesiazusae* the breakdown of distinctions between male and female leads to a situation in which "private property is abolished and all is held in common. Exclusive relationships between men and women are forbidden; sexual access is open for all. Dichotomies between male and female, public and private, old and young no longer control the relations of citizens and all (except, of course, slaves) become part of one unified family, eating, drinking, and sleeping together," thus restoring a sort of primeval utopia before the "fall" into gender (Saxonhouse 1992, 2–3). I have suggested that this narrative of a fall haunts the metaphysics of gender exemplified by Wittig. Rabbinic discourse on sex/gender refuses this narrative of oneness fallen into twoness, insisting on a twoness of humanity in the flesh from the very beginning, from the conception by God, as it were. To the extent that there is a fall in the rabbinic reading, it is a fall into sexual domination, a/k/a gender, and not into sexuation or sexuality. Two sexes exist from the beginning and sexual joining does also; what ensues from the "eating of the apple," the primal disobedience, is not sex but male domination and the apparent essences of maleness and femaleness. It is these, and not the division into sexes, that are to be overcome in the drive to redemption.

In their refusal to read sexual difference as secondary and fallen, the Rabbis anticipate, I suggest, the same refusal on the part of the feminist thinker who typifies the tradition of opposing the (masculinist) metaphysics of substance, Luce Irigaray. "The human species is divided into *two genders* [sic] which ensure its production and reproduction. To wish to get rid of sexual difference is to call for a genocide more radical than any form of destruction there has even been in

History" (Irigaray 1993, 12). What precisely does Irigaray mean by this surprising statement? Can she simply mean that the suppression of sexual difference through the achievement of even a masculine-neutral androgyny will lead to an end to physical reproduction? Even disaggregated bodies, however, can get pregnant, even the body of the radical constructivist theorist who claims that "she" "has" no vagina could presumably give birth. The radical decentering of desires/pleasures that Wittig calls for does not preclude desires and pleasures that would result in human births in sufficient numbers to forestall "genocide"—indeed, the result might be births in sufficiently reduced numbers to make another kind of genocide, ecocide, less likely. This, then, can't be what Irigaray means. I suggest, therefore, that the genocide to which Irigaray refers is not the end of humanity but the end of women, their disappearance into the "masculine-neutral," which would be the ultimate triumph of the masculinist economy and the fulfillment of a masculinist dream of a world without women.

Perhaps in tacit recognition of the collapse of the most obvious reading of this Irigarayan passage, Goux reads this apocalyptic formulation as effectively providing a near mythic statement of her philosophy of gender which he, with his usual clarity, reduces to two strong statements of conviction: "1. To overthrow patriarchal and phallocentric power does not mean denying the difference between the sexes but living the relation between them differently. 2. To assert the difference between the sexes is *not* at all the same thing as positing an essential femininity (or masculinity). . . . It is sexuation that is 'essential,' not the content of dogmas fixing once and for all, in an exhaustive and closed definition, what for eternity belongs to the masculine and what belongs to the feminine" (Goux 1994, 181). Another way of saying this would be that while there is no fixed essential nature to either woman or man (indeed, there is no woman per se, no man per se), there are material differences between being a man and being a woman that are productive of different (but not fixed or essential) subjectivities and relations to language and sexuality: "Woman's being is acquired, won, determined, invented, produced, created. Not by totally denying its biological preconditions (which would be both absurd and dangerous—not to say unjustified in its complicity with an ancient patriarchal ideology that has devalued in advance this natural substratum), but through an elaboration of the sexuate" (Goux 1994, 182). Different attitudes of the body in sexual intercourse (one enclosing, the other being enclosed), the capacity to menstruate, gestate, and lactate, all of these form a sort of material base for a subjectivity that is different from that of men *but do not prescript what that subjectivity will consist of or how it will be lived*. As a final way of conceptualizing this, I propose the following formulation: There is nothing in the being of a male or female body that prescribes a particular way of conceiving of the world or a particular relation to language, but the use of the male genital (the sex that is *one*—already a heavily ideologized construct in its eclipse of the testicles) as the primary symbol of language and thought has produced, of course, the masculinist economy of the same. As

Irigaray herself has put it, she invokes not anatomy (as destiny) but the "morphology of the female sex" (1990, 51) as the organizing metaphor. Imagining a symbolic organized around female genitals ("this sex that is not One") could lead to a different subjectivity and thus to a different politics of desire and of the social organization of the life of sexual difference (including "love") (Burke 1994, 43–4). Irigaray's project of the installation of a female alternative to the phallus and the logos has been read as a classically Derridian move. By reversing the polarity of the valued and devalued terms of a binary opposition, the very terms of that opposition are set into oscillation and destabilized. In other words, Irigaray's insistence on the irreducibility of sexual difference while at the same time reimagining a symbolic (not an imaginary) of fluids, lips, and concrete language to displace the symbolic of the column, the unit, the abstract and transcendent phallo-logos is not an essentialism but a deconstruction (Schor 1994). Rabbinic Judaism, it can plausibly be claimed, operates without the notions of logos and phallus that inscribe the male genital as the anchor of the symbolic system. Thus Goux's Beauvoirian/Wittigian, ultramodern masculine neutral, which is resisted by an Irigarayan postmodern, is revealed as the logic of an ancient Christian drive for the universal that is resisted by rabbinic Judaism, just as midrash, for instance, has been interpreted as an ancient resistance to the logos (Boyarin 1990).

Rabbinic Judaism did, however, implacably and oppressively prescribe women's roles even as it avoided and resisted the essentialist dualism that in the West almost always constructed the spirit as masculine (even in a woman) and the body as feminine (even in a man) (Lloyd 1984). Owing to its ironclad insistence on universal marriage (for men and for women), it differentiated gender roles more sharply certainly than Christianity, perhaps even than many cultures have done. When we compare it with much of historical Christianity, we find that within historical Judaism women have been much more powerfully constrained to occupy one and only one position entirely, namely, that of wife and mother. Interestingly enough, this constraint did not preclude public economic activity (Boyarin 1997b, xxii–xxiii and passim), but unfortunately this fact only disproves the hopeful contention of Schor in the name of de Beauvoir that "by leaving behind the unredeemed and unredeemable domestic sphere of contingency for the public sphere of economic activity, women too can achieve transcendence" (Schor 1994, 63). Even if any theory of transcendence were already appropriated by the male, there was somehow in the Christian world an opportunity for women to achieve it (Burrus 1987). Not so in Judaism. There are virtually no Jewish equivalents of Thekla, Hildegard, Claire, or even Heloise. While the theory of dualism was lacking in Judaism, in practice women were nevertheless confined exclusively within bodily realms, whle men were afforded the realms of the body (sexuality, parentage), the intellect (study of Torah), and the spiritual (full religious lives). There was no pregendered, postgendered, androgynous, or even male space to which a woman could escape. A story like the famous one of Yentl (by Isaac Bashevis Singer and Streisand) who dressed as a boy in order to study exemplifies the frustrations and pain felt by many women occupying this society as late as the nineteenth century (Boyarin 1997, 172–85). Women were trapped within the category of gender precisely because it was understood as ontologically primary, as definitional for what it is to be a human being. Difference, opposition to the universal same, it seems, potentially (perhaps always) also portends enormous dangers for women, the dangers, precisely, of essentialism (Plaza 1980), while universalism seems to threaten an end to woman entirely.

The two representative feminist thinkers that I have concentrated on here seem to closely reproduce the terms of a very ancient dilemma of our culture with respect to gender. Insistence on the value of sexual dimorphism, with its recognition of sexual intercourse as pleasure for both male and female, of the value of the female body in reproduction, indeed of reproduction itself, seems fated always to imprison women within a biological role, while transcendence, liberation of the female, seems always to be predicated on a denigration of the body and the achievement of a male-modeled androgyny, a masculine neutral. The latter seems as implacable as the former. See for instance the inscription of this dualism in the following statement: "For them [the Shakers], celibacy implied communal familial and economic systems, unified social classes, and, most important to this discussion, *equality along with genuine, spiritual (rather than false, physical)* unity of males and females" (Kitch 1989, 3, emphasis added). I am neither unconvinced nor unmoved by Kitch's demonstration of the genuine feminist commitments of the Shakers. The opposition between "genuine, spiritual" and "false, physical" seems to me, however, no comfort but simply a reinstatement of masculinism by other means. My "old Adam," it appears, is not superseded. If we speak of a pregendered person, a universal subject, necessarily, it seems, disembodied, then we are implicitly valorizing the very metaphysics that causes all of the gender trouble in the first place; and in the bargain, we are problematizing (hetero)sex (and perhaps sexual pleasure itself) beyond retrieval. If, on the other hand, we insist on the corporeality and always already sexed quality of the human being, then it appears that we trap (one half of) the human race in the (necessarily?) hierarchical category of gender. I question whether this is necessary, because empirically it seems that no society has yet been found in which gender is not a hierarchical category. The question of whether hierarchy is a necessary consequence of "intercourse" or only a contingent one remains (for me) open. I certainly hope that it is the latter, for otherwise we may indeed be led to seek such extreme "solutions" as those of the Shakers. I refer again to Kitch (1989, 23-73) and especially her comment that "in fact, women's exclusion from cultural prestige systems is a direct result of reproductive/sexual relationships to men" (32). If that be true, are Irigaray's apocalyptic fears valid after all in their simplest and most direct sense? I hold out some hope here that the empirical given that men dominate women in almost all societies is factitious, that is, contingent on specific historical, material conditions. That, for instance, Irigaray essentializes only sexual difference itself but does not ascribe an essential nature to either male or female holds out much hope for change in an altered material world, hope that indeed the sexual relation may not have to be destroyed but may be livable in a radically different fashion. Until that (messianic?) moment, it seems we are required to maintain the two poles of this dialectic, the "Christian" and the "rabbinic" understandings of gender, in tension and in suspension such that neither of them can overwhelm the other. "Christianity" and "Judaism" are names, then, for the poles of an irresolvable antinomy or aporia; neither can sublate the other, nor is there yet any third term that can clearly resolve this antithesis. Even in the absence of the synthesis, the thesis and the antithesis themselves can perhaps protect us each from the excesses of the other.

Suggested Readings

Butler, Judith. 1990. *Gender Trouble: Feminism and the Subversion of Identity.* Thinking Gender.

de Beauvoir, Simone. 1952. *The Second Sex,* translated and edited by H. M. Parshley.

Delphy, Christine. 1984. *Close to Home: A Materialist Analysis of Women's Oppression,* translated and edited by Diane Leonard.

Goux, Jean-Joseph. 1994. "Luce Irigaray Versus the Utopia of the Neutral Sex." In *Engaging with Irigaray: Feminist Philosophy and Modern European Thought,* edited by Carolyn Burke, Naomi Schor, and Margaret Whitford.

Irigaray, Luce. 1985. *Speculum of the Other Woman,* translated by Gillian C. Gill.

———. 1996. *I Love to You: Sketch of a Possible Felicity in History,* translated by Alison Martin.

Wittig, Monique. 1981. "One is not Born a Woman." *Feminist Issues* 1(2).

———. 1992. "The Category of Sex." In *"The Straight Mind" and Other Essays.*

References

Boyarin, Daniel. 1990. *Intertextuality and the Reading of Midrash.* Bloomington: Indiana University Press.

———. 1997a. "Torah-Study and the Making of Jewish Gender." *The Feminist Companion to Biblical Approaches and Methodologies,* edited by A. Brenner and C. Fontaine. Sheffield: Journal for the Study of the Old Testament.

———. 1997b. *Unheroic Conduct: The Rise of Heterosexuality and the Invention of the Jewish Man.* Contraversions: Studies in Jewish Literature, Culture, and Society. Berkeley and Los Angeles: University of California Press.

Bruns, J. E. 1973. "Philo Christianus: The Debris of a Legend." *Harvard Theological Review* 66.

Burke, Carolyn. 1994. "Irigaray through the Looking Glass." In *Engaging with Irigaray: Feminist Philosophy and Modern European Thought,* edited by Carolyn Burke, Naomi Schor, and Margaret Whitford. Gender and Culture. New York: Columbia University Press.

Burrus, Virginia. 1987. *Chastity as Autonomy: Women in the Stories of the Apocryphal Acts.* Studies in Women and Religion. New York: Edwin Mellen Press.

Butler, Judith. 1990. *Gender Trouble: Feminism and the Subversion of Identity.* Thinking Gender. London: Routledge.

Castelli, Elizabeth A. 1991. "'I Will Make Mary Male': Pieties of the Body and Gender Transformation of Christian Women in Late Antiquity." In *Body Guards: The Cultural Politics of Ambiguity,* edited by J. Epstein and K. Straub. New York: Routledge.

Clement, of Alexandria. 1989a. "The Instructor," edited by A. Roberts and J. Donaldson. In *The Fathers of the Second Century. Vol. 2 of The Anti-Nicene Fathers.* Grand Rapids, Mich.: Eerdmans.

———. 1989b, "The Stromata; or, Miscellanies," edited by A. Roberts and J. Donaldson. In *The Fathers of the Second Century. Vol. 2 of The Anti-Nicene Fathers.* Grand Rapids, Mich.: Eerdmans.

Cohen, J. 1989. *"Be Fertile and Increase, Fill the Earth and Master It": The Ancient and Medieval Career of a Biblical Text.* Ithaca, N.Y.: Cornell University Press.

D'Angelo, M. R. 1995. "Veils, Virgins, and the Tongues of Men and Angels: Women's Heads in Early Christianity." In *The Female Head: Pub(l)ic Meanings of Women's Hair, Faces, and Mouths,* edited by H. Eilberg-Schwartz and Wendy Doniger O'Flaherty. Berkeley: UC Press.

Delphy, Christine. 1984. *Close to Home: A Materialist Analysis of Women's Oppression,* translated and edited by Diane Leonard. Amherst: University of Massachusetts Press.

Dworkin, Andrea. 1974. *Woman Hating.* New York: Dutton.

Fiorenza, Elisabeth Schüssler. 1983. *In Memory of Her: A Feminist Theological Reconstruction of Christian Origins.* New York: Crossroad.

Fuss, Diana. 1989. *Essentially Speaking: Feminism, Nature, and Difference.* New York: Routledge.

Goux, Jean-Joseph. 1994. "Luce Irigaray versus the Utopia of the Neutral Sex." In *Engaging with Irigaray: Feminist Philosophy and Modern European Thought,* edited by Carolyn Burke, Naomi Schor, and Margaret Whitford. Gender and Culture. New York: Columbia University Press.

Halperin, D. M. 1990. *"One Hundred Years of Homosexuality" and Other Essays on Greek Love.* New York: Routledge.

Harrison, Verna E. 1990. "Male and Female in Cappadocian Theology." *Journal of Theological Studies* 41 (2).

———. 1991. "A Gender Reversal in Gregory of Nyssa's First Homily on the Song of Songs." Paper presented at the Eleventh International Conference on Patristic Studies, Oxford, 19–24 August.

Irigaray, Luce. 1990. "Women's Exile," translated by C. Venn. In *The Feminist Critique of Language: A Reader,* edited by D. Cameron. London: Routledge.

———. 1993. *Je, Tu, Nous: Toward a Culture of Difference,* translated by Alison Martin. New York: Routledge.

King, Karen L. 1988. "Sophia and Christ in the *Apocryphon of John.*" In *Images of the Feminine in Gnosticism,* edited by Karen L. King. Philadelphia: Fortress Press.

Kitch, S. L. 1989. *Chaste Liberation: Celibacy and Female Cultural Status.* Urbana: University of Illinois Press.

Kraemer, R. 1989. "Monastic Jewish Women in Greco-Roman Egypt: Philo on the Therapeutrides." *Signs: A Journal of Women in Culture and Society* 14 (1).

Kürzinger, Josef. 1978. "Frau und Mann nach 1 Kor 11, 11f." *Biblische Zeitschrift* 22 (2).

Lloyd, G. 1984. *The Man of Reason: "Male" and "Female" in Western Philosophy.* Minneapolis: University of Minnesota Press.

Macdonald, Dennis Ronald. 1987. *"There Is No Male and Female": The Fate of a Dominical Saying in Paul and Gnosticism.* Harvard Dissertations in Religion. Philadelphia: Fortress Press.

———. 1988. "Corinthian Veils and Gnostic Androgynes." In *Images of the Feminine in Gnosticism,* edited by Karen L. King. Philadelphia: Fortress Press.

Meeks, Wayne A. 1973. "The Image of the Androgyne: Some Uses of a Symbol in Earliest Christianity." *Journal of the History of Religions* 13 (1).

Pardes, I. 1989. "Beyond Genesis 3." *Hebrew University Studies in Literature and the Arts* 17.

———. 1992. *Countertraditions in the Bible: A Feminist Approach.* Cambridge: Harvard University Press.

Philo. 1929. "Legum allegoria." In *Loeb Classics Philo,* vol. 1, translated by F. H. Colson. London: Heinemann.

Plaza, M. 1980. "'Phallomorphic Power' and the Psychology of 'Woman': A Patriarchal Vicious Circle." *Feminist Issues* 1 (1).

Rapoport-Alpert, A. 1988. "On Women in Hasidism." In *Jewish History: Essays in Honour of Chimen Abramsky,* edited by A. Rapoport-Alpert and S. J. Zipperstein. London: Polity Press.

Saxonhouse, A. W. 1992. *Fear of Diversity: The Birth of Political Science in Ancient Greek Thought.* Chicago: University of Chicago Press.

Schor, Naomi. 1994. "This Essentialism That Is Not One: Coming to Grips with Irigaray." In *Engaging with Irigaray: Feminist Philosophy and Modern European Thought,* edited by Carolyn Burke, Naomi Schor, and Margaret Whitford. Gender and Culture. New York: Columbia University Press.

Shell, M. 1988. *The End of Kinship: Shakespeare, Incest, and the Religious Orders.* Stanford: Stanford University Press.

Sissa, G. 1992. "The Sexual Philosophies of Plato and Aristotle." In *A History of Women in the West,* edited by G. Duby and M. Perot. Cambridge: Harvard University Press.

Sly, D. 1990. *Philo's Perception of Women.* Brown Judaica Series. Atlanta: Scholars Press.

Smith, Jonathan Z. 1966. "The Garments of Shame." *History of Religion* 5.

Theodor, J., and H. Albeck, eds. 1965. *Genesis Rabbah.* Jerusalem: Wahrmann.

Tobin, T. H. 1983. *The Creation of Man: Philo and the History of Interpretation.* The Catholic Biblical Quarterly Monograph Series, no. 14. Washington, D.C.: The Catholic Biblical Association of America.

Turcotte, L. 1992. "Changing the Point of View," foreword to *"The Straight Mind" and Other Essays,* by Monique Wittig. Boston: Beacon Press.

Wittig, Monique. 1981. "One Is Not Born a Woman." *Feminist Issues* 1 (2).

———. 1992a. "The Category of Sex." In *"The Straight Mind" and Other Essays.* Boston: Beacon Press.

———. 1992b. "The Straight Mind." In *"The Straight Mind" and Other Essays.* Boston: Beacon Press.

SEVEN

God

Francis Schüssler Fiorenza and Gordon D. Kaufman

The term taken up in this chapter is one of the most complex and difficult in the English language. "God" is a word rich with layers and dimensions of meaning. It is full of problems and difficulties—for religious believers as well as unbelievers—and is susceptible to many sorts of interpretation. "God" is a term used to name the ultimate reality, value, and meaning for humans more often than any other in the language, but one that has also been employed frequently in thoroughly dehumanizing ways. "God" is a word known and used (in one way or another) by everyone who speaks English: in everyday exclamations of surprise as well as in religious meditation, in cries of despair as well as in worship, in curses as well as in prayers. It is a word that, more than any other, is at the center of many of the problems with which religion studies must come to terms, although, and perhaps for just this reason, it is often bypassed by religionists today instead of straightforwardly faced and carefully examined. It will not be possible, of course, to explore all the complexity and richness of the meanings and uses of "God" within the compass of this chapter. The most that can be hoped for here is a sketch that suggests some of the intricacy of meaning along with some of the reasons for it, and which attempts to show the significance of these matters for the field of religion studies.

Although all religion scholars are well aware that the word "God" has been central to Western religious traditions, in recent decades this term has not often been given the kind of careful examination and analysis devoted to many other features of human religiousness. There have been, of course, many studies of the idea of God characteristic of this or that historical period, or found in the work of one or another philosopher or theologian. But comprehensive, focused attention on the way in which this symbol developed in the course of the past four thousand years or so, its enormous influence on human life and culture throughout that period, and its continuing significance today is scarcely to be found. For some, perhaps, it is simply assumed that "God is dead," and, therefore, it is no longer necessary to attend carefully to this symbol (even though it obviously still has great power in popular religion); others, who count themselves as "believers" in God, may take one or another more or less traditional understanding so much for granted in their own personal lives that it does not occur to them that this ambiguous, complex, much contested symbol demands at least as careful study as any other aspect of human religiousness. It might be thought that the guild of professional theologians pursues investigations of the term "God" of the sort we call for in this chapter; but that is not the case. Most theologians concentrate their attention largely on explication of symbolizations and interpretations found in one particular religious tradition (or a relatively narrow family of religious traditions); the enormous diversity and complexity that this symbol actually carries in our languages and cultures is, in consequence, rarely regarded as being of central importance for their work. Despite its continuing importance in human life, serious study of this term is hard to find. In this chapter we shall try to suggest what might be involved in such study.

I. Linguistic and Biblical Backgrounds

The English language word "God" (spelled with a capital *G*, and with cognates in other Indo-European languages) functions most commonly as a proper name: God is one on whom humans can call in a time of desperate need; God is the creator of the world and of all that is in it, the protector and savior who provides for creaturely wants and who sustains women and men undergoing evil of all sorts; God is one to whom humans should give thanks for the many blessings of life. In the major Western religious traditions, God is the central object of worship and the ultimate court of appeal in all major crises of life.

But who or what is this "God"? According to the *Oxford English Dictionary*, the proper name "God" (as used in English speech and writing) is linguistically derived from earlier uses (usually indicated by a lowercase *g*) in which the word designates a "superhuman person (regarded as masculine . . .) who is worshipped as having power over nature and the fortunes of mankind; a deity" (1971, compact ed., 1:1168). "Deity," in turn, is defined as the "estate or rank of a god; godhood; . . . godship. . . . The divine quality, character, or nature of God" (*OED*, s.v. "deity"). We begin our reflections here with "God" as a proper name since "throughout the literary period of English [this has] been the predominant" usage, and what had been "the original heathen sense" of the word came to be "apprehended as a transferred use of this; 'a *god*', in this view, is a supposed being put in the place of *God*, or an imperfect conception of *God*" (*OED* 1: 1168). In "the specific Christian and monotheistic sense" of this word, which has long been standard in written English, the name "God" has designated the "One object of supreme adoration; the Creator and Ruler of the Universe"; and it was often used "in contexts where the One True God is contrasted with the false gods of heathenism" (1:1168). As these quotations from the *OED* suggest, the text of the Bible has been the principal source of the conceptions of God that have dominated spoken and written English; and radical departures from biblical notions (whether in reflective philosophical or theological works, or in esoteric [religious or other] writings)—though often incorporating metaphors, images, and concepts drastically different from any found in the Bible—nevertheless have always (in significant respects) depended for their intelligibility in English-speaking cultures on the force of the basic biblical images and conceptions.

The Bible is a collection of writings produced over at least two millennia, and as such includes many different images, concepts, and ways of thinking about what is referred to therein as "God." Though the conception of God that dominates biblical texts as they have been appropriated in English-language usage is monotheistic, traces remain of earlier polytheistic and henotheistic uses out of which biblical monotheism gradually emerged. During the early period, when the tribes of Israel lived a nomadic life, God was understood as the god of the tribe. A plurality of gods was envisioned, as suggested, for example, by reference to "the God of Abraham and the God of Nahor" (Gen. 51:53). The first commandment also presupposes this view: "I am Yahweh your God . . . ; you shall have no other gods before me" (Exod. 20:23; Deut. 5:6–7); this commandment does not dispute the existence of other gods but demands exclusive veneration of Yahweh by the Israelite tribes. A god *(El)* of this sort was usually associated with a particular location and its traditions. The development and spread of the *Sinai* traditions led to an understanding of God as *Yahweh,* the local god of Mount Sinai who was honored by Kenites and Midianites. In the later exilic and postexilic periods, the belief in God as creator became established, as Israel articulated its convictions about Yahweh in confrontation with the cosmogonic notions of its new cultural and religious environment. Thus, the claim to Yahweh's exclusiveness eventually developed into Israel's monotheism.

In English language Bible translations the image/concept "lord" is used most frequently (much more frequently than "God") to characterize God; in many versions of the biblical text, this term is used to translate "Yahweh," a name that traditional Jews have regarded as too holy to pronounce. This dominant use of "lord" (a title rather than a name) to refer to God connects directly, of course, with the *OED*'s basic characterization of God as the "Creator and Ruler of the Universe." Many other images and concepts, which deepen and expand the notion of God the Lord—nearly all of them male-gendered—are also found in the Bible. Some of these are essentially extensions of the notion of lord (e.g., king, mighty one, creator, father, shepherd); others, however, bring in strikingly different metaphorical meanings (e.g., the first and the last, the most high, the holy one, spirit, love). For the most part the Bible presents readers with an essentially andromorphic image/concept of God: God is sometimes pictured as having arms and legs, eyes and ears, a nose, a mind, a will, a voice; God has feelings of anger, kindness, vengeance, mercy; God's actions are purposive and creative, and they manifest righteousness and justice, faithfulness, strength of will, loving kindness, care for God's creatures, a strong commitment to keep promises made in covenants with them. In short, God is presented as an all-powerful, all-knowing *moral agent* who has brought the world into being and who is continually working in that world—especially with men and women—to carry out the purposes for which it was created.

These largely anthropomorphic images are, however, significantly qualified by a number of profoundly *abstract* metaphors that give the biblical image/concept of God its sense of utter difference from the human, its sense of overwhelming authority and power: that is, that enable this symbol to refer to *deity* (as contrasted with all finite realities). God is portrayed as saying, for example, "I am the first and I am the last" (Isa. 44:6 [cf. 48:12, 41:4]; Rev. 1:17, 2:8, 22: 13); God is said to be the reality "in [which] we live and move and have our being" (Acts 17:28), a reality present everywhere (apparently at all times), not only in heaven above or "at the farthest limits of the sea" but even "in Sheol" (Ps. 139:8f.), the last place of the wicked and the dead; God is frequently referred to as the "Most High"; God is presented as having created the heavens and the earth, as being the ultimate source of all that is. None of these expressions and conceptions are anthropomorphic or anthropocentric (although the activity of *creating* is depicted in anthropomorphic terms in Genesis 1 and 2); all are quite abstract, so much so that, taken simply by themselves, they present no specific *content* at all. What they express is God's *unsurpassability,* God's *uniqueness.* God is *eternal,* a uniqueness of an entirely different order from that of any finite being.

In consequence, what would otherwise appear to be quite straightforward anthropomorphic or anthropocentric locutions frequently become qualified in rhetorically powerful ways: "For as the heavens are higher than the earth [says the Lord], so are my ways higher than your ways and my thoughts than your thoughts" (Isa. 55:9). God's profound incomprehensibility to humans thus becomes an important theme. In the New Testament, for example, Paul writes that God "has mercy on whomever he chooses, and he hardens the heart of whomever he chooses. . . . who . . . are you, a human being, to argue with God?" (Rom. 9:18, 20; cf. Job 38–42). And Jesus is reported to have reminded his followers that many of God's activities are not what humans would regard as morally discriminating: "your Father in heaven . . . makes his sun rise on the evil and on the good, and sends rain on the righteous and on the unrighteous" (Matt. 5:45). It is often suggested in the Bible that no one ever has direct or immediate contact with or experience of God: in the Gospel of John (1:18) and again in 1 John (4:12), it is stated flatly that, "No one has ever seen God." The figure of God as portrayed in the Bible (even though in many respects it is quite anthropomorphically conceived) remains to very deep levels beyond human comprehension or understanding: "How unsearchable are his judgments and how inscrutable his ways!" (Rom. 11:33).

In the Bible itself, thus, the anthropomorphic and anthropocentric qualities so important to those who pray to and worship God are not what in fact establish God's *deity;* it is, rather, those locutions that drastically *qualify* these humanlike characteristics which distinctively identify God as *God.* And it is their presence as essential components of the biblical image/concept of God that makes it possible for worshippers to employ this symbol in directing their feelings and thoughts and activities toward what they regard as ultimate reality, power, and meaning. Nonetheless, the anthropomorphism of the biblical God and the overall anthropocentrism of the biblical story of God's activities remain throughout; and in some Christian texts these are strongly accentuated: "God so loved the [human] world," we are told, "that he gave his only Son, so that everyone who believes in him may not perish but may have eternal life" (John 3:16).

The biblical God has been regarded, in many quite different sociocultural contexts, as the ultimate reality and power, and thus the ultimate authority figure with which women and men have to do in life. There have always been, however, sharp disagreements about how God is to be conceived and understood, due at least in part to the great diversity of images and concepts that (as we have seen) are used to characterize God in the Bible, and the tensions of many sorts to which this diversity inevitably gives rise. Heretics were burned at the stake or drowned, and terrible wars were fought over such issues; so-called unbelievers were persecuted, tortured, killed; and campaigns of enslavement and genocide were undertaken—all in the name of the holy and righteous God of the Bible. The God who claimed to be the creator, sustainer, and savior of humans from all manner of evils to which they are subject has, on many occasions, been thought to have authorized utterly bloodthirsty crimes of humans against each other. This God has also, of course, frequently provided the inspiration for resistance to injustice and tyranny as well as movements toward more responsible and humane patterns of human life.

II. Three Strands of Meaning in the Term "God"

We have thus far considered only one of the strands that constitute the meaning of the word "God" as it is employed in English speaking societies: the *biblical* strand, which contributed the basic structure and many of the images that comprise this meaning-complex, providing it with much of its sociocultural, personal, and religious-spiritual energy, creativity, power, and authority. The Christian movement (the principal bearer of this symbol during the formative period of Western culture), however, grew into a major religious and sociocultural force largely within Hellenistic culture, and was heavily shaped in many ways—including in its use and understanding of the image/concept "God"—by Greek and Roman (in addition to Jewish) traditions and practices. Thus the term "God"—already a very complex one, as we have noted—was to become much more elaborate and complicated in its strands of meaning and in its uses than has so far been suggested.

It has sometimes been supposed that the great diversity of thinking and feeling and attitudes respecting God could be sorted out and assessed by distinguishing sharply what Pascal (1623–62) called "the God of Abraham, Isaac, and Jacob" (i.e., the God of biblical traditions) from "the God of the philosophers and scholars" (*Memorial* [1654]). But the intermixing of Greek and Hebraic traditions in Western religious history has become so intricate and intraconnected that such simplistic attempts to disentangle the various dimensions of meaning that this word now bears inevitably fail. Consider, for example, the uses to which the word "trinity" (a term central in Christian understanding of God) has been put. "Trinity" is not a biblical word at all but acquired its meaning originally in highly technical, theologicopolitical discussions of a range of terms drawn from Greek (and Latin) philosophical reflection (*ousia,* hypostasis, substance, essence, persons, modes, etc.). Nevertheless, in such phrases as "Blessed Trinity" it is widely used in the liturgies and prayers of many ordinary worshippers. Similarly, in the historic creeds (often given a central place in worship), technical philosophical language about "two natures" in "one person" and the like is to be found. Not only have philosophical ideas been integrated in this way into central devotional activities and practices but in the Bible itself profoundly abstract notions, deeply qualifying the prevailing anthropomorphic imagery, also perform indispensable functions. Claims that Greek conceptions of God are philosophical—and hence conceive of God as immutable—while biblical understanding is anthropomorphic and more suitable in worship are inadequate on other counts as well: they overlook the extent to which the Bible, especially the Christian writings, is itself permeated with Hellenistic cultural and philosophical views, and they fail to take account of the anthropomorphic polytheistic images in Greek mythology.

Though some might still wish to separate out these various historical strands in the meaning that the symbol "God" has come to carry in Western languages and cultures, this is not likely to illuminate matters much since the word "God" itself, as employed today, inevitably carries traces of all this complex weight of meaning. A more adequate approach recognizes that both anthropomorphic and philosophical ideas and images of God are to be found in every historical period in Western history—Judaic, Hellenistic, and Roman antiquity as well as the medieval, Reformation, and modern periods. It is precisely this richness and intricate complexity of meaning that gives this word its continuing significance in human life and praxis, thus also making it an important theme in religion studies.

Instead, therefore, of attempting to identify the exact historical roots of various strands of meaning borne by the word "God," we will discuss here three of the complex patterns of or tensions in meaning that have emerged in the course of Western history, each of which contributes significantly to the meaning(s) that "God" bears today. The first complex is concerned with the distinction we have already begun to discuss, between, on the one hand, popular images and models for conceiving God and, on the other, more reflective and philosophical language. Some popular images seem to dominate certain periods but may not be employed much in others, and these differences are themselves often correlated with the social and political practices and beliefs characteristic of each period. Philosophical categories, attitudes, and questions also change drastically over time. Consider, for example, the enormous impact modern science and philosophy have had on reflective, as well as popular, thinking about God.

The second complex of meaning to which we shall attend concerns the relation of language about God to the understanding of human subjectivity and creativity. Whereas in antiquity it was often assumed that the reality of God is interior to, and thus directly present within, the soul (e.g., Plotinus, Augustine), in modernity this way of thinking has become both more complex and more problematic. Human subjectivity (from Descartes to Rahner) is thought of as permeated by an awareness of infinity (not "God" as such), and a critical awareness of the creative and constructive roles that human language itself plays in precisely this consciousness increasingly emerges.

These developments prepare the way for consideration of our third complex of meaning, which is concerned with "negative theology," the awareness and articulation of the inadequacy of *all* human language and ideas about God. This is a theme going back to the first centuries of the common era, which has reappeared in every period and found new forms of articulation in modernity/postmodernity. There have been, however, significant changes along the way, with emphasis shifting from a focus on the attributes of the *object* of theological inquiry—God—to the intrinsic limitations of all human knowledge.

These three complexes of meaning in concert contribute significantly to the tensions, complexity, and force of the term "God" today, as well as to an intrinsic indeterminateness in its meaning that makes agreement on its proper specification and articulation difficult to reach.

III. The Conflict between Philosophical and Popular Images of God

The early Christian theologians appropriated Greek philosophical thinking in a very selective manner to elaborate their understanding of God. They criticized the Skeptics and Epicureans but took over elements of Stoic speech and thought about divine providence. Above all they appropriated Platonic and neo-Platonic ideas about the divine that were regarded as useful in criticizing popular Greek and Roman mythological language. The emphasis on unity in neo-Platonic philosophy was employed in criticizing Greco-Roman polytheism, for God conceived as one and unchangeable stood in sharp contrast with popular language about the actions of various deities on behalf of particular cities, locales, or persons. The early Christians were called "atheists" because, in denying the existence of the gods of the polis, they undermined popular beliefs in Greco-Roman deities. However, this embrace of Platonic philosophy by Christians also presented some large problems. For example, the incarnation of God in Jesus meant that God *changed* through entering the world of time, history, and matter. The attempt to understand this led to the gradual development of the concept of the trinity (often regarded as the most distinctive mark of Christian thinking about God). But Christian belief in the trinity had then, in turn, to be reconciled with the Hellenistic idea of God's oneness.

The Greek affirmation of the oneness of God goes back to Plato's adoption of the Pythagorean method of seeking explanation in mathematical terms. The ultimate principle of all reality, order, and goodness is to be found in the origin of all numbers, the *One*. God, the originative source of all being, was not dependent upon any other being, and was thus the sole ultimate, without beginning, without change, without parts, existing from all eternity. This Greek understanding was linked with the biblical God of Exodus, "He Who Is" (cf. 3:14), in both Jewish (Philo of Alexandria [c. 20 B.C.E. to 54 C.E.]) and Christian theology. The philosophical emphasis on oneness also had a popular political connotation since it was associated with the Roman monarchy: the one divine ruler of the universe and the one emperor on earth were seen in intimate connection. In the East, the debate about the trinity, therefore, was not only an issue about Christian orthodoxy but involved a critique of political monotheism as well.

The distinction between everyday popular usage of the term "God" and philosophical language using other terms became important in the medieval period. Anselm of Canterbury (1033–1109) consistently replaced the popular term "God" with philosophical terminology more appropriate to his argumentation. He used such terms as *summa essentia, summus spiritus,* and *ipsum bonum* to refer to the divine. This distinction between a philosophical and a popular use of language is also evident in Thomas Aquinas (1225–74). The individual "proofs" or "ways" to God's existence resulted in a philosophical principle, such as unmoved mover or first cause. Aquinas concluded that these refer to "what everyone calls God."

At the same time, popular thinking about God in terms drawn from the feudal social system was current even among sophisticated theologians. Anselm's classic theory of satisfaction is based upon a feudal conception of justice with its emphasis on honor and debt: the human debt to God is infinite because human sin went against the (infinite) honor of God and therefore can be satisfied only by an incarnate God. And Thomas Aquinas explained divine providence in terms of the popular imagery of a king setting goals, even though he thought of the divine causality in neo-Platonic and Aristotelian conceptions. Jean de Gerson (1363–1429) not only argued that one had to keep to the traditional term "God" but also affirmed the importance of the sovereignty of God who ruled the world with the control of an absolute ruler. Nicholas of Cusa (1401–64), however, underscored the inadequacy of all language respecting God, even the term "God." He argued that it is necessary to have the greatest number of descriptions, of which he preferred the terms *maximum pariter et minimum* and *unum absolutum* (1:4).

Medieval theology thus sought a synthesis between philosophical ways of speaking/thinking and the God of revelation. But the rise of medieval nominalism, represented especially by William of Ockham (c. 1285–1347), led to a breakdown of this synthesis. For Ockham, not only does God's free will determine what is necessary for salvation but God's free choice can be discerned only through divine revelation. This voluntarism provided a philosophical context for the Protestant Reformation, which emphasized the radical corruption of human nature through sin and the conviction that humans know God only through revelation. In Martin Luther (1483–1546) the causal ontological grounding of theological and philosophical speaking and thinking of God recedes in favor of an emphasis on God's free activity. Although John Calvin (1509–64) acknowledges a sense of the divinity within humans and the witness of creation to God's existence, all such natural knowledge is considered confused, hindered by sin, and thus incapable of leading to true knowledge of God. The latter, to be found only in the scriptures, was available to all believers and not simply to academic theologians or spiritual mystics. The Reformers thus conceived God less in categories such as absolute simplicity or principle of unity of being and more as the Divine Monarch with a sovereign will (in keeping with the political context of the increasing power of national monarchies). Here the inscrutable will and freedom of the sovereign God, rather than the simplicity and unity of the uncreated principle of all Being, came to the forefront of language and conceptions about God.

The religious wars of the sixteenth and seventeenth centuries led to the acceptance of religious tolerance as a necessity for political life. They also led to a critique of the dogmatic claims in the religious confessions (most of which were formulated largely in "popular" terms). Two movements in this early modern period, the Enlightenment and pietism, are important for our concerns here. Though pietism is often seen as a reaction to the Enlightenment, the two developments nevertheless had similar features in their thinking about God: they both emphasized religious subjectivity (either through an analysis of consciousness or through emphasis on the believer's religious experience), and they underscored the practical relevance of faith. The use of more personal language about God, strongly emphasized in the Reformation period (especially in left-wing groups), steadily increased, with deism using the image of God as watchmaker and pietism employing personalistic familial metaphors. Despite these commonalities, however, sharp differences between Enlightenment and pietistic rhetoric and thinking led to a decisive split between popular imagery of God and the philosophical critique of such language. Hegel's (1770–1831) philosophy of religion attempted to overcome this, but a dualism between philosophical reflection and popular religious language became dominant in the modern period; in addition, a great proliferation of ways of speaking and thinking of God have appeared.

Although Darwinism sounded the death knell for a natural theology of design, attempts to conceive God in philosophical categories based on a scientific understanding of the world have continued. William James's writings on pragmatism and religion, for example, present a scientific democratic conception of religion and divinity. *The Varieties of Religious Experience* (1985, pub. 1902) points to the specific and irreducible nature of religious experience and its enlargement of human consciousness. In *A Pluralistic Universe* (1977, pub. 1909), James advances the notion of the divine as finite (as had John Stuart Mill [1806–73]) within a pluralistic universe: "'God,' in the religious life of ordinary men, is the name not of the whole of things, heaven forbid, but only of the ideal tendency in things" (124). James regards the idea of an omniscient and omnipotent God as the "disease of the philosophy-shop." In his view of the universe as pluralistic, "God" signifies a reality that is finite in both knowledge and power but calls forth an active human response; humans can cooperate with God in effecting changes in the world.

Quantum theory brought an end to the mechanistic worldview of Newtonian physics and thus encouraged the development of notions of God as in process. In contrast to the emphasis of traditional theism on the divine simplicity that entails immutability and infinity, the process theisms of Alfred North Whitehead (1861–1947) and Charles Hartshorne (b. 1897) distinguish between the abstract essence of God (as absolute, eternal, unchangeable) and God's concrete actuality, which is temporal, relative, changing, and dependent on decisions made by finite actualities. Hartshorne, moreover, claims his language about God is more biblical and personal than that evoking the God of classical theism. In Whitehead's understanding, God offers each "actual occasion" that possibility which would be best but does not control or determine the finite occasion's self-actualizing; God works by persuasion and is not in total control of the events of the world. The existence of evil in the world is thereby compatible with the divine beneficence toward the world.

In these and other similar developments, there is a continual criss-crossing of popular and reflective images and conceptions nurturing and fertilizing each other, giving birth to widely different ways of speaking and thinking of God. So the meaning(s) of the word "God" have expanded in many directions, producing rich new possibilities for its employment but also much disagreement about how it is to be used; and many have begun to wonder whether it can any longer be usefully employed. Nevertheless, the power of this symbol remains great in popular Western culture, particularly in North America, and theologians and philosophers of quite diverse commitments continue to struggle with its meaning for human life in today's world.

IV. Subjectivity and the Word "God"

In the classical tradition, in keeping with the prevailing anthropomorphism and androcentrism of earlier conceptions and images of God, the spirituality of the soul was regarded as the avenue to knowledge of God as Spirit, and this influenced decisively the way in which the term "God" was employed (especially in "reflective" uses). This focus continues, although now the emphasis is placed more on the dynamism of the human intellect, which in its striving to unify experience is taken to be the source of our ideas of God. This modern development opened the door for historical studies and the sociology of knowledge to call attention—in connection with their exploration of the social and linguistic character of all human knowing—to certain social and political features of language about God as well as to the practical consequences in human life of the diverse images employed in this language. These all have had their effects on the meaning and uses of the term "God" today.

The idea of God as Spirit, pure Being without material parts, led classical

Christian authors to approach the understanding of God largely through reflection on the self. In his *On Free Choice of the Will*, Augustine (354–430), for example, holds that human intelligence is the highest and best of human attributes. This intelligence is dependent upon a reality that is higher than itself, the spiritual, eternal, and unchanging God (1993, 2:37–15:39). Since the soul is the image of God, Augustine asserts in *On the Trinity* that the mystery of the trinity can be understood (to some extent) through analogy with the human soul: just as self-knowledge, self-memory, and loving self-affirmation are interrelated, so too are Father, Son, and Holy Spirit (1963). The soul's knowledge of itself leads to knowledge of God and to a true idea of being.

This approach to God through subjectivity, however, undergoes a decisive shift in the transition to modernity. René Descartes (1596–1650), seeking to establish knowledge upon a secure foundation, called into question everything that could be doubted until he reached an indubitable proposition: "I think, therefore, I exist." Then, through establishing a criterion of truth (what is clearly and distinctly perceived) and the existence of God (as an infinitely perfect being who cannot deceive), he made the idea of the infinite the condition of the knowledge of all finite objects (since these objects are delineated as limited only in relation to this idea). Descartes's approach left the modern West with a twofold legacy: (1) a *foundationalism* that equates knowledge with secure foundations and clear and distinct ideas, and (2) an emphasis on subjectivity that anchors the knowledge of God but leaves the world of nature "godless."

This decisive shift in the understanding of subjectivity's importance is connected with other cultural developments. As the Newtonian and mechanical worldview was increasingly established as the only legitimate scientific position, a move from theism to deism took place. The terms "deism" and "theism" were originally synonymous, but "deism" came to refer to the view that the divine lacks an immediate ongoing personal relation to the world. God was often pictured as a watchmaker: once the watch is made, it runs according to its own mechanism. Having established natural laws, God does not intervene in ways that are contrary to them, that is miraculously. David Hume's (1711–76) critique of the metaphysical view of causality and his demolition of the argument from miracles advanced a naturalistic view of the world; and in the nineteenth century, Charles Darwin's theory of evolution further undercut natural theologies, with evolution providing an alternative explanation to divine teleology. These developments in the natural sciences eliminated God entirely from the order and design of the material world. Christian theology had long distinguished the traces of God in the sensible and material world from the image of God in the soul, but in modernity this distinction became a rupture, with the locus of God for humans restricted to subjectivity—pious subjectivity without objectivity.

Schleiermacher (1768–1834) sought a post-Enlightenment understanding along this line by locating religion in human feeling, not understood as an emotion but rather as an immediate self-consciousness or a mode of experiencing oneself in relation to the totality of the universe. This religious dimension of experience became, then, the locus for language about the divine. In his *On Religion: Speeches to Its Cultured Despisers* (1958, pub. 1800), he uses such terms as "universum," "infinite," "world-soul," "All" to replace the idea of an all-powerful person. Such terms focus attention more on the unity and infinity of the universe than on a personal God (thereby picking up on widely influential ideas earlier developed by Spinoza [1632–77]). G. W. F. Hegel, however, argued that both the Enlightenment critique of metaphysics and the location of language about God in religious feeling robbed the idea of God of its proper meaning: in Christianity the divine idea is the unity of the divine and human natures, not as a static structure but as a trinitarian *movement* of self-othering and self-reconciliation. Thus, what is originally present in religious belief as a "representation" and objectification becomes elevated into a (philosophical) *concept* that transcends the representational in its validity. God as spirit is triune, a conception of the divine that enabled Hegel to overcome dichotomized understandings of the relationship between God and the world, between the infinite and the finite.

In the left-wing Hegelian movement, however, the social construction of language about the divine came to the fore, exemplified in the critiques of religion found in Bruno Bauer (1809–82), Karl Marx (1818–83), and Ludwig Feuerbach (1804–72). In his *Essence of Christianity,* Feuerbach argues that when humans attribute qualities to God, they are actually calling attention to those human qualities they consider most valuable. To affirm that God is love, for example, is to affirm that love is divine. However, by projecting these qualities onto an object other than the human species, one alienates the human species from itself as well as from the world of nature. Feuerbach thus brings out not only the constructive character of language about God but also the alienating effects of such language. Friedrich Nietzsche (1844–1900) further radicalizes the critique of religious belief in his proclamation that "God is dead" (a phrase already used by Hegel) and his critique of Christian theism as a popularized Platonism. His analysis of the "will to power" shows how theistic valuations and beliefs introduce dominative powers that alienate humans from nature and life.

In the period following World War I, under the impact of the cultural crisis it provoked, a strong "neo-orthodox" protest against these sorts of developments occurred, beginning with Karl Barth's (1886–1968) emphasis, in his *Epistle to the Romans* (1933, pub. 1918), on the "infinite qualitative distinction" (a Kierkegaardian phrase) between God and everything human. Given this understanding, Barth claimed that God could be known only through God's own activity, that is, divine revelation. Though Barth's intent was to overcome in this way the human-centeredness of theologies rooted in human subjectivity and religious experience, he accomplished this by employing a concept of God (held to be drawn from the Bible) as a fully self-conscious, volitional, self-revealing being, a supreme *Subject*. That is, he built on central human metaphors. Thus, though neoorthodoxy criticized modern theology for its emphasis on subjectivity and its "humanization" of language about God, it too mirrored this emphasis by employing the categories of modern (androcentrically conceived) subjectivity in its understanding of God. Whereas the medieval tradition interpreted God as the "to be of being," Barth, though seeking to demolish the modern theological emphasis on the human subject, nevertheless conceived God essentially in these modern terms.

During the same period that Barth was working out his theology of revelation in Europe, Shailer Mathews in the United States was proposing in *The Faith of Modernism* (1924) and *The Growth of the Idea of God* (1931) that the social scientific study of religion investigate the relation between social mind-sets and religious beliefs. Mathews surveyed the idea of God through seven social mind-sets: Semitic, Hellenistic, imperial, feudal, nationalist, bourgeois, and scientific democratic. Whereas the Semitic mind-set views Christ as a messianic king within the scenario of the world drama between God and Satan, the Hellenistic mind-set recasts the messianic expectation in terms of the *logos*. The imperial mind-set casts God as a universal emperor, the feudal mind-set sees redemption in terms of the honor due God as a feudal lord, and the nationalist mind-set envisions God as a political monarch with absolute authority. Mathews ends his survey with the scientific-democratic social mind-set. The task of theology is to understand God in a way that coheres with this current dominant way of thinking; in 1915 Mathews emphasized the democratic pattern, whereas in 1930 he emphasized the scientific pattern. His proposals made explicit the modern awareness of the interrelation between human consciousness and religious language, between social mind-sets and religious beliefs. His work not only shows the extent to which conceptions of God are always built out of the metaphors in the environing culture but also underscores the necessity for theological methodological reflection and construction to take into account the current social and political institutions and conditions, as theologians and others attempt to ascertain (i.e., construct) the meaning of the term "God" in a specific historical context.

This methodological awareness of the social and linguistic conditioning of language about God has come to the fore in this century in discussions of the nature of religious language. Some seek to explore what is distinctive about religious language or about "God talk" by examining specific types of language, such as "limit" expressions; others ask whether religious language involves speech acts that entail a specific existential commitment of the speaker as well as propositional affirmations. According to another approach, religious language cannot be defined in essentialist terms. It is a mistake, thus, to speak and think of it in any of these essentialist ways: religious language is always part of a life praxis and can be understood only within that specific context (Wittgenstein). Yet another approach emphasizes the openness and creativity of all metaphors: Paul Ricoeur has proposed that biblical language about God be explored in terms of the creativity of its literary forms and its metaphors, while Sallie McFague's *Models of God* (1987) and Gordon Kaufman's *In Face of Mystery: A Constructive Theology* (1993) present programs of God talk in basically metaphorical terms.

The images and metaphors used to express the divine are taken from several areas: the family and personal relations, various occupations, political life, the world of nature, modern scientific thinking. Images from the family often convey the intimacy of a personal relation (God as father, mother, friend, helper). Images drawn from occupations provide examples of particular activities that may be regarded as important ways of viewing the divine (shepherd or caretaker, potter, builder, warrior or commander). Other images are drawn from political life (king, lord, master), from nature (spirit [wind], force, power, ground), and from science (evolution, ecology, field of force). The use and implications of these images may be quite diverse. On the one hand, to imagine God as king encourages attitudes of submission and obedience (to God) in ways that the images of friend or comforter do not. On the other hand, images of Christ as king or lord have often served to draw contrasts with totalitarian regimes, as in the anti-Nazi position of the German Confessing Church; the allegiance to the divine ruler serves, in this case, not as a source of submission but as a resource for resistance.

H. Richard Niebuhr has emphasized that more fundamental than the question of God's existence is the question of the *kind* of God we have. In *Radical Monotheism and Western Culture* (1960), he points to God as a transcendence that undercuts all human idols, including church, the Scriptures, and Christ. Niebuhr explicates Christian belief in the trinity by showing how it protects against various sorts of one-sidedness in life. If God is identified only as father, then one tends to see the created order in terms of the will of God (creator of that order) and its fulfillment; however, if God is identified mainly as Christ the savior, then salvation and redemption, in contrast to the present created order, are emphasized; if God is viewed exclusively as spirit, the ecstatic elements in religious life become highlighted. Here the trinity, with its images of God as father, son, and holy spirit has implications not only for the conception of God but also for the understanding of human life.

Contemporary feminist theology has challenged the largely male-gendered traditional imagery of God because of its reinforcement of patriarchal institutions and values. In *Beyond God the Father* (1973), Mary Daly not only criticizes the system of patriarchy entailed in this image but also attacks the static and dualistic metaphysics implicit in it. In seeking to overcome the inadequacies of exclusively identifying the symbol "God" with such symbols as father and lord, feminist theologians have taken different directions. Sallie McFague has sought to offer alternative images such as mother, friend, and lover (cf. the classic trinitarian imagery of father, son, and holy spirit). Elisabeth Schüssler Fiorenza (1983), a New Testament scholar, highlights the role of the feminine Sophia-God within the Wisdom traditions of the Bible, and the identification of Jesus in the early strands of the New Testament traditions as the messenger of this Sophia-God, and then later with Sophia herself. In a different direction, Carol Christ (see esp. 1997) and others argue for the necessity of a post-Christian approach to God language. They retrieve the image of the Goddess from non-Christian, especially pre-Christian, traditions and argue for its significance. Rosemary Ruether (1992) explicates the notion of Gaia in relation to the understanding of God (a name that she frequently writes as God/ess).

All of these more recent approaches ask what kind of God we have, thus exploring further the meaning and use of God language. The increasing proliferation of metaphors and images, of course, and the growing critical awareness that each has significant limitations raise the question of the adequacy of all God talk—an issue at the center of the tradition of negative theology to which we now turn.

V. *Negative Theology and the Word "God"*

As reflective modes of thinking about God develop, awareness of the limitations of human knowledge of God becomes increasingly acute; already in the Bible there are poignant references to the hiddenness and inscrutability of God, as we earlier observed (section 1). It is not surprising, then, that early Christian writers, alongside their positive theological speaking and thinking, developed a negative theology as well. The Cappadocians, especially Gregory of Nyssa (c. 335–94), underscored the inaccessibility of God to human knowing; the spirituality and infinity of God makes God inaccessible to human knowledge. Pseudo-Dionysius (sixth century) goes further: God's incomprehensibility does not flow from the limitations of the human mind but is a quality of God. John of Damascus (c. 675–740) in *Concerning Orthodox Faith* and Pseudo-Dionysius in *The Divine Names* (1.4) and *The Mystical Theology* affirm that one can only posit negative statements about God. Moses Maimonides (1135–1204), an influential medieval Jewish thinker, argues similarly: the oneness of God means not only that there is not a plurality of gods but also that God as unique is beyond all human creatures; propositions about God are, therefore, negations (1963, 1:58). For both Pseudo-Dionysius and Maimonides we can affirm what God is not, not what God is; similar conclusions are reached by Islamic philosophers such as Avicenna (980–1037) and al-Ghazzali (1058–1111).

Medieval theology developed an explicit theory about the uses of analogical language in speaking of God, and this doctrine of analogy is often contrasted with negative theology, in that analogy entails not only negative but also positive affirmations about God. Correctly understood, however, the theory of analogy does not so much affirm the adequacy of positive affirmations as the imperfection of all language about God; and it should be seen, thus, not as rejecting but as continuing the tradition of negative theology. Thomas Aquinas (1964, I, Q. 13) distinguishes between an analogy of attribution and an analogy of proportionality. An analogy of attribution is based on similarity between cause and effect:

eating vegetables, for example, can be called healthy because it produces health. An analogy of proportionality, however, points only to a proportion between two elements in realities that are to be sharply contrasted with each other. Thus, God's understanding and wisdom are proportionate to God's being, and human understanding and wisdom are proportionate to the being of humans. This type of analogy underscores *dis*similarity rather than similarity, when human language and images are applied to God. God is infinite and human beings are finite and limited: no proportionality exists between God and humans. In applying propositions to God, one is indeed making an affirmation but only imperfectly; and what is affirmed has to be affirmed in a way that negates and transcends the finite analogue. As Aquinas noted in the introduction to Question 3 of the *Summa Theologiae:* "Now we cannot know how God is, but only how God is not; we must therefore consider the ways in which God does not exist, rather than the ways in which he does exist" (*ST* I, Q. 3). The theory of analogy is thus close to a negative theology.

A more radical negative theology is found in the writings of the mystics. Meister Eckhart (c. 1260–1328), for example, holding that being and knowing are identical, noted that what has most being is most known. But from this he concludes that, "Because God's being is transcendent, he is beyond all knowledge" (1941, 142). Nicholas of Cusa takes negative theology in a speculative direction, going beyond medieval thinking with his notion of "learned ignorance." This was not simply a Socratic not knowing but rather the assertion that one knows *because* one does not know. Since nothing can be greater than the "Absolute Maximum" or less than the "Absolute Minimum," God is beyond all opposition, for in God these opposites coincide (*coincidentia oppositorum*).

In modernity, a distinctive sort of negative theology emerges. It is not so much based on the spiritual nature of God or the infinity of God's being in contrast to human finiteness as on the limits of human reason. Immanuel Kant (1724–84) sought to provide a firm foundation for rationality by examining the proper use of human reason within its limits. He shows that the cosmological, teleological, and ontological proofs of God's existence all presuppose an ability that the human mind does not have: to go *beyond* experience and give content to the idea of an absolutely necessary being. Kant's critique of natural theology is not simply that one cannot theoretically demonstrate the existence of such a being; it is the more basic claim that the very notion "existence of God" ensnares speculative philosophy in the dialectical illusion of assuming that God is the sort of object that can be characterized as existing. The concept of God for Kant, thus, becomes a regulative idea or transcendental ideal. "What this primordial ground of the unity of the world may be in itself, we should not profess to have thereby decided, but only how we should use it, or rather its idea, in relation to the systematic employment of reason in respect of the things of the world" (1929, B727). Kant thus develops a negative theology based on the limitations of human knowledge. At the same time, however, his understanding of the function of the transcendental, and of God as a postulate of practical reason and morality, opens the way for a pragmatic and self-critical reflection on our use of language, images, and metaphors about God.

Johann G. Fichte's (1762–1814) critique of traditional theism goes further than Kant's. Fichte argues that qualifications or determinants such as substance, consciousness, and personhood are all finite and therefore cannot be applied to God. Personhood is finite, for example, since a personal subject is determined by things outside of itself and becomes conscious of itself only in relation to other finite objects. To transfer the anthropomorphic category of personhood (an individual self-conscious self) to God goes against the infinitude of the divine. Fichte's conclusion led to misunderstanding and to the charge of atheism.

Influenced by Kant's critique of theistic metaphysics and Fichte's critique of personhood, Friedrich Schleiermacher sought to redefine the understanding of religion and the divine in his *On Religion* (as noted above). In his *Christian Faith* and *Dialektik,* Schleiermacher explicates the believer's immediate self-consciousness as an experiencing of the self as "utterly dependent." As he goes on to note, the "whence" of this utter dependence is what religious persons and believers name God, but what a nonreligious interpretation calls nature. In his discussion of the adequacy of religious statements about this "whence," Schleiermacher is conscious of the Kantian critique: Religious affirmations are more properly propositions about the human condition than metaphysical descriptions about God or the world; the attributes of God thus do not refer to something specific in God but rather express our relation to God. Schleiermacher does go beyond this, however, insofar as he views the diverse divine attributes as expressing the one divine causality. ("Causality," of course, is simply the correlate of the sense of a "whence.")

In postmodern philosophers and theologians a more radical critique is advanced. Here it is not simply the epistemological issue that is raised but the "onto-theological" question. (Behind this postmodern challenge stands the influence of Martin Heidegger [1889–1976] with his view that the distinguishing characteristic of modern philosophy is its tendency to think of Being in terms of subjectivity and its search for an indubitable certitude [Descartes].) The problem becomes, How does one think of God, or otherwise use the word "God," without reducing God to a being like other beings or an object like other objects? The concern with overcoming these objectifying tendencies so characteristic of the onto-theological tradition is evident in such postmodern thinkers as Marion, Lévinas, and Derrida.

Jean-Luc Marion criticizes the metaphysical conception of God as idolatry. In *God without Being* (1991), he argues that to think of God as the all-comprehensive concept and as a free-willing ground of everything is idolatrous, for it fails to eliminate empirical threads from the supersensible notion of God. Emmanuel Lévinas (1906–95) also criticizes the Western philosophical tradition for its conception of God as a being with certain ontological qualities.

For him even Western mysticism sees God as, however mysterious, nevertheless comprehensible by some elect few; this is still to conceive God anthropomorphically, and fails to comprehend the otherness of God. In *Totality and Infinity* Lévinas uses the word "Infinity" rather than God to express this otherness. For him the Holocaust reveals the failure of theodicy and the God of ontology, and he proposes that God is known through the ethical relation of our responsibility for others. He finds "traces" of the Good, of the transcendent Other, in our responsibility for the other. Jacques Derrida criticizes attempts to appeal to a negative theology and to seek to distinguish God from being in his argument that such attempts are still onto-theologies. They continue to use the conceptuality of Platonic and neo-Platonic philosophy even in arguing that God is not being or is beyond being. Though negative theologies seek to go beyond the alternatives of theism and atheism, they are tied to an onto-theology to the extent that they seem to retain a being beyond Being, some hyperessentiality that is beyond all negation and positive predication.

Such critiques radicalize negative theology. They suggest that even in its negations all negative theology is tied to an ontology that presupposes the being of the divine. We seem here, with respect to God, to end up with utter speechlessness. But we should not forget that it has been only through *speaking*—through uttering this enormously complex word "God" and speaking about God, and through speaking in critique of all such speaking—that we may be led to this conclusion.

VI. The Symbol "God" and the Study of Religion

Our sketch of these three meaning complexes connected with Western employment of and reflection on the term "God" shows how complicated, difficult, but rich this word has been, and indeed still is. As an ultimate point of reference for all that is (and, indeed, is *not*), the term seeks to gather up, comprehend, and hold together in a meaningful interconnection that can orient human life, all reality and experience, all possibilities and imaginings—intentions surely transcending human capabilities of knowing, conceiving, or imagining. It is hardly surprising, therefore, that the "death" of God has frequently been proclaimed in modern times. And yet, speaking the word "God," worshipping God, thinking about God, all continue. The long history of negative theology, and alongside it and coexisting with it the regular renewal of reflective positive theologies as well as much popular imagery and language about God, testifies to the continuing importance of this term for religion studies today. The full meaning of these conflicted ways of speaking to and about God, evident throughout the history of God talk, is still far from clear.

Much of this chapter has been devoted to sketching the complexity that the word "God" has come to have in the course of Western history; it is the central, most powerful symbol in terms of which human life in the West has been ordered and oriented. In modern times, however (as we have noted), although it has become highly contested (not only among intellectuals in the universities but in wide sectors of Western culture at large), this symbol is still very much alive; and it falls to religion studies to assess its continuing import and significance. No other academic discipline is in a position to bring to bear the wide range of approaches (historical, psychological, sociological, anthropological, linguistic, comparative, feminist, ethical, aesthetic, philosophical, theological) necessary to sort out the nuances and complexities of meaning that are intricately bound up in it.

Other terms, such as the "holy," the "sacred," "divinity," the "supernatural," the "mystical," and so on, have been proposed as articulating what is at the heart of all religion, and thus as best denoting the proper object of religion studies. None of these common nouns, however, can or does contain either the comprehensiveness or the specificity of meaning to which the proper name "God" adverts, with its positing of an ultimate point of reference in terms of which all realities must be understood, and its claim that all aspects of human life therefore—and not only religious and moral practices and experiences—should be oriented in terms of this reference point. This ultimate point of reference (God) *relativizes* all present human practices, ideologies, and institutions, calling them all into question critically, while demanding their transformation in more *humanizing* and *humane* directions. It is not evident that the meaning and uses of this rich and complex symbol can be properly grasped through subsuming it under one or more such general concepts as those mentioned above; rather, it should be carefully examined in its own right, not reduced to something else quite different. Otherwise, we may in our religion studies programs be missing something at the very heart of certain important strands of human religiousness.

What kind of study is required to bring this enormous complexity of meaning into proper focus? How can religion studies contribute most effectively to the exploration, understanding, and interpretation of this symbol? We suggest here the usefulness of three different approaches. Each of these can help bring into view important dimensions of the symbol "God" and the way it functions; and all of them taken together, and as interconnected with each other, should produce a richer and more profound understanding than anything now available. Only an interdisciplinary "field-encompassing field" such as religion studies has the capability of pursuing a project of this scope and depth. In view of the power and significance this symbol has had in the past, and, indeed, continues to have, this sort of concentrated effort would seem to be appropriate.

1. *Historical, sociological, and other analytical studies of the symbol "God."* One sort of study that needs to be pursued much further is of the sort which this present essay begins to sketch: much fuller and more careful analysis of the origins of this symbol, the various streams of tradition that have contributed to its development, and the many diverse cultural and linguistic contexts in which it has played a significant role in ordering and orienting human life is needed.

In addition to such historical studies, we need much fuller knowledge than we presently have of the way in which the word "God" continues to function in a range of cultural contexts today. There are, for example, those popular religious movements for which "God" is a central rallying cry and focus for devotion as well as for political action, movements including (but not limited to) some that are often designated as "fundamentalist" or "evangelical." Many persons, however, who are not directly associated with such movements, also count themselves "faithful believers" in God. What does this word mean to such believers? How do they understand the God in whom they place their faith? Why do they regard faith in God as important? How do they relate themselves to their neighbors who do not profess such faith? Does their faith lead them to church involvement, regular biblical study? And so on. Nonreductive sociological, psychological, linguistic, and other studies of what "God" actually means to diverse groups of modern/postmodern people, and what importance (or lack of importance) this word has for them, are much needed.

2. *Comparative studies of "God" and/or "the gods."* Much academic study of religion is being directed today by interest in history of religions and comparative religions. Earlier in this century comparative studies of the symbol "God" (and "the gods") were beginning to get under way, but for many decades these have been in abeyance, perhaps in part because of the Western bias evident in many of those earlier studies. Properly done, such studies would involve not only comparative examination of the diversity of linguistic traditions involved—their grammatical and syntactical practices and their uses of various sorts of metaphor, the differing ways in which major ordering symbols (like "God") function in these diverse traditions, and so on—but also the ritualistic, moral, and social contexts with which these linguistic practices are connected. Comparative studies of this sort should help to call into question and challenge Western theistic and atheistic biases that may still be operative in the studies proposed under (1) above, by introducing totally different conceptual frameworks for ordering, orienting, and reflecting on human existence and activities. One thinks, for instance, of the illumination the Buddhist notion of *sunyata* (emptiness) could bring to the problems posed by Western substantialist thinking about God, a way of thinking that has given rise (as we have seen) to the long critical tradition of negative theology.

These two sorts of studies taken together should bring fuller understanding of the diverse ways in which (at least some) religious symbol systems have actually functioned in a range of sociocultural contexts, thus providing a basis for developing more adequate theories of religious symbolization than are now available. Such theories, in turn, should facilitate more disciplined examination of the alleged uniqueness of the symbol "God" as well as more adequate assessment of its actual strengths and weaknesses. Without better understanding of these issues the questions regarding this symbol posed by, for example, today's growing consciousness of the significance of religious pluralism, can scarcely be addressed intelligently.

3. *Constructive work.* With these various sorts of studies all in mind, a further question needs to be addressed: Can (or should) the symbol "God" be deliberately *re*constructed today in ways that will enable it to order and orient the lives of modern/postmodern people more effectively? Attempts to construct imaginatively new, more viable, meaningful, and self-critical ways to conceive, understand, and employ the symbol "God" in today's world make up the central task of *constructive* theology (Kaufman 1993, 1995). Theological work has always been a constructive and/or reconstructive (Fiorenza 1984) activity, engaged in imaginatively as women and men have had to come to terms with new contingencies, new issues, new problems. Today many different sorts of issues call into question various features of traditional (Western) understandings of God: issues posed by religious pluralism; by scientific cosmologies; by the increasing economic, political, cultural, and religious tensions between the powerful "first world" societies and other less powerful sectors of our global village; by the moral, intellectual, religious, philosophical, and other forms of criticism (including, most recently, feminist criticism) to which the symbol "God" has been subjected in the last two or three centuries, both in the West and in parts of the world that the West colonized; and so on. These can be taken up in more deliberate and self-conscious fashion now than has ever before been feasible. Radical, far-reaching deconstructive work, together with highly imaginative fresh construction and reconstruction, is beginning to appear in the studies of theologians of many different stripes. In due course all of this should have significant effects on the way the word "God" is understood and used in the future, though doubtless much "popular" religion will continue to be resistive to these developments.

The significance of constructive work with the symbol "God" can be considered from another vantage point. What bearing (if any) do the various sorts of technical studies described as analytical (1) and comparative (2) have for the actual *faith in God* of thoughtful women and men in today's world? That is, reflective members of churches, synagogues, and mosques, as well as interested persons who do not have communal or institutional religious commitments? Should those involved in the academic study of religion be concerned with "practical" questions of this sort? Do religionists have responsibilities to the wider society and culture that sustains them, to assist in the address of major problems faced in that society and culture? Or is the study of religion a "purely academic" exercise? The natural and social sciences, as well as some of the humanities, are drawn upon in diverse ways for the knowledge and understanding necessary to address major problems that today's societies confront. Religion studies might also have much to offer if they focused attention more directly on sociocultural problems in which religion, and religious symbols, are deeply implicated; and if they sought to address more directly some of these matters. We think that scholars in the study of religion do have responsibilities of this kind. They ought, therefore, to be developing proposals about how the enormous confusions concerning God, and faith in or loyalty to God, might be addressed in modern/ postmodern societies.

Are some ways of thinking of God today more responsible than others? Is it important (or feasible) for modern societies to address sensitive theological questions of this sort (in view of the enormous sociopolitical power that the symbol "God" still commands)? In what ways do some of the individuals and groups that use the word "God" quite freely in fact seriously *misuse* it? And what sorts of sociocultural consequences does this have? Is it appropriate to speak of "proper" and "improper" uses of this word? What should loyalty to God today involve? These questions call attention to important issues that should be much more freely discussed and debated in the public square than they commonly are; and such discussions should in no way be foreclosed by governmental or ecclesiastical authorities. In American society—with its well-known "wall" separating church (or religion) and the state, even while the name of God is widely invoked in contexts (often government-sponsored) of "civil religion"—surely more public attention to what is involved when the word "God" is employed is called for. Should such questions continue to be largely avoided by religion scholars? More direct address of this deep *theological* root of public life in this society might help soften some of the hard-edged discourse becoming increasingly prominent in our public life.

The study of religion is one of the few disciplines that is in a position to begin addressing the problems that arise in connection with the centrality of the symbol "God" in our historical past and its continuing force in public life. But taking up this social/cultural/political task has rarely been considered by scholars in this field to be their responsibility, and hence studies in religion have not been organized in ways that focus directly on these matters. Religion scholars should, we believe, at least ask themselves whether they may not have some distinctive responsibilities, qua religion scholars, with respect to these central problems in our society about which they are almost alone in having expertise. As Robert Bellah said years ago, "in the last analysis [humans are] responsible for the choice of [their] symbolism" (1970, 42). In our opinion religion scholars have a special obligation to help modern societies exercise that choice responsibly.

Suggested Readings

Armstrong, Karen. 1993. *A History of God: From Abraham to the Present.*

Barth, Karl. 1960. *Anselm: Fides Quaerens Intellectum.*

Buber, Martin. 1927. *I and Thou.*

Buckley, Michael. 1987. *At the Origins of Modern Atheism.*

Burrell, David. 1986. *Knowing the Unknowable God: Ibn-Sina, Maimonides, Aquinas.*

Christ, Carol. 1997. *Rebirth of the Goddess: Finding Meaning in Feminist Spirituality.*

Farley, Edward. 1996. *Divine Empathy: A Theology of God.*
Hartshorne, Charles. 1948. *The Divine Relativity.*
Jüngel, Eberhard. 1983. *God as the Mystery of the World.*
Kaufman, Gordon D. 1995. *An Essay on Theological Method.* Third Edition.
McFague, Sallie. 1987. *Models of God.*
Miles, Jack. 1995. *God: A Biography.*
Pannenberg, Wolfhart. 1988. *Metaphysics and the Idea of God.*
Rahner, Karl. 1978. *Foundations of Christian Faith.*
Rubenstein, Richard. 1992. *After Auschwitz.* Second Edition.
Sells, Michael. 1992. *Mystical Languages of Unsaying.*
Tillich, Paul. 1951. *Systematic Theology,* vol. 1.

REFERENCES

Aquinas, Thomas. 1964. *Summa Theologiae.* New York: McGraw-Hill.
Augustine. 1963. *The Trinity,* translated by Stephen McKenna. Vol. 45 of *Fathers of the Church.* Washington, D.C.: Catholic University of America Press.
———. 1993. *On Free Choice of the Will,* translated by Thomas Williams. Indianapolis: Hackett.
Barth, Karl. 1933. *Epistle to the Romans.* London and New York: Oxford University Press.
Bellah, Robert. 1970. *Beyond Belief.* New York: Harper and Row.
Christ, Carol. 1997. *Rebirth of the Goddess: Finding Meaning in Feminist Spirituality.* Reading, Mass.: Addison-Wesley.
Daly, Mary. 1973. *Beyond God the Father: Toward a Philosophy of Women's Liberation.* Boston: Beacon Press.
Eckhart, Meister. 1941. *Meister Eckhart: A Modern Translation,* edited and translated by Raymond B. Blakney. New York: Harper.
Feuerbach, Ludwig. 1957. *The Essence of Christianity,* translated by George Eliot. New York: Harper.
Fiorenza, Francis. 1984. *Foundational Theology.* New York: Crossroad.
James, William. 1977. *A Pluralistic Universe.* Cambridge: Harvard University Press.
———. 1985. *The Varieties of Religious Experience.* Cambridge: Harvard University Press.
John of Damascus. 1899. *Exposition of the Orthodox Faith.* In *Select Works,* by Hilary of Poitiers and John of Damascus. Vol. 9 of A Select Library of Nicene and Post-Nicene Fathers of the Christian Church, second series. Oxford: Parker.
Kant, Immanuel. 1929. *Critique of Pure Reason,* translated by Norman Kemp Smith. New York: St. Martin's Press.
Kaufman, Gordon. 1993. *In Face of Mystery: A Constructive Theology.* Cambridge: Harvard University Press.
Lévinas, Emmanuel. 1969. *Totality and Infinity.* Pittsburgh: Duquesne University Press.
Maimonides, Moses. 1963. *The Guide of the Perplexed,* translated and edited by Shlomo Pines. Chicago: University of Chicago Press.
Marion, Jean-Luc. 1991. *God without Being.* Chicago: University of Chicago Press.
Mathews, Shailer. 1924. *The Faith of Modernism.* New York: Macmillan.
———. 1931. *The Growth of the Idea of God.* New York: Macmillan.
McFague, Sallie. 1987. *Models of God: Theology for an Ecological, Nuclear Age.* Philadelphia: Fortress Press.
Nicholas of Cusa. 1954. *Of Learned Ignorance.* New Haven: Yale University.
Niebuhr, H. Richard. 1960. *Radical Monotheism and Western Culture.* New York: Harper.
Pascal, Blaise. 1995. *Pensées and Other Writings,* translated by Homer Levi. New York and Oxford: Oxford University Press.

Pseudo-Dionysius. 1987. "The Divine Names" and "The Mystical Theology." In *Pseudo-Dionysius: The Complete Works*. New York: Paulist Press.

Ruether, Rosemary. 1992. *Gaia and God: An Ecofeminist Theology of Earth Healing*. San Francisco: Harper.

Schleiermacher, Friedrich. 1928. *The Christian Faith*, translated by H. R. Mackintosh and J. S. Stewart. Edinburgh: Clark.

———. 1958. *On Religion: Speeches to Its Cultured Despisers*. New York: Harper.

———. 1976. *Dialektik*, edited by Rudolf Odebrecht. Darmstadt: Wissenschaftliche Buchgesellschaft.

Schüssler Fiorenza, Elisabeth. 1993. *In Memory of Her*. New York: Crossroad.

EIGHT

Image

Margaret R. Miles

Augustine remarked in his *Confessions* that he knew what time was until he tried to explain it. Similarly, "image" is a perfectly transparent and straightforward term, until one begins to consider its complex past and present usages. Affected not only by inevitable drifts in denotation and connotation but also by technological changes, the meanings of image have changed dramatically from ancient times to the modern West. Moreover, changes not only in meaning but also in the value ascribed to image complicate the term. As a critical term in religious studies, "image" is singularly difficult to define, even if the discussion is confined, as is this essay, to the Christian and post-Christian West.

In the fifth century B.C.E. Plato wrote, "I strain after images" (*Republic* 488a). He defined philosophy as the search for images that give a more or less adequate picture of the world in which human beings live, relate to one another, struggle for sustenance, and face inevitable death. His description of philosophy has strikingly postmodern resonances in its confession that discursive prose is ultimately unable to represent simultaneously the commonalities and the particularities of human experience, the "big picture" and the delicate shade of nuance. No one image can do this either, of course; rather, a repertoire of images must supplement and correct one another as the philosopher struggles to gather the most evocative, accurate, and fruitful images. Plato also suggests that the search for images is necessarily ongoing; as experience changes continually, the images that seek to describe it must change. No perfect and final image can be imagined. In Plato's usage, both the provocativeness and the volatility of images are emphasized.

Plato's understanding of images and their uses, however, was not normative for the idea of image in antiquity. Plotinus and the Christian theologians influenced by him used the word to define the metaphysical status of living beings and the visible entities of the natural world in relation to God. A complete history of the uses of image cannot be attempted in this essay. I will, instead, divide my task into two parts, first discussing theological uses of the term in the early centuries of the common era culminating in an eighth-century controversy concerning images and their religious use in the Eastern Orthodox Church. Second, a description of twentieth-century understandings of image in American media culture will demonstrate a sharp contrast with earlier theological uses. Finally, I will indicate the importance of "image" as a critical term in contemporary religious studies.

Image in Antiquity

Plotinus was the first ancient philosopher to use a concept of image as the center-piece of his metaphysics. His usage was later adopted and adapted by Christian theologians who incorporated Plotinus's metaphysics into the account in Genesis of humanity's creation "in the image and likeness of God." I begin, then, with Plotinus.

In Plotinus's picture of the universe each entity has a place where it may stand in its own light. Each living being is protected from either being flooded by chaos or marginalized by stronger realities. Plotinus's conceptual scheme has frequently been diagrammed as a ladder: underneath, matter defines the limit of the One's emanations and supports the myriad forms of life. Body lies on the first rung, and so on "up" through Soul to Intellect and on to the One, the source of the whole. The ladder image, however, is accurate only if one focuses on the uprights or sides of the ladder, the parts that hold the whole together, rather than on the distinct rungs. Although he was not averse to saying that some entities are higher and some are lower, it was the interconnection of the whole that interested Plotinus. For each entity, informed to the full extent of its capacity by the being, goodness, and reality that emanate from the One, participates in a continuous circulation of life through all beings. Each catches, absorbs, is formed by, and reflects the being above it.

Above the ladder, the One emanates its undifferentiated rays to Intellect spontaneously, effortlessly, and without diminishment. Intellect contains thoughts, differentiations, movement and rest, qualities and quantities, and the forms of everything that exists. Intellect localizes the energy of the One, making with it the myriad forms of the world we see and experience. Plotinus (1966–88) describes Intellect as "boiling with life" (6.5.2, 6.7.12). Intellect beams the forms it contains to the common Soul of all living creatures, and Soul places those forms into bodies. Bodies are created and supported in life because "the One does not give, and pass, but gives on forever" (6.9.9). For Plotinus, life is not biodegradable; even at death it does not perish but spins off to animate other forms. Like light, life depends on its source, not on the body illuminated or animated by it (4.5.7, 1.9.1, 3.2.15).

Because each sphere both creates and is mirrored by the sphere beneath it, all the forms of life contained by Intellect must also exist in the world of the senses (Plotinus 1966–88, 4.8.1):

> Does the world there have everything that is here? Yes, everything that is made by forming principle and according to form. . . . Certainly the sky there must be a living being, and so a sky not bare of stars. . . . But obviously there is earth there too, not barren, but much more full of life, and all animals are in it. . . . and, obviously, plants . . . and sea [are] there, and all water in abiding flow and life,

161

and all the living beings in water . . . and air, and aerial living things. (6.7.11)

Plotinus's vision of the universal life permeating everything is expansively inclusive; even rocks partake of the universal life (6.7.11, 4.4.27). "These things here below are carried along with those things in heaven, and those in heaven with these on earth, and both together contribute to the consistency and everlastingness of the universe" (3.3.6).

Each entity is an image of the one above it. It lives because of its ability to reflect. Because the concept of image is so crucial to his metaphysics, Plotinus carefully specifies what he means by it. He does not intend the kind of image that is created when a painter creates a portrait, for the person sitting for the portrait can disappear or even die while her image remains. He means, rather, the kind of image that depends at each moment upon the *presence* and reality of its original, like an image reflected in a mirror or a pool of water (1966–88, 6.2, 6.4.10). For "it is not possible for what has come to be to exist cut off from it" (6.4.10).

What is supremely important for Plotinus is that one discern the entities of the sensible world as *images*. Seen as image—at several removes—of the One, the sensible world becomes not mere image but perfect image:

> Surely, what other fairer image of the intelligible world could there be? For what other fire could be a better image of the intelligible fire than the fire here? Or what other earth could be better than this, after the intelligible earth? And what sphere could be more exact or more dignified or better ordered in its circuit [than the sphere of this universe] after the self-enclosed circle there of the intelligible universe? And what other sun could there be which ranked after the intelligible sun and before this visible sun here? (1966–88, 2.9.4)

Despite Plotinus's use of the term to emphasize not only resemblance but near perfect copy, an ambiguity adheres to the term "image": on the one hand, it indicates the closest possible relation; on the other, the conception of image always carries a sense of something inferior in relation to its model.

Patristic authors simplified Plotinus's complex universe but retained his understanding of the pivotal function of image as well as its ambiguity. For Christian authors, life and being no longer circulate through an intricate series of differentiations from the One to the visible bodies of the sensible world but from Creator to the created world.

The Christian Scriptures claimed not only that humanity was created in God's image but that Jesus Christ, as God's first image, had come to the human world to share the human condition, to participate directly in the human experiences of ordinary birth and painful death. The trinitarian and christological controversies of the fourth and fifth centuries arose because of the difficulty, in an intellectual context heavily influenced by Platonism, of imagining a God who bypassed

Plotinus's gradations of being to enter the visible world in a human body. Surely a God compromised by the necessities and limitations of human flesh could not be equal to the transcendent God. And how could entities as vastly different as human and divine coexist as a unity in which neither dominated? Such assertions were inconsistent and profoundly uncomfortable to minds influenced by the subtle distinctions of Platonic philosophy.

Christian beliefs raised multiple questions and intellectual quandaries. What is the status of human beings in a universe in which God acts directly in the world of bodies and senses? How is evil to be explained in a world governed by such a hands-on God? These were the burning and much contested questions of the first five hundred years of Christian theology. Augustine inherited the problems and made some suggestions that, while not fully resolving them, reformulated them in ways that both incorporated and adapted Plotinus's conceptual scheme. His doctrine of original sin locates the origin of evil in the willfulness of the progenitors of the human race, relieving God of responsibility for the suffering of humanity. And his mature belief in miracles acknowledges God's prerogative of acting directly in the world of bodies. But I must return to earlier patristic authors in order to identify the importance of image as Augustine inherited it.

The Hebrew Bible account of creation was appropriated by Christians as the decisive statement about human nature. According to Gen. 1:26, God created humans in God's own "image and likeness." But a vast crevasse separates the original condition of humanity from its present condition. Patristic authors developed the idea of a distinction between the Greek terms "image" *(eikon)* and likeness *(homoiosis)*. After the Fall caused by Adam and Eve's disobedience, they said, humanity lost its likeness to God, retaining only the image of God irreversibly given with creation. Origen's treatment of image was decisive for Greek Christian authors like Gregory of Nyssa as well as for Latin authors like Ambrose and Augustine. He insisted that humanity's imaging of God was purely spiritual, and he emphasized that the restoration of image and likeness depended on the Christian's conscious imitation of Christ, God's first image.

Patristic authors believed, however, that even the image exhibits signs of deterioration. In his treatise *On the Incarnation of the Word*, Athanasius used a metaphor common to patristic authors to describe humanity's present condition:

> For as, when the likeness painted on a panel has been effaced by stains from without, he whose likeness it is must needs come once more to enable the portrait to be renewed on the same wood, for, for the sake of the picture, even the mere wood on which it is painted is not thrown away, but the outline is renewed upon it; in the same way also the most holy Son of the Father, being the image of the Father, came to our region to renew man, once made in his likeness, and find him, as one lost, by the remission of sins; as he says himself in the Gospels, "I came to find and to save the lost." (1954, 68)

In Athanasius's account of humanity's need for reformation, Plotinus' essential *connection* between the source of life and its myriad forms is lost. Plotinus's image required the continuous informing presence of its original (as does a mirror or a pool of water). For Athanasius, even though the damaged painting is still arguably an image of its original, restoration of the likeness requires that the absent original return to provide a model for the renovations. It is not enough, as it was for Plotinus, for human beings to turn toward the source of their being, strengthening a connection that is unbroken but is cluttered and overgrown through lack of use. Athanasius taught that without God's initiating action, humans are helpless.

Augustine was a bit more optimistic about the condition of God's image, humanity, in a fallen world than were Greek authors. *De trinitate (On the Trinity),* a treatise of his maturity, explores the possibility of discovering knowledge about the Trinity from an extended investigation of human nature: "What we have tried to do," he writes at the end of the treatise, "is to gain through this image which is ourselves some vision, as though in a mirror, of him who made us" (1954, 15.14). He explores myriad "trinities" within human beings, deciding finally that knowledge, memory, and will are both decisive for human functioning and direct reflections of the triune God.

Augustine's optimism about the possibility of deducing knowledge of God from human nature should not, however, be overestimated. At best such knowledge will be approximate, its clarity clouded by humanity's limited visibility. The Scripture Augustine quoted most frequently throughout his writings was evidently a reminder to himself not to hope for much clarity in present knowledge: "For now we see through a glass darkly; but then face to face" (1 Cor. 13:12). In *Beauty and Revelation in the Thought of St. Augustine,* Carol Harrison (1992, 1) comments on Augustine's metaphor of a spotted and cloudy mirror as characteristic of human beings:

> Ancient mirrors . . . were simply polished pieces of metal. They did not, therefore, give a very clear reflection. Looking *into* a mirror and trying to make out the reflection was something more than simply looking *at* a mirror, a distinction almost elided by the fine quality of most modern mirrors. Augustine makes this distinction: . . . looking into a mirror is an act of discernment, an attempt to make out the shapes and forms in the mirror and grasp what they signify. This looking through cloudiness and obscurity to make out shapes and forms is, for Augustine, a powerful metaphor of human life following the Fall, where man no longer looks at God *facie a faciem,* but *per speculum.*

Augustine acknowledges that "our struggle to see at all must be a hard one" (1963, 15.16), since it is "through a mirror and in an enigma" (15.44). But for Augustine, as for Plotinus, the crucial thing is not to be "unaware that the mirror seen *is* a mirror," for "even in obscurity, the form is God's image" (15.14). For most historical Christians, however, the theology of image was intricately related to the use of actual images in liturgical and devotional practice.

The Practice of Image Use

In seventh- and eighth-century Eastern Orthodoxy, in controversy over the use of religious images, a theology of image was articulated. The practice of image use was by then well established, but as occurred repeatedly in the history of Christianity a fully rationalized theology emerged only when questions arose about practice, in this case the legitimacy of venerating icons of Christ, the Virgin Mary, the apostles, and the saints, both in communal liturgies and in private devotions.

Charles Murray (1977) was the first scholar to point out that it is likely that images were used from the earliest days of Christian worship. Although others had assumed that the absence of massive evidence for image use indicated that the second commandment's proscription of images was adopted by Christians as it had been by Jews, Murray surveyed the extant literature of the Christian movement to show that no such general proscriptions existed. Indeed, in every known worship setting before the Peace of the Church, traces of wall paintings can be seen, while the underground catacombs of the Roman Empire preserve figures and scenes from the third century forward.

The Eastern iconoclastic controversy seems to have arisen only when portrait busts came to predominate over narrative representations in the sixth century. An increment of viewer engagement, and thus of potential for worship of the icon itself, was inaugurated by the frontal presentation of holy figures. In frontal presentation, the icon's large eyes held the worshipper's gaze, encouraging devotion to the icon rather than to its prototype. Beyond the politics and practices of icon use, however, lay the issue of an icon's relationship to its prototype. The iconoclast controversy was the first debate over representation:

> The iconoclasts held that a material object could be the habitation of a spiritual being—that the *ousiai* of both coalesced into one *ousia*— thus worship of any image was inevitably . . . idolatry. Against this the Iconodules [icon-lovers] laboured to show that, however close the connection between image and original, their *ousiai* were different—hence the worship of images was legitimate, as this worship would be referred to the prototype. This was essentially a Platonic view. (Barnard 1977, 10)

Traces of the Platonic idea of image underlie this rationale for the legitimacy of image use. In C.E. 787, the Second Council of Nicaea successfully reestablished the liturgical and devotional use of icons in the Eastern churches, defining carefully the kind of veneration allowable for icons of divine figures, apostles, and saints. For Christians of the Eastern Churches, the issue was settled; it arose again in the West, however, in the Protestant Reformation with an intensity equal to that of the iconoclast controversy. Moreover, although the Platonic basis has disappeared from contemporary discussion, many of the issues and arguments of iconoclasm are still detectable in twentieth-century debates over the power of images in media cultures.

The Image in the Twentieth Century

In historical Christianity, image was seen as dependent (in varying degrees) on its original. Its primary use was in describing humanity's relationship to God through Christ. In twentieth-century media culture, however, the meaning and value of image have altered dramatically. The media image often stands alone, without a referent, reflecting nothing but its creator's imagination. Even if, as in photojournalism, an image still represents a scene or a person, the image is equally capable of *mis*representing or falsifying the original. It can present a prettified and superficial representation, misleading the viewer; or it can focus on or eliminate features of the original scene according to a political agenda. Mass-produced images create their own "world," or "reality," unconnected, or only tangentially connected, to a referent. Images, produced from "miniaturized units" by simulation, have no origin or reality, but are, in Jean Baudrillard's term, hyperreal (1994, 2–3). In political campaigns, entertainment, and news coverage, the image has become a focus of concern about manipulation of a public with no access to realities other than the image.

Augustine's concept of image as a cloudy mirror in which, nevertheless, traces and suggestions of its original can be found has come under serious question in twentieth-century discussions of images. Baudrillard sketches the "successive phases of the image":

> it is the reflection of a profound reality;
> it masks and denatures a profound reality;
> it masks the *absence* of a profound reality;
> it has no relation to any reality whatsoever; it is its own pure simulacrum. (1994, 6)

Contemporary debate over representation in the fields of art history and literary and critical studies reiterates some of the terms of the iconoclastic controversy but with a different underlying concern, namely, the social effects of representation. Relying on "religious terminology which defines representation as . . . a 'picture language' that embodies, expresses, and transmits otherwise inexpressible truths," modernists claim that representation possesses "truth content" or epistemological value. Postmodernists, on the other hand, use "representation against itself to destroy the binding or absolute status of any representation" (Jameson 1981, 102), examining the "invisible strategies and tactics whereby representation achieves its putative transparency" (Owens 1982, 13). "The postmodern critique of representation undermines the referential status of visual imagery, its claim to represent reality as it really is—either the appearance of things or some ideal order behind and beyond appearance" (21). Both the status and the effects of media images are presently disputed.

While traditional art historians believe representation "to be a disinterested and therefore politically neutral activity," poststructuralists (like Michel Foucault) believe that representation is an integral "part of social processes of differentiation, exclusion, incorporation, and rule." Cultural critics are less interested in *interpreting* works of art and popular culture, that is, in revealing what they *say,* and more interested in analysis of what they *do.* They "explore representational systems as apparatuses of power" (Owens 1982, 10).

For postmodern critics, public self-representations take on a more than casual importance, not because they represent a referent and therefore embody a truth but because they have concrete social *effects.* Foucault defined "strong power" as power to attract to imitation; "weak power"—coercion or force—comes into operation when societies have lost the ability to attract their population to the behavior and values needed for society's perpetuation (1979, 27). According to this view, media representations play a major role in maintaining American society's strong power, designating the economic and social rewards for incorporating the values of a consumer society. Foucault's intent was neither to designate villains who appropriate power for personal or political gain nor to detect hidden ideological messages embedded in public representations but, rather, to see how power *works,* from myriad tiny points within society, to achieve broad consensus on matters as visible as social arrangements and as concealed as values and attitudes. Foucault proposed that the dangers and potential destructiveness of power could be mitigated by its continual distribution throughout society.

Although the power of vision to attract to imitation has been recognized from Plato forward, it remains difficult to say how powerful vision is without either overestimating or underestimating the case. Throughout Christianity, the ability of religious images to attract and augment devotion was acknowledged, but the power of images was thought of at various times and places either as strength or as danger. Iconoclasts and iconodules argued about images because they acknowledged their power, disagreeing only about the religious implications of that power.

The controlled studies are not yet in place that would demonstrate, for example, not only whether the violence regularly viewed on television and movie screens by popular audiences exacerbates actual violence but what kinds of screen violence are likely to affect particular individuals. Lacking such studies, commentators either dismiss screen violence as entertainment or exaggerate its effects. Yet a careful comparison of the practices of historical and contemporary image use can, I believe, illuminate the vexed question of media images' power.

Consider first the effects of realistic representation in religious images and in media. David Freedberg (1989) has described the attraction realistic sacred scenes held for many historical Christians, an attraction that continues in our own time. Many historical and contemporary examples of tableau scenes with naturalistic figures, often with real hair and clothing, attest to the fascination they still hold for devotees. For example, at St. Anne de Beaupré near the city of Quebec, a million visitors each year enter a huge round cyclorama to view a realistic representation of the day of Jesus's Crucifixion. Visitors circumambulate the scene, pausing to pray at stations overlooking the central events of the Crucifixion day. In so doing, they imitate medieval Christians who undertook arduous travel in order to be present, physically and emotionally, at the holy places, primarily to see but also to touch and to smell the alleged scenes of scriptural events. For fifteenth-century Christians, participating in a religiously momentous scene was an achievement, the result of long instruction and practice in the devotional use of vision. It required training, exercise, and concentration. The image acted as a catalyst and focus, providing complex information and instruction.

By contrast, twentieth-century Americans are usually unaware of the extent to which our own visual practice is trained. Yet spectatorship requires visual training at least as complex as that of religious devotion but very different in its goal. Realist narrative film in theaters or on television implicitly claims to function as a window; the eye of the camera seems to record—without distortion and without selection—a "real world." Moreover, realist film locates its characters and action in a particular social and historical setting that adds to the illusion of the screen's transparency. The spectator consents to see, in grainy marks on a flat screen, characters acting and interacting in a three-dimensional world. In short, realist illusions are so effective that spectators must train themselves in detachment. The first film spectators were unable to do so; several reportedly ran from the theater screaming when an on-screen train threatened to overrun them.

Is representation substitution or replacement? Is it "a stand-in or replacement for someone who would not otherwise appear," or does it symbolize a *presence,* imitating and localizing an unseen reality? (Owens 1982, 13). In contrast to the modernist claim that media images present the world of experience, postmodernist critics claim that they actually represent, or replace, a world that is missing. One early film spectator is said to have walked to the front of the theater to look behind the screen for the people displayed on the screen. But there is nothing but light beams; there is nothing to touch, and there are no bodies. Film theorist Dudley Andrew has called film "the presence of an absence" (1984, 44). Again, comparison with a devotional image user will be instructive. Christians, past or present, who use images religiously believe that their images represent a "world" that is not absent but invisible: a world that is present but unseen. For believers, the religious image configures a world that is more real than the visible world, a reality that has created and that informs and sustains the visible world.

Another difference between religious image use and media viewing may be even more decisive. It is ultimately not the image itself but the viewer's committed and trained labor of imagination that connects the devotee to the religious painting. It is neither the subject nor the style of the painting that makes its use religious but the viewer's conceptual and emotional investment in it. Looking at a painted narrative scene in the context of devotional practice, the devotee must imaginatively reconstruct a moment in a story, a moving scene. What gives the captured moment its intensity is the viewer's knowledge of what came before and what will come after. In the case of a scene in which sacred figures are posed for the viewer's gaze (a Christ in Majesty or a Madonna and Child, for example), she must reconstruct in imagination the figures' heavenly context and their import for human life (Hollander 1991, 7). By contrast, media images usually require little engagement of the imagination; the possibility of watching them passively, with little investment of imaginative embellishment, is greater.

Contemporary theories of vision that emphasize the viewer's distance or separation from the object do not describe adequately the religious use of vision. Rather, the use of religious images presumes an ancient theory of vision in which a quasi-physical visual ray streams from the eye of the viewer to touch its object. The form of the object then moves back along the visual ray to imprint itself in the memory of the viewer. This theory of vision emphasizes the viewer's initiative and active engagement, an intentional appropriation of the object that permanently connects viewer and object (in memory). Lacking such concentrated attention, a religious painting is simply a painting with a religious topic. The location of an image is also important to the use made of it. Paintings that once aroused religious devotion in churches now, on museum walls, attract artistic appraisal and admiration that may have nothing at all to do with religious interest.

Like paintings, media images do not function iconically unless viewers augment the image, that is imagine how it would feel to be in the protagonist's situation, imagine the smells, the tastes, the touch the film character experiences. In fact, some spectators do contribute sensory imagination and reflection to film viewing. It is not, then, impossible for media images to act iconically, attracting the viewer to imitation; it is just less likely that they will do so. Moreover, Christians who use icons gaze at the same image again and again; most people see a film only once, though some people see a few films again and again.

Orthodox Christians make the connection between icon and viewer even more explicit than does visual ray theory, by kissing their icons, thereby acknowledging the presence of the icon's prototype and establishing an intercorporeal connection between the once-living bodies of the sacred figures and their own living bodies. The ultimate goal of religious desire is not vision but touch, the metaphoric touch of the visual ray or the literal touch of a kiss. In turn, the worshipper expects to be touched by the object of vision as its image moves back along the visual ray to impress itself on the soul through memory.

In short, though media spectatorship and devotional image use are formally similar, their differences are substantial. Most of us do not imitate the violence we may see repeatedly, though a troubling number do. But people who are alarmed enough about the effects of media to urge censorship do so because they assume that spectators relate to media images as an Eastern Orthodox or Roman Catholic Christian relates to an icon. This, I believe, exaggerates the power of media images.

What, then, *is* the real power of images in a media culture? No image, I have said, has iconic power unless it is related to rather atypically. Assuming that the worshipper's imitation of the virtues and values suggested by a religious image was an incontrovertible good, historical Christians did not examine the social effects of their religious images. But the repetitious representation of similar images *across* media weaves those images into the fabric of the common life of American society, influencing everything from clothing styles to accepted and expected behavior. Media conventions, of which most spectators are never consciously aware, cumulatively affect Americans' self-esteem, expectations, attitudes, and relationships. Moreover, media culture has established global networks with the capacity to export images around the world. That is why it is important to examine and question them, to ask of them the ancient question of the Holy Grail: Whom does it serve? Responses to this question define the importance of image to religious studies.

One answer, of course, is that a few writers, actors, directors, and studios make a lot of money from them. But a more accurate and complex answer is that, to a greater or lesser extent, to paraphrase Plotinus, "we [as a society] are what we look upon and what we delight in" (1966–88, 4.3.8). Roland Barthes once said that we "get" the cultural message when we get the pleasure. Coated and masked by the pleasure, the cultural message slides across without conscious consideration. But we *are* what we see, not once or several times, but repeatedly, and media conventions guarantee that Americans will repeatedly gaze upon similar images of beauty, success, and happiness. These images usually ignore the actual diversity of American society.

Who is the "we" in a pluralistic society? Americans need images that help us picture religious, racial, and cultural diversity not merely as tolerable but as irreducible and delightful. Media images could help all Americans imagine difference that is neither overcome nor transcended, difference that is evenly distributed rather than posited of anyone who diverges from a repetitiously reiterated norm. Moreover, the globalization of media images exports American consumer values worldwide, complexifying and multiplying interpretations of the same image by people with other cultural interpretive repertoires.

In societies in which functional illiteracy is high, images are an important source of information and socialization. The twentieth-century philosopher Suzanne Langer (1962) said that the primary function of a society's art is to educate the emotions, to train the sensibilities to a rich range of feeling and to a perceptual life that misses nothing of importance. To the extent that the images we live with identify our quandaries and supply stimulation, articulation, and perceptive delicacy to our relational lives, we are well served. If, however, we find our society's public images are governed by a narrow emotional repertoire, repetitive images, and unimaginative narratives, we are not well served. Ultimately, stocking one's imagination with the rich and diverse images that are capable of criticizing and enhancing relationship, community, and society will require more than the media (Miles, 1996, 192).

When critical religious studies attend only to language and texts, we ignore a central feature of the historical and contemporary societies we study. Postmodern criticism has articulated and specified the ancient question "Whom does it serve?" in a way that is useful for religious studies. Analysis of historical religious images in relation to their societies of origin can lead to recognition of the perennially central role played by public images in informing, socializing, and attracting. Scrutiny of the images with which Americans live on a daily basis reveals the social assumptions and political allegiances on which media images are based. By analyzing and criticizing public images, religious studies can serve religious institutions that seek to propose images representing values alternative to those of a culture based on entertainment and consumption. Like Plato, we still "strain after images" that help us to imagine our lives fruitfully, enjoy our differences, and relate lovingly to one another and the natural world.

SUGGESTED READINGS

Baudrillard, Jean. 1994. "The Precession of Simulacra." In *Simulacra and Stimulation,* translated by Sheila Faria Glaser.

Bryson, Norman. 1983. *Vision and Painting: The Logic of the Gaze.*

Dagron, Gilbert. 1991. "Holy Images and Likeness." *Dumbarton Oaks Papers* 45.

Foucault, Michel. 1979. *Discipline and Punish: The Birth of the Prison,* translated by Alan Sheridan.

Frary, Joseph. 1972. "The Logic of Icons." *Sobornost* 6 (6).

Hollander, Anne. 1991. *Moving Pictures.*

Jameson, Fredric. 1981. "In the Destructive Element Immerse." *October* 17.

Ladner, Gerhart B. 1953. "The Concept of Image in the Greek Fathers and the Byzantine Iconoclastic Controversy." *Dumbarton Oaks Papers* 7.

———. 1967. *The Idea of Reform: Its Impact on Christian Thought and Action in the Age of the Fathers.*

Langer, Suzanne. 1962. "The Cultural Importance of Art." In *Philosophical Sketches.*

Miles, Margaret R. 1983. "Vision: The Eye of the Body and the Eye of the Mind in Saint Augustine's *De Trinitate* and the *Confessions.*" *Journal of Religion* 3 (2).

———. 1985. *Image as Insight: Visual Understanding in Western Christianity and Secular Culture.*

———. 1988. *Carnal Knowing: Female Nakedness and Religious Meaning in the Christian and Postchristian West.*

REFERENCES

Andrew, Dudley. 1984. *Concepts in Film Theory.* New York: Oxford University Press.

Athanasius. 1954. *On the Incarnation of the Word,* translated by Archibald Robertson. In *Christology of the Later Fathers.* Philadelphia: Westminster Press.

Augustine. 1963. *On the Trinity,* translated by Stephen McKenna. Washington, D.C.: Catholic University of America.

Barnard, Leslie. 1977. "The Theology of Images." In *Iconoclasm,* edited by Anthony Breyer and Judith Herrin. Birmingham: University of Birmingham.

Baudrillard, Jean. 1994. "The Precession of Simulacra." In *Simulacra and Stimulation,* translated by Sheila Faria Glaser. Ann Arbor: University of Michigan Press.

Bryson, Norman. 1983. *Vision and Painting: The Logic of the Gaze.* New Haven: Yale University Press.

Foucault, Michel. 1979. *Discipline and Punish: The Birth of the Prison,* translated by Alan Sheridan. New York: Vintage.

Freedberg, David. 1989. *The Power of Images: Studies in the History and Theory of Response.* Chicago: University of Chicago Press.

Harrison, Carol. 1992. *Beauty and Revelation in the Thought of St. Augustine.* Oxford: Oxford University Press.

Hollander, Anne. 1991. *Moving Pictures.* Cambridge: Harvard University Press.

Jameson, Fredric. 1981. "In the Destructive Element Immerse." *October* 17.

Ladner, Gerhart B. 1953. "The Concept of Image in the Greek Fathers and the Byzantine Iconoclastic Controversy." *Dumbarton Oaks Papers* 7.

———. 1967. *The Idea of Reform: Its Impact on Christian Thought and Action in the Age of the Fathers.* New York: Harper and Row.

Langer, Suzanne. 1962. "The Cultural Importance of Art." In *Philosophical Sketches.* Baltimore: Johns Hopkins University Press.

Miles, Margaret R. 1996. *Seeing and Believing: Religion and Values in the Movies.* Boston: Beacon.

Murray, Charles. 1977. "Art and the Early Church." *Journal of Theological Studies* 28 (October).

Owens, Craig. 1982. "Representation, Appropriation, and Power." *Art in America* 70 (5).

Plato. *The Republic,* translated by Paul Shorey, *The Collected Dialogues of Plato,* Edith Hamilton and Huntington Cairns, editors (Princeton, 1961).

Plotinus. 1966–88. *Enneads,* translated by A. H. Armstrong. Vols. 1–7. Cambridge: Harvard University Press.

NINE

Liberation

Kenneth Surin

"Liberation" has several cognate or semantically adjacent expressions, as do a number of the terms featured in this volume. In English alone, "salvation," "redemption," "freedom," "emancipation," "purification," "absolution," "illumination," and "enlightenment" are relatively closely related terms (and inspire images associated with these terms). The differences of signification between these terms are sometimes slight. However, depending on the case, significantly different kinds of practice and conviction can correspond to this or that term, depending on the particular configuration of practice and belief that gives the term (or image) in question its conditions of intelligibility and validity. To get a sense of what these differences are, and what they typically involve, the person engaged in the academic study of "religion" has to attend to the conditions that give such terms their always dense particularities of meaning. Two major difficulties are likely to surround any such attempt.

The first problem is the now fairly commonplace realization that expressions such as "religion," "culture," "society," and so forth, are abstractions that, irreducibly, have a historically and geographically specific character. A great many cultures, including the not so distant predecessors of our regnant "Western" culture, have organized and conceived of relations between their members without employing anything approximating our notion of *the social,* just as they have created overarching systems of meaning without needing to make any sense of the category of *culture.* (For a discussion of culture, see Herbert [1991].) The same is true of the term "religion." Thus, the Buddhist, say, does not necessarily understand what she or he adheres to as amounting to something that constitutes "religion" or "religiosity," in the way that, say, Durkheim or Hume employ this term in *The Elementary Forms of the Religious Life* or *Dialogues Concerning Natural Religion,* respectively.

Even if we are willing to overlook this particular difficulty (which enjoins us to be nominalists where the term "religion" is concerned), a second problem arises when we acknowledge that it is not clear if, for instance, the Hindu notion of *moksha* is adequately expressed by the English term "liberation," or the Homeric *moira* by the English "destiny," and so forth. This is because any commonly received English rendition is almost inevitably permeated by elements derived from a tacitly (if not explicitly) normative Christianity. The same would more or less be true of someone seeking to find a similar translation scheme for Christianity, since that person would be using terms taken from traditions or standpoints not necessarily congruent with a Christian conception of things.

It is not obvious, in other words, that the translatability of concepts between different religious traditions and communities can be accomplished in the way presumed by someone eager to establish commonalities and affinities between the practices and beliefs constitutive of the various religious traditions. Historians, philosophers, and sociologists of religion tend to be more mindful these days that these convergences are what we take them to be precisely because we are beholden to a *discourse* or *theory* (taken from comparative mythology, phenomenology, psychology, etc.) that gives us the requisite assumptions, modes of procedure, heuristic and analytic principles, and forms of writing and imagery needed to identify and speak of the convergences in question. Such putative convergences reflect a triumph of statement, of discourse, that necessarily has to be left undeclared in order to function as a kind of enabling illusion, in the way that, say, the Durkheim of *The Elementary Forms of the Religious Life* (1965) had to invoke (or invent, according to less charitably disposed critics) a "totemic principle" or "force" to establish what he took to be commonalities between "the gods in Samoa, the wakan of the Sioux, the orenda of the Iroquois, the mana of Melanesia," and of course the spirits of the aboriginal people of Australia.

A General Theory of Salvation

The above caveats notwithstanding, the student of the concept of liberation may find it helpful to begin by considering the pioneering general theory of salvation formulated by Max Weber (1864–1920). A general theory of this kind, as long as it keeps in mind the potentially insurmountable differences that exist among peoples, their communities, and their traditions, is likely to be more interesting and productive than its less theoretically ambitious counterparts because of the inherent qualities that reside in any attempt to bring ostensibly disparate phenomena into relationship with each other: while it may be salutary to heed Gertrude Stein's injunction that "[a] rose is a rose is a rose," the attempt to provide a narrative that, say, links the story of a rose to the history of a group of people to the story of a certain ideology of courtly love is, "all else being equal," going to be of greater intellectual import for the person who is curious about all kinds of relationships between phenomena (and the principles that make such relationships possible) than is a statement of the form "[an] *x* is an *x* is an *x*." This is perhaps why there is, in the academy at any rate, an abiding interest in the great philosophical elaborations of the natures and forms of such relationships, the exemplary instances perhaps being Aristotle's *Metaphysics,* Spinoza's *Ethics,* Hegel's *Phenomenology,* Whitehead's *Process and Reality,* Heidegger's *Being and Time,* and Deleuze and Guattari's *Thousand Plateaus.* These ambitious undertakings may be claimed by their detractors to be the failures they were doomed in the end to be (according to these critics, this is the inevitable fate of narratives that aspire to be a "story of everything"—philosophy as the mastery of the Whole and the Remainder, in Henri Lefèbvre's lapidary phrase), but such "grand narratives" can be powerful intensifiers of thought nonetheless. A theory of liberation, one that approaches liberation as a *concept,* will have something of the quality of such grand narratives; it has in some sense to aspire to be a "story of everything." The first grand or overarching narrative of liberation as a concept is to be found in Max Weber's sociology of religion.

In his general sociology of religion, and thus in his formulation of what he intended to be a comprehensive scheme for understanding the different conceptions of religious salvation, Weber uses the concept of an "ideal-type" to isolate and characterize features from the different "religions" he took to manifest certain transhistorical and transcultural principles. The ideal-type is an analytical construct *(Gendankenbilder)* that isolates and synthesizes certain moments and aspects of the phenomenal or historical world, forms an abstraction from these observable processes, and then returns the abstraction to the historical and observable world in order to yield interpretations of it. Using the ideal-type in conjunction with what is in effect a comparative mythology of salvation, Weber creates a series of linked and overlapping typologies that enable him to formulate a number of theses about salvation in the different religions.

Weber develops his theory of salvations by making a number of distinctions that are now well known: religions that take salvation to require the assistance of supernatural powers (such as the religions of the so-called Abrahamic traditions) versus those that do not (such as ancient Buddhism); paths to salvation based on "ethical demands" versus ones based on "pure faith"; salvation based on a "world-rejecting asceticism" *(weltablehnende Askese)* versus that of a "this-worldly asceticism" *(innerweltliche Askese)*; "contemplative" versus "active" religious practices; and so forth. Further demarcations are made within these divisions. Another important strand in Weber's analysis of the different soteriological principles is provided by schemas of the form "salvation from . . ." and "salvation [attained] for . . . ," as in, for example, "salvation from the machinations of Satan" or "salvation from the wheels of *karma* causality" and "salvation [attained] for the eternal rest that is *nirvana*" or "salvation (attained) for the bliss that is heaven" (see Weber 1963).

Wolfgang Schluchter (1987) has encapsulated most of these distinctions in a useful chart (figure 9.1).

While Weber's formulations have an undeniable importance for the comparative sociology of religions, and have provided the basis for some of his most significant theses (e.g., *The Protestant Ethic and the Spirit of Capitalism* could not have been written without the complementary analysis of the affinity between capitalism and the "this-wordly asceticism" of Puritanism), some of his commentators have made the obvious point that these typologies are not as "ideal-typical" as Weber himself presumed them to be. For instance, the distinction between "pure faith" and "ethical demands" (or "works") is fairly obviously Christian in its provenance (and confined basically to post-Reformation Christianity at that). Therefore, the attempt to apply it to other religions, even if only as a heuristic principle, can involve a possible misrepresentation of their soteriological systems. The same could also be said to a greater or lesser degree of sev-

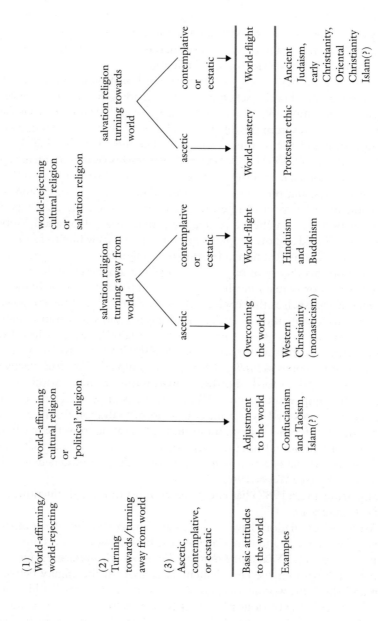

Fig. 9.1. A synopsis of the distinctions Max Weber makes with regard to his theory of salvations. From Schluchter 1987.

eral of the other components of Weber's typologies, for example, the distinctions between "the divine," "the human," and "the world" that Weber clearly regarded as unproblematic. (We shall see below that this set of distinctions may no longer be tenable.) All of these caveats notwithstanding, Weber's theory of religious salvation is the first great attempt to say what is happening "conceptually" when religious traditions make their various affirmations about the means to attain salvation, the states that coincide with its attainment, and the figures or forms instrumental to this attainment. At any rate, Weber was certainly the first to try to conceptualize, at the most general level, the different dispositions toward "the world" that are motivated by the religious traditions.

Of particular interest to the student of religions is Weber's claim that the fundamental aspiration of the various doctrines of salvation is to provide a solution to the "problem" of the world, it being the goal of the seeker of salvation or liberation to find a way of resolving the problem of a basic recalcitrance of the world. (Liberation or salvation here is typically understand as liberation *from* some unacceptable state of the world or condition attendant upon one's being in the world.)

Liberation, then, is the name of a desire, in this case the desire to overcome, circumvent, or ameliorate an unacceptable condition of being, whether individual or transindividual or both. It can also be the name of the extinction of that desire: the desire to end desire is also "simply" that, a desire, albeit one of a peculiar kind, as we known from certain schools of Buddhist philosophy. Liberation is thus a *concept* internally related to that desire (including the desire for the cessation of desire itself), and as such has to be approached through an analysis of the conditions and functions of that primordial desire, its names, its situations, its outcomes, its productions. The production of our world begins with desire, as indicated by a remark from Spinoza's *Ethics* that is central to this account of liberation as a concept: "We neither strive for, nor will, nor want, nor desire anything because we judge it to be good; on the contrary, we judge something to be good because we strive for it, will it, want it, and desire it" (1994, 160). In such a case, an ethics of liberation depends on a prior ontology of human constitutive power, since it is this ontology that charts the various trajectories of our desire, and thus allows an ethics to emerge as a kind of reflection based on this (prior) knowledge of desire (this in a nutshell being Spinoza's own program). This ontology of human constitutive power will delineate what it is that the ensembles of desire that go by the name "human" are capable of, what their aversions and attractions are, including those that, however troublingly, point to something that seems to be beyond what is now taken to constitute "the human."

The Desire that Grounds Liberation and Truth

It is being suggested here that an ontology of human constitutive power is a necessary prolepsis to an ethics of liberation, an ethics that is in turn inextricably bound up with the way of life whose name is this or that "religion." It is not being claimed, however, that there is a kind of progression that has to begin from this ontology and that culminates in religion, with the ethics somehow mediating between the ontology and the religion. Quite the reverse is the case, for it is inevitably in the nature of the religious traditions to provide for their adherents something like this ontology, that is, to say who or what we are, whether in the form of a cosmography (as in a doctrine of creation) or an anthropology. But in reflecting on liberation as a *concept*, this ontology has to be accorded priority, if only because a religious tradition is a system of truth effects, and any truth effect (or amalgam of truth effects) can, depending on historical and social circumstances (these of course always being political), be prevented from displaying itself (or themselves). A truth effect does not produce automatically, and hence cannot guarantee its own mode of actualization; it cannot of itself banish the historical conditions, whatever they may be, that could in principle preempt its realization as a truth effect. (This of course is true of any system of thought, including this ontology of constitutive power: as a regime of truth effects it too cannot institute its own modes of existence, and it too can be prevented from realizing its truth effects. On truth effects, see Balibar [1995, 162]). A truth effect, on this account, is the product of desire, often having the force and character of a "project," in this case a project motivated by a particular arrangement of this constitutive desire or striving. For instance, Nelson Mandela desiring his freedom (and thus the abolition of apartheid) is a truth effect because this desire functions as an enabling (though of course not a sufficient) condition for the removal of all that stands in the way of the realization of that desire. We could call this a "truism" of the logic of desire, inasmuch as to desire x is to aim to make true all that conduces to the attainment of x. More will be said about the ontology of constitutive power later.

The Production of Truth Effects and Liberation

It is clear from the above that any treatment of liberation as a concept has to place an undeniable centrality on the conditions underlying the production of the truth effects of this or that system of liberation. Weber, for all his deserved influence, simply took for granted the effectiveness, in whatever way or ways, of the truth effects of what he referred to as the "salvation religions": for him it was simply a matter of identifying and categorizing the various "dispositions toward the world" of these religions, the presumption being that their truth effects were already in place (as a condition of possibility for the "dispositions" noted by Weber). By the terms of our account, therefore, Weber could be said to have unsatisfactorily conflated "dispositions toward the world" with truth effects, for such dispositions are essentially what each system of salvation has to announce for itself simply in order to be what it is. It would after all be pragmatically futile for a religious tradition to fail to presume the existence, indeed the effectuality, of dispositions associated with its own affirmations, which perforce have to be given the title "truth" by its adherents. But since Weber did not see himself as doing more than providing a typological framework for classifying the "dispositions toward the world" of the various salvation religions, it was natural that he did not think there was any necessity of posing the question of the conditions that enabled systems of liberation or salvation to have truth effects of the kind mentioned here.

But why is it important for this question to be raised? It behooves the writer on liberation as a concept to pose this question because no practice of liberation, nor any theoretical formulations stemming from that practice, can see the seeker of liberation as someone who settles for life just as it is. Even those conceptions of liberation that advocate, or perhaps promote in more active ways, an "acceptance" of the world (as in many versions of stoicism) invariably affirm the need, whether "real" or merely felt, for the protagonists involved to come actively to the point of such an acceptance. That is, inherent in these conceptions of liberation is the presumption that these individuals or collectivities have at least to change, practically and in the end decisively, their dispositions toward the world (i.e., their "subjectivity"), even if not the world itself. This is precisely the point at which the question of the conditions that subtend the production (or the dissolution) of truth effects arises in all its force, for the difference made to life by any practice conducing to liberation is something that depends crucially on the emergence or the suppression of the conditions that effectuate "truth."

Also important for any "thematics" of liberation is the insight that there is a need for liberation only because something about the world is distorted, because the world is a place of catastrophes, whether big or little, potential or real. This basic distorted quality of the world, or one's being in the world, which for this thematics propels the quest for liberation, can have another consequence: for a number of religious or ethical traditions that take the realities of a catastrophic world as their starting point when thinking about liberation, it is invariably the case that hope or the potential for change can survive (or become effective) only if the figures of redemption are hidden or expressed indirectly by other means. This is especially true of the many apocalyptic or messianic traditions. These concealed or partly shrouded figures can then be retrieved only through the use of interpretive resources that have been refined and attuned in suitably complex ways. The exemplary instance of this strand of messianic thinking is provided by Walter Benjamin, who in his "Theses on the Philosophy of History" used the code of a historical materialism to express, allegorically, utopian and messianic (and therefore "theological") impulses that for him were forced out of sight by a history taken over by an unremitting barbarism. For Benjamin the truth effects of these hidden utopian propensities are marked by untimeliness and discontinuity, and thus can only be registered allegorically. A more complicated form of attention then needs to be paid to these characteristic discontinuities and their associated untimeliness, since a broken history discredits all conceptions of inexorable progress and teleology, and ensures that any transcodings of potential images of liberation (and the truth effects that go with these images) will be unfamiliar and hard to retrieve.

The implementation of truth effects depends crucially on the active presence of conditions of possibility for a project of liberation. This is something of a conceptual requirement, since truth has value only because we first deem it valuable to get to know the truth, to continue to seek the truth, to avoid deception of oneself in regard to what is considered true, to heed those who are in the best position to find truth, and so forth. Thus, for instance, there may be someone who, contrary to the available evidence and contrary to the convictions of everyone else, happens to believe that her child survived the avalanche. She happens to be right, it is true that her child survived the avalanche, and it is a good thing that this belief is true. But what makes it a good thing that this belief is true is simply that it is good that the child survived. Here the value of truth (its effects, in other words) is clearly dependent on the value of survival. (This formulation and example are taken in slightly modified form from Williams [1995, 230–31].) If truth effects and the value of truth are inextricably bound up with the value attached to the relations that we have to the conditions that underlie these effects, then the value of the truth effects associated with any presumptive project of liberation will depend crucially on the conditions, always but not solely political, that subtend these projects.

Identifying and characterizing these conditions of possibility for a particular quest of liberation will require the kind of dense specificity that only an ethnographic description can aspire to provide: philosophy (or "theory" as it is called in some circles) aims at something more general and in a sense more problematic, that is, conditions given in advance of their appearance in the realm of phenomena. Nevertheless, it can be said that a "logic" of these conditions, of the kind being sought here, will contain a number of features intrinsic to the concept of liberation. These include the axiom that those engaged in a quest for liberation have at least to be possessed of a desire for the new or different, inasmuch as for these protagonists there is necessarily a contrast between a prevalent state of affairs (one held to be in need of liberation, i.e., "the old") and one that represents a supersession of this state (liberation itself, i.e., that which supplants the old). This "desire for the new" is thus the primary, though not the exclusive, defining characteristic of liberation. (It should be mentioned here that there are religious traditions that provide an apparent exception to this axiom, in that they posit the liberation or redemption of, for example, an entire people, an elect, a community of the devout, and this even for those who are not in a position to evince any desire for the new, such as the unborn, infants who die, the brain damaged, and so on. In such cases, this desire for the new has clearly to be predicated on the collectivity involved, and not on specific individuals belonging to it.)

The crux for this desire for the new comes when there is a situation in which this desire is confronted with the total absence of any conditions that conduce to its fulfillment. What happens to liberation when the desire for liberation is confronted with the impossibility of its realization? Liberation here has necessarily to become the desire or the thought of the new in the absence of all conditions (Negri 1996, 54). Negri here is discussing a line of reflection involving revolutionary thought and practice pursued by Louis Althusser in the writings of the last few years of his life. My next few paragraphs are indebted to Negri. Walter Benjamin's remark that "only for the sake of the hopeless are we given hope," though not mentioned by Althusser or Negri, also reflects this crux of liberation: for Benjamin, liberation can only be expressed in terms of what T. W. Adorno has called an "impossible possibility" (see Adorno 1981, 241).

The absence of its historical conditions represents a powerful and decisive intensification of liberation as a concept and as practice. Reflection may go beyond the boundary represented by these historical conditions, but it does so only as thought, as empty speculation. The futility of any speculative practice having liberation as its object in the absence of its historical conditions of possibility means that liberation has to be lodged in nothing else but a countervailing power that is expressed bodily and only bodily. Thought founders on this impossibility, but the body remains to confront what defeats thought. This prompts a turning to the directly lived, to zones of viscerality as yet not permeated by the powers that destroy. Here is the core of a constitutive ontology of practice, one that furnishes the basis for resistance and the continued mobilization of the desire for the new. (Spinoza provides an exemplary formulation of this ontology of the desire for liberation in his *Ethics.*)

This only provides a horizon, albeit one that is salutary and absolutely indispensable, for a resuscitation or sustaining of the desire for the new. Something more needs to be said about this ontological horizon and its relation to its precursors as horizons for the constitution of practices of liberation.

The Conditions of Possibility for Liberation and the Future

Using the most general terms, it could be said that prior to the onset of modernity (bearing in mind of course that this is preeminently a category defined by and for Europeans and North Americans), *infinity* and *perfection* were the primary forces that shaped human beings. Liberation, in this epoch that extended from antiquity until its demise in the European eighteenth century, was understood as the quest for perfection and the transcending of finitude. In modernity, a relatively brief epoch that reached a point of culmination in the European nineteenth century, *finitude* became the primary norm for envisioning the textures of human life, these textures extending across a space of contiguous domains that could be termed "life," "labor," and "language." (For these terms see Foucault (1971), whose account of the three *epistēmēs*—classical, modern, and current— is being invoked here and in the following paragraphs. See also Rabinow (1992), whose line of argument regarding Foucault is being followed very closely here.) The horizon whose name is modernity, and whose mark is *finitude*, marks a crisis for religious sensibilities, perhaps most tellingly reflected in the "works of suspicion" associated with Marx, Nietzsche, and Freud. However, and this continues Foucault's periodization, this postclassical horizon or *epistēmē* itself went into crisis, and modernity was supplanted in turn by the current or postcontemporary *epistēmē*.

The onset of the current *epistēmē* was heralded by Nietzsche, but for Foucault it is still an *epistēmē* of the future. In it, *finitude* (understood typically as empirical constraint) is displaced by a ceaseless flux of forces and their mutations, a flux that Foucault's interpreter Gilles Deleuze calls an "unlimited finity" (*fini-illimité*) (1988, 131). In this new formation, beings do not approximate to or depart from perfect forms (as they did in the classical horizon or *epistēmē*), nor are they epistemically recalcitrant (as they were in the modern *epistēmē*, which viewed them as a problem for the constitution of knowledge). Instead, the current *epistēmē* views beings as ensembles of forces arranged algorithmically. The "unlimited finity" that marks these configurations of forces allows a "finite number of components [to yield] a practically unlimited diversity of combinations" (131). Recursiveness in the mode of an "unlimited finite" is thus, "emblematically," the modus operandi of the epoch that comes after modernity.

Foucault of course had a narrative that purported to account for the displacement or supersession of modernity along with its pivotal creation, the figure of man. In Foucault's famous image, man would be erased in the way that a wave washes away the drawing of a face at the edge of the sea (1971, 387). Moreover, as Foucault saw it, of the three components of the anthropological triad—*life*, *labor*, and *language*—it would be language that would pave the way for the *epistēmē* that would supersede modernity and man. Man would be undone or overcome by the "enigmatic and precarious being" of the word. Here, as Deleuze has argued, Foucault got it wrong, or at least he was somewhat off track: as Foucault himself came subsequently to acknowledge, the practices and forms that are shaping the new *epistēmē* are arising not so much in the area of language as in those of life and labor. Deleuze's position on the practices of the emerging dispensation is clear:

> The forces within man enter into a relation with forces from the outside, those of silicon which supersedes carbon, or genetic components which supersede the organism, or agrammaticialities which supersede the signifier. In each case we must study the operations of the superfold, of which the "double helix" is the best known example. What is the superman? It is the formal compound of the forces within man and these new forces. It is the form that results from a new relation between forces. Man tends to free life, labour and language within himself. (1988, 132)

It is important to be cautious about all such pronouncements about the character of epochal shifts and transformations, of the spirit of this or that age, and so on, even if they come from Foucault or Deleuze or Hegel. After all, even

Foucault lived long enough to see that he did not get it right about language and the emergence of the postcontemporary horizon or *epistēmē*. But let us assume that the new practices that have emerged, and are still emerging, in the domains of life and labor are clearly significant for any understanding of post-contemporary knowledges and powers, and thus for the concept of liberation.

Deleuze makes a concluding comment about the superman, or the "para-human" as I prefer to call it, who comes to exist in our postcontemporary *epistēmē* that forms a threshold for the next part of my account:

> The superman . . . is the man who is even in charge of the animals (a code that can capture fragments from other codes, as in the new schemata of lateral or retrograde). It is man in charge of the very rocks, or inorganic matter (the domain of silicon). It is man in charge of the being of language (that formless, "mute, unsignifying region where language can find its freedom" even from whatever it has to say). As Foucault would say, the superman is much less than the disappearance of living men, and much more than a change of con-cept: it is the advent of a new form that is neither God nor man and which, it is hoped, will not prove worse than its two previous forms. (1988, 132; the embedded quotation is from Foucault 1971, 38)

"The advent of a new form that is neither God nor man." In other words, the dawning of times in which the desire for the new that prompts our searchings for liberation will take the form of a movement beyond the dialectic of perfection (God) and finitude (man), these forms having been surpassed as modernity has been displaced by the postcontemporary, just as modernity itself once succeeded the classic *epistēmē*. (Weber's typologies of salvation depend on this dialectic and presume it to be completely unproblematic. To this extent, therefore, they can only be viewed with circumspection.) So, what is it to conceive of liberation as desire but always as politics, without the forms of God and man, or perhaps more precisely, God or man? What happens to liberation as a category in this epoch of radically new practices of life and labor?

Michel Serres has often made the point that philosophy traditionally speaks in substantives or verbs, and not in terms of processes and relationships (1995, 105; a similar criticism is to be found in the writings of Henri Bergson and Alfred North Whitehead). Several of these substantives give philosophy its best-known organizing principles or its defining "origins": Being, existence, God, commu-nity, law, the polis, causality, immanence, transcendence, and so forth. These substantives are also integral to a great many mythographies and narratives of liberation. Serres has proposed that philosophy should instead start with preposi-tions, because prepositions are best able to express the character of relationships (some examples he gives are *between, with, across, beside*). A philosophy of libera-tion that constructs itself out of these prepositions will be postmetaphysical, be-cause prepositions have no place in them for the rational subject (this subject being presumed throughout by the organizing principles for philosophy that congregate around the above-mentioned substantives). This rational metaphysical subject was later transmuted into the subject of bourgeois rationalism, with its epistemologies and political and economic philosophies, and so a postmetaphysical philosophy of liberation that hinges itself on the prepositional form will also be postbourgeois.

Our new epochal practices are conducing toward forms of thought that proceed vectorially, that move along a myriad number of lines of movement or of transformation, and all of these have their linguistic counterparts in the prepositional forms adverted to by Serres. The model for these forms of thought is not the code but topology, the science of proximities and ongoing or disrupted transformations, transformations that are never in equilibrium and have ill-defined edges and "fuzzy" logics. Relations, and their attendant manifestations and articulations, far outnumber subjects and objects. Obviously a great deal more can be said about the implications, for philosophy and the study of religions, of these immense changes in the landscapes of knowledge. These changes continually construct new worlds, environments of fluctuations and interferences that we create, but which in turn produce us. The truth effects associated with these new knowledges, truth effects produced by our chartings of the always broken symmetries of these new worlds, will be "obscure, confused, dark, non-evident" (Serres 1995, 148). Serres calls this a theory of "adelo-knowledge . . . [that is] something that is hidden and does not reveal itself."

The practices and the needs of the subjects of these new postmetaphysical worlds will be the practices and needs of beings who take the aleatory and the material (Negri 1996) as the basis of their self-constitution. Desire, or *conatus* in Spinoza's terms, is what constitutes human subjects, and desire only exists in exteriority, the surpassing of itself in the always changing movement. *That* is the basis for a conception of liberation, one that can never find adequate figuration but which, it is hoped, is likely to be satisfactory because it opens its subjects to the urgency and bareness of the never predictable event, "the new."

SUGGESTED READINGS

Durkheim, Emile. 1965. *The Elementary Forms of the Religious Life.*

Foucault, Michel. 1971. *The Order of Things: An Archaeology of the Human Sciences.*

Schluchter, Wolfgang. 1996. *Paradoxes of Modernity: Culture and Conduct in the Theory of Max Weber.*

Weber, Max. [1922] 1963. *The Sociology of Religion.*

REFERENCES

Adorno, Theodor W. 1981. "A Portrait of Walter Benjamin." In *Prisms,* translated by Samuel and Shierry Weber. Cambridge: MIT Press.

Balibar, Etienne. 1995. "The Infinite Contradiction," translated by Jean-Marc Poisson, with Jacques Lezra. *Yale French Studies* 88.

Benjamin, Walter. 1976. "Theses on the Philosophy of History." In *Illuminations,* translated by Harry Zohn. New York: Schocken.

Deleuze, Gilles. 1988. *Foucault,* translated by Sean Hand. Minneapolis: University of Minnesota Press.

Durkheim, Emile. 1965. *The Elementary Forms of the Religious Life,* translated by Joseph Ward Swain. New York: Collier.

Foucault, Michel. 1971. *The Order of Things: An Archaeology of the Human Sciences,* unidentified collective translation. New York: Pantheon.

Herbert, Christopher. 1991. *Culture and Anomie: Ethnographic Imagination in the Nineteenth Century.* Chicago: University of Chicago Press.

Negri, Antonio. 1996. "Notes on the Evolution of the Thought of Louis Althusser," translated by Olga Vasile. In *Postmodern Materialism and the Future of Marxist Theory: Essays in the Althusserian Tradition,* edited by Antonio Callari and David F. Ruccio. Hanover, N.H.: Wesleyan University Press.

Rabinow, Paul. 1992. "Artificiality and Enlightenment: From Sociobiology and Biosociality." In *Incorporations,* edited by Jonathan Crary and Stanford Kwinter. New York: Zone.

Schluchter, Wolfgang. 1987. "Weber's Sociology of Rationalism and Typology of Religious Rejections of the World." In *Max Weber, Rationality, and Modernity,* edited by Sam Whimster and Scott Lash. London: Allen and Unwin.

———. 1996. *Paradoxes of Modernity: Culture and Conduct in the Theory of Max Weber,* translated by Neil Solomon. Stanford: Stanford University Press.

Serres, Michel, with Bruno Latour. 1995. *Conversations on Science, Culture, and Time,* translated by Roxanne Lapidus. Ann Arbor: University of Michigan Press.

Spinoza, Benedict de. [1677] 1994. *Ethics.* In *A Spinoza Reader,* edited and translated by Edwin Curley. Princeton: Princeton University Press.

Weber, Max. [1922] 1963. *The Sociology of Religion,* translated by Ephraim Fischoff. New York: Beacon Press.

———. [1922] 1978. *Economy and Society: An Outline of Interpretive Sociology,* edited by Guenther Roth and Claus Wittich. 2 vols. Berkeley and Los Angeles: University of California Press.

Williams, Bernard. 1995. "Truth in Ethics." *Ratio* 8.

TEN

Modernity

Gustavo Benavides

Most of the essays in this book deal with concepts that can be used without great difficulty to understand religious and other developments at various times and in many parts of the world. Some of the essays may challenge this assumption by attempting to show, for example, that religion itself may be a category of dubious usefulness, one whose domain has been delimited by the Enlightenment. On the other hand, the subject matter of this essay, modernity confronts us with a concept that most readers, and most authors as well, will consider as having an identifiable place and time of birth. Whereas the time will be debated—ranging from the beginnings of Christianity, or even earlier, through the discovery of America, the Reformation, the English Civil War, the French Revolution, or even the nineteenth century—the place of birth, the West, will be relatively uncontroversial. That the situation is not actually that simple, particularly when the connection between modernity and religion is examined, will become clear as we proceed. But before doing so, it is necessary to examine the origin and career of this critical term.

I

The term "modern" and its equivalents in other European languages derive from the Latin *modernus,* which itself derives from the adverb *modo,* a term that since the fifth century C.E. was equivalent to *nunc,* "now." Considering that over the centuries *modernus* has been used to refer to that which is new, *novus,* a newness that has seldom been approached in a neutral manner, it is significant that by the end of the fifth century Pope Gelasius used the term *novus* to refer to that which differed from what is regular and expected, while employing *modernus* in a neutral manner to allude to recent events. Four centuries later in Carolingian times, some authors, aware that they lived in an age different from that of early Christianity, used *modernus* in a way that emphasized the difference between their own and other historical periods. This awareness led finally to the coining of the term whose English equivalent we are exploring: in the eleventh century St. Peter Damian (1007–72) derived *modernitas* from *modernus,* and around 1075 Berthold of Regensburg referred self-consciously to "our modernity" *(modernitas nostra).* But, since signification takes place within a system of oppositions, in order to count oneself among the *moderni* one had to distinguish oneself from the *antiqui.* As Chenu (1928) and Freund (1957) have shown, this medieval, self-conscious marking of the new—which does not quite correspond to our perception of a medieval period from which we, the true moderns or postmoderns, must necessarily want to distinguish ourselves—led theologians of the first half of the thirteenth century to consider those of the last third of the previous century as belonging to the *antiqui*. The value attached to the labels *modernus* and *antiquus* could, however, be reversed; thus in the eleventh century, in the context of controversies concerning the Eucharist, being *modernus* was used against Berengar of Tours, while *antiquus* was regarded positively as referring to the early Fathers (Hartmann 1974).

The problematic character of the perception, and above all the valorizacion, of the past and the present, the old and the new, can be seen at work in what has come to be known as the Renaissance, the self-conscious attempt to recapture the presumed values of Greece and Rome, bypassing what would be known as the Middle Ages. (It must be remembered, however, that the noun "renaissance" appeared in the mid-sixteenth century, and that the term "Middle Ages" was not used in Germany until 1601 and in France until 1640.) Where does one place the beginning of modernity, then? Koselleck (1977, 1987) has proposed the mid-eighteenth century and has provided six reasons in support of his position, all of them involving the problematization of one's relation to time. These include the sense that history takes place through time rather than in time; the idea of an open future; the use of "centuries" *(saecula)* to refer to independent periods different from previous ones; the sense that events, even if taking place at the same time, belong to different stages of cultural development; the realization that one's perspective is unavoidably subjective; and the experience of living in a time of transition. But, as Koselleck himself recognizes, even though it was in the eighteenth century—during an Enlightenment that proudly and self-consciously declared itself to be such—that these perceptions became truly self-reflexive, the changes to which he refers began taking place in the sixteenth century. Indeed, the realization of the contemporaneity and noncontemporaneity of Europeans and the inhabitants of the New World goes back to the late fifteenth and early sixteenth centuries, while the awareness of the role that one's historical location plays in one's judgment of exotic customs was as clear to Descartes in the seventeenth century as it was to Robinson Crusoe in the eighteenth. In any case, it is a peculiarity of this way of looking at the world that the self-monitoring in which one must engage involves the awareness that such a quest is condemned to be subject to continuous scrutiny and correction. This includes the realization, expressed by La Bruyère in 1688, that those who now consider themselves as being *modernes* will be *anciens* in a few centuries, as well as Wilhelm von Humboldt's extraordinary statement at the turn of the eighteenth century to the effect that the ancients were just what they were, whereas the moderns, knowing what they are, are able to see beyond themselves and have through reflexion made double beings out of themselves (Gumbrecht 1978, 101, 106).

II

As we just saw, a condition of modernity presupposes an act of self-conscious distancing from a past or a situation regarded as naive. This self-extrication, however, is in principle an endless task, for just as the term naive may be applied, for example, to an organic conception of the social order that is rejected in favor of one built around mechanistic metaphors (Borkenau 1980, pub. 1934; Jauß 1964), it may also be applied to the rejection of an understanding of a reality built around science, proof, and experimentation; in this case, such a presumably ingenuous view could be replaced by a nonnaive one built around indeterminacy, irony, and the like. Now, if we understand modernity as involving a kind of perpetual critique, the parallels with the distancing techniques and polemical intent of aesthetic modernism become apparent (Marino 1974); indeed, literary, and aesthetic modernism in general, can help us grasp the oppositional, distancing, and self-referential nature of modernity. We must be aware, however, that the existence of these parallels points in the direction of an atemporal modernity, or at least of multiple modernities, some of which may have reached their various self-reflexive heights in political, philosophical, or purely aesthetic terms. We must also keep in mind that, despite their parallel careers, aesthetic modernity has frequently been at odds with its technological counterpart, a fact that, given the prestige of technological achievements (and the increased power of social arrangements based on them), has contributed to intensifying the oppositional character of the former (Bradbury and McFarlane 1976; Calinescu 1987). One could argue in fact that the tension between the two has delimited the aesthetic realm, a development that parallels the one involving the delimiting of religion that we will examine later.

Thinking in terms of multiple modernities forces us to consider the differences between a modernity understood mainly in cultural terms and one that combines heightened reflexiveness with technological development, and to reflect on the approach proposed by Elvin (1986), who in attempting to provide a working and value-free definition of modernity has suggested paying more attention to the role played by power in European modernity. Elvin singled out the following characteristics: power over other human beings, practical power over nature in terms of the capacity for economic production, and intellectual power over nature in the form of capacity for prediction. We should in fact consider that it is the interaction between the exercise of reflexivity and the capacity to exercise power—in other words between modernity and modernization—that has led to the emergence of the peculiar configuration known as Western modernity. This means that while the proclivity to think that the world could be otherwise has positive effects on scientific development and economic advancement, the accelerating speed at which scientific knowledge changes reinforces the generalized cognitive instability that characterizes modernity. It is necessary, therefore, to pay attention to the connections between the processes of social differentiation that made possible the emergence of universities as corporate entities, and the development of Western science (see Huff 1993). Conversely, even though it would be unwise to accept fully attempts to establish causal connections between Israelite and Christian religious representations and attitudes towards nature (Benz 1964; White 1971; Hooykaas 1972; Preus 1972), it would be equally misguided to ignore the articulations between religion and conceptions of nature. Particularly important are the links between the twelfth-century renaissance and fourteenth-century nominalism and Western attitudes towards a world understood as God's creation (Stiefel 1977; Dales 1978, 1980; Grant 1979; Taylor 1989; Dupré 1993; Huff 1993). Moving on to the seventeenth century, we must follow Jacob's advice (1988, 1997) and pay more attention to the line that leads from the scientific to the industrial revolution.

In cultural terms, the constant awareness of the contingent nature of the social arrangements of which one is a part, of the contested nature of their sources of legitimation, and of the accelerated pace of change (Koselleck 1977, 1987; Gumbrecht 1978) leads to a way of life in which, as with our own, everything seems to be framed by quotation marks. Recent theories of modernity, such as Giddens's (1990) (and, more thoroughly, Wagner's [1994]), have stressed precisely the issues of separation and recombination: the separation of time and space and the disembedding of social relations from local contexts, along with their reflexive ordering and reordering. Similarly, in an influential paper (1993a, pub. 1967) Horton, himself influenced by Popper's ideas, presented the differences between traditional (mainly African) and nontraditional societies in terms of the absence or presence of alternative views of reality, and, more important, of second-order intellectual activities, a view he would modify later. In his second formulation, Horton (1993b, pub. 1982) abandoned the closed/open dichotomy, emphasizing rather the contrasts between faith in tradition and faith in progress and between consensual and competitive ways of theorizing. This latter concern has resulted in a divorce of theory from practical considerations, a fact that allows theorizing for its own sake. As we shall see below, it is this divorce and this agonistic attitude that Lloyd (1987, 1990) has identified as two of the sources for the development of Greek science in the sixth century B.C.E. Ultimately, it is the presence of the oppositional attitude towards the given and the differentiation of domains in the West and its absence in China and the Islamic world that Bodde (1991) and Huff (1993) have singled out when contrasting Western, Chinese, and Islamic developments (but see Lapidus 1975).

In any event, even as we identify the characteristics that constitute modernity, we must keep in mind, first, that those characteristics are not found all at once; second, that they tend to coexist with and in some cases generate opposite forces, namely, a countermodernity; third, that instead of a modernity we may find modernities; and fourth, that the concept should not necessarily be understood in a teleological manner. One of the characteristics of modernity is the existence of certain points of reference around which social relations are built. Thus Bidet (1990) speaks of a social order prevalent since the seventeenth century, a "matrix of modernity" constituted by a market in which individuals engage in contractual relations, the contract being the pivot around which everything gyrates. The role of contracts is indeed crucial, for, even though contractuality as such may be regarded as an absolute value, the temporal duration and the characteristics of the contracts themselves are contingent upon the agreement of the contracting parties. Bonds involving a supernatural agent are quite different: neither the covenant between the god of the Hebrew scriptures and his people nor the effects of the Christian sacraments nor the Muslim formal acceptance of Islam can be dissolved at the request of the human contracting party. Neither can a limiting clause be part of the covenant (in this respect, as in others, Buddhism constitutes an exception). It is not surprising, therefore, that in the seventeenth and eighteenth centuries Descartes placed "among the excesses all of the promises by which one curtails something of one's freedom," that Milton wrote a treatise on divorce, and that Kant condemned the covenants that bind one's descendants.

III

In terms of religion, modernity has generally been identified with the resolute rejection of a sacramental view of reality and of anthropomorphic conceptions of the divinity, as well as even more radically with an outright rejection of any notion of transcendence. But, once again, the self-questioning nature of modernity may lead to a situation in which such rejections are replaced by an essentially aesthetic attitude ruled either by a so-called second naïveté or by irony, with the former allowing one to engage in the reenchantment of reality, and the latter making it possible for one to entertain simultaneously conflicting conceptions of the world. In general, however, Western modernity has involved the first kind of distancing: from the organic to the mechanic; from the corporate to the individual; from hierarchy to equality; from an understanding of reality in which everything resonates with everything else (or, more radically, in which everything is present in everything: the medieval mystical formula *quodlibet in quolibet*), to one built around precision and the increasing differentiation of domains (Dumont 1983; Kula 1986; Frey 1995; Gurevich 1995; Crosby 1997). In the West, the movement from one pole to the other has been regarded as involving a motion away from religion. Such a view is problematic to the extent that the process of differentiation, studied by among others Böckenförde (1981, pub. 1967; 1977) and Kaufmann (1989), involved less a movement away from religion than the coming into being of two separate domains, the religious and the secular, whose tensions contributed to the peculiarly dynamic character of the West. Furthermore, the bureaucratic and rational organization of the emerging religious domain—religious understood here in the narrow sense of clerical—appears to have served as a model for the centralization and bureaucratization of the emerging European states.

We do not have to assume that the process of differentiation proceeded in a linear fashion; what seems more plausible is that desacralizing and resacralizing tendencies coexisted, and that in certain periods one or the other gained the upper hand. According to Weber (1920–21; see also Winckelmann 1980), the rejection of an enchanted worldview and its replacement by a rational and instrumental approach to reality can be traced to the relationship established between the transcendent and jealous god portrayed in the Hebrew Scriptures and his people. This exclusive relationship would have made impossible, or at least illegitimate, any attempts to manipulate the world through magical means, thus setting the stage for the disenchanted *(entzaubert)* world of Western modernity. In fact, according to Gellner (1988, 82–4), "it was jealous Jehovah who taught mankind respect for the Principle of Excluded Middle," while "the logic of the promise of salvation as a reward . . . required free will." But even if Weber's and Gellner's assessments of the implications of Israelite theology were correct, one would have to consider this primordial disenchantment (*Entzauberung*) as but one of many, in some cases contradictory, acts of a drama. For, in opposition to both Israelite views of transcendence and Jesus's acknowledgment of the difference between Caesar's realm and that of his god, what we encounter in late antiquity is a sacralization of the political sphere: the divinization of the Roman emperors and then the intimate connections between the church triumphant and Christian rulers who, like Justinian, were referred to by the title "most holy emperor" (*sacratissimus princeps*) (Hiltbrunner 1968). It would be only during the investiture conflict of the eleventh century that the struggle between emperor and pope would call into question the legitimizing function of the church, forcing the political domain to validate itself and assert its rights. Unlike the situation that prevailed in the Byzantine Empire and in its spiritual heir, Moscow, the "Third Rome," where the emperor continued to exercise supremacy over the church, in the Latin West the investiture conflict contributed to the opening up of a conceptual space, to the delimitation of two domains, and to the exacerbation of the conflicts (but also the mutual borrowing) without which Western modernity would have been impossible.

We cannot examine in any detail here the many aspects of the rational-bureaucratic character of the Roman church. It should be pointed out, however, that the remarkable institutional stability and effectiveness of the church is not unrelated to the development of canon law, an example of a rational and all-encompassing approach to life with parallels to the Buddhist rules of discipline that would require extended treatment. More important, by creating an autonomous legal order, canon law may have contributed not just to the institutional longevity of Catholicism but also to the emergence of independent legal institutions. One must pay attention also to the way in which this hierarchical system has approached the recruitment, training, performance, and loyalty of its members. Worth stressing is the fact that early on, positions in the ecclesiastical hierarchy were independent from those who held them, and that the holders of the positions lived in a way that made it impossible for them to have legally recognized offspring; to do so would have made members of the clergy part of kinship networks, a fact that would have weakened their exclusive loyalty to their only real family, the church (the reasons for priestly celibacy are to be sought less in doctrine or in corporate or individual psychology than in institutional needs). In intellectual terms, we should pay attention to the long-term effects of the adversarial character of the intellectual disputations held during the high scholastic period (and to the parallels between this practice and the one still found among Tibetan monks living in exile). Indeed, some of the questions asked during the high scholastic period—for instance, whether the principle of natural law would be valid even if God did not exist—may be viewed less as intellectual hairsplitting and more as explorations of the limits of thinking itself.

IV

Important as the role of the Hebrew Scriptures or of the Roman church may have been, it would be unwise to regard them as the only two sources of Western modernity. Indeed, if we were to think in terms of modernities rather than of a single modernity, we ought to pay attention to the modernizing characteristics of Buddhism (and Jainism). But even if we were to remain within the confines of the West, we would find that the situation is more complicated. Against claims that technological progress derives from the conception of the transcendent god of the Hebrew Scriptures, Cancik (1979) has shown that many of the traits associated with modernity, namely, the beliefs in progress and in a rational approach to a nature that is to be the object of one's *imperium* and entrepreneurship, can be found in Rome. It is also to Rome that we can trace approaches to law, fixity of contract, absolute property, and work that we tend to associate with a modern approach to the economy, and which in fact was revived in the urban centers of northern Italy and northern Europe in the early modern period. Thus we find the concept of absolute property— Quiritary ownership—which by establishing an absolute (but not universal) realm contributed to the process of differentiation of domains without which individualism and modernity would have been impossible (Anderson 1974a, 1974b). As a contrast to this crucial element of Roman law, we may recall the almost complete absence of private property of land in a much later empire, the Ottoman. This absence, which sixteenth- and seventeenth-century authors such as Machiavelli, Bodin, and Bacon singled out when they contrasted Europe and Islam, had important consequences for economic development, namely, the lack of entrepreneurship and accumulation at the time when Europe was developing its mercantile capitalism and increasing the general rights of private property. Furthermore, the lack of private property had important consequences in terms of the understanding of individual freedom. As Anderson (1974b, 367) has pointed out, referring to the Ottoman Empire, "once any strict juridical concept of ownership was suspended in the fundamental domain of the basic wealth of the society, the conventional connotations of possession in the domain of manpower were by the same stroke diluted and transformed."

Belief in the freedom and equality of human beings qua human beings can be traced not to Christianity, as claimed by Löwith, Moltmann, and others, but to Hellenistic philosophy, particularly to Zeno and the other Stoics, who were propounders of an ideal of world citizenship and who Diderot quoted approvingly in the eighteenth century. As Cancik (1983) has shown in another of his remarkable studies, despite the well-known prevalence of slavery in Rome, Roman law considered slavery to be *contra naturam.* It is also in republican Rome that we find ideals such as *parsimonia, frugalitas, abstinentia,* and *continentia,* all of which are easily recognizable, although with shifting meanings, in English and other European languages, and all of which refer to the deferral of satisfaction that would be required much later by capital accumulation. Another important component of Western modernity, which is sometimes traced back just to the seventeenth century, especially to Descartes, but which is to be found in early Greek science, is the sharp distinction between rhetoric and science, and, as Lloyd has put it, the demand for ultimate, absolute, impersonal justifiability (1987, 1990). There are several noteworthy aspects of Greek science that are related to our concerns and which are similar to those identified by Horton as characterizing nontraditional ways of thinking; among them is the fact that this desire for rigorous proof emerged in part as a result of the polemical style of Greek politics and in part as a self-conscious attempt to engage in a new form of inquiry that moved beyond rhetoric. No less important was the concern not just with results but with procedural questions, with second-order questions and, in more general terms, with abstract theorizing for its own sake.

V

Moving back from the Christian to the non-Christian West or to the Hebrew Scriptures is not, however, sufficient. A study of the so-called world religions, a term used to refer to those religions that do not serve primarily as vehicles for ethnic identification, shows that many of the concerns that characterize Western modernity appeared as the result of the caesura established by the religious founders' skepticism toward received ideas and practices, as well as by the transcendentalization of norms, and by the second-order questions asked by some of them. In order to do justice to these developments it would be necessary to engage in the never-ending controversies about the causal or noncausal effects of religious beliefs and practices; however, such a discussion—related in many ways to the very concept of modernity—is not within the purview of this essay. Suffice it to say first that, whatever position one adopts, the emergence of these religions cannot be understood apart from large social changes such as the ones that took place in northern India or in the eastern Mediterranean world; and second, that the very positing of the question about the causal status of religion presupposes the radical critical attitude that characterizes modernity (and which one can see already at work in Greece in the sixth century B.C.E., in Xenophanes's critique of anthropomorphism). In general terms, one ought to pay attention to the role played by cities in the development of Buddhism, Christianity, and Islam, and to the role played once again by urban centers in the emergence of Western modernity (Braudel 1981; Huff 1993). Further, we may consider

Mann's (1986) thesis concerning the affinity between a transcendent god and individuals belonging to interstitial, and to that extent transcendent, trading networks (in the case of Buddhism and Jainism, the goal, rather than a god, in theory at least, would be a transcendental state, nirvana or *kaivalya*).

The changes that were taking place in the Gangetic plain around the time the Buddha was preaching the Dharma—disappearance of a tribal order, emergence of large states, urbanization, and a new economy in which coins, invented in the late sixth century B.C.E., played an important role—seem to have required a soteriology that by emphasizing interiorization and discipline would have served both as a commentary on, and a refuge from, the new order. These developments parallel the interaction in twelfth-century Europe between the centralization of power and the increase in the use of money on the one hand, and the differentiation between magical and religious domains with the concomitant spiritualization, interiorization, and disciplining of religion, on the other. The connection between money and asceticism, difficult to perceive at first, becomes clear when one realizes that both have to do with the resisting of desire and thus with the disciplining of life. In the case of asceticism, discipline and self-control defer the satisfaction of desire or even annihilate it; the very existence of money, on the other hand, represents the postponement of the satisfaction of desire. In the India of the Upanishads and early Buddhism, the desire to overcome one's cravings, especially the greatest craving of all, the attachment to an illusory ego, required a highly developed sense of individuality and subjectivity; it required also a world in which one's cravings could be satisfied in principle. The exploration of this subjectivity was, in turn, the precondition for the elaborate meditational techniques devised for the use of the monks. Paralleling their concern with the exploration and regulation of their psychological life, early Buddhists developed equally elaborate regulations of the social lives of the monks. The fact that such regulations, while demanding constant self-control and self-examination, forbade monks to engage in work and the handling of money can be understood not as a refutation of the connection between Buddhism and modernity, but rather as an example of a rational division of labor that rendered visible certain crucial aspects of the new social order. The monks could be understood as introspection specialists, that is, as able to carry to virtuoso levels what ordinary people could expect to cultivate to a limited degree only; likewise, the highly regulated life of the monks could be regarded as a model for rational behavior, above all the management of time, which among other things produced the wealth that made donations to the Buddhist community possible. More speculatively, we could consider whether the prohibition against the monks working and handling money rendered visible the autonomy of the economic realm, as well as the relatively new reality of money as the embodiment of labor. However, it is necessary to point out that, as in the case of the medieval West, despite the early prohibitions, the monasteries became, particularly in medieval China, centers of "rational" economic activity.

No less important than the above developments is the attitude of the Buddha, and of Buddhist philosophy in general, toward the mythological legitimation of the social order, toward ritual, and toward what is generally understood as magic. As opposed to the legitimation of the caste system found in the Rig-Veda, according to which the universe is understood as an anthropomorphic organism out of which the various groups emerge, early Buddhism postulated a form of social contract. Although it would be a mistake to present Buddhism as a soteriological system unconcerned with the mastery of physical reality (as was done by early scholarship and also, it should be remembered, by twentieth-century Buddhist reform movements), according to early scriptures the Buddha's attitude toward what is generally considered magic was at least ambivalent: he acknowledged having supernatural powers *(ṛddi)* but made a point of denying being a magician, a *māyāvin*, a possessor of *māyā* (Benavides 1997).

To be sure, one must distinguish between doctrinal statements produced by monks or other religious virtuosi and religion in practice; nevertheless, it would not be unjustified to regard the emergence of the world religions, and certainly of Buddhism, as inextricably linked to a process of differentiation, and in more general terms of skepticism towards the prevailing social order, which in some cases has been as strong as that associated with the rise of Christianity. In some respects, indeed, systems such as Buddhism went much further than philosophies developed in the Christian world in their approach to philosophical problems. Thus one can regard Buddhist conceptions of language as having recognized the arbitrary and relational character of the linguistic sign. Similarly, the attempts to move beyond the infatuation with the illusory ego can be considered as the most consistent rejection of reification before Marx (one which, it ought to be remembered, seems to have been as problematic to some early monks as it is to contemporary Buddhists and non-Buddhists). Finally, the concept of *dharma* and the concern with causality allow one to analyze all of reality in its constitutive aspects as well as to determine the mechanisms through which these principles relate to each other. Still, if we ask ourselves why the types of social arrangements that characterize Western modernity did not emerge in the Buddhist world, we must remember Bendix's (1967), Wilson's (1987), and Kaufmann's (1989) warnings about modernity referring not to a clearly delimited formation but rather to a bundle of elements, not all of which can be expected to be present at the same time; above all, we must keep in mind that the emergence of Western modernity required the confluence of a constellation of technical, institutional, and ideological developments (Hall 1985; Baechler 1986; Gellner 1988; Huff 1993). Otherwise, early Buddhist skepticism and its concern with causality would have led us to expect a flourishing technology in the Buddhist world; similarly, the fact that membership in the community of monks is regulated in a contractual rather than in a sacramental manner would have led us to anticipate generalized democratic social arrangements resembling our own throughout Buddhist Asia, when what we find, on the contrary, are democratic arrangements such as voting that apply only to the community of monks (Dumont [1983] reminds us that majority vote was discovered independently by Buddhist and Christian monks).

VI

The relationship between religion and modernity has frequently been approached in terms of the process of secularization, that is, of the progressive disappearance of religion. After several decades of popularity, the concept of secularization itself has been subject to critical examination. However, as stressed most recently by Casanova (1994), both the uncritical acceptance and the no less uncritical rejection of the concept ought to be avoided, since, properly understood, secularization refers not to a process that will lead to the disappearance of religion but to one of differentiation and narrowing of the institutional religious realm. This is a twofold process: On the one hand is the inverse relationship between the delimitation of institutional religion and the increasing importance of subjective religion, and on the other are the narrowing and ultimate repression of the belief that religious rituals can influence physical reality. The interiorization and subjectivization of Western religion can be traced back to the High Middle Ages (Dinzelbacher 1981, 1987), and can be seen at work in the emphasis on religious experience found in Bernard of Clairvaux's commentaries on the Song of Songs, and in women mystics such as Hadewijch (keeping in mind the differences between the spiritualized and Scripture-centered experiencing of Bernard and the passionate physicality of Hadewijch). The extravagant emotional vocabulary and sexual imagery used in the twelfth and thirteenth centuries—one need only think of Rupert of Deutz's exchange of deep kisses with his god—at first appear to be incongruous with the increased control exercised by ecclesiastical authorities and with the emergence of centralized states. In reality, setting limits forces a turning inward, and the exploration of one's subjectivity can be seen as necessarily linked, if perhaps only negatively, to the control exercised not just by ecclesiastical and political authorities but also by monetarization (Kaye 1988), by the new ways of measuring time, and by the ongoing rationalization of everyday life, particularly of economic activities (Le Goff 1977). This rationalization of economic ideas led in Protestant countries to the denunciation of ritual and in Catholic ones to the curtailing of ritual and to its being placed under tighter clerical control. This process would be repeated many times, most notably in eighteenth-century England during the period of domestication of everyday behavior required by capitalism, to which E. P. Thompson has devoted several studies (1993, pub. 1967). But one finds it also in Asia, for instance in nineteenth- and early-twentieth-century Thailand, where Kings Mongkut (Rama IV) and Chulalongkorn (Rama V), seeking to centralize power, modernize the state, and rationalize the economy, had to create a modern bureaucracy, reform the community of monks, and try to control what they considered to be "grossly expensive and unremunerative ritual" (Tambiah 1976). The rationalization of everyday life, however, is always challenged, either by the utopian materiality of popular ritual or by the equally utopian emphasis on subjectivity and inner freedom cultivated by intellectuals and artists (the delimitation of the aesthetic realm itself having to be regarded in the context of the emergence of modernity). In any event, the fundamental ambiguity at the core of modernity is revealed by the tension between the two strands at work in the cultivation of subjectivity: on the one hand the self-centered rationality of individualism (Gurevich 1995), and on the other the ideal of internal freedom and ceaseless self-exploration exemplified by medieval mystics, romantics, and pietists: Does anyone doubt the tense coexistence of those two passions in our own world?

VII

The control of everyday, particularly ritualistic behavior for economic and other reasons can be seen to be at work in sixteenth-century Spain, where ecclesiastical and civil authorities sought to abolish certain forms of ritual. The authorities explicitly stated their desire to put an end to the illegitimate "mixing of sacred and profane things" and to the wasteful use of economic resources (Christian 1981). In so doing, they were attempting to redraw and solidify the hitherto relatively flexible boundaries between what students of religion since the days of Durkheim, Söderblom, and Otto have called the sacred and the profane. At the same time, the attempts to curtail wasteful economic expenditures—reminiscent of the already mentioned Southeast Asian developments as well as of current theories about conversion to Protestantism in Latin America—are consonant with the rationalization of economic behavior and interiorization of religion that are hastily identified with Protestantism, being in fact, as Trevor-Roper (1969) has put it, commonplace before the Reformation. In any event, insofar as the delimitation of a religious realm under the control of ecclesiastical authorities has as its counterpart the creation of a profane one, we can speak of a process of secularization. This secularization, however, does not result in the disappearance of religion but rather in its consolidation; similarly, the rationalization of economic and other types of behavior, exemplified by the denunciation of certain rituals, helps to delimit a subjective realm, one whose importance increases in direct proportion to the rationalization and instrumentalization of the social world. It is not surprising, therefore, that the development of Western modernity has been accompanied by an emphasis on the experiential aspects of religion, even when this emphasis has been explicitly intended to counteract the deleterious effects of the Enlightenment. The cultivation of subjectivity found among the romantics, the pietists, and the theorists of religion who flourished during the first few decades of this century can be seen as a response to the Enlightenment, and then to the accelerating urbanization, industrialization, and above all to the disciplining of everyday life (Berman 1982; Frisby 1986). According to Lefebvre (1962, 174), in fact, nineteenth-century aesthetic modernity masked the failure of revolution, whose parody it became. As we have seen already, the flourishing of subjectivity within, or against, the constraints of social modernity may be found again at the end of the nineteenth and the beginning of the twentieth century in the ferment of literary modernism (all these developments are examples of the tense relationship between freedom and discipline).

Related to the process of secularization and the control of ritual activities is the attitude towards the role religion plays in the management of physical reality, including one's health, sexuality, and wealth. Besides articulating social cohesion, or, perhaps more frequently, functioning as a vehicle for the negotiation of social tensions, ritual activity has taken place within calendars that were used to regulate the activities that made possible the physical survival of individuals and communities. Since in nonindustrial societies those activities had to do mainly with agriculture, cattle herding, and the like, ritual activities have been generally connected, although in some cases in a loose way, with the agricultural calendar and with the well-being of livestock and domestic animals. That connection requires what could be called a symbolic, or perhaps more accurately a sacramental view of reality, that is, one in which the various aspects of reality are not regarded as constituting discrete domains but are seen as relatively unified and therefore accessible to control through a variety of means. The differentiation of domains that characterizes modernity made it in the long run impossible, or at least illegitimate, to engage in activities that mingled the increasingly distinct religious and material realms. But it is necessary to emphasize that the extrication of religion from the material world was, and still is, a contested process. If we limit ourselves to Western Christendom, we encounter in the early Middle Ages an assimilation of pagan practices. However, already by the beginning of the eleventh century, the generalized, open use of magic, common in the early Middle Ages, had come to a stop. Contemporary with the interiorization of religion, eleventh-century condemnations of magic were succeeded in the twelfth century by more comprehensive condemnations such as those issued by Hugh of St. Victor. On the other hand, the ritual activities of the Catholic church continued to comprise a range of activities involving the manipulation of physical substances. These went from the sacraments, which were subject to strict clerical control, to the sacramentals. Sacramentals were objects or elements such as candles, images, and water, which were subject to minor rites and benedictions, but which, after the clerical blessing, could be used outside the church, generally in apotropaic rituals or, in general, to ensure the health and fertility of humans and animals. In the context of our concern with the dematerialization and interiorization of Western modern religion, it is necessary to stress that the physicality of religious practices was inversely related to the degree of clerical control. Therefore, a clerically controlled liturgical activity such as the mass involved a lesser degree of materiality than a sacred performance such as washing the feet of paupers. More extremely, popular rituals free from ecclesiastical supervision involved an even greater degree of physicality, both in terms of goals and means, in that they had to do especially with bodily processes such as eating, excretion, and sexuality (Benavides 1997).

The legitimate or illegitimate character of certain practices was determined by the drawing of boundaries, with the boundaries themselves being a response to the requirements of emerging social formations, particularly to the need to discipline all aspects of life. This disciplining has been identified with the Protestant Reformation, especially with its Calvinist version. But one must reject sharp dichotomies between Catholic and Protestant approaches to materiality and, in more general terms, to the control of religious activities. For if it is true that we find Luther condemning magical practices as papist superstition, we also encounter attempts to remove religion from the physical realm in a papist country such as Spain. Therefore, the complex nature of the relationships between religious and other social processes should force us to avoid facile equations between Protestantism and modernity, on the one hand, and Catholicism and antimodernity, on the other. Indeed, we must confront the fact that just as "magical" practices persisted in post-Reformation Germany (as shown by Scribner in several studies), the renewed bureaucratization of the Catholic church, the rationalization of its procedures, and its largely successful attempts to control the lives of the Catholic flock—or more radically, if we follow Delumeau, to Christianize Europe in the first place—provided a model for the totally administered world of modernity. In fact, it has been claimed that one of the consequences of the Counter Reformation was the dissolution of the old European kinship-based social arrangements and their replacement by new arrangements built around the individual (Gellner 1988; Frey 1995). Thus, for example, confession went from being an act of reconciliation between adversarial groups to one that emphasized the psychological aspects of individual conversion. A further internalization of religion, combined with activism, can be seen at work in the case of the Company of Jesus—the Counter Reformation order par excellence. What, using Weber's terminology, Reinhard (1977) has called the "inner-worldly" asceticism of the Company of Jesus, that is, their belief in the sanctity of secular work, led Trevor-Roper (1969) to speak not just of their economic but of their general modernity. Indeed, it appears that both the rationalization of the structure of the Catholic church and the influence of church organization on the development of European states, to which we have already referred, were developments that did not begin as a result of the Counter Reformation but were simply revivals of ecclesiastical procedures.

It is impossible even to begin reviewing the literature concerning Max Weber's thesis about the affinity between capitalism and Protestantism in its Calvinist version here. But, even if one rightly rejects a causal connection between Protestantism and capitalism, the fact remains that Protestantism contributed to the destabilization of the traditional order and therefore to the restructuring and realigning of European societies. At least, once the opening caused by the Reformation as a political fact had occurred, the Protestant combination of "inner-worldliness" and transcendence—what Eisenstadt (1983) has called the transformative capacities of Protestantism—played a modernizing role in northern Europe. In line with our above discussion of Horton's theory about closed and open societies, it is important to mention that these transformative capacities were smallest in the cases where the Protestant groups attained full powers. This indicates that one should pay less attention to a group's doctrine than to its position within a social configuration; the same applies to individuals, for as Trevor-Roper (1969) has shown, what the great Calvinist entrepreneurs of the mid-seventeenth century had in common was that they were not natives of the country in which they worked. In addition, many Catholic, Lutheran, and Jewish entrepreneurs in the capitalist cities of the seventeenth century had emigrated from four areas: Flanders, southern Germany, Seville and Lisbon, and northern Italy. In general, thinking in structural terms rather than in terms of religious representations when considering the causes of economic change, besides allowing us to understand European developments, permits us to make sense of the already mentioned discrepancy between the "modern" conceptual world of Buddhism and the lack of modernization in Buddhist Asia. For, if religious representations functioned as independent variables, one would expect, for example, that the Indian ideology of the four stages and the four aims of life would have caused the scientific and the industrial revolutions (Baechler 1986, 54).

VIII

At the beginning of this essay we saw that, in order to think about the concept of modernity, one has to make use of it, and that modernity therefore is unavoidably self-reflexive. This reflexivity appears to have reached new levels of intensity during the last decades of the nineteenth and the first decades of the twentieth centuries, as shown, among other exercises in self-examination, by the consolidation of sociology, by the emergence of psychoanalysis, and later by the appearance of the sociology of knowledge, as well as by the self-reflexive character of literary modernism demonstrated, for example, in novels such as Gide's *Counterfeiters* (*Les faux-monnayeurs,* 1926). Now, in the closing years of the twentieth century, with an urgency caused perhaps by the proximity of the new millennium, the levels of self-reflexivity have reached an even greater intensity. The characteristic self-examination of modernity has led some to regard it as having constituted a new period—a "post"-modernity—which by engaging in relentless self-examination will be able to keep itself free from the hubris of modernity; however, postmodernity should not be regarded as the transcending of a supposedly monolithic modernity but rather as the intensification of modernity—as an unavoidable exercise in self-examination and even self-denunciation. Postmodernism's irony, signaled by the automatic placement of literal or figurative quotation marks that characterizes much of contemporary writing and speech, is actually older than the German romantics or Sterne's *Tristram Shandy:* it goes back to the self-conscious concern with writing and narrative found in Cervantes' *Don Quixote,* and in the *Arabian Nights.* Indeed, our examination of medieval conceptions of time should remind us that the concern with being "post" is as novel as the Carolingian Renaissance. As a further exercise in reflexivity, it may be salutary to remember once more that already in the first half of the thirteenth century, theologians of the last third of the twelfth century were considered as belonging to the *antiqui.*

We could say that in examining the concept of modernity we have confronted a concept whose very substance is an act of self-reflection—indeed, it is the reflexivity of modernity that has generated the present book. To the extent that this is the case, each of these critical terms in religious studies, beginning with "religion" itself, appears as modern, as problematic, as requiring an exercise in self-reflection whose result may be the recognition that the realities they are believed to delimit could be otherwise or not at all.

SUGGESTED READINGS

Berman, Marshall. 1982. *All That Is Solid Melts into Air: The Experience of Modernity.*

Calinescu, Matei. 1987. *Five Faces of Modernity: Modernism, Avant-Garde, Decadence, Kitsch, Postmodernism.*

Dumont, Louis. 1983. *Essais sur l'individualisme: Une perspective anthropologique sur l'idéologie moderne.*

Dupré, Louis. 1993. *Passage to Modernity: An Essay in the Hermeneutics of Nature and Culture.*

Eisenstadt, S. N. 1983. *Tradition, Change, and Modernity.*

Freund, Walter. 1957. *Modernus und andere Zeitbegriffe des Mittelalters.*

Frey, Herbert. 1995. *La arqueología negada del Nuevo Mundo: Europa, América y el surgimiento de la modernidad.*

Giddens, Anthony. 1990. *The Consequences of Modernity: Self and Society in the Late Modern Age.*

Habermas, Jürgen. 1985. *Der philosophische Diskurs der Moderne.*

Herzog, Reinhart, and Reinhart Koselleck, eds. 1987. *Epochenschwelle und Epochenbewusstsein.*

Horton, Robin. 1993. *Patterns of Thought in Africa and the West: Essays on Magic, Religion, and Science.*

Kaufmann, Franz-Xaver. 1989. *Religion und Modernität: Sozialwissenschaftliche Perspektiven.*

Kolakowski, Leszek. 1990. *Modernity on Endless Trial,* translated by Stefan Czerniawski, Wolfgang Freis, and Agnieszka Kolakowska.

Koselleck, Reinhart, ed. 1977. *Studien zum Beginn der modernen Welt.*

Lloyd, G. E. R. 1990. *Demystifying Mentalities.*

Taylor, Charles. 1989. *Sources of the Self: The Making of the Modern Identity.*

Wagner, Peter. 1994. *A Sociology of Modernity: Liberty and Discipline.*

Zimmermann, Albert, ed. 1974. *Antiqui und Moderni: Traditionsbewußtsein und Fortschrittsbewußtsein im späten Mittelalter.*

REFERENCES

Anderson, Perry. 1974a. *Lineages of the Absolutist State.* London: Verso.

———. 1974b. *Passages from Antiquity to Feudalism.* London: Verso.

Baechler, Jean. 1986. "Aux origines de la modernité, castes et féodalité: Europe, Inde, Japon." *Archives européennes de sociologie* 27.

Benavides, Gustavo. 1997. "Magic, Religion, Materiality." *Historical Reflections/Réflexions historiques* 23.

Bendix, Reinhard. 1967. "Tradition and Modernity Reconsidered." *Comparative Studies in Society and History* 9.

Benz, Ernst. 1964. "I fondamenti cristiani della tecnica occidentale." In *Tecnica e casistica: Tecnica, escatologia e casistica,* edited by Enrico Castelli. Rome: Istituto di studi filosofici.

Berman, Marshall. 1982. *All That Is Solid Melts into Air: The Experience of Modernity.* New York: Penguin.

Bidet, Jacques. 1990. *Théorie de la modernité* suivi de *Marx et le marché.* Paris: Presses Universitaires de France.

Böckenförde, Ernst-Wolfgang. 1977. "Zum Verhältnis von Kirche und Moderner Welt: Aufriß eines Problems." In *Studien zum Beginn der modernen Welt,* edited by Reinhart Koselleck. Stuttgart: Klett-Cotta.

———. [1967] 1981. "Die Entstehung des Staates als Vorgang der Säkularisation." In *Säkularisierung,* edited by Heinz-Horst Schrey. Darmstadt: Wissenschaftliche Buchgesellschaft.

Bodde, Derk. 1991. *Chinese Thought, Science, and Society: The Intellectual and Social Background of Science and Technology in Pre-modern China.* Honolulu: University of Hawaii Press.

Borkenau, Franz. [1934] 1980. *Der Übergang vom feudalen zum bürgerlichen Weltbild: Studien zur Geschichte der Philosophie der Manufakturperiode.* Darmstadt: Wissenschaftliche Buchgesellschaft.

Bradbury, Malcolm, and James McFarlane, eds. 1976. *Modernism, 1890–1930.* New York: Penguin.

Braudel, Ferdinand. 1981. *Civilization and Capitalism, Fifteenth to Eighteenth Century.* Vol. 1, *The Structures of Everyday Life,* translated by Siân Reynolds. New York: Harper and Row.

Calinescu, Matei. 1987. *Five Faces of Modernity: Modernism, Avant-Garde, Decadence, Kitsch, Postmodernism.* Durham, N.C.: Duke University Press.

Cancik, Hubert. 1979. "Römische Rationalität: Religions- und kulturgeschichtliche Bemerkungen zu einer frühform des technischen Bewußtseins." In *Gottesvorstellung und Gesellschaftsentwicklung,* edited by Peter Eicher. Munich: Kösel-Verlag.

———. 1983. "Gleichheit und Freiheit: Die antiken Grundlagen der Menschenrechte." In *"Vor Gott sind alle gleich": Soziale Gleichheit, soziale Ungleichheit, und die Religionen,* edited by Günter Kehrer. Düsseldorf: Patmos Verlag.

Casanova, José. 1994. *Public Religions in the Modern World.* Chicago: University of Chicago Press.

Chenu, Marie-Dominique. 1928. "Notes de lexicographie philosophique médiévale: Antiqui, moderni." *Revue des sciences philosophiques et théologiques* 17.

Christian, William. 1981. *Local Religion in Sixteenth-Century Spain.* Princeton: Princeton University Press.

Crosby, Alfred W. 1997. *The Measure of Reality: Quantification and Western Society.* Cambridge: Cambridge University Press.

Dales, Richard C. 1978. "A Twelfth-Century Concept of the Natural Order." *Viator* 9.

———. 1980. "The De-Animation of the Heavens in the Middle Ages." *Journal of the History of Ideas* 41.

Dinzelbacher, Peter. 1981. "Über die Entdesckung der Liebe im Hochmittelalter." *Saeculum* 32.
———. 1987. "Pour une histoire de l'amour au moyen âge." *Le Moyen Age* 93.
Dumont, Louis. 1983. *Essais sur l'individualisme: Une perspective anthropologique sur l'idéologie moderne*. Paris: Editions du Seuil.
Dupré, Louis. 1993. *Passage to Modernity: An Essay in the Hermeneutics of Nature and Culture*. New Haven: Yale University Press.
Eisenstadt, S. N. 1983. *Tradition, Change, and Modernity*. Malabar: Krieger.
Elvin, Mark. 1986. "A Working Definition of 'Modernity'?" *Past and Present* 113.
Freund, Walter. 1957. *Modernus und andere Zeitbegriffe des Mittelalters*. Münster: Verlag Aschendorff.
Frey, Herbert. 1995. *La arqueología negada del Nuevo Mundo: Europa, América y el surgimiento de la modernidad*. Mexico City: Consejo Nacional para la Cultura y las Artes.
Frisby, David. 1986. *Fragments of Modernity. Theories of Modernity in the Work of Simmel, Krakauer, and Benjamin*. Cambridge: MIT Press.
Gellner, Ernest. 1988. *Plough, Sword and Book: The Structure of Human History*. Chicago: University of Chicago Press.
Giddens, Anthony. 1990. *The Consequences of Modernity: Self and Society in the Late Modern Age*. Stanford: Stanford University Press.
Grant, Edward. 1979. "The Condemnation of 1277, God's Absolute Power, and Physical Thought in the Late Middle Ages." *Viator* 10.
Gumbrecht, Hans Ulricht. 1978. "Modern, Modernität, Moderne." In *Geschichtliche Grundbegriffe: Historisches Lexikon zur politisch-sozialen Sprache in Deutschland*, edited by Otto Brunner, Werner Conze, and Reinhart Koselleck. Stuttgart: Klett-Cotta.
Gurevich, Aaron. 1995. *The Origins of European Individualism*, translated by Katherine Judelson. Oxford: Blackwell.
Hall, John A. 1985. *Powers and Liberties: The Causes and Consequences of the Rise of the West*. Berkeley and Los Angeles: University of California Press.
Hartmann, Wilfried. 1974. "'Modernus' und 'antiquus': Zur Verbreitung und Bedeutung dieser Bezeichnungen in der wisseschaftlichen Literatur vom 9. bis zum 12. Jahrhunderts." In *Antiqui und Moderni: Traditionsbewußtsein und Fortschrittsbewußtsein im späten Mittelalter*, edited by Albert Zimmermann. Berlin: Walter de Gruyter.
Herzog, Reinhart, and Reinhart Koselleck, eds. 1987. *Epochenschwelle und Epochenbewusstsein*. Munich: Wilhelm Fink.
Hiltbrunner, Otto. 1968. "Die Heiligkeit des Kaisers (Zur Geschichte des Begriffs *sacer*)." *Frühmittelalterliche Studien* 2.
Hooykaas, A. 1972. *Religion and the Rise of Modern Science*. Edinburgh: Scottish University Press.
Horton, Robin. [1967] 1993a. "African Traditional Thought and Western Science." In *Patterns of Thought in Africa and the West: Essays on Magic, Religion, and Science*. Cambridge: Cambridge University Press.
———. [1982] 1993b. "Tradition and Modernity Revisited." In *Patterns of Thought in Africa and the West: Essays on Magic, Religion, and Science*. Cambridge: Cambridge University Press.
Huff, Toby. 1993. *The Rise of Early Modern Science: Islam, China, and the West*. Cambridge: Cambridge University Press.
Jacob, Margaret C. 1988. *The Cultural Meaning of the Scientific Revolution*. New York: McGraw-Hill.
———. 1997. *Scientific Culture and the Making of the Industrial West*. New York: Oxford University Press.
Jauß, Hans Robert. 1964. "Ursprung und Bedeutung der Fortschrittsidee in der 'Querelle des Anciens et des Modernes.'" In *Die Philosophie und die Frage nach dem Fortschritt*, edited by Helmut Kuhn and Franz Wiedman. Munich: Anton Pustet.
Kaufmann, Franz-Xaver. 1989. *Religion und Modernität: Sozialwissenschaftliche Perspektiven*. Tübingen: Mohr (Paul Siebeck).
Kaye, Joel. 1988. "The Impact of Money on the Development of Fourteenth-Century Scientific Thought." *Journal of Medieval History* 14.

Kolakowski, Leszek. 1990. *Modernity on Endless Trial,* translated by Stefan Czerniawski, Wolfgang Freis, and Agnieszka Kolakowska. Chicago: University of Chicago Press.

Koselleck, Reinhart. 1977. "'Neuzeit': Zur Semantik moderner Bewegungsbegriffe." In *Studien zum Beginn der modernen Welt,* edited by Reinhart Koselleck. Stuttgart: Klett-Cotta.

———. 1987. "Das achtzehnte Jahrhundert als Beginn der Neuzeit." In *Epochenschwelle und Epochenbewusstsein,* edited by Reinhart Herzog and Reinhart Koselleck. Munich: Wilhelm Fink.

———, ed. 1977. *Studien zum Beginn der modernen Welt.* Stuttgart: Klett-Cotta.

Kula, Witold. 1986. *Measures and Men.* Princeton: Princeton University Press.

Lapidus, Ira M. 1975. "The Separation of State and Religion in the Development of Early Islamic Society." *International Journal of Mideast Studies* 6.

Lefebvre, Henri. 1962. *Introduction à la modernité.* Paris: Editions de Minuit.

Le Goff, Jacques. 1977. *Pour un autre Moyen Age: Temps, travail et culture en Occident.* Paris: Gallimard.

Lloyd, G. E. R. 1987. *The Revolutions of Wisdom: Studies in the Claims and Practice of Ancient Greek Science.* Berkeley and Los Angeles: University of California Press.

———. 1990. *Demystifying Mentalities.* Cambridge: Cambridge University Press.

Mann, Michael. 1986. *The Sources of Social Power.* Vol. 1, *A History of Power from the Beginning to A.D. 1760.* Cambridge: Cambridge University Press.

Marino, Adrian. 1974. "Modernisme et modernité, quelques précisions sémantiques." *Neohelicon* 3–4.

Preus, James S. 1972. "Theological Legitimation for Innovation in the Middle Ages." *Viator* 3.

Reinhard, Wolfgang. 1977. "Gegenreformation als Modernisierung? Prolegomena zu einer Theorie des konfessionellen Zeitalters." *Archiv für Reformationsgeschichte* 68.

Scribner, Robert W. 1990. "The Impact of the Reformation on Daily Life." In *Mensch und Objekt im Mittelalter und in der frühen Neuzeit. Leben, Alltag, Kultur.* Wien: Österreichische Akademie der Wissenschaften.

———. 1993. "The Reformation, Popular Magic, and the 'Disenchantment of the World.'" *Journal of Interdisciplinary History* 23.

Stiefel, Tina. 1977. "The Heresy of Science: A Twelfth-Century Conceptual Revolution." *Isis* 68.

Tambiah, S. J. 1976. *World Conqueror and World Renouncer: A Study of Buddhism in Thailand against a Historical Background.* Cambridge: Cambridge University Press.

Taylor, Charles. 1989. *Sources of the Self: The Making of the Modern Identity.* Cambridge: Harvard University Press.

Thompson, E. P. [1967] 1993. "Time, Work-Discipline and Industrial Capitalism." In *Customs in Common.* New York: New Press.

Trevor-Roper, H. R. 1969. "Religion, the Reformation and Social Change." In *"The European Witch-Craze of the Sixteenth and Seventeenth Centuries" and other essays.* New York: Harper and Row.

Wagner, Peter. 1994. *A Sociology of Modernity: Liberty and Discipline.* London: Routledge.

Weber, Max. 1920–21. *Gesammelte Aufsätze zur Religionssoziologie.* 3 vols. Tübingen: Mohr (Paul Siebeck).

White, Lynn. 1971. "Cultural Climates and Technological Advance in the Middle Ages." *Viator* 2.

Wilson, John F. 1987. "Modernity and Religion: A Problem of Perspective." In *Modernity and Religion,* edited by William Nicholls. Waterloo: Wilfred Laurier University Press.

Winckelmann, Johannes. 1980. "Die Herkunft von Max Webers 'Entzauberungs'-Konzeption." *Kölner Zeitschrift für Soziologie und Sozialpsychologie* 32.

ELEVEN

Performance

Catherine Bell

S cholars use many terms to talk about religious activity, most basically, liturgy, worship, ritual, and recently performance. Although these terms reflect different perspectives and assumptions, they share the supposition that ceremonial actions characterized by a self-conscious formality and traditionalism are a primary aspect of religion and an important focus in any project to understand religion. Nonetheless, most theories of religion since the Enlightenment have tended to emphasize the more cognitive aspects of religion no matter how rooted these were thought to be in emotional, doctrinal, or communal experience. In the last several decades, however, religious studies has become (as have other fields such as anthropology, history, and psychology) increasingly concerned to give more attention to the actual "doing" of religion. In this venture, the term "ritual," which pioneered the attempt to get beyond confessional perspectives by suggesting a nearly universal structure to religious activities, has attracted some criticism. Major critiques note its long-standing complicity in bifurcating thought and action, its unilateral imposition of symbolic intentionality, and the "globalization" by which nearly everything becomes some sort of ritual (Bell 1992; Asad 1993; Goody 1977).

The term "performance" attempts to minimize these problems and explore religious activity more fully in terms of the qualities of human action. Interest in the language of performance has been multifaceted, explicitly experimental, and occasionally quite idiosyncratic. While there are some islands of consensus, there is little systematic direction or assessment. Indeed, an exclusive emphasis on performance has receded in favor of a broader set of terms used alongside performance, notably "ritualization" and "ritual practice." Yet by virtue of a shared concern to deal with action as action, all of these theoretical orientations can be loosely grouped as "performance approaches" to the study of religion. Moreover, despite their heterogeneity, they have been sufficiently coherent and dynamic to influence fundamental orientations in the study of religion today.

The terminology of performance harbors some basic ambiguity. The oldest meanings of the noun denote the accomplishment or execution of a specified action, most notably a command or a promise. Similarly, performance has also come to mean the enactment of a script or score, as in a theatrical play or musical recital. More recent uses, however, emphasize a type of event in which the very activity of the agent or artist is the most critical dimension and not the completion of the action. With this repertoire of meanings, religious studies uses the language of performance to stress the execution of a preexisting script for activity (as in conducting a traditional church service) or the explicitly unscripted dimensions of an activity in process (as in the spirit or quality of the service). While the former sense of enacting a script captures much of how ritual activity has been traditionally viewed, the latter sense of focusing on the qualities of ritual action is the concern of current approaches. Overall, usage remains diverse and ambiguous: To speak of ritual performances or the performance of worship can imply a tradition-oriented execution of established codes of behavior, an action-oriented perspective focused on the doing itself, or both.

The notion of performance became popular in the late 1960s. At that time several well-known sociologists and anthropologists began to embrace such terminology as a means of sidestepping the mind/body and thought/action dichotomies that previous approaches to ritual appeared to impose. Among the most influential formulations were Victor Turner's ethnographic descriptions of ritual as a processual form of "social drama," J. L. Austin's linguistic theory of "performative utterances," and Erving Goffman's analyses of the scenarios of "social interaction." This general direction found further amplification in the work of Stanley Tambiah and Clifford Geertz. Tambiah explicitly focused on performance as a way to rectify the devaluation of action that occurs when it is contrasted with thought, while Geertz argued for the necessity of "blurred genres" of interpretation in order to do justice to the ways in which a ritual may be like a game, a drama, or an "ensemble of texts" (Geertz 1983; 1973, 452). In this vein, Richard Schechner's writings on anthropology and theater offered provocative connections among ritual, experiments in performance art, and cross-cultural dimensions of expressive physical movement (1977, 1993). Before long, there were enthusiastic suggestions that the notion of performance was a conceptual and methodological "breakthrough," possibly able to reintegrate the bifurcated disciplines of the humanities and the social sciences (e.g., Hymes 1975, 11).

While reflecting some of the ambiguities in the term itself, these new methods employed the language of performance to try to decode action as action by going beyond the textual framework standard to decoding analysis. That is, the challenge was to grasp the logic of the provisional, instinctive, and performative in social action without translating it into something else in the very act of analyzing it. Many prominent "practice" theorists like Marshall Sahlins, Sherry B. Ortner, and Pierre Bourdieu shared this concern, although they did not emphasize performance terminology per se. Their formulations of the dynamics intrinsic to how people do things in culturally effective ways have delineated a surer focus on the expedient and negotiated dimensions of human activity or, in other words, the play of power in the micropolitics of all social action. In this context, power refers less to physical control of people than to social prestige or the concern to secure the dominance of models of reality that render one's world coherent and viable.

In the field of religious studies in particular, the language of performance is usually invoked to counter the scholarly tendency to approach religious activity as if it were either a type of scriptural text to be analyzed or the mere physical execution of a preexisting ideology. Although Paul Ricoeur proposed the text metaphor for the analysis of meaningful action as late as 1971, the concern in religious studies soon paralleled that of other fields, namely, how to get beyond textual metaphors for action and the particular practices of decoding that such a metaphor implies. The goal has been an analytic orientation truer to the nature of human activity, or at least one less patently reflective of the hermeneutical stance and agenda of the textual scholar. Hence, the interdisciplinary developments noted above influenced religious studies as much as any other field. However, religious studies also registered another sort of influence with the major upheavals in liturgical traditions that began to occur in the late 1960s and 1970s. Liturgical experiments in more open-ended forms of communal performance underscored dimensions of ritual activity that had been relatively inaccessible to those looking at religious action as the execution of a "script" of doctrines, beliefs, and traditions. Particularly hidden from that older view were the dynamics of ritual change; despite the condemnation of some experts, projects to redesign familiar ritual conventions were radically shifting the formal religious experiences of most Americans. The terminology of performance not only appeared better able to appreciate these shifts in contemporary religious practice but also seemed to provide fresh justification for them (Bell 1997).

Influenced by these developments, work on performance in religious studies has been quite varied. For example, there are the more theologically oriented studies of Thomas F. Driver (1991) and Theodore Jennings (1982), with their respective pastoral and philosophical emphases. In the history of religions, Jonathan Z. Smith's rereading of traditional texts demonstrates the importance of the exact historical-political context of the ritual over phenomenological form, a conclusion also borne out by the more anthropological studies of Bruce Lincoln (Smith 1982, 53–65, 90–101; Lincoln 1989, 53–74). In a very different key, the work of René Girard (1977) on ritual scapegoating or Walter Burkert (1996) on the biological roots of sacrifice weave psychology, folklore, literature, and sociobiology into grand syntheses about religion and civilization that are reminiscent of Sigmund Freud or the Cambridge myth-and-ritual school.

With the publication of *Beginnings in Ritual Studies* in 1982, Ronald L. Grimes attempted to lay the groundwork for ritual studies as a field in itself, albeit an overtly interdisciplinary one. The *Journal of Ritual Studies,* founded a few years later, particularly encouraged multidisciplinary approaches to ritual performances, setting aesthetic and biological analyses alongside cultural, political, and liturgical ones. Although interdisciplinary approaches have increasingly become the rule since the early 1980s, it is not clear to what extent new topics like performance have led the way or emerged as a result, but it has probably been a bit of both. In any case, this embracing of methodological diversity brought new groups into a wide-ranging conversation. For example, liturgical studies became closely involved in the theoretical developments described above and began to articulate ritual as a primary medium for communal renewal that had major implications for theology, scriptural studies, and liturgy (Collins 1981; Collins and Powers 1983; Kelleher 1993). Indeed, one could argue that the influence of performance terminology in religious studies has come full circle from seeing action as a type of text to seeing the text as a type of activity. At times the enthusiasm for bringing a performance approach to bear on various aspects of religion has appeared to push sober discretion aside. Recently, some para-linguistic models of ritual action that focus in various ways on the prior cognitive competence of the agent who produces an act have emerged in opposition to some forms of performance theory (Staal 1989; Lawson and McCauley 1990).

The most significant contributions of performance theory involve a cluster of interrelated themes that embody important dimensions of recent thinking about religion and culture. In fact, the rubric of performance has been indispensable to the articulation of the specifically cultural dynamics involved in religious activity, thereby recognizing religious life as more than a functional expression of concep-tual beliefs or social relationships. This focus on cultural dynamics fueled specu-lation about just what these activities actually signify or mean. Questions of meaning led, in turn, to concerns with how performative actions produce a cul-turally meaningful environment as opposed to simply communicating ideas or attitudes. The anthropologist Milton Singer, for example, described a number of Hindu ritual festivals as "cultural performances" that do not express social rela-tions so much as the more hidden structures of the Hindu cultural system (1972, 64–7). Turner (1969) went further in arguing that Ndembu rituals not only give dramatic form to underlying social tensions in such a system, they orchestrate a resolution of these tensions. Both Singer and Turner represented a shift from seeing ritual performances as projections of an existing system of social relations to seeing them as modes of expressing cultural ideas and dispositions. They also pointed the way to a further perspectival shift that would view such cultural expressions as the very activity by which culture is constantly constructed and reproduced. No longer would religious ritual be understood simply as a means of transmitting ideas or molding attitudes, either by explicit socialization or implicit coding. Performance approaches seek to explore how activities *create* culture, authority, transcendence, and whatever forms of holistic ordering are required for people to act in meaningful and effective ways. Hence, by virtue of this underlying concern, performance terminology analyzes both religious and secular rituals as orchestrated events that construct people's perceptions and interpretations.

By logical extension, performance theorists are also concerned with the pecu-liar efficacy that distinguishes ritual activities from related activities such as literal communication, routine labor, or pure entertainment. There is less consensus in this area, however, than in some others. Schechner and Appel suggest that ritual performance achieves a distinctive type of psychological transformation, some-times described as an intensity of "flow" or "concentration" (1989, 4). Others argue that the efficacy of ritual performance resides in the reorchestration of the meanings of symbols, which is accomplished by the nondiscursive, dramaturgical, and rhetorical dynamics of the performance (Schieffelin 1985, 707–10). Geertz compares these dynamics to the transformative abilities of dramatic theater, where the impact is "neither a persuasion of the intellect nor a beguiling of the senses. . . . It is the enveloping movement of the whole drama on the soul of man. We surrender and are changed" (Geertz 1983, 28, citing Charles Morgan). Another argument links the efficacy of ritual to what is called its emergent qualities, that is, its ability to bring about social and ontological change by virtue of the doing itself: a child is now recognized as an adult, prestige has accrued to some but not others, certain social relationships or alliances have been strengthened while others are undermined (Bauman 1975, 302–5). However embryonic, these attempts to explore the peculiar efficacy of performance illustrate a major goal of performance theory: to show that ritual action does what it does by virtue of its dynamic, diachronic, physical, and sensual characteristics.

Intrinsic to these concerns with the dynamics of performance is a fresh awareness of human agents as active creators of both cultural continuity and change rather than passive inheritors of a system who are conditioned from birth to replicate it. This emphasis is often a self-conscious development of Marx's insight that people make their own history, even if they do not make it exactly as they please (1948, 15). From this perspective, change is a dynamic process integral to how persons live and reproduce culture and not the disruption of some intrinsically static state of affairs. In other words, performance theory is more likely to eschew concerns with how ritual molds people to maintain the status quo, looking instead at how individuals fashion rituals that shape their world, with some theorists describing a complex interaction of these forces (Handelman 1990). This emphasis on both the impetus of individual agency as well as its constraints has led to a new sociological engagement of power, politics, negotiation, and appropriation. The work of Bourdieu, Michel de Certeau, and Michel Foucault is frequently invoked to elaborate this view of agency.

Performance imagery also employs an analytic vocabulary that attempts to go beyond primarily intellectual assessments of what ritual does for a better appreciation of the emotional, aesthetic, physical, and sensory aspects of religion. This means special attention to the bodily (broadly defined) dimensions of ritual activity. Some theorists appeal to *kinesthesia*, the sensations experienced by the body in movement, or *synesthesia*, the evocation of an integrated and overwhelming sensory experience (Schechner 1977, 99–107; Sullivan 1986, 6–8). Others see this physical dimension as the site for many more "senses" than the usual five, such as beauty, duty, direction, balance, and common sense (Bourdieu 1977, 124). With a more taxonomic perspective, Grimes catalogs a spectrum of physical styles and cognitive sensibilities invoked in ritual activities (1985, 1–7; 1995, 24–57).

Performance approaches are also involved in reconsiderations of the cultural ramifications of orality and literacy. The rubric of performance appears to facilitate greater anthropological attention to literate cultures, while supporting more attention to oral practices by the traditionally text-based scholars of religious studies. For example, recent studies identify the importance of performative dimensions found in various scriptural and textual traditions (Krondorfer 1992; Graham 1987; Blackburn 1988; Lutgendorf 1991). Wilfred Cantwell Smith's rather simple contrast of the literate/textual and oral/performative media—"what theology is to the Christian Church, a ritual dance may be to an African tribe"—has given way to an awareness of a more complex interaction of oral and literate forms (1979, 15). Some ethnographic analyses specifically explore ritual performances as the source of key religious concepts for nonelite social classes, as in Chinese notions of spirit and ghost, in contrast to which elite classes would tend to create and use more literary formulations (Weller 1987, 86). Other arguments demonstrate the impossibility of making any simple distinctions between oral and literate societies or media, pointing to multiple and complex dynamics among degrees of literacy, types of texts, and forms of textual authority (e.g., Gill 1985). Certainly performance theories appear to encourage scholars of religion to pay more attention to those practices that have no scriptural basis, such as domestic practices and local religion in both routine and anomalous examples (Orsi 1985; Christian 1992).

Finally, a greater awareness of the scholar's own position is intrinsic to the performance approach, articulating postmodernist concerns for reflexivity, critiquing claims to simple objectivity, and sometimes systematically deconstructing the whole scholarly stance. In describing the ritual construction of new cultural images, dispositions, or situations, various performance analyses have also focused attention on concomitant processes of indigenous self-reflection and self-interpretation. As a distinctive quality of performance, wherein people become an audience to themselves, reflexivity has invited further speculation on the comparable role of the theorist observing and studying ritual (Bourdieu and Wacquant 1992). The provocative claim that the epistemological concerns of those who *study* ritual parallel the epistemological concerns of those who *perform* ritual, giving theorists and performers much in common, is an interesting focus of some debate (Jennings 1982; Bell 1992, 29). Turner, for his part, saw the dramatic dimension of social action as affording both personal and public forms of reflexivity, a type of "mirroring" that enables the community to stand back and reflect upon their actions and identity (Turner 1990, 8; Kapferer 1984). Yet later in his career he suggested that scholars, joined by performers and artists, should supplement their ethnographic study of ritual with actual performances of them (Turner 1982, 89–101). These suggestions were picked up by others eager to experiment with interweaving the study and the practice of ritual (MacAloon 1984, 3). A handful of laboratories for experiments in ritual and theatrical performance have been set up at various universities, although the published results have not yet had a great impact on theoretical developments. In a related development, Grimes coined the term "ritology" to denote the activity of ritual criticism whereby experts in ritual theory help communities to reflect on their own rites and design improvements (Grimes 1990, 109–44; 1995, 7–23). Hence, while some forms of reflexivity invite greater self-consciousness of the theorist's impact on the performance phenomenon he or she is studying, other forms attempt to break down such pretenses at demarcating boundaries so as to pull the theorist into an active role in the phenomenon itself. Performance theory invites experimentation with any number of these configurations. So far, however, the most positive effect has been to keep such issues open to lively debate.

As a result of these explorations, performance approaches have little concern for preliminary definitions of ritual action, especially in terms of any particular mental states (such as expressing or reflecting belief) or specific choreographic structures (such as a three-stage rite of passage). For some, this apparent logical laxity merely condones general methodological subjectivity. Yet this retreat from prior definitions may also reflect a major shift in understanding how to go about wielding analytic categories. Performance theory does not analyze the phenomenal data by shepherding it into preliminary categories; rather, it tries to ask questions that disclose the holistic dynamics of the phenomenon in its own terms as much as possible. Most radically, it does not start out assuming what religion and ritual are; it attempts to let the activities under scrutiny have ontological and analytic priority, while the scholar deploys tools to untangle those activities in ways that can inform and modify his or her notions of religion and ritual and not simply attest to them.

A classic study of cultural performance describes Jacob Kovitz's ninety-fifth birthday party at a Jewish senior citizens center. In this analysis, Barbara Myerhoff (1984) focuses on the way ritual action could construct collective interpretations of reality even in the face of the unexpected, specifically, Jacob's demise in the course of the festivities. While Jacob had wanted to make the occasion an affirmation of his hopes, the community of elderly, Yiddish-speaking Jews, all immigrants from Eastern European *shtetles* that no longer existed, sought to construct from it a validation of lives on the brink of personal and communal obliteration. With his well-to-do sons attentively at his side, Jacob had hosted a generous community-wide party on his birthday for several years running, ostensibly as a way to raise funds for Jewish causes but actually as a central event in the psychological and social life of the senior citizens' center. His ninety-fifth birthday celebration, like the others, was not a ritual in the formal Jewish tradition. It was a secular event that made use of a combination of ritual formulas, opening with a Hebrew blessing, followed by traditional toasts, introductions of family and important guests, festive kosher food, after dinner folk songs, speeches, announcements of donations, and finally, a birthday cake with candles and the customary song. Jacob, the oldest member of the community, fell seriously ill in the months before his last party but was resolved to hold the event as usual. It began on his exact birth date amid rumors about his health and a sense of foreboding. Whispering that the Angel of Death was at his side, Jacob himself hurried people through their parts but did not otherwise curtail the familiar routine. Finally, after the food was cleared away, he took the microphone, spoke haltingly of his love for the community, and announced a special gift to the community that would enable them to continue their annual party in the future. Then, falling back into his seat, he dropped his chin on his chest and died.

At that point, those present had to draw upon their sense of what was psychologically and socially needed in order to improvise an appropriate form of closure and meaning for the wayward event. Conscious of the need to say and do something that would make things right for the several hundred anxious elderly in the room, all the participants drew on multiple cultural strategies for redefining the situation. Jacob's oldest son, for example, instinctively refused to let the drama of sudden death overwhelm the celebration. Instead, he and others used a series of ritual-like activities and step-by-step interpretive processes to frame the death as a culmination of the significance of the birthday party itself, that is, as a testimony to the fullness of life and how meaningful its ending can be. "It was a good death," many murmured by the end (Myerhoff 1984, 167). Ritual dramatization, Myerhoff points out, is a flexible if delicate process capable of constructing meaningful events from the raw happenings of life.

It is unlikely that Jacob Kovitz's party would have figured as data in the rubric of many earlier approaches to the study of religion and ritual. In Myerhoff's framework, however, it is an event that reveals a number of distinct dynamics, both personal and communal, by which people knit together an empowering view of their lives, traditions, communities, and futures. Yet Jacob's birthday certainly remains an atypical example of religious ritual. While more standard examples of simple, routine, and overtly religious ritual may present greater challenges to a performance approach, they may also reveal more of its methodological ramifications. An appropriately routine and ubiquitous ritual for this purpose is the Chinese practice of making daily domestic offerings of incense to the ancestors, a ritual deeply embedded in complex textual and oral traditions.

Until the middle of this century, almost every Chinese home had a domestic altar, usually located opposite the main door into the central room or hall. Such altars are still found in Chinese communities around the world, although significantly less so among urbanized generations who have left the land. The standardization of this custom is such that any sort of exception to it in otherwise traditional communities attracts much attention. Usually the altar is a high, narrow table pushed against the wall that holds the main ritual paraphernalia; a lower square-shaped table in front of it holds the more extensive offerings made on special occasions. Like the main door of the house, the altar faces south while the worshipper in front of it faces north. The altar itself is divided roughly in half. Its right side (stage right, the subordinate position) accommodates several generations of ancestor tablets in the form of names and dates on a large paper scroll, a wooden board, or smaller individual tablets for each person or couple. Traditionally a red dot next to the name denotes the installation of the soul of the deceased in the tablet. On the left side (stage left, the superior position), there are paper images and often a statue or two of the more popular deities in the region. Each side of the altar has a small incense burner placed in front of the ancestral tablets or god images, and it is customary to have two candlesticks (or electric candles) and a vase for flowers as well (Doolittle 1986, 217–25; Hsü 1967, 184; Freedman 1979, 275–7).

Usually twice a day, before breakfast and in the evening, the senior woman of the house offers incense in each burner. Typically she lights three sticks of incense, bows with the incense sticks held fanlike in her clasped hands, then places one in the incense pot for the gods, another in the pot for the ancestors, and the third in a pot just outside the main door to placate various types of ghosts. Small offerings of food or spirit money may be added on the new and full moons of each lunar month, while more substantial food offerings are made on special occasions, such as death day anniversaries, rites of passage (marriages, births, etc.), and particular festivities of the lunar year (the New Year Festival, the Spring Festival, and the Festival of the Hungry Ghosts). While the male head of the household is in charge of the more formal rites when the food offerings are made and the ancestors are addressed, the daily offerings are typically left to an older (usually postmenopausal) woman as a type of household duty. Her ritual routine takes less than two minutes to perform.

This simple act has been the subject of intense and profuse speculation about Chinese culture in particular and the essential nature of religion in general. It was at the heart of the famous seventeenth-century "rites controversy," when various Catholic missionary factions argued whether such practices were simply a matter of social morality or real (and hence pagan) religion. European scholars later pioneering the comparative study of religion collected this ritual alongside others as evidence for the origins of religion in primitive notions of the soul and fear of the dead. Today there is an enormous body of sophisticated ethnographic and historical studies relevant to any interpretation of this brief scenario. The following descriptive frameworks attempt to set out the interpretive schemes in this scholarship as efficiently as possible before explicating the specific contributions of a performance approach.

The most immediate framework for analyzing the daily incense offering has been to connect these actions with Chinese ideas concerning the nature of the living and dead, the body and soul(s), gods and ghosts, the family and lineage, filial piety, and so on. From this basic perspective, the ritual reflects preexisting beliefs about the nature of reality; when expressed in action, these beliefs are reaffirmed and transmitted to subsequent generations. At this point, however, an interpreter must decide the degree of contextualization that further interpretation of the ritual requires. If the interpreter is seeking to understand what this practice contributes to a more generalized notion of ritual or sacrifice or performance, then he or she will tend to see it as a freestanding representation or even archetypal example of the religious belief system in practice. As such the interpreter can conceptualize various cross-cultural comparisons. The meaning of the practice will be closely tied to how it helps to define a more universal analytical category, such as ritual, or to illuminate a more universal phenomenon, such as reciprocal bonds between the living and the dead. This type of analysis, a style quite characteristic of religious studies, generates a particular body of knowledge that is clearly more geared to thinking about religion in general than about the woman's daily routine.

If the interpreter seeks a fuller understanding of what the ritual means for its Chinese practitioners, then the rite's cultural context is most important and the ritual is best viewed as inextricably linked to a larger set of ritual activities. Such a set would be comprised of other ritual practices involving gods, ghosts, and ancestors, such as the domestic cult of the Stove God, grave-based geomancy, the surname lineage hall, temple-based regional festivals, spirit mediums, and the division of temple incense. The pertinent context might extend to include imperial rites, sectarian movements that initiate followers into entirely new lineage relationships, or various other dimensions of Chinese social and political organization. One widely cited conclusion that emerged from just this type of analysis is the theory that the pantheon and practices involved in rites as simple as the daily incense offering effectively replicate the basic hierarchical principles and bureaucratic structures of Chinese society as a whole. Hence, even small-scale domestic religious ritual mirrors the organization and values of the culture (Wolf 1974).

Going beyond ritual as a simple reflection of religious beliefs or the sociopolitical organization, some analyses have also attempted to decode the symbolic structure of regional versions of this ritual in order to elucidate an underlying system, that is, a set of cultural assumptions that can account for the meaning of variations. Such studies have demonstrated strong links between these daily domestic offerings and the construction of jural authority, lineage organization, residence, property inheritance rights, and regional-national politics. From this perspective, the incense ritual is primarily a medium for constructing and reproducing a specific lineage culture, both in terms of dispositions and institutions. Nevertheless, it is far from clear there exists in practice any single underlying system of acts, symbols, or meanings from which this rite derives its significance (Li 1985).

Explicitly historical-textual approaches also contribute an important framework within which such domestic offerings can be analyzed. Starting with the early Chinese classics on ritual—the *Book of Rites (Li-chi)*, the *Book of Etiquette and Ceremonial (I-li)*, and the writings of the Confucian ritualist Hsün Tzu— it is clear that the elite perspective on ancestor worship saw it as closely connected to the regulated expression of the social distinctions that ordered society. Social status, for example, determined the degree to which a family could perform ancestral rites (Watson 1963, 91–2, 97–8). By the medieval period, however, there was a variety of popular guides to family ritual that were less tied to the prescriptive Confucianism of the classics and more concerned to systematize what people were actually doing (Ebrey 1991, 37 f.; 1995). In response, the Neo-Confucian revival begun in the eleventh century attempted to revitalize the classical rites (and social order) with new guidelines that eliminated class distinctions and accommodated some of the popular proliferation of ancestral offerings in the home and at the grave. As a result, the relationship of ritual activity to a pervasive tradition of textual prescriptions is an important dimension of cultural practice in China, not only for the social location of the actors but for the larger significance of the ritual to those involved in it—most simply, whether they see themselves as part of the so-called great tradition or as simply upholding local and familial customs in ignorance of, or resistance to, this tradition.

These frameworks for analyzing the daily incense offerings approach this particular religious activity as an instance of a definable, unified, and coherent phenomenon known as ritual, that is, as a matter of relatively scripted actions, structurally distinct from nonritual action and possessing certain apparently universal properties (like formality, repetition, and divine beings). Although it is widely understood that any particular ritual practice or corpus changes over time and place, the identity of ritual as a phenomenon is usually taken for granted. This set of assumptions may be responsible for making ritual—and specifically this ritual—important to arguments concerning the underlying unity of Chinese culture or religion.

A performance approach to the daily domestic incense offerings ritual might well include some or all of the above frameworks, but it would be characterized by a few other emphases as well. First of all, a primary concern with performance would attempt to approach this humble act in terms of a specific ethnographic instance instead of a generalized description in the abstract. By using a particular ethnographic instance, the researcher is able to minimize the assumptions that any observer brings to the action. Yet this can be a very difficult requirement, and perhaps no more so than in the case of this specific rite, which is so commonplace that no one has recorded a routine instance of it. The most detailed descriptions available generalize the activities of whole villages or all ancestor rites; the most careful ethnographic studies assume some such general model and then search out variations from it, such as families without any domestic worship, those with more than one lineage on the altar, or atypical behavior attributed to the ancestors (Ahern 1973; Harrell 1976; Li 1985; Wolf 1976). While such studies may build on observations of numerous particular instances, subsuming the specific into a generalized model can suggest more of an underlying system or structure than there actually is, as well as divert attention from the way any ritual performance does what it does precisely because of its more specific qualities.

A performance analysis of Chinese domestic offerings might also pay particular attention to the movements of the body in space and time, notably the way these movements define a total cosmic orientation at the heart of the home. The relative positions of gods, ancestors, human beings, and ghosts do not only organize spatial relations (north, south, east, and west) but qualify and hierarchize them as well (north of oneself is superior, the left position facing south dominates the right, etc.). The woman's mute movements in these directions create a holistic set of values embodied in a very tangible orientation to a structured cosmos. The temporal sequence of activities at the altar similarly defines the coming and going of the day, year, and generation. Even use of the incense burner, which transforms matter into smoke that ascends into the invisible world, effectively defines the universe into bifurcated realms and powers to be properly mediated. Intrinsic to this sort of performance is the actor's assumption that she is not *creating* this environment but simply *responding* to a de facto organization of reality. In the same way, the senior citizens interviewed by Myerhoff did not see themselves constructing the meaningfulness of Jacob's death at his birthday party; even as they helped orchestrate the event, they saw themselves as responding to what unfolded with its meaningfulness impressing itself on them from without, by the hand of God, the virtue of Jacob, or the destiny of the Jewish people. The Chinese grandmother who lights incense and distributes the sticks in their various pots does not see herself reconstructing a complex cultural system of binary categories—living descendent/dead ancestor, benevolent gods/malevolent ghosts, family deities/community deities, high/low, superior/inferior, female routine care/male formal ceremony, and so on (Ebrey 1995, 107). Yet performance analysis suggests that the particular efficacy of her actions as action lies in how she creates and modifies such realities while never quite seeing the creation or the system as such.

The third emphasis of a performance approach is the rather different orientation toward questions of context and agency that follows from a primary focus on a specific set of actions. At its extreme, which may not always be useful, such a focus highlights what is most distinctive about the situation—how *this* woman lights incense in *her* house *today*—and downplays any prior notion of ritual, duty, or textual prescriptions as the most significant context for analyzing her actions. Therefore, the interpreter is able to define the context in ways that have more to do with the specific actions, such as all the other routine tasks in this woman's day, or all the other activities involving incense, or even table tops. When the specific performance is the starting point of the analysis, the relevant context within which to analyze the actions is no longer automatic. Of course, the full context of this woman, her family, and her culture is inexhaustible and not amenable to analysis without radical reductionism. But the principle of reductionism must be determined as part of the analysis; it should not be imposed by invoking ritual or religion, the social or the sacred. This emphasis on the particular repositions the researcher to explore as context whatever sets of relations, symbols, and attitudes the activities themselves imply. In other words, performance analysis shifts the emphasis from how some system is expressed in these activities to how this performance simultaneously invokes (and thereby both constructs and plays off) a strategically defined set of terms, values, and activities. A performance does this by means of various personal (conscious and unconscious) and cultural strategies that the actor uses in what she does and how she does it. Since this particular type of incense offering has been one of the most uniform practices in Chinese religion ritual in recent centuries, there is only a little room for personal or local flourishes. Nonetheless, by virtue of small emphases in the performance, the woman's routine will evoke her obedience to lineage demands, her prestige in a partnership with that lineage, a deep devotion to a deity in contrast to token respect to the ancestors, fears about grandchildren, or a socialist impatience with superstitious nonsense.

A performance approach is alert to the micropolitics that are always involved in these routine acts, the ways in which people manipulate traditions and conventions to construct an empowering understanding of their present situation. For example, the daily incense offering has been called an "act of obeisance" of junior to senior, living to dead, woman to male lineage (Wolf 1974, 159). Although offerings to her husband's ancestral lineage are a significant part of the marriage ritual, a woman usually assumes the daily routine of tending the altar when the ancestors on the altar have become the kin of her own children. And such duties inevitably involve a negotiation of power. For example, her care of these nonblood kin is thought to have important consequences for the well-being of the family, and there is some suggestion that her role in this activity could be used to make her influence felt (Freedman 1979, 272; Ahern 1975, 175–8, 180–2). The textual history of these offerings suggests that the two-minute performance also harbors long-standing tensions between canonical practices to the ancestors and more popular worship of gods, while what are understood as canonical practices are themselves shaped by tensions between dyadic descent-line practices that give a prominent place to women and collective descent-group practices that banish women from all rites save this routine care (Ebrey 1995, 126).

Basic to this woman's understanding of her own activities is a series of unsystematic cultural classifications that have little to do with a broad category like ritual. Self-conscious participants in the classical tradition have distinguished between *li* (usually translated as ritual, propriety, or etiquette), a term with major political ramifications that denotes authentic and orthodox ceremonial based on clear textual sources, and *su*, the popular customs of the people so often deemed vulgar and improper (Ebrey 1991, 11). According to many of the textual authorities that this woman or her family could consult, offerings to the ancestors should have nothing to do with belief in their existence and ability to make a return on one's piety; only the common people regarded worship as a medium for influencing spirits. Moreover, in the context of *li* and *su*, domestic use of the incense burner has been a highly contested symbol in power struggles between local cults and the state. One recent study argues that the presence of an incense burner defines a local cult as an autonomous institution structurally opposed to imperial power and the bureaucratic system (Feuchtwang 1992, 126–49). Ostensibly classical and orthodox worship of the ancestors can be performed and interpreted in ways that make it deeply resistant to major aspects of the political and cultural unity identified by other interpretations.

In the end, a performance approach does not usually offer a definitive interpretation of a set of ritual actions. Indeed, it is better at conveying the multiple ways in which such activities are meant and experienced, as well as how such multiplicity is integral to the efficacy of ritual performances. This approach can, therefore, actually undermine reliance on concepts like ritual, especially the notion of ritual as a universal phenomenon with a persistent, coherent structure that makes it tend to work roughly the same way everywhere. One could even push the current state of performance theory further to argue that the imposition of an unduly predefined concept of ritual to activities in Chinese culture could threaten our ability to recognize and analyze how these activities actually work. Outside of the prescriptive literature, for example, Chinese domestic offerings show regularities and some systematic features, but there is no evidence of a system or model as such. Attempts to formulate a system run into counter-examples and regional differences very quickly. In the words of one experienced ethnographer, we must confess our failure to find adequate generalizations and hold to "the stubborn facts" (Wolf 1974; 1976, 339).

The terminology of performance emerged partly as a logical corrective to flaws in other approaches and partly as a response to new experiences and evidence concerning ritual action. Nonetheless, many of its basic ideas are not new; more than a few voices in the older literature set out similar ideas. What is new is the holistic framework based on metaphors of performance (as well as action and practice) and the ease with which this framework has been broadly accepted. However, when performance becomes a dominant metaphor that is systematically developed and applied, its insights may begin to cost more in terms of systematic oversights.

Perhaps the greatest challenge to current performance theory lies in its tendency to flirt with universalism, that is, to substitute performance for older notions of ritual in order to create a new general model of action. This tendency toward universalism and essentialism spawns many of the smaller problems afflicting performance analyses, such as the tendency to assume that performance is a single, coherent thing, sufficiently the same everywhere, that to approach something as "performance" implies a general formula for explaining it. Indeed, several attempts to get beyond earlier universals have ended up rooting performance in prelinguistic grammars or the biogenetic legacy of the reptilian brain (Staal 1989; Turner 1983, 226). Without denying the value of further exploration of generative linguistics or sociobiology, such conclusions may fail to include any significant cultural basis for ritual action.

Other analyses are apt to see a performative dimension to everything. In the more sophisticated versions of this argument, theorists find a wide variety of activities—theater, sports, play, political spectacles, and so on—to be similarly structured media that draw upon universal qualities of performance. Unquestionably, the processes of creative socialization seen in cultural patterns of play, theater, and sports are very relevant to understanding religion. As noted earlier, these studies have made important contributions by seeing beyond the cultural boundaries that sharply distinguish all these genres of activity. In particular, they point to the significance of a deliberate, self-conscious "doing" of highly symbolic actions in public as key to what makes ritual, theater, and spectacle what they are. Yet such studies often fail to deal with the accompanying issue, namely, why it is that societies draw their own distinctions among these activities. To conclude that Chinese domestic offerings demonstrate aspects of a human proclivity for performance can illuminate certain aspects of these offerings, but it will tell us nothing about how Chinese practitioners of these offerings might compare their actions to those of a local theatrical production (Ward 1979).

Performance terminology is also used to illuminate fundamental similarities in the enterprise of the "observing scholar" and the "performing native." Some analyses attempt to collapse this dichotomy, while others try to create a third place where the two parties can meet in a more egalitarian series of exchanges. Yet the value of these explorations is severely constrained by their failure to pursue the source and significance of the differences that really exist between such enterprises. Universalism also pays little attention to important historical differences in how people perform their customary activities, the significance they ascribe to them, or the ways they re-create them. For example, a scholar of Chinese imperial history wonders if our modern category of ritual can do justice to events in the reign of the Chinese emperor Ming Shih-tsung (1524), whose ministers risked their careers and lives by objecting to plans to change the titles by which the imperial ancestors were ritually addressed. Is our understanding of ritual able to explain the full moral, political, and cosmic ramifications of such titles for these people (Fisher 1979, 84–5)? The same sort of question is raised by the anthropologist Talal Asad (1993), who suggests that the tendency to analyze ritual in terms of decoding the symbolic cannot do justice to the way in which religious activity in the medieval European church was understood as a matter of discipline for the development of virtue.

Asad's concern is borne out by a recent ethnographic study of table rituals in a modern Catholic convent. The researcher found an enormous emotional and intellectual gap between an older generation who grew up understanding ritual to be a matter of repentance and self-discipline, and a younger generation that saw ritual as an opportunity for communal and celebratory expression of shared values and bonds (Curran 1989). Similarly, an analysis of the ceremonies by which the European nations in the fifteenth through seventeenth centuries claimed hegemony over what was to them "the new world" finds activities with utterly different styles, logic, references, and symbols. While the French arranged courtly processions, the Spanish made formal speeches, the Dutch drew up maps, and the British set up fences and hedges. Moreover, the cultural bricolage that made these newly devised ceremonies authoritative to their compatriots made them completely impenetrable and irrelevant to everyone else (Seed 1995). The most basic models of ritual—what constitutes it, its purpose, and how to go about it—can differ dramatically in one small community and in a seemingly obvious "class" of activities. Any analysis of underlying commonality must also provide a complementary study of the significance of the historical or perceptual differences. Otherwise, and more subtly, universalistic tendencies end up valorizing what is identified as the panhuman dimension, accessible only to the scholar, in contrast to the secondary, even problematic, status of what becomes the culturally specific site of difference. Nostalgia for the ethnic wisdom of vanishing customs and ceremonials will do nothing to redress this type of asymmetry.

There is much that we do not yet understand about the construction of categories and the formation of frameworks for analysis and knowledge. It is sobering, for example, to consider the evidence that scholarly promotion of the concept of ritual, which some would replace with the term "performance," has significantly affected how many people today think about and engage in their own religious activities. Popularly understood as a dimension of all human religiosity that transcends specific forms of cultural and confessional activity, the notion of ritual has effectively relativized the internal authority of long-standing liturgical traditions and emerged as the basis for revising canons and fostering new styles of ritualization—notably styles that emphasize the communal, the performative, and the symbolic. It is this popular understanding of ritual in America today, which assumes cross-cultural similarities in how people seek the spiritual, that brings Protestant suburbanites to embark on Native American vision quests and mainstream churches to offer classes on Zen meditation (Bell 1997). Indeed, the general openness to performance terminology among scholars today may be rooted in many factors other than the logical improvements this term offers over others. It may be related to the politics of negotiating less reductive and arrogant relationships between the people who study and the people who are studied. It may also reflect a more thoroughgoing secularism (and disenchantment?) that minimizes religion as any sort of distinct cultural system.

Programmatically, there is nothing that performance theory can do to solve all these issues. Critical terms are not critical because they contain answers but because they point to the crucial questions at the heart of how scholars are currently experiencing their traditions of inquiry and the data they seek to encounter. Performance theory—broadly conceived, flexible, hospitable to difference and experimentation—needs to resist becoming a formula with which to process the data of difference into some premature vision of universal humanity. We are entering an era in which what we want to learn cannot be learned if our terminology overdetermines the theater of engagement. It is an era in which our terms are best used as a minimalist set of props with which we can begin to engage ideas and inquire into practices that may well modify the surroundings. If performance terminology can evoke this type of open stage as well as it has evoked the dramatic fullness of human action, it will continue to be a vital asset in modern discourse on religion.

SUGGESTED READINGS

Bell, Catherine. 1992. *Ritual Theory, Ritual Practice.*
———. 1997. *Ritual: Perspectives and Dimensions.*
Grimes, Ronald L., ed. 1996. *Readings in Ritual Studies.*
MacAloon, John J. 1984. *Rite, Drama, Festival, Spectacle: Rehearsals toward a Theory of Cultural Performance.*
Moore, Sally F., and Barbara G. Myerhoff, eds. 1977. *Secular Ritual.*
Schechner, Richard, and Willa Appel, eds. 1989. *By Means of Performance: Intercultural Studies of Theater and Ritual.*
Sullivan, Lawrence E. 1986. "Sound and Senses: Toward a Hermeneutics of Performance." *History of Religions* 26 (1).
Turner, Victor. 1987. *The Anthropology of Performance.*

REFERENCES

Ahern, Emily M. 1973. *The Cult of the Dead in a Chinese Village.* Stanford: Stanford University Press.
———. 1975. "The Power and Pollution of Chinese Women." In *Women in Chinese Society,* edited by Margery Wolf and Roxane Witke. Stanford: Stanford University Press.
Asad, Talal. 1993. "Toward a Genealogy of the Concept of Ritual." In *Genealogies of Religion: Discipline and Reasons of Power in Christianity and Islam.* Baltimore: Johns Hopkins University Press.
Austin, J. L. 1962. *How to Do Things with Words.* Cambridge: Harvard University Press.
Bauman, Richard. 1975. "Verbal Art as Performance." *American Anthropologist* 77 (1).
Bell, Catherine. 1992. *Ritual Theory, Ritual Practice.* New York: Oxford University Press.
———. 1997. *Ritual: Perspectives and Dimensions.* New York: Oxford University Press.
Blackburn, Stuart H. 1988. *Singing of Birth and Death: Texts in Performance.* Philadelphia: University of Pennsylvania Press.
Bourdieu, Pierre. 1977. *Outline of a Theory of Practice,* translated by Richard Nice. Cambridge: Cambridge University Press.
Bourdieu, Pierre, and Loïc J. D. Wacquant. 1992. *An Invitation to Reflexive Sociology.* Chicago: University of Chicago Press.
Burkert, Walter. 1996. *Creation of the Sacred: Tracks of Biology in Early Religions.* Cambridge: Harvard University Press.
Christian, Jr., William A. 1992. *Moving Crucifixes in Modern Spain.* Princeton: Princeton University Press.
Collins, Mary. 1981. "Critical Ritual Studies: Examining an Intersection of Theology and Culture." In *The Bent World: Essays on Religion and Culture,* edited by John R. May. Missoula, Mont.: Scholars Press.

Collins, Mary, and David N. Power, eds. 1983. *Liturgy: A Creative Tradition.* Edinburgh: Clark.

Curran, Patricia. 1989. *Grace before Meals: Food Ritual and Body Discipline in Convent Culture.* Urbana: University of Illinois Press.

de Certeau, Michel. 1984. *The Practice of Everyday Life,* translated by Steven Rendell. Berkeley and Los Angeles: University of California Press.

Doolittle, Rev. Justus. 1986 [1865]. *Social Life of the Chinese.* 2 vols. Singapore: Graham Brash.

Driver, Thomas F. 1991. *The Magic of Ritual: Our Need for Liberating Rites That Transform Our Lives and Our Communities.* San Francisco: HarperCollins. Rpt. 1997 as *Liberating Rites: Understanding the Transformative Power of Ritual.* Boulder, Co.: Westview Press.

Ebrey, Patricia Buckley. 1991. *Confucianism and Family Rituals in Late Imperial China: A Social History of Writing about Rites.* Princeton: Princeton University Press.

———. 1995. "The Liturgies for Sacrifices to Ancestors in Successive Versions of the *Family Rituals.*" In *Ritual and Scripture in Chinese Popular Religion: Five Studies,* edited by David Johnson. Berkeley: Institute for East Asian Studies.

Feuchtwang, Stephan. 1992. *The Imperial Metaphor.* London: Routledge.

Fisher, Carney T. 1979. "The Great Ritual Controversy in the Age of Ming Shih-Tsung." *Bulletin of the Society for the Study of Chinese Religion* 7 (fall).

Foucault, Michel. 1977. *Language, Counter-Memory, Practice: Selected Essays and Interviews,* edited by Donald F. Bouchard, translated by Donald F. Bouchard and Sherry Simon. Ithaca, N.Y.: Cornell University Press.

———. 1979. *Discipline and Punish: The Birth of the Prison,* translated by Alan Sheridan. New York: Vintage Books.

———. 1980. *Power/Knowledge: Selected Interviews and Other Writings, 1972–77,* edited and translated by Colin Gordon. New York: Pantheon.

Freedman, Maurice. 1979. *The Study of Chinese Society: Essays by Maurice Freedman,* edited by G. William Skinner. Stanford: Stanford University Press.

Geertz, Clifford. 1973. *The Interpretation of Culture.* New York: Basic Books.

———. 1983. "Blurred Genres: The Reconfiguration of Social Thought." In *Local Knowledge: Further Essays in Interpretive Anthropology.* New York: Basic Books.

Gill, Sam D. 1985. "Nonliterate Traditions and Holy Books." In *The Holy Book in Comparative Perspective,* edited by Frederick M. Denny and Rodney L. Taylor. Columbia: University of South Carolina Press.

Girard, René. 1977. *Violence and the Sacred,* translated by Patrick Gregory. Baltimore: Johns Hopkins University Press.

Goffman, Erving. 1967. *Interaction Ritual.* Chicago: Aldine.

Goody, Jack. 1977. "Against 'Ritual': Loosely Structured Thoughts on a Loosely Defined Topic." In *Secular Ritual,* edited by Sally F. Moore and Barbara G. Myerhoff. Amsterdam: Van Gorcum.

Graham, William A. 1987. *Beyond the Written Word: Oral Aspects of Scripture in the History of Religion.* Cambridge: Cambridge University Press.

Grimes, Ronald L. 1982. "Defining Nascent Ritual." *Journal of the American Academy of Religion* 50 (4).

———. 1985. *Research in Ritual Studies: A Programmatic Essay and Bibliography.* Metuchen, N.J.: Scarecrow Press.

———. 1990. *Ritual Criticism: Case Studies in Its Practice, Essays on Its Theory.* Columbia: University of South Carolina Press.

———. 1995. *Beginnings in Ritual Studies.* Rev. ed. Columbia: University of South Carolina Press.

Handelman, Don. 1990. *Models and Mirrors: Towards an Anthropology of Public Events.* Cambridge: Cambridge University Press.

Harrell, C. Stevan. 1976. "The Ancestors at Home: Domestic Worship in a Land-Poor Taiwanese Village." In *Ancestors,* edited by William H. Newell. The Hague: Mouton.

Hsü, Francis L. K. 1967 [1948]. *Under the Ancestors' Shadow.* New York: Anchor Books.

Hymes, Dell. 1975. "Breakthrough into Performance." In *Folklore: Performance and Communication,* edited by Dan Ben-Amos and Kenneth S. Goldstein. The Hague: Mouton.

Jennings, Theodore W. 1982. "On Ritual Knowledge." *Journal of Religion* 62 (2).

Kapferer, Bruce. 1984. "The Ritual Process and the Problem of Reflexivity in Sinhalese Demon Exorcisms." In *Rite, Drama, Festival, Spectacle,* edited by John J. MacAloon. Philadelphia: Institute for the Study of Human Issues.

Kelleher, Margaret Mary. 1993. "Hermeneutics in the Study of Liturgical Performance." *Worship* 67 (4).

Krondorfer, Bjorn, ed. 1992. *Body and Bible: Interpreting and Experiencing Biblical Narratives.* Philadelphia: Trinity Press.

Lawson, E. Thomas, and Robert N. McCauley. 1990. *Rethinking Religion: Connecting Cognition and Culture.* Cambridge: Cambridge University Press.

Li, Yih-yuan. 1985. "On Conflicting Interpretations of Chinese Family Rituals." In *The Chinese Family and Its Ritual Behavior,* edited by Jih-Chang Hsieh and Ying-chang Chuang. Taipei: Academia Sinica, Institute of Ethnology.

Lincoln, Bruce. 1989. "Ritual, Rebellion, Resistance: Rethinking the Swazi Ncwala." In *Discourse and the Construction of Society.* New York: Oxford University Press.

Lutgendorf, Philip. 1991. *The Life of a Text: Performing the "Ramcaritmanas" of Tulsidas.* Berkeley and Los Angeles: University of California.

MacAloon, John J. 1984. *Rite, Drama, Festival, Spectacle: Rehearsals Toward a Theory of Cultural Performance.* Philadelphia: Institute for the Study of Human Issues.

Marx, Karl. 1948 [1852]. *The Eighteenth Brumaire of Louis Bonaparte.* Moscow: Foreign Languages Publishing House.

Myerhoff, Barbara G. 1984. "A Death in Due Time: Construction of Self and Culture in Ritual Drama." In *Rite, Drama, Festival, Spectacle,* edited by John J. MacAloon. Philadelphia: Institute for the Study of Human Issues.

Orsi, Robert Anthony. 1985. *The Madonna of 115th Street: Faith and Commitment in Italian Harlem, 1880–1950.* New Haven: Yale University Press.

Ortner, Sherry B. 1989. *High Religion: A Cultural and Political History of Sherpa Buddhism.* Princeton: Princeton University Press.

Ricoeur, Paul. 1971. "The Model of the Text: Meaningful Action Considered as a Text." *Social Research* 38 (autumn).

Sahlins, Marshall. 1976. *Culture and Practical Reason.* Chicago: University of Chicago Press.

———. 1981. *Historical Metaphors and Mythical Realities.* Ann Arbor: University of Michigan Press.

Schechner, Richard. 1977. *Essays in Performance Theory, 1970–1976.* New York: Drama Book Specialists.

———. 1993. *The Future of Ritual: Writings on Culture and Performance.* London: Routledge.

Schechner, Richard, and Willa Appel, eds. 1989. *By Means of Performance: Intercultural Studies of Theater and Ritual.* Cambridge: Cambridge University Press.

Schieffelin, Edward L. 1985. "Performance and the Cultural Construction of Reality." *American Ethnologist* 12.

Seed, Patricia. 1995. *Ceremonies of Possession in Europe's Conquest of the New World, 1492–1640.* Cambridge: Cambridge University Press.

Singer, Milton. 1972. *When a Great Tradition Modernizes.* New York: Praeger Publishers.

Smith, Jonathan Z. 1982. *Imagining Religion: From Babylon to Jonestown.* Chicago: University of Chicago Press.

Smith, Wilfred Cantwell. 1979. *Faith and Belief.* Princeton: Princeton University Press.

Staal, Frits. 1989. *Rules without Meaning: Mantras and the Human Sciences.* Bern: Peter Lang.

Sullivan, Lawrence E. 1986. "Sound and Senses: Toward a Hermeneutics of Performance." *History of Religions* 26 (1).

Tambiah, Stanley J. 1979. "A Performative Approach to Ritual." *Proceedings of the British Academy*

65. Reprinted in *Culture, Thought, and Social Action: An Anthropological Perspective.* Cambridge: Cambridge University Press, 1985.

Turner, Victor. 1969. *The Ritual Process: Structure and Anti-Structure.* Ithaca, N.Y.: Cornell University Press.

———. 1974. *Drama, Fields, and Metaphors: Symbolic Action in Human Society.* Ithaca, N.Y.: Cornell University Press.

———. 1982. *From Ritual to Theater: The Human Seriousness of Play.* New York: Performing Arts Journal Publications.

———. 1983. "Body, Brain, and Culture." *Zygon* 18 (3).

———. 1987. *The Anthropology of Performance.* New York: Performing Arts Journal Publications.

———. 1990. "Are There Universals of Performance in Myth, Ritual, and Drama?" In *By Means of Performance: Intercultural Studies of Theater and Ritual,* edited by Richard Schechner and Willa Appel. Cambridge: Cambridge University Press.

Ward, Barbara E. 1979. "Not Merely Players: Drama, Art, and Ritual in Traditional China." *Man* 14 (1).

Watson, Burton, trans. 1963. *Hsün Tzu: Basic Writings.* New York: Columbia University Press.

Weller, Robert P. 1987. *Unities and Diversities in Chinese Religion.* Seattle: University of Washington Press.

Wolf, Arthur P. 1974. "Gods, Ghosts, and Ancestors." In *Religion and Ritual in Chinese Society.* Stanford: Stanford University Press.

———. 1976. "Aspects of Ancestor Worship in Northern Taiwan." In *Ancestors,* edited by William H. Newell. The Hague: Mouton.

TWELVE

Person

Charles E. Winquist

Toute métaphysique est à la première personne du singulier. Toute poésie aussi.

—Louis Aragon

The word or concept "person" in ordinary usage is familiar and unambiguous because of its close association with the indexical presence of the word "I." We think we know what we mean when we say *I* and that this *I* is a *person,* which, in turn, gives a substantial meaning to the word "person." There is in the study of religion, because of this certitude of a substantial meaning, a sense that if we talk of the person, persons, or people that our study is concrete and real in a way that theoretical reflection is not. This naïveté or nostalgic positivism is, of course, a choice to be forgetful of the etymology of the word and genealogy of the concept person and its complexification through notions of self and subjectivity.

The word "person" is derived from the Latin *persona,* "mask," which many scholars think is from *personare,* "to sound through." The long *o,* however, creates some difficulties in this derivation (see the Oxford English Dictionary, s.v. "person"). When the concept of person is thought of in relation to the etymology of the word, it carries associations of both masking and sounding through. The person is not a simple I. Grammatical simplicity is pressured by an ontological complexity in the antique understanding of person.

It is a commonplace in scholarship to recognize that words, ideas, or concepts are embedded in historical and cultural settings and cannot be isolated or abstracted without being misplaced, or translated without accounting for the transformation of or difference in the cultural milieu into which the word is rendered or onto which it is inscribed. It is especially important to keep the problematic issue of cultural translation in mind when a word is as important and as familiar as person. What is particularly difficult is that important words, words that orient thinking, can function differently and take on different meanings when there is an epochal shift within a culture of what is meant by intelligibility and reality. In the Western philosophical tradition, the shifts in dominance from philosophies of being to philosophies of consciousness to philosophies of language correspond to such epochal shifts that entail transformations of the meaning of meaning itself. The referentiality and materiality of meaning are differently located such that the ability to think intelligibly about the person, the self or the I of experience, is significantly altered. As we explore the history of Western philosophy, it is ambiguous whether the person or self is rooted in the "I think," is

225

rooted in the "I" that is thought, or involves some combination of the two. Is it a notion of being, consciousness, or language that makes intelligible the experience of reality? These are not, of course, exclusive options in thinking but can be characterized as dominances and alternatives in any particular grammar of assent. When do we say "yes, I understand" or "yes, I know"? It is especially important in the study of religion to know that the yes I pronounce in the late twentieth century may not be the same yes that was spoken in the first century. This, however, does not preclude the possibility that a twentieth-century yes could correspond to a first-century yes.

In the christological and trinitarian controversies during the third to fifth centuries of Christian theological thinking, the intertwining of the questions of person and being is expressed in extremis and provides an important contrast with thinking on questions of personal identity in later periods dominated by philosophies of consciousness and language. In this early period of Christian theology, the two themes of masking and sounding through are thought of in the context of the central affirmation of the Incarnation. The formulas for understanding personhood are explicitly theological and only secondarily psychological. Theologically, the essential meaning of person is in its application to the three hypostases of the Trinity. In the third century, Tertullian claimed that the Father, the Son, and the Holy Ghost were three personae of one and the same substance. Since Jesus as the Christ, God incarnate, is fully human and fully divine, there is within history the realized possibility of the *ecstasis* of the person with the oneness of the Logos. The self-communication of God in the Trinity must be proper to God as the absolutely unoriginate origin of the plenitude of being itself. In the personae of the Trinity, this being is communicated and yet undiminished. What *sounds through* the trinitarian personae is the Logos of being.

If the trinitarian formulation is paradigmatic of communicative salvation, it also appears that the authentication of the person is in the transcendence of finitude, through the union with God, the original plenitude of being. The finite person, in other words, is not a self-sufficient reality. The person is the persona, mask, or hypostasis of a reality that sounds through it.

It may be an oversimplification but not inaccurate to say that the person of philosophies of being is a metaphysical I. It is a notion that is incomplete in itself. The recognition of its completeness is always elsewhere in a realm of essences or in the purity of being or in the presence of being.

The *person* of Western antiquity and the middle ages was profoundly different from the *self* of philosophies of consciousness that emerged in the Reformation and in the Age of Reason. Although less specifically philosophical than their predecessors and successors, the reformers shifted the authorization of Christian experience from an institutional base to the experience of the individual. Reformation themes such as *sola scriptura, sola fides, sola gratia,* and the priesthood of all believers theologically enfranchised a concept of an experienced self that is consciously reflexive. In the Reformation, what was reflected in this reflexivity was not simply the consciousness of consciousness but the consciousness of guilt. Luther and Calvin brought consciousness to a mindfulness of freedom but also to a recognition of human misery. Paradoxically, the Reformation enfranchised the concept of the self by putting the self into question. Calvin's *Institutes of the Christian Religion* (1960, pub. 1559) begins by explicitly claiming that there is no knowledge of God or self unless there is a knowledge of both. To look upon oneself is to turn thinking into a contemplation of God, and it is the knowledge of God that convinces us of our "unrighteousness, foulness, folly, and impurity" (37). The Reformation valued the concept of the self in a soteriological problematic. With the Age of Reason, the self came to be understood primarily within an epistemological problematic.

There is no one event or thinker that can be definitively identified with an epochal epistemic shift in a culture. However, it is convenient to read Descartes's *Meditations on the First Philosophy* (1960, pub. 1641) as synechdochically emblematic of the epistemic shift initiating the Age of Reason. The heuristic use of radical doubt to clear away any uncertainties was, as Descartes suggested, a removal from below of the foundation of the whole edifice of thinking and believing. This deracination meant that thinking had no recourse to notions of being other than itself or to those given within itself. What Descartes discovered is that when thinking is radical enough in the employment of methodical doubt, it can suspend judgment on all existence and any specific formulations of being. The philosophy of being is bracketed in and by the darkness of doubt. In its awakening, doubt suppresses the appeal of the self beyond itself.

Within this framework, the point of reference for the determination of meaning is consciousness, the I *thinking* rather than *being*. Being is methodologically subordinate to consciousness when thinking incorporates its capacity for radical doubting. This doubting, which is a thinking, is also a consciousness of thinking. Descartes can affirm that he is not nothing because he is conscious of being something in and through the very act of consciousness itself. The "proposition I am, I exist, is necessarily true each time it is expressed by me, or conceived in my mind" (1960, 79). *I think* and *I am* are affirmed together. Since being is not known as independent of thinking, it is known in the being of the self. The being of the self is known as subjectivity. Accordingly, the problem of the person is the problem of the *subject*. Even the metaphysical I is now thought in the first person singular.

The importance of this shift can be thought of as the transmogrification of transcendent concepts of philosophies of being into transcendental concepts in the development of Enlightenment philosophies of consciousness. This move might be conceived of as a disfiguration, for all thinking has to think and justify itself on a plane of immanence. Transcendence is reinscribed as a formulation of immanence. Numerous formulations of minimal units of intelligibility were made during the Enlightenment that are restricted to a plane of immanence.

Locke's *idea* was such a minimal and aporetic formulation that we cannot get behind or beyond it. Berkeley further radicalized a rational empirical vision when he proclaimed that experience will only allow us to affirm that *esse* is *percipi*. Essence is bound to immanence of perception. There is no justification for talk about a concrete realm of essences or concrete realm of things independent of experience. This is an epistemological constraint that recognizes subjectivity as the arbiter of meaning and not an ontological constraint. This epistemological shift leaves no justification for talk of a pure subjectivity. This was made clear in Descartes's third *Meditation* and was further developed and problematized by Hume and Kant. Kant's *Critique of Pure Reason* (pub. 1781, rev. 1787) is as emblematic of the close of the Enlightenment project as Descartes's *Meditations* is emblematic of the opening of the Age of Reason. The notion of a pure subjectivity is immediately compromised by the quality and range of subjective experience and by the interrogation of the conditions that make subjective consciousness possible.

The impurity of the self noted by the Reformers in a quest for salvation was noted by Enlightenment philosophers in a quest for knowledge. Consciousness can be reflexive but its reflexivity is an aftereffect. Consciousness is conscious of something before it can be conscious of itself. Thinking is implicated in an otherness that is constitutive of its presentment. The status of concepts of otherness in the processes of thinking is not immediately self-evident. In the mediated reality of thinking, it is not clear whether the experience of otherness is an experience of what is transcendent of the self or is an experience of what is transcendental to consciousness.

A problem to be recognized is that the beginning of an epistemological interrogation is not a pure beginning but is a beginning in a middle. Techniques like Descartes's radical doubt can only simulate a pure beginning. Descartes only works toward a beginning as he ends his first evening of meditation. In most cases, a radical bracketing or suspension of judgment is actually a methodological sleight-of-hand rather than a suspension of belief. The *cogito* of Descartes's second night of meditation acknowledges that we never really stop thinking the "I think."

Saying the "I" of "I think" appears to be a habit (an insight of David Hume). There are tendencies of mind that repeat themselves and have formed habits that we know as subjectivity. We say "I" in the ordinariness or vulgarity of consciousness before consciousness is able to fold on itself and think of itself as a subject. We are always already in language and are always already in the habit of subjectivity before constructing a notion of the self as subjectivity. Hume's investigation of the laws of association on which we base complex ideas does not yield an immediate experience of a *necessary connection* in a nexus of a subjective and objective world. It is repetition and the constant conjunction of saying the "I" with phenomenal presentation of experience that give force and vivacity to a probable assertion that there is an "I" that thinks a world. The Humean world is an immanent world of surface effects whose foldings constitute the objective subject.

Kant's transcendental questioning of the conditions that make knowledge of an object possible is not an unreasonable step beyond Hume's modest notion of a habit of subjectivity. Kantian idealism, like Berkeleyan idealism, is first of all a radical empiricism. The emergent concept of self is a qualification of empiricism. The importance of this observation emerges when it is recognized that the self is unavoidably implicated in an alterity. Thus, alterity will be immanently experienced rather than transcendentally augmented as philosophers of being insist. When the constitution of identity is thought through categories that are transcendental and hence transcendent and inaccessible in any directly objective way, there is transformation in the notion of the person-self and its complex relationship with otherness. Transcendence in thinking does not guarantee a relationship to any transcendent reality. Kant's active faculties of thought, imagination, understanding, and reason most importantly reference the *processes* of thinking and thereby compromise the meaning of external referentiality.

Transcendental inquiry in an empirical frame develops a formal aesthetic that reveals the constructedness or phenomenality of the world and the constructedness of the subject in the knowing of the world. Just as there is no easy access to a world of things-in-themselves, there is no easy access to a pure subjectivity behind the identity of a person. The notions of a pure and true world or pure and true self are suspended in the suspicion that the processes constitutive of the phenomenality of experience are themselves complex and impure. Experiential intuition is compromised by the formal conditions of its possibility, and the transcendental unity of apperception is conditioned by the heterology of forces and things known a posteriori, although it contributes to the constitution of this unity. The transcendental unity of apperception is not a substance but a ghostly substrata known only in the aftereffects of thinking. We are able to exercise the habit of saying "I" and "I think" even when what is thought is diverse and fragmented. The subject experienced in the transcendental unity of apperception, which is itself an effect of a differential series of active formal processes, can then be asserted as the basic meaning of the person in an epistemological construct.

This self or person of pure reason was certainly not satisfying to Kant. There is a legitimate and illegitimate employment of the active faculties and what is clear is that only phenomena can be subject to the faculties of knowledge. The dreams of the imagination, the transcendental employment of understanding to things-in-themselves, and the speculative illusions of reason all neglect the limits of thinking revealed in his critique. The subject can be known as object only in the phenomenality of experience. Kant sought to resolve the attenuation of the meaning of the self and the inaccessibility of the thing-in-itself in pure reason by turning to practical reason.

Reason has a practical as well as a speculative interest. As a thing-in-itself and not an object understood, the self can be thought of as spontaneous and free. Reason can legislate the faculty of desire, which is an act of the will. That is, the faculty of desire finds its determination in itself as will and not as an object or content of thought. When pure practical reason is uncontaminated by sensible interest, it can direct the will to think a logical absolute, defining a moral action as an action whose maxim can be conceived without contradiction. The moral law is a pure form of universal legislation; it is reason in its extreme accomplishment. The freedom that can will a categorical imperative is legislative and not sensible. This freedom of the will is a thing-in-itself, *being* a thing-in-itself instead of being reduced to a *knowing* of a thing-in-itself.

The relationship between pure and practical reason is always problematic, and in some ways reinscribes the problem of the *Critique of Pure Reason* by separating suprasensible nature from sensible nature, the noumenal from the phenomenal worlds. Kant wants to fill the abyss separating these worlds. He thought the suprasensible will could influence the sensible world. The suprasensible world must have sensible effects. The moral law would be empty and collapse if there were no conditions by which the faculty of desire could legislate over objects. Kant does not and perhaps cannot establish an objective accord between the faculties of knowledge and desire. It is almost as if he believes in the efficacy of the reason of will in the sensible world, which is not knowable to the reason of understanding in the sensible world. In an odd way the suprasensible is the unknowable substratum of the sensible, a reality that can only be felt. In that it forces one to think, feeling is an intuition for which no concept is adequate. The Kantian person-self is not less than rational but more than rational. The faculties of the self are known representationally as knowing, desiring, and feeling. Their accord is their discord in as much as they complement each other by pointing to an otherness that is profoundly manifest in their differences. They jointly refute the fullness of the phenomenality of the world.

There is always something other about the self when it is interrogated transcendentally, and this opened a door to suspicions and problems deeper than Kant even thought. Kant gave articulate expression to what Calvin called the fallibility of thinking; but Calvin also wrote of the perversity of the intellect that, in the wake of Kant, was given diverse and perplexing expression by Marx, Nietzsche, and Freud. Illusion can be more than error or the illegitimate use of reason. It can be cunning distortion arising out of the ideologies of class interests, the weakness of resentment, or the vagaries of desire.

The hermeneutics of suspicion announces a new sensibility that alters what we can mean by a *person*. The problematics of representation identified with the shift from philosophies of being to philosophies of consciousness certainly are not resolved by a new shift to philosophies of language but instead are comingled with a problematics of communication. Representation is complicated by the recognition of the materiality of its expression. What we learned from Kant is that objective knowledge is not intuitively immediate, and what we learned from

Marx, Nietzsche, and Freud is that many of the mediating conditions for the expression of knowledge are not disinterested elements or parts of a neutral substratum. Thinking is marked on a plane of immanence that is not a tabula rasa. The self of the Enlightenment lost its innocence in the nineteenth century.

It appears that the infrastructure of consciousness is heterological and is not composed of pure a priori forms. Kant's critical philosophy could never come to a simple closure. The notions of *subject* and *person* associated with the bedrock of the *I think* are too often paralogistic arguments confusing a substantial identity with processes of subjectivity. His own notion of the sublime was a notion of experience that involved more than the understanding, a notion of an intuition to which no concept is adequate. The formal determinations of the a priori are not adequate to the experience of the sublime and perhaps not adequate for a broad range of experiences. The inability to achieve closure anywhere in the experience of consciousness opens a very large door to other complexifications of experience. It is at least possible, and even probable after the critiques of Marx, Nietzsche, and Freud, that there are if not other transcendental structures at least quasi-transcendental structures that suggest that illusion is less benign than error.

Kant, using the criteria of apodictic certainty and universality to identify and understand the a priori structures and procedures of thinking, curiously and perhaps unwittingly undid the confidence and sense of certainty that characterize the spirit of the Enlightenment. By deracinating and regulating reason, he became a direct benefactor to the nineteenth-century hermeneutics of suspicion. The Kantian problematic separating representation and referentiality was reinscribed in the troubled awareness of the philosophies of language.

The Nietzschean understanding of all philosophy as interpretation and truth as metaphorical, followed by the positivist inability to reduce language usage to the univocity of a perfect dictionary, heralded the coming of a new sensibility sometimes now characterized as postmodern. The move to philosophies of language became a move to a culture of signs or simulacra. According to Paul Ricoeur, "for Marx, Nietzsche and Freud, the fundamental category of consciousness is the relation hidden-shown or, if you prefer, simulated-manifested" (1970, 33). This binary tension was not resolved by the reduced empiricism or refined logic of positivist sensibilities. Incompleteness, undecidability, indeterminancy, contingency, relativity, and the overdetermination of meaning are terms that can be more easily indexed to the reflexivity of consciousness thinking about its use of language in language than can clarity, distinctness, and univocity. From a traditional perspective, postmodernism speaks a language of *irrevocable loss* and *incurable fault* (Taylor 1984, 6). Mark C. Taylor further extends these characteristics of postmodernism by thematically amplifying the noted rift in thinking and saying that a postmodern a/theological agenda must address (1) the death of God, (2) the disappearance of the self, (3) the end of history, and (4) the closure of the book (19–97). These themes implicate each other, and anyone of them can be a starting point for assessing the epochal shift that is the shift to philosophies of language or, more generally, postmodernism.

It is the disappearance of the self that is most immediately related to our *subject*, person. More precisely, it is the definition of self as *subjectivity* that is obscured by the notion of the disappearance of the self. The problem is that the person as a self is dispersed and disseminated over a range of experience that is subsumable under the transcendental unity of apperception. There are experiences that mark discontinuities or ruptures in our thinking in which the ruptures can be thought as wounds but not thought in themselves. I can think about there being a fissure, but I do not think the fissure itself. What is present to consciousness is an absence or a deformation such that what is present is in fact absent. The subject is subjected to what it is not and does not control.

The assault on the adequacy of modern conceptions of the self can be seen as a minimum Nietzschean thematic; but, it was with the development of psychoanalysis by Freud that these themes entered the mainstream of culture. It is Freud who brought a not fully assimilable *it* to the thinking of the self that thickly overdetermined the meaning of self or person for the twentieth century. The Marxist critique is probably too much compromised by the political need for a scientific materialism for a clear sense of the epistemological and linguistic dilemma of a postmodern sensibility.

Although there is very little in the Freudian corpus to suggest that he thought he was addressing an epistemological problem in philosophical language, he reinscribed the Kantian critique with guile and cunning. The Freudian subject constructs a world and a self without innocence. It is not the self of pure practical reason that is enunciated in the faculty of desire. It is, instead, the polymorphously perverse child of the body that pressures the formation of ego consciousness in diverse and sometimes distorted representational schemes that have to be accounted for in the presentment of the world and the self.

The displaced subject of postmodernism in philosophies of language involves a reversal of Enlightenment notions of referentiality that is as radical as the moves that gave primacy to the self as subjectivity from Descartes to Kant. The "I think" of the cogito is not an adequate container for the increasingly complex "I am" that emerges from the legacy of the nineteenth-century hermeneutics of suspicion. The dependence of rationality for a linguistic exfoliation in its expression subjects the subject to all of the ambiguities of language in its primary metaphoricity and in its overdetermination in a venue that is not always or fully conscious. There is no return to a singular concept of being or any univocal understanding of language subordinate to a notion of being. Instead, the subject is disseminated beyond itself in realities that are not under its control even though the primary reference of experience remains in the notion of the self as subject. The postmodern person is an amalgam of the person of philosophies of being and philosophies of consciousness without either the transcendent unity of being or the transcendental unity of apperception in consciousness.

Who is this person? It is not the person of psychoanalytic adaptations to ego psychology or object relations theory. It now appears that Freud's work was more important in marking a cultural epistemic shift than in providing a viable psychotherapeutic model for the twentieth century. The various attempts to present psychoanalysis as a science have too often obscured Freud's troubling discovery or construction of a notion of a dynamic unconscious implicating the experience of the person in both primary and secondary processes of thinking. The identity of the self as subjectivity is now only part of the human story. Since Nietzsche and Marx it is obvious that there are social and linguistic formations that are known subjectively but do not derive from subjectivity. However, with Freud there is a psychological urgency to recognizing that there are processes contributing to the being there of the self, processes that are other than those of subjective consciousness. From as early as Freud's "Project" of 1895, there has been a recognition of what Ricoeur calls a nonhermeneutic state of the system (1970, 69). Freud's first topography of systems, conscious/preconscious and unconscious, introduces relations of force or an energetics that marks discourses of meaning that are not identical with the representation of meanings. The questions of meaning and force collide or coincide in the psychic representation of force. A biological reality is thought in the language of psychic reality. What goes on in the primary work that brings a drive to differential psychic representation is known not in itself but only as a trace, aftereffect, or symptom in the secondariness of conscious thinking. The forces that Freud introduces into the equation of becoming conscious are not the procedural actions of the schematism for the universal or necessary formal conditions or considerations introduced by Kant and knowable through a transcendental critique. The paradigm for interpretation that Freud thought would usher in the twentieth century was not an explicitly epistemological critique but was instead his self-analysis articulated in *The Interpretation of Dreams*. Formal considerations are only a part of the model introduced by Freud.

Freud inserts formulations of thinking about thinking in the darkness of desire. The dream is a "royal road" into the unconscious because in the dream the stratagems of desire are writ large and are at least analogically exemplary of the formation of culture, including religion. It is not so much the dream but the "dream-work" that complicates or deepens the epistemological crises of postmodernism. The separations of the phenomenality of experience are complicated beyond the demand to account for the formalization of spatial and temporal determinations by the possibility of disguise. There are psychological as well as transcendental illusions. The "dream-work" adds to the Kantian problematic of considerations of representability the possibilities of displacement, condensation, and secondary revision as procedures for making manifest a content to be known. The "dream-work" is an architectonic elaboration of what we know as a language of desire. In Freud, "The entire drama of dreams is . . . generalized to the dimensions of a universal poetics. . . . [A]rt, morality and religion are analogous figures or variants of the oneiric mask" (Ricoeur 1970, 162).

Psychoanalysis may be thought of as an epistemology of the darkness of desire, which transforms the hermeneutics of culture in general and the assessment of the person within culture in particular. It is the organic complex of the person that always makes the idealization of meaning in consciousness suspect. The force of desire is not so much a problem of valuation within conscious deliberation as it is a problem because of its inaccessibility and its inassessability in conditioning the presentations that come to consciousness. Some of the work of desire is already done by the time we have the privileged moments of consciousness. Consciousness, therefore, cannot tell the tale of its origination. Nor can it immediately witness to the forces of desire in its own originating meaning. The meaning that consciousness knows is a deferred meaning. Its presentment is secondary.

A complicating factor in assessing the importance of Freud's understanding for a twentieth-century conception of *person* or *self* is that the cultural implications of his basic insights were too dark or nihilistic for those who followed in the wake of his thinking. *Civilization and Its Discontents* is uncompromising in maintaining a tension in the middle of any human pursuit of happiness. The Freudian promise of transforming "hysterical misery into common unhappiness" is not a sufficient palliative for many people.

The goal of a well-adjusted personality became a therapeutic desideratum, allied with demands of the ego, that was sometimes forgetful of the importance of Freud's emphasis on the *it* of the unconscious (*es* is translated as "id" in common practice but "it" is closer to Freud's meaning). In its rejection of the abjection of the real, psychoanalytic thinking became increasingly and curiously forgetful of Freud. What has been forgotten, we might now say, is what was most postmodern and theological about Freud in his challenge to the completeness and adequacy of a refined modern philosophical notion of a pure subject and its capacities for intuition, understanding, and reason.

The return to Freud is a theme that is most notable in French discussions of psychoanalysis and is particularly associated with the work of Jacques Lacan. His understanding of the subversion of the subject, or what we have earlier called "the disappearance of the self," is a recognition of originary wounds where Freud marked the *it* of the unconscious. Lacan returns to that which in Freud's understanding of the unconscious is inassimilable in consciousness. However, Lacan does not make a simple return to Freud. Rather, he uses the linguistic theory of Saussure and poststructuralist philosophical theory for an interpretation that he understands as a return to Freud. In one of his most remarkable formulations, Lacan claims that the Freudian "unconscious is structured like a language" (1978, 20). With this suggestion, the importance of psychoanalysis is immediately extended into discussions of language, discourse theory, textuality, and text production. Psychoanalysis is interpreted "postmodernly," thereby giving its character to what is meant by postmodern discourse.

Lacan's words are not Freud's words in some very important ways. Freud's two topographies, first the systems preconscious/conscious and unconscious and later the id, ego, and superego, are replaced or subordinated to a topography of orders of the real, the imaginary, and the symbolic. The real includes the unconscious or "the order of the unrealized." The infantile dynamic focuses especially on a "mirror stage" that ironically is a specific refutation of the ideal of thinking being a mirror of nature. During the mirror stage, sometime in the interval of infancy between six and eighteen months, the reflected image of the whole body is substituted for the "I," which was primordially precipitated in the autoerotic relationship to the partial objects of the fragmented body. The image of the I is separated from the subjective primacy of perception of the fragmented body. The *I-image* can only be indexed on an imaginary register. What is lost is the body and with it the intentional molecular multiplicity of the subject.

In Lacan's understanding, there is no simple epistemological or psychological access to the order of the real. There is no thinking that can contain the real. The imaginary "I" is a substitution for the "I" that is disseminated throughout the polymorphously erotic body of infancy and constitutes a fundamental loss of the real. The body of the imaginary "I" is a body without organs. That is, the body of the imaginary "I" is a body that is not an organism. For these reasons, there is, Jane Gallop notes, an implicit imperative in Lacan's writings "to break the mirror, an imperative to disrupt the imaginary in order to reach the symbolic" (1985, 59). The symbolic order is an order of discourse in which we move from imaginary wholes to a differential sign system. The differential play in the symbolic order is closely akin to what Saussure described as the determination of meaning in the interrelationship and play of differences between signifiers. Lacan accepts Saussure's distinction between signifiers and the signified but emphasizes the bar separating the signifiers from the signified. The signified is absent in the present play of signifiers, and thus there is no mimetic reference to the real. The bar in the Saussurian algorithm is for Lacan an *aporia,* so that identity is absolutely only in difference.

As Freud clearly stated, we can only know the unconscious as it manifests itself in consciousness. For Lacan this occurs in the symbolic order. But, since the unconscious is what is unthought in thinking, it can manifest itself in the symbolic order only through lacuna, fissures, gaps, and deformations. The unconscious inscribes a lack in the symbolic order. It manifests itself in language but is both anticonceptual and unassimilable. In this way it is the other of language in language.

The immediate problem for the study of religion implied by this line of analysis is that this is not an other that can be thought. The concept of the "person" is implicated in an other that is not the other that is thought theologically in articulations instantiating the negativity of the *wholly other* for consciousness or in the more ethnological thinking about the others of different cultures. Lacan's unthinkable other is the other of the *work* of the imagination, which functions analogously to Freud's dream-work, bringing things (experiences) into consciousness and making it possible to think them in consciousness through the differential possibilities of discursive formations. This is how we know what we do not know in the phenomenality of mind. Lacanian alterity implies an ignorance that echoes in the insistent question, "Who is speaking?" Not knowing how to answer the question "Who is speaking?" with any confidence—since thinking and speaking have become such a complex affair as we pass through philosophies of being to philosophies of consciousness to philosophies of language—is a problem if we are trying to understand ourselves or understand someone else.

While the notion of "person" is obviously an existential and psychological issue, it also poses a methodological problem for thinking theologically and for the study of religion. Who is speaking or writing in theological text production? Who is speaking or writing in studies of religion in which there is also the question of the identities of voices of witnesses within the traditions being studied?

These questions do not imply a *simple* loss of the subject or disappearance of the self. There are ideas that are thought, there are books that are written, and there are feelings that are felt. The "I" is complex and may be displaced in its complexification, but there is still an existential or felt significance in being able to say "I think" or "I feel." We can still say "I think" even when we ask "Who is speaking?" What is lost or displaced is the notion of a pure subject as the referential correlative of the "I think." The "I think" of the cogito has always been impure because it has always been implicated in the complexity of the "I am." In a simple formulation, the Cartesian subject is compromised by Gertrude Stein's "I am I because my little dog knows me." Being complicates thinking and little dogs complicate being.

The ancient themes of "masking and sounding through" associated with the notion of the persona are reinscribed in the contemporary moment with added ambiguities or difficulties in the concepts or notions of "self," "subject," "person," or "I." The mask is not singular but is the all pervasive culture of the simulacra elaborated by Nietzsche, in the tropic transformation of all discourse, and deeply psychologized by Freud, in the elaboration of the dream-work as constitutive processes in the making of all culture. What sounds through is not a clarion call of being to being but a cacophony of voices including all the little things and little histories marked by diverse interests and the vagaries of desire.

As we go forward in trying to understand culture and religion, the notion or concept of the person is not simply a problem or solution to the difficulties of problems in thinking about culture. The "I think" insists on its importance in any equations of thought that formulate orientations to reality. At the same time the "I am" insists on its presence and complexity within these same equations. Cultural and religious studies have to define themselves within the tension of this double insistence.

There are some obvious pragmatic responses to this recognition. Kant, through the power of his own criticisms, saw that in their highest expressions there was a discord among the faculties of knowing, desiring, and feeling. The practical question is whether there can be an accord in the midst of this discord. Can there be a complementarity of thinking strategies or heuristic arrangements that access the diverse empiricities that complicate the definition of the person?

The cathartic power of radical postmodern criticism in writing unreadable texts, forcing recognition of the opaque materiality of texts, or giving a carnival-esque crazing to the surface of thinking in the valuation of an errant thinking all contribute to a style of noncontainment of thinking without silencing its voice. Thinking instantiates an experience of the person even when it is not the pure thinking of philosophies of consciousness or even when it is not a response to the call of being with or without angelic and other complicated mediators in philosophies of being.

The genealogical legacy of the concept of person means that thinking cannot exclusively fixate its interrogation on either the importance of *masking* or *sounding through* without trivializing its own capacities. It would be a mistake to con-struct a margin of safety by too narrowly defining the parameters of what think-ing cannot think, just as it would be a mistake to let thinking uncritically ignore its finite limitations.

Who is speaking? In the philosophies of being, this was most commonly a theological question with psychological shadows. In the philosophies of con-sciousness, this was most commonly an epistemological question that cast shad-ows internal to its own interrogations, always threatening the containing power of its self-imposed boundaries. In the philosophies of language, this is most commonly a linguistic and psychological question with unrecognized theologi-cal shadows.

The concept of person with all of its limitations and complications enfran-chises a theological exigency in thinking. The concept of person implicates phi-losophies of being, consciousness, and language in soteriological questions even when they modestly prescind from these questions. It is a concept that has a history of not being contained. It insinuates itself on the other side of any pro-visionally defined boundaries and is itself the explicit or shadowed presence of the theological question of what makes a life significant. The continual presence of this concept is the richness of a trace of the other in and of any discipline of language.

Suggested Readings

Deleuze, Gilles. 1983. *Nietzsche and Philosophy.*
Gallop, Jane. 1985. *Reading Lacan.*
Gellner, Ernest. 1985. *The Psychoanalytic Movement: The Cunning of Unreason.*
Habermas, Jürgen. 1992. *Postmetaphysical Thinking: Philosophical Essays.*
Haar, Michel. 1996. *Nietzsche and Metaphysics.*
Lacan, Jacques. 1977. *Ecrits: A Selection.*
Ricoeur, Paul. 1970. *Freud and Philosophy.*

Taylor, Mark C. 1984. *Erring: A Postmodern A/theology.*
Wyschogrod, Edith; D. Crownfield; and C. Raschke, eds. 1989. *Lacan and Theological Discourse.*

REFERENCES

Calvin, Jean. 1960. *Institutes of the Christian Religion,* translated by Ford Lewis Battles. Philadelphia: Westminster Press.

Descartes, René. 1960. *"Discourse on Method" and "Meditations,"* translated by Laurence J. Lafleur. Indianapolis: Liberal Arts Press.

Gallop, Jane. 1985. *Reading Lacan.* Ithaca, N.Y.: Cornell University Press.

Kant, Immanuel. 1965. *Critique of Pure Reason,* translated by Norman Kemp Smith. New York: St. Martins Press.

Lacan, Jacques. 1978. *The Four Fundamental Concepts of Psycho-Analysis,* translated by Alan Sheridan. New York: W. W. Norton and Co.

Ricoeur, Paul. 1970. *Freud and Philosophy: An Essay on Interpretation,* translated by Denis Savage. New Haven: Yale University Press.

Taylor, Mark C. 1984. *Erring: A Postmodern A/theology.* Chicago: University of Chicago Press.

THIRTEEN

Rationality

Paul Stoller

I n December of 1979 I set out for the town of Wanzerbe in the western
region of the Republic of Niger. For centuries Wanzerbe-le-magique, as the
French filmmaker and anthropologist Jean Rouch once called it, had been
a village widely known throughout West Africa for its sorcerers. Indeed, the
seemingly inexplicable feats of Wanzerbe sorcerers had long triggered great
fear—and respect—in the hearts and minds of Nigeriens. In a decidedly patriarchal society, it was perhaps ironic that the most powerful sorcerer in this fabled
city was Kassey, a diminutive grandmother. People warned me not to seek out
Kassey. "She can transform herself into a vulture," they told me. "She can maim
or kill you," they cautioned, "by reciting a few verses." "She'll make you disappear if she doesn't like you."

Despite these warnings, I went on to Wanzerbe, and sought out the illustrious
woman. Having heard through the grapevine of my imminent arrival, Kassey left
town. Dejected at Kassey's refusal to meet with me, I wondered what to do.
People suggested that I see Dunguri, also a woman, who was Kassey's powerful
associate. And so I did.

Even when material conditions are dire, the Songhay people have a tradition
of great generosity. But Dunguri's rudeness during my visit shocked me and
my Wanzerbe host. Our meeting was an abject failure. And so I returned to my
host's house, ate dinner, and went to bed.

In the middle of the night I awoke to the tattoo of steps on the roof and
became aware of a presence in the room. Frightened, I wanted to bolt from the
house. I started to get up but could not move. I pinched my thighs and felt
nothing. And then I remembered what my teacher, Adamu Jenitongo, had told
me, "Whenever you feel danger, recite the *genji how*," the Songhay incantation
that by harmonizing the forces of the bush protects the person reciting it. And
so I recited it until I began to feel sensation in my feet and legs. In time, I rolled
off my mat and stood up. The presence I had sensed had left the room (Stoller
and Olkes 1987: 148). The next day I again went to confront Dunguri, for I
sensed her responsibility for the events of the previous night. Her smile came as
a surprise. She said, " 'Now I know you are a man with a pure heart.' She took
my left hand and placed it in hers. 'You are ready. Come into my house and we
shall begin to learn.' " (149).

This story from Niger, of course, begs the question of rationality, a problem
that has long been at the forefront of scholarly debate in anthropological, philosophical, and religious studies. Is it indeed possible for Kassey of Wanzerbe to
transform herself into a vulture, the familiar of Songhay sorcerers? Could she

actually maim or kill someone with her magical words, words so precious that they are passed from master to apprentice only at death? Could Kassey make a person disappear?

Many Songhay people, especially Kassey's neighbors in Wanzerbe, believe firmly in her sorcerous capacities. Given the checkered history of how and to whom rationality has been attributed, many people in Europe and North America might expect Songhay peasants in the Republic of Niger to harbor, to borrow a phrase from Dan Sperber (1985), "apparently irrational beliefs." Rationality, by contrast, has been a central component of Western analytical thought, meaning that scholars are usually expected to provide cogent and consistent rational explanations for sets of tangled and inconsistent irrational beliefs.

More disquieting, of course, are cases in which "rational" scholars report on "irrational" beliefs or events *as if* they are rational or real. What can one make of the events I described in Wanzerbe? Reports of Songhay beliefs about the magical power of words hardly raise an eyebrow. But what of my sensing a presence in a dusty and dark Wanzerbe room? What of my temporary paralysis? One reader of *In Sorcery's Shadow* (Stoller and Olkes 1987), who has never lived in Niger, explained the entire episode simply by suggesting that it was a compellingly vivid dream. Another reader suggested that the presence I felt resulted from a chemically induced hallucination. As of this writing no one has rationally accounted for Dunguri's overnight change of heart. Did she really send me "terror in the night"? These kinds of questions have long triggered debate among anthropologists and philosophers. What is important about them, however, is not the content of their specific answers, but how they challenge our thinking about rationality and why we find these challenges so unsettling.

In this essay I discuss three approaches to rationality: universalist, relativist, and phenomenological. While the universalists attempt to evaluate beliefs through a set of logical criteria free of local context, the relativists concentrate on differences to the exclusion of common connections. The phenomenological approach, which I have used in my own work, creates space for multiple realities in a given belief system; it attempts to circumvent the logical conundrums of the interminable debates waged between the universalists and relativists. After sketching the development of and analyzing the three scholarly approaches to rationality, I conclude that in the future the phenomenological approach might lead us to more embodied rationalities that are intellectually and personally transformative.

Historical Antecedents to Rationality

The concept of rationality lies at the core of the Western epistemology. The *Shorter Oxford Dictionary* not only defines it as "reasonableness," "acceptability to reason," "having reasoning power" but also as "the distinguishing character of man." The notion of rationality surfaced rather recently in the stream of European intellectual history. Although the concept of reason is the foundation of Enlightenment thinking, a term like "rationalism . . . was not christened till very late in the nineteenth century" (Tambiah 1994, 89).

Given this intellectual time line, early considerations of rationality constituted an extension of the nineteenth-century debate about human evolution. Indeed, unilineal evolutionism marks one of the major intellectual paradigms of the nineteenth century. Put simply, unilineal evolutionism is the idea that human society has progressed from a relatively primitive stage of savagery through more complex barbarism to nineteenth-century European civilization. Thinkers of this era wondered what factors—race or religion, for example—prompted the progression of some societies and the stagnation of others. Unilineal evolutionism shaped the thinking of Sir James Frazer; Lewis Henry Morgan; Sir Edward Tylor, the first professional anthropologist; and such Social Darwinists as Herbert Spencer. It also influenced the historical materialism of Marx. In one way or another these thinkers saw some fundamental connection between primitive and modern, past and present. Accordingly, they found antecedents of modern thinking in what they called primitive thought.

Not so Lucien Lévy-Bruhl, a French philosopher, who saw little evolutionary connection between the thinking, the rationality, if you will, of primitive and modern. In his earlier writings, Lévy-Bruhl "proposed the challenging thesis that the primitive mentality is not to be considered an earlier, or a rudimentary, or a pathological form of the modern civilized mentality, but as a manifesting of processes and procedures of thinking that were altogether different from the laws of modern logical rational scientific thought" (Tambiah 1994, 85). Lévy-Bruhl called this decidedly distinct set of thought processes "prelogical mentality," which he sometimes referred to as "mystical mentality." He criticized the arguments of Auguste Comte, Tylor, and Frazer that so-called primitive mentality was "irrational," suggesting instead that "prelogical mentalities" had their own distinct logical systems in which what he called the law of participation played a central role (see Tambiah 1994, 86–8). For Lévy-Bruhl the primitive fused into one mystic universe what Europeans would consider logically distinct. Put another way, in Lévy-Bruhl's scheme of primitive thought there is no distinction between science and religion. The key notion here is that in "primitive mentality" elements are linked exclusively through association, the kind of cognitive move that Foucault would one day call "resemblance," the central *epistēmē* of Renaissance thinking (see Foucault 1970).

Lévy-Bruhl's notion of a separate "primitive mentality," which could be used by some Social Darwinists as evidence for the intellectual inferiority of the non-white races, provoked much commentary, especially from E. E. Evans-Pritchard, whose monumental *Witchcraft, Oracles, and Magic Among the Azande* was to become the first—and perhaps the best—empirically grounded disputation on rationality. Lévy-Bruhl's critics argued for the psychic unity of human kind and against hermetically sealed notions of collective mentalities. They saw the distinct separation of the mystical and scientific as empirically fallacious. Evans-Pritchard argued that in their everyday lives, so-called primitives behaved empirically, especially to solve practical problems. By the same token, Europeans, he argued, often behaved in a manner that Lévy-Bruhl would call mystical.

To his credit, Lévy-Bruhl accepted many of these criticisms and in his last work, *Les Carnets de Lucien Lévy-Bruhl*, he reconsidered many of his ideas. Despite these changes, however, Lévy-Bruhl never gave up the Durkheimian notion of other mentalities based on separate collective representations—symbols, emblems, and objects that reinforced the recognition of a person's connection to a social whole. Although he accepted the premise of the psychic unity of human kind, Lévy-Bruhl still believed in the existence of diverse cultural logics distinct from our own thought. Western scholars, he argued, should not denigrate these other ways of fashioning a world. Lévy-Bruhl, then, was an early relativist.

Lévy-Bruhl's most vociferous critic, as previously mentioned, was Evans-Pritchard, whose chef d'oeuvre, the above-mentioned *Witchcraft, Oracles, and Magic Among the Azande,* first published in 1937, remains a primary resource for arguments about rationality that are still being debated today (see Evens 1996). Evans-Pritchard putatively adhered to a universalist epistemology, and yet a close reading of the work reveals a text that is laced with equivocations. Evans-Pritchard criticizes a Zande reasoning that is filled with contradictions, fundamental violations of the universal principles of symbolic logic, and then argues why and how sociocultural contexts reduce these logical flaws to insignificance. "Contradictions between their beliefs are not noticed by the Azande because the beliefs are not all present at the same time but function in different situations" (Evans-Pritchard 1937, 475). Put in more contemporary language Evans-Pritchard argued "that, in a sense, among the Azande a contradiction may not be a contradiction, because their beliefs are not primarily matters of theory but of practice" (Evens 1996, 30–1).

The equivocations continue as one probes deeper into Evans-Pritchard's analysis of the Zande poison oracle. Among the Azande, the oracle works in the following manner. A specialist poses a question to the poison oracle. He then administers a dose of poison to a chick. The chick's survival or death determines the affirmative or negative answer to the question posed. Based on his reading of Evans-Pritchard, Evens isolates five features of the oracle that according to him conform to a strict sense of Western rationality:

> 1) Azande test their oracle for reliability; 2) they do not ignore contradictions resulting from these tests, but rather seek to account for them; 3) in explaining them, they appeal to specific initial conditions that can deductively generate the explicandum; 4) these initial conditions do admit of independent testing; and 5) in arriving at their explanations, Azande appeal not only to initial conditions but also to universal laws or regularities. (1996, 32)

For all his efforts to describe a parallel system of belief that adhered to a universalist rationality, an effort that would establish respect for alternate epistemologies, Evans-Pritchard found Zande logic deficient. Despite his profound experiences among the Azande, Evans-Pritchard could not easily extricate himself from the universalist belief that there existed an ultimate reality, the truth of which could be established through scientific procedures and logical processes independent of context.

> It is an inevitable conclusion from Zande descriptions of witchcraft that it is not an objective reality. The physiological condition which is said to be the seat of witchcraft, and which I believe to be nothing more than food passing through the small intestine, is an objective condition, but the qualities they attribute to it and the rest of their beliefs about it are mystical. Witches, as Azande conceive them, cannot exist. (1937, 63)

Despite the firmness of Evans-Pritchard's beliefs about universal objective reality, one sees between the lines of his text how much the power and presence of Zande beliefs challenge and disturb him:

> I have only once seen witchcraft on its path. I had been sitting late in my hut writing notes. About midnight, before retiring, I took a spear and went for my usual nocturnal stroll. I was walking in the garden at the back of my hut, amongst banana trees, when I noticed a bright light passing at the back of my servants' hut towards the homestead of a man called Tupoi. As this seemed worth investigating I followed its passage until a grass screen obscured the view. I ran quickly through my hut to the other side in order to see where the light was going to, but did not regain sight of it. I knew that only one man, a member of my household, had a lamp that might have given off so bright a light, but the next morning he told me that he had neither been out late at night nor had he used his lamp. There did not lack ready informants to tell me that what I had seen was witchcraft. Shortly afterwards, on the same morning, an old relative of Tupoi and an inmate of his homestead died. This event *fully* explained the light I had seen. I never discovered its *real* origin, which was possibly a handful of grass lit by someone on his way to defecate, but the coincidence of the direction along which the light moved and the subsequent death accorded well with Zande idea. (1976, 11, emphasis added)

Nothing in Evans-Pritchard's analysis logically explains what he saw that night. These anomalies haunt Evans-Pritchard's text and compromise his sense of universal rationality. Can one reconcile rationality with experience?

Universalist Rationality

Scholars who take a universalist position on rationality are less equivocal than either Lévy-Bruhl or Evans-Pritchard. Many of them maintain an overriding passion to isolate Truth through the precision of language and logic. For them rationality has been a matter of the coherence and logical consistency of statements. Rational beliefs, for example, are those that would adhere to the universal rules of coherence and logical consistency.

> Logical inconsistency may seem the core of our concept of irratio-
> nality, because we think of the person who acts irrationally as having
> the wherewithal to formulate maxims of his action and objectives
> which are in contradiction with each other. (Taylor 1982, cited in
> Tambiah 1994, 117)

Viewed in this manner, it is clear that a universalist rationality is an extension of the intellectual hegemony of the Enlightenment project in which universally applied Reason is used to constitute authoritive knowledge.

Although there has been much agreement about the centrality of consistency to the constitution of universally rational statements and beliefs, there is divergence on three related issues about how rational thought might explain human behavior, how it might account for human choices:

1. Can rational intentionality explain social behavior?
2. Do individual predispositions affect rational choice?
3. Is rational choice free of social context?

The first two questions are fascinating but less germane to a discussion of rationality in anthropological and religious studies than the third question, which confronts the seemingly unending debate about relativism in the human sciences.

As already stated, the universalists, Tambiah (1994, 115–6) calls them "lumpers," believe in a singular rationality founded upon universal principles of logic that are universally applicable no matter the sociocultural context. Armed with these context-free rules, universalists believe they can make sense of any phenomenon they encounter. Further, using logical criteria, universalists attempt to measure the relative rationality/irrationality of a system of belief. Assessing evidence consisting of a set of statements about belief, they make judgments. In the end, universalists seek to transform the tangle of irrational beliefs into a coherent set of logical explanations.

Robin Horton, an anthropologist who has lived for many years in West Africa, takes a universalist position on rationality. Horton admits that African systems of thought are capable of what he calls cohesive "theoretical" thinking. He suggests that African traditional thought is rational. But, like the good universalist, he wonders if it is rational enough? "At this stage of the analysis there is no need for me to insist further on the essential rationality of traditional thought. I have already made it far too rational for the taste of most social anthropologists. And yet, there is a sense in which this thought includes among its accomplishments neither Logic or Philosophy" (1970, 159). For Horton, African systems of thought are sophisticated but closed, unable "to . . . formulate generalized norms of reasoning and knowing" (160). Horton's take on African thought is curiously similar to that of Evans-Pritchard. Both scholars applaud the previously overlooked sophistication of African thinking, but in the end, they maintain a universalist rationality in which they find African systems of thought logically and philosophically inferior.

Dan Sperber (1985), also an anthropologist, unequivocally embraces a universalist rationality that he seeks to refine. He pinpoints weaknesses in what he calls the intellectualist orientation (a strict universalism). Surveying the ethnographic literature, Sperber finds many cases that defy a strict universalist rationality. By expanding the horizons of a universal rationality, Sperber contends, one can make sense of "apparently irrational beliefs." Sperber's primary criticism of relativists is that they are blithely unaware of the psychological ramifications of their views. In Sperber's universe, relativism fares badly when confronted with the universal realities of cognitive development. One of the most essential of these is that all normal children acquire language at the same pace, and that by the age of four the language capacities of normal children are well formed. "Far from illuminating new areas and solving more problems than those which suggested its adoption in the first place, relativism, if taken seriously, would make ethnography either impossible or inexplicable, and psychology immensely difficult. It is the kind of theory any empirical scientist would rather do without" (49). How might the human sciences adjust to the demise of relativism? Sperber proposes a universal rationalist approach that embraces both propositional and semipropositional representations as well as factual and representational beliefs. Propositional representations, according to Sperber, are fully understood ideas; the semipropositional idea is one that is partially understood. Factual beliefs are the sum of representations in a person's memory as well as the representations that he or she is able to infer from that which is stored in memory. Representational beliefs, by contrast, consist of a nebulous set of linked attitudes that usually lack universal application (54–7).

Sperber uses a matrix of these elements to assess the rationality of reported beliefs. Factual beliefs based upon propositional content are rational. Factual beliefs based on semipropositional content are irrational. Representational beliefs based on propositional content are weak candidates for rationality. Representational beliefs based on semipropositional content are very weak candidates for rationality. "That cultural beliefs are representational is almost tautologous; that they are semipropositional is implicit and even sometimes explicit in the way people express and discuss them. There are many implications to this view of cultural beliefs . . . but only one concerns us here: relativism can be dispensed with" (60). In sum, Sperber goes to elaborate lengths to clear rational space for cultural beliefs within a rigidly formulated universalist/rationalist paradigm. In the end, however, Sperber's project is a psychologically sophisticated extension of Evans-Pritchard's and Horton's universalist positions on rationality.

Although the work of Horton and Sperber has been significant in anthropology, it is the monumental work of Claude Lévi-Strauss that extends the project of universalist rationality to all of the human sciences. Although Lévi-Strauss's work has concerned such diverse subjects as kinship, totemism, myth, and art, the central thesis of his structuralism is to uncover "elementary forms," abstract structures of categorization that underlie all social and cultural diversity. In structuralism Lévi-Strauss extends the structural methods of linguistics to cultural analysis. In phonology, for example, an individual phoneme, /p/, is meaningless in and of itself. Its meaning is contingent upon its relation to the other phonemes in a language. By extension, an individual cultural datum—the power of an individual shaman or a particular marriage or kinship practice—is an isolated element, the true meaning of which becomes clear only when it is situated in a system of relations.

In his first major work, *The Elementary Structures of Kinship*, Lévi-Strauss presents a mind-boggling array of kinship and marriage practices. In his thorough analysis, he seeks unity in diversity, and at the end of the volume he isolates what he calls the "atoms of kinship," a core, universal structure to which all forms of kinship and marriage can be reduced. In his influential essay "The Sorcerer and His Magic," Lévi-Strauss argues that the various individual acts of sorcerers are less important than how they fit into a system that relates sorcerer, patient, and group traditions of health and sickness. In his study of myth, Lévi-Strauss suggests that "if there is a meaning to be found in mythology, it cannot reside in isolated elements which enter into the composition of the myth, but only in the way those elements combine" (1967, 206). In analyzing how the elements combine, Lévi-Strauss isolates in mythical thought a "kind of logic . . . as rigorous as that of modern science" (227). He suggests further that the only difference between mythical and scientific thought lies "in the nature of things to which it is applied" (227). Although human thought patterns, like human practices of kinship, marriage, and sorcery, may vary considerably, there exist for Lévi-Strauss abstract universal structures of human cognition.

In sum, Lévi-Strauss's structuralism constitutes one of the most powerful arguments for a universalist rationality. Although Lévi-Strauss does not deny sociocultural difference, he reduces its specificity to theoretical insignificance. In his scheme the diversity of local nuance is lost in the unity of universal systematicity.

Relativist Rationalities

In contradistinction to Lévi-Strauss, the relativists, whom Tambiah (1994, 115–6) calls "splitters," believe in the diversity of rationality. There can be many rationalities, based upon diverse sets of rules, distinct Wittgensteinian language games, specific "ways of worldmaking," many of which may prove to be inconsistent (see Goodman 1978; Wittgenstein 1953). Relativists seek to understand the nuances of local context to avoid making insensitive analytic errors. Given the density of other systems of belief, they believe that it is best not to make judgments of relative rationality/irrationality. One of the great achievements of Evans-Pritchard's Zande work is that it was the first scholarly treatise to consider a set of non-Western beliefs as something more than a jumble of irrational superstitions. In so doing he demonstrated that non-Western systems of beliefs could be highly sophisticated in their own right.

Many contemporary scholars who are relativists no longer adhere strictly to an absolute relativism. They are, however, consistently critical of an absolute universalist rationality, and attempt to temper their relativism with good sense.

Stanley Tambiah (1994) provides an ecumenical discussion of relativism. Like many contemporary relativists, he considers an uncritical cultural relativism untenable. Using Hilary Putnam's quip that if all is relative, then the relative is relative too, Tambiah suggests that in radical relativism critical judgments are impossible. Can we excuse, he wonders, the Holocaust or apartheid in the name of cultural relativism? In contrast with Sperber, however, Tambiah believes that all symbolic expression or action cannot be transformed into some form of logical proposition, a key criterion for a universalist rationality. He cautions scholars about the dangers of using the criteria of Western rationality as a judgmental yardstick: "[T]he universal rationalist should beware of too cavalierly underrating the difficulties that have to be surmounted in the process of translation between cultures, or of artificially overrating the status requirement that all discourse be reduced or transformed into the verifiable propositional format of logicians" (129). Given these difficulties, Tambiah steers a moderate course through the debate. He believes that scholars should strive for comparisons and generalizations where they are appropriate, but he urges patience. He writes that "to declare that two phenomena seem incommensurable in our present state of knowledge does not automatically put you in the relativist camp or deny the possibility of measurement at some future time" (129). Such a position enables the scholar to maintain that religions adhere to a set of existential universals and constraints and yet differ in fundamental ways (130).

Clifford Geertz, for his part, is less ecumenical in his assessment of a universalist rationality. In his well-known and much cited essay "Anti-anti Relativism," he criticizes the attempts by Sperber and Horton to erase relativism from the anthropological landscape. Although he believes that relativism is an ill-defined and tired concept, he objects to the moves of Ernest Gellner, another well-known universalist; Horton; and especially Sperber "to save us from ourselves" (1984, 274). Evoking the universality of cognitive processes, rationalist antirelativism for Geertz is the attempt to undermine cultural diversity. "As with 'Human Nature,' the deconstruction of otherness is the price of truth. Perhaps, but it is not what either the history of anthropology, the materials it has assembled, or the ideals that have animated it would suggest" (274–5): "The objection to anti-relativism is not that it rejects an it's-all-how-you-look-at-it approach to knowledge or a when-in-Rome approach to morality, but that it imagines they can only be defeated by placing morality beyond culture and knowledge beyond both. This, speaking of things which must needs to be so, is no longer possible. If we wanted home truths, we should have stayed at home" (276). Indeed, the major projects of a universalist rationality, like those of Lévi-Strauss, have been by and large developed, according to Geertz, by scholars who have indeed stayed at home. Can a universalist rationality be reconciled with experience? Geertz says no.

In his thoughtful essay "Witchcraft and Selfcraft," Terrence M. S. Evens speaks to the epistemological importance of experience. He thinks that the anthropological record productively—based upon (field) experience—confounds the neat and tidy distinctions drawn by such universalists as Sperber. For him otherness should not be obliterated by narrowly drawn rules of reason. Evens suggests that scholars approach the quandaries of otherness through the philosophy of Emmanuel Levinas in which the difference between self and other is "no less reducible than relative, such that it can be meaningfully engaged but not finally resolved" (1996, 29). Distancing himself from the universalist rationalists, Evens finds in such exotic systems of belief as the Azande, a truth worth knowing. It is, however, an inassimilable truth that is beyond our world, beyond our reason, which exacts a fundamental cost—"the cost of the world as we know it, which is to say, not the enrichment, as one may be used to hearing, but the veritable transformation of our-selves" (30). Here Evens takes the relativist position that other systems of knowledge contain much wisdom, that we have much to learn from the likes of the Azande or the Songhay, and that such learning may well be transformative (see Stoller 1989, 1997).

Phenomenological Rationalities

One of the great problems of the debate about rationality is that it ultimately boils down to whether one can accept some version of relativism or universalism. This either/or impasse often results in published hand wringing. Relativists complain that universalists are insensitive, Eurocentric, or even racist. Universalists chide the relativists for their scientific naïveté and epistemological imprecision. The hand wringing continues today in the pages of *Anthropology Newsletter,* which in 1995–96 were littered with debate about the scientific status of anthropology. In this debate unapologetic universalists tended to criticize the fuzziness of the radical relativists whom they labeled postmodernists. For their part, relativists often considered the intellectualist "scientific" principles of the universalists as mere illusion. Even the more thoughtful considerations of Geertz, Tambiah, and Evens do not advance our comprehension beyond the narrowly defined boundaries of the original debate. The same can be said for the recent rationality debates between Marshall Sahlins and Gananath Obeyesekere about whether Hawaiians murdered Captain Cook because they "irrationally" mistook him for the Hawaiian god Lono.

This intellectual version of serve and volley tennis often becomes frustrating. One path out of the unproductive debate on rationality may be to change perspective and consider it from a phenomenological vantage that engages the issues of multiple realities and experience. Phenomenology starts with Edmund Husserl who charted a rigorous methodology, the *epochē*, that would enable observers to apprehend lived reality. This process, which takes several steps, enables the observer to move through several levels of consciousness until he or she grasps the immediacy of the object of observation.

> The strategy for beginning, in Husserl's case, was one which called for the elaboration of a step-by-step procedure through which one viewed things differently. His model was one of analogy to various sciences, often analytic in style; thus he built a methodology of steps: *epochē*, the psychological reduction, the phenomenological reduction, the eidetic reduction and the transcendental reduction. At the end of this labyrinth of technique what was called for was a phenomenological attitude, a perspective from which things are to be viewed. (Ihde 1976, 19)

In the end, the *epochē* was an effort to return "to the things themselves" (Husserl 1970, 12), to let things speak, to let them show themselves. Put another way, phenomenology "is an attempt to describe human consciousness in its lived immediacy before it is subject to theoretical elaboration or conceptual systematizing" (Jackson 1996, 2). Indeed, in some of the most influential work in religious studies, scholars like Mircea Eliade have employed the phenomenological *epochē* to assess data from the history of religions.

And yet Husserl's ideas proved to be problematic. Although Husserl influenced a whole generation of philosophers, many of his descendants rejected his inattention to how one lives in the everyday world. They wondered how observers might so purify their perception to experience "lived immediacy." Taking many of these criticisms into consideration, Alfred Schutz transformed Husserl's ahistorical abstractions into a set of concrete conceptions that would enable observers to apprehend the chaos of what he, like Husserl, called the "lifeworld."

For Schutz (1962) the description of social reality involves neither a singular intellectualist move to transform sets of beliefs and behaviors into universally verifiable propositions that *mirror* reality nor the naive relativist move to accept the complete incommensurability of differing systems of belief. For Schutz the individual's interpretation of any event entails the apprehension of multiple realities. The most essential of these realities is what Schutz called the "natural" attitude, which consists of the socially conditioned mechanisms we use to experience the immediacy of everyday life. The natural attitude shapes the contours of interaction between self and other and is therefore mediated through culture as well as a person's "biographically determined situation." The natural attitude delimits intersubjectivity. It also enables us to tiptoe through the unending sociological complexities of the quotidian to make sense of what Schutz called the "paramount" reality.

Although Schutz problematically privileges the everyday as paramount, he also writes about other attitudes that flesh out our experience of social reality. These other "attitudes" include dreams, fantasy, science, and religion. Schutz demonstrated how these various attitudes interpenetrate as we experience the flux of social life.

Critics have faulted Schutz for placing so much emphasis on the "paramount" reality of everyday life. Such a logic parallels the rationalist contention that there is a transcendent reality that is prior to other realities. If we equalize the weights of the various attitudes, however, the epistemological flexibility of Schutz's approach becomes constructive. By employing a multiple realities approach to the question of rationality, one can avoid the niggling problem of how to evaluate what is and what is not rational. In a world of multiple realities, there are several paths to the apprehension of social reality.

An Azande following the interpretive procedures of the poison oracle, for example, might employ personally and culturally conditioned aspects of the natural, scientific, and religious attitudes in trying to grasp the social reality of witchcraft. By the same token, an anthropologist, like Evans-Pritchard or Terrence Evens, would also need to apply a range of personally and culturally contoured attitudes to make sense of Zande witchcraft. The quality of social description, then, would depend on how well the Zande and anthropological multiple realities of the Zande world might be reconciled.

Multiple realities, of course, exist within distinct and permeable universes of meaning. From a phenomenological perspective, the nature of one's experience is the key to reducing distances between universes of meaning. As experience expands with time, the boundaries of the universes may begin to intersect, creating an arena of shared space and interpretation. Some critics argue, of course, that experience may or may not result in increased awareness, let alone personal transformation. And yet, some of the best, and most disturbing, descriptions of religious practices come from scholars, like Evans-Pritchard, who have spent long periods in the field.

Evans-Pritchard's textual equivocations, as I have intimated, may well have resulted from the troubling nature of his experiences among the Azande. He admits to using Zande logic to run the day-to-day affairs of his household. He waffles about the "soul of witchcraft," writing passages filled with the very logical contradictions he denigrates. Perhaps Evans-Pritchard kept his silence about what Evens (1996, 30) states directly: that there is a profound truth about the world as the Azande know it and that truth exacts a high price, a personal transformation. Given the irreducible nature of these kinds of experiences, the world we thought we knew may no longer exist.

Such a realization does not mean that there is no place for universalist or relativist practices in the apprehension of the social worlds of diverse peoples; rather, it means that there are several interpretive moves scholars can employ to make sense of the multiple realities of their experience. Such a practice compels scholars to be humbled by the complex forces of the world.

Embodied Rationalities

The specter of phenomenology in the human sciences has attracted much scholarly criticism. Lévi-Strauss, for one, finds the phenomenologist's foregrounding of experience troubling. He thinks that reality and experience must remain discontinuous. Pierre Bourdieu (1990) criticizes the ahistorical nature of the phenomenological *epochē*, which, he suggests, ignores the historical and cultural context of the social. Although Bourdieu's conception of the habitus seems similar to the phenomenological notion of lifeworld, he sees the move to phenomenology as a descent into the solipsistic subjectivism of the autonomous subject. Indeed, one central tenet of poststructuralist thought is the problem of the subject. In Foucault's work, for example, the idea of the *epistēmē*, the formation and structure of historically situated discourses, excludes the autonomous subject.

Many of these criticisms, however, focus on such classical phenomenological practices as the *epochē*, which many phenomenologists have also criticized. They also mistakenly believe that phenomenologists retain outmoded concepts of the self derived from the Romantics. As Jackson recently argued, "no matter what constituting power we assign the impersonal forces of history, language and upbringing, the subject always figures, at the very least, as the site where these forces find expression and are played out" (1996, 22). From Jackson's vantage, phenomenology is more than simply a philosophy of the subject: "Insofar as experience includes substantive *and* transitive, disjunctive *and* conjunctive modalities, it covers a sense of ourselves as singular individuals as well as belonging to a collectivity" (26).

Perhaps one of the most essential aspects of phenomenology for an approach to the study of non-Western religions is its emphasis on embodiment. First and foremost, phenomenological embodiment is a rejection of the Cartesian separation of mind and body. For Merleau-Ponty, whose work has become increasingly important to anthropologists, consciousness devolves from embodiment: "Consciousness is in the first place not a matter of 'I think that' but of 'I can.' . . . [it is] a being-towards-the-thing through the intermediary of the body" (1962, 137). Although it could be argued that such a view of embodied consciousness is too subjective and ahistorical, it can also be argued that "the orderly systems and determinate structures we describe are not mirror images of social reality so much as defenses we build against the unsystematic and unstructured nature of our experiences within that reality" (Jackson 1989, 3). It can be further argued that although one's embodied perception of an encounter may well be unsystematic and unstructured, it is always historically, socially, and politically situated.

As Jackson suggests, scholars often avoid acknowledging the contingent nature of situated experience, an avoidance that distances us from the ambiguous, the tangential, and the external textures and sensuous processes of our bodies. The full presence of the scholar's body, in turn, demands a fuller sensual awareness of the smells, tastes, sounds, and textures of the lifeworld. Such an embodied presence also means that scholars open themselves to others and absorb their worlds. Embodiment is therefore more than the realization that our bodily experience gives metaphorical meaning to our experience; it is rather the realization that we too are consumed by the sensual world. Such is the scope of an embodied rationality (see Stoller 1997).

To accept an embodied rationality, then, is to eject the conceit of control in which mind and body, self and other are considered separate. It is indeed a humbling experience to recognize, like wise Songhay sorcerers and griots, that one does not master sorcery, history, or knowledge; rather, it is sorcery, history, and knowledge that master us. To accept an embodied rationality is, like the Songhay spirit medium or diviner, to lend one's body to the world and accept its complexities, tastes, structures, and smells.

Such humility does not mean that scholars ignore historical and political contexts or relinquish their agency. An embodied rationality can be a flexible one in which the sensible and intelligible, denotative and evocative are linked through a profound respect for the world. It is an agency imbued with what the late Italo Calvino called "lightness," the ability to make intellectual leaps to bridge gaps forged by illusions of disparateness (see Merleau-Ponty 1962; Stoller 1997). In the future, such an embodied rationality may well expand the scope of religious studies.

The Man Who Walked on Water

In a kingdom of long ago, there was a dervish from a very strict school who was one day strolling along a river bank. As he walked, he pondered great problems of morality and scholarship. For years he had studied the world of the Prophet. Through study of the Prophet's sacred language, he reasoned, he would one day be blessed with Mohammed's divine illumination and acquire the ultimate Truth.

The dervish's ruminations were interrupted by a piercing noise: Some person was reciting a dervish prayer. "What is the man doing?" he wondered to himself. "How can he be mispronouncing the syllables? He should be saying 'Ya hu' instead of 'U ya hu.'"

It was his moral duty, he thought, to correct his brother, to set him straight on the path of piety. Accordingly, he hired a boat and rowed his way to an island, the source of the errant incantation. He found a man dressed in frayed wool sitting in front of a hut. The man swayed in time to his rhythmic repetitions. He was so engrossed in his sacred incantation that he did not hear the first dervish's approach.

"Forgive me," the first dervish said. "I overheard your prayer. With all due respect, I believe you have erred in your prayer. You should say 'Ya hu' instead of 'U ya hu.'"

"Thank you so much for your kindness," the second dervish said. "I appreciate what you have done."

Pleased with his good deed, the first dervish boarded his boat. Allah, he reasoned, would take notice of his pious efforts. As it was written, the one who can repeat the sacred incantation without error might one day walk upon water. Perhaps one day he'd be capable of such a feat.

When the first dervish's boat reached midstream, he noticed that the second dervish had not learned his lesson well, for once again the latter continued to repeat the incantation incorrectly. The first dervish shook his head. At least he had made the proper effort. Lost in his thoughts about the human penchant for error, the first dervish then witnessed a bizarre sight. Leaving the island, the bumbling second dervish walked on the water and approached the first dervish's boat.

Shocked, the first dervish stopped his rowing. The second dervish walked up to him and said, "Brother, I am sorry to trouble you, but I have to come out to ask you again the standard method of making the repetition you were telling me about. I find it difficult to remember it" (adapted from Shah 1993).

*　　*　　*

No matter the logical consistency of our propositions and semipropositions, no matter how deeply we think we have mastered a subject, the world, for the embodied scholar, remains a wondrous place that stirs the imagination and sparks creativity. Those who struggle with humility, no matter their scholarly station, admit willingly that they have much to learn from forgetful old men and women who, at first glance, seem to have little knowledge to impart. In the end these kinds of people not only have precious knowledge to convey but can teach us much about living in the world.

Among the Songhay of the Republic of Niger it is usually this kind of person who has been mastered by the sacred words of history and the powerful secrets of sorcery. It is their humility, developed through a locally contoured embodied rationality, I think, that enables them to receive knowledge and transform it into wisdom.

The key test for a future rationality, then, may well be whether its processes and procedures can lead us not only to increasingly insightful truths but also to wisdom. My own guess is that if we allow humility to work its wonders, it can bring embodiment to our scholarly practices and expression. It can also enable us to live well in the world.

Like the unmistakable "presence" in my Wanzerbe room, the temporary paralysis I suffered that faraway night in Western Niger remains a mystery to me. I may never discover reasonable explanations for my experiences there. And yet those experiences have kept me suspended in uncertainty and ambiguity that have fired my imagination and fed my hunger for knowledge. They have taught me the intellectual and personal rewards of acknowledging what Keats called "negative capability," that is, the capability of "being in uncertainties, mysteries, doubts, without any irritable reaching after fact or reason." The book of my experiences in Niger remains open. Perhaps I will learn more about "presences" and "paralysis" the next time I return to Niger to sit with and listen to the elders.

SUGGESTED READINGS

Evans-Pritchard, E. E. 1937. *Witchcraft, Oracles, and Magic among the Azande.*

Evens, Terrence M. S. 1996. "Witchcraft and Selfcraft." *Archives of European Sociology.*

Foucault, Michel. 1970. *The Order of Things.*

Geertz, Clifford. 1984. "Anti-anti Relativism." *American Anthropologist.*

Goodman, Nelson. 1978. *Ways of Worldmaking.*

Hollis, Martin, and Stephen Lukes, eds. 1982. *Rationality and Relativism.*

Jackson, Michael, ed. 1996. *Things as They Are: New Directions in Phenomeno-logical Anthropology.*

Lévi-Strauss, Claude. 1973. *The Savage Mind,* translated by John Weightman and Doreen Weightman.

Lévy-Bruhl, Lucien. 1949. *Les Carnets de Lucien Lévy-Bruhl.*

Merleau-Ponty, Maurice. 1962. *The Phenomenology of Perception,* translated by Colin Smith.

Obeyesekere, Gananath. 1992. *The Apotheosis of Captain Cook: European Myth Making in the Pacific.*

Sahlins, Marshall. 1995. *How "Natives" Think: About Captain Cook, For Ex-ample.*

Schutz, Alfred. 1962. *Collected Papers.* Vol. 1, *The Problem of Social Reality.*

Sperber, Dan. 1985. *On Anthropological Knowledge.*

Tambiah, Stanley J. 1994. *Magic, Science, Religion, and the Scope of Rationality.*

Wilson, Bryan R. 1970. *Rationality.*

REFERENCES

Bourdieu, Pierre. 1990. *The Logic of Practice,* translated by Richard Nice. Stanford: Stanford University Press.

Evans-Pritchard, E. E. 1976. *Witchcraft, Oracles, and Magic among the Azande.* Oxford: Clarendon Press.

Evens, Terrence M. S. 1996. "Witchcraft and Selfcraft." *Archives of European Sociology* 37 (1).

Foucault, Michel. 1970. *The Order of Things.* New York: Pantheon Books.

Geertz, Clifford. 1984. "Anti-anti Relativism." *American Anthropologist* 86 (2).

Goodman, Nelson. 1978. *Ways of Worldmaking.* Indianapolis: Hackett.

Horton, Robin. 1970. "African Traditional Thought and Western Science." In *Rationality,* edited by Bryan Wilson. New York: Harper and Row.

Husserl, Edmund. 1970. *Logical Investigations,* translated by J. N. Findlay. London: Routledge and Kegan Paul.

Ihde, Don. 1976. *Listening and Voice: A Phenomenology of Sound.* Athens: Ohio University Press.

Jackson, Michael. 1989. *Paths toward a Clearing: Radical Empiricism and Ethnographic Inquiry.* Bloomington: Indiana University Press.

Jackson, Michael, ed. 1996. *Things as They Are: New Directions in Phenomenological Anthropology.* Bloomington: Indiana University Press.

Lévi-Strauss, Claude. 1967. *Structural Anthropology.* Garden City, N.J.: Doubleday.

———. 1969. *The Elementary Structures of Kinship,* translated by James Harle Bell, John Richard von Sturmer, and Rodney Needham; edited by Rodney Needham. Rev. ed. Boston: Beacon.

———. 1973. *The Savage Mind,* translated by John Weightman and Doreen Weightman. Chicago: University of Chicago Press.

Lévy-Bruhl, Lucien. 1949. *Les Carnets de Lucien Lévy-Bruhl.* Paris: Presses Universitaires de France.

Merleau-Ponty, Maurice. 1962. *The Phenomenology of Perception,* translated by Colin Smith. London: Routledge.

Obeyesekere, Gananath. 1992. *The Apotheosis of Captain Cook: European Myth Making in the Pacific.* Princeton: Princeton University Press.

Sahlins, Marshall. 1995. *How "Natives" Think: About Captain Cook, For Example.* Chicago: University of Chicago Press.

Schutz, Alfred. 1962. *Collected Papers.* Vol. 1, *The Problem of Social Reality.* The Hague: Nijhoff.

Shah, Idries. 1993. *Tales of the Dervishes.* New York: Arcana.

Sperber, Dan. 1985. *On Anthropological Knowledge.* Cambridge: Cambridge University Press.

Stoller, Paul. 1989. *The Taste of Ethnographic Things: The Senses in Anthropology.* Philadelphia: University of Pennsylvania Press.

———. 1997. *Sensuous Scholarship.* Philadelphia: University of Pennsylvania Press.

Stoller, Paul, and Cheryl Olkes. 1987. *In Sorcery's Shadow: A Memoir of Apprenticeship among the Songhay of Niger.* Chicago: University of Chicago Press.

Tambiah, Stanley J. 1994. *Magic, Science, Religion, and the Scope of Rationality.* Cambridge: Cambridge University Press.

Wittgenstein, Ludwig. 1953. *Philosophical Investigations,* translated by G. E. M. Anscombe. New York: Macmillan.

FOURTEEN

Relic

Gregory Schopen

Scholars of religions have generally been more comfortable with ideas than with things, more comfortable with what they thought others thought than with what they knew they did. They have been particularly uncomfortable, perhaps, when people touched or rubbed or hugged or kissed things, especially when those things were themselves somewhat disconcerting—dead bodies, bits of bone or cloth, dirt or fingernails, dried blood. This unease itself may go a long way toward explaining why we still understand little about relics. And this lack of understanding may represent a serious gap since these bodies and bits of bone and otherwise seemingly dead matter have played a lively role in the history of several major religions, in religious architectures and arts, in religious practices, economies, and institutions. They have discomfited some and consoled many. They have challenged official doctrine, created conflict, and quite literally brought diverse types of people together. They have changed secular laws and even rearranged landscapes, and we still do not understand exactly how. Even the etymology of the term, which should be the easiest part of any discussion of relics, immediately lands us in both conceptual and crosscultural difficulties.

Whether it be the English word "relic" or the Sanskrit originals that it almost always translates, it is clear that etymologies and literal meanings can only represent a small part of what the terms mean. The English "relic" is derived from Latin *relinquere,* "to leave behind"; the same Latin verb has also produced English "relinquish." A relic, then, is something left behind. But the two Sanskrit terms that are taken to correspond to the English word relic do not mean this at all. The etymology of the most common of the two terms, *śarīra,* is unsettled. Its most common usage, however, is not. In the singular it means "the body, bodily frame." It is when it is used in the plural that it comes to have some of the senses of the English word relic. The other Sanskrit word that is usually translated by relic is *dhātu.* Its basic meanings are "constituent part," "ingredient," "element," "primitive matter," or "constituent element or essential ingredient." It is, for example, the word used for a primary element of the earth: a metal, mineral, or ore; it is also the word used to designate what we call a verbal root. If we assume for the moment that the process we call biological death must intervene between a living person and at least the bodily relics of that person, then these lexical differences become interesting. In the West, death—and usually burial—produces remains, "remaining fragments; surviving parts," or "the body, or parts of the body, of a dead person." The latter two meanings are the only ones recorded for "relic" in the plural in *Webster's Unabridged Dictionary.* But in Buddhist sources, in Sanskrit, death—and usually cremation—produces not remains of a body but a plurality of bodies. The language moves from singular *śarīra,* "body," to the plural *śarīrāṇi,* "bodies." Alternatively, death and cremation reduce the person to its "essential ingredient," *dhātu.* They extract— to exploit a pun used by the Buddhist poet Aśvaghoṣa—the ore (*dhātu*) from the dross. These would appear to be very different conceptions. However, etymological meanings, like appearances, are often deceiving.

If the literal meanings of relic and *śarīra* or *dhātu* are clearly different, what is done for or to them, what is said about them, and what they themselves do are very often not. There is, moreover, an enormous body of material bearing on all these things, but once again, any approach to it lands us in immediate difficulties, most of which are of our own making or—to shift the blame—our forefathers' and predecessors'. The Protestant reformers were, for example, no friends of relics (see Eire 1986, 40–3, 96–7, 211 ff.; cf. Delumeau 1989, 234– 42). Calvin's *Admonition Showing the Advantages which Christendom might Derive from an Inventory of Relics* (Beveridge 1844, 289–341), a characteristically vituperative tract, is peppered with descriptions of relics as "frivolities," "absurdities," with repeated references to "superstition," "corrupt practice," "the excessive zeal of rude and ignorant men or old women," "ignorant people," "the wretched populace," "the stupidity of men," and "monkish and priestly impostors." Although he lets slip that he himself—of course "long ago"—kissed a portion of St. Ann's body, he concludes with the hope that others will not, that "every man, who is not obstinately determined against the truth, though he may not yet clearly perceive that the worship of any relics, of whatever kind they be, whether genuine or spurious, is execrable idolatry, yet seeing how clear this falsehood is, will have no desire to kiss them any more."

If Calvin, then, would have us believe that he believes that relics are humbug, that is well and good. We are simply dealing with his beliefs, and as a theological position they are as good or bad as any other. But as a representation of the beliefs of all those "rude and ignorant men or old women" who were going around kissing such things—and Calvin's polemic established, if anything, that they were—as a representation, in short, of history and actual practice, they will not do, in spite of the fact that until recently, given the enormous influence of Calvinism and Protestantism on Western intellectual values, they often have. *That* they have probably needs little demonstration. If it does, two entries in what was—and in important ways remains—the most authoritative and learned encyclopedia of religion and ethics will suffice.

When the history of twentieth-century religious studies is written, Hastings' *Encyclopaedia of Religion and Ethics* will undoubtedly be seen to have played a very important role. The first volume was published in 1908, the last in 1921. It therefore summarized the great richness of nineteenth-century scholarship and values, and set the agenda for much of the twentieth century. It is, then, a little disconcerting to see what it says under the heading "Relics," and it is probably no accident, and certainly symptomatic, that the topic of Christian (here called "Western") relics is treated together with what is called "Primitive." The actual rubric is "Relics (Primitive and Western)." The entry was written by J. A. MacCulloch and contains a great deal of interesting material, with an equal number of unbecoming adjectives and phrases: the views of early Catholic fathers "differ little from the theory implicit in savage magic, as far as that concerns the use of relics"; he refers to "the extent and the absurdity of the cult," "abuses," "the credulity of the people," "superstition," and "many anomalies and absurdities," all of which should have a familiar ring, as does his conclusion: "the admitted great uncertainty which surrounds any relic, the certainty of impudent fraud in the case of many, the gross superstitions and abuses to which they have given rise and which have attended the cult from early times, far outweigh any positive good which they may ever have done." MacCulloch did not invent his vocabulary nor, it seems, did he arrive at it through a disinterested study of his sources. This is even more obvious in the second entry that follows immediately.

The noted historian of India, Vincent A. Smith, wrote that second entry under the title "Relics (Eastern)." In fact it is almost entirely devoted to Buddhist South Asia and here too is the familiar litany: "rank superstition, open to every kind of abuse and fraud"; "superstitious veneration"; "disgusting extreme." MacCulloch, writing about Christian relics, could call up Christian critics for his talk, and there was thereby at least a certain theological continuity, even if it had crept noiselessly into scholarship. The language at least came from a part of the tradition itself. Smith could do no such thing. Although *śarīra* had had their challengers in the Indian Buddhist tradition, they had never had these sorts of rabid detractors. In fact, the only individuals who had ever said this sort of thing about Buddhist relics were outsiders—European travelers and missionaries. In this sense the sources of Smith's evaluations are clear: They could not have been either Buddhist or Indian. Though some things have changed, these views—now perhaps in more cleverly disguised forms—are still sometimes with us, and both MacCulloch's and Smith's entries are cited, for example, in the new *Encyclopedia of Religion* as "still useful, although dated." But the problems, surely, are more than simply chronological, and the language of abuse and stupidity surely is only one part of a complex set of conceptual clutter that, like their "virtues," still clings to relics.

Without, of course, wanting to follow out their logical implications, both MacCulloch and Smith, for example, "explain" the use of relics as the result of natural "affection" or "instinctive reverence": "reverence for the remains of the dead or the treasuring of some of their more personal belongings is natural and instinctive"; or it "is a natural exhibition of emotion." Since, again according to both, this natural and instinctive reverence invariably leads to abuse, superstition, and fraud, we are invariably led to a rather unflattering anthropology, and there we sit. This unflattering anthropology is also almost as invariably associated with the appearance of a particular species of, or particularly specious, explanatory deus ex machina: need. People do and think these sorts of stupid things because various needs make them: the need for reassurance, the need for physical contact with what is thought sacred, the need to locate that curious commodity (the list is long). We are an alarmingly needy bunch. But that there is something to all of this is almost as certain as the fact that it so far has been badly expressed. To do better, however, is not necessarily an easy task.

There is both a startling precision and a maddening conceptual fuzziness in what Christians and Buddhists say about relics and *śarīras;* and both, it seems, are here to stay. Like it or not, when we are dealing with *śarīras* and relics we are, it seems, dealing *both* with conceptions of something like what Bergson called "élan vital," Dylan Thomas called "the force that through the green fuse drives the flower," or your grandmother called "life," *and* something that remains stubbornly material, something that is transmissible and has weight. The latter, for example, was already demonstrable — or thought to be so — in the time of Gregory of Tours. In his *Liber in gloria martyrum,* with regard to the tomb of St. Peter, he says,

> But if someone wishes to take away a blessed relic, he weighs a little piece of cloth on a pair of scales and lowers it into [the tomb]; then he keeps vigils, fasts, and earnestly prays that the power of the apostle will assist his piety. [What happens next] is extraordinary to report! If the man's faith is strong, when the piece of cloth is raised from the tomb it will be so soaked with divine power *[imbuitur divina virtute]* that it will weigh much more than it weighed previously. (van Dam 1983, 45–6)

That such hard-nosed empiricism is not just ancient, and that we are indeed dealing with "the force that through the green fuse drives the flower," seems to be confirmed by the Boston *Globe* for 19 December 1972:

> A medical man in Düsseldorf . . . claimed to have measured the weight of the human psyche. He placed the beds of his terminal patients on ultra sensitive scales and claimed that as they died he found that the needle dropped 21 grams. (MacGregor 1992, 16n.1)

We of course do not like this sort of thing much because it confounds our categories, but our preferences cannot — however humbling — prevent our sources from saying what they do. Indian Buddhist sources — epigraphical, canonical, and learned; early and late — are all but unanimous that relics are, if you will pardon the etymological pun, animate. What is probably the earliest actually datable reference to a Buddhist relic occurs in what is known as the "Bajur Inscription of Menandros" (Schopen 1997, 126 and n.49) and may be as early as the second century B.C.E. Although it refers to what we *now* would call the deposition of a "relic," it calls what we call a relic "the body of the Blessed

One Śākyamuni which is endowed with life [literally, breath]" (*prāṇasametaṃ śarīraṃ bhagavataḥ śākyamuneḥ*). Oddly enough, however, the cognitive fact that relics were alive should, by necessity, also put them at risk: If relics lived they could also, it seems, die and—more importantly—be killed. This seemingly necessary corollary is also found in Buddhist sources. First of all, the destruction of a *stūpa* or monumental reliquary was ruled a particularly heinous crime and, when classified, it occurred alongside several other forms of murder. Probably the most dramatic example of the latter is recorded in a collection of rules for monks belonging to the Mūlasarvāstivādin Order.

A group of nuns had built a *stūpa* or monumental reliquary for the relics of a monk who had died, and had instituted a cult with regard to it. Another monk came along and, thinking it was a *stūpa* of the Buddha, paid worship to it. When he was informed of the *stūpa*'s "contents" he was furious—a rather unseemly state of mind for an *arhat*—tore the *stūpa* down, and threw the "bones" away. When they were told what had occurred, the nuns did not understand it as the destruction of a structure but as the death of the monk whose relics had been enshrined. They said, "Our brother is from today truly dead! (*bdag cag gi ming po deng gdod shi ba lta zhes . . .*)." He had, it seems, been murdered (see Schopen 1996). Similarly, in the much later Sri Lankan monastic chronicle called the *Cūlavaṃsa,* a group of Tamil invaders is said to have wrecked image houses and monasteries, destroyed sacred books, and torn down reliquaries, destroying relics that were "the veritable life of them" (*teṣaṃ jīvitasaṃnibhe . . . dhātū sārīrike;* Geiger 1953, vol. 1, 133). The similar actions of the opponents of Christian relics probably should also be read in this way. When Julian the Apostate, for example, destroyed chapels containing the "bodies" of martyrs or, more particularly, removed the "remains" of St. Babilas from his church and had them carried away in a wagon to a cemetery (Ricciotti 1959, 210–13), he was almost certainly attempting to kill him, if by no other means than by dumping his remains unceremoniously in a wagon and relocating "him." The equation seems clear: that which is in a church or *stūpa* is alive; that which is dumped in a cemetery or thrown away is dead. Relics, then, are defined as much by where they are located and what people do with them as they are by what they physically are. And this idea is only narratively rephrased in two dramatic events, one in Kusinārā immediately after the death of the Buddha and one in Milan in 385 C.E.

Although St. Ambrose was by no means the first churchman to take an active role in the relic cult, and although his translation of the newly discovered bodies of the martyrs Gervasius and Protadius to his basilica "had thus failed to breach the ultimate barrier," that is, the city walls (Harries 1992, 61), still "he had been prepared both to move bodies and to link them decisively to the altar of a new church" (Brown 1981, 37). This move was—or more accurately has come to symbolize—the crucial moment in what came to be a full-scale Christian rearrangement of Late Antique urban landscapes. After Ambrose, "dead" bodies came to be ever more commonly housed in urban churches in the very midst of the living, and the old Roman separation of the living and the dead was gone. Sort of.

What has generally been presented as the breakdown of the Roman separation of the living and the dead effected by Ambrose and other Christian worthies has more recently been remodulated in an interesting way by Jill Harries. Harries (1992) argues that in regard to the common dead, there was initially no change at all: "Christian promoters of martyrs did not directly challenge assumptions about the common dead" (59). The separation here, at least initially, remained. What Christians succeeded in doing, she argues, was to change notions of who was and who was not dead. They did not break down the separation but rather succeeded in shifting certain individuals from one category to another: "Their point about the martyrs was that they were not dead at all; like Christ they were historical people who had died as witnesses to their faith and were now alive. Their relics therefore could not be classified among the remains of dead people" (59). It was this shift and reclassification that Christians "had succeeded in imposing on the world of Late Antiquity" (59). The separation here too still remained.

Something like this reclassification seems already to have been narratively articulated in the *Mahāparinirvāṇa Sūtra,* the well-known early Buddhist canonical text dealing with the death of the Buddha. There the Mallas, the people in whose territory the Buddha had died, intend to carry the body "by the south and outside, to a spot on the south, and outside of the city." The gods, however, have other ideas and the Mallas cannot lift the body. The gods want the body to be carried out "by the north to the north of the city, and entering the city by the north gate, let us [the gods] bring it through the midst of the city into the midst thereof. And going out again by the eastern gate . . . to the east of the city . . ." (Rhys Davids and Rhys Davids 1910, 181). And so it is done. Although the directional symbolism here remains obscure, one thing is certain: to carry a *dead* body into the city would have been unheard of. Indian notions of death pollution were, if anything, even stronger than Roman. The narrative fact that this was what the gods not only insisted on but effected can only mean, it seems, that *this* body was not—on divine authority—to be classified as dead. Here too there is no breakdown of separation but a selective reclassification using old categories.

If Christian and Buddhist relics are defined by where they are put or allowed to enter, and by what people do in regard to them, they are also defined by what is said about them. And here too the language used is sometimes hauntingly similar. Buddhist sources—again early and late, inscriptional and learned—talk about *śarīras* or *dhātus* as, for example, "infused with morality, infused with concentration, infused with wisdom," infused, in other words, with the three things that define a living Buddha or saint. They are also described as "full of virtue" or "informed with universal benevolence" (see Schopen 1997, chap. 7). Sometimes too the Buddha himself is described as "the Perfectly Enlightened One who is enclosed within the most excellent relic" (Schopen 1997, chap. 8);

or it is said that worship directed toward the relic is the same as worship directed toward the living Buddha; or, finally, it is simply said that "when relics are present the Buddha is present."

For the language used by Christians in regard to their relics, we might simply cite some examples from Victricius of Rouen's *De laude sanctorum* written at the end of the fourth century. Victricius was a bishop speaking of relics he had just received. For example, he says that the saints "inhabit forever the Holy Relics" *(semper sacratas reliquias possidetis)*, that "in these relics perfect grace and virtue are contained" *(in istis reliquiis perfectam esse gratiam perfectamque uirtutem);* and that "he who cures lives. He who lives is present in his relics" *(qui uiuit, in reliquiis est)* (Hillgarth 1986, 23–8; Mulders and Demeulenaere 1985; cf. Bynum 1995, 106–8; for later conceptions of relics, see Delumeau 1989, 228–33).

In both traditions, then, the relic is or has virtue, grace, benevolence, and life. It is also important to keep in mind that in both traditions virtue, grace, benevolence, and life are transmittable by touch or through less direct contact. In the passage cited above from Gregory of Tours, we saw that a cloth that comes into contact with St. Peter's tomb is soaked with divine virtue, and much the same is said in the Georgian and Arabic versions of a text ascribed to John Moschos (McCulloh 1976, 183–4). In the Buddhist case the transmission is sometimes even articulated by a shadow. In the monastic code of the Mūlasarvāstivādin Order, for example, monks who are charged with sweeping the compound refuse to walk on the shadow cast by the *stūpa,* and in the *Sarvatathāgatoṣṇīṣavijayadhāraṇī*—a much later text—it is said that "those who are touched by the shadow of the *stūpa,* or sprinkled with its dust, will not go to an unfortunate destiny" (Suzuki 1955–61, vol. 7, 173.3.1). Something moves from A to B and B, it seems, is the beneficiary even if, in at least one very important case, B is supposed to be dead.

The case in point brings together, summarizes as it were, much of what we have already seen in regard to relics, but it does so in such a way as to make problematic both *their* meaning and *our* typical approach to the study of religion. The case concerns what in the Latin West came to be called burial or deposition *ad sanctos,* "near to, by, close by, a saint." This practice produced a typical archaeological configuration succinctly described by Philippe Ariès:

> Over the saint's tomb a basilica would be built. . . . Christians sought to be buried close to this structure. Diggings in the Roman cities of Africa or Spain reveal an extraordinary spectacle concealed by subsequent urban growth: piles of stone sarcophagi in disorder, one on top of the other, several layers high, especially around the walls of the apse, close to the shrine of the saint. (1974, 16, 17)

This, again according to Ariès, "is what one finds in Tipasa, Hippo and Carthage. The spectacle is just as striking in Ampurias, in Catalonia . . . [and] . . . the same situation is found in our Gallo-Roman cities" (1981, 34). To these observations should be added the more recent remarks of Yvette Duval:

> So very soon relics also attract the dead, and not just the holy tombs as in the first inhumations *ad sanctos* attested in Africa and Italy: moreover the same terms—*memoria,* then *reliquiae*—designate the "remains" whether they are the whole or a part of the body or just contact relics of the second degree. . . . [T]he dead are said to be buried "near the martyrs" even when, after the 4th Century, only a little of their ashes or tiny relics are alone deposited under the altar of the edifice that shelters the burial. It is necessary to emphasize, finally, that one also buried someone *ad sanctos* around places that were sanctified by the life (or the death) of the martyrs and saints, but that had never contained their tombs or even their material relics . . . these places which were sanctified by only the presence of the martyrs and saints during their passage on this earth *(loca sancta)* and were charged with their *virtus.* (Duval 1988, 56–7; cf. Bynum 1995, 200–25)

Duval also points out that burial *ad sanctos* was a "mass phenomenon," but also "a 'praxis' fully participated in by the highest authorities of the church." This is what the highest authorities did. It is not, however, what they talked about. Apart from stray references in literary sources, Augustine alone among the church fathers wrote a small treatise—*De cura pro mortuis gerenda,* little more than a long letter in response to a question by Paulinus of Nola who himself had buried his own son near the saints of Aecola—dealing with the *problems* this practice created. The *De cura* has been variously described. MacCulloch says the treatise was written "in support of the practice" (Hastings 1908–21, 657); Brown (1981) refers to it as a "clear answer." But neither seems to be entirely true. More than anything it seems to be hesitant, at times tortured. Augustine says, for example, "If . . . supplications which are made with true faith and devotion for the dead should be lacking, there would be no advantage to their souls, I think, however holy the places be in which their lifeless bodies are buried" (Lacy 1955, 359). But later he says, "This question as to how the martyrs aid those who certainly are aided by them surpasses the powers of my intelligence" (379). These latter sentiments are in fact something of a leitmotif running throughout the work: "Somehow or other . . ." "I might believe that this is done by the workings of angels." "In what way such things happen I do not know." "This question is so deep that I cannot comprehend it, and so complex as to defy all my efforts to scrutinize it successfully." Augustine here, perhaps uncharacteristically, is struggling. He has a problem, and so do we.

Part of our problem is that Augustine's *De cura* is the only extended discussion that we have; and part of our problem is that—as in this case—the religious elite, those who wrote for and of the tradition, did not always write about what they and others did. We often know—again as in this case—what religious people did, not from learned treatises and official writings, but from archeology and epigraphy. It is on the basis of Christian archeological and epigraphic sources that Duval "knew" that burial *ad sanctos* was a "mass phenomenon . . . fully participated in by the highest authorities of the Church," knew, in fact, what people did (see also Duval and Picard 1986). And here we have several more problems.

Those sources that allow us to see at least something of what religious people did are the same sources that until recently have not been allowed a full voice in the histories of religious traditions. We can track this slow and sometimes grudging development in the historiography of Christianity, for example, in W. H. C. Frend's recently published *Archaeology of Early Christianity* (1996). Frend notes that Harnack, still a name to be reckoned with, used little archeological material in his "monumental" *Die Mission und Ausbreitung des Christentums in den ersten drei Jahrhunderten,* and says that Benjamin Kidd's *History of the Church to A.D. 461,* published in three volumes in 1922, "remains the last (if not also the greatest) history of the early Church that relied almost exclusively on patristic texts" (213–4). "Henceforth," Frend says, "no study of early Christianity could afford to neglect the wealth of evidence from archaeology." The definitiveness of this remark, however, is considerably blunted by others: "Even Hans Lietzmann, archaeologist at heart though he was, kept closely to his literary texts in the first two volumes of his masterly *Geschichte der Alten Kirche,* published in 1930 and 1936" (251). "The year 1961 had seen the first textbook designed to correlate literary with archaeological remains. . . . his [M. Gough's] *The Early Christians* was a pioneering work, a pointer to future writing of early Church history, which integrated literary and archaeological studies" (327). In fact, it is only in reference to work published in the 1970s and 1980s that Frend can finally say "Archaeology and literary studies are now seen as inextricably linked" (362).

It is hard to believe that this long exclusion, and then the slow and grudging admittance of archeological and epigraphic sources into the study of Christianity, is completely unrelated to theological controversies within the tradition itself. Archeological and epigraphic sources tell us, after all, what people did, but this was almost precisely what the Protestant reformers who were concerned with locating "true" religion in sacred texts were trying to exclude from their definition of religion. What people did and had been doing was in fact a large part of the Protestant problem: what had "been practiced in some ages, and is now practiced wherever Popery prevails," and what "have been admitted into the general belief and practice" (both from Calvin). Suffice it to say that the Protestant position won and, although it has been diluted, residual, and secularized, "a basically Whiggish and ultimately 'Protestant' view of things is still a potent influence on our thinking" (Scarisbrick 1984, 1), and especially on Western intellectual understandings of what religion is. Since these understandings excluded from the definition of "true," what we would probably now refer to as "real," religion those things that people did, would it be surprising if those sources that told us about such things were to be marginalized? (cf. Geary 1994, 30–45).

All of this, and the meanings of relics and burial *ad sanctos,* might merely be considered a bizarre and long episode in the history of Christianity but for one thing: we have seen other religions—as indeed we only can—through our own eyes. And that has often meant that for a long time we might not have seen some things at all.

When what was considered early Buddhist literature was first read, it contained so little about disposal of the dead that it was almost assumed that Indian Buddhists did not do it. Buddhist scholastic literature also did not address the question. Since Buddhism was identified as a religion, and since religion was by then all but assumed to be located in texts, and especially sacred texts, this almost clinched it. The fact that even very early archeological work at Buddhist sites suggested otherwise counted for very little because, as in the Christian case, archeological material could only show what Buddhists did, and it had already been culturally decided in the West that that was at best marginal to "real" religion. Though the archeological evidence constantly increased, its admission into the study of Indian Buddhism has been even slower and more grudging than in the case of the Christian West (see Schopen 1997, chap. 1). However, it too revealed a typical and repeated configuration, and it was almost exactly the same as that found in Tipasa, Hippo, and Carthage, in Ampurias and Catalonia, and in our Gallo-Roman cities.

As at Christian sites, so too at Buddhist sites the presence of a relic permanently housed in ever more elaborate *stūpas,* or spots sanctified by the former presence of the Buddha, also usually marked by a *stūpa,* drew to themselves an equally disorderly array of secondary deposits, several layers high, of mortuary remains. Though often poorly excavated, poorly reported, or both, there can be no doubt about the basic pattern. What remains unsure is the lower chronological limit of the practice (although it appears to have been in full swing at early sites like Sāñcī and common even in Sri Lanka in the first few centuries of the Common Era) and its extent: it may have been far, far more common than at first thought (see Schopen 1994). Although this pattern has only recently been brought into something like focus, it had not gone entirely unnoticed. C. Duroiselle, for example, had said long ago in speaking about Buddhist Burma that the Burmese have "a curious custom, which is similar to that which is in vogue in Christian countries, of turning the sacred precincts of a pagoda *[stūpa]* into a cemetery" (1915, 147). It is indeed curious and from several points of view.

What we have bumped up against here are two religious traditions that differ radically in formally expressed and "official" doctrine, in worldview and orientation, and very largely in institutional organization. Still, they share similar understandings of a relic and their sacred sites reveal the same archeologically determinable spatial configuration or distribution of mortuary deposits crowded around that permanently housed relic. What are we to make of this since in neither tradition has the practice that produced these configurations been subjected to emic exegesis, discussion, or rationalization. We can, I think, only describe in culturally specific terms, insofar as that is possible, what is there. But that itself turns out to be interesting.

There is at the center or focal point of both configurations usually a relic or tomb or *stūpa*. These are all considered to be or contain the holy person: "He who lives is present in his relics." "When relics are present the Buddha is present." The center is culturally alive, and it is permanently and architecturally located—it does not move. Its life is transmittable by contact, closeness, and shadow. In both cases mortuary deposits are permanently and definitively placed within its range. They too do not move. In the Buddhist case, for example, mortuary remains are permanently—dare we say eternally—in the shadow of the presence of the Buddha. If the bones and ashes and broken bodies in these deposits are also alive—and must they not be to be affected by the shadow—then we have a materially constructed, articulated, and assured permanent state of, if not "salvation," then heaven or paradise: the conventionally dead have been permanently placed in the presence of the Holy.

Duval in her important study has come close to these kinds of conclusions. She has suggested that burial *ad sanctos* "is evidently based on the certitude that the dead body is not entirely *exanimum* [dead], it has been 'in-formed', modeled by the soul which during its lifetime had given it form, and after death it guards the imprint of its soul *(vestigia animae suae)*." "One is here," she says, "far from the doctrine hammered out by Augustine" (xl), but that is another matter. She also says in regard to the "themes" expressed in Christian epitaphs that "One sees without going further, that these themes, certainly tied to the material situation of the tomb and the relics nearby have a resonance that is above all spiritual; they refer to the links in the hereafter which are prefigured by burial *ad sanctos* and which, by so doing, it favors" (134). We need only add that in the mind of the believer, burial *ad sanctos* may not simply favor it. It may effect it.

And what of the fact that all of this would seem to fly in the face of formal doctrine, both Buddhist and Christian? It may well be that scholars of religion have not yet sufficiently distinguished formal doctrine from belief. In may well be that large numbers of religious men and women knew little and cared much less for formal doctrine than have modern scholars. It may well be that religious women and men—even those who did not know they had a metaphysics—followed Emerson's suggestion: "In your metaphysics you have denied personality to the Deity: yet when the devout motions of the soul come, yield to them heart and life, though they should clothe God with shape and color. Leave your theory, as Joseph his coat in the hand of the harlot, and flee" (Gilman 1965, 269). It may well be that many did just that, and so might we.

SUGGESTED READINGS

Ariès, Philippe. 1974. *Western Attitudes toward Death: From the Middle Ages to the Present,* translated by Patricia M. Ranum.

———. 1981. *The Hour of Our Death,* translated by Helen Weaver.

Bareau, André. 1960. "La Construction et le culte des stūpa d'après les vina-yapiṭaka." *Bulletin de l'école française d'extrême-orient* 50.

Dooley, Eugene A. 1931. *Church Law on Sacred Relics.*

Duval, Yvette. 1988. *Auprès des saints corps et âme: L'inhumation "ad sanctos" dans la chrétienté d'orient et d'occident du IIIe au VIIe siècle.*

Faure, Bernard. 1991. *The Rhetoric of Immediacy: A Cultural Critique of Chan/Zen Buddhism.*

Geary, Patrick J. 1978. *Furta Sacra: Thefts of Relics in the Central Middle Ages.*

———. 1994. *Living with the Dead in the Middle Ages.*

Lacy, John A., trans. 1955. *The Care to Be Taken for the Dead.* Vol. 27 in *The Fathers of the Church,* edited by Roy J. Deferrari.

Schopen, Gregory. 1994. "Ritual Rights and Bones of Contention: More on Monastic Funerals and Relics in the *Mūlasarvāstivāda-vinaya.*" *Journal of Indian Philosophy* 22.

———. 1994. "Stūpa and Tīrtha: Tibetan Mortuary Practices and an Unrecognized Form of Burial Ad Sanctos at Buddhist Sites in India." In *The Buddhist Forum.* Vol. 3, *1991–1993,* edited by Tadeusz Skorupski.

———. 1997. *Bones, Stones, and Buddhist Monks: Collected Papers on the Archaeology, Epigraphy, and Texts of Monastic Buddhism in India.*

REFERENCES

Ariès, Philippe. 1974. *Western Attitudes toward Death: From the Middle Ages to the Present,* translated by Patricia M. Ranum. Baltimore: Johns Hopkins University Press.

———. 1981. *The Hour of our Death,* translated by Helen Weaver. New York: Alfred A. Knopf.

Bareau, André. 1960. "La Construction et le culte des stūpa d'après les vinayapiṭaka." *Bulletin de l'école française d'extrême-orient* 50.

Beveridge, Henry, trans. 1884. *Tracts Relating to the Reformation,* by John Calvin. Edinburgh: Calvin Translation Society.

Brown, Peter. 1981. *The Cult of the Saints: Its Rise and Function in Latin Christianity.* Chicago: University of Chicago Press.

Bynum, Caroline Walker. 1995. *The Resurrection of the Body in Western Christianity, 200–1336.* New York: Columbia University Press.

Delumeau, Jean. 1989. *Rassurer et protéger: Le Sentiment de sécurité dans l'occident d'autrefois.* Paris: Fayard.

Duroiselle, C. 1915. "Excavations at Hmawza, Prome." *Annual Report of the Archaeological Survey of India for 1911–1912.* Calcutta: Government of India.

Duval, Yvette. 1988. *Auprès des saints corps et âme: L'inhumation "ad sanctos" dans la chrétienté d'orient et d'occident du IIIe au VIIe siècle.* Paris: Etudes Augustiniennes.

Duval, Yvette, and J.-Ch. Picard, eds. 1986. *L'Inhumation privilegiee du IVe au VIIIe siecle en occident.* Paris: De Boccard.

Eire, Carlos M. N. 1986. *War against the Idols: The Reformation of Worship from Erasmus to Calvin.* Cambridge: Cambridge University Press.

Frend, William H. C. 1996. *The Archaeology of Early Christianity: A History.* Minneapolis: Fortress Press.

Geary, Patrick J. 1994. *Living with the Dead in the Middle Ages.* Ithaca: Cornell University Press.

Geiger, Wilhelm, trans. 1953. *Cūlavaṃsa: Being the More Recent Part of the Mahāvaṃsa.* Colombo: Ceylon Government Information Department.

Gilman, W. H., ed. 1965. *Selected Writings of Ralph Waldo Emerson.* New York: Penguin Group.

Harries, Jill. 1992. "Death and the Dead in the Late Roman West." In *Death in Towns: Urban Responses to the Dying and the Dead,* edited by Steven Bassett. London: Leicester University Press.

Hastings, James. 1908–21. *Encyclopaedia of Religion and Ethics.* Edinburgh: Clark.

Hillgarth, J. N. 1986. *Christianity and Paganism, 350–750: The Conversion of Western Europe.* Philadelphia: University of Pennsylvania Press.

Lacy, John A., trans. 1955. *The Care to Be Taken for the Dead.* Vol. 27 of *The Fathers of the Church,* edited by Roy J. Deferrari. New York: Fathers of the Church.

MacGregor, Geddes. 1992. *Images of Afterlife: Beliefs from Antiquity to Modern Times.* New York: Paragon House.

McCulloh, John M. 1976. "The Cult of Relics in the Letters and 'Dialogues' of Pope Gregory the Great: A Lexicographical Study." *Traditio* 32.

Mulders, I., and R. Demeulenaere, eds. 1985. *Victricii Rotomagensis: De Laude Sanctorum.* In *Corpus Christianorum.* Series Latina 64. Turnhout: Brepols.

Rhys Davids, T. W., and C. A. F. Rhys Davids. 1910. *Dialogues of the Buddha,* part 2. London: H. Frowde.

Ricciotti, Giuseppe. 1959. *Julian the Apostate,* translated by M. Joseph Costelloe. Milwaukee: Bruce.

Scarisbrick, J. J. 1984. *The Reformation and the English People.* Oxford: Basil Blackwell.

Schopen, Gregory. 1994. "Stūpa and Tīrtha: Tibetan Mortuary Practices and an Unrecognized Form of Burial Ad Sanctos at Buddhist Sites in India." In *The Buddhist Forum.* Vol. 3, *1991–1993,* edited by Tadeusz Skorupski. London: School of Oriental and African Studies.

———. 1996. "The Suppression of Nuns and the Ritual Murder of Their Special Dead in Two Buddhist Monastic Texts." *Journal of Indian Philosophy* 24.

———. 1997. *Bones, Stones, and Buddhist Monks: Collected Papers on the Archaeology, Epigraphy, and Texts of Monastic Buddhism in India.* Honolulu: University of Hawaii Press.

Suzuki, D. T., ed. 1955–61. *The Tibetan Tripitaka.* Peking Edition. Kyoto: Otani University.

Van Dam, Raymond, trans. 1988. *Gregory of Tours, Glory of the Martyrs.* Liverpool: Liverpool University Press.

Religion, Religions, Religious

Jonathan Z. Smith

In the second earliest account of the "New World" published in English, *A Treatyse of the Newe India* (1553), Richard Eden wrote of the natives of the Canary Islands that, "At Columbus first comming thether, the inhabitantes went naked, without shame, religion or knowledge of God." In the same year, toward the beginning of the first part of his massive *Crónica del Perú* (1553), the conquistador historian Pedro Cieza de León described the north Andean indigenous peoples as "observing no religion at all, as we understand it *(no . . . religion alguna, à lo que entendemos)*, nor is there any house of worship to be found." While both were factually incorrect, their formulations bear witness to the major expansion of the use and understanding of the term "religion" that began in the sixteenth century and anticipate some of the continuing issues raised by that expansion: (1) "Religion" is not a native category. It is not a first person term of self-characterization. It is a category imposed from the outside on some aspect of native culture. It is the other, in these instances colonialists, who are solely responsible for the content of the term. (2) Even in these early formulations, there is an implicit universality. "Religion" is thought to be a ubiquitous human phenomenon; therefore, both Eden and Cieza find its alleged absence noteworthy. (3) In constructing the second-order, generic category "religion," its characteristics are those that appear natural to the other. In these quotations this familiarity is signaled by the phrases "knowledge of God" and "religion . . . as we understand it." (4) "Religion" is an anthropological not a theological category. (Perhaps the only exception is the distinctively American nineteenth-century coinages, "to get religion" or "to experience religion.") It describes human thought and action, most frequently in terms of belief and norms of behavior. Eden understands the content of "religion" largely in the former sense ("without . . . religion or knowledge of God"), whereas Cieza articulates it in the latter ("no religion . . . nor . . . any house of worship").

The term "religion" has had a long history, much of it, prior to the sixteenth century, irrelevant to contemporary usage. Its etymology is uncertain, although one of the three current possibilities, that it stems from the root *leig* meaning "to bind" rather than from roots meaning "to reread" or "to be careful," has been the subject of considerable Christian homiletic expansion from Lactantius's *Divine Institutes* (early fourth century) and Augustine's *On True Religion* (early fifth century) to William Camden's *Britannia* (1586). In both Roman and early Christian Latin usage, the noun forms *religio/religiones* and, most especially, the adjectival *religiosus* and the adverbial *religiose* were cultic terms referring primarily to the careful performance of ritual obligations. This sense survives in the

English adverbial construction "religiously" designating a conscientious repetitive action such as "She reads the morning newspaper religiously." The only distinctively Christian usage was the fifth-century extension of this cultic sense to the totality of an individual's life in monasticism: "religion," a life bound by monastic vows; "religious," a monk; "to enter religion," to join a monastery. It is this technical vocabulary that is first extended to non-Christian examples in the literature of exploration, particularly in descriptions of the complex civilizations of Mesoamerica. Thus Hernán Cortés, in his second *Carta de Relacíon* (1520, 64), writes of Tenochtitlan:

> This great city contains many mosques *[mezquitas,* an eleventh century Spanish loan word from the Arabic, *masjid],* or houses for idols. . . . The principal ones house persons of their religious orders *(personas religiosas de su secta).* . . . All these monks *(religiosos)* dress in black . . . from the time they enter the order *(entran en la religión).*

Cortes's relatively thoughtless language of assimilation is raised to the level of a systemic category two generations later in the encyclopedic work of the Jesuit scholar Joseph de Acosta, *The Natural and Moral History of the Indies* (1590; English translation, 1604). While the vast majority of the occurrences of the term "religious" refer to either Catholic or native members of "religious orders," sometimes expanded to the dual category, "priests and monks of Mexico" *(los sacerdotes y religiosos de México),* a number of passages strain toward a more generic conception. The work is divided into two parts, with the latter, "moral history," chiefly devoted to religion, governance, and political history. "Religion" per se is never defined. Its meaning must be sought in words associated with it as well as its synonyms. For Acosta, "religion" is the belief system that results in ceremonial behavior. "Religion" is "that which is used *(que usan)* in their rites." "Custom" *(costumbre),* "superstition" *(superstición),* and "religion" *(religión)* form a belief series in conjunction with the action series of "deed" *(hecho),* "rite" *(rito),* "idolatry" *(idolatria),* "sacrifice" *(sacrificio),* "ceremony" *(ceremonia),* and "feasts" *(fiestas y solemnidades).*

"Religion" in relation to ritual practice became an item in an inventory of cultural topics that could be presented either ethnographically in terms of a particular people, as in Eden or Cieza with reference to the "Indies," or in a cross-cultural encyclopedia under the heading of "ritual" or "religion." The encyclopedic version is illustrated by Joannes Boemus's popular *Omnium gentium mores, leges et ritus* (1520), in which *ritus* was translated as "customs" in the English translations by William Watreman, *The Fardle of Facions, Conteining the Aunciente Manners, Customes and Lawes of the People Inhabiting the Two Partes of the Earth* (1555) and by Edward Aston, *The Manners, Laws and Customs of all Nations* (1611), and by Sebastian Muenster's *Cosmographiae universalis . . . : Item omnium gentium mores, leges, religio* (1550). This focus on ritual had an unintended consequence. The myths and beliefs of other folk could simply be recorded as "antiquities," to use the term employed by Columbus. They raised no particular issues for thought. But ritual, especially when it seemed similar to Christian practice or when it illustrated categories of otherness such as "idolatry" or "cannibalism," gave rise to projects of comparative and critical inquiries. Similarity and difference, with respect to ritual, constituted a puzzle that required explanation by appeals to old patristic, apologetic charges of priestly deceit or to equally apologetic, patristic theories of accommodation, demonic plagiarism, diffusion, or degeneration. In the case of belief and myth, "their" words were primary; with ritual, "our" account superseded theirs.

Some two centuries later, this essentially Catholic understanding of "religion" in close proximity to ritual has been decisively altered. Samuel Johnson, in his *Dictionary of the English Language* (1755), defines "religion" as "virtue, as founded upon reverence of God, and expectations of future rewards and punishments." The first edition of the *Encyclopaedia Britannica* (1771) titled its entry "Religion, or Theology," defining the topic in the opening paragraph: "To know God, and to render him a reasonable service, are the two principal objects of religion. . . . Man appears to be formed to adore, but not to comprehend, the Supreme Being." Terms such as "reverence," "service," "adore," and "worship" in these sorts of definitions have been all but evacuated of ritual connotations, and seem more to denote a state of mind, a transition begun by Reformation figures such as Zwingli and Calvin who understood "religion" primarily as "piety." The latter term takes on a less awesome cast in subsequent Protestant discourse, for example, "Piety, a Moral vertue which causes us to have affection and esteem for God and Holy Things" (Phillips 1696).

This shift to belief as the defining characteristic of religion (stressed in the German preference for the term *Glaube* over *Religion*, and in the increasing English usage of "faiths" as a synonym for "religions") raised a host of interrelated questions as to credibility and truth. These issues were exacerbated by the schismatic tendencies of the various Protestantisms, with their rival claims to authority, as well as by the growing awareness of the existence of a multitude of articulate, non-Christian traditions. The former is best illustrated by the first attempt to provide a distribution map for the various European Protestantisms: Ephraim Pagitt's *Christianographie, or The Description of the Multitude and Sundry Sorts of Christians in the World Not Subject to the Pope* (1635). The latter is the explicit subject of the anthropological work by Edward Brerewood, *Enquiries Touching the Diversity of Languages and Religions through the Chiefe Parts of the World* (1614), which distinguished four "sorts" (i.e., "species") of the genus "religion"—"Christianity, Mohametanism, Judaism and Idolatry"—and provided statistical estimates for "the quantitie and proportion of the parts of the earth possessed by the several sorts" (118–19). It is the question of the plural *religions* (both Christian and non-Christian) that forced a new interest in the singular, generic *religion*. To cite what is perhaps the first widely read English book to employ the plural in its title, *Purchas His Pilgrimage; or, Relations of the World and the Religions Observed in All Ages and Places Discovered,* "The true Religion can be but one, and that which God himselfe teacheth[,] . . . all other religions being but strayings from him, whereby men wander in the darke, and in labyrinthine errour" (Purchas 1613, sig. D4r). What is implicit in Purchas becomes explicit in later seventeenth- and eighteenth-century debates concerning "natural religion," a term that became common only in the latter half of the seventeenth century, beginning with works such as the one by the prolific Puritan controversialist Richard Baxter, *The Reasons of the Christian Religion* (1667), in two parts: "Of Natural Religion, or Godliness," and "Of Christianity, and Supernatural Religion." (Compare Baxter's earlier but congruent terminology, *Of Saving Faith, That It Is Not Only Gradually but Specifically Distinct from All Common Faith* [1658]).

As David Pailan (1994) has demonstrated, the notion of natural religion has been employed in the literature "to designate at least eleven significantly different notions, some of which have significant sub-divisions" ranging from "religious beliefs and practices that are based on rational understanding that all people allegedly can discover for themselves and can warrant by rational reflection" to "that which is held to be common to the different actual faiths that have been and are present in the world." The former definition largely grew out of intra-Christian sectarian disputation and relied primarily on processes of introspection; the latter arose from study of the "religions," and involved processes of comparison. The essentially anthropological project of describing natural religion privileged similarity, often expressed by claims of universality or innateness; the explanation of difference was chiefly historical, whether it emphasized progressive or degenerative processes. This double enterprise had the effect of blurring the distinctions between questions of truth and questions of origins. For example, the title of Matthew Tindal's fairly pedestrian but widely read treatise, published anonymously as *Christianity As Old as the Creation; or, The Gospel, a Republication of the Religion of Nature* (1730; six printings by 1732, and the *British Museum General Catalogue* lists more than forty replies in the 1730s), contains early English uses of the terms "religion of nature" and "Christianity." Tindal argues:

> If God, then, from the Beginning gave Men a Religion[,] . . . he must have giv'n them likewise sufficient Means of knowing it. . . . If God never intended Mankind shou'd at any Time be without Religion, or have false Religions; and there be but One True Religion, which ALL have been ever bound to believe, and profess[,] . . . All Men, at all Times, must have had sufficient Means to discover whatever God design'd they shou'd know and practice. . . . [He] has giv'n them no other Means for this, but the use of Reason. . . . There was from the Beginning but One True Religion, which all Men might know was their Duty to embrace. . . . By [this] *Natural Religion,* I understand the Be-

lief of the Existence of a God, and the Sense and Practice of those Duties, which result from the Knowledge, we, by our Reason, have of
Him and his Perfections; and of ourselves, and our own Imperfections;
and of the Relations we stand in to him, and to our Fellow-Creatures;
so that the *Religion of Nature* takes in every Thing that is founded on
the Reason and the Nature of Things. (pp. 3–7, 13)

While Tindal acknowledges some relativity—"I do not mean by This that All
shou'd have equal Knowledge; but that All shou'd have what is sufficient for the
Circumstances they are in" (p. 5)—his usual explanation for variation is the historical institution and wiles of "priestcraft":

Religion either does not concern the Majority, as being incapable of
forming a Judgement about it; or must carry such internal Marks of
its Truth, as Men of mean Capacity are able to discover; or else notwithstanding the infinite Variety of Religions, All who do not understand the Original Languages their traditional Religions are written
in, which is all Mankind, a very few excepted, are alike bound in all
Places to pin their Faith on their Priests, and believe in Men, who
have an Interest to deceive them; and who have seldom fail'd to do
so, when Occasion serves. (p. 232)

In Tindal's self-description,

He builds nothing on a Thing so uncertain as *Tradition,* which differs in most Countries; and of which, in all Countries, the Bulk of
Mankind are incapable of judging; but thinks he has laid down such
plain and evident Rules, as may enable Men of the meanest Capacity,
to distinguish between *Religion,* and *Superstition.* (p. iii)

When Tindal argued on logical grounds, the presumption of the unity of
truth, that natural religion "differs not from *Reveal'd,* but in the manner of its
being communicated: The One being the Internal, as the Other the External
Revelation" (p. 3) he signaled the beginning of the process of transposing "religion" from a supernatural to a natural history, from a theological to an anthropological category. This process was complete only when the distinctions between questions of truth and questions of origin were firmly established. While
not without predecessors, the emblem of this transposition is David Hume's essay *The Natural History of Religion,* written between 1749 and 1751 and first
published in his collection *Four Dissertations* (1757).

The question Hume sets out to answer in the *Natural History* is that of religion's "origin in human nature." He begins by disposing of the innateness thesis. If "religion" is defined as "the belief of invisible, intelligent power," then,
although widely distributed, it is not universal, nor is there commonality: "no
two nations, and scarce any two men, have ever agreed precisely in the same

sentiments." "Religion" fails the minimal requirements for innateness, that it be "absolutely universal in all nations and ages and has always a precise, determinate object, which it inflexibly pursues." Therefore, "religion" is not "an original instinct or primary impression of nature," and "the first religious principles must be secondary." In addition, because they are "secondary," religious principles "may easily be perverted by various accidents and causes" (p. 25). In this opening move, a major thesis is forecast. There may well be a primary and valid human experience that gives rise to the secondary religious interpretation, but the truth of the experience is no guarantee of the validity of the interpretation.

The rich details of Hume's exposition need not concern us here but only the argument with respect to this issue. "Polytheism or idolatry was . . . the first and most antient religion of mankind." Its origin must be sought in "the ordinary affections of human life." Filled with anxiety, human beings seek the "unknown causes" that "become the constant object of our hope and fear." The primary human experience, "hope and fear," becomes a secondary religious interpretation when these "unknown causes" are personified through "imagination" (pp. 26, 31–33).

> There is a universal tendency amongst mankind to conceive all beings like themselves, and to transfer to every object those qualities, with which they are familiarly acquainted, and of which they are intimately conscious. . . . No wonder, then, that mankind, being placed in such an absolute ignorance of causes, and being at the same time so anxious concerning their future fortunes, should immediately acknowledge a dependence on invisible powers, possest of sentiment and intelligence. The *unknown causes,* which continually employ their thought, appearing always in the same aspect, are all apprehended to be of the same kind or species [as themselves]. Nor is it long before we ascribe to them thought, and reason, and passion, and sometimes even the limbs and figures of men, in order to bring them nearer to a resemblance with ourselves. (pp. 33–34)

What Hume here raises is the issue of the adjectival form "religious." What sort of primary human experience or activity does it modify? What constitutes its distinctive secondary interpretation? How may religious interpretation be assessed in relation to other sorts of interpretation of the same experience or activity? The "religious" (the unknown that the scholar is seeking to classify and explain) becomes an aspect of some other human phenomenon (the known). As Walter Capps (1995, 9) has argued, in the eighteenth-century Enlightenment debates "the goal of the inquiry was to make religion intelligible by discovering precisely where it is situated within the wide range of interactive human powers and faculties." In which of the genera of common individual human capacities is the religious a species? Most frequently, the religious is identified with rationality, morality, or feeling.

A different set of taxonomic questions were raised by the "religions" and became urgent by the nineteenth century: Are the diverse "religions" species of a generic "religion"? Is "religion" the unique beginner, a *summum genus,* or is it best conceived as a subordinate cultural taxon? How might the several "religions" be classified?

The question of the "religions" arose in response to an explosion of data. Increased mastery of non-European languages led by the latter part of the eighteenth century to a series of translations and editions of religious texts. Missionaries, colonial officials, and travelers contributed ethnographic descriptions. Encyclopedias of religions, lexica, and handbooks (the latter, frequently bearing the title "History of Religions") were produced to organize these materials. One of the earliest handbooks, *Historische-theologische Bericht vom Unterschied der Religionen die Heute zu Tage auf Erden sind,* by the Lutheran scholar Johann Heinrich Ursin (1563), focused heavily on the various Christian denominations, establishing a pattern that holds to the present day: that the history of the major "religions" is best organized as sectarian history, thereby reproducing the apologetic patristic heresiological model. By the time of Brerewood's *Enquiries Touching the Diversity of Languages and Religions* (1614) this horizon had been extended to require inclusion of not only Christian data but also Jewish, Muslim, and "idolatry." This fourfold schema was continued by other writers from the seventeenth century (for example, Guebhart Meier, *Historia religionum, Christianae, Judaeae, Gentilis, Mahumedanae* [1697]) until well into the nineteenth century (Hannah Adams, *A Dictionary of All Religions and Religious Denominations, Jewish, Heathen, Mahometan, and Christian, Ancient and Modern* [1817]; David Benedict, *History of All Religions, As Divided into Paganism, Mahometism, Judaism, and Christianity* [1824]; J. Newton Brown, *Encyclopedia of Religious Knowledge: or, Dictionary . . . Containing Definitions of All Religious Terms; An Impartial Account of the Principal Christian Denominations that have Existed in the World from the Birth of Christ to the Present Day with their Doctrines, Religious Rites and Ceremonies, as well as those of the Jews, Mohammedans, and Heathen Nations, together with the Manners and Customs of the East* [1835b]; Vincent Milner, *Religious Denominations of the World: Comprising a General View of the Origin, History and Condition of the Various Sects of Christians, the Jews, and Mahometans, As Well as the Pagan Forms of Religion Existing in the Different Countries of the Earth* [1872]). The bulk of the subsequent expansion occurred in Brerewood's fourth category, "Idolatry," with data added on Asian religions and on those of traditional peoples. Beginning with Alexander Ross, *Pansebeia; or A View of All Religions in the World from the Creation to These Times* (1614), there was a steady stream of reference works that undertook this task, including Bernard Picart and J. F. Bernard, *Cérémonies et coutumes de tous peuples du monde* (1723–43); Antoine Banier, *Historie général des cérémonies, moeurs, et coutumes religieuses de tous les peuples du monde* (1741); Thomas Broughton, *An Historical Dictionary of All Religions, from the Creation of the*

World to the Present Time (1742); Christopher Meiners, *Grundriss der Geschichte aller Religionen* (1785) and *Allgemeine kritische Geschichte der Religionen* (1806–7); John Bellemy, *The History of All Religions* (1812); and Benjamin Constant, *De la religion considérée dans sa source, ses formes et ses développements* (1824–31). This undertaking invented the familiar nomenclature, "Boudhism" (1821), "Hindooism" (1829, which replaced the earlier seventeenth-century usages "Gentoo [from "gentile"] religion" and "Banian religion"), "Taouism" (1839), and "Confucianism" (1862). The urgent agendum was to bring order to this variety of species. Only an adequate taxonomy would convert a "natural history" of religion into a "science."

The most common form of classifying religions, found both in native categories and in scholarly literature, is dualistic and can be reduced, regardless of what differentium is employed, to "theirs" and "ours." By the time of the fourth-century Christian Latin apologists, a strong dual vocabulary was well in place and could be deployed interchangeably regardless of the individual histories of the terms: "our religion"/"their religion," with the latter often expressed through generic terms such as "heathenism," "paganism," or "idolatry"; "true religion"/"false religion"; "spiritual (or "internal") religion"/"material (or "external") religion"; "monotheism" (although this term, itself, is a relatively late construction)/"polytheism"; "religion"/"superstition"; "religion"/"magic." This language was transposed to intrareligious disputation with respect to heresies, and later revived in positive proposals of originary recovery in Christian Renaissance hermetism as well as, most massively and insistently, in Protestant polemics against Roman Catholicism. As such, it was at hand for the evaluation of the newly encountered religions beginning in the sixteenth century. Lifting up the fourfold enumeration of religions—Christianity, Judaism, Islam, and "Idolatry"—Christianity, in some imagination of its ideal form, became the norm in which Judaism and Islam problematically share. Adopting a term from Muslim discourse, these three "Abrahamic religions" form one set over and against an undifferentiated other:

> It is indeed probable, that all the idolatrous systems of religion, which have ever existed in the world, have had a common origin, and have been modified by the different fancies and corruptions of different nations. The essence of idolatry is every where the same. It is every where "abominable" in its principles and its rites, and every where the cause of indescribable and manifold wretchedness. (Brown 1835a, 229)

The initial problem for a classification of the religions is the disaggregation of this category.

One of the more persistent stratagems was the conversion of the epistemological duality natural/supernatural into a characterization of the object of belief (as in "nature worship") and the placement of these two terms in a chronological relationship.

> The elements of nature were . . . the first divinities of man; he generally has commenced with adoring material beings. . . . Everything was personified. . . . Natural philosophers and poets [later distinguished] nature from herself—from her own peculiar energies—from her faculty of action. By degrees they made an incomprehensible being of this energy, which as before they personified: this abstract metaphysical being they called the mover of nature, or God. (Mirabaud 1770, 2:4)

This simple schema of two religions could be greatly extended by the addition of intermediate stages in the temporal series.

Nineteenth-century anthropological approaches focused on increasing the number of "natural" religious categories, especially for "primitive" peoples, those held to be "nature peoples" *(Naturvolker)*. Often mistermed evolutionary, these theories conceded no historical dimensions to those being classified but rather froze each ethnic unit at a particular "stage of development" of the totality of human religious thought and activity. "Natural" religion was segmented into fetishism, totemism, shamanism, anthropomorphism, preanimism, animism, family gods, guardian spirits, ancestor worship, departmental gods, to name but a few. If the category "natural" were to be taken as including not only "primitives" but "antiquity," a set of peoples with whom the scholar more readily identified, then a meager note of historical dynamism would be introduced. For example, A. M. Fairbairn in his *Studies in the Philosophy of Religion and History* (1876) divided "Spontaneous or Natural Religions" into two classes, "Primitive Naturalisms" (which included, among others, "primitives" and the "early" Greeks, Hindus, Teutons, and Slavs) and "Transformed Naturalisms" (e.g., "later" Greeks and Romans, Egyptians, and "ancient" Chinese).

The "high religions," which could be designated "spiritual," required a different technique for their division, one that recognized history. One proposal, establishing an alternative duality that remains current to this day, was set forth by the distinguished American Sanskritist, W. D. Whitney (1881, 451): "There is no more marked distinction among religions than the one we are called upon to make between a race religion—which, like a language, is the collective product of the wisdom of a community, the unconscious growth of generations—and a religion proceeding from an individual founder." He cites as examples of the latter, Zoroastrianism, "Mohammedanism," Buddhism, and Christianity, noting that the latter may be described as "growing out of one [Judaism] that was limited to a race." Whitney here makes clear the dilemma posed by the study of the "religions" from the perspective of the spiritual. The older fourfold enumeration of the three "Abrahamic religions" plus "Idolatry" required revision.

Judaism was to be demoted in that from a Christian apologetic perspective, it was the very type of a "fleshly religion"; Buddhism was to be promoted because in the two-century history of the Western imagination of Buddhism, it had become the very type of "spiritual religion."

Fairbairn adjusted his model such that the ultimate duality was between "spontaneous or natural religions" and "instituted religions," with the latter having two classes, each characterized by the same powerfully positive Protestant term: "Reformed Natural" (including the archaic religion of Israel ["Mosaism"], Zoroastrianism, Confucianism, Taoism), and "Reformed Spiritual," limited only to the new triad (Buddhism, "Mohammedanism," and Christianity). All other "religions" fell into one of three classes of "natural," the replacement term for the older category, "idolatry."

The most enduring device was the invention of the taxon "world" or "universal religions," a division that appeared to recognize both history and geography. The term was introduced and placed in a classificatory scheme that synthesized previous taxonomic divisions in a work that stands as the first classic in the science of religion, Cornelius Petrus Tiele's work *Outline of the History of Religion to the Spread of Universal Religions* (1876), and was reworked in Tiele's article "Religions" in the ninth edition of the *Encyclopaedia Britannica* (1884). Tiele's "morphological" classification, which schematizes the "stage of development" each religion has "attained," has as its fundamental principle of division "natural religion" and "ethical religion," which he self-consciously correlates with Whitney's distinction between "race religion" and "founded religion." "Natural religion" has three families, one of which has two genera. The first family comprises "polydaemonistic magical religions under the control of animism." To this class "belong [all] the religions of the so-called savages or uncivilized peoples." Recognizing, perhaps, the effects of colonialism, he adds that their present forms are "only degraded remnants of what they once must have been."

The second family of "nature religions" is that of "purified or organized magical religions," which Tiele terms "therianthropic polytheism," according to which the "gods are sometimes represented in human form, more frequently in that of an animal." These are politically divided into two families, "unorganized" (tribal) and "organized" (imperial). The "unorganized" include the Japanese *kami* traditions, the Dravidians, the Finns, the "old Arabic religions, old Pelasgic religion, old Italiote religions, Etruscan religion before its admixture with Greek elements, [and] the old Slavonic religions." The "organized" include "the semi-civilized religions of America, . . . the ancient religion of the Chinese empire, ancient Babylonian (Chaldaean) religion, [and] the religion of Egypt."

The third family, "anthropomorphic polytheism," is characterized by the "worship of manlike but superhuman and semi-ethical beings" (the latter indicating that while the gods are often represented as being concerned with good and evil, they are also depicted as essentially amoral). Belonging to this class are "the ancient Vaidic religion (India), the pre-Zarathustrian Iranic religion, the younger Babylonian and Assyrian religion, the religions of the other civilized Semites, the Celtic, Germanic, Hellenic and Graeco-Roman religions."

Distinct from these "nature religions" are those belonging to the second major division, "ethical religions," which are subdivided into "national nomistic (nomothetic) religious communities" characterized by being "founded on a law or holy scripture," that is, "Taoism and Confucianism . . . Brahmanism, with its various ancient and modern sects, Jainism and primitive Buddhism, Mazdaism (Zarathustrianism) with its sects, Mosaism [and] Judaism," and "universalistic religious communities," a class with only three members: Islam, Buddhism, Christianity. They are distinguished in not being devoted to the special interests of a nation or people but to humankind in general; they are proselytizing traditions.

After discussing at some length the relative merits of the labels "universalistic," "universal," and "world religions," Tiele employs blunt imperialistic language to defend his use of "world religions" to

> distinguish the three religions which have found their way to different races and peoples and all of which profess the intention to conquer the world, from such communities [that is, "national, nomistic religions"] as are generally limited to a single race or nation, and, where they have extended farther, have done so only in the train of, and in connection with, a superior civilization. Strictly speaking, there can be no more than one universal or world religion, and if one of the existing religions is so potentially, it has not yet reached its goal. This is a matter of belief which lies beyond the limits of scientific classification. . . . Modern history of religions is chiefly the history of Buddhism, Christianity and Islam, and of their wrestling with the ancient faiths and primitive modes of worship, which slowly fade away before their encroachments, and which, where they still survive in some parts of the world and do not reform themselves after the model of the superior religion, draw nearer and nearer to extinction.

Furthermore, he apologetically insists, the three "world religions" are not on an equal plane. Islam "is not original, not a ripe fruit, but rather a wild offshoot of Judaism and Christianity," "in its external features [it] is little better than an extended Judaism." Buddhism "neglects the divine" and while "atheistic in its origin, it very soon becomes infected by the most fantastic mythology and the most childish superstitions." Christianity "alone preaches a worship in spirit and in truth . . . the natural result of its purely spiritual character, Christianity ranks incommensurably high above both its rivals." Despite the latter assertion, Tiele insists that "we are giving here neither a confession of faith nor an apology. . . . we have here to treat Christianity simply as a subject of comparative study, from a scientific, not from a religious point of view." (Tiele 1884, 20:358–71.)

Later scholars expanded the number of world religions to seven by collapsing Tiele's two classes of "ethical religions" in an odd venture of pluralistic etiquette: if Christianity and Islam count as world religions, then it would be rude to exclude Judaism (ironically, the original model for the opposite type, "national nomistic religions"). Likewise, if Buddhism is included, then Hinduism cannot be ignored. And again, if Buddhism, then Chinese religions and Japanese religions.

It is impossible to escape the suspicion that a world religion is simply a religion like ours, and that it is, above all, a tradition that has achieved sufficient power and numbers to enter our history to form it, interact with it, or thwart it. We recognize both the unity within and the diversity among the world religions because they correspond to important geopolitical entities with which we must deal. All "primitives," by way of contrast, may be lumped together, as may the "minor religions," because they do not confront our history in any direct fashion. From the point of view of power, they are invisible.

Attempting to avoid such strictures and suspicions, other scholars have turned to alternative modes of classification. Following the implied correlation in Brerewood's *Enquiries Touching the Diversity of Languages and Religions*, F. Max Müller (1873, 143) argued "that the only scientific and truly genetic classification of religions is the same as the classification of languages," while Brerewood's interest in statistics has led to geographical taxonomies, either demographic (Haupt 1821 is an early example) or in terms of spatial distribution (for example, Deffontaines 1948). Others combine these elements with ethnographic classifications maintaining that any particular "religion derives its character from the people or race who develop it or adopt it" (Ward 1909, 64). All of these result in projects describing "the religion of" such and such a geographical region or folk, arguing that these eschew the imposed universalisms or barely disguised apologetics of their predecessors in the name of a new ethic of locality that often favors native categories. Thus, Clifford Geertz introduces his early work *The Religion of Java* (1960) by emphasizing the copresence of nativistic, Islamic, and "Hinduist" elements, arguing that "these three main subtraditions . . . are not constructed types, but terms and divisions the Javanese themselves apply. . . . Any simple unitary view is certain to be inadequate; and so I have tried to show . . . variation in ritual, contrast in belief, and conflict in values" (pp. 6–7). What remains uncertain is what he intends by the singular religion in his title.

As in the eighteenth century, so too in the late twentieth do the issues attending the religions force the definitional question of religion. Two definitions command widespread scholarly assent, one essentially theological, the other anthropological. Paul Tillich, reversing his previous formulation that religion is concern for the ultimate, argued that

> religion, in the largest and most basic sense of the word, is ultimate
> concern . . . manifest in the moral sphere as the unconditional seri-

ousness of moral demand[,] . . . in the realm of knowledge as the passionate longing for ultimate reality[,] . . . in the aesthetic function of the human spirit as the infinite desire to express ultimate meaning." [Religion is not a] special function of man's spiritual life, but the dimension of depth in all its functions. (1959, 7–8)

As Tillich's earlier concern with topics such as idolatry and the demonic should suggest, this is not as generous and open ended a definition as might seem to be implied. There are insufficient, inadequate, and false convictions of "ultimacy." Tillich has in fact provided a definition of the religious, as a dimension (in his case, the ultimate, unconditioned aspect) of human existence. This is explicit in William A. Christian's reformulation: "Someone is religious if in his universe there is something to which (in principle) all other things are subordinated. Being religious means having an interest of this kind" (1964, 61). If one removes Tillich's and Christian's theological criteria (as, for example, Robert D. Baird suggests in *Category Formation and the History of Religions* [1971]), then it becomes difficult if not impossible to distinguish religion from any other ideological category. This would be the direction that Ninian Smart (1983) points to in suggesting that religion be understood as "worldview," with the latter understood as a system "of belief which, through symbols and actions, mobilize[s] the feelings and wills of human beings" (pp. 2–3).

The anthropological definition of religion that has gained widespread assent among scholars of religion, who both share and reject its functionalist frame, is that formulated by Melford E. Spiro (1966, 96), "an institution consisting of culturally patterned interaction with culturally postulated superhuman beings." This definition requires acceptance of a broad theory of cultural creation, signaled by the phrases "culturally patterned" and "culturally postulated," and places human cultural activities or institutions as the *summum genus* and religion as a subordinate taxon. This is made plain in Spiro's formulation that "religion can be differentiated from other culturally constituted institutions by virtue only of its reference to superhuman beings" (p. 98). Subsequent reformulations by scholars of religion have tended either to remove this subordination (for example, Penner 1989) or to substitute "supernatural" for "superhuman" (as in Stark and Bainbridge 1987).

It was once a tactic of students of religion to cite the appendix of James H. Leuba's *Psychological Study of Religion* (1912), which lists more than fifty definitions of religion, to demonstrate that "the effort clearly to define religion in short compass is a hopeless task" (King 1954). Not at all! The moral of Leuba is not that religion cannot be defined, but that it can be defined, with greater or lesser success, more than fifty ways. Besides, Leuba goes on to classify and evaluate his list of definitions. "Religion" is not a native term; it is a term created by scholars for their intellectual purposes and therefore is theirs to define. It is a second-order, generic concept that plays the same role in establishing a disciplinary horizon that a concept such as "language" plays in linguistics or "culture" plays in anthropology. There can be no disciplined study of religion without such a horizon.

SUGGESTED READINGS

Almond, Philip C. 1988. *The British Discovery of Buddhism.*
Bianchi, Ugo, Fabio Mora, and Lorenzo Bianchi, eds. 1994. *The Notion of "Religion" in Comparative Research: Selected Proceedings of the Sixteenth Congress of the International Association for the History of Religions, Rome, 3–8 September 1990.*
Capps, Walter H. 1995. *Religious Studies: The Making of a Discipline.*
Despland, Michael. 1979. *La Religion en Occident.*
Feil, Ernst. 1986. *Religio: Die Geschichtes eines neuzeitlichen Grundbegriffs vom Frühchrisentum bis zür Reformation.*
Harrison, Peter. 1990. *"Religion" and the Religions in the English Enlightenment.*
Manuel, Frank E. 1959. *The Eighteenth Century Confronts the Gods.*
Pailan, David A. 1984. *Attitudes to Other Religions: Comparative Religion in Seventeenth- and Eighteenth-Century Britain.*
Penner, Hans H. 1989. *Impasse and Resolution: A Critique of the Study of Religion.*
Preus, J. Samuel. 1987. *Explaining Religion: Criticism and Theory from Bodin to Freud.*
Smith, Wilfred Cantwell. 1963. *The Meaning and End of Religion.*
Spiro, Melford E. 1966. "Religion: Problems of Definition and Explanation." In *Anthropological Approaches to the Study of Religion,* edited by Michael Banton.

REFERENCES

Acosta, Joseph de. 1604. *The Natural and Moral History of the Indies,* translation of the original Spanish edition, published in Seville in 1590. London: V. Sims for E. Blount and W. Aspley.
Adams, Hannah. 1817. *A Dictionary of All Religions and Religious Denominations, Jewish, Heathen, Mahometan, and Christian, Ancient and Modern.* 4th ed. Boston: Cummings and Hilliard.
Aston, Edward, trans. 1611. *The Manners, Laws, and Customs of All Nations,* by Joannes Boemus. London.
Baird, Robert D. 1971. *Category Formation and the History of Religions.* The Hague: Mouton de Gruyter.
Banier, Antoine. 1741. *Histoire générale des cérémonies, moeurs, et coutumes religieuses de tous les peuples du monde.* Paris.
Baxter, Richard. 1658. *Of Saving Faith, That It Is Not Only Gradually but Specifically Distinct from All Common Faith.* London.
———. 1667. *The Reasons of the Christian Religion.* London: Printed by R. White for Fran. Titon.
Bellemy, John. 1812. *The History of All Religions, Comprehending the Different Doctrines, Customs, and Order of Worship in the Churches . . . from the Beginning of Time to the Present Day.* London.

Benedict, David. 1824. *History of All Religions, As Divided into Paganism, Mahometism, Judaism, and Christianity.* Providence, R.I.

Bernard, J. F. 1723–43. *Cérémonies et coutumes de tous peuples du monde.* Amsterdam.

Boemus, Joannes. 1520. *Omnium gentium mores, leges, et ritus.* Augsburg.

Brerewood, Edward. 1614. *Enquiries Touching the Diversity of Languages and Religions through the Chiefe Parts of the World.* London.

Broughton, Thomas. 1742. *An Historical Dictionary of All Religions, from the Creation of the World to the Present Time.* London.

Brown, J. Newton. 1835a. "Buddhism." In *Encyclopedia of Religious Knowledge.* Brattleboro, Vt.

———. 1835b. *Encyclopedia of Religious Knowledge; or, Dictionary . . . Containing Definitions of All Religious Terms: An Impartial Account of the Principal Christian Denominations That Have Existed in the World from the Birth of Christ to the Present Day with Their Doctrines, Religious Rites, and Ceremonies, and Heathen Nations, Together with the Manners and Customs of the East.* Brattleboro, Vt.

Camden, William. 1586. *Britannia.* London.

Capps, Walter H. 1995. *Religious Studies: The Making of a Discipline.* Minneapolis: Fortress Press.

Christian, William A. 1964. *Meaning and Truth in Religion.* Princeton, N.J.

Cieza de León, Pedro. 1553. *Crónica del Perú.* 4 vols. Seville. Reprint 1918, edited by D. Enrique de Vedia, *Historiadores primitivos de Indias,* 2 vols. Madrid: Imprenta de los Sucesores de Hernando.

Constant, Benjamin. 1824–31. *De la religion considérée dans sa source, ses formes, et ses développements.* Paris.

Cortés, Hernán. 1520. *Cartas de Relacíon.* Reprint 1971, edited by Manuel Alcalá. Sepan Cuantos, no. 7. Mexico City: Editorial Porrúa.

Deffontaines, Pierre. 1948. *Géographie et religions.* Paris.

Eden, Richard. 1553. *A Treatyse of the Newe India.* London.

Encyclopaedia Britannica. 1771. 1st ed. Edinburgh.

Fairbairn, A. M. 1876. *Studies in the Philosophy of Religion and History.* London.

Geertz, Clifford. 1960. *The Religion of Java.* Glencoe, Ill.: Free Press.

Haupt, Karl G. 1821. *Tabellarischer Abriss der vorzüglichsten Religionen und Religionsparteien der jetzigen Erdebewohner.* Leipzig.

Hume, David. 1757. *The Natural History of Religion.* In *Four Dissertations.* London: Printed for A. Millar. Variorum edition, 1976, edited by A. Wayne Colver, Oxford, Clarendon Press. (Page numbers cited in text are from the Variorum ed.)

Johnson, Samuel, comp. and ed. 1755. *A Dictionary of the English Language.* London: W. Strahan, for J. and P. Knapton.

King, Winston L. 1954. *Introduction to Religion.* New York: Harper and Row.

Leuba, James H. 1912. *A Psychological Study of Religion.* New York: Macmillan.

Meier, Guebhart. 1697. *Historia religionum, Christianae, Judaeae, Gentilis, Mahumedanae.* Helmstadt.

Meiners, Christopher. 1785. *Grundriss der Geschichte aller Religionen.* Lemgo.

———. 1806–7. *Allgemeine kritische Geschichte der Religionen.* Hannover: Helwing.

Milner, Vincent. 1872. *Religious Denominations of the World: Comprising a General View of the Origin, History, and Condition of the Various Sects of Christians, the Jews, the Mahometans, as well as the Pagan Forms of Religion Existing in the Different Countries of the Earth.* Philadelphia.

Mirabaud, M. [Paul Henry Thiery, Baron d'Holbach]. 1770. *Système de la nature; ou, Des lois du monde physique et du monde moral.* [First English translation 1820, n.p.]

Muenster, Sebastian. 1550. *Cosmographiae universalis . . . : Item omnium gentium mores, leges, religio.* Basel.

Müller, F. Max. 1873. *Introduction to the Science of Religion.* London: Longmans, Green.

Pagitt, Ephraim. 1635. *Christianographie; or, The Description of the Multitude and Sundry Sorts of Christians in the World Not Subject to the Pope.* London.

Pailan, David. 1994. "Natural Religion." Paper presented at the annual meeting of the American Academy of Religion, Chicago.

Penner, Hans H. 1989. *Impasse and Resolution: A Critique of the Study of Religion.* New York: Peter Lang.

Phillips, Edward. 1696. *A New World of English Words; or, A General Dictionary Containing the Interpretation of Such Hard Words As Are Derived from Other Languages.* London: E. Tyler for Nathanael Brooke at the Sign of the Angel in Cornhill.

Picart, Bernard, and J. F. Bernard. 1723–43. *Cérémonies et coutumes de tous peuples du monde.* Amsterdam.

Purchas, Samuel. 1613. *Purchas His Pilgrimage; or, Relations of the World and the Religions Observed in All Ages and Places Discovered, in Foure Parts.* London.

Ross, Alexander. 1614. *Pansebeia; or, A View of All Religions in the World from the Creation to These Times, Together with the Discovery of All Known Heresies, in All Ages and Places.* London.

Smart, Ninian. 1983. *Worldviews: Cross-Cultural Explorations of Human Beliefs.* New York: Scribner's.

Spiro, Melford E. 1966. "Religion: Problems of Definition and Explanation." In *Anthropological Approaches to the Study of Religion,* edited by Michael Banton. London: Tavistock.

Stark, Rodney, and William S. Bainbridge. 1987. *A Theory of Religion.* New York: Peter Lang.

Tiele, Cornelius Petrus. 1877. *Outline of the History of Religion to the Spread of Universal Religions,* translation of the original Dutch edition, published in Amsterdam in 1876. London.

———. 1884. "Religions." In *Encyclopaedia Britannica.* 9th ed.

Tillich, Paul. 1959. *Theology of Culture,* edited by Robert C. Kimball. New York: Oxford University Press.

Tindal, Matthew. 1730. *Christianity As Old As the Creation; or, The Gospel, a Republication of the Religion of Nature.* London.

Ursin, Johann Heinrich. 1563. *Historische-theologische Bericht vom Unterschied der Religionen die Heute zu Tage auf Erden sind.* Nuremberg.

Ward, Duren J. H. 1909. *The Classification of Religions.* Chicago: Open Court.

Watreman, William, trans. 1555. *The Fardle of Facions, Conteining the Aunciente Manners, Customs, and Lawes of the People Inhabiting the Two Partes of the Earth,* by Joannes Boemus. London.

Whitney, W. D. 1881. "On the So-Called Science of Religion." *Princeton Review* 57, pt. 1: 429–52.

SIXTEEN

Sacrifice

Jill Robbins

While a comprehensive treament of the term, not to mention a theory of, "sacrifice," is not possible here, it will be useful to indicate the parameters and the points of reference that such a term and such a theory would comprise. After a general discussion of a historical and critical nature, I will turn briefly to an exemplary text from the Hebrew Bible, the binding of Isaac recounted in Genesis 22, in order to determine some of the questions it poses about sacrifice.

In the Hebrew Bible and in the cultic context of ancient Israelite religion, sacrifice, the offering up of slain animals for sacred purposes, holds a prominent place, although its full significance is not entirely understood. Leviticus, especially chapters 1 through 7 (generally attributed to the biblical author "P" or the Priestly source), details the laws of sacrifice. It makes distinctions between such categories as propitiary offerings (as atonement for sins and as a purification ritual) and dedicatory offerings (gifts for the deity). In the practice known as the sin offering, *hatta'at,* the offering must be the property of the person making the sacrifice. The sacrificer lays his hand on the offering, thus identifying it with himself. The idea behind this practice was explained by the medieval commentator Nachmanides in his commentary on Lev. 1:9 as follows: the sinner's life is forfeit to God, but by a gracious provision, he is permitted to substitute an animal victim in his place. Lev. 17:11 explains that the substitution occurs precisely by the extraction of the animal's blood: "For the life of the flesh is in the blood, and I have given it for you upon the altar to make atonement for your souls: for it is the blood that makes atonement, by reason of the life that is in it." While the idea of substitution and expiation is prominent in these cases, the dedicatory offerings convey primarily the idea of gift giving, which will later be explored within anthropological theories of sacrifice. These offerings are distinguished in terms of the matter, the mode, and even the place of sacrifice. For example, there is the meal offering, the *minha,* sometimes translated as "gift." In Genesis 4, Cain brings such a gift to God, who in turn indicates his preference for Abel's animal sacrifice over Cain's cereal offering. The burnt offering, the *olah,* which means literally "that which goes up," namely, the smoke, describes the mode of delivery of the sacrifice. It refers to an offering that is entirely consumed in the fire, what the Septuagint translates as *holokaustus,* and the King James, in its English equivalent, as "holocaust." (I will return later to the problematic use of this term to refer to the Nazi genocide of the Jews.) *Olah* is the word that is used in Genesis 8 for Noah's sacrifice, the odor of which is "pleasing" to God; it is also the word used in Genesis 22 when God commands Abraham to sacrifice his son. The term *zebah* is used in the Hebrew Bible for the slaughter of animals both for religious purposes and for the purposes of ordinary consumption. In the communion meal associated with the *zebah,* the animal victim is presented at the altar, but part of the flesh returns to the worshipper, to be eaten by him under special rules. Finally, the term *korban,* exclusively used for sacrifice, expresses the idea of "approach" or "bringing near," possibly to the altar.

What is described in the Book of Leviticus ceased to be practiced after the destruction of the second temple in 70 C.E., even though the material continued to be studied by rabbinic commentators on the Bible and is still studied by contemporary biblical scholars. Hence, one of the reasons why sacrifice remains enigmatic is that the old sacrifice is no longer practiced. Its "original," cultic meaning was already to some extent lost at the time of the redaction of the Hebrew Bible. Moreover, the relation of the Hebrew sacrificial system to the practices of neighboring cultures in the ancient Near East is interpreted in divergent ways. The medieval Jewish philosopher Maimonides argued that, since sacrifice was a universal custom among all peoples at the time of Moses, the laws pertaining to sacrifice in the Hebrew Bible were given to counteract the attractions of contemporary "paganism" and are of no intrinsic value. Yehezkel Kaufmann represents a contemporary prolongation of this view when he argues that sacrifice in the Hebrew Bible is a legacy of Israel's "pagan" environment but without the mythological and magical framework that lent cosmic significance to it. There are two issues here. First is the irreducible enigma of sacrifice as if it were the sign of something, the explanation of which has been lost. As Kaufmann puts it, "religion customarily conserves forms that have become emptied of meaning" (Kaufman 1972, 111). Second, such a scheme for the interpretation of sacrifice invariably describes Hebraic monotheism as a repudiation of mythology, a sober and rational reaction to the polytheistic, prelogical, "primitive" religions that are deemed inferior. Howard Eilberg-Schwartz recently argued that the twentieth-century preference for studying Israel in relation to contiguous cultures replicates the same evolutionary biases that caused anthropologists to reject the comparative method in the first place. What persists in any case, and especially as regards the question of sacrifice, is an unwillingness to acknowledge the commonality between the Israelite sacrificial system and those of so-called primitive cultures.

The prophetic critique of sacrifice in the Hebrew Bible concerns the hypocrisy involved in the performance of sacrifice when it is not accompanied by righteous deeds and by a sense of obligation towards the most defenseless members of the community. In Isaiah we read, "What to me is the multitude of your sacrifices? say the Lord. I have had enough of the burnt offerings of rams and the fat of fed beasts; I do not delight in the blood of bulls, or of lambs, or of he-goats. . . . Cease to do evil, learn to do good; seek justice, correct oppression, defend the fatherless, plead for the widow" (1:11, 16–17). The argument, which we also find in Jeremiah, Amos, Hosea, and Micah, is not necessarily a denunciation of the Israelite sacrificial system as such. However, it does denounce the kind of sacrifice practiced by the prophets' contemporaries, in which sacrifice is no more than an empty form or formalism, contravened as it is by the actual content of Israel's deeds. Hence there arises the emphasis on the relation between the *outer* form of sacrifice and the *inner* attitude, which will become especially important in the New Testament and Christian context. "For I desire steadfast love rather than sacrifice, the knowledge of God, rather than burnt offerings," we read in Hos. 6:6, which is later cited in the Gospel of Matthew.

It is precisely this interiorization of the sense of sacrifice that characterizes the New Testament's discourse on sacrifice, which is organized around the difference between content and form, outer and inner, old and new, bad and good, carnal and spiritual. These oppositions make possible the New Testament's claim not only to go beyond the Hebrew Bible's conception of sacrifice but to supersede what it refers to as the "Old Testament." In Heb. 10:1, such a claim is explicitly connected to a typological or figural understanding of the relationship between the two testaments, namely, to an interpretation in which the persons and events in the Old Testament prefigure and are fulfilled by those of the New: "For since the law has but a shadow of the good things to come, instead of the true form of these realities, it can never, by the same sacrifices which are continually offered year after year, perfect those who draw near." The claim, which is not without a certain interpretive violence, is to "transcend" the old sacrifice of the older Scripture. Jesus's occupation or "cleansing" of the temple, found within the synoptic as well as the Johannine Gospels, is generally seen as an accomplishment of this. As Bruce Chilton suggests (1992), Jesus's action, which interfered with the habitual course of worship, represents an attempt to possess the temple within his own program of sacrificial purity. It turns on a disagreement (already articulated by Rabbis Hillel and Shammai) as to how inherently acceptable offerings are to be presented. But it may be a distortion of Jesus's position to see this as a concern only with inner, moral purity as distinguished from cultic (or external) purity. This interpretation is a residue of the anti-Judaic, anticultic rhetoric of the Gospels. Jesus's position can be read, rather, as speaking to the need for continuity between inner and outer purity.

In more general terms, the New Testament brings the problem of sacrifice into association with the Christ event. The expiatory death of the servant of God (depicted in Isaiah's fourth servant song) was already regarded as a sin offering, a *hatta'at*: "It was the will of the Lord to bruise him; he has put him to grief when he makes himself an offering for sin" (Isa. 53:10). The Christ event is also put into the context of the salvation history that the Passover commemorates, as when Paul says in 1 Cor. 4:7: "Christ was offered as our pascal lamb." The certain return here to a nonfigured usage would seem to result from a double metaphorical substitution: the substitution of Christ's perfect (self-)sacrifice (man for animal) for the Passover sacrifice's initial substitution of animal for man. In any case, such a typological understanding is also reflected in the connection between the Last Supper and the sacrificial connotation of the Passover seder, in Jesus's eucharistic words and in their subsequent theological development. Finally, and as a further instance of the New Testament's interiorization of the sense of sacrifice, the sacrificial self-offering of Christ becomes associated, especially in the Pauline letters and in Hebrews, with the practical and ethical demands of the life of apostleship, the sacrifice performed by (that is) the Christian life.

Already within the Judeo-Christian background to which I have limited myself in the exploration of the term "sacrifice," several key features announce themselves. First, sacrifice, especially after the destruction of the temple, is more of an interpretive construct than an event to be apprehended. It occurs as something that is always already past, the significance of which is always already lost (and preserved *as* lost) from the point of view of the redaction of the Hebrew Bible, the rabbinic commentary, the prophetic criticism, and the New Testament supersessionary discourse. Second, the West's discourse on sacrifice would seem to rest on a foundation in which sacrifice has been surmounted and gone beyond. This is the case with the sacrifice of Christ, who according to the author of Hebrews, offered once and for all a single sacrifice for sins, as opposed to the priest who repeatedly offers the same meaningless sacrifices. One could also point to the Greek example here. Socrates, condemned to death, drinks the cup of hemlock in Plato's *Phaedo* after having designated his death as a liberation from the prison of earthly life. Jean-Luc Nancy (1991) shows that in the *Phaedo*, Socrates's self-sacrifice, as he lies at the point of death, is framed by references to "the older sacrifice": "Crito, we ought to offer a cock to Asclepius. See to it and don't forget." Both the figure of Christ and of Socrates propose a transfiguration and a transcendence of sacrifice. They detemine it as autosacrifice, namely, not only as a sacrifice of the self that is willed and desired, but also, it will be shown, self-sacrifice on its way to becoming the very sacrifice of sacrifice. They determine it by a repetition of the old sacrifice that reveals an entirely new content, as when the New Testament understands itself as the revelation of what was concealed in the Old. Both claim to have acceded to the truth, hitherto concealed, of sacrifice. That is why in the West, the movement of going beyond, or the transcendence of sacrifice, is foundational. Nancy comments in a reference to Hegel, "the truth of sacrifice sublates the sacrificial moment of sacrifice itself" (24). That is to say that for Hegel, the negativity of the finite can only be produced in a finite way, namely, as sacrifice, as the surrender of an immediate finitude. But by "sacrificing" itself as sacrifice, the dialectical transcendence of sacrifice "reabsorbs the finite moment of sacrifice" in order to accede to its infinite truth.

Many of the theoretical treatments of sacrifice are found in the literature of the anthropology of religion. Edward Tylor in 1871 understood sacrifice as a gift made to a deity as if he were a man, a tribute. In the *Lectures on the Religions of the Semites* (1890), William Robertson Smith, inspired by the discovery of totemism, described sacrifice as a communal meal where gods are present. In this the idea of communion becomes closely related to sacrifice, as does its social dimension. Robertson Smith's contemporary James G. Frazer conceived of sacrifice as the driving out or exorcism of an evil spirit. (This tendency to describe sacrifice in apotropaic terms will be seen, three-quarters of a century later, in E. E. Evans-Pritchard's position, and more recently, in René Girard's account of the violent roots of religion.) The most influential anthropological theory of sacrifice was formulated in 1898 by Henri Hubert and Marcel Mauss in the essay "Sacrifice: Its Nature and Function." For Hubert and Mauss, sacrifice mediates the arrival of or departure of the divine: "Sacrifice is a procedure which consists in establishing a communication between the sacred and the profane worlds, by the intermediary of a victim, that is, a consecrated thing which is destroyed in the course of the ceremony" (1964, 97). In every sacrifice an object passes from the common into the religious domain; it is consecrated. The subject who sacrifices "communicates" with the divine. Sacrifice modifies the condition of the person who performs it. Ultimately, sacrifice serves to balance the always possible disequilibrium between the sacred and the profane. Hubert and Mauss drew on older theories of ritual in order to emphasize that within sacrifice both communion and the expulsion of the sacred spirit are primordial.

As in the case of the gift, about which Mauss also wrote a famous essay, there is a tension between understanding sacrifice as a form of exchange or barter (in Robertson Smith's formula, *do ut des,* "I give in order that you may give"), that is, within an economic circuit, and as something that is not exhausted by a process of exchange. In a comprehensive study influenced by the French sociological and phenomenological methods, Georges Gusdorf attempts to describe sacrifice as an a priori structure within the affirmation of personal life. He too is caught up in the tension between its economic and aneconomic meanings: "Sacrifice realizes a kind of commerce between man and the gods, but the economic sense of this commerce masks in reality a deeper sense"; or "Sacrifice puts us in the presence of a 'paradoxical' form of exchange" (Gusdorf 1948, 86, 67). Following Jacques Derrida's reflections on the gift in *Given Time,* one could argue that perhaps, at the limit, sacrifice *must* be aneconomic, gratuitous, indeed excessive. Nonetheless, within all theoretical discourses about sacrifice, there is a tendency to think of "primitive religion" as economic in nature, which modern religious sensibility, even as it projects its own conception of commercial exchange onto "primitive culture," claims to go beyond.

Part of the difficulty here stems from the way in which the seeming circuit of sacrificial exchange is embedded in an affective space or network proper to "primitive mentality" that Lucien Lévy-Bruhl in 1923 called "participation." (Gusdorf had called it "possession.") The metaphysics of participation (or methexis) assumes the interpenetration between the unseen and seen worlds, the presence of the supernatural in the natural. It appears to confuse the distinctions between persons, between the one and the many; it appears not to operate

289

according to the principle of identity or the logic or noncontradiction. For Lévy-Bruhl, who shares with Robertson Smith an evolutionary bias, the history of religion, and of sacrifice along with it, assumes a rupture with the affective matrix of "prelogical," magical consciousness when it begins to conceive of the separation between man and the transcendence of a personal god. This would be to say, once again, that the old sacrifice is no longer practiced. But, in fact, we do not know what participation is; we know only our representations of it from the perspective of modern mentality, when we consider such thinking as "erroneous." As Lévy-Bruhl himself emphasizes, the "logic" of primitive mentality is, ultimately, heterogeneous to modern mentality and ways of conceptualizing. But precisely in this conceptual heterogeneity lies the interest and the influence of the concept of participation. Emmanuel Lévinas contends that the certain transcendence *within* immanence that it articulates would seem to go beyond a binary opposition of transcendence and immanence, and to anticipate, especially in its analysis of affective states, twentieth-century philosophies of finitude.

In his *Theory of Religion,* written in 1948, Georges Bataille defines the essence of religion as "the return to *intimacy,*" understood as an "immanence between man and the world," a "trembling of the individual" which is "holy, sacred, and suffused with anguish" (1992, 44, 52). Bataille's theory needs to be fully explored in the context of his other writings and of his reading of Hegel, especially as it is influenced by Alexandre Kojève's lectures, which interpret Hegel's operative concept of negativity as a passage through death. Bataille writes, "to sacrifice is not to kill but to abandon and to give" (Bataille 1992, 48–9). The sacrificer belongs to the world of violent and uncalculated generosity and consumption, namely, a realm of unlimited expenditure where utilitarian relations are suspended. Sacrifice, which can no longer be understood in terms of sublation, thus represents a certain departure from the boundaries of the restricted economy, from the enclosed system of reciprocal relations reducible to a utilitarian logic of means and ends.

In this respect sacrifice appears in Bataille's theory as something of a desideratum. Would this not be open to the kind of ethical objection to sacrifice that Emmanuel Lévinas mounts when he refers to its "nostalgia for mythology and the cruelty it perpetuates in morality"? (1991, 67). In one of his essays on Judaism, in a phrase cited from Leon Brunschvig, Lévinas also asks if there is not "in sacrifices joyously consented to, heroically offered in the exaltation of faith, a necessary turning away from the sufferings violently imposed by that same exaltation" (1991, 48). Lévinas's ethical objection to sacrifice here is at least as much a response to the events of the Second World War as it is a refusal of the Christian economy of personal salvation, with its splendors, its levitations, and its "egoism," in that it elides the Hebraic priority of obligation to others. But while Lévinas's objections to an apparent "retrieval" of sacrifice are important (as are his objections to the mystical and ecstatic "possession" implied in participation), this does not mean that we can assume that we know what the term "sacrifice" in Bataille's text means. As Maurice Blanchot cautions, within Bataille's writings the term undergoes "a slippage" from a historical and religious interpretation to something that is neither historical nor religious. This is, as Maurice Blanchot puts it, "the infinite exigency to which it is exposed in that which opens it to others and separates it violently from itself" (1988, 15). To be understood more fully, Blanchot's assertion would have to be explored in the context of the writings of Bataille, Nancy, Heidegger, and Lévinas. But suffice it to say here, that as Blanchot reads Bataille, sacrifice is no less than the condition of possibility of community as such, a curious condition, or *in*condition, which "founds community by undoing it," "an ordeal which exposes community to its necessary disappearance" (1988, 15). Consequently, sacrifice, understood on this originary level and thus rethought and revised, would not be altogether incompatible with what Lévinas calls ethics, namely, a radical putting into question of the self and the subject in the presence of the other.

* * *

The Hebrew Bible's exemplary story of sacrifice, the *Akedah* or "the binding" of Isaac recounted in Genesis 22, has a great deal to say regarding these questions about the relationship of ethics to sacrifice. It too recounts the "end" of sacrifice, the end of the practice of human sacrifice, according to the etiological interpretation proposed by Hermann Gunkel, E. A. Speiser, Klaus Westermann, and numerous others. According to Eilberg-Schwartz, the story reflects the idea that God is willing to accept an animal sacrifice in the place of a human. But these etiological interpretations (perhaps another interpretive instance of the "transcendence" of sacrifice) far from exhaust the meaning of this text. Indeed, the proportion of commentary that this text has received is staggering in relation to its nineteen verses:

> [1]And it came to pass after these things that God tested Abraham. And he said "Abraham, Abraham," and he said "Here I am." [2]He said, "Take now thy son, thine only son, whom thou lovest and get thee into the land of Moriah and take him up there as a burnt offering on one of the mountains that I will tell thee of." [3]And Abraham rose early in the morning, and he saddled his ass, and he took two of his young men with him, and Isaac his son, and he split the wood for the burnt offering, and arose and went to the place of which God had told him. [4]On the third day Abraham lifted up his eyes and saw the place afar off. [5]And Abraham said to his young men: "Stay here with the ass and I and the lad will go yonder, we will worship and we will return to you." [6]So Abraham took the wood for the burnt offering, and he placed it upon Isaac his son, and he took in his hand the fire and the knife. And they went the two of them together. [7]And Isaac said to Abraham his father, saying, "My Father." And he said, "Here

I am, my son." He said, "Behold the fire and the wood, but where is the lamb for the burnt offering?" [8]Abraham said, "God will provide the lamb for the burnt offering my son." And they went the two of them together. [9]And they came to the place of which God had told him, and Abraham built an altar there and cleaved the wood and bound Isaac his son and placed him on the altar atop of the wood. [10]And Abraham stretched out his hand and took the knife to slay his son. [11]But the angel of the Lord called to him from heaven, saying "Abraham, Abraham," and he said, "Here I am." [12]And he said, "Lay not your hand upon the lad, nor do anything at all to him for now I know that one fearing of God are you, seeing that you have not withheld your son, your only son from me." [13]And Abraham lifted up his eyes and behold, a ram caught behind in the thicket by its horns. And Abraham went and he took the ram and offered it up as a burnt offering instead of his son. [14]And Abraham called the name of the place "God will provide," as it is said to this day "On the mountain of the Lord it shall be provided." [15]And the angel of the Lord called to Abraham a second time from heaven [16]saying, "By myself I have sworn, says the Lord, because you have done this, and have not withheld your son, your only son, from me, [17]I will multiply your descendants as the stars of heaven and as the sand which is on the seashore. And your descendants shall possess the gates of their enemies. [18]And by your descendants shall all the nations of the earth bless themselves, because you have obeyed my voice. [19]And Abraham returned to his young men, and they arose and went together to Beersheba; and Abraham dwelt at Beersheba.

I will not attempt an account of the history of interpretation of this biblical chapter but will indicate only a few of the nodal points in the text that give rise to questions and commentary. The readiness that characterizes Abraham's response to God's call, conveyed by the phrase "here I am" (hineni), is by all accounts extraordinary. God commands him to sacrifice his son, and Abraham is so obedient that he even gets up early in the morning to fulfill the command. Erich Auerbach noted, in a famous contrast between the styles of biblical and Homeric narrative, that what the text does *not* say is enormous. It gives no description of Abraham's psychology, his state of mind regarding God's command that he sacrifice his only son (by his wife Sarah), for whom he had waited one hundred years, whom he received by divine intervention, and through whom God had promised, in Genesis 17, his seed would be blessed. Rather,

> A journey is made because God has designated the place where the sacrifice is to be performed; but we are told nothing about the journey except that it took three days, and even that we are told in a mysterious way. Abraham and his followers rose "early in the morn-

ing" and "went unto" the place of which God had told him; on the third day he lifted up his eyes and saw the place from afar. That gesture is the only gesture, is indeed the only occurrence during the whole journey of which we are told. . . . it is as if, while he travelled on, Abraham had looked neither to the right nor to the left, had suppressed any sign of life in his followers and himself save only their footfalls. . . . Three days! Three such days positively demand the symbolic interpretation which they later received. (Auerbach 1953, 9–10)

Auerbach's literary critical and philological interest is largely in the Christian allegorical interpretations that this text from the Hebrew Bible has received. The sacrifice of Isaac prefigures the Gogoltha event, to take just a few examples, in the symbolism of the three days, in Isaac's carrying the wood of his sacrifice (as Christ carried his own cross), and most prominently, in the free consent of the sacrificial victim. But Auerbach's central observation here concerns the distinctive features of biblical style. He proposes that the text's very sparseness and economy, its persistent obscurity, the presence of gaps and lacunae, "demand interpretation," even, at the limit, the kind of transgressive or supersessionary interpretation that Christian figural reading implies. That the Hebrew Bible's absolute claim to truth would be connected to the possibility, indeed the necessity, of transgressive interpretation is paradoxical, but this is one of the reasons why the story of Isaac is foundational for Christianity and for its "sacrificial soteriology" (Daly 1978, 3). It is thus also foundational for the difference (or the differend, the conflict) between the Hebrew Bible's self-understanding, and the Christian figural understanding of it.

Søren Kierkegaard is also preoccupied with the questions that the story, in its reticence and its obscurity, poses. In *Fear and Trembling,* he generates several imaginative responses to the following questions: What was Abraham's state of mind? Did Abraham communicate the purpose of his journey to Isaac? Where was Sarah and what did she know about it? and, ultimately, What is God doing? In Kierkegaard's reading, what God asks of Abraham is no less than the sacrifice of the ethical itself, namely, the universally recognized duty that a father should love his son, in the name of the religious relation, namely, the absolute relation to the absolute. With this "teleological suspension of the ethical," Abraham also sacrifices all possibility of making himself intelligible to Isaac and Sarah, his family, or to the community. But he does not lose his faith that in Isaac his seed shall be blessed, nor does he lose the possibility of living happily with Isaac and Sarah again when he is returned to him. Hence Abraham is "a knight of faith" who not only sacrifices the finite (which requires a movement of infinite renunciation of the things of this world) but gains it back, whole and intact.

This emphasis on Abraham's faith follows to some extent that of Heb. 11:8 and 11:17–9: "By faith Abraham obeyed when he was called to go out to a place which he was to receive as an inheritance, and he went out, not knowing where he was to go. . . . By faith Abraham when he was tested offered up Isaac and he who had received the promises was ready to offer up his only son." However, for Kierkegaard, understanding what the author of Hebrews calls faith is not a given but a task. This task is as difficult, as enormous, and as potentially interminable as the task of understanding Abraham. For simply to call Abraham's experience "a test" or "an ordeal," in the words of verse 1 ("And God tested Abraham"), or to understand it in the didactic terms of verse 12 ("For now I know that one fearing of God are you"), is to risk reducing the radicality of Abraham's position:

> An ordeal, this word can say much and very little, and yet the whole thing is over as soon as it is spoken. We mount a winged horse, in the same instant we are at Mount Moriah, in the same instant we see the ram. We forgot that Abraham only rode an ass, which trudges along the road, that he had a journey of three days, that he needed some time to chop the firewood, to bind Isaac, and to sharpen the knife. (Kierkegaard 1983, 52)

Hence Kierkegaard's retellings, as well as his entire exposition, are motivated by an extreme desire to fill in the gaps between verses 3 and 4, between Abraham's "early rising" and "the third day," to draw out "the anxiety" inherent in Abraham's situation.

It is arguable that the gaps and lacunae in the text, its contradictions, and the questions that it poses are precisely what commentators throughout the history of the text's interpretation have always responded to. The earliest form of Jewish commentary on Scripture, known as midrash (from the root word "to study, to search"), denotes a genre of rabbinic exegesis practiced during the first five centuries of the Christian era, and a "searching" attitude toward Scripture. By way of a juxtaposition of scriptural verses, midrash searches out the text of the past for its present relevance. In its patient attention to details of language and to every diacritical mark in Scripture, in its at times playful designation of scriptural problems and their solutions, in its frequent use of wordplay, it resembles what literary critics call "close reading." Its radically text-bound procedure, its open-endedness, and its blend of commentary and creativity has also been seen to herald developments in poststructuralism in significant ways.

Within the rabbinic interpretation of Genesis 22, God's command to Abraham in verse 2 ("Take thy son, thine only son, whom thou lovest . . . and get thee into the land of Moriah"), as well as Abraham's extraordinary response, is always read together with God's command to Abraham in Gen. 12:1 ("Get thee from thy homeland, from thy kindred, and from thy father's house, to a land of which I will tell thee"), a tradition that the author of Hebrews no doubt knew. Jacob Halevi even argues that Kierkegaard's emphasis on Abraham's "teleological suspension of the ethical" is already contained in the rabbinic reading of Gen. 12:1:

When Abraham heard the command of God to forsake his father's house . . . he recognized at once the irony and ambiguity of his position. In God's command there was implicit the command to leave his father in his old age. Thus in the name of the religious he was bidden to suspend a basic ethical principle, the honor and respect which a son owes to his parents. (1953, 19).

According to *Genesis Rabbah* 39:7, and the dialogue between Abraham and God that it imaginatively interpolates, when Abraham remonstrated with God about this, God answered, "I exempt thee from the duty of honouring thy parents, though I exempt no one else from this duty." The midrashic response to Gen. 22:9, "And he bound Isaac his son," ranges from an image of the angels weeping because, in the words of Isa. 33:7–8, "Behold the valiant ones cry without . . . He is breaking the covenant," to a realization that Isaac is hardly a helpless lad at the time of the episode: "Can one bind a man thirty-seven years old (another version: twenty-six years old) without his consent?" (*Genesis Rabbah* 56:8). The same midrashic unit portrays Isaac, in his conscientious concern that his self-oblation and self-sacrifice will be acceptable, asking to be bound firmly. Shalom Spiegel shows how, in various times of persecution within Jewish history, when Jews have taken their own lives rather than commit apostasy, Isaac's self-sacrifice has become a paradigm for Jewish martyrdom. This paradigm is built on a very early tradition (which, according to Spiegel, was largely suppressed as Christianity gained historical prominence) that Isaac was actually sacrificed. In the *Mekilta de-Rabbi Ishmael,* there are references to "the blood of the sacrifice of Isaac" and to "the ashes of Isaac." Even the concluding line of the scriptural episode yields this possible interpretation: "And Abraham returned [in the singular] to his young men" (Gen. 22:19). Where was Isaac? While we know that the sacrifice was interrupted and that a ram was offered in Isaac's stead, is not the omission of his name in verse 19 somewhat alarming under the circumstances?

In sum, the very way in which Genesis 22 is referred to is significant, and reveals much about the interpreter's emphasis and assumptions. Whose story is it, and whose ordeal? For the allegorical and typological reading, Isaac's role must be emphasized. Auerbach refers to the text variously as "the story of Isaac," "the story of Abraham and Isaac," "the sacrifice of Isaac," "the story of Abraham's sacrifice." Westermann (1985) calls it "Abraham's sacrifice," which emphasizes that Abraham, in his willingness to sacrifice his son, also sacrifices himself and all hope for the future. Speiser (1964) in entitling this scriptural chapter "the ordeal of Isaac" announces a tendency to view the episode from Isaac's point of view. And surely, for Kierkegaard, the "ordeal"—if we can even call it that—is Abraham's. "But who, Abraham?" to pose again a question that I ask in *Prodigal Son/Elder Brother* (Robbins 1991, 73). How to understand him? How to understand his extraordinary response to God's call (also apparent in Genesis 12), through which merit accrues to future generations: "Cheerfully, freely, confidently, loudly he answered: Here I am" (Kierkegaard 1983, 21). Of course, the Jewish tradition is careful to refer to the story simply as "the binding," the *Akedah,* after the words of verse 9 with its verb's unusual conjugative form: "And he bound Isaac his son." In my view, this last naming preserves the way in which what one improperly calls "the sacrifice of Isaac" is in fact the story of *an event that does not take place.* This is to say that sacrifice is impossible.

There are several registers of this impossibility that I would let resonate in closing. When Abraham is ready to put to death his one and only son, the unique, and to give that death to God, sacrifice can no longer be understood in terms of substitution, because it concerns precisely that which is unsubstitutable. Sacrifice, as an *an*economic phenomenon, necessarily takes place and becomes legible in a domain that we call the impossible. This is the sense in which it can be understood as an ordeal that exposes community to its necessary disappearance. Sacrifice is also impossible in ethical terms, insofar as it is abhorrent, as the etiological interpretations of the *Akedah* maintain. Finally, that sacrifice is impossible does not mean that it has not always already occurred. This tension is apparent in the use of the term "holocaust," namely, an offering that is wholly burnt in the fire, to refer to the Nazi genocide of the Jews. The term no doubt makes reference to something darkly obscure in the *Akedah* narrative to explain something that is also inexplicable, and the previous tendency to use the story of the binding of Isaac in response to catastrophe in Jewish history has been noted. But in the context of the Nazi genocide of the Jews, the term "holocaust" can no longer have the sacrificial, indeed sacramental connotations that it may have in the biblical account (See Wiesel 1985). What happened was not sacrifice, but murder, which aims at, but always misses, the alterity of the other. In the impossibility of sacrifice, cannot the beginning of the thinking of responsibility toward the other be found?

Suggested Readings

Auerbach, Erich. 1953. "Odysseus's Scar." In *Mimesis,* translated by Williard Trask.

Bataille, Georges. 1992. *Theory of Religion,* translated by Robert Hurley.

Chilton, Bruce. 1992. *The Temple of Jesus.*

Daly, Robert J. 1978. *The Origin of the Christian Doctrine of Sacrifice.*

Derrida, Jacques. 1992. *Given Time,* translated by Peggy Kamuf.

Eilberg-Schwartz, Howard. 1990. *The Savage in Judaism.*

Gusdorf, Georges. 1948. *L'Expérience humaine du sacrifice.*

Halevi, Jacob L. 1955. "Kierkegaard and the Midrash." *Judaism* 4 (1).

Hubert, Henri, and Marcel Mauss. 1964. *Sacrifice: Its Nature and Function,* translated by W. D. Halls.

Kaufmann, Yehezkel. 1972. *The Religion of Israel,* translated by Moshe Greenberg.

Kierkegaard, Søren. 1983. *Fear and Trembling,* translated by Howard V. Hong and Edna H. Hong.

Midrash Rabbah: Genesis. 1977. Translated and edited by Rabbi Dr. H. Freedman and Maurice Simon.

Nancy, Jean-Luc. 1991. "The Unsacrificeable," translated by Robert Livingston. *Yale French Studies* 79.

Robbins, Jill. 1991. *Prodigal Son/Elder Brother.*

Spiegel, Shalom. 1993. *The Last Trial,* translated by Judah Goldin.

References

Auerbach, Erich. 1953. "Odysseus's Scar." In *Mimesis,* translated by Willard Trask. Princeton: Princeton University Press.

Bataille, Georges. 1992. *Theory of Religion,* translated by Robert Hurley. New York: Zone.

Blanchot, Maurice. 1988. *The Unavowable Community,* translated by Pierre Joris. New York: Station Hill.

Chilton, Bruce. 1992. *The Temple of Jesus.* University Park: Pennsylvania State University Press.

Daly, Robert J. 1978. *The Origin of the Christian Doctrine of Sacrifice.* Philadelphia: Fortress Press.

Derrida, Jacques. 1992. *Given Time,* translated by Peggy Kamuf. Chicago: University of Chicago Press.

———. 1995. *The Gift of Death,* translated by David Wills. Chicago: University of Chicago Press.

Eilberg-Schwartz, Howard. 1990. *The Savage in Judaism.* Bloomington: Indiana University Press.

Gusdorf, Georges. 1948. *L'Expérience humaine du sacrifice.* Paris: Presses Universitaires de France.

Halevi, Jacob L. 1955. "Kierkegaard and the Midrash." *Judaism* 4 (1).

Hubert, Henri, and Marcel Mauss. 1964. *Sacrifice: Its Nature and Function,* translated by W. D. Halls. Chicago: University of Chicago Press.

Kaufmann, Yehezkel. 1972. *The Religion of Israel,* translated by Moshe Greenberg. New York: Schocken.

Kierkegaard, Søren. 1983. *Fear and Trembling,* translated by Howard V. Hong and Edna H. Hong. Princeton: Princeton University Press.

Lévinas, Emmanuel. 1990. *Difficult Freedom,* translated by Sean Hand. Baltimore: Johns Hopkins University Press.

———. 1991. "Lévy-Bruhl and Contemporary Philosophy." In *Entre Nous.* Paris: Grasset.

Lévy-Bruhl, Lucien. 1966. *Primitive Mentality,* translated by Lilian A. Clare. Boston: Beacon Press.

Midrash Rabbah: Genesis. 1977. Translated and edited by Rabbi Dr. H. Freedman and Maurice Simon. London: Soncino Press.

Nancy, Jean-Luc. 1991. "The Unsacrificeable," translated by Robert Livingston. *Yale French Studies* 79.

Robbins, Jill. 1991. *Prodigal Son/Elder Brother.* Chicago: University of Chicago Press.

Speiser, E. A. 1964. *Genesis.* New York: Doubleday.

Spiegel, Shalom. 1993. *The Last Trial,* translated by Judah Goldin. Woodstock, N.Y.: Jewish Lights.

Vermes, Geza. 1973. *Scripture and Tradition in Judaism.* Leiden: Brill.

Westermann, Claus. 1985. *Genesis 12–36,* translated by John J. Scullion. Minneapolis: Augsburg.

Wiesel, Elie. 1985. "The First Survivor." In *Against Silence,* edited by Irving Abrahamson. New York: Holocaust Library.

SEVENTEEN

Territory

Sam Gill

Archie marked the key sites in the dirt, and drew a line between them. Then
he indicated how a second rain track, belonging to Jakamarra-Jupurrurla/
Nakamarra-Napurrurla, split off from the main one and ran to a place called
Wingkiyi. Still other tracks converged on Kulpulurnu from the west. I recognized enough of the site names to realize that Archie's sand diagram was
an objectification of how he *thought* of their relationships: the tracks would
actually meander and dogleg in linking all the places he had named.
— Michael Jackson, *At Home in the World*

"Territory" is not a term commonly used in the academic study of religion. It does not appear among the 3,200 articles in *The HarperCollins
Dictionary of Religion*. Space, time, and place, particularly when qualified by the adjective "sacred," are commonly used terms. While territory, in this
sense, may refer to concrete space and time, to the specific geographical, physical, and temporal structuring of actual religious traditions, it is also used meta-
phorically to refer to a wide range of theoretical issues. For example, the complicated theoretical issues regarding the relationship between the concrete materials
considered by students of religion and some supposed corresponding religious
reality, understood as either a spiritual realm or an academic construct, have been
addressed in the metaphorical terms of the relationship between map and territory. Reflection upon the term "territory" provokes a wide-ranging critical discussion of academic method.

The concerns regarding territory serve the correlation of meaning with order.
Distinctions made in spatial and temporal terms are often assumed to be fundamental to the way humans designate meaning, create order. Certainly it is a
central theme in Western thought to make sense of the world by correlating
meaning with order using the terms associated with space, shape, and body. As a
product of this propensity, virtually every aspect of religion, both within specific
traditions and academic categories, is articulated using a vocabulary of territory.
Issues regarding territory must also address the even more fundamental academic assumption that reality invariably exhibits some meaningful order or plan
(for an interesting discussion of the expectation that reality presents itself to us
as an exhibit, see Mitchell 1988). This assumption motivates the persistence of
academic methods to prescribe where to stand to "get the picture," to see the
underlying plan or intention of reality.

One of the primary means of individual and group identity for the aboriginal
cultures in Central Australia is the complex concept often rendered as "the

dreaming," though the English term all too often suggests unfounded Western romantic projections. Each language has its own term, for example, the Warlpiri call it *jukurrpa* while the Arrernte call it *altjira*.

The people of these cultures are divided into subgroupings, often referred to as totems, and each group is identified with mythic figures who are recognized, in some sense, as their ancestors. These ancestors are identified in the terms of a natural form, that is, they are called by the name of a plant, an animal, or even a meteorological phenomenon like rain. Songs sung during rites tell the actions of the ancestors. They arose from the earth at a particular geographical location. They journeyed across the land, camping at a variety of named places where they performed rites and sometimes interacted with others. Eventually they returned to the earth. These ancestors are not deities (in any sense of being numinous, transcendent, cosmic creators, or sky dwellers), though they are heroic and mythic in being credited with engaging in formative acts, establishing rites, and identifying themselves and their actions with the territory they traveled through. Aborigines do not have accounts of cosmic creation or origination.

Jukurrpa or *altjira* can refer variously to these mythic ancestors, to their actions, to the accounts told of their actions, to graphic depictions of ancestral journeys, and to the country defined by the itinerary taken by these ancestors. *Jukurrpa* or *altjira* also denotes one of the ways all human beings are identified, including one's responsibilities (one's dreaming is the law) and the potential of one's opportunities (particularly in terms of the potential for forming new relationships). For aborigines, identity is inseparable from territory and, as Tony Swain (1993) has shown, their ontology is strongly spatial, rather than temporal, in character.

Aborigines identify with country, but it is a conception of country that differs from the boundaried understandings by which cartographers customarily circumscribe countries. Country, to aborigines, is designated by a track across the land. It is a series of nameable geographical locations interconnected as the itinerary of ancestral travels. The totem identity—that is, the identity with a plant, animal, or natural form—designates a track (a song line) and one's country.

The groups of people who are identified with a given country have the responsibility to "hold up" that country, which they do by traveling to specific locations along the track where they perform song and dance dramas that refresh the knowledge of the actions performed by their ancestors at this location. Over a period of years, each track is retraced by the group whose members identify with the country.

Unlike countries that mutually exclude one another, this aboriginal conception of country allows one country to span the territory occupied by peoples who speak mutually unintelligible languages or different dialects, and who have different social structures and kinship systems. It also allows for countries, tracks, to cross one another, to occupy the same objective space. Typically one country crosses another at a specific location that is important to both. Each group's story of their dreaming tells of the encounter with the other group at the place of intersection. When a group performs rites at a totem location shared by other groups, they all meet together, share their knowledge through dance drama performances, and form relationships based on the terms of these crossings.

Jukurrpa, altjira, country, totem, dreaming, law (all more or less synonymous) define a person's identity, her or his descent (though not consanguineous). Each person receives this identity at birth, and it is immutable. However, the aboriginal conception of territory interplays with complex consanguine relationships providing the foundation for aboriginal society and religion.

Nineteenth-century colonialism and the rise of modern anthropology with its vast ethnographic project challenged accepted, basically theological views of the world by introducing evidence and experience of human diversity. Distinctions in space and time were employed as fundamental to the social sciences informed by the powerful presumption of evolution developed by the natural sciences. The evolutionist assumption demanded that the territory of human existence be presented as a sequence of developmental stages. The quest, distinctive to the social sciences during this late-nineteenth- and early-twentieth-century period, often took the form of a concern with beginnings that frequently included the search for the origin of religion. Emile Durkheim (1965, pub. 1912) found the origin of religion in society as expressed in his famous statement that "the 'sacred' is society." Sigmund Freud (1913) articulated his understanding of origination in terms of "the primal scene." Phylogenetically this primal event occurred "one day" and was distinguished by brothers killing and eating their father because of their sexual desire for their mothers and sisters. The proposition of this event endeavors to explain the origin of sacrifice, taboos, and belief in gods. Ontogenetically this primal scene is inseparable from the dynamics of infant sexuality; it designates a child's observation of her or his parents in coitus. Both Durkheim and Freud depended heavily on Australian aboriginal ethnography for the development of their theories of origination. All of the classical works in the social sciences during this period were influenced to some extent by the evolutionist assumptions and an essentialist/objectivist epistemology.

The emergence of the modern academic study of religion in the nineteenth century correlates with the realization that religion might be understood in such a way as to be useful in accounting for the development, classification, and distinction of being human. Since the academic study of religion developed from Western intellectual roots, with Christianity (and, to a lesser extent, other Abrahamic traditions) functioning as the categorical prototype, religion was, as it continues to be, understood in largely theological terms, that is, religion has to do with beliefs in the existence of God. A broad and concerted effort was made in the late nineteenth and early twentieth centuries to retain belief in God as the distinctive characteristic of religion by seeking high gods among so-called primitive and archaic peoples to show that these peoples, considered as representative of the earliest stages of human development, believed in a creator god. The belief of the first peoples in a high god arguably confirmed the Christian under-standing of religion, the early existence of the Christian god, and the definition of religion as belief in god.

The academic study of religion began to emerge as a distinctive enterprise with the shifting from theologically based to territorially based understandings of religion. Concerns with documenting the high god and original monotheism blended into more neutral, less theological concerns with a study of religion centered on beginnings or origins. In the nineteenth century, religion, seen on a worldwide stage, began to be thought of in terms of classifications in space and time. While these territorial classifications simply overlay the underlying theological assumptions, they established the taxonomy of religion that remains broadly accepted today. The most fundamental classification in this taxonomy is world religions. World religions are those that, like Western religions, transcend national boundaries and are inclusive with respect to national and ethnic identity. World religions contrast with national and ethnic religions in terms of their relationship to territory. Though world religions transcend national boundaries, they continue to be identified in terms of basic relative territorial categories: Western and Asian or Eastern, which are further subclassified East Asian, South-east Asian, Middle Eastern, American, and so forth. Temporal distinctions have also been important. Archaic and ancient religions are distinguished from mod-ern or living religions. Primitive religions, though temporally contemporary, are commonly correlated with the archaic. Further, historical methods have consti-tuted the primary approaches used to study world religions. Studies of religion are commonly distinguished in terms of a particular historical period as more fundamental even than the designation of geographical place. So-called primitive religions, being made to correlate with the time of origination, have been typi-cally considered, following the logic of the temporal assumption, ahistorical.

The shift to concerns with territory—space, time, and place—and away from theological interests corresponded with the shift from understanding religion as principally Christian or Western to acknowledging religion as a distinct aspect of being human. It corresponded with the growing awareness that comparison among religions serves the endeavor of understanding the human world rather than advancing the understanding of a particular religious tradition or people. Still, analysis of these often self-contradictory and illogical divisions of the terri-tory of religion reveals the persistence of the powerful historical and ideological assumptions of the Western prototype for the category religion. The academic study of religion has yet to free itself from its roots in a colonial territorial ideology.

Territory as it is and has been engaged by the academic study of religion can be effectively presented through the critical examination of the contribution of two religion scholars to the concept "territory": Mircea Eliade and Jonathan Z. Smith.

Numbakulla arose "out of nothing" and traveled to the north, making mountains, rivers, and all sorts of animals and plants. He also created the "spirit children" *(kuruna)*, a very large number of whom were concealed inside his body. Eventually he made a cave or storehouse, [in which] to hide the *tjurunga* [oblong decorated ritual object] that he was producing. At that time men did not yet exist. He inserted a *kuruna* into a *tjurunga*, and thus there arose the first Achilpa (mythical) Ancestor [the Achilpa, or *tjilpa*, are the wild cat totem group of the Arrernte]. Numbakulla then implanted a large number of *kuruna* in different *tjurunga*, producing other mythical Ancestors. He taught the first Achilpa how to perform the many ceremonies connected with the various totems. (Eliade 1967, 50–1)

Mircea Eliade has been the most influential proponent of focusing on territory as the basis for the academic study of religion. The modern comparative study of religions that Eliade introduced when he arrived midcentury in the United States broadly transformed the academic study of religion. Developing upon the Durkheimian distinction between the sacred and profane, Eliade recognized a correlation between this distinction and distinctions in space and time (see esp. Eliade 1959). Informed about religious traditions the world over and throughout history, Eliade argued that religious values are imprinted as distinctions in space and time. These distinctions owe their existence to some nonhuman other, often termed "the sacred," which manifests itself in what Eliade referred to as "hierophanies," eruptions of the sacred into the world as acts of creation and orientation resulting in distinguishing a territory as qualitatively different from all other places. Human beings do not construct their world so much as they discover or recognize the distinctions, the sacred places, that supernatural beings introduced in the world.

The presence of the supernaturals in the human world occurred "in the beginning." Events designated as "sacred" correspond with "the beginning time" (*in illo tempore*), which Eliade understood as constituting a distinct kind of time, a "sacred time." Through their actions supernaturals created and ordered the world as it is now known. Their deeds are recounted as "sacred history" in the mythology of a tradition. Human time and history, if they are to be meaningful, must reflect and stem from this sacred time. It is to this time that religious practitioners eternally return in the performance of rituals, the reenactments of the actions of the gods. The actions of the gods, the events of sacred time, distinguish the sacred from the profane, the real from the chaotic, the meaningful from the meaningless. Rather than freedom and creativity, the human modes of engaging reality and meaning are repetition and participation. Eliade focused his attention on the analysis of mythology recounting the sacred history, the ritual "reactualizing" of those events, and the cosmic distinctions borne often symbolically in the structure of the world. Because of what he believed was their proximity with the sacred time of the origins, Eliade held that the archaic traditions and those contemporary religions he classified as primitive are more prototypically religious in character than the world religions bearing long histories. History, in the sense of ongoing accumulating human action, is, to Eliade's view, a degenerative process in that it moves progressively away from the sacred events of the beginning. Sacred time is, however, circular or reversible, indefinitely recoverable and repeatable through reenacting the cosmogonic acts (see Eliade 1954). Australian aborigines were highly important to Eliade because their preagricultural lifestyle as hunter-gatherers and their absence of writing and technical history indicated to him that, structurally speaking at least, they live in close temporal proximity to the realm of the gods. Aborigines were to Eliade truly *ab origine*.

> Numbakulla had planted a pole called *kauwa-auwa* in the middle of a sacred ground. . . . After anointing it with blood, he began to climb it. He told the first Achilpa Ancestor to follow him, but the blood made the pole too slippery, and the man slid down. Numbakulla went on alone, drew up the pole after him and was never seen again. (Eliade 1967, 51)

The world created by the supernaturals in the beginning sacred time constitutes "the real," "home," or cosmos. Any territory lying outside this world is considered chaotic, uncreated, dangerous, and unreal. The creation of "sacred space" is synonymous with establishing orientation. Such spatial distinctions invariably correlate with the points of entry into the world of the supernatural creators. These places continue to function as the locations where humans may communicate with the gods. In Eliade's analysis, the strongest place, the place giving orientation to all space, is the center. Structurally the center can have no other valuation than sacredness since it is the locus of all creative and thereby religious activity, both divine and human. Thus "sacred space" is focused upon and is oriented by "the sacred center." As Allah revealed himself to Muhammad at Mecca, Mecca is the center of the Muslim world. It is the orientation for daily prayer for Muslims throughout the world and the destination of religious pilgrims. By following the model of creation, human beings may replicate the sacred center in architectural forms such as dwellings and places of worship. The spires, poles, towers, inner sanctuaries, and altars of religious architecture replicate the sacred centers as do designated mountains, trees, and water places in nature. These places thus become openings to the transcendent. Eliade (e.g., 1958), as have those who have followed his approach, tirelessly described and amassed the evidence of this religious patterning throughout human history.

> One day an incident befell one of these mythical groups: while pulling up the *kauwa-auwa,* which was very deeply implanted, the old chief broke it just above the ground. They carried the broken

pole until they met another group. They were so tired and sad that they did not even try to erect their own *kauwa-auwa* "but, lying down together, died where they lay. A large hill, covered with big stones, arose to mark the spot."

Seldom do we find a more pathetic avowal that man cannot live without a "sacred center" which permits him both to "cosmicize" space and to communicate with the transhuman world of heaven. So long as they had their *kauwa-auwa*, the Achilpa Ancestors were never lost in the surrounding "chaos." Moreover, the sacred pole was for them the proof par excellence of Numbakulla's existence and activity. (Eliade 1967, 52–3)

With religion being recognized as having the quality distinguished as "sacred," the study of religion was thus the study of territorial distinctions made significant by sacred events, "the center" (or "the sacred center") in spatial terms and "the beginning" in temporal terms. Eliade showed that one approach to understanding the religion of another people is to appreciate their characterization of territory, especially in terms of space and time.

Eliade's influence on the shape of the academic study of religion has been extensive. The establishment of a large number of religion programs in American state-supported institutions of higher education was an important consequence of the mid-1960s U.S. Supreme Court decision in the cases of *Engel* and *Schempp* that distinguished between teaching religion and teaching *about* religion. In institutions that had to carefully avoid the theological terms associated with seminary education and the teaching of religion that would be considered illegal in these new programs, Eliade's seemingly nontheological terms based in the apparently neutral and universal categories of territory were broadly embraced.

While Eliade's terms and approaches continue to shape the study of religion, they have not gone without challenge. Jonathan Z. Smith has been an outspoken critic, and he has presented important alternatives. Smith's criticism has shown that Eliade's territorial categories, while promising nontheological and religiously neutral terms for the comparative study of religion, stem from an essentialist presumption that does little more than disguise their theological character.

Smith began with queries and concerns (1972), largely pertaining to the narrowness and historical applicability of Eliade's categories, and in time (1987) presented a full critical discussion of Eliade's program focused on examination of his territorial language regarding the sacred center. In examining the principal historical and cultural examples on which Eliade constructed his notion of the sacred center, Smith shows that the center "is not a secure pattern to which data may be brought as illustrative; it is a dubious notion that will have to be established anew on the basis of detailed comparative endeavors" (Smith 1987, 17).

Smith's critique of Eliade presents a fundamental anthropological and epistemological alternative in the academic study of religion. Eliade's discourse on territorial categories is basically a consideration of the morphology, the structure, of the phenomenological world. He ultimately rejected the Kantian view that to be human is to be a constructor of worlds; he was opposed to the relativism suggested by such a view. For Eliade, the presence that marks some times and places as sacred establishes an objective, dependable grounding beyond all human creativity. Smith's response to Eliade is more than a rational criticism of Eliade's scholarship, it is a challenge to his understanding of the world; it exposes it as grounded in belief that is, finally, religious in character.

> By focusing on the false causal relationsip—from broken pole to corporate death—Eliade has missed the actual structure of the narrative. . . . The horizon of the Tjilpa myth is not celestial, it is relentlessly terrestrial and chthonic. The emphasis is not on the dramatic creation of the world out of chaos by transcendent figures, or on the "rupture" between these figures and man. Rather, the emphasis is on transformation and continuity, on a world fashioned by ancestral wanderings across the featureless, primeval surface of the earth. (Smith 1987, 9–10)

Smith does not reject territorial categories of space, time, and place as important to the academic study of religion. Rather he sees territory as offering the basic world-building tools used by all human beings. Religion, for Smith, is a mode of creating and discovering worlds of meaning and the discourse upon territory is the enterprise of creativity and discovery. For Eliade, the student of religion shares the anthropology of all human beings in that he or she must discover the sacred in the world of the academic subject and report upon its existence: an academic method that seems to require certain human qualities more than rational procedures. Smith's anthropology, also encompassing students of religion as well as religious peoples, sees humans as constructing their worlds of meaning. For Smith there is no objective territory; religion is not sui generis; and no data are essentially religious. The discourse on territory is then a discourse on mapping. Distinctions in space, time, shape, and body are the human methods of constructing reality, of engaging the world meaningfully. To recognize something as a center or an originating event is not to locate a hierophany, a point of rupture, but to participate in a mode of human creativity. The academic student of religion assumes no being presence, no essential sacredness, yet such beliefs may exist among the people of the traditions studied.

> The Tjilpa conceive of the world as a landscape whose distinctive features were formed by ancestral activity. . . . for the Australians, the world was a "man-made world" and summarized the mythology. . . . A topographic feature was not deliberately constructed by the ancestors. In most cases, it appeared as a sort of accidental by-product of their journeys. The feature records, permanently, the transitory act

of their passing-through in a manner similar to a photograph of the movement of charged particles in a cloud chamber—a solemn and important graffito, "Kilroy was here." (Smith 1987, 17–18)

In the territorial terms of the received tradition of studying religion—the academic tradition in which religion is inseparable from the sacred and where Christianity is the operative prototype for the category religion—the alternative presented by Smith's approach can only be recognized as an act of profanation. The word "profane" comes from the Latin *profanum,* the place in front of the temple, outside the temple. The historical, psychological, anthropological study of myths, scriptures, and rites renders these religious forms profane. The comparative study of human culture in the academically constructed terms of religion requires the profanation of the religious. The academic study of religion demands the removal of the sacred from the temple, or at least the examination of the temple and what takes place inside the temple from the perspectives of the world outside. The morality of the academic study of religion corresponds with the morality of the novel, a genre distinctive of Europeans, which Milan Kundera identifies as the suspension of moral judgment (1995, 7). That is, the morality of the academic study of religion, as of the novel, requires the suspension of all moral judgments with respect to the study of all religions. Where, other than outside the temple, can religion be studied without making moral judgments?

Smith differs markedly from Eliade regarding comparison, the most fundamental method of the academic study of religion. Eliade's work proceeded from the assumption that, structurally speaking, the sacred is everywhere essentially the same as is the structure of the human response to the sacred. Thus the student of religion knows at the outset the structure and pattern of the sacred. The sacred is synonymous, in territorial terms, with the beginning time and the place designated as the center. The principal comparative method of the study of religion is, then, the identification of the phenomenological examples of this pattern. Comparison is, as it is broadly understood in folk usage, the discovery of sameness.

> The fact that Numbakulla disappeared into the sky after climbing it suggests that the *kauwa-auwa* is somehow an *axis mundi* which unites heaven and earth. Elsewhere, and particularly in the Oriental cultures and areas under their influence, the *axis mundi* (conceived as a pillar, a tree, a mountain, etc.) actually constitutes a "center of the world." This implies, among other things, that it is a consecrated place from which all orientation takes place. (Eliade 1973, 50)

In contrast, Smith's study of religion proceeds from no essential structures that define religion, but rather from the conviction that religion is a mode of creating meaning. The possible weakness here, it seems, is the failure to distinguish a religious mode of world creating from other modes. The tendency is to consider any construction of meaning potentially religious. Smith is interested in the diverse ways in which this world construction is practiced. Religion is always application, never essence. For Smith the task of understanding religion is not the recognition of some essential structure wherever it occurs; rather it is constantly to expand one's understanding of religion by the way observed applications reshape and challenge some aspects of the academically constructed concept of religion.

> To return to Numbakulla. The 1927 version of the myth appears to be an awkward hybrid. A common corporate name for ancestors has been reinterpreted as the proper name of a single figure who has been given a number of characteristics more typical of a celestial high god than an Australian totemic ancestor.
>
> Such an odd combination raises the possibility of Christian influence, of a Christianized reinterpretation of Arandan [Arrernten] myth. This supposition is strengthened by the fact that the putative deity's full title, . . . *Injkra Altkira Njambakala,* was an Arandan phrase created by local Christian missionaries to translate the liturgical acclamation, "Lord God Eternal." (Smith 1987, 5)

Smith offers a discussion of territorially oriented strategies to map the world: "locative," which emphasizes place, and "utopian," which values being in no place (Smith 1978). These mapping strategies can be discerned from an examination of the myths and rituals of a religious tradition. The locative approach is identifiable as the attitude of attempting to "overcome all incongruity by assuming the interconnectedness of all things, the adequacy of symbolization . . . and the power and possibility of repetition" (308). To the utopian approach, interconnection and repetition spell terror and confinement. This strategy "turns in rebellion and flight to a new world and a new mode of creation" (309). Smith warns that these mapping strategies are not adequate to classify religions, yet he notes that the academic study of religion has been most successful at describing traditions characterized by a locative mapping, a territory oriented to a center and an origin.

Smith's important contribution is less in the categories he introduces than in the difference represented by his attitude towards territory. Smith recognizes that the materials publicly available to the academic endeavor—materials such as myths and the descriptive accounts of ritual—are equivalent to maps and, like maps, they are significant only in terms of their use in making sense of some territory. Advancing this metaphor, as maps are used by travelers to negotiate some territory or are constructed by cartographers to chart the significance of a territory from some perspective, so too function the myths and rituals that play major roles in religious traditions. As there are endless ways to map a territory and to use maps to negotiate a territory, there are endless ways to perform rites and apply myths in the effort to construct meaning in life. What is important to

Smith is application. Application always involves the issues of correspondence, the fit or lack of fit, between map and territory; it is an enterprise of negotiating and manipulating the incongruities between the exigencies of life and the expectations of tradition. For Smith, then, religious meaning is not accomplished through an endless repetition of the sacred events but through the manipulation and negotiation of myths and rites in the attempt to apply them to the situations of life and to adjust life to these maps. Comparison, in Smith's view, is always motivated by, made interesting because of, difference. "The Tjilpa do not build; Mesopotamia did" (1987, 17, referring to the two principal cultural examples Eliade used to establish his notion of the "sacred center").

While the locative and utopian maps discussed by Smith have commonly been used by students of religion as interpretive categories, the fullness of Smith's views on territory can be gained only by heeding his warning that these are not intended as categories by which to classify religions and by paying careful attention to a third, usually overlooked, mapping strategy that Smith describes. This strategy amounts to the recognition that religion may be meaningfully considered as a process of negotiating among mapping or map-using strategies. When the locative and utopian mapping strategies are pushed to their limits, it is clear that neither is ever more than momentarily achievable and that one is but the flip side of the other. Logically the two mapping approaches are inseparable. Both strategies are intent upon overcoming the separation between map and territory, the locative by making the map correspond perfectly with the territory, the utopian by eliminating map (and for that matter territory) altogether. Acknowledging that the locative and utopian visions are strategies that shape ongoing processes is tantamount to seeing religion and the religious in more process-conducive terms, allowing "the incongruous elements to stand . . . [and admitting] that symbolism, myth, ritual, repetition, transcendence are all incapable of overcoming disjunction" (Smith 1978, 309). In other words, religion is a map-making and map-using process characterized by differing attitudes toward the inevitable difference between maps and territories. Whatever the attitude, the difference must remain. The title of Smith's seminal essay on this topic, "Map Is Not Territory," clearly states his position. Later, Smith writes: "What does such [aboriginal ancestral] activity mean in such a context? It is clearly more a matter of marking than of making, of memorializing than of constructing. It is not a language of edifices, but of 'tracks,' 'paths,' 'traces,' 'marks,' and 'prints'" (1987, 18).

Smith further utilizes the same map-territory metaphor to discuss the task of the academic student of religion. The work of the study of religion is borne in the juxtaposition of the interpretive frame of the student (the mapping strategy) with the data (the territory), such as rites and myths that present a religious tradition, in the attempt to manipulate and negotiate the incongruities between theory and data in the construction of meaning (a map), making an interpretation or reading. While, if one is unable to free oneself from the former essentialist position, it might be thought that the goal of this process is to reveal the religious territory of the subject studied (which might be designated "the sacred"), Smith cuts short any hope for closure in a further application of the metaphor: "'Map is not territory'—but maps are all we possess" (1978, 309). In other words, as religion is the continuing process of negotiating the application of elements of a tradition with the ongoing lived history of the tradition, the academic study of religion is the continuing process of negotiating the application of academic theories and expectations with the historical and culturally specific evidence of the traditions studied. Both map and territory are real in both cases and both are being constantly re-created.

Smith cites Archimedes, "Give me a place to stand on and I'll move the world," reflecting a classical perspective and one common to many religions. But he denies students of religion the possibility of a firm place to stand. According to Smith, students of religion have no place to stand "apart from the messiness of the given world. . . . There is . . . only the plunge which he takes at some arbitrary point to avoid the unhappy alternatives of infinite regress or silence" (1978, 289–90). It is in this dilemma that the student of religion bears kinship with the novelist.

The more fully we appreciate the operative uses of territorial terms, the clearer it is that they have yet to realize fully the morality of the academic study of religion; they remain terms used within the temple, at least the temple of colonialism. In this respect territory is a political term. The search for neutral language has served as a disguise, though doubtless most often unwittingly, for knowing the other in the sense of controlling the other.

Jean Baudrillard uses the map-territory metaphor to describe the process in which the map becomes the only reality, a process he sees as increasingly characterizing the modern West. Applying his perspective to the academic enterprise suggests that abstractions, models, academic constructs of the generic are no longer maps that reflect a real territory. They are not used as maps to direct the inquiry of historically and culturally real territories, nor are they the products of such inquiries. Rather they amount to a hyperreality without the traditional correspondence of a represented territory. As Baudrillard puts it, "Today abstraction is no longer that of the map, the double, the mirror, or the concept. Simulation is no longer that of a territory, a referential being, or a substance. It is the generation of models of a real without origin or reality: a hyperreal. The territory no longer precedes the map, nor does it survive it. It is nevertheless the map that precedes the territory—*precession of simulacra*—that engenders the territory" (1994, 1).

Doubtless Baudrillard's broad analysis of Western culture applies, to a degree not yet appreciated because it would be too damning, to the academic study of religion. The implication is that we may have come to rely so deeply on our maps, on our generic ideas regarding religion, that our presentations of religion are simulations of culture and history; hyperrealities with few territorial or referential realities beyond the simulation.

Territorial terms that are used in the analysis of phenomena considered to be religious remain largely those of space and time. Terms that are used in conjunction with territory—such as perspective, worldview, insight, outlook, landscape—all privilege the visual sense. Both in its literal and figurative senses, the visually dominated sensorium subtly transforms the world senses, to use Walter Ong's term, of others into the familiar Western concept of worldview. Studies in sensory anthropology show that the visual is not primary to the sensoria of many cultures. For the Arrernte and Warlpiri, while their dreamings are represented in diagrams etched on *tjurungas* (oval-shaped ritual objects) and in the designs of body painting, these markings are not pictures, maps, or even representations. They are themselves presentations, something more akin to embodied poetry. They correspond with the poetic songs sung in dance dramatic performances. An important use of *tjurungas* is to rub them with fat and ochre and press them to the human body, particularly the stomach. "Painting up," that is, body painting in preparation for dancing, requires extensive touching of the body. Sight is no more important than other senses to aboriginal understandings of territory. While travel literature is brimming with descriptions and personal responses to the stimulation of the nonvisual senses, suggesting that the full sensorium can hardly be suppressed when one is in another's territory, students of religion have given little attention to the sensoria of others.

Many of the limitations on the present conceptions of territory stem from the Western style of separating mind and body that elevates the mind over the body. The privileging of sight is associated with this devaluation of body. Sight is understood to be the objective sense: seeing is believing. The other senses are more personal and, therefore, more subjective. Territory, though the key to cultural differences, tends to be considered as objectified and impersonal. But Merleau-Ponty insisted that lived space is different from objective uniform space. Territory is perceived and experienced differently with respect to gender, culture, age, and bodily ability. Lived territory, as evidenced by human action, does not appear much in analyses or descriptions of territory. The terms of territory in use in academic analyses have focused largely on the designation of objective structual categories that distinguish religion. However, territory is always significant only as the setting for action, only as the background against which action engages the motion that is life. The dream tracks of aborigines are useless and meaningless to them without the movement and actions of the mythic ancestors and without the weight of the law these actions bear upon the people. It is fitting that aborigines present dreamings in the dynamic form of dance dramas. Students of religion must conceive anew the terms of territory using enriched metaphors. The map-territory metaphor, as powerful and effective as it has been, tends to support the comprehension of territory as static, as stable, as mappable, as graspable from some view. Smith's attention to application implies the importance of movement and process. Journey or story may serve more effectively to stimulate a richer conception of territory, and these active terms are now receiving increasing attention.

As suggested throughout this essay, the aborigines of Central Australia may inspire, as they have in the past, the rethinking of our present approaches to territory, and they may stimulate our imaginations with regard to developing new concepts. Their conception of dreamings as designating countries overlying one another, as mythic ancestral journeys that crisscross one another, and as webs of storytracks, as well as the way these notions of territory facilitate human relations is powerfully provocative.

> The Warlpiri social universe was made up of skeins of relationships, not just songlines. A Dreaming defined a person's descent. It was immutable and given. But during the course of a lifetime, a man made contacts with others outside of his own home area. Networks of ties developed which were different for each person, reflecting the contingencies of where he traveled, lived, worked, married, and learned ceremony. It went without saying that alliances shifted, things changed. (Jackson 1995, 64–65)

Warlpiri networks of relationships, which Jackson aptly describes as "skeins," suggest something akin to the structure of the Internet and other postmodern models of communication and interaction. Among Internet users, each person has a distinctive point of access, a way of entering, a motivating idea or need, and a strategy of interacting. Cyberspace is an incredibly complex dynamic field of play in which personal interests, personal whim, and pure coincidence greatly influence the way relationships are made, the way one travels (surfs), works, and learns.

These examples suggest a number of shifts presently under way in our conception of territory. The traditional conception of territory as space and time divided into jigsaw puzzle-like maps in which every division is entirely separate from all others is a less and less useful model. These traditional expectations of territory correspond with traditional conceptions of categories as containers whose members all share a common definitive trait that is the essential feature of the category. We have held such a categorical expectation with regard to religion. Discussions of the definition of religion have been battles over territory. Even identifiable religious traditions—such as Buddhism, Judaism, Islam—are often presented in terms of this understanding of category. Each tradition is identified, despite all of its manifestations and subdivisions throughout history, in terms of a single distinctive trait.

The sociology of knowledge is a discourse on territory. The frequent discussions of the appropriateness of studying religion from the inside as opposed to the outside reflect a traditional understanding of category and associated concepts of power. That the lion's share of the study of religion has been done by insiders (a trend that continues), that is, by members of the tradition studied, has received little critical attention. Being a member of a tradition or gender or ethnicity, being an insider, is often a major criterion for academic authority and authenticity. Strategies of field study are often directed towards making the scholar in some respects an insider of the religion studied and thus to win the associated authority.

The studies of religious phenomena such as myth, ritual, rites of passage, and pilgrimage are often approached on the basis of a classical theory of category, a traditional understanding of territory directed toward discovering the essential distinctive feature for all phenomena so classified. Unlike the Warlpiri, academic students of religion have not known how to deal with territorial designations that overlap one another, that have fuzzy or fluid boundaries.

If the examples of the Warlpiri and the Arrernte dreamings are not adequate stimulation for imagining an enriched vision of territory, George Lakoff's discussion of category theory in *Women, Fire, and Dangerous Things: What Categories Reveal About the Mind* (1987) may be: "The Australian Aboriginal language Dyirbal . . . has a category, *balan,* that actually includes women, fire, and dangerous things. It also includes birds that are *not* dangerous, as well as exceptional animals, such as the platypus, bandicoot, and echidna" (5). Lakoff proposes a prototype theory of category along with a variety of principles by which prototypes are extended and expanded to bring inclusion of other items into a category. This theory of category helps us understand the richness and apparent conflicting character of such categories as *balan,* and it has promise to do the same for the terms "territory" and "religion."

There is an odd intertwining of Western academic conceptions of territory and Australian aborigines. Doubtless to some extent this has occurred because in being considered *ab origine,* "from the origin," aborigines have been imagined into existence, hyperrealities, in the terms that have satisfied Western territorial needs, whether colonial, conceptual, or observational (sensorial). While this process has been actively imaginative, it has not been interactive. Imaginative constructs of aborigines have been inadequately constrained by the independent reality of the aborigines; they are often preceding simulacra. Perhaps the greatest challenge facing the conception of territory is how to foster the creative interpretation of others based on appreciating their lived territory, without the accompanying need to control them and their territory.

> Archie stared somberly at Japanangka's diagrams, "That's the whitefella way," he said irritably, "fixing boundaries." (Jackson 1995, 64)

SUGGESTED READINGS

Baudrillard, Jean. 1994. *Simulacra and Simulation,* translated by Sheila Faria Glaser.

Eliade, Mircea. 1954. *Cosmos and History: The Myth of the Eternal Return,* translated by Willard R. Trask.

———. 1958. *Patterns in Comparative Religion,* translated by Rosemary Sheed.
———. 1959. *The Sacred and the Profane: The Nature of Religion,* translated by
    Willard R. Trask.
Smith, Jonathan Z. 1972. "The Wobbling Pivot." *Journal of Religion* 52.
———. 1978. "Map Is Not Territory." In *Map Is Not Territory: Studies in the
    History of Religions.*
———. 1987. "In Search of Place." In *To Take Place: Toward Theory in Ritual.*
Swain, Tony. 1993. *A Place for Strangers: Towards a History of Australian Ab-
    original Being.*

REFERENCES

Baudrillard, Jean. 1994. *Simulacra and Simulation,* translated by Sheila Faria Glaser. Ann Arbor:
    University of Michigan Press.
Durkheim, Emile. [1912] 1965. *The Elementary Forms of the Religious Life,* translated by Joseph
    Ward Swain. New York: Free Press.
Eliade, Mircea. 1954. *Cosmos and History: The Myth of the Eternal Return,* translated by Willard R.
    Trask. Princeton: Princeton University Press.
———. 1958. *Patterns in Comparative Religion,* translated by Rosemary Sheed. London: Sheed
    and Ward.
———. 1959. *The Sacred and the Profane: The Nature of Religion,* translated by Willard R. Trask.
    London: Harcourt Brace Jovanovich.
———. 1967. *Australian Religions: An Introduction.* Ithaca, N.Y.: Cornell University Press.
Freud, Sigmund. 1913. *Totem and Taboo: Some Points of Agreement between the Mental Lives of Sav-
    ages and Neurotics,* translated and edited by James Strachey. Vol. 13 of *The Complete Standard
    Edition of the Works of Sigmund Freud.* New York: Norton.
Jackson, Michael. 1995. *At Home in the World.* Durham, N.C.: Duke University Press.
Kundera, Milan. 1995. *Testaments Betrayed: An Essay in Nine Parts,* translated by Linda Asher. San
    Francisco: HarperCollins.
Lakoff, George. 1987. *Women, Fire, and Dangerous Things: What Categories Reveal about the Mind.*
    Chicago: University of Chicago Press.
Mitchell, Timothy. 1988. *Colonizing Egypt.* Cambridge: Cambridge University Press.
Smith, Jonathan Z. 1972. "The Wobbling Pivot." *Journal of Religion* 52 (2).
———. 1978. "Map Is Not Territory." In *Map Is Not Territory: Studies in the History of Religions.*
    Leiden: Brill.
———. 1987. "In Search of Place." In *To Take Place: Toward Theory in Ritual.* Chicago: University
    of Chicago Press.
Swain, Tony. 1993. *A Place for Strangers: Towards a History of Australian Aboriginal Being.* Cam-
    bridge: Cambridge University Press.

EIGHTEEN

Time

Anthony F. Aveni

F ew words in the dictionary are as monopolized by the sciences as the word "time." On the one hand, time is the idea of successive existence, the recognition of an order of sequence in our states of consciousness, as nineteenth-century physicist James Clerk Maxwell put it. To use a spatial metaphor, we can think of time as a continuous running line to which recognizable events are pegged as a series of moments. On the other hand, time is the measure of duration, a metric quantity that is continuous, homogeneous, unchangeable, and never ending. In both these senses time becomes a reality that lies outside of human existence. Like tangible things, it is already there to waste, spend, kill, or lose. This so-called classical idea of time is best expressed in Newton's *Principia Mathematica*. Time is absolute, "of itself," as Newton put it, and "flows equably without relation to anything external" (Cajori 1947, 6). When the notion of physical absolutism was attacked by Bishop Berkeley on the grounds that it led to atheism, Newton, a profoundly religious man, added in a later edition of the *Principia* his belief in a God that endures everywhere and always. His being thus encompasses every indivisible moment of time. Therefore, what Newton could not establish by scientific empiricism he managed to certify by the tenets of religion.

We sense time by taking the measure of its duration with our instruments. Generations of watching natural phenomena like the heavens turning, the moon's phases waxing and waning, flower petals opening and shutting at dawn and dusk, respectively, together with the pre-Socratic and Aristotelian conviction that time is related to motion, led to time measurement through *mechanical* models that oscillate. Western chronology begins with concrete models, or simulacra as the Greeks called them, that further concretize time: sand falling through an overturned hourglass, a pendulum bobbing back and forth, or an encased vibrating crystal wrapped about one's wrist. But it was the demands of precise religion, not quantitative science, that later led to the creation of more elaborate machines that mimic time. The medieval Christian way demanded a controlled and disciplined life. It was a strict rule in the monasteries that the call to prayer be made at the correct times of day. Historian David Landes (1983) regards the mechanical clock as the *result* of an interest in measuring time, not the *origin* of that interest. The one-hand version of the clock gave rise to two, and in the age of expansion of trade and commerce that followed, it was not long before the hours and their parts chimed, gonged, and clattered their way into our cycle of daily activities.

The high-speed twentieth century has caused us to rethink the meaning of time, to make it less absolute and more relative, less objective and more subjective. The special theory of relativity recognized that experimental facts admit a joint definition of distance and time based upon the dynamics of a particular situation. This led to the conclusion that whether two events can be conceived as having occurred at the same time depends on where in the universe one witnesses them. The standard classroom example involves a moving train, the opposite ends of which are struck by lightning. Though an observer standing trackside might witness the flashes impinging on the train simultaneously, an observer in the train would see each one occur at a different time for he or she moves away from one signal and toward the other as news of each event travels at a finite speed toward him or her. This is, of course, pure physics, but such considerations would have a decided impact on the interpretation of causality and free will. That time is discontinuous at the microscopic as well as the macroscopic levels was another revolutionary development that took place at the borderline between nineteenth- and twentieth-century physics. Implicating the observer of atomic events as a participant in their ultimate outcome further eroded scientific confidence in the ability to pin down natural phenomena in a fully determined chronological framework.

Under the domain of nineteenth-century science, history too was regarded as a chain of events, a process whereby every happening contributed to the causation of future events. Like the scientists, historians of the nineteenth century seemed confident in their ability to give definite, objective answers to the questions they entertained. One supposedly studied archival documents without preconceptions, then wrote a story about them "attested to by the documents in such a way as to make the story itself the explanation of 'what happened' in the past" (White 1973, 141).

By the beginning of the twentieth century, the realistic apprehension of time in history lay on no more solid ground than the positivist's comprehension of time in the natural world. Historians came to realize that there is a difference between a chronology, or the simple arrangement of facts on a time line, and a narrative, or the story one writes about them. Hayden White (1973), for example, analyzed historical discourse in terms of metaphorical strategies. Like the physicist who perturbs an electron when attempting to observe and describe its position by illuminating it with a single photon of light, each storyteller affects the meaning of a set of facts by "emplotting" the events with his or her own "viewpoint." It is in the plot, wrote Ricoeur (1984, xi), that we "reconfigure our confused informed and at the limit mute temporal experience."

Rooted in the late-nineteenth- and early-twentieth-century German and French schools of philosophy, and central to modern philosophical debates concerning temporal consciousness, is the issue of whether there can be a transcendental phenomenology of time; that is, can there be a direct intuitive access to time's essential structure and meaning? Rejecting scientific objectivism,

Edmund Husserl (1965) argued that the essence of time can be discovered by examining the structure, and that God is both the end and the motivating force of consciousness and reason. Martin Heidegger (1985) and Maurice Merleau-Ponty (1962) extended Husserl's analysis by subjectivizing time. Heidegger desubstantialized time, laying heavy accent on the past by viewing all temporal experience as part of the dialectical process of coming into being. Rather than viewing oneself as helplessly sliding along a teleological temporal pathway toward death, one participates in constituting temporality. One manages time by taking action along with others who share a communal heritage. Accordingly, I do not merely exist as a moment in the world but bring myself into being in and through the tradition I choose to carry on.

There has been much written on the subject of whether time is linear or cyclic (or both). In the Old Testament, for example, the people of the covenant advance from a given point in time to another such point in the future. During the Enlightenment, the notion of progress led to a refinement of this linear model by slanting time's arrow in an ascending direction. Located within this time line are the rhythmic processes of natural order, which recur at regular intervals and which serve as the basis for cultic festivals. The synthesis of linear and cyclic notions of time leads to a helical model of sacred historical time in which short duration cycles are conceived as loops or turns in a forward (upward) advancing time coil. Taking the extreme position, Mircea Eliade (1954) argues that only in the Western literate tradition is there actually a notion of linear time. All other cultures, he contends, perceive time as cyclical. The link between humanity and the sacred is forged by a ritual reenactment of events believed to have brought about creation. Thus, the heroic past of the gods remains alive in the present, perpetuated by the human reactualization of their deeds. The holder of an office does not *represent* the power of nature that governed all people, but *manifests* it. Archaic preliterate societies, Eliade maintains, lived in a "paradise of archetypes" governed by time structures based on the renewal of the regenerative powers observable in all biorhythms. This periodic regeneration presupposes that all personal and cosmic re-creation repeats the first act of genesis or becoming. By re-actualizing creation, the believer relives over and over the oscillation between chaos and order. Past events never become a part of history and thus do not create the burden of time that characterizes linear development. Though some historians (e.g., Farriss 1987) have challenged this dichotomy between preliterate cyclic and literate linear views of time, the idea that earlier cultures think about time frozen in an unalterable sequence of events still permeates a good deal of the literature (cf. Hallpike 1979; Ricoeur 1975).

Western time also separates human history from events in the history of nature, which appear to be strung out on a different, far lengthier processional pathway. By creating a history of nature, scientific empiricism effectively robbed theology of any hold it once had on the notion of one-way development through linear time. At the start of the twentieth century, all the sciences, with the exception of physics (which still primarily concerned itself with the discovery of im-mutable laws), were dealing with temporal processes, the determination of which was guided in the already well-established empirical tradition by the observation and evaluation of physical evidence: what Toulmin and Goodfield (1965) aptly call the "testimony of things" (as opposed to human history or the testimony of people). Thus the fossil record, along with the observation of the variation of extant biological species, led to the notion of life as an extraordinarily lengthy developmental chain of being. Geological evidence on stratigraphy and sedimen-tation pushed the traditional linear time barrier back even further, and the later cosmological discovery of the expansion of the universe, revealed through the redshifts measured in the spectra of distant galaxies, wrenched away any remain-ing theological grip on the word "time." Like the new interstate highway run-ning alongside the old state road connected by neither exit nor entry ramp, the development of nature, like that of humanity, came to be viewed as a one-way process. The discovery of the New World, the assassination of Lincoln, the fall of the Berlin Wall—all blips on one time line—can never be related causally to the eruption of Mount Vesuvius, the appearance of Halley's comet, or the blizzard of 1888, which are event markers on the other road of time. There is an arrow of time, and it points toward the future. But there is no forward pull or purpose to nature's arrow. Instead, it is pushed from behind. What we see before us is the ever-changing eventuality that results from events or circumstances traceable to the past.

Having highlighted a range of views on the meaning of time espoused by a variety of Western disciplines, I would next like to explore time's meaning in a comparative context by considering the Maya of Central America. I will conclude by returning briefly to persistent questions about time that continue to emerge in cross-cultural studies.

I choose the Maya and this particular course of reflection for several reasons: First, like all New World cultures, these people were hermetically sealed from outside cultural intervention prior to European contact. This gives us the rare opportunity to inquire, in our search for cultural universals, whether under such circumstances a civilization would develop similar ideas and practices in dealing with the problem of time. If other cultures really did have different ideas than we do about time—if they were unfamiliar with any of the imagery we use to articu-late the nature of time—we would be unable to communicate with them. Does all of humanity think of time as duration and of duration as either cyclic or linear, the former static and ritually motivated and the latter dynamic and practical? A second reason for considering the Maya lies in the possibility of exploring how the clash of two cultures at the time of contact between Europe and America altered indigenous views of temporality. The third reason for focusing on the Maya is that more than any other non-Western culture, they seem to have exhib-ited an obsession with time. We can trace this obsession to both the monuments they carved and the few surviving books they wrote in hieroglyphic script, which have survived for us to decipher. Their dalliance with celestial movement and the way they incorporated events from unimaginably early times—times before creation—into the history they wrote offers a contrast with our own ancient roots concerning the comprehension of time. Fourth, even though they fully exploited a strategy of discovering mathematically expressible accounts of how nature behaves, the Maya, in stark contrast to the West, seem never to have separated science from religion. A study of their way of knowing time is central to this development. And last, an interdisciplinary discourse on Maya time permits some of the major questions and problems about time, which arise from the interplay of anthropology and the sciences, to impinge upon questions emanating from the more purely reflective canon of literature with which students and scholars of religious studies are more familiar.

The Maya culture of the Yucatan peninsula rose to prominence around the beginning of the Christian era and flourished until well into the ninth century. Compared to the civilizations of the ancient Middle East, we still know relatively little about these people, for the New World archaeological record has only begun to be unraveled. When Heinrich Schliemann dug up Troy and Sir Arthur Evans unearthed the Mycenean remains of Crete, the Maya ruins lay undisturbed, blanketed by the Guatemalan rain forest. In the twentieth century, however, investigators discovered, firmly embedded in the topsoil of pre-Columbian America, evidence of the identical sort of dialogue with nature that their predecessors had encountered in ancient Babylonia: records pertaining to celestial timing schemes that were perceived to trigger omens about the future course of human events and mythological creation episodes featuring the sun, moon, and planets in starring roles. "It is as if the world was [sic] perceived as being magically charged, inherently alive in greater or lesser degree with this vital force. Everything in the world was potentially a hierophany: things, animals, people, transitory phenomena had the capacity to manifest some aspect of the sacred" (Townsend 1970, 28). Richard Townsend's assessment of the Aztec perception of the universe may apply equally well to that of the Maya. Nonetheless, there is a debate over whether classic Maya religion was devoted to the worship of specific gods or based upon the worship of a *mana*-like force or spirit extant in the material world. Supernatural beings depicted on artistic works seem to consist of a combination of parts of different animals, which display no stable associations or patterns (Taube 1992).

The ancient Maya do not appear to have believed that they lived in an indifferent, deterministic universe that operated on its own, totally devoid of any linkage with the human spirit. Rather, they conceived of an everyday human world that was intimately related to nature. When all was well, the natural and the human worlds functioned in perfect harmony. This universe was a distinct whole, with all parts intricately laced together, each aspect influencing every other—animate, breathing, teeming, vibrant, and interactive. Celestially based myths explained the unfolding of history, politics, social relations, and ideas about creation and life after death. In a manner similar to that used by present day astrologers, the Maya forged links between the sky and just about every phase and component of human activity. They celebrated this knowledge not only in texts but also in art, architecture, and sculpture.

The starting point for any inquiry into the nature of Maya time resides in the codices. To judge from their content, these folding screen, painted bark books were filled with numbers, hieroglyphs, and pictures depicting the Maya reverence for *kin,* a single word in their language, which meant sun, day, and time. The sixteenth-century Spanish chronicler Diego de Landa, bishop of Yucatan, who purged the idolatrous Maya as devil worshippers by burning their books, none-theless respectfully described the exalted religious leaders of the day who once toted their texts under their arms from town to town heralding time's message:

> The natives of Yucatan were as attentive to the matters of reli-gion as to those of government, and they had a high priest whom they called *Ah Kin Mai* [Lord of the Days, or "daykeeper" named *Mai*]. . . . In him was the key of their learning and it was to these matters that they dedicated themselves mostly; and they gave advice to the lords and replies to their questions. . . . They provided priests for the towns when they were needed, examining them in the sci-ences and ceremonies, and committed to them the duties of their office, and the good example to people and provided them with books and sent them forth. And they employed themselves in the duties of the temples and in teaching their sciences as well as in writ-ing books about them. (Tozzer 1941, 27–8)

Anyone who has even glanced at replicas of these calendrical almanacs filled with grotesque zoo- and anthropoform imagery, can imagine their impact on a Roman Catholic prelate of the sixteenth century who was already preoccupied with combating the devil's work in Reformation Europe. Most of the almanacs are highly prescriptive; they contain invocations and divinatory procedures that deal with weather and agriculture, disease and medicine. These invocations are intended to bring all natural and human activity into relationship with a sacred round of time they termed the *tzol kin,* or the "count of the days." This round of 260–day duration consisted of a pair of shorter cycles made up of the num-bers one to thirteen and 20 named days. Scholars hotly debate the origin of the *tzol kin,* which is unique to Mesoamerica (for a summary of relevant arguments see Aveni 1980, 148–53). For example, this period has been related to the hu-man gestational cycle (average 255 days), the nine-month lunar phase cycle, the average interval of the appearance of Venus as the evening or morning star (263 days), the eclipse year (the average period separating the seasons during which eclipses occur), and the simple multiplication of the sacred number thir-teen (the number of layers in the Maya heaven) by the number of fingers and toes on the human body. (The use of a base twenty counting system all over

Mesoamerica is archaeologically documented to 600 B.C.E. The most likely conclusion is that, like the universal constants of Western physics (e.g., the constant of gravitation or the speed of light), which become manifest in a variety of physical measurements, the number 260 was recognized as central in linking humanity and temporality precisely because its duration could be equated with each of these natural cycles, and in addition could be expressed in a counting system that resided in the human body.

The Maya broke down time and they built it up. Some divinatory almanacs in the codices fracture the 260-day cycle into shorter intervals (e.g., there are many 5 times 52– and 4 times 65–day almanacs). After each subinterval, one learns, through picture and prescriptive glyphic statement, which offering to make, where to make it, and to what deity. As the reader's eye passes from pictorial panel to panel, from left to right in these texts, time rolls inexorably forward. At the end of the panel, the user is instructed to return to the beginning of the table and may do so without missing a day. Other almanacs constitute an effort to accumulate cycles by multiplying the *tzol kin:* thus, 2 times 260, 4 times 260, 7 times 260, 9 times 260, and so on. Evidently these almanacs were carefully updated, for later editions reveal when "uncontrollable" events such as planetary conjunctions or eclipses had intervened during several of the interval courses.

A few almanacs indicate direct timing by the course of celestial bodies, and some of these efforts border on extravagant precision. One of them deserves a closer look for it captures the essence of the meaning of time in this extraordinary culture. The Venus Table in the Dresden Codex (1975), so called after the library in which it now resides, is both a historical record of what the Maya had observed concerning the motion and timing of the planet Venus, and an ephemeris capable of generating scientific predictions about the future course of that celestial body. Moreover, the text frames the observations in the context of the perceived relationship between a people and their gods. Those who could read the Venus Table would know precisely where the great luminary would be in the near or distant future to a tolerance of a single day over a period of five centuries. Given their penchant for temporal commensurabilities, Maya infatuation with the Venus time period likely stemmed from their recognition of the perfect fit between its visible cycle of appearances and disappearances (584 days) and the 365-day seasonal year, in the perfect ratio of 5 to 8. Ever mindful of the necessity of wedding Venusian timings to the sacred *tzol kin,* the day keeper was careful to run the full length of this recyclable table to 37,960 days, the lowest whole multiple of 584, 365, and 260.

Venus's proximity to the sun, which led the ancient Babylonians to view the planet as Ishtar, the goddess of love who courted the solar deity, seems instead to have evoked a metaphor for resurrection on the part of Mesoamerican sky watchers. Venus symbolized Quetzalcoatl, the quasi-mythical ruler of the Toltec empire, from whom the Aztecs say they drew their right to govern all peoples of Mexico. Exiled from office, he vowed to return from the east to resurrect his empire. Wrote one Spanish chronicler, at the time when the planet was visible in the sky (as evening star) Quetzalcoatl [Venus] died. And when Quetzalcoatl was dead he was not seen for 4 days; they say that then he dwelt in the underworld, and for 4 more days he was bone (that is, he was emaciated, he was weak); not until 8 days had passed did the great star appear; that is, as the morning star. They said that then Quetzalcoatl ascended the throne as god. (Seler 1904, 364–5)

At midpage the subject of the Dresden Venus text abruptly passes from precise numerical calculation and detail of celestial observation—what we would call scientific astronomy—to matters that deal with the veneration of the deity. The set of pictures that always follows the (average) eight-day disappearance before first morning appearance of Venus refers to the five manifestations of Venus as the shield-wielding Kukulcan or feathered serpent god (as Quetzalcoatl is called in Yucatan). He is depicted flinging his spears (Are they the brilliant darts of light we see emanating from Venus when it reappears from the underworld?) at victims who lie impaled at the bottom of each page. In one picture, for example, Kukulcan is a long-nosed god. A jaguar, represented below him with a spear through his cringing body, is his sacrificial victim. Between pictures of Kukulcan and his victim, a block of a dozen glyphs encode the omens he brings with this particular set of his Venus appearances.

To judge from what the Spanish chroniclers who first encountered this culture in the mid-sixteenth century have to say, the response to this omen had a dual purpose. First, it signaled the time to pay one's debt to the god, presumably to avert any prognostication that might connote evil. And second, the day keeper would need to compute a more propitious fateful day for the sacrificer to conduct the appropriate offertory rite. While many scholars tend to view the Maya calendar as a paragon of scientific timekeeping, it is also constrained by ritual dictates, for example, the need to set the celebration of the arrival of the deity on his special name days in the *tzol kin*. A sacred round of 260 days was intimately involved in a complex numerological rhythm making associated with this doubly difficult priestly duty.

Unfortunately, many scholars exhibit a tendency to think of those who handled the codices as mystical number jugglers who dealt in arbitrary, whimsical machinations. Even the dean of Maya epigraphers, Sir Eric Thompson, once commented that Maya astronomy was astrology pure and simple. But the challenge to the ancient calendar keeper was an intellectual one. Given his many prognosticatory tables, he needed to determine, in the march of time, which cosmic forces would rear themselves up on any given day and to gauge the resulting influence in the computation of the fates. Solving the puzzle—finding order in the perceived chaos of natural time—was vital in promoting methodical living.

To our knowledge, no chronicler of the New World ever recorded the performance of a Maya Venus ritual; therefore, we can never know the details of what happened once Venus omens were cast. But contemporary anthropologists who have worked with the living descendants of the ancient Maya believe that the extant process of divining, which consists of a dialogue between person and deity, may not be so different from, if somewhat less elaborate than, what went on during the Maya classical period. For example, Barbara Tedlock (1982) has carefully followed and recorded the action of a contemporary master day keeper from the highland Guatemalan town of Momostenango. She discovered that not only did the day keeper actively work with the ancient *tzol kin* but also he seemed to exhibit both rigor and reason in his ritual practice, which linked the divine with every conceivable category of social structure.

Today's keeper of the day sits at a table, which he carefully aligns with the cardinal directions and arrays with lighted candles, bowls of incense, pieces of woven cloth, and other amulets withdrawn from his divining bag. Unlike his ancient predecessor, he has neither codex to guide him nor precise knowledge of celestial orbits, which might make a difference in his predictions. The day keeper arranges piles of seeds and crystals in separate groups consisting of equal numbers of elements. Then he "uses his blood," the place where his spirit is located and described by Tedlock (1982, 136–8) as a certain feeling in his upper and lower arms, to tell when something is about to happen. He speaks of borrowing *kin*—the power of certain days—to make his predictions. His performance is based on reading the seeds and crystals, which represent the names and numbers in the still extant 260-day sacred round, as he answers a series of questions posed by his clients, for example: Will the marriage of our daughter be successful? Is my dead father truly at rest? Reading Tedlock's contemporary account of a modern diviner, one wonders how much subjectivity was present in his performance, which is missing in written accounts from antiquity.

The Maya notion of borrowing time attributes an inherent power to temporality that escapes those who insist on seeing time as empty and contentless, as does Sartre (1956) in his existential notion of temporality in which consciousness (the "For-itself") continually annihilates the flow of time that arises solely out of that which is (the "In-itself") or as have we in coming to view pure number as void without reference to context or that which is to be counted. Appearing to summon the cosmos, the Maya diviner borrows not only time (the days) but also space (the directions) as he engages in an exchange with the numinous forces of nature through the crystals and seeds on his table. When he later pays a visit to each of the mountains of the four directions, the day keeper symbolically aligns himself with the universe on a larger scale. Thus he goes forward to the eastern mountain on the *tzol kin* day 11 *Quej*, a day associated with the ability to see into the future; backward to the mountain in the west on 11 *Junajpu*, a day associated with the ancestors; and to the mountains located laterally on the south and north, which are said to benefit the male (right) and female (left) sides of his body, respectively. Front side (forward) and back side (backward) have obvious experiential temporal associations, but they also represent the flow of time from ancestors to descendants, who correspond respectively to east (where the sun rises) and west (where it sets). The right and left directional pairs deal with questions of marriage and lineage. These are not simply binary oppositions but represent a dialectical complementarity like the terms male-female and right-left, which encompass rather than oppose one another.

The study of the Maya diviner's actions clearly demonstrates that the tendency to attach a spatial component to time is not unique to the West. This setting up of quadripartite space-time orientation has an analog in the codices. Many of the almanacs picture rituals taking place in each of the four directions (e.g., 4 times 65 equals 260 days), and in one instance (pp. 75–7 of the Madrid Codex [1967]), a four-directional calendrical diagram shows various gods/rituals framed within the flaps of a Maltese cross cosmogram, each arm of which is assigned a spatial direction. In contrast to the Western view of time as process, these spatial arrangements seem to emphasize time as pattern.

One of the defining principles in the Maya philosophy of history is the belief that the pattern of the past operates in a literal sense as a framework for the future. The twelve surviving *Books of Chilam Balam,* "Spokesmen of the Jaguar," colonial documents from the cities of Yucatan, give *katun* by *katun* histories. A *katun* is a period of 20 times 360 days, and a *katun round* consists of thirteen such periods. This cycle returns the same day and number of the *tzol kin* to the beginning of the *katun*. A good analogy in our calendar would be the time required to bring New Year's Day back to, say, Sunday. The narrative contained in these books interweaves recent events with like events from the distant past. All are united by faith that if a priest makes the correct calendrical calculations, he will be able to predict the fate of the next cycle. While these prophecy/histories refer to particular people, places, and events, all phenomena are configured in the *katun* in which they occurred rather than in linear temporal order. As an analogy, imagine discussing the assassinations of Lincoln and Kennedy in the same chapter of a history book because both occurred in a decade of the sixties. In mixing people of one epoch with gods of another and in being cast in typical elliptical language, this section of a lengthy *katun* prophecy from the *Book of Chilam Balam* of [the city of] *Tizimin,* is exemplary:

> The captain in the woods
> was Ma Zuy [military commander of an anti-Christian phratry]
> And Elom Tzitz' [community ruler]
> At the new count of Pop [the first month of the year];
> And the Tun [the year belonging to Tzitź]
> Had its thirteenth burden, . . .
> Because Lahun Chan [a deity, but also the name of a pro-Christian
>   leader]
> Was destroyed by the east sacrificial
> priest.
> It dropped fire
> And poured down steam.
>
> (Edmonson 1982, 35–6)

Yet the Maya were entirely capable of writing historical narrative in a linear mode, as one learns from the record of the Long Count, or the time lapsed since the most recent putative creation thousands of years in the past. We find evidence of this linear view of time both written in the codices and carved in stone (*tun*, the Maya word for stone, is also the word for year). Bishop Landa (Tozzer 1941, 38) recalls seeing public stone monuments (stelae) at Mayapan, a city only recently abandoned at the time of the conquest:

> There are in the plaza of that city seven or eight stones, each about ten feet long and rounded on one side, well worked and containing several lines of the characters which they use, and which cannot be read from their having been worn away by water, but it is thought that it is a memorial of the foundation and the destruction of that city, and there are others like them in Dzilan, a town of the coast, although they are taller and the natives when asked about this, reply that they were accustomed to erect one of these stones every twenty years.

Once thought to be Maya gods, the effigies on the stelae now being restored by archaeologists to their once-standing positions in front of the temples today are interpreted as real people who ruled these ancient city states. Scholars have only recently begun to decipher their exotic names from the phonetically based hieroglyphs written on their funerary monuments: Stormy Sky of Tikal, Bird Jaguar of Yaxchilán, and New-Sun-at-Horizon of Copan. (For a colorful recounting of the exciting story of glyphic decipherment, see Coe 1992). The stelae offer a long-term public record of dynastic accomplishments—birth, marriage, battles, and captures—interwoven with ritual events that celebrate the passage of cycles of time, the way we mark our decade, century, and other anniversaries with tangible mileposts such as world's fairs, expositions, and exhibits.

The carved monuments authorize the *k'ul ahau* (holy lord) or ruler as the conduit of the incarnation of nature's forces, the one in whom is invested the defining relationship between the natural and supernatural worlds. In the blood sacrifice of the Maya king lay the channel of communication with the gods and the dead ancestors. As art historians Linda Schele and Mary Miller (1986, 301) put it: "The king acted as a transformer through whom, in ritual acts, the unspeakable power of the supernatural passed into the lives of mortal men and their works. . . . The king ensured that the heavens would rotate in perpetuity through the rituals of sacrifice and bloodletting." He literally kept time in motion.

The stela script records a sacred religious foundation, for gods of time and number are included in the texts of most carved monuments. Pure number was accorded considerable potency in ancient Maya religious thought. Each number was conceived as a god with particular characteristics: youth or old age, gender, degree of sexual prowess—just about every range of human personality trait that one could catalog. For example, thick-lipped, his face spotted with tattoos, the god of the number two symbolized death and sacrifice; and the wrinkled countenance of number five reminds us of the wisdom of old age. Zeroes are represented by full figures with their hands clasped against their jaws to denote completeness of a full body count of twenty. Like the codices, the stelae evoke both performance and poetics. People once likely stood in the vast open spaces in front of these number gods chanting their names in the hope that their intervention in daily affairs would lead to a better life.

Divine number seems to have made the passage of time possible, for the number gods often are depicted in full figure carrying the burden of the days. The weight of time is parceled out into *tuns, katuns,* and *baktuns* (scores of *katuns*), with the gods of number sharing the load in the relay. (Recall the use of the word burden in the aforementioned *katun* prophecy.) Maya transcriptions from the colonial period document such imagery. They tell of bearers who let fall their burdens of time, tie on their burdens, travel the road, and so on. Ends-of-time cycles are equated with resting places, where one lays down the load. And the burden of time came to be signified as the anticipated good or bad fortune associated with the benevolent or malevolent aspect of the god who bore it.

Is Maya history purely fatalistic? So it might seem from the above description; however, there is considerable latitude for interpretation provided we widen our perspective. Maya historian Nancy Farriss argues that as with the metastructure to universal history disclosed by modern chaos theory, if a long enough period of Maya history is observed, one will discover that a pattern exists. One need only devise "a cycle so large that it could in theory encompass any conceivable linear sequence, to account for any contingency" (Farriss 1987, 574). The story is told of one of the last Maya kings who in 1697 sent his delegation to announce to the provincial governor that the *katun* 8 Ahau, normally associated with conflict and political change, deemed it was time to submit to Spanish rule, just as his ancestors had capitulated to a precontact foe on the previous such *katun* 260 cycles earlier. Even as late as the seventeenth and eighteenth centuries, resistance to Spanish rule was based on the cyclic rotation principle of the Maya return to rule—the bigger the cycle, the more time in which to maneuver, and the lengthier the period, the stronger the collective forces would be from the combination of smaller cycles. Like so many odometer readings that record seminal events on a journey through time, five-digit long counts pile up as they conflate contemporary events with those that transpired in the past.

As in codices, the historical chronology carved on Maya monumental sculpture is imbued with an aura of extraordinary precision and detail. Long count tabulations on some of the monuments project history far backward to a time that transcends the creation of the existing world. It is as if the day keeper were trying to iron out time's biggest loop, the way some of our modern cosmologists speculate about time before the "big bang" creation, a previous epoch in which the universe might have contracted in the aftermath of an earlier expansion. This way of thinking about time as a series of enormously long cycles linked together is reminiscent of the Hindu and Buddhist traditions, with their emphasis on reincarnation and eternal repetition, or the Babylonian "Great Year," which was marked by long-term recurrences of observational and computational astronomy that reset the hands of the cosmic creation clock. In one well-documented Maya example, the initiation date of the seventh-century ruler Chan Bahlum of the city of Palenque (near Mexico's gulf coast) has been linked to a dramatic sequence of repeatable natural events. In 690 C.E., Jupiter and two other planets that move in a similar way had been dancing around together. First, over the course of a few weeks, Mars and Jupiter entered into conjunction; then, on 20 July 690 C.E., the equivalent of a date written several times in the Palenque inscriptions, all three coincided rather closely.

What could such a rare sky phenomenon documented in the Maya chronicles have meant to the believer? The visible heavenly triad was likely taken to celebrate the foundation event in the story of the creation of the Maya world: the birth of the gods written in the inscriptions of Palenque. The mid-seventh century was a time of great tumult in western Yucatán. Toniná and Yaxchilán, rival cities of the rain forest, had been vying with Palenque for supremacy. Shield Pacal, the old king of Palenque, had recently succumbed after six decades on the throne. His was a reign of triumph and success in battles with neighboring city-states. But now he was gone, and the Maya, like the Egyptians, needed a "Horus principle," that is, some assurance that his son and successor, Chan Bahlum, then in his late forties, would be a god incarnate just like his father. Thus the history of the gods at Palenque was inscribed in hieroglyphs alongside the dynastic family genealogy, all freshly carved in stucco on a tablet about to be installed in Chan Bahlum's first temple. Recently deciphered, the text tells of the descent of the ruling dynasty from three creator gods born at Palenque nearly four thousand years before. Each deity had been born of a father and mother who came into being several hundred years earlier, shortly before the commencement of the most recent cycle of creation, just after the world had been destroyed by floods (11 August 3114 B.C.E. by our calendar). According to the Popol Vuh, "The Mayan Book of the Dawn of Life," the world initially consisted only of water. A male-female creator god spoke and land appeared. The creator covered the land with trees and animals and then proceeded to create, destroy, and recreate, through successive approximations, people who would be adequate to serve them. The desiderata: intelligent, red-blooded worshippers able to genuflect and show gratitude to their creators, required several tries. In the present creation cycle, people were fashioned of blood and maize, the staple food of Mexico even today. Then the gods sent forth twin heroes, the last of their generation, who descended into the underworld to make final preparations for the present creation. They waged war on the underworld deities, thus depriving them of the ability wantonly to wreak pestilence upon the earth. Their work concluded, they ascended into the sky to become the sun and moon (or Venus according to some accounts). These people made of corn became the ancestors of all Maya people, who still worship their makers. Though this creation story is infused with ancient Israelite religious elements derived from the colonial Spaniards, who extracted the story from the natives (the creation of a failed generation of people made out of mud is an amusing parody on the second creation story in Gen. 2:7), unique to the tempo of this narrative is the repeated and successive creation and destruction of the world.

A hieroglyphic statement on a stucco plaque at Palenque accompanying the date of the last creation seems to verify the astronomical manifestation of the second coming of the gods. It reads, "the three gods joined who cross the sky." Several of Palenque's inscriptions indicate that Chan Bahlum had conducted certain rites of renewal commemorating the anniversary of the birth of the gods, his presumed ancestors, at Palenque. These events, like *katun* endings, were not wholly subject to human control but depended on certain computed numerical concordances. Such was the scientific, mathematical backdrop in the making of a religious hierophany—a manifestation of the sacred in the ceremonial landscape.

Ordinarily one would not tend to think of the built environment as a vehicle for expressing the meaning of time, though European religious architecture, examined carefully, does exhibit examples of encoded celestial timing. For example, in an obscure poem William Wordsworth claims to have witnessed the event of the laying out of the baseline of Rydal Chapel in England to the position in which the sun rose on the day of its patron saint:

> Then to her Patron Saint a previous rite
> Resounded with deep swell and solemn close,
> Through unremitting vigils of the night,
> Till from his couch the wished-for Sun uprose.
>
> He rose, and straight—as by divine command—
> They, who had waited for that sign to trace
> Their work's foundation, gave with careful hand
> To the high altar its determined place.
>   (Selincourt 1969, 417)

Given what we have learned of the hierophany of the birth of the gods at Palenque along with the predominance of exterior monumental design and inscriptions incorporated in Maya sacred architecture, it would not be at all surprising to discover that astronomical phenomena above the local horizon fronting a Maya place of worship would be taken into account in the architectural planning of sacred places and in the timing of rites conducted therein.

One example of time-fixed architecture from the Maya world can be found in Temple 22 at Copan, Honduras, now known to have been built at the northern end of a huge open courtyard by the eighth-century ruler 18 Rabbit (New-Sun-at-Horizon's grandfather). Closs, Aveni, and Crowley (1984) have argued that worship and observation of the planet Venus may have been a special feature of this structure. The key to the astronomical argument rests upon an observational relationship between the position of the planet Venus on the horizon and the direction of the single narrow window located on the west side of the structure. Venus could be glimpsed through this narrow window during our months of April and May while it was on its way to or returning from one of its standstill positions on the local horizon. Like the rising or setting sun, Venus oscillates along the horizon between standstills except that it takes considerably longer (eight years) for the planet to complete its cycle. Specifically, when the temple was built, in the year prior to a standstill, the first day of visibility of Venus always fell within or very close to an eight-day period ranging between 25 April and 3 May; moreover, in a year following a standstill, the last day of visibility of Venus possessed essentially the same property. These standstills occurred at the same time of the year as the traditional period associated with the onset of the rainy season. Since the ethnohistoric and ethnographic records reveal a coherent pattern that connects rain, maize planting, and Venus, the window could have served as a device to aid in marking the exact time when Venus would reappear in the sky following its last appearance in the west during the rainy season.

The iconography on the frieze of Temple 22 also calls attention to Venus. For example, the same hieroglyphs that appear in the Dresden Venus Table also can be found on the two-headed sky serpent sculpted in high relief over the doorway. Precisely what human events transpired in the open space fronting Temple 22 when Venus appeared? Having analyzed its inscriptions, Miller (1988) interprets the Venus temple to be part of the ritual complex of the royal family. She suggests that the ruler literally sat over the glyphic text of the temple, elevated and enframed by the bicephalic serpent as he appeared within the interior chamber of the temple. Here youthful rulership was celebrated and symbolized as one of the stages of the growth of the maize plant. The ruler would have entered this space through the mouth of the serpent (the doorway). As if planted like a kernel of corn, he became enthroned; then he sprouted and grew. The maize metaphor of the flourishing career of the sun god ruler is consistent with the hypothesis that attempts to tie celestial representations of the king to the act of sowing maize and the apparition of Venus in the temple to the timing of the sowing of maize. While in mythological time the Venus and sun symbols appear in stucco carvings at opposite ends of the bicephalic serpent, in the real time framework of the hierophany, the sinuous serpent reveals its celestial counterpart in the twisting motion of the visual line that connects Venus to the sun over the course of its evening star appearance.

Viewing at the appropriate time, the eye is confronted with two kinds of visual imagery, which for the Maya may have conveyed identical notions of reality. Private knowledge about Venus-sun timings would have been known only to the priests, encapsulated in the view that appeared to them through the window of the temple, as well as in the appellations associated with the ascension to rulership that appear in the hieroglyphic inscriptions at the top of the building. Pivoting about the king, religious ceremonies (whatever they might have been) that attended the astronomical phenomena surely would have impressed anyone standing in the vast, open east court of the acropolis of Copan fronting Temple 22 to watch the sky serpent appear more than a millennium ago.

Not until he had spent years visiting the Mesoamerican sacred sites did the author realize that one of the differences between the environment in which one worships in Christian Europe as opposed to precontact Central America has to do with the fact that the latter religion developed in a tropical climate. The sixteenth-century Spanish chapel at the ruins of Dzibilchaltun in north Yucatan is decisive for this insight. It frames an altar, which is entirely open to the western horizon, and faces the same direction, the place where the sun sets on the equinoxes, as the nearby House of the Seven Dolls (so called because of the cache of seven miniature icons found in its basement), which predates it by nearly 2,000 years. In early colonial times, believers stood in the open air to worship the new Christian god, in the same way their Maya ancestors once must have worshiped the sky gods in front of the Seven Dolls Complex. The accommodating nature of the tropical climate to outdoor worship makes it clear that Maya architects never would have dreamed of developing either a Roman arch or a flying buttress. Theirs was a sacred architecture that emphasized exterior space, as the visitor to Palenque, Copan, or any other Maya ruin for that matter will readily observe. There is simply no need of large enclosed interior spaces in buildings, sacred or otherwise, built at twenty-degrees latitude (the absence of which critics of those who extol Maya architecture are always quick to point out). But the large open courtyards in front of their temples once used for processionals and gatherings like the one discussed above do have their parallel in the atria of the sixteenth-century Spanish church, a fact that was employed to the fullest extent in the appropriation of sacred sites by the first Roman Catholic priests who entered the New World to convert the natives (McAndrew 1965, 187).

Few cultures in the world have exhibited such an absorbing interest in time as the Maya. But what are we to make of these Maya studies of time in relation to problems and questions about this subject that have confronted students of religion? Is time a transcendent principle? What is the essence of time and of those who live in it? How is past related to present and future? How do chronology, history, and narrative interact in the Maya view of temporality?

One hallmark of the Maya philosophy of time, which clearly emerges from the foregoing discussion, is its past directedness. Future time seems of little interest because of the Maya belief that events will recur provided the same balance of cosmic influences is attained. Just as Merleau-Ponty (1962, 69) has argued that "past time is wholly collected up and grasped in the present," each moment in time calling all the others that preceded it to witness, so too the Maya philosopher of time discerns the essence of present being as an aggregate of happenings that have gone before. The Maya present and future, however, are viewed as a configuration of particular combinations and sets of past phenomena and events.

Maya time is regarded not as an abstract concept but according to the way it affects the lives of individuals. The cosmology woven around Maya time is decidedly participatory, a far cry from its role in twentieth-century scientific cosmologies that prompt even their designers to remark, "The more the universe seems comprehensible, the more it also seems pointless" (Weinberg 1988, 154). For the Maya, one must assume responsibility for continuing the present form of the world, for it is only through human action that things will stay on course. Such action, however, is collective; there is no evidence that the concept of personal salvation ever had existed among the Maya before Hispanic contact. One petitioned the gods through the group, and each individual bore responsibility to contribute to the communal litany.

But how much of what modern scholars read into the chronicle of Maya history is a fabrication? After all, much of the record was destroyed by the very Spanish holy men who reinterpreted the portion that survived. Literary critic Tzvetan Todorov (1985, 116–9) believes that the narrative of Quetzalcoatl's return may have been part of a ploy by the Spanish to justify their claim to New World territory by deluding the natives into believing that Cortez was Quetzalcoatl. (There is no messiah in all of Mexican mythology, and this deity is simply one among many who do not occupy a privileged position.)

The dramatic discovery of the Maya hieroglyphic record and the story of its decoding have no doubt altered our interpretation of its content. Prior to the 1960s, scholars engaged in recovering the Maya inscriptions focused so heavily on the notion of the so-called Maya obsession with time that they interpreted the totality of the record to pertain to astronomy, legend, and the world of the supernatural. Only when it was recognized that the duration between dates tied to specific anthropomorphic figures carved on the stelae approximated the length of a human lifetime, and that the arrangement of such dates could reasonably be made to chronicle significant events in the lives of rulers (e.g., accession, marriage, victory in battle) did the pendulum of the interpretation of Maya chronology swing over to dynastic history.

By the early 1980s, a few scholarly narratives claimed the Maya inscriptions represented exactly what the monuments stated. Some interpreters almost seemed to profess a personal level of acquaintance with the ancient Maya lords portrayed on the stelae. Thus, "Chan-Bahlum tasted the salty sweat that rolled into the corner of his mouth as he lowered himself to the last of the high slippery steps that descended down through the rock of his fathers [sic] sacred mountain" (Schele and Freidel 1990, 228). More recently, anthropologist Joyce Marcus (1992, 15) has envisioned the pendulum swinging back to embrace a position in which one thinks of the written record as an amalgam of myth, history, and propaganda, "both a tool and a by-product of . . . competition for prestige and leadership positions." For example, the ruler places himself in the most favorable light, Marcus argues, by enhancing his record through the manipulation of a particular date, which enables him to claim to have accomplished a great act on the anniversary of a mythical ancestor.

Above all, we have learned that nature's cycles underlie the basis of Maya chronology. We need to think of these cycles as more than a set of convenient, recognizable periods whereby the Maya attempted to anticipate war, drought, or a coronation ceremony. Just as the medieval concept of geocentric spheres went beyond pure materialism and spatiality and penetrated far into the realm of the spiritual, so too was there more to the mathematics of Maya sky timing than pure science. The behavior of Venus, as I have stressed, was a microcosmic mirror of the long era cycles of which the Maya believed time to consist. The great conjunctions of the planets constituted an experiential application in miniature of the philosophy of repetition and recursiveness inherent in Maya creation narratives. These cycles were among a rather large number of lived temporal rounds (of which I have mentioned only a few) the Maya employed to give structure to their history. This allowed them to survive as active organizers and mediators against the chaotic forces of nature. What the Maya gave back to nature was a similar structuring principle, a framework for time. Their heavens consisted of cosmic cycles that, if charted closely and understood correctly, would ultimately be found to interlock commensurately not only with one another but also with the cycles of human life—all conceived in a kind of unity and harmony that we, in our most candid moments, must admit we can never really hope to fully comprehend.

One's comprehension of time, then, is conditioned by the world one experiences, together with the ways in which one articulates that which is experienced. Connecting the telling of stories about everyday affairs with the witnessing of changes in the world of nature is a coherent way to lend a meaningful structure to the Maya concept of time. With the process of storytelling comes the expansion into more fundamental and speculative questions, questions, which in our Western taxonomy of disciplines, we insist on relegating to the domain of religion. Where did we come from? What will happen to us in the future? In some instances—and this was especially so in certain highly structured hierarchical societies like the ancient Maya—the relationship between people and the things they saw in the sky became formalized through the ruling class. Cosmic myths expanded to extraordinary proportions, and so did the temporal cycles that framed them. Today scholars may debate where myth and history intersect in the ancient writings they decipher in the material record the Maya have left behind, but we can be sure the rhyme and meter of these texts have their origin in the cosmos.

The study of other cultures, a famous anthropologist once remarked, gives us a chance to expose what we think we know to a buffeting by other ideas and customs best able to rebut it. As an outsider to the discipline, it strikes me that the literary canon of religious studies insofar as it pertains to the study of time is confined largely to philosophical reflection, much of it directed toward the denial of an earlier generation's thought on the matter. I hope the comparatively based material brought together in this essay will offer alternative substance to reflect upon.

SUGGESTED READINGS

Aveni, Anthony. 1989. *Empires of Time: Calendars, Clocks, and Cultures.*

Farriss, Nancy. 1987. "Remembering the Future, Anticipating the Past: History, Time, and Cosmology among the Maya of Yucatan." *Comparative Studies in Society and History* 29.

Landes, David S. 1983. *Revolution in Time: Clocks and the Making of the Modern World.*

Tedlock, Barbara. 1982. *Time and the Highland Maya.*

Weinberg, Steven. 1988. *The First Three Minutes: A Modern View of the Origin of the Universe.*

White, Hayden. 1973. *Metahistory: The Historical Imagination in Nineteenth-Century Europe.*

REFERENCES

Aveni, Anthony. 1980. *Skywatchers of Ancient Mexico.* Austin: University of Texas Press.

———. 1989. *Empires of Time: Calendars, Clocks, and Cultures.* New York: Basic.

Cajori, Florian, trans. 1947. *Sir Isaac Newton's Mathematical Principles of Natural Philosophy and His System of the World.* Berkeley and Los Angeles: University of California Press.

Closs, M.; A. Aveni; and B. Crowley. 1984. "The Planet Venus and Temple 22 at Copan." *Indiana* 9.

Codex Dresden (Dresdensis). 1975. Royal Public Library Dresden. Codices Selecti, vol. 53. Graz: Akademische Druck- und Verlagsanstalt.

Codex Madrid (Tro-Cortesianus). 1967. Museo de América, Madrid. Codices Selecti, vol. 8. Graz: Akademische Druck- und Verlagsanstalt.

Coe, Michael. 1992. *Breaking the Maya Code.* London: Thames and Hudson.

Edmonson, Munro S., trans. 1982. *The Ancient Future of the Itza: The Book of Chilam Balam of Tizimin.* Austin: University of Texas Press.

Eliade, Mircea. 1954. *Cosmos and History: The Myth of the Eternal Return,* translated by Willard R. Trask. Princeton: Princeton University Press.

———. 1959. *The Sacred and the Profane: The Nature of Religion,* translated by Willard R. Trask. New York: Harcourt Brace.

Farriss, Nancy. 1987. "Remembering the Future, Anticipating the Past: History, Time, and Cosmology among the Maya of Yucatan." *Comparative Studies in Society and History* 29.

Hallpike, C. R. 1979. *The Foundations of Primitive Thought.* Oxford: Clarendon Press.

Heidegger, Martin. 1985. *History of the Concept of Time.* Bloomington: Indiana University Press.

Husserl, Edmund. 1965. *The Phenomenology of Internal Time Consciousness,* translated by James S. Churchill, edited by Martin Heidegger. New York: Harper.

Landes, David S. 1983. *Revolution in Time: Clocks and the Making of the Modern World.* Cambridge: Harvard University Press.

Marcus, Joyce. 1992. *Mesoamerican Writing Systems: Propaganda, Myth, and History in Four Ancient Civilizations.* Princeton: Princeton University Press.

McAndrew, John. 1965. *Open-Air Churches of Sixteenth Century Mexico: Atrios, Posas, Open Chapels, and Other Studies*. Cambridge: Harvard University Press.

Merleau-Ponty, Maurice. 1962. *Phenomenology of Perception,* translated by Colin Smith. London: Routledge and Kegan Paul.

Miller, Mary. 1988. "The Meaning and Function of the Main Acropolis, Copán." In *The Southeast Classic Maya Zone,* edited by Elizabeth Hill Boone and Gordon R. Willey. Washington, D.C.: Dumbarton Oaks Research Library and Collection.

Ricoeur, Paul. 1984. *Time and Narrative*. Vol. 1, translated by Kathleen McLaughlin and David Pellauer. Chicago: University of Chicago Press.

———, ed. 1975. *Les Cultures et le temps: Etudes preparées pour l'UNESCO*. Paris: Payot.

Sartre, Jean-Paul. 1956. *Being and Nothingness: An Essay on Phenomenological Ontology,* translated by Hazel E. Barnes. New York: Philosophical Library.

Schele, Linda, and David Freidel. 1990. *A Forest of Kings: The Untold Story of the Ancient Maya*. New York: Morrow.

Schele, Linda, and Mary Ellen Miller. 1986. *Blood of Kings: Dynasty and Ritual in Maya Art*. Ft. Worth: Kimbell Art Museum.

Seler, E. 1904. "Venus Period on the Picture Writings of the Borgian Group." *Bureau of American Ethnology Bulletin* 28.

Selincourt, E. de, ed. 1969. "Preparing for the Erection of Royal Chapel, Westmoreland." In *Wordsworth: Poetical Works*. Oxford: Oxford University Press, 1969.

Taube, Karl. 1992. "The Major Gods of Ancient Yucatan." Studies in Pre-Columbian Art and Archaeology, no. 32. Washington, D.C.: Dumbarton Oaks Center for Pre-Columbian Studies.

Tedlock, Barbara. 1982. *Time and the Highland Maya*. Albuquerque: University of New Mexico Press.

Thompson, J. E. S. 1972. *A Commentary on the Dresden Codex: A Maya Hieroglyphic Book*. Philadelphia: American Philological Society.

Todorov, Tzvetan. 1985. *The Conquest of America: The Question of the Other,* translated by Richard Howard. New York: Harper.

Toulmin, Stephen, and June Goodfield. 1965. *The Discovery of Time*. Chicago: University of Chicago Press.

Townsend, R. F. 1979. "State and Cosmos in the Art of Tenochtitlan." Studies in Pre-Columbian Art and Archaeology, no. 20. Washington, D.C.: Dumbarton Oaks Center for Pre-Columbian Studies.

Tozzer, Alfred M. 1941. *Landa's "Relación de las Cosas de Yucatán."* Cambridge: Peabody Museum, Harvard University.

Weinberg, Steven. 1988. *The First Three Minutes: A Modern View of the Origin of the Universe*. New York: Harper.

White, Hayden. 1973. *Metahistory: The Historical Imagination in Nineteenth-Century Europe*. Baltimore: Johns Hopkins University Press.

NINETEEN

Transformation

Bruce B. Lawrence

This essay has three equivalent but uneven parts: a broad historical review of transformation, followed by a specific pedagogical use of the term, and finally a proscriptive hope for its future invocation in scholarship generally and religious studies in particular.

Historical Treatment

Of all the terms considered in this volume, perhaps only three others have such a specific modern connotation that some readers would be surprised even to find them included in a volume dealing with critical terms in religious studies. Those other three are modernity, nature, and rationality, each of which evokes a broad, diverse set of reflexes, actions, and outlooks that in many cases have nothing to do with religion—or at least appear not to be related to religion on first, second, or even third readings.

Transformation is so far removed from what many folk think about in connection with religion that it does not even merit an entry in some very recent one-volume reference books on religion(s) (see Crim 1981; Pye 1994; Hinnells 1995). In the one reference work where it does appear (Smith 1995), it rates such an insignificant entry that it may be quoted here purely for comic relief. The entry "transformation" is cross-referenced to "shape shifting," where we are told, "shape shifting [is] the capacity to change bodily form at will. It is a common characteristic of gods, spirits and religious functionaries (e.g., shamans). In folklore, magical objects can shape shift" (Smith 1995, 982).

Two other specifically Christian usages of transformation are coded in technical language that suggests their special theological significance: one is transfiguration, the changing of Jesus's form on the mountain, and the second is transubstantiation, the changing of his body into the bread consecrated for Holy Communion. Much has been written about both topics; what interests us is the common thread that links them to "shape shifting" as described above. Both are evidences of good magic, but they are still magic from a phenomenological viewpoint.

Indeed, all the above instances of transformation presuppose that the form being changed or the shape being shifted is bodily or at least physical. Shamans take on different forms, as do demons in Hindu mythology or Mara in Buddhist lore or the devil in Christianity. Indeed, one of the skills in means *(upaya)* in Buddhism is to take on different forms.

But the most dramatic instance of bodily transformation in a religious context may belong to Taoism. While there is a Vedic creation myth linked to Purusa as a cosmic being who instantiates Indian society, including its well-known class hierarchies, the Taoist creation myth has Lao Tzu not only becoming the universe in a once-and-for-all transformation but also becoming something new in a continuous transformation. Both processes are described by a European Taoist priest:

> Lao Tzu transformed his body. His left eye became the sun; his right eye, the moon; his head became mount K'un-lun; his beard, the planets and constellations; his bones, dragons; his flesh, four-footed creatures; his intestines, snakes; his stomach, the sea; his fingers, the Five Peaks; his hair, trees and grasses; his heart, the Flowery Dais; as to his two kidneys, they were united and became one, the Real and True Father and Mother. (Schipper 1993, 114)

But elsewhere in one of the oldest extant Taoist texts, appropriately titled *Book of the Transformation of Lao Tzu,* the Old Master is alleged to have said, "I transform my body, passing through death to live again. . . . I die and am reborn, and each time I have a [new] body" (116). And this same passage not only signifies a cosmological dimension but also a ritual process, since the one energy *(ch'i),* while one, becomes manifest as three, whether three colors, three spheres, three stages, or three hypostases of the Taoist pantheon: anterior to this world, they "appear in groups and function as rhythmic, structuring elements of ritual time" (119).

Yet Lao-Tzu is also said to have gone through nine inner transformations (Schipper 1993, 171), and in this sense he represents another equally valid and widely known usage of transformation in a religious context, namely, to describe the real or apparent change from one state to another. By this approach, bodily shifts, however multiple or spectacular, are but incidental to the internal transformation experienced. It is internal transformation at the deepest level that becomes the most sought after religious experience.

It is also a transformation often linked to magic. The link is made explicit by no less renowned a modern explorer of the human psyche than Carl Jung. While transformation through a magical potent or elixir is common to many classical texts, including those from Taoism (see Schipper 1993, 170f.), Taoists are careful to distinguish between internal and external alchemy in the ceaseless quest for immortality. In a part of Carl Jung's writings, however, alchemy is radically inner directed. It comes to symbolize the quest that for Jung is tantamount to the quest for immortality, namely, the quest for the collective unconscious. Only by foregrounding and eliding their own identity with a collective unconscious can human beings—or at least some human beings—achieve profound inner transformation (Schwartz-Salant 1995, 139–55).

Jung selects an illustration from Islam to specify how he believes the individuation process "takes place entirely outside the sphere of consciousness." He draws on one of the richest allegorical substrata from the Qur'anic narrative, the story of Moses and Khidr in sura 18, in which the senior prophet in the Abra-hamic cycle (after Abraham himself) is upbraided and then transformed by a mysterious stranger from the Unseen (Khidr). To be sure, Jung's reflections on Moses and Khidr are more modest than those of other polymaths, notably Norman O. Brown, who used this same sura to prove his own apocalyptic specu-lations, pairing James Joyce's *Finnegans Wake* and the Qur'an as equivalent provo-cations of simultaneous totality (1991, 88–9). For Jung the key to the Khidr story is "merely" its alchemical connection; it becomes a pathway to disclosing the true self, showing "how ego-consciousness reacts to the superior guidance of the self through the twists and turns of fate." As such, therefore, the Khidr story is more than scriptural; it is therapeutic. It becomes "a comforting tale to the initiate who is capable of Transformation" (Jung 1969, 141).

Still a different, but widely recognized, dimension of religious transformation is conversion, that is, the explicit shape shifting or form changing from one reli-gious tradition to another. It can also be conversion to a new identity within a single tradition, whether given or received. The late Cardinal Bernadin of Chi-cago talked of being converted to a new sense of apostolic truth *after* he had been promoted to the office of archbishop. Much earlier in this century, the late Norman Vincent Peale used similar language in describing how he overcame severe depression at his early failure in the ministry: he went overseas to England during the mid-1930s when his self-esteem had plummeted along with the size of his Sunday congregations. There he discovered an alter ego that allayed his fears and precipitated what his biographer calls "another spiritual Transforma-tion, a 'conversion'" (George 1993, 82). And there is also extensive evidence of conversion as perceived transformation within the new religious movements. Not only is converson required of new adepts but it has come to mean total departure from a traditional religious orientation in order to embrace its oppo-site, namely, a total commitment, usually to one godlike religious leader who demands of his or her followers a total transformation of their outlook and praxis, as well as a transference of their residence, employment, and also fre-quently bank accounts (Pye 1994, 53–4 for further references).

Less widely recognized but still operative within religious scholarship is the notion of reflexive transformation. A modern day Roman Catholic theologian, for instance, proposes that all notions of male deity have proven static and their persistence is threatening to marginalize religion, at least in America, from the lives of would-be believers, and relegating it to the private sphere. Instead of a privatized male deity he proposes a publicized female deity, pervading all rela-tionships of value and enthroning religious norms in the lives of a twenty-first-century believers. His thesis provides the title for his book, *When God Becomes Goddess: The Transformation of American Religion* (Grigg 1995). While the claims may be exaggerated, and the process overly schematized, the basic notion of a flux, transmutation, or transformation undergirds the thesis of this and other works on feminist theology. A better contextualized instance comes from the feminist theologian Mary McClintock Fulkerson. In her pioneering monograph, one chapter is entitled, "Decently and in Order: Discourses of Self- and World-Transformation" (Fulkerson 1994). The need for middle-class, white Presbyterian women in late-twentieth-century America, argues Fulkerson, is not to liberalize readings of scripture but rather to challenge the ideology of domesticity. To the extent that these women resist patriarchal capitalism even while being marked by their location on its leading edge, "Presbyterian women transgress the constraints that construct their subject positions" (Fulkerson 1994, 237). In transforming themselves, they try also to transform the world that has both shaped and constrained them.

* * *

Though varying in subject matter, perspective, and method, all the above instances of transformation circulate within a dichotomous band of time, space, and identity. They tend to presuppose that a single form or shape can change inalterably into a new, identifiably different being. Transformation may also, however, be considerably more nuanced and perplexing. It may mean, for instance, the adaptation of one group to another group, which shifts its formal identity but perhaps does not shift its indigenous or autochthonous self-expression. Such is the case with voodoo and Catholicism. On one reading Haitians and Haitian Americans are practicing Catholics, but on another reading what they practice is voodoo under the capacious canopy of Catholicism (see esp. Brown 1991; Hurston 1990; Mulrain 1984). Another example of transformation as a complexly coded ritual is Bun Bangfai or Rocket Festival celebrated throughout Laos and northern Thailand. It has been described as "a fertility cult that honors the spirit of a particular village" that also becomes the site of competition between neighboring villages. Since the Buddha is seen to be at the top of both the spiritual and political cosmologies of these villages, it is Buddhist monks from their respective villages who serve as both ritual specialists and conflict resolution mediators during the Rocket Festival (Condominas 1975, cited in Strong 1995, 222–6).

Still another example of transformation as elision or bricolage rather than dramatic, wholesale change concerns Bengali Islam. In this case, a universalizing religious community (Islam) expands to northeast India through the appropriation of new cultural markings (Bengali). This case, however, illustrates just how difficult it is to separate indigenous from "foreign" elements. Asim Roy (1983) has argued that the two are inseparable and are fused into a Bengali Muslim identity that is dominated by Bengali (Hindu) cosmological beings, but Eaton (1993) more recently has asserted the opposite, namely, that the transposition of Muslim prophetic figures onto Bengali creation myths amounts to the mutual transformation of Bengali Muslims and Islamic Bengal:

> The success of Islam in Bengal lay ultimately in the extent to which superhuman beings that had originated in Arab culture and subsequently appropriated (and been appropriated by) Hebrew, Greek,

and Iranian civilizations, succeeded during the sixteenth through the eighteenth centuries in appropriating (and being appropriated by) Bengali civilization. Initially, this involved the association of Islamic with Bengali superhuman beings. But when figures like Adam, Eve, and Abraham became identified with central leitmotifs of Bengali history and civilization, Islam had become established as profoundly and authentically Bengali. (303)

* * *

All the above historical usages of transformation expand the range of the term and ensure its viability in religious discourse. The majority presuppose that transformation is (1) largely individual, (2) markedly voluntary, and (3) avowedly positive. But there is another, more drastic case of transformation, at once collective, compulsive, and negative (except for the elect few). It concerns predictions and preparations for the end of the world. The notion that there will be a final cataclysmic finale to human existence as we know it is the most radical expression of transformation; it is linked to the trope of apocalypse and rapture especially by groups drawn to the significance of millennial calculations of doom (see O'Leary 1994, 212 on the rhetoric of apocalyptic ideology). While most often identified with evangelical Christian groups, it can also be found in numerous other traditions. As the year 2000 inevitably approaches, some are daring to hope that millennial fever will subside, but the greater likelihood is that hope deferred will give rise to new future datings, as has already become the case in the vast literature announcing global proselytization (see Barrett and Reapsome 1988).

There are other, more docile invocations of transformation that permeate popular literature while feeding on, and also stoking, millennial fever. The prospect of a dramatic time shift, and with it the vision of a daunting future for a deeply fractured and dangerously unstable humankind, has caused some to seek radical change before the end, a transformation bordering on epiphany. Consider the following three secenarios:

1. *Transformation as a plea for ecumenical unity.* One might find this from several sources, but the one at hand comes from an American cleric, the Episcopal bishop of California. Bishop Swing invites others to share his vision and change the world for the better in the next millennium. Committed to the notion of a major shift that comes with the calendrical move from the second to the third millennia C.E., he issues an appeal for united religions. The appeal ends with these words:

> A commitment to participate is rooted in each of our own unique traditions; it honors each other's traditions, and it calls us to risk moving beyond ourselves to a common ground where the world might be transformed. I have committed myself to this spirit and this process, and invite your commitment in return. (Swing 1996)

2. *Transformation as a directive to raise local into international, parochial into universal modes of spiritual orientation.* The key word, as for Jung, is consciousness or self-consciousness. What is espoused is a rigorous, self-conscious repositioning vis-à-vis both time and space, one that changes the very nature of religious loyalty and spiritual commitment. It has been expressed by the Catholic theologian Ewert Cousins with reference to both Karl Jaspers and Teilhard de Chardin:

> If we shift our gaze from the first millennium B.C.E. to the eve of the twenty-first century, we can discern another Transformation of consciousness. It is so profound and far-reaching that I call it the Second Axial Period. Like the first it is happening simultaneously around the earth, and like the first it will shape the horizon of consciousness for future.... [At heart it requires] that religions must make every effort to ground themselves in their own traditions and at the same time to open themselves to other traditions. In concert with the other religions they should commit themselves to creating the new complexified global consciousness we have been exploring. (Teasdale and Cairns 1996, 162, 166)

3. *Transformation as a concrete reality in terms of individual praxis.* Wayne Teasdale suggests, when he appeals to other like-minded religious persons to face the millennial challenge, that they respond by pursuing

> spiritual practice, which of course includes and demands self-knowledge. It manifests a realized or transformed being, or nature in the latter three aspects of spirituality—that is, simplicity of life, selfless service, and prophetic action. These are some of the fruits of Transformation in the domain of action, and no genuine spirituality today would be without them. They represent inner resources needed for changing the direction of the human family so that it can accept its universal responsibility. (Teasdale and Cairns 1996, 215)

This view has perhaps been best summarized by a quotation credited to the Dalai Lama, which appears frequently, though without reference, on the Internet: "Now, and in the near future, there are but two options available to humankind: fundamentalism or inter-religious dialogue," with dialogue presuming a radical inner transformation of the individual akin to that urged by Teasdale and Cousins and others.

* * *

What is glossed in the above appeals and is intrinsic to each is the need for a reconvergence of religion and politics, such that the next millennium might witness a world transformed through the simultaneous religious reorientation of public agencies, especially the state, and political engagement of private communities, including religious organizations.

The difficulty here is the long legacy of modern research and common usage: both see state and church as separate nodes. Many also see the state as modern and the church as traditional, so that the yardstick for measuring good or bad religion is the flexibility or compliance of the religious body (here designated "church" for shorthand) with the modernizing goals of the bureaucratic state.

The word "transformation" can no longer be isolated to refer to religious or quasi-religious practices, dispositions, or outcomes; it also has to take account of the ambiguity in which religion as a category is lodged. In addition, it must be ratcheted with claims about a process of change that is neither exclusively individual nor reflexively voluntary; and as a process itself, it might be labeled negative rather than positive in its outcome.

To begin to consider transformation on this broad scale gradient, one must reexamine its relationship to the word most often paired with religion: tradition. Religion as tradition is thought to embody stasis or rigid embrace of custom and ascriptive norms. The spoken or unspoken "other" to religion qua tradition is modernity. In this usage transformation, rather than being individual, voluntary, and positive, can also be collective, imposed or determinate, and often negative, though in a very different sense from that intended by the Christian millennialists cited above.

But does transformation have to be the opposite of tradition? In the minds of some social scientists, tradition and modernity are not necessarily antithetical, and transformation can even occur within the boundaries of what is presumed to be tradition. Insofar as science, meaning Western science, is the linchpin of modernity, Robin Horton (1967) has explored the relationship of traditional African medicine to modern science in ways that are still worth noting. Also, Hobsbawm and Ranger (1983) show the extent to which tradition itself, far from being stable and static, is constantly invented or reinvented. Much of this literature has been ably summarized and reviewed in Waldman (1986). The second part of her often brilliant, always lively article suggests that what seem to be traditional projections of age-old values are often the means for legitimating extensive, even radical change. Her example is the hotly debated notion of Muslim women's dress codes.

The outcome of Waldman's argument is to suggest that transformation of Muslim societies may be as thorough as other non-Muslim societies, but the evidence has to be sought through other indices than the most obvious, dress codes. Her arguments developed *in nuci* can now be expanded with reference to several books (among them MacLeod 1991, especially chap. 5 and following, and Moghadam 1994).

Related to Waldman's argument, and also those of MacLeod and Moghadam, though more by inference than by direct citation, is the contention that religion is the key variable to effecting transformation of numerous societies in the aftermath of the Cold War and the collapse of the U.S.-Soviet rivalry. The case for religion as a positive transforming agent comes in Piscatori and Rudolph (1997), and is summarized in Rudolph (1996). Several contributors make the seemingly counterintuitive argument that although "religion can be an opiate that reconciles humans to injustice, it can also provide the vision and energy that makes for collective action and social Transformation" (Rudolph 1996, 27).

It is too early, however, to be euphoric that a new wave of social scientists will begin to see religion as a positive and enabling rather than a negative and retarding agent for cultural and social change. Even Rudolph has heavily qualified the seemingly positive role of religion, warning that "religious formations and movements may share analytic membership in a 'religion' sector but will have good reasons to differ. Transnational pluralism is likely to result in both benign and non-benign outcomes" (Rudolph 1996, 29).

Insofar as "transnational pluralism" will be transformative because of religious factors, however, it may reinscribe premodern, ascriptive identities that do not admit of modern norms or values. This reasoning would project the likely, albeit harsh, judgment stemming from the weight of German scholarship in this century. For, from Max Weber to Jürgen Habermas, an influential segment of German scholarship continues to argue that transformation is above all an Enlightenment-specific potential, that is, the coefficient of a structural process that elides with modernity, at once confirming its power and accelerating its impact. The liberal bourgeois public sphere rivals, even as it dislodges, the reduced and redirected private sphere. Genuine transformation by this logic projects a secular, state-oriented agency of the enlightened few opposed to the religious, civic agency of the preenlightened masses.

No social scientist has more directly criticized Habermasian notions of religion than the sociologist José Casanova. Habermas's theory of modernity, asserts Casanova, is rigidly secularist because "in Habermas's model, conventional religion ought to be superseded by postconventional secular morality" (Casanova 1994, 231). Yet Casanova himself at the decisive point in his argument limits the possible benefit of religion to its positive role in furthering processes of practical rationalization. Only a religion, he concludes, that

> reformulates its relationship to modernity by incorporating reflexively the three dimensions of the Enlightenment critique of religion—cognitive, ideological and moral—while also upholding publicly the sacred values of modernity, that is, human life and freedom, may contribute to the revitalization of the modern public sphere. For the very reassertion of religious traditions may be viewed as a sign of the failure of the Enlightenment to redeem its own promises in each of these spheres (cognitive, ideological and moral). Religious traditions are now confronting the differentiated secular spheres, challenging them to face their own obscurantist, ideological and unauthentic claims. In many of these confrontations, it is religion which, as often as not, appears to be on the side of human enlightenment. (233–4)

What Casanova proposes is to retrieve enlightenment in terms of religion and not the reverse; so he mitigates the autonomous function of religion that seemed possible in Weber. It is from Anglo-American sources that one finds a greater resilience accorded religion in the march up to the next temporal watershed, whether it be the new millennium, the Asian century, the postmodern world system, or simply the age of the Internet (which has already arrived). The British social historian Terence Ranger, for instance, shows less animus than Habermas against conventional or traditional religion. Both Hobsbawm and Ranger (1983) and Ranger (1985) demonstrate how fluid and autonomous religious movements can be, whether their leaders and followers attempt to uphold and affirm a traditional pattern of society, or attempt to retain traditional values in a transformed setting where socioeconomic groups advocate religious values that cannot be deemed "rational" from a Weberian perspective.

Yet the most thorough, all-out attack on Weberian notions of calculating rationalism comes from an American scholar. Marshall Hodgson remains the premier American Islamicist of the twentieth century. We examine Hodgson's views in depth both to challenge Weberian assumptions and to establish a prognosis for transformation on a different calculus. One might assume that Hodgson speaks only on behalf of Islamic evidence, and favors Islamic over other civilizations, but in fact, Hodgson was a world historian and the arguments he makes for transformation apply to a broad spectrum of humankind, redefining religion as the catalyst for hopeful change and genuine transformation.

The Hodgson Case versus Medjugorje

For Hodgson the major question always posed, either directly or indirectly, is "Does religion assist or impede the modernization process?" The assumption is that in the final analysis, only modernization works, and that religions must be judged good or bad by how congruent or dissonant they are with the forces, structures, and goals of modernization.

Hodgson, however, stands this question on its head, suggesting that modernization—the most radical expression of ineluctable transformation in the past three to four centuries—is neither monolithic nor inevitable. It is not monolithic because it did not affect all parts of Euroamerica with equal success. It is not inevitable because it was a concatenation of circumstances rather than a single cluster of ideal traits or the convergence of such traits with technical discoveries that produced the Great Western Transmutation. What the Great Western Transmutation overlooked is what had forged all the great civilizations of premodern history: individual initiative and cultural creativity. These two remain the twin ideals for Hodgson that caused him to describe the most recent axial shift as the Great Western Transmutation.

Why does Hodgson use transmutation and not transformation or transition? A brief comparison illumines both Hodgsonian and subsequent uses of transformation. Of the key words used to qualify transformation, even while they are often confused with it, transition is the lower-set term and transmutation the higher-set term. Transition implies a much less radical form of change, one that is almost unintentional, imperceptible, or insignificant, while transmutation suggests ineluctable but also irreversible change. It is a much more freighted term than transformation, which might be seen as the middle term, at once more expressly intentional and of greater consequence than transition but not as wholesale or consequential as transmutation.

It is for this reason that Hodgson, with deliberate foresight, describes the process inaugurating the modern world not as the Great Western Trans*forma-tion* but as the Great Western Trans*mutation*. On the one hand, he was invoking Jaspers's notion of axial shift covering not only centuries but millennia of historical variation and also affirming Weber's insight into the distinctive character of modern European technicalism. On the other hand, Hodgson was intent not to slight either the social achievements or the cultural norms of non-Western societies by highlighting what they had deemed to be both creative and productive. Therefore, in his major essay on the ambiguous character of modernity, first published over thirty years ago (1967), Hodgson drew attention not to Euroamerican global dominance but to the downside of this dominance for the dominated or marginalized:

> It was part of the transmutational character of the new Transformation that it broke down the very historical presuppositions in terms of which gradual diffusions had maintained parity among Afro-Eurasian cited societies. In the new pace of historical change, when decades sufficed to produce what centuries had produced before, a lag of four of five centuries was no longer safe. The old gradual diffusion or adjustment was no longer possible. . . . Those untransmutated agrarianate-level societies that did not share Western cultural presuppositions had perforce to continue developing in their own traditions at their own pace, adopting from alien traditions only what could be assimilated on that basis. Hence the Western Transmutation, once it got well under way, could neither be paralleled independently nor be borrowed wholesale. Yet it could not, in most cases, be escaped. The millennial parity of social power broke down, with results that were disastrous almost everywhere. (1993, 70–1)

Hodgson's perception of global disjunctures is hardly unique. Ernst Bloch spoke of "the simultaneity of the non-simultaneous," or "the synchronicity of the non-synchronous," and Fredric Jameson (1991, 307) uses Bloch to set forth his own prognosis of the tensions and ambiguities of late global capitalism. Hodgson's bleak vision of a dominant West gone awry is also shared by numerous others. The lament has frequently been made of a Western colossus that has either lost its religious roots or trammels others in the name of a Christianity that is itself the accomplice of global hegemony—socioeconomic, political, and military.

What Hodgson traces as a global pattern is what has also emerged in a number of disparate sources as a reflection of three centuries of European colonial expansion coincident with the rise of the West. The major outcome has been to challenge the twin assumptions that the West (1) rose by itself and (2) achieved global dominance on its intrinsic merits. Dominance and hegemony are closely allied to imperialism and colonialism. Religion is deeply implicated in the debate about the origin and scope of Euroamerican global influence. Insofar as resistance to that influence can be theorized and traced in multiple cultural contexts, it is represented in voices ranging from the Martinican psychiatrist Frantz Fanon to the American political theorist James Scott. While Fanon advocated the use of violence against colonial impositions in Algeria and elsewhere, James Scott demonstrated the sophistication of resistant strategies (which he identifies as hidden transcripts) against postcolonial state structures in Southeast Asia as well as in the American South.

In this reading, transformation is at best ambiguous and at worst nefarious. It is the rhetorical capstone of victors "inasmuch as the major historical forms of domination have presented themselves in the form of a metaphysics, a religion, a worldview." However, to oppose domination others have resorted to religion as a symbolic capital, such that the discourse of the victors has "provoked the development of more or less equally elaborate replies in the hidden transcript (of those oppressed or marginalized)" (Scott 1990, 115).

But what has also emerged more recently from within the social sciences is a means of showing how resistance to Western global influence, including Christian missionary activity, persists often in forms that must be detected at the microlevel of social analysis. Again, the effort is to complicate, if not eradicate, misleading antinomies, such as animism/magic versus rationality/religion. Jane Schneider in "Spirits and the Spirit of Capitalism" both invokes Weber and subverts him. She invokes him by suggesting how the notion of convergence between economic practices (capitalism) and religious dispositions (Protestant reformers) is still valid, but she supersedes him by showing the extent to which competing centers of economic and political power often create a reverse flow of energy from the so-called periphery of societies to the putative core, pointing out contradictions within the core's self-representation and projection of its power. What results is a much broader, more nuanced understanding of global transformation in late capitalism, with "genuine cultural change relevant to the rise of capitalism only in relation to circumscribed times and places, and only with the caveat that the change would forever be resisted and undermined" (Schneider 1991, 183).

While Schneider claims a partially hopeful role for religion among African animists and their Christian missionary inquisitors, Mart Bax, the Dutch anthropologist, takes a much more sinister view of the work of the Catholic Church in the former Yugoslavia. Unlike others who have tried to explain complex ethnoreligious relations in Bosnia through juxtaposed narratives told from "opposite" viewpoints, Mart Bax uses few narrative details. His project instead is to demonstrate how Marian cults, such as the one at Medjugorje, are subject to both sacralization and barbarization. Ostensibly Medjugorje is a huge religious success story. Its primary consumers are the sixteen million pilgrims who have journeyed there since 1981 seeking a direct, unmediated contact with the holy that will empower, through healing or hope, lives riddled with disease, despair, and often the prospect of imminent death. Yet there is another side to the Medjugorje success story: since the outbreak of war in April 1992, many of the shrine's supporters have been openly motivated by ethnonationalist ideology. Whereas they formerly used the Virgin's support to fight communists, they now use it to fight enemies other than communists, whether the Orthodox in nearby Serbia or Muslims concentrated in Bosnia. Socially implicated in the Medjugorje shrine are all the groups that contest the shrine's power, some within and others beyond the Roman Catholic fold. Franciscans versus Papists, Orthodox versus Catholic, ethnonationalists versus pluralists—all have a stake in Medjugorje, but it is a different stake, and the dominance of one group over its rival alters the outcome for all. As Bax wryly notes, barbarization as much as sanctification will likely continue to mark the youthful Medjugorje complex in its next phase, with consequences for other sites dotting the frontiers of official versus popular Catholicism (Bax 1995, 101–2).

And so the most important as well as the most sinister transformation at Medjugorje may not be the shrine itself and its immediate boosters, but the long-term implications of this and other shrines for perpetuating ethnonationalist rivalries. All religion epitomizes exclusion as well as inclusion, opposition as well as affirmation, and what is important to note for both anthropologists and historians is how deeply implicated religion is at the local level in perpetuating conflict. In rural Bosnia Medjugorje symbolizes the perceived wrongs that motivate not only spiritual solace but also an urge to avenge. How then can one talk of religiously derived transformation when the most visible change in western and southern Hercegovina is the continuing domination of Croat communities by Serbian power centers? (See Wolf 1991, 7–53 and Bax 1995, 125–6)

The Medjugorje example helps to put in perspective the achievements of Hodgson. What persists as part of his legacy, and also the legacy of others who work within the structures of late capitalist society and its academic appendages, is an awareness of the fragility of transformation as a durable, once-and-for-all achievement representing the dominance of one culture or religious ideology over competing others. Instead, competition itself is the only winner, with transformation remaining partial, circumscribed, and fragile.

Proscriptive Conclusion

Religion will continue to be a major part of the future hope for both the dominators and the resisters. One might deduce from Hodgson's prescient reflections on world history a subdued vision of spiritual recuperation, a kind of rear guard transformation of humankind that will emerge only piecemeal and will often provoke its own violent suppression. While the threats both internal and external of the Great Western Transmutation will command the most public attention and preempt genuine alternatives to its own hegemony, human culture is not monolithic nor is the ascendancy of one group or region or outlook irreversible. Neither the Great Western Transmutation nor its successors can finally prevail against the human spirit, or a chain of human spirits, alert to the twin pitfalls of blind scientism and multinational corporativist capitalism.

It is by subverting transformation in its overtly evolutionary, determinist sense that one can reclaim its validity for religion and religious studies. Above all, one must resist the move to make transformation a fail-safe term. Too often, as we have seen in many of the examples above, the word "transformation," like other such seemingly affirmative yet vague words, for example, "experience" and "spirituality," is made to bear an impossible burden. Its mere invocation is supposed to provide closure to competing options. To claim transformation, for oneself or for others, is to preempt speculation and forestall criticism. Much better is the approach of the Taoist adepts and the Christian spiritualists with whom this essay began. Like Marshall Hodgson, they believe in the power of internal transformation, not once and for all, not a do-or-die conversion but rather a rigorous, persistent opening from within to the creative potential of a divine source that resists exclusive identification with any name or nation: common to all religions, it can never become the sole possession of one except as its antithesis. It will always remain both collective and individual, surrendering neither to the tyranny of apparatchiks nor to the romanticism of sky gazers nor to the doomism of apocalypticists. That perhaps is the final hope for transformation as a cultural/religious/spiritual category in the next millennium, whether it be the third on a Christian calendar or the fifth on a Chinese calendar.

SUGGESTED READINGS

Bax, Mart. 1995. *Medjugorje: Religion, Politics, and Violence in Rural Bosnia.*

Casanova, José. 1994. *Public Religions in the Modern World.*

Fanon, Frantz. 1971. *The Wretched of the Earth,* translated by Constance Farrington.

Hodgson, Marshall G. S. 1993. *Rethinking World History: Essays on Europe, Islam, and World History.*

Piscatori, James, and Susanne Rudolph, eds. 1997. *Recent Trends in Transnational Religion.*

Scott, James C. 1990. *Domination and the Arts of Resistance: Hidden Transcripts.*

Waldman, Marilyn. 1986. "Tradition as a Modality of Change." *History of Religions.*

Wolf, Eric R., ed. 1991. *Religious Regimes and State Formation: Perspectives from European Ethnology.*

REFERENCES

Barrett, David B., and James W. Reapsome. 1988. *Seven Hundred Plans to Evangelize the World: The Rise of a Global Evangelization Movement.* Birmingham, Ala.: Foreign Mission Board of the Southern Baptist Convention.

Bax, Mart. 1995. *Medjugorje: Religion, Politics, and Violence in Rural Bosnia.* Amsterdam: VU University Press. [Special thanks to Menno Kruk for the reference and also the book]

Brown, Karen McCarthy. 1991. *Mama Lola: A Vodou Priestess in Brooklyn.* Berkeley and Los Angeles: University of California Press.

Brown, Norman O. 1991. *Apocalypse and/or Metamorphosis.* Berkeley and Los Angeles: University of California Press.

Casanova, José. 1994. *Public Religions in the Modern World.* Chicago: University of Chicago Press.

Condominas, Georges. 1975. "Phiban Cults in Rural Laos." In *Change and Persistence in Thai Society,* edited by G. W. Skinner and A. T. Kirsch. Ithaca, N.Y.: Cornell University Press.

Crim, Keith, ed. 1981. *Abingdon Dictionary of Living Religions.* Nashville: Abingdon.

Eaton, Richard M. 1993. *The Rise of Islam and the Bengal Frontier, 1204–1760.* Berkeley and Los Angeles: University of California Press.

Fulkerson, Mary McClintock. 1994. *Changing the Subject: Women's Discourses and Feminist Theology.* Minneapolis: Fortress Press.

George, Carol V. R. 1993. *God's Salesman: Norman Vincent Peale and the Power of Positive Thinking.* New York: Oxford University Press.

Grigg, Richard. 1995. *When God Becomes Goddess: The Transformation of American Religion.* New York: Continuum.

Habermas, Jürgen. 1992. *The Structural Transformation of the Public Sphere: An Inquiry into a Category of Bourgeois Society,* translated by Thomas Burger. Cambridge: MIT Press.

Hinnells, John R., ed. 1995. *A New Dictionary of Religions.* Oxford: Blackwell.

Hobsbawm, Eric, and Terence Ranger, eds. 1983. *The Invention of Tradition.* Cambridge: Cambridge University Press.

Hodgson, Marshall G. S. 1993. *Rethinking World History: Essays on Europe, Islam, and World History.* Cambridge: Cambridge University Press.

Horton, Robin. 1967. "African Traditional Thought and Western Science." *Africa* 38.

Hurston, Zora Neale. 1990. *Tell My Horse.* New York: Harper and Row.

Jameson, Fredric. 1991. *Postmodernism; or, The Cultural Logic of Late Capitalism.* Durham: Duke University Press.

Jung, Carl G. 1969. "A Typical Set of Symbols Illustrating the Process of Transformation." In *Collected Works,* vol. 9, pt. 1. Princeton: Princeton University Press. [Special thanks to H. T. Halman for the reference]

MacLeod, Arlene. 1991. *Accommodating Protest: Working Women, the New Veiling, and Change in Cairo.* New York: Columbia University Press.

Moghadam, Valentine M., ed. 1994. *Identity Politics and Women: Cultural Reassertions and Feminisms in International Perspective.* Boulder, Colo.: Westview Press.

Mulrain, George MacDonald. 1984. *Theology in Folk Culture.* New York: Peter Lang.

O'Leary, Stephen D. 1994. *Arguing the Apocalypse: A Theory of Millennial Rhetoric.* New York: Oxford University Press.

Piscatori, James, and Susanne Rudolph, eds. 1997. *Recent Trends in Transnational Religion.* Boulder, Colo.: Westview Press.

Pye, Michael, ed. 1994. *The Continuum Dictionary of Religion*. New York: Continuum.

Ranger, Terence. 1985. "Religious Movements and Politics in Subsaharan Africa." Unpublished paper.

Roy, Asim. 1983. *The Islamic Syncretistic Tradition in Bengal*. Princeton: Princeton University Press.

Rudolph, Susanne. 1996. "Transnational Religion and Fading States." In *ITEMS* [Social Science Research Council] 50, 2–3.

Schipper, Kristofer. 1993. *The Taoist Body*, translated by Karen C. Duval. Berkeley and Los Angeles: University of California Press.

Schneider, Jane. 1991. "Spirits and the Spirit of Capitalism." In *Religious Regimes and State Formation: Perspectives from European Ethnology*. Albany: State University of New York Press.

Schwartz-Salant, Nathan. 1995. *Jung on Alchemy*. Princeton: Princeton University Press.

Scott, James C. 1990. *Domination and the Arts of Resistance: Hidden Transcripts*. New Haven, Conn.: Yale University Press.

Smith, Jonathan Z., ed. 1995. *The HarperCollins Dictionary of Religion*. San Francisco: HarperCollins.

Strong, John S. 1995. *The Experience of Buddhism: Sources and Interpretations*. Belmont, Calif.: Wadsworth.

Swing, William E. 1996. *United Religions*. San Francisco: United Religions Board.

Teasdale, Wayne, and George Cairns, eds. 1996. *The Community of Religions*. New York: Continuum.

Waldman, Marilyn. 1986. "Tradition as a Modality of Change." *History of Religions*.

Wolf, Eric R., ed. 1991. *Religious Regimes and State Formation: Perspectives from European Ethnology*. Albany: State University of New York Press.

TWENTY

Transgression

Michael Taussig

At first sight it seems strange if not absurd and confusing to claim that transgression is a key component of religion: *strange* because mainstream religions in our time seem more concerned with controlling and eliminating transgression; and *confusing* because transgression turns out to be the quintessence of intellectual and emotional uncertainty, and this must be of great significance for what is referred to as sacred. Doubtless these issues would be best explored and enunciated through historical study of a particular religion in a particular location in order to eschew the universalizing pseudotruths that plague the study of religions. But because historical and concrete exploration itself presupposes a dialectical dependence on principles of analysis, it is my aim, in the limited space here, to provide an elaboration of transgression in terms of negation and its connection with taboo.

Much has been made of the implications in Latin-derived languages, and hence in Christianity, of the negation built into the word "sacred" in its meaning of accursed as well as holy, impure as well as pure, and thus its suggestion, at least poetically, of a deep wound and the necessity thereof in holiness per se. This sense of negation as within and constitutive of the sacred has been most widely explored in modern Western discussions of the concept of *taboo* at the turn of the century, for example, Freud's elegant summary of its connotations *combining* sacredness, purity, danger, the unclean, the uncanny, and the forbidden (1958, pub. 1913, 20). The salient property of danger present in this fascinating complex of negation, with its mutually nourishing oppositions, is its considerable if undefinable power to attract and repulse (compared by numerous authors with electricity!).

Another striking instance of the dominant role of negation is Emile Durkheim's obsessive discussion of the sacred as that which (1) is not profane and exists separated and set apart and (2) is hedged in by prohibitions, as if the sacred is first and foremost the worshipful negative. Whether one agrees or not, one can only be struck full of wonder at the perverse and unexpected nature of this carefully worked out framework for analysis, and stand perplexed at the dizzying logic unleashed as the negative negatively defines something ineffable (we recall the "electricity").

The power of the negative, however, cannot be construed as a simple barrier, because in being separated, something is connected as much as it is dislocated from that which it is set apart from, and it is on the curious tension of negations embodied in this relationship that we need to focus attention. Nor can such tension be assimilated to the telos of order characteristic of both the semiotic paradigm of French structuralism (as in the work of Claude Lévi-Strauss) and the scaled down version of this semiotics emerging from the British structural functionalism apparent in Mary Douglas's elaboration of the idea that impurity is disorder, and that "ideas about separating, purifying, demarcating and punishing transgressions have as their main function to impose system on an inherently untidy experience"(1966, 4). What emerges from this is what a tough time transgression is going to have of it intellectually, in that its very being transgresses deeply embedded norms of intellection, of making sense through making order.

But would we have gotten into the issue of transgression if we hadn't expected a rough ride? As a first approximation we have to consider that the barrier crossed by transgression does not so much exist in its own right as erupt into being on account of its being transgressed. Second, we have to try to understand that this barrier is one of repulsion and attraction, open and closed at the same time. On this basis, then, in which we can see the encounter of Nietzsche with Hegel, negation should be understood as an endlessly discharging circuit of taboo and transgression, as if fearsome barriers were erected precisely in order to be crossed. Moreover it is in the charged space thus opened up by transgression that we encounter empowering and sacred ritual, caused by and causative of this "space."

Take for example the initiation rites for young men and boys described for the turn-of-the-century Thonga (present day Mozambique) by the Swiss missionary Henri Junod in his *Life of a South African Tribe*. Junod relates how the boys are placed in a self-contained, separated, and heavily tabooed fenced-in compound for three months, during which time serious transgressions of other taboos, including sexual transgressions, have to occur to bring about the mystical transformation of the boys into men. Important too are the secret formulae transmitted by the older men to the initiates, which include what are considered obscene images and ideas. Girls are subject to similar rites on a reduced scale, and we see the same curious logic of transgression involved in funerals, war, and the moving of a village.

In post–World War II anthropology, Victor Turner (1966) built on Junod's work and the latter's use of Arnold Van Gennep's idea of rites of passage to accentuate the importance of a so-called liminal period outside normality, a period involving an enclosed, set-apart, theatrical-like space of make-believe for the representation and visceral realization of sacred force. It is striking how in Turner's hands this liminal period has been V-chipped or censored such that the force of negation, and hence of transgression, is virtually erased. Indeed, with the passage of time and the further development of the idea, his depictions became increasingly balmy and innocent, with erotic, obscene, sadistic, cruel, and licentious features bleached out—much like the trajectory described by Nietzsche and Bataille for the evolution of Christianity itself. Even more important is that Turner was by no means alone among anthropologists in consciously or unconsciously avoiding transgressive features and their importance in reli-

gion, even though the material that came to light around this time from serious ethnographic work in highland New Guinea (let alone what existed in the
earlier ethnographic record in general) could hardly be accommodated to such a
genteel view.

It is useful philosophically to speculate as to why there has been such aversion
to meeting the transgressive material head-on and analyzing its religious significance. The sort of detail brought to light by Junod, or the (admittedly cursory)
questions posed decades later in 1929 by Evans-Pritchard in his brief paper
"Some Collective Expressions of Obscenity in Africa," were rapidly forgotten
(but not by that oddball nonanthropologist and one-time member of the recently resurrected College of Sociology, Paris, 1937–39, Roger Caillois, in his
Man and the Sacred). Likewise pushed aside for serious consideration were the
presence and crucial importance of transgression in the Christian church of the
Middle Ages with regard to liturgy as well as to feasts such as carnival, no less
than in the Dionysiac elements in the religion of ancient Greece and Rome, and
the tantric and "left-handed" currents of Hinduism and Buddhism and Islam.

A telling symptom of the evasion was the virtual torrent of enthusiastic publications such as Max Gluckman's "Licence in Ritual," which concerns "rituals
of reversal" in which, for a brief time of licensed transgression, rulers become
servants, kings or queens are humiliated, men dress as women or vice versa, and
things serious are exposed to ridicule and monstrous reflection. In the writings
of modern scholars, it is impossible to escape the utilitarian theme that such
excitements were merely part of a social narrative whose function was to enforce
the status quo, yet such analyses in themselves, so to speak, were generally enlivened by a surreptitious countermove as these same scholars, searching for an
escape from such a tedious conclusion, identified with the temporary madness
and ecstasy of that which they were writing about. In other words, the claims
to stability and function were not completely containable. There was always
this excess creeping out from under the scholarly depictions with their inevitable
functionalist stamp of approval. Could the reversal and the transgression expressed beckon to another world altogether different and no less wonderful than
terrifying?

This dilemma was especially marked in reactions to the celebrated work of
Mikhail Bakhtin on Rabelais and carnival. Here the "licensed transgression" of
another era, early modern Europe, becomes nostalgically wrought by Bakhtin's
reading into carnival and the poetics of the laughing belly the heroically lost
cause of humor and dream in the struggle against Stalinism that was taking place
as he was writing his study in semiexile in the far reaches of the Soviet Union in
the 1930s. The pathos of the Cold War ensured that Bakhtin's "message," once
translated decades later into English, would be purified in scholarly reflection on
laughter, while the horror of the gulag would remain unexamined as no less a
mark of transgression than carnival. For all his references to the belly, the genitals, piss, and shit, Bakhtin's sense of the transgressive was interpreted as allied

with the angels and eminently respectable, while writers in the tradition of de Sade or Bataille, for instance, can never be assimilated in this or any other way, and their laughter remains mired in death, the corpse, and eroticism. Indeed, here we are forcefully made aware that transgression necessarily finds terrible application in the study of the sacred dimensions of violence in our time, as with the Holocaust and the ever increasing ethnic conflicts of the late twentieth century.

In most instances it would seem that the aversion to trying to think through the nature of transgression in religion was not directly due to the analytic predilections of any particular theoretical school but could be attributed to the influence of taste and morality in modern times simply closing down massive areas of human experience as consolidated by the combined action of Christianity and Enlightenment in harness with the utilitarian postulates of capitalist common sense. It is this blocking of feeling and the capability of expression that Georges Bataille identifies as his subject and the source of his anxiety in his preface to his *History of Eroticism*, where he describes how we "manage in any case to substitute empty thinking for those moments when it seem[s] to us, however, that the very heavens [are] opening." As against this he wanted to "lay out a way of thinking that would measure up to those moments." This representational pathos will forever remain the challenge that is transgression.

Surrealism and Profane Illumination

We can gain some insight into this representational pathos by invoking surrealism (with which Bataille was closely associated), as with André Breton's concepts (in *Mad Love*) of "convulsive beauty" and the "fixed-explosive." For not only do these concepts convey the dilemma in representing transgression, but in their art-practice surrealists resurrected the stimulating impact of the unsayable through cunningly crafted contradiction in visual image, poetry, and unusual forms of narrative. At its best this amounted to what the extraordinary modernist critic Walter Benjamin (1978b), in his essay on surrealism, termed "profane illumination," playing off against the mystical sense of *illumination* (rather than *Enlightenment*) so as to give it a sense at once secularized and materialist while maintaining something mystical as well.

Moreover, such an illumination was in Benjamin's eyes dependent upon a nondiscursive reality emphasizing image and viscerality, and amounting to a specific challenge to the meaning of meaning. For surrealism, life "only seemed worth living," he wrote, "where the threshold between waking and sleeping was worn away in everyone as by steps of multitudinous images flooding back and forth, language only seemed itself where sound and image, image and sound interpenetrated with automatic precision and such felicity that no chink was left for the penny-in-the-slot called meaning" (1978b, 178–9). It is only from an epistemological enthusiasm such as this that we can begin to follow Bataille's astonishing essays of the 1930s (*Visions of Excess*), as much exemplary of transgression as of the problem of its representation, let alone do justice to those aspects of religion and ritual energized precisely on account of the representational dilemmas thus made manifest.

Body and Image

Let us therefore take up body and image not as symbols or as symptoms but as vehicles for the transgressive in religion. Pride of place should be given first to the cadaver and then to menstrual blood, compared with which polluting and hence sacred power, other components and features of the body, female or male, are usually quite inferior in terms of sacred, transgressive potential. Yet so as to grasp something of the scope with which human cultures have endowed what we might call the religious or religiously worked upon body as the sacred art form, let us not overlook the removal of the clitoris; circumcision; cutting into the underside of the penis; masking; body painting; covering the face with tattoos; cranial "deformation"; flattening the forehead; letting of blood; knocking out teeth; filing the teeth; carving the teeth; scarifying the body, arms, and legs; human sacrifice; eating the body of the other; and hacking off a finger joint while praying to the sun (an automutilation figured by William Burroughs [1964] and of consummate interest for Bataille [1985b] as shown in his study of relating Vincent van Gogh's amputation of his ear and suicide to the sun and to the evacuation of mythic meaning from such acts by modern life).

During the years 1907 to 1916 when he visited the Crow Indians, the esteemed anthropologist Robert Lowie says he saw few old men with their left hands intact. In the early 1830s after visiting the Crow, George Catlin saw young Mandan braves of the upper Missouri River place their left hands on buffalo skulls and chop off the little finger. Some then also amputated the forefinger, leaving the two middle fingers and thumb as essential for handling a bow. Several of the chiefs and dignitaries had in years past also cut off the little finger of the right hand as an even greater sacrifice. But this was as nothing to what immediately went before when the young braves had the musculature of their upper torsos skewered with stakes to which ropes were attached, allowing them to swing free suspended from the rafters of the medicine lodge while their companions on the ground twirled their bodies around until they fainted with pain. This was accompanied by four old men "incessantly beating upon the sacks of water and singing the whole time, with their voices strained to the highest key" (Catlin 1973, 173). Then followed something between a race and a dance in which heavy buffalo skulls were attached to the stakes through the ligaments of the leg and arm muscles—not through the muscles themselves—which the young men had to drag while running until the flesh was torn out with the splint.

Then there is human blood, not just the fearsome blood of menstruation, which becomes its own sacred theater and the epicenter of pollution in general, but men's attempts at equivalence to such bleeding as in the scene well portrayed in Kenneth Read's *High Valley*, which recounts his experiences, in 1950, among the Gahuku people in the Asaro River valley in the eastern highlands of New Guinea. Read saw initiated men standing in the brightly lit shallows of the river ostentatiously displaying their genitals and masturbating in front of hordes of other brilliantly painted and feathered men, the sacred flutes crying. Then one by one, each man stepped forward with rolls of razor sharp leaves, "flourishing them like a conjurer in a spotlight," and plunged this vicious instrument up his nose so as to tear at the mucous membrane and force blood to flow. The watching men ululated while the wounded man himself was so distraught with pain that, strong as he was, his knees were trembling and it seemed as though his legs would buckle under him (1965, 131). It was this act, understood by Read as in part motivated by a need to exorcise the polluting effects of women, that the male initiates had then to succumb to for the first time in their lives, following which they were forced to swallow large canes doubled over into a long narrow U-shape. Read experienced it this way:

> Leaning forward from the waist, he placed the rounded section in his mouth, straightened, tilted his head, extended the line of his neck, and fed it into his stomach. My throat contracted and my stomach heaved, compelling me to look away. When I turned to him again most of the cane had disappeared, only two small sections, the open ends of the U, protruding from the corners of his mouth.
>
> I have no idea how long he held this grotesque stance, his straining abdomen and chest racked with involuntary shudders. Already sickened by the display, I stiffened with shock as he raised his hands, grasped the ends of the cane and sawed it rapidly up and down, drawing it almost free of his mouth at the peak of every upward stroke. The fervor of the crowd mounted to a clamorous pitch, breaking in wave upon wave of pulsing cries, the final surge matching my own relief when he dropped the cane, bent from the waist, and vomited into the river. (133–4)

Examples of such uses of the body could be multiplied, but the very notion here of an example seems to miss the point. The performances are so shocking as to transcend their being examples of anything other than what Read calls "the Gahuku's exhausting tendency to seek excess." It would be a cold fish indeed who would not stand in awe of these ever more ingenious games with the body demanded to serve a sacred and supernatural purpose in which ritual gives way to theatricality, and the leading performer and most stunning prop is the human and all too profane body with its various appendages, fluids, undulating surfaces, folds, exits, and entrances.

Secrecy

A crucial conceptual point provided by Read's depiction of initiation here is the role of secrecy, or rather public secrecy, as with the secret sacred Nama flutes played only by initiated men. What is important is to realize how *secrecy* is intertwined with *taboo* (and hence transgression) to create a powerful yet invisible presence (indeed, the presence of presence itself), and how essential this seems to what we generally might mean by religion. For example, the circumcision lodge as described by Junod is taboo to women and the uninitiated, and a woman who has seen the dressing used for the penile wound must be killed. In their 1899 description of the sacred *churinga* objects of the Aranda of Central Australia, Spencer and Gillen (1968) claimed that death or blinding by firestick awaited any woman or uninitiated man who saw such an object, and I would imagine that this sort of sanction and the fear and danger it articulates would have been found across much if not all of that continent.

These dramatic examples give us insight into the strategic role of secrecy within the sacred propounded by the great world religions as well. "Not only is there no religion without secrecy," writes Kees W. Bolle (1987), "but there is no human existence without it," and he is concerned to evoke a nonpositivist and self-reflexive view of the secret here at stake, as when he talks of limits, special mystery, caution, and self-restraint. He asks the pertinent question of the believer no less than of the scholar, "How do we become fully aware of [the secret] without distorting it?"

Here we could say that the power of negation built into the secrecy depends upon the fearsome expectation of its transgression as indicated by the threatened penalties. Transgression, we could say, exerts its tremendous and tremendously creative force through its threat rather than its actualization. And this is more than sufficient. Yet there is an additional feature to consider, and that is that the anxiety illustrated in the two examples above with regard to *visual* manifestation of the mystery is of note, as it is the act of *uncontrolled* seeing that is prohibited in these and countless other examples, because the secret (and hence the transgression that has to break through it) has in fact *to be not only concealed but revealed as well*—in keeping with the logic of the negative in which transgression and taboo artfully play off one another in what I have described above as an endlessly discharging circuit. This negation of the negation is spectacularly illustrated by the *unmasking* of men masked as spirits in many societies across the globe, and in the showing of the sacred flutes or bull roarer as in central Amazonia, New Guinea, central Africa, and Australia.

To illustrate the importance of revelation in a studied back-and-forth movement between concealment *and* revelation as art forms generating a fund of power from taboo and transgression, let us first note that it is the drama involved in the revelation of the mysteries that ensures a person's initiation. In addition, such revelation ensures not disenchantment but further enchantment thanks to a mystical illumination. In this sense revelation leads to further concealment. Showing the secret leads to another if not deeper secret.

But there is even more to this. Let us turn our attention to the wider context, to the women and children left in the village and kept away from the sacred precinct of the circumcision lodge described by Junod, or to those who have to hide in their huts when the *molimo* trumpet plays among the Mbuti in central Africa (Turnbull 1962), the sacred flutes play in central Amazonia and highland New Guinea (Bamberger 1974; Crocker 1983; Gillison 1980; Berndt 1962; Hays 1988; Gregor 1985), or the masked figure of the *Shoort* spirit enters the camp of the Selk'nam in Tierra del Fuego (described for the early 1920s in vivid detail by Martin Gusinde [1982]). Here too we find an exceedingly powerful but quite different expression of negation, because it is the task of the uninitiated persons (read generic woman) to form the *absent presence* and *active unknowing* as to what goes on in the lodge. Note how this absent presence and active un-knowing is in itself, in its very makeup, a subtle expression of revelation and concealment, for the women know they must not know but in fact do "know" a good deal. In other words, while the powerful drama of revelation within the secrecy of the lodge can only be achieved by concealing it and all that goes on in the lodge from uninitiated others, such concealment is itself part of a larger scheme of revelation in that the secrecy at issue is strategically incomplete, being an open or public secret to some extent shared by all—once again displaying the artful play of negation as concealment *and* revelation, taboo *and* transgression.

"Secrecy lies at the very core of power" wrote Canetti (1962, 290) and to that we must add that this power very much includes the power of make-believe essential to religious force and without which there can be no religion. Hence as Huizinga (1955) instructed in his work on play, the term "artful play" (as I deploy it for the work of negation) has to be seen as a precise characterization of transgression, as both utmost seriousness and gay abandon, thus making secrecy (that "lies at the very core of power") a potent stimulus to creativity, to what Simmel (1950) called "the magnification of reality," by means of the sensation that behind the appearance of things there is a deeper, mysterious, reality, that we may here call the sacred, if not religion.

This same play with secrecy of things sacred and the controlled transgression of their revelation is forceful in discussions of medicine men and women and of so-called *shamanism* (an essentializing term sanctioned more by conventional usage than the facts merit), it being repeatedly pointed out by anthropologists that, although it is widely suspected that such magic is fraudulent, it is neverthe-less believed to be efficacious or potentially so. "It is perfectly well-known by all concerned," wrote Franz Boas towards the end of his long career, "that a great part of the shamanistic procedure [among the Kwakiutl] is based on fraud; still it is believed in by the shaman as well as by patients and their friends. Exposures do not weaken the belief in the 'true' power of shamanism. Owing to this pecu-liar state of mind, the shaman himself is doubtful in regard to his powers and is always ready to bolster them up by fraud" (1966, pub. 1930, 121). What Boas refers to as a "peculiar state of mind" is this form wherein "fraud" and "belief" in "magic" are so many (inadequate) expressions not of skilled concealment but of skilled revelation of skilled concealment—this in atmospheres of expectation made dense by the seesawing contradictions built into the labyrinth that is the public secret of knowing what not to "know" about the practices in question. "Indeed, scepticism is included in the pattern of belief in witch-doctors. Faith and scepticism are alike traditional," wrote Evans-Pritchard in his 1937 book on Azande medicine men (p. 193).

Sound and Song as Invisible Presence That Has to Be Transgressed

Here is where *sound* as with bull roarers, sacred flutes, and singing, becomes important because, unlike the prohibition on the *visual manifestation* of the secret, the sound, whose whole purpose is to be public, evokes the secret's presence without otherwise manifesting it. Therefore, sound provides a perfect vehicle for absent presence. Sound is like a metasecret or the "skin" of the secret, announcing but concealing its content, and it is precisely this skin that represents the mysterious line of transgression which has to (yet must not) be breached.

With the sacred flutes of highland New Guinea or central Amazonia, the crucial mise-en-scène is men playing secret sacred flutes while the women and children must hide their eyes, secreted in their homes and gardens as an absent presence that augments the power of the invisible force of spirit manifested by the sound of the invisible flutes. Kenneth Read's description of human-made sounds during the three months' long Gahuku male initiation in New Guinea strikingly conveys this. For example, there was an overwhelming sense of noise in the initial stages of male initiation—the women's keening cries "stabbing into the din around me"; men ululating in synchrony with their chests thumped in counterpoint to the crashing of feet on the bare ground; "and rising above it all, . . . the cries of the flute, which I heard at close quarters for the first time, a sound like great wings beating at the ear drums, throbbing and flapping in the hollow portions of the skull" (1965, 126–7, 117). He notes the men's "ecstatic communion with an invisible force" at this point and states that although it was impossible for him to tell what they felt, "I was struck by the thought that they may have wanted to be seen [by the women]."

In another sensitive and well-known account, *The Forest People,* which concerns the secret sacred *molimo* trumpet and its associated songs of the Mbuti "pygmies" of the Ituri Forest of central Africa, Colin Turnbull describes in unforgettable terms this same sort of invisible presence evoked by an instrument belonging to the men, seeing which, women are supposed to believe, will bring their death. With Turnbull, or should we say with the Mbuti, at that time at least, this is all the more exemplary in that it is this sound, this invisible musical instrument, that virtually is the religion providing comfort and beauty, mystery and efficacy, an ethical system and a sense of rootedness in "Being" in the forest. Above all, religion is the secret, carefully concealed *and* revealed.

> For a month I sat every evening at the kumamolimo [rite of the
> *molimo*]; listening, watching, and feeling—above all, feeling. If I still

had little idea of what was going on, at least I felt that air of importance and expectancy. Every evening, when the women shut themselves up, pretending that they were afraid to see "the animal of
the forest"; every evening, when the men gathered around the fire,
pretending they thought that the women thought the drainpipes
were animals; every evening, when the trumpet drainpipes imitated
leopards and elephants and buffalos—every evening, when all this
make-believe was going on, I felt something very real and very great
was going on beneath it, something everyone else took for granted,
and about which only I was ignorant. (1962, 88)

In the Putumayo shamanism with which I was connected in the 1970s and
1980s in southwest Colombia, the shaman's singing is both his way of reaching
out to and connecting with powerful spirits, just as it is those very same spirits
that are singing through him, by means of the vehicle that is his body. He thus
breaches the wall of the secret shrouded in taboos against spirit contact, and
therewith presences them invisibly through a mystery of sound working dialec-
tically between person and spirit (Taussig 1987).

The hallucinogenic yagé-inspired visions that follow give visual form to this
sonically formed but otherwise invisible spiritual presence, it being precisely the
point, however, that while enormously inspiring, hallucinogenic images are only
precariously real. They are the epitome of what in modernity came to be called
collage and montage. They come and go, they contradict one another, they are
emotionally polarized, they may be sent by another, hostile shaman, and they
may be deliberately misleading—in this form is created, thus, another mode of
revelation and concealment, and of concealment through revelation. In addition
to recognizing the curative function of visual exposure, we should also be mindful of how the danger and intensity of feelings associated with the taking of drugs
such as yagé indicate the depth of the transgression involved in breaking through
into the otherwise forbidden domain of spirits. (And we might note, inter alia,
the overarching taboos here against women, menstrual blood, and pregnancy
as fearsome states that can physically destroy the shaman when he is engaged in
his work.)

Along with this presencing of the invisible through song and music is the way
the human body serves as a philosophical "device," theatricalizing and ponder-
ing innerness and veiling as the inviolable element of Truth. Here I am thinking
not only of the aforementioned use of the body as a sacred staging ground of
religious rituals such as initiation but of the worldwide use of the human body
for the staging of insided/outsidedness, of penetration and retrieval, and hence
of evisceration and exposure of hidden depth in often spectacular performances
of concealment and revelation. Healing someone of sorcery, for instance, generally involves the extraction of an object, a splinter or a worm or an animal, from
the inside of the body, just as sorcery—an intrinsic part of religion and perhaps

its most "transgressive" part—involves the placing of these things in that body. (Christian notions of exorcism, confession, catharsis, and purgation, as well as the ready use of Christian concepts to translate key elements of so-called primitive religions, the soul, for instance, are parallel phenomena energized by insided/outsidedness.) Also of note here is the play with being and nothingness, as exemplified by the skill with which objects appear and disappear in and from the body in remarkable changes of pace, together with the often ontologically undefinable nature of the substances involved.

In many societies, as in Asia and Africa and Latin America, it is not a sorcery substance but the spirit of a dead human through which notions of insided/outsidedness are staged. Powerful traces of this enormously widespread phenomenon, often categorized as "spirit possession," underlie the Christian liturgy, specifically the Holy Spirit and the cult of the saints. Similarly, this use of the body to mark the drama and mystery of concealment has been called *physiognomy*—the ancient science of reading insides from outsides, character and soul, no less than the future, from external bodily features—and as such became a basis for theorizing the (magical) power of film, especially the close-up of the face. The point to dwell upon with embodied insided/outsidedness is not, however, the triumph of a catharsis with the eventual bringing to light of hiddenness, but rather the performance of hiddenness itself in an eternal and unstable movement with a continuously discharging circuit of taboo and transgression, concealment and revelation.

Negation and the Exhausting Tendency to Seek Excess

In drawing attention to the "exhausting tendency to seek excess," Kenneth Read unintentionally and hence all the more convincingly underscores Georges Bataille's 1933 theory of *dépense* or "expenditure" (1985a), which is no less relevant for religion than for economics, and which later became more fully elaborated in Bataille's three-volume work, *The Accursed Share* (1988). Postulating a built-in need in all human societies for going over the top, for wasteful and lavish spending for the hell of it, for a "toomuchness" (in the phrasing of Norman O. Brown [1991]) and hence for expenditure without motive of gain other than sheer loss, Bataille suggested a way of reading world history that was especially relevant to sacrifice, a most important feature of many religions whose defining features are (1) the presence of an intermediary as victim between the sacrificer and the god, and (2) the destruction of the intermediary. "Sacrifice destroys that which it consecrates," emphasizes Bataille searching for a formula that in negating utility and profit would give rise to the sacred quality of *dépense* in intimate relation to transgression (1988, 1:58).

This view of sacrifice is intimately bound to a philosophical dispute Bataille had with Hegel as to the meaning of the death space in Hegel's famous operation of *Aufhebung*, whereby a concept or event is transcended by its negation yet preserved within it. In Bataille's view Hegel did not know to what extent he was right in his emphasis on death and dismemberment, as in the famous passage in the latter's preface to *The Phenomenology of Spirit* wherein Spirit "attains its truth only by finding itself in absolute dismemberment. It is not that prodigious power by being the Positive that turns away from the negative. . . . Spirit is that power only to the degree in which it contemplates the Negative face to face and dwells with it. This prolonged sojourn is the magical force which transposes the negative into given-Being" (1977, 19). Against this sort of magic, Bataille sees the negation at work in human history and Spirit as a sort of derailed *Aufhebung* neither achieving redemptive closure nor interested in it. To close the dialectical would in fact be nondialectical. To the contrary, negation is a sacrifice of the very idea of closure in a continuous face to facedness with death and dismemberment (Bataille 1990).

Automutilation and the Killing of the God

Death and dismemberment return us to the human body as a privileged theater of sacred activity in a way that makes it hard to avoid the topics of automutilation, of the killing of the god, and of the god killing himself. The basis of Christianity, and implicating extraordinary degrees of transgression at the core of that religion, these actions bear heavily on Nietzsche's famous concept of enlightenment as synonymous with the death of God in which the God killing himself is taken to new heights, actually defining the place, character, and meaning of transgression in modernity.

This God did not die from senescence. Murder is how Nietzsche sees it. And it is murder by society as a whole, by the era in an act of such enormity that he asks in *The Gay Science,* "How did we do this?" "How could we drink up the sea? Who gave us the sponge to wipe away the entire horizon?" Uncertainty reigns, the earth unchained from the sun. "Whither is it moving now? Whither are we moving?" (Nietzsche 1974, 181–82). Moreover the event is not recognized for what it is—perhaps the most telling feature of all as regards transgression. The bearer of the news throws his lantern to the ground, and it breaks into pieces. "I have come too early," he says. "My time is not yet. This tremendous event is still on its way, still wandering; it has not yet reached the ears of men. Lightning and thunder require time" (181).

So fundamental is this death of God that in 1963, in "A Preface to Transgression," Michel Foucault defined modernity itself in terms of transgression as a prelude to his all-consuming project for a new philosophy to be built around the poetic logic of experience at the Limit in a world evacuated of the sacred (the Infinitude of the Limit replacing the rule of God with His Limit of Infinity). The key insight here as I understand it, and one of great significance for the study of religion, is that the sacred, itself a staging ground of transgression (as the aforementioned examples are intended to indicate), is not so much *erased* by modernity, as is suggested by the famous notion of the disenchantment of the world, but is instead itself *transgressed*. Paradoxically this transgression of transgression can be viewed as the ultimate sacred act but one in which *sacrilege* becomes the place where the sacred is most likely to be experienced in modernity, sacrilege being the inverse of sacrifice, a charged space of negative holiness characterized by the meeting of extremes in unending waves of metonymic proliferation. For Foucault this charged space of transgression in modernity is sex, or should we say sex and language, located not in God but in his absence. With this a unique twist is given to transgression, demanding a fundamentally new "nondialectical philosophy" bound to an effervescent, impossible language of the limit reminiscent of Bataille's death space of excess and of laughter tracing, as Foucault puts it in terms no less lyrical than forlorn, "the line of foam showing just how far speech may advance upon the sands of silence." Everything here rests on language, this language-as-philosophy, language-as-being, language-as-transgression (taking us back to the issue of surrealism, Benjamin, and representational pathos): it is the "product of fissures, abrupt descents, and broken contours, this misshapen and craglike language describes a circle; it refers to itself and is folded back on a questioning of its limits" (1980, 44).

A leading but rarely acknowledged motif in Foucault's final project on the history of sexuality is that this sacred force of transgression bound to sexuality is intimately bound not only to language at the limit, but to secrecy, and more particularly to the play of concealment and revelation. "What is peculiar to modern societies," he repeatedly wrote in *The History of Sexuality* fourteen years later, "is not that they consigned sex to a shadow existence, but that they dedicated themselves to speaking of it *ad infinitum,* while exploiting it as *the* secret" (1980, 35). That this is the crossroads where surrealism comes to bear on the new mix modernity makes of religion and transgression, image and body, was one of Benjamin's insights, evident in his advice, in speaking for *profane illumination,* that "we penetrate the mystery only to the degree that we recognise it in the everyday world, by virtue of a dialectical optic that perceives the everyday as impenetrable, the impenetrable as everyday" (1978b, 189–90).

Intoxication

Benjamin's sagacious recommendation, written in 1928, was inspired by the issue of *intoxication* as a mystical force all too ready at hand in the anarcho-communist class struggle; intoxication as the realm in which the maker of images may thus work, explosively dislocating and reconfiguring body and image; and intoxication in its more literal meaning of inspiration through drugs, which Benjamin regarded as weakening the profane element in profane illumination. This is dangerous territory but one we cannot avoid in discussing transgression and modernity at the end of the twentieth century, with drugs as much if not more than sex occupying a strategic position in politics, revolution, counter-revolution, and the sacred, in modern times, canonized in the extensive writing and painting of William Burroughs (for whom the taking of yagé with Indian shamans in Colombia and Peru was a formative experience). In referring to religion as the opiate of the masses, Karl Marx could not have known how literally correct his assessment would become, only that the equation could be read backwards as well as forwards. It is the early Foucault, in the wake of Nietzsche and Bataille, who has opened eyes to what a religion/philosophy of transgression would be like without an obvious church or priesthood, and who thus allows us to understand the concepts of the sacred and the marvellous in modernity to which drugs may provide (or are thought to provide) access, complete with all the trappings of automutilation and self-sacrifice. This is obvious enough in Burroughs whose work, beginning with *Naked Lunch,* problematizing image and word in obscene and transgressive forms, together with flights of great lyrical beauty, brings religion, sex, drugs, and montage together. That such transgressive phenomena are seen as the antitheses of religion is testimony to the narrow moralism of organized religions today. Such organization finds its counterpart in the fact that modern societies and especially the United States, having made drugs illegal and attached extraordinary penalties to their use and sale, bring the fearsome logic of taboo and transgression underlying the sacred to its terrible perfection.

SUGGESTED READINGS

Bakhtin, Mikhail. 1968. *Rabelais and His World,* translated by Helene Iswolsky.
Bataille, Georges. 1985. "The Notion of Expenditure." In *Visions of Excess: Selected Writings, 1927–1939.*
———. 1985. "Sacrificial Mutilation and the Severed Ear of Vincent van Gogh." In *Visions of Excess: Selected Writings, 1927–1939.*
———. 1990. "Hegel, Death, and Sacrifice," translated by Christopher Carsten. In *Yale French Studies.*
Benjamin, Walter. 1978. "Hashish in Marseilles." In *Reflections.*
———. 1978. "Surrealism." In *Reflections.*
Brown, Norman O. 1990. "Dionysus in 1990." In *Apocalypse and/or Metamorphoses.*
Burroughs, William. 1964. *Naked Lunch.*
Durkheim, Emile. 1965. "The Negative Cult and its Functions." In *The Elementary Forms of the Religious Life.*
Foucault, Michel. 1977. "A Preface to Transgression." In *Language, Counter-Memory, Practice: Selected Essays and Interviews.*
———. 1980. *The History of Sexuality.* Vol. 1, *An Introduction.*
Hegel, G. W. F. 1977. Preface to *The Phenomenology of Spirit.*
Hollier, Denis, ed. 1988. *The College of Sociology, 1937–1939.*
Junod, Henri. 1962. *The Life of a South African Tribe.* Vol. 1, *Social Life.*
Kristeva, Julia. 1982. *Powers of Horror: An Essay on Abjection,* translated by Leon S. Roudiez.

Sobieszek, Robert A. 1995. *Ports of Entry: William S. Burroughs and the Arts.*
Stallybrass, Peter, and Allon White. 1986. *The Politics and Poetics of Transgression.*

REFERENCES

Bakhtin, Mikhail. 1984. *Rabelais and His World,* translated by Helene Iswolsky. Bloomington: University of Indiana Press.

Bamberger, Joan. 1974. "The Myth of Matriarchy: Why Men Rule in Primitive Society." In *Women, Culture, and Society,* edited by Michelle Z. Rosaldo and Louise Lamphere. Stanford: Stanford University Press.

Bataille, Georges. 1985a. "The Notion of Expenditure." In *Visions of Excess: Selected Writings, 1927–1939,* edited by Allan Stoekl, translated by Allan Stoekl, with Carl R. Lovitt and Donald M. Leslie, Jr. Minneapolis: University of Minnesota Press.

————. 1985b. "Sacrificial Mutilation and the Severed Ear of Vincent van Gogh." In *Visions of Excess: Selected Writings, 1927–1939,* edited by Allan Stoekl, translated by Allan Stoekl, with Carl R. Lovitt and Donald M. Leslie, Jr. Minneapolis: University of Minnesota Press.

————. 1988. *The Accursed Share,* translated by Robert Hurley, 3 vols. New York: Zone.

————. 1990. "Hegel, Death, and Sacrifice," translated by Christopher Carsten. In *Yale French Studies* 78.

Benjamin, Walter. 1978a. "Hashish in Marseilles." In *Reflections,* edited by Peter Demetz, translated by Edmund Jephcott. New York: Harcourt Brace Jovanovich.

————. 1978b. "Surrealism." In *Reflections,* edited by Peter Demetz, translated by Edmund Jephcott. New York: Harcourt Brace Jovanovich.

Berndt, Ronald. 1962. *Excess and Restraint: Social Control among a New Guinea Mountain People.* Chicago: University of Chicago Press.

Boas, Franz. 1966. *Religion of the Kwakiutal Indians.* In *Kwakiutal Ethnography,* edited by Helen Codere. Chicago: University of Chicago Press.

Bolle, Kees W. 1987. "Secrecy in Religion." In *Secrecy in Religions,* edited by Kees W. Bolle. Leiden: Brill.

Breton, André. 1987. *Mad Love,* translated by Mary Ann Caws. Lincoln: University of Nebraska Press.

Brown, Norman O. 1991. "Dionysus in 1990." In *Apocalypse and/or Metamorphoses.* Berkeley and Los Angeles: University of California Press.

Burroughs, William. 1964. *Naked Lunch.* London: Calder.

Caillois, Roger. 1950. *L'Homme et le sacre.* Paris: Gallimard.

Canetti, Elias. 1962. *Crowds and Power,* translated by Carol Stewart. New York: Farrar Straus Giroux.

Catlin, George. 1973. *Letters and Notes on the Manners, Customs, and Conditions of the North American Indians.* 2 vols. New York: Dover.

Crocker, Christopher. 1983. "Being and Essence: Totemic Representation among the Eastern Bororo." In *The Power of Symbols: Masks and Masquerade in the Americas,* edited by N. Ross Crumrine and Marjorie Halpin. Vancouver: University of British Columbia Press.

Douglas, Mary. 1966. *Purity and Danger: An Analysis of the Concepts of Pollution and Taboo.* London: Routledge.

Durkheim, Emile. 1965. "The Negative Cult and Its Functions." In *The Elementary Forms of the Religious Life.* New York: Free Press.

Evans-Pritchard, E. E. 1929. "Some Collective Expressions of Obscenity in Africa." *Journal of the Royal Anthropological Institute* 59.

————. 1937. *Witchcraft, Oracles, and Magic among the Azande.* Oxford: Clarendon Press.

Foucault, Michel. 1977. "A Preface to Transgression." In *Language, Counter-Memory, Practice: Selected Essays and Interviews,* edited by Donald F. Bouchard, translated by Donald F. Bouchard and Sherry Simon. Ithaca, N.Y.: Cornell University Press.

———. 1980. *The History of Sexuality.* Vol. 1, *An Introduction,* translated by Robert Hurley. New York: Vintage.

Freud, Sigmund. 1958. *Totem and Taboo: Some Points of Agreement between the Mental Lives of Savages and Neurotics.* Vol. 13 of *The Standard Edition of the Complete Psychological Works of Sigmund Freud,* edited and translated by James Strachey. London: Hogarth.

Gillison, Gillian. 1980. "Images of Nature in Gimi Thought." In *Nature, Culture, and Gender,* edited by Carol P. MacCormack and Marilyn Strathern. Cambridge: Cambridge University Press.

Gluckman, Max. 1960. "The Licence in Ritual." In *Custom and Conflict in Africa.* Oxford: Blackwell.

Gregor, Thomas. 1985. *Anxious Pleasures: The Sexual Lives of an Amazonian People.* Chicago: University of Chicago Press.

Gusinde, Martin. 1982. *Los Indios del Tierra del Fuego.* Vol. 1, *Los Selk'nam.* Buenos Aires: Centro Argentino de Etnología Americana.

Hays, Terence. 1988. "'Myths of Matriarchy' and the Sacred Flute Complex of the Papua New Guinea Highlands." In *Myths of Matriarchy Reconsidered,* edited by Deborah Gwertz. Oceania Monographs, no. 33. Sydney: University of Sydney.

Hegel, G. W. F. 1977. Preface to *The Phenomenology of Spirit,* translated by A. V. Miller. Oxford: Oxford University Press.

Huizinga, Johannes. 1955. *Homo Ludens: A Study of the Play-Element in Culture.* Boston: Beacon.

Junod, Henri. 1962. *The Life of a South African Tribe.* 2 vols. New Hyde Park, N.Y.: University Books.

Kristeva, Julia. 1982. *Powers of Horror: An Essay on Abjection,* translated by Leon S. Roudiez. New York: Columbia University Press.

Lowie, Robert H. 1948. *Primitive Religion.* New York: Liveright.

Nietzsche, Friedrich. 1974. *The Gay Science,* translated by Walter Kaufmann. New York: Vintage.

Read, Kenneth. 1965. *The High Valley.* New York: Scribners.

Simmel, Georg. 1950. "Secrecy." In *The Sociology of Georg Simmel,* translated and edited by Kurt H. Wolff. New York: Free Press.

Sobieszek, Robert A. 1995. *Ports of Entry: William S. Burroughs and the Arts.* Los Angeles: Los Angeles County Museum of Art/Thames and Hudson.

Spencer, Baldwin, and F. J. Gillen. 1968. *The Native Tribes of Central Australia.* New York: Dover.

Stallybrass, Peter, and Allon White. 1986. *The Politics and Poetics of Transgression.* Ithaca, N.Y.: Cornell University Press.

Taussig, Michael. 1987. *Shamanism, Colonialism, and the Wild Man: A Study in Terror and Healing.* Chicago: University of Chicago Press.

Turnbull, Colin. 1962. *The Forest People.* New York: Simon and Schuster.

Turner, Victor. 1966. "Betwixt and Between: The Liminal Period in Rites de Passage." In *The Forest of Symbols: Aspects of Ndembu Ritual.* Ithaca, N.Y.: Cornell University Press.

TWENTY-ONE

Value

Edith Wyschogrod

Ordinary usage confers a double meaning on the verb "to value," that of prizing and of assigning worth. When valuing is envisaged as cherishing or holding dear, emphasis falls upon preference or inclination, its affective aspect, but when valuing is interpreted as the activity of rating in the sense of ascribing place in a hierarchy or as assessment construed in terms of money, goods, or services, it is conceived of as entailing an intellectual component. "To value" expresses, at least in part, the distinction between the verbs "to esteem" and "to estimate," the former designating respect or regard, the latter signifying gauging or calculating in order to arrive at a judgment. Thus, when Democrats and Republicans endorse family values, they express a consensus about what they believe is socially prized. Queries about the value of a given stock, by contrast, are demands for calculation of its monetary worth, and a discussion of the value of a college education may be an inquiry about both its meaningfulness and the income it is likely to generate. Because the same value-laden object may become nomadic, migrate from one framework to another, sociocultural setting determines whether a value is to be construed as aesthetic, cognitive, religious, or moral.

Since the field of religious studies cannot be univocally conceived, a wide-angle lens is needed to see how these tendencies enter into interpretation. Value construction inheres in the most diverse subject matters ranging from detailed inquiries into what is sung about, prayed over, or fasted for in the world's religions to abstract discussions of God in process theology or postmodern theory. Because present-day study brings a high degree of reflexivity to scholarly undertakings, value-laden presuppositions are brought to the fore, sometimes in confessionlike statements preceding a concrete description or analysis. By examining transformations in the notion of value, we may come to see how valuing, in its meanings as both prizing and assessing, has entered into recent studies. We will consider, for example, cases in which a belief or rite is interpreted as a way of managing desire. To understand such value-laden terms as management and desire into which psychological and social meanings enter requires painstaking genealogical tracking.

Never wholly isolable, the emotive and calculative aspects of valuing often work in tandem, especially in the glossing of religious doctrines and practices. As early as the fifth century B.C.E., the connnectedness of affect and reasoned calculation was brought out in Plato's dialogue *Euthyphro,* a discussion about the relation between humans and gods. Socratic questioning focused on the issue of whether a religious act has value because it is approved by the gods or is approved by the gods because it is inherently valuable. Euthyphro is made to see that divine approbation is contingent upon the intrinsic value of a given act. What appears to be an abstract theological issue may generate political consequences. In Plato's *Apology*, Socrates is accused of atheism in a trial that can be interpreted as the political fallout of a theological debate about religious values. If the jury were to decide that Socrates preached value as intrinsic to the object valued rather than as divinely conferred, then it would have to conclude he believed the gods to be subservient to the higher power of reason, an act that could be construed as treason. Even when divested of theological content, the affective and rational dimensions of valuing persist in modern philosophical accounts. The term "value" as a key construct of ethics is in fact applied anachronistically to premodern discussion even if the concept was functionally present in classical antiquity.

In contrast to those who adhere to the rational determination of value, biblical religions depict the possession of value as deriving from the divine singling out of an object or act because God prizes or loves it, even if the object of such love is expected subsequently to live up to or become worthy of the affect that God has bestowed on it. Although there are occasional intimations that the object first must be at least potentially worthy of God's affect—the election of ancient Israel, the consecration of Levite priests, and the calling forth of the prophets are cases in point—value is essentially the result of God's actions.

In the history of Western religion, modernity's shift from a theocentric to an anthropocentric construal of value as prizing is especially evident in the sea change initiated by David Hume. He urges upon his eighteenth-century readers a view first ascribed to Francis Hutcheson, that judgments of right and wrong are attributable to irresistible feeling, the products of moral sentiment rather than of rational reflection. On Hume's account, the will is not tossed about in a sinister war between reason and passion; volition is freely acknowledged to be governed by feelings of pleasure and pain. Even if moral judgments appear to result from the application of universally binding rational criteria, this semblance of rationality is attributable to sentiment of a particular type, a "calm passion," an amalgam of aversion to controversy and sympathy for others.

This perspective would later be framed in linguistic terms in the claims of the unreconstructed positivists of the 1930s. A. J. Ayer, in accordance with what is called his "boo-hooray" theory, contends that moral judgments are no more than ejaculatory, emotive utterances that have no cognitive standing. While C. L. Stevenson claims that such utterances are attempts to persuade one's auditors, Rudolf Carnap sees statements in the form of "ought to" or "should" as disguised imperatives. For positivists, theological statements are either intended as statements of fact that are inherently unverifiable and therefore meaningless or as emotive utterances.

It would be simplistic to associate the identification of value with desire in recent French thought as deriving principally from Hume's account of the desire for pleasure as motivating moral conduct. Nevertheless, French poststructuralists Gilles Deleuze and Felix Guattari in *Anti-Oedipus: Capitalism and Schizophrenia* see the conferring of value as a "plugging into desire, effectively taking charge of desire" (1982, 166). In prescriptions proferred in the manner of spiritual exercises, desire is coupled with social control. In an independently written work, Deleuze supports Hume's view that "the passional" and the "social" determinations of value are reciprocally implicated in one another (1991, 21). Hume is, for Deleuze, one of several misunderstood thinkers whose moral philosophy is seen as premonitory of his own reconfigured post-Nietzschean values. These include the encouragement of the joyful and celebratory, an animus against interiority, and the substitution of the exteriority of forces and relations for the idea of underlying metaphysical principles. Thus Humean *philosophemes*, conceptual elements that enter into an analysis or systematization, have become subjects of discussion among the notable voices of continental thought: Jacques Derrida, Julia Kristeva, and Jean-Luc Marion (France); Peter Sloterdijk (Germany); and Gianni Vattimo and Giorgio Agamben (Italy).

Having recognized the role of emotions in rendering moral judgments, Hume saw their deployment in the world's religions as strengthening the disvalues of superstition and fanaticism. Rejecting the Scottish Calvinism that sees the refusal to interpret Scripture as the Word of God as a vice, and which posits a double predestinarianism, the election to salvation or damnation, Hume decided that religion as practiced from antiquity to his own time exerted a malign influence upon human affairs. Philosophy did not escape the shackles of superstition in that it had been historically co-opted to defend dogmas whose presuppositions it dared not question. Repudiating a belief in miracles, revelation, and an afterlife, Hume concluded in his epistemological writings that true religion is a species of disinterested philosophy, and more important, that genuine religion cannot exceed the deliveries of experience or provide standards of conduct apart from what can be gleaned from the observations of ordinary life. This contention contradicts that of the theist Cleanthes, often considered the fall guy in Hume's *Dialogues Concerning Natural Religion*, that religion humanizes conduct and provides the affective impetus for morality and justice.

Yet it is Cleanthes' position that reflects a transformation in the metaphysical ground of religious debate from that of doctrinal truth to social utility. Religion is valued not because its claims are necessarily true but because it is an effective instrument of social control. Freud, for example, derogates Western religion as a group neurosis but upholds the view that religious beliefs may be instrumental in maintaining social order. The utility argument is not without potentially incendiary political consequences. Those who endorse a religion because it may help to achieve some desired social value might, in the interest of consistency, be cornered into supporting practices they perceive as undesirable but which are approved by that religion. For example, those who find a given religion useful as a support for the ecological movement may feel obliged to endorse its stand on abortion. Studies in the sociology of religion uncover and help to explain such cognitive dissonances in belief systems.

In the context of the argument for God's existence based on the order of the world, the design argument, Hume makes another startlingly contemporary move. By privileging biological generation over reason as a cosmogonic principle ("[T]he latter arises from the former, never the former from the latter" [1947, 179–80]), Hume anticipates the cosmologization of desire even if what was intended was merely a philosophical alternative to the mechanistic rational teleology of the day.

What has gone largely unnoticed is Hume's revaluation of desire as a cosmological principle. In his laudatory preface to Deleuze and Guattari's *Anti-Oedipus*, Michel Foucault notes that in the late 1960s the symbiosis of Marx and Freud that predominated in the West from 1945 to 1965 was far from replicated; rather, an experience and technology of desire was born making desire a locus of value and the linchpin of a new ethics. What Foucault does not say is that desire as a psychological, libidinal force can be reborn, as it is in Deleuze and Guattari, as a metaphysical and cosmological construct, an eroticized earth envisaged as "a body without organs" and arranged into strata that constrain pulses of energy. In a striking passage that could pass for one written by Deleuze and Guattari, Hume declares, "These words, *generation, reason,* mark only certain powers and energies in nature, whose effects are known but whose essence is incomprehensible" (1947, 178). In *A Thousand Plateaus: Capitalism and Schizophrenia,* Deleuze and Guattari deploy such expressions as "unstable matters," "flows in all directions," "free intensities," "nomadic singularities," and "passional assemblages" (1987, 409, 219, 153, 405, and 399) in order to depict the earth as a minefield of unrestrained desire. "Copulation" and "generation" (Hume's terms) construed as the modus operandi of the cosmos lose their explanatory role and become a locus of value in a philosophy of desire.

Similarly numerous feminist theological writings trope sexual experience in terms of earth and cosmos and, conversely, describe cosmology in erotic terms. Reworking desire as a woman-centered "geography" of pleasure alters not only the way in which the motifs of sexual psychology are construed but helps to recodify the anthropomorphic language that designates transcendance. Any simplistic reading of woman as earth mother can only serve to sanction traditional values, the nexus of discursive practices that reenforce the view of "the feminine" as a passive material substratum to be shaped by "masculine" reason. By situating value in the eros of woman, the legacy of this phallagocentric account may be overturned and a new sense of body/cosmos ascribed to the theological themes of creation and redemption in Western religion.

The locus classicus for considering values as the end result not of affect but of an uncompromising rational regimen is to be found in the moral philosophy of Immanuel Kant. Individuals act in accordance with maxims, subjective rules of conduct, Kant contends. The maxim that guides a given act is to be elicited and the worth of the action mandated by the maxim judged in accordance with an easy-to-apply litmus test: Ask yourself if the rule upon which you mean to act ought to become a universal law, one binding on all rational agents. If so, act on it. In addition, the motive for an act must be duty and the will that determines it that of the agent alone.

Although the limitations of Kant's moral philosophy have been roundly criticized on a variety of grounds by analytic philosophers from the 1950s to the present, as well as by recent poststructuralist theorists, residues of Kantian moral reasoning resist subversion even among Kant's most formidable critics. Thus Jacques Derrida, whose powerful arguments against logocentrism—the claim that Western metaphysical thought identifies being with presence—have undermined many of the pretensions of rational discourse, nevertheless finds it morally incumbent upon participants in intellectual public debate to affirm the value of the "principle of reason" and "the spirit of Enlightenment." To profess the contrary in a media-dominated culture invites assertions that are immune to correction. Yet paradoxically the value of the obligatoriness that is said to attach to rational discourse cannot be asserted on rational grounds, because these grounds have already been forfeited. Instead, value must flow from preference or prizing, as Derrida concedes in expressing his admiration for those who take the trouble to justify their discourse (1995, 427).

Most contemporary criticisms of Kantian ethics that both appropriate and displace it derive their trenchancy from the recognition that the subject of ethics is also that of history. Hegel's recognition of Spirit as coming to reflective self-awareness in the course of a succession of historical moments that arise, persist for a time, and pass away, and Marx's contention that the subject is a material being having needs and class interests open the way for interpreting value as determined by socially constructed and distributed constellations of power. No longer is the subject one from whom gender, economic, social, and cultural circumstances have been eliminated; conceptual categories themselves are seen as indices of power. In an influential work, *The Differend: Phrases in Dispute,* Jean-François Lyotard sees value as determined by the power structure embedded in a juridical language that penalizes the deprived so that they are in effect silenced. It follows that the problem of marginalization cannot be resolved in juridical terms if the plaintiff or accuser lacks the instruments of arugment. Forced to accede to the dominant language, he or she is transformed from accuser into victim. As opposed to the life situations envisaged in Kant's examples, a case exhibiting an asymmetry of power, what Lyotard calls "a differend," remains irresolvable (1988, 13). Transcending the mere assertion of power discrepancies, the differend offers a paradigm for the exploration of religious differences that resist adjudication.

The implications for religion of the anthropocentric turn in Kant's account of value formation are staggering. Moses Maimonides and Thomas Aquinas had earlier argued that divine commands do not contradict reason, but Kant issues a far stronger claim. Because God's will is foreign to that of the agent, the introduction of divine commands into the forming of moral decisions taints those decisions and the acts that flow from them. The individual subject alone is both producer and product of what she or he is ethically to become; good or evil actions are the outcome of autonomous acts, acts freely chosen. In *Religion within the Limits of Reason Alone,* Kant declares "man himself must make himself into whatever in a moral sense, whether good or evil, he is to become. Either condition must be an effect of his free choice; for otherwise he could not be held responsible for it and could therefore be morally neither good nor evil" (1960, 40). The autonomy claim still haunts contemporary phenomenologies of religion in that beliefs and practices may be evaluated in terms of consent or its absence.

Even if, for Kant, no action can be justified by an appeal to God's wishes or commands, he does not entirely abandon Christian teachings but rather refigures them to reflect the primacy of the moral law. Thus the kingdom of God, depicted in Matt. 6:10 or Luke 11:2 as a state of being that will prevail when God's will comes to pass on earth, is redescribed in political terms as an ethical commonwealth under God who now is seen as an ideal moral ruler. Such a commonwealth is not an object of possible experience but rather an archetype of the church invisible, "a mere idea of the union of all the righteous under direct and divine world government" (Kant, 92). Is there anything left in the contemporary study of heterogeneous religions of this Kantian heritage?

Although nineteenth- and early-twentieth-century liberal Christian theologians such as Albrecht Ritschl, Rudolph Hermann Lotze, and Adolph von Harnack were influenced by Kantian thought, nowhere was the transformation of religious into ethical values more wholeheartedly embraced than in the German Judaism of the period. The concern with Jewish ritual law that remained an important deposit in Moses Mendelssohn's accommodation of Judaism to the Enlightenment is, in Hermann Cohen's *Religion of Reason out of the Sources of Judaism,* historicized and recast as ethical monotheism, a tradition that, somewhat refurbished, remains alive today in Reform and Reconstructionist Judaism. Rabbinic accounts of revelation or "the giving of the Torah" are, in Cohen's reconfiguring, God's coming into relation with human beings insofar as they are rational and the bearers of morality. Although Cohen maintains that the laws of logic hold for both ethics and the knowledge of nature, ethics is considered an infinite task and nature is seen as providing the field for the realization that ethics strives to attain. From the standpoint of traditional Jewish doxology, Cohen concludes shockingly that the possibility for the realization of values in the world is underwritten by a God who is neither person nor infinite substance in an Aristotelean sense but a postulate whose function is to guarantee the realization of the moral law. In neo-Kantian theologies, being collapses into value and ontology into axiology, a position that remains attractive to a number of contemporary Jewish thinkers who fear the excesses of a romanticism that is seen to have played a role in the ideology of Nazism and in the creation of violence generally. Thus L. E. Goodman, endorsing a value-laden and ontologically attenuated God, writes the following in *God of Abraham:* "In violence or violation, or the romantically appealing notions of the arbitrary, actively uncaring or chaotic, I encounter nothing divine. . . . It is the goodness of God that renders the God of Abraham universal" (1966, 28).

Still another present-day legacy of Kant's description of the ethical subject is the issue of whether the world's religions have a common core. If all human beings, insofar as they are rational, are essentially alike, there are strong grounds for questioning the hegemony of Christian values. Although Kant himself eschewed such skepticism, it was no longer possible for his successors to regard Jewish and Muslim monotheism, and the religions of Asia and Africa that were yielding to scholarly inquiry, as subject to hierarchical arrangement. Although Hegel derogated non-Christian religions as lower rungs on the ladder of Spirit's ascent, Kant's nonhistorical ethics provided an entering wedge for the democratization of religions based on the commonality of moral values grounded in practical reason.

While universalism was not without precedent in the Stoicism of the ancient world, only in the nineteenth century did scholars develop what they believed to be the objective study of religion. Calling for dispassionate inquiry, systematic analysis of data, and the creation of a classification system that would crosscut cultural differences, it was hoped that the new science of religion would provide a value-free grid for analyzing the beliefs and practices of the world's religions. No longer could the differences among religions weigh in as arguments for older accounts of religious multiplicity, such as the view that multiple religions presupposed the degeneration of an aboriginal monotheism or that the evolution of primitive religions culminated in Christianity. By mapping the spiritual terrain of Indian religions, Max Müller, nineteenth-century translator and interpreter of ancient Indian texts, could dispense with the claim that biblical religion alone instantiatied ethical norms. More recently, Carl Gustav Jung explained the recurrence of motifs in religious narratives in terms of unconscious collective archetypes, while the comparative phenomenological studies of Gerardus van der Leeuw and Mircea Eliade elicit the patterns inherent in myths, rites, and symbols that segregate the sacred from the profane world. Although differences in approach are obvious, these thinkers presuppose that what they have exhumed is founded on a common human nature.

Similarly, sociology and anthropology as modern disciplines that have transformed the study of religion retain traces of their Kantian lineage. The comprehension of value acts in the social scientific studies from the late-nineteenth to early-twentieth century exhibited on the one hand an often unconscious rendering of value judgments about a belief or practice, coupled with the insistence that the investigator's research is value-neutral, and, on the other hand, the claim that objects of inquiry hold values to which they are oblivious but which are open to the disinterested gaze of the observer. Schooled in Kant's theory of knowledge, Emile Durkheim, a founder of modern sociology, argued that the structures of thought posited by Kant as prior to experience, space, time, and causality, are actually socially derived. Against this view, Ernst Cassirer, in his influential midcentury *Philosophy of Symbolic Forms,* sought a "purer" Kantianism by asserting that society is not the cause but rather the effect of religious and spiritual categories. Lacking the capacity to frame the ideal, Cassirer contended, mythic thought transforms ideal meanings into material substances such that image, object, and rite become indistinguishable from the reality they represent.

In spite of a professed indebtedness in these studies to Kant, who saw the categories of the understanding as universal, the Kantian legacy had been undermined by nineteenth-century historicism. These analyses manifested an ofen uncomprehending ascription of simplemindedness to nonwestern cultures, while attributing superiority to the viewpoint of the investigator. In a move intended to redress the inequity of an alleged inferiority of "primitive" relative to "civilized" societies, an inequity embedded in a perceived overvaluation of scientific reason, Claude Lévi-Strauss posited a difference not in caliber of intellect but in perspective. Nonliterate societies develop taxonomies of plants and animals within an environing nature not only to satisfy basic human needs but to indulge in the pleasure of knowing. These cognitive acts meet intellectual requirements as complex in their own way as those of scientific observation. The thought of primitives works in the manner of the *bricoleur,* a versatile jack-of-all-trades who makes do with available materials as opposed to the engineer who follows a master plan. A more graphic analogy familiar to the camping enthusiast is the difference between one who follows a trail and the improvisatory hiking of the bushwhacker.

Lévi-Strauss does not worry about the moral acceptability of articulating the values of others as a destruction of indigenous values, which is a matter of some apprehension in the academic study of Asian, African, and Native American religions. While remaining unsympathetic to this concern, Clifford Geertz, in a memoir of his life as an anthropologist, nevertheless describes it graphically as "ventriloquizing others, making off with their words" (1995, 129). Current text-based scholarship and fieldwork in the study of religion generally reflect the view that differences among peoples go all the way down, and that the ambiguities flowing from differing value configurations should be made explicit in scholarly analysis. At the same time, a promising direction is taken in the history of theory by focusing not on Durkheim, Freud, and other patriarchical figures as magisterial founders of the social sciences but rather on the salubrious critical intelligence they wielded against their predecessors, "the quests of yesteryear that can threaten the very configuration of positions that legitimate 'Western man's' occupation in science/knowledge," as Tomoko Masuzawa shows (1993, 5).

Discomfiture with the disinterested subject is further expressed by Paul Ricoeur who endorses the existential involvement of the inquirer. Yet he concedes in his influential *Symbolism of Evil,* a methodologically eclectic study of defilement, sin, and guilt, that his account is a transcendental deduction, an effort to construct a domain of objectivity in the Kantian sense. By interpreting human nature through an analysis of the symbols of chaos and fall, the meanings of human evil will be deduced. While promising, Ricoeur's study of disvalues implicates the subject in a system of voluntary commitments that await the correctives of Foucault's relating of values to power, as well as of feminist theorists' analyses of gender construction, and of Jean Baudrillard and Paul Virilio's depiction of the loss of the sense of history and the attendant day-to-day shifting of values fabricated by the new information culture.

Although Kant's account of values has greatly influenced the study of religion, no view of the calculative aspect of value has had more earthshaking consequences than Karl Marx's description of the transmutation of value into price by modern capitalism. Marx (1906) presupposed that the means of subsistence are at first produced and consumed within the limited horizons of small communities for which objects have an essential nature defined by their use. With the invention of barter, value took on an independent form as exchange value and was added on to that of use. When entities are traded for other entities, quantification becomes necessary: a coat may be traded for five bushels of corn. The understanding of objects as expressing unique essences is supplanted by a new fluidity based on quantifiability, a development that came to a head with the invention of money. Already strained by the exchange value introduced with the barter system, the use value of objects was further eroded when money, circulating continuously, provided a permanent system of translation that controls the relation among objects.

At first money in the form of precious metals provided the standard of exchange. Because of their natural uniformity, gold and silver could be weighed and units of weight transposed into measures of value. The invention of paper money advanced the process of abstraction by replacing gold and silver with what lacks intrinsic value. The ethical force of Marx's analysis lies in its application to human labor, "the aggregate of those mental and physical capabilities existing in a human being, which he exercises whenever he produces a use value of any description" (1906, 186). Capitalism translates labor into monetary terms. The Christianity of the bourgeoisie that Marx excoriates is but a reflex, a projection of this world.

Far from having vanished as a resource for religious thought, Marxism has shown itself to be remarkably resilient. The Latin American liberation theologies of Gustavo Guttierez, Jon Sobrino, Leonardo Boff, Juan Luis Segundo, and Victorio Araya maintain that in order to live the Christian message, one must do so in the determinate context of the poor and economically oppressed, to hear, accept, and serve the poor. These theologians function as "whistle blowers" or denouncers who keep alive the hope for social, economic, and political justice.

Marx has been criticized by feminists in various religious traditions who contend that the oppression of women and class oppression differ significantly, and that Marxist atheism is both incompatible with theological values and insufficiently critical of the values of patriarchy. Yet it is also generally conceded that Marx's focus on actual material conditions opens the way for social change. Thus, thinkers such as Mary Daly identify the unfolding of woman consciousness with God's self-unfolding but speak appreciatively of contemporary Marxist atheism as castigating reified conceptions of God deployed to justify the exploitation of women.

The calculative strain in both the Kantian and Marxist views should not lead us to the erroneous conclusion that ascriptions of value in late-nineteenth and early-twentieth-century thought are rationally derived. Beginning with Kierkegaard's critique of rational ethics and continuing through Nietzsche's genealogical deconstruction of traditional morality, the notion of value as that which is prized, esteemed, or held dear becomes the counterpoise to various manifestations of ethical rationalism. By showing that the singularity of the existing individual not only is in excess of the moral law but that singularity itself is destroyed in the straitjacketing operation of universalization, Kierkegaard offers a devastating critique of a rationalism that undermines the existing individual. He turns instead to a faith that is both within and beyond reason, one destined to generate paradox and absurdity rather than moral norms. Yet faith is irreducible to nonsense because reason, powerless to tamper with faith, is unable to unsay it. Not only does Kierkegaardian faith reinstate the heteronomous will of God as the wellspring of value, but it attributes worth to what, from the ethical standpoint, must appear as heinously transgressive—Abraham's willingness to sacrifice his son Issac. What is prized is an obedience to divine command that does not render Abraham's prizing of Isaac nugatory but rather demonstrates his compliance all the more forcefully.

That Kierkegaardian attentiveness to Scripture is reflected in neoorthodox Protestant theology is hardly surprising. Despite a paucity of reference to Kierkegaard, Karl Barth's *Church Dogmatics* mirrors his uneasiness with Kierkegaard's emphasis on *der Einzelner,* "the Single One," because singularity appears to inhibit the development of an ecclesiology. The non-Pauline character of Kierkegaard's biblicism is evident in the difference between Barth's view of obedience to God's commands and the perceived nonscipturalism of Kierkegaard's concept of the leap of faith. At the same time, Barth's stress upon faith as always already offended, and his depiction of faith as loving obedience to the word of God, palpably manifests Kierkegaardian tendencies. It is precisely what Barth eschews in Kierkegaard that becomes a driving force in Mark C. Taylor's a/theology, a contemporary conceptual rendering of the impossible that invites the re-figuring of justice, law, and religion. By eliciting what is encrypted in Kierkegaard's marginalia, Taylor opens the way not only to transgressive rereadings of Western theology but also to an a/phenomenological reading of the excesses of contemporary cultural practices.

When the ascription of values is the result of cherishing or prizing, the issue of method, how moral principles are to be derived, is displaced by the question, "Says who?" where "who" is not to be regarded as an ego, that is, a substantive self. This destabilization of the self reorients, indeed revolutionizes, value determination. Although Kierkegaard and Nietzsche focus on authorship, each has argued compellingly for the undecidability of authorial identity. Never claiming ownership of the values embedded in works written pseudonymously, Kierkegaard refers to himself as a *Janus bifrons* in that the life options depicted in the psuedonymous texts wander errantly from the personae of the pseudonymous authors to Kierkegaard's *propria persona*, one who is indeterminable. Similarly Nietzsche, the philosopher of masks, does not envisage the mask as camouflage for a hidden ontological ground but rather as attesting to the ambiguity of phenomena, the unreality of the real. The enigmatic character of phenomena disrupts the subject who now sees the world from differing perspectives. On the face of it, there would appear to be some specifiable cognitive yield in answers to the question "Says who?" Can it not be said that values are lodged in the commands of God (Kierkegaard), or in the significations of good and bad conferred by an aristocratic caste (Nietzsche)? Yet these alleged values are fissured, for Kierkegaard by that which must remain inexplicit because of its uncontainability in language, and for Nietzsche, because of the imbrication of caste in the transgressive web of ancestral misalliances that poison the *Ursprung* of morality.

In spite of their differences, both Kierkegaard and Nietzsche excoriate the embourgeoisement of Christendom. "All the concepts of the church have been recognized for what they are, the most malignant counterfeits that exist, the aim of which is to devalue nature and natural values; the priest himself has been recognized for what he is, the most dangerous kind of parasite, the real poison-spider of life," Nietzsche contends in *The Antichrist* (1982a, 611). In *The Gay Science* (1982b), he concludes, rebarbatively, that the God of classical Christian faith, the source of values, is dead and the churches are merely "the tombs and sepulchers of God" (1982b, 96).

Although the post-Christian death-of-God theologies of the 1960s promulgated by Gabriel Vahanian, Paul van Buren, William Hamilton, and the post-Holocaust theologian Richard Rubenstein challenge biblically endorsed values on Nietzschean grounds, nowhere is Nietzschean influence more pronounced than in the radically new and forward-looking romantic apocalypticism of Thomas J. J. Altizer. What the *Genealogy of Morals* is to Kantian axiology, Altizer's reinscription of the metaphysics of creation is to biblical ontology—an inversion of what had heretofore been named and valued as God but is now manifested as emptiness or abyss. The fallout of this total and radical overturning is the collapse of God's creative acts into the emptiness of apocalypse such that creation and apocalypse are nondifferent. It is as total presence that we encounter this abyss and name it in the only way possible, through silence. Hope lies in both negating and affirming this void by an absence of speech that is nevertheless language, even if the subject of language disappears. With the help of Madhyamika Buddhism's teaching of emptiness and its dissolution of the I, the question "Says who?" is rendered nugatory. Yet even in the absence of the subject, there is a prizing of the apocalyptic ending, of the process of inversion itself. If void and abyss, the total presence of an absence, as Altizer would have it, are not simply the negation of a Hegelian Absolute, the process of inversion itself and its instantiation in politics and culture invite future exploration.

Rarely has the critique of interpreting value as a function of assessment or calculation been more insistent than in Heidegger's philosophy. His interpretation of human being has profoundly influenced such midcentury religious thinkers as Paul Tillich and Rudolph Bultmann. Has the last word then been said in this already extensive body of Heidegger-inspired theology or can a wider range of issues relevant to the study of religion still arise from Heidegger's thinking? His narrative of the conversion of Being into value, into what first has to be unsaid, must be explored before the resources for such expansion can be seen. For Heidegger, deficiencies of judgment-based ethics are seen to result from a turn in the history of metaphysics that transformed the Being of beings into the being of the subject that constitutes the objects of perception and knowledge, a view that comes to a head in Kant. If an act of knowing is to occur, Kant thinks, the faculty of sensible intuition must cooperate with the understanding which, without it, would be empty, just as intuition bereft of concepts would be blind. Both faculties are contained within the essential unity of the subject, an "I think." Even if Kant's account of cognition has uncovered the temporal character of the subject, thus linking time and finitude, time remains a property of the subject and cannot provide a horizon for thinking the meaning of Being.

With the progressive loss of the meaning of Being, Heidegger views philosophy as striving to make up for the resulting degradation by setting something above Being, the ought. For Kant, Being is interpreted as the being of nature determinable by theoretical reason, as opposed to the ought, the domain of practical reason ascertainable by reason and as reason. To understand philosophy's move of compensation, its substitution of value for Being, it is useful to think of the process Heidegger depicts in much the same way as Europeans envisage the value-added tax. In the manufacture of a product, each change added by the producer is seen as adding to the value of the object and is taxed accordingly. The increase in cost resulting from each tax increment is incorporated into the final price but is invisible to the consumer. Analogously, the modern subject creates values and superimposes them upon Being as if value were extraneous to Being and could be added and made intrinsic to it in the manner of the tax.

Heidegger could not be more forceful in his castigation of ethics based on self-justifying values when he declares in *An Introduction to Metaphysics* that,

Obligation, the ought, could emanate only from something which in itself raised a moral claim, which had an intrinsic *value* which was itself a value. The values as such now become the foundations of morality (the ought). But since the values are opposed to the being of the essent in the sense of facts they themselves cannot *be*. Therefore they were said to have validity. The values became the crucial criteria for all the realms of the essent, i.e., of the already-there. History came to be regarded as a realization of values. (1959, 198)

Heidegger's contemporary Max Scheler attempted to overcome the formalism of Kantian ethics by showing that values are objective and intuitable. Heidegger believed that Scheler inverted Kant's thought, thereby reducing values rather than the subject to the being of things.

After it is demonstrated that in the modern world beings are encountered as scientific objects or in a businesslike way, the question remains as to whether Heidegger provides a substitute for the Kantian conception of value or whether value has indeed become a moot question. In his "Letter on Humanism," a response to this issue as posed by French philosopher Jean Beaufret, Heidegger renounces the idea of value, yet makes specific recommendations that, astonishingly, resemble moral imperatives: recognize the blandishments of the public realm and the impotence of the private; speak and dwell in the nearness of Being. The critique of values, he avers, is not intended to deprecate the dignity of human beings but to suggest that dignity is misunderstood by humanism. Heidegger does not say what is meant by dignity in this context. We may assume that such elevation occurs as the end point of a process described as a transformation of thinking in which language is envisaged as the house of Being and humans are regarded as dwellers in this house and as the guardians of Being.

It is here that Heidegger's analysis becomes suggestive for the contemporary study of religion. If mortals are those who have been granted speech (Is language not Being's abode?) a human being's cultural and linguistic site is more than a feature added on to a common nature. Instead language and culture determine differences among human beings not in the sense of the cliché "worldviews differ" but rather as meaning that difference goes all the way down. Once the notion of a common human nature is abandoned, difference becomes primordial. This is precisely the premise with which much current sophisticated comparative study of world religions begins.

From Heidegger's perspective, ontological difference is not embedded in a politics but rather the converse is true. If the difference between Being and beings is more primordial than political activity, attentiveness to this difference, listening and waiting, implies a certain quietism. Such irenicism on Heidegger's part has been challenged on contradictory grounds: First, it is argued, he has refused to see that an apolitical stance is already embedded in a politics, that of silence and nonparticipation. Second, far from renouncing politics, Heidegger is known to have been a member of the Nazi Party and never to have retracted his praise for its "inner truth and greatness" (1959, 199), a claim that has been seen as bearing on the interpretation of his philosophy and has resulted in a fracas that has engaged the attention of Jürgen Habermas, Philippe Lacoue-Labarthe, Lyotard, and Derrida, to name a few. At the forefront of a contemporary discussion, "*l'affaire* Heidegger" opens the question of whether Heidegger's thought should continue to be appropriated in the study of religion.

What has gone unnoticed in earlier theological uses of Heidegger's account of valuing from 1945 to 1968 is his suggestive description of the being of things. In a move reminiscent of Taoist thought, the thing-being of a jug is seen to depend upon the void or emptiness that both takes and keeps what is poured. The meaning of this taking and keeping lies not, as might be supposed, in the function of storing or retaining but rather in its character as an outpouring that is also a gesture of giving. The act of pouring, Heidegger proclaims in the essay "The Thing," is essentially one of gift giving, a libation for the immortal gods "who receive back the gift of giving, as the gift of donation. . . . In the gift of the outpouring, earth and sky, divinities and mortals dwell together all at once" (1971, 173). The student of the history of Christianity may recognize in the emphasis on self-emptying and filling, not the libations of Heidegger's Hellenes but the metaphor of the soul's emptiness that will be filled by divine love. The link is made explicit in Heidegger's remark that for Meister Eckhart the word "thing" is applied to the soul, that "love is of such a nature that it changes man into the thing he loves" (1971, 176).

Derrida, following Heidegger's promising lead, suggests that one is no longer to ask the Kantian question about the conditions of possibility of the gift but rather whether giving itself is possible. The moment that a gift enters into the circle of exchange, whether of commodities or signs, it loses the gratuitousness that gift giving implies. Derrida writes that "The gift, if there is any, does not even belong to practical reason. It should remain a stranger to morality, to the will, . . . to the law or to the *il faut* (you must, you have to) of practical reason. It *should* surpass *duty* itself: duty beyond duty" (1992, 156). Beyond discourse and economy, the gift cannot appear, exist, mean anything: that is, it cannot embody value. If there is anything that can count as a gift, then we must acquiesce to a transcendental illusion of the gift, not in a straightforwardly Kantian way but rather by acknowledging the unforeseeability, the chanciness of giving. The imperative to commit oneself to this illusion is to agree to the necessity of a return to the sphere of economy. No longer is the gift to be troped in terms of Eckhart's description of an outpouring of love in the soul-thing. Instead, the student of religion may think of Mahayanna Buddhist descriptions of the Boddhisattva who agrees to remain within the world illusion in order to bestow upon others the sacrifical gift of a self that is itself no-self, an illusion. Not only is the calculative view of value as grounded in judgment contested by the ambiguity of the gift, but the alternative view of value, prizing, holding dear, founders in that there may be nothing to prize, no giver or recipient to treasure it.

Unaffected by the radical critiques of value by continental thinkers, many Anglo-American philosophers continue to regard moral behavior as bound up with judgments that depend on normative constructs even if there is considerable disagreement about how these constructs are derived and applied. While it is impossible to do justice to the vast literature that has emerged in this area since 1971, the publication date of John Rawls's landmark *Theory of Justice,* Rawls's perspective and that of ethicist Alan Gewirth exemplify an important trend: the locating of value in the social and economic good conferred upon others. Like a classical social contract theorist, Rawls contends that unlimited self-interest must give way to the more modest claims of self-preservation and social order if the parties are to reach an agreement. In a well-worn parable, Rawls describes the principles of justice as those a rational agent situated behind a veil of ignorance would choose. Behind the veil are concealed the future social and economic status and the talents of the agent as well as the type of society he or she will inhabit. Confronted with the problem of apportioning a society's goods, a rational agent will choose rules that are likely to insure that "all social primary goods—liberty and opportunity, income and wealth are to be distributed equally unless an unequal distribution is to the advantage of the least favored" (1971, 302). In criticism of this position, Alasdair MacIntyre contends that Rawls's asocial self could hardly understand social needs or the importance of conferring rights upon others and would be unlikely to enter into an agreement to benefit the less favored.

Like Kant, Alan Gewirth contends that there is a supreme principle of morality, denial of which is self-contradictory. The PGC or Principle of Generic Consistency is a call to "Act in accord with the generic rights of your recipients as well as of yourself" (1978, 135). Positively it enjoins people to help others attain necessary goods when it causes no personal harm and negatively to refrain from doing harm to or coercing others. It has been argued against Gewirth that he has not established that agents have a right to freedom but only that they desire it, and that no responsibility can be shown to follow from desire. Appeal to universalizability does not help because need and desire are precisely what cannot be universalized.

These criticisms reflect *in nuce* difficulties bound up with an issue that remains marginal to Anglo-American value theory, that is, the meaning of alterity, of the otherness of the other person. The theories cited allow for inequities resulting from social and economic difference but see in the development of conceptual instruments a possibility for creating corrective measures. Yet in the absence of a more primordial analysis of otherness, doing good to others is at bottom grounded in self-interest such that value inheres in the self. The agent conceives of the other as another myself, numerically distinct but otherwise like me, to whom rights and goods must be extended. But the term "other" loses its force unless self and other are radically incommensurable. The meaning of alterity as applied in the study of ethics and religion is at the forefront of current debate.

Heidegger's account of social existence as being-with-others offers a starting point for addressing the issue but is insufficiently radical in that the other and the I are merely coequals in common undertakings in a shared world. In the thought of Emmanuel Lévinas, the other is given its most extreme articulation in that the other and I are different *en principe*. Even the effort to know the other reduces her or his otherness in that objects of cognition become a property of one's own consciousness. The other is not first apprehended and moral value added on, but rather the other is given in the formless immediacy of a moral intuition that proscribes violence against her or him. Neither the object of sexual intention nor of knowledge, the other imposes a demand for self-sacrifice. With the concentration of value in the other, theorizing about morality is bypassed.

The view that theory cannot provide the underpinnings for moral conduct is challenged on other grounds by Richard Rorty who argues in *Contingency, Irony, and Solidarity* (1989) that values cannot be grounded and that theories are abstractions about values that fail to motivate moral behavior, whereas a society's beliefs and practices are better suited to insuring such behavior. This attack on theory has been criticized on the grounds that historical experience provides ample evidence that societies will underwrite genocide, racism, gender inequities, and other practices and, moreover, that such values can be invalidated only by appealing to values held by other societies in what would appear to be an infinite regress. This is especially vexing when appeals to one religion are invoked to uphold some given value of another.

As an alternative to ethical theory and total relativism, some ethicists, for example, MacIntyre, Martha Nussbaum, and Stanley Hauerwas, turn to narrative as a discursive framework that exhibits concrete lives in moral contexts. Not only is a narrative an emplotting of events in time enacted by its protagonists but, as Derrida insists, it is a juridical discourse in which a demand is made on someone to recount something that is true. Even nondidactic narratives exhibit values. Narratives do not mirror but orchestrate events in the interest of the story's point. Unlike the relation of theory to example in which the temporality of the example is suppressed in the interest of the theory, narrative, like life, is temporal. Even when recounted in the indicative, narrative episodes may exert what J. L. Austin calls perlocutionary (imperative) force such that values espoused by a story's characters may be read as demands for imitation.

It has been argued against a narrative ethic that in the absence of a non-narrative plane of morality there is no way to select among competing stories those that promote desirable values. The printed or filmed story that treats murder as an expression of freedom may invite imitation, but such an assessment can only be made on the basis of a rule or of some competing narrative. It is just here that otherness may be invoked as a promising locus of value to shore up this weakness in narrative ethics: the otherness of the narrative subject constitutes an exhortation to elude violence and to refrain from the abuse of power. It can be said that narratives of violence fail to exhibit this proscription. Yet, it can be responded, the other as other (like the gift) *simulates* a "transcendental condition" or a "master signifier" that guides but does not mandate juridical norms. In response to their awareness of the caveats surrounding claims to objectivity, scholars of religion generally recognize the mandate of alterity in depicting the beliefs and practices that embody values.

In sum, the interpretation of value remains a focal point for the study of religion even if the ways of attributing worth have changed. Refusing to consign the ascription of values to the limbo of emotive utterances in the manner of early and midcentury positivism, Anglo-American philosophers now debate the manner in which value should be determined in particular situations, as well as methodological issues bound up with how value is to be ascribed generally. Community consensus, personal and communal narrative, and juridical models play significant roles in this process.

Taking a different tack, continental thinkers and those influenced by them see acts of valuing as driven by power constellations, desires, or hidden ontological claims. At the same time, these accounts themselves reflect ascriptions of value, for example, the view that desire can be commodified suggests that one ought to value the liberation of desire from commodification. If value is seen as determined by power, the question of how a society's assigning of value might benefit those who are powerless inevitably arises. This worry has prompted some thinkers to propose that the other, whether construed individually or collectively, is to be understood as the ultimate source of worth. Claims of otherness bring to bear interests apart from those of the investigator who inquires into the beliefs and practices of the world's religions. Neither prizing nor holding dear disappear from contemporary accounts of value; rather, the multiple ways in which these attitudes function in a variety of contexts is brought to the fore.

Suggested Readings

Cooey, Paula. 1994. *Religious Imagination and the Body: A Feminist Analysis.*
Cornell, Drucilla, Michel Rosenfeld, and David Gray Carlson, eds. 1992. *Deconstruction and the Possibility of Justice.*
Hick, John. 1985. *Problems of Religious Pluralism.*
MacIntyre, Alasdair. 1988. *Whose Justice? Which Rationality?*
Paden, William E. 1988. *Religious Worlds: The Comparative Study of Religion.*
Peperzak, Adriaan T., ed. 1995. *Ethics as First Philosophy: The Significance of Emmanuel Lévinas for Philosophy, Literature, and Religion.*
Rorty, Richard. 1989. *Contingency, Irony, Solidarity.*

Taylor, Mark C. 1987. *Altarity*.
Wyschogrod, Edith. 1990. *Saints and Postmodernism: Revisioning Moral Philosophy*.

REFERENCES

Cohen, Hermann. 1972. *The Religion of Reason out of the Sources of Judaism,* translated by Simon Kaplan. New York: Fredrick Ungar Publishing Co.

Deleuze, Gilles. 1991. *Empiricism and Subjectivity: An Essay on Hume's Theory of Human Nature,* translated by Constantine T. Boundas. New York: Columbia University Press.

Deleuze, Gilles, and Guattari, Felix. 1982. *Anti-Oedipus: Capitalism and Schizophrenia,* translated by Robert Hurley, Mark Seem, and Helen R. Lane. New York: Viking Press.

———. 1988. *A Thousand Plateaus: Capitalism and Schizophrenia,* translated by Brian Massumi. Minneapolis: University of Minnesota Press.

Derrida, Jacques. 1992. *Given Time I: Counterfeit Money,* translated by Peggy Kamuf. Chicago: University of Chicago Press.

———. 1995. "The Work of Intellectuals and the Press." In *Points: Interviews, 1974–1994,* translated by Peggy Kamuf. Stanford: Stanford University Press.

Geertz, Clifford. 1995. *After the Fact: Two Countries, Four Decades, One Anthropologist.* Cambridge: Harvard University Press.

Gewirth, Alan. 1978. *Reason and Morality.* Chicago: University of Chicago Press.

Goodman, L. E. 1996. *God of Abraham.* Oxford: Oxford University Press.

Heidegger, Martin. 1947. "Letter on Humanism," translated by Frank A. Capuzzi and J. Glenn Gray. In *Basic Writings,* edited by David Farrell Krell.

———. 1959. *An Introduction to Metaphysics,* translated by Ralph Mannheim. New Haven: Yale University Press.

———. 1971. "The Thing." In *Poetry, Language, Thought,* translated by Albert Hofstadter. New York: Harper and Row.

Hume, David. 1947. *Dialogues Concerning Natural Religion.* Indianapolis: The Library of Liberal Arts.

Kant, Immanuel. 1960. *Religion within the Limits of Reason Alone,* translated by Theodore M. Greene and Hoyt H. Hudson. New York: Harper and Row.

Kierkegaard, Søren. 1970. *Fear and Trembling,* translated by W. Lowrie. Princeton: Princeton University Press.

Lyotard, Jean-François. *The Differend: Phrases in Dispute,* translated by Georges Van der Abeele. Minneapolis: University of Minnesota Press.

MacIntyre, Alasdair. 1988. *Whose Justice? Which Rationality?* Notre Dame: Notre Dame University Press.

Marx, Karl. 1906. *Capital,* translated by Samuel Moore and Edward Aveling. New York: Modern Library.

Masuzawa, Tomoko. 1993. *In Search of Dreamtime: The Quest for the Origin of Religion.* Chicago: University of Chicago Press.

Nietzsche, Friedrich. 1974. *The Gay Science,* translated by Walter Kaufmann. New York: Random House.

———. 1982. *The Antichrist.* In *The Portable Nietzsche,* translated by Walter Kaufmann. New York: Penguin.

Rawls, John. 1971. *A Theory of Justice.* Cambridge: Harvard University Press.

Ricoeur, Paul. 1967. *The Symbolism of Evil.* Boston: Beacon Press.

Rorty, Richard. 1989. *Contingency, Irony and Solidarity.* New York: Cambridge University Press.

TWENTY-TWO

Writing

David Tracy

The three Western monotheistic religions, Judaism, Christianity, and Islam, are sometimes described as the religions of the book. In one sense the designation is accurate enough. Unlike such traditions as Buddhism, Hinduism, and Confucianism, the three Abrahamic religions understand their sacred written texts not as classics, nor even as sacred texts, but as Scripture and thereby as somehow participatory in what is construed as the revelation of God. To focus upon the presently much discussed role of writing, it is useful to notice first the role of written texts in certain religions, especially those with Scriptures in the strict sense.

There is a new need to reflect upon the nature of writing and religion, in both the empirical and the theoretical senses. For example, the role of the Vedas as sacred texts in that complex of Indian religions often named Hinduism (ritualistic, mythological, or speculative) or the role of the "classics" in both Confucianism and neo-Confucianism occasions hermeneutical perplexity concerning the empirically different roles of writing in the various religions. Judaism, Christianity, and Islam, on the other hand, provide distinct hermeneutical puzzles on the relationship of writing and written texts relative to what is construed as divine revelation. In one sense, Islam is both the clearest and the most perplexing of the monotheistic religions on the issue of writing, for in Islam (alone among the monotheistic religions) the written text (the Qur'an) *is* the revelation. Thus the role of writing is particularly acute for the hermeneutics of Islamic texts. In Judaism, there are kabalistic and some rabbinic interpretations that express a position analogous to the Islamic concentration on the role of writing in written texts insofar as the written scriptural texts somehow "participate" in the divine reality. Indeed, in some forms of Kabalah, even the very materiality of the letters of the text at times have this function. Writing as such is thereby revelatory. Part of the flourishing interest in kabalistic methods of interpretation since the major surge of contemporary scholarship initiated by Gershom Scholem stems from the surprising similarities between some kabalistic theories of materiality and writing and some contemporary theories on the interpretation of writing and materiality.

However, the more usual rabbinic formulation of Jewish hermeneutics hesitates to affirm the kabalistic position on the revelatory role of the materiality of writing. Instead, classical Jewish biblical and rabbinic modes of interpretation, in contrast to Islamic hermeneutics, do not ordinarily affirm the written text as, in the strict sense, revelation. Instead, in biblical and rabbinic interpretations, Jewish hermeneutics more often concentrates on a dialectic between oral Torah and written Torah. Some contemporary Jewish thinkers propose that a relationship of both oral Torah and written Torah may be found in either a revelatory event as encounter (Buber) or in the revelatory "founding events" occurring at Mount Sinai and during the Exodus (Fackenheim). The biblical texts (in the latter view) are interpreted as witnesses or testaments to founding revelatory events like Mount Sinai and the Exodus and not as the revelation itself. Franz Rosenzweig's complex and increasingly influential position (especially through the work of Emmanuel Lévinas) is far closer to contemporary discussions of the centality of writing (and thereby, for Lévinas, of the centrality of ethics over ontology and, one might add, the superiority of Jewish modes of interpretation over classical Greco-Christian interpretations of both Scripture and philosophy). The exceptional complexity and variety of Jewish hermeneutics on writing, written and oral tradition, and revelation are well documented in the many debates in biblical, rabbinic, and kabalistic hermeneutics, as well as in such distinctly modern notions of the relationship of revelation and text in the differing positions of Rosenzweig and Buber, of Lévinas and Fackenheim, and of Cohen, Handelmann, and Kepnes.

Focusing on the role of written texts in the different religions is one of the more fruitful and complex scholarly possibilities for comparative religious hermeneutics, both *within* and *among* traditions. For example, note the differences in Judaism among biblical, rabbinic, and kabalistic positions on writing or the equally acute differences among the contemporary Jewish thinkers mentioned earlier. Similarly, note the differences among the three Western monotheistic traditions, which acknowledge certain written texts as "Scripture" in contrast to either Hinduism, with its sacred but not strictly scriptural texts, or Confucianism, with its classical texts.

It is also the case, as such historians of religions as Lawrence Sullivan have justly insisted, that writing (especially in the form of written texts, whether scriptural, sacred, or religious classical) has often played too central a role in scholarship on religion with unfortunate results, namely, disregard for the fact that many religious traditions (sometimes named primal or indigenous or local) *highlight* material realities other than writing to play the central role in the religion. The result is clear. Many religious traditions in which writing does not play the central role are often, even in major scholarship, misinterpreted as "archaic" or even "primitive" when they are merely different from religions in which writing (especially in the form of written texts) *does* function as the central material reality. Indeed, these other traditions have often been seriously misinterpreted and, even more seriously, marginalized as not among the "classic" universal religious traditions or ways. The emphasis on written text in so much religious scholarship as well as in most contemporary hermeneutics needs its own hermeneutics of suspicion, to which point we will return later, after a more detailed study of writing, written text, and Scripture in one religious tradition, Christianity. A future comparative hermeneutics of writing in the religions also needs to direct attention to the radical differences among the three Western monotheistic traditions themselves on the issues of writing, word, and revelation, as well as on the distinct role of writing in nonscriptural traditions and, even more so, in traditions not centered around a written text.

In the meantime, as a partial contribution to future comparative hermeneutics of writing and written texts in religion, I shall spend the bulk of this essay attempting to clarify the hermeneutics of writing, written text, and revelation-as-presence in the complex case of Christianity (or, perhaps more accurately, Christianities). Here the greatest puzzle and complexity lie not in traditional Christian theological debates on "Scripture alone" versus "Scripture and tradition" but, rather, in Christian self-understanding of the hermeneutical relationship of the presence-oriented category "Word" to Scripture as *written* text and, thereby, to writing. *The* decisive revelation in the Christian construal of reality is understood to be the self-manifestation, or self-presencing, of God in the Logos, the Word—Jesus Christ believed present to the Christian community in word and sacrament as well as in communal and personal experience.

The importance in Western culture of this Christian understanding of revelation as God's self-presencing in Word as it is rendered in writing in the different forms of Scripture would be difficult to overemphasize. The recent theoretical work on Western "logocentrism" and writing (especially Jacques Derrida) in Western philosophy and culture needs to be explicitly related to a study of Christian self-understanding within the discipline designed for critical self-understanding—that is, theology, the discipline that asks "Greek" (logocentric) questions of Jewish and Hellenistic Jewish scriptural texts, especially (for the early Christian communities) narrative "gospel" texts. This traditional Greco-Christian alliance on the centrality of Word-as-presence and divine self-manifestation, and, as a consequence, the traditional Greco-Christian characterization of writing as derivative, has clearly helped to occasion such hierarchically paired Western religious and cultural categories as spirit over letter, ideality over materiality, reason over feeling, content in written sign over form, signified over signifier, identity over difference, and self-presence in self-understanding over all "derivative," distancing forms of writing.

Historically, the first Christian temptation was to misread Judaism, its parent religion, as legalistic and materialistic under newly forged Greco-Christian rubrics like "letter" (materiality) and "spirit" (ideal self-presence). The second Christian temptation was to misunderstand itself hermeneutically by denying the importance of writing for Christian self-understanding and thereby for Christian critical thinking (theology) as distinct from Greek philosophy. The third Christian temptation has been to misread the complexity of Islamic hermeneutics (on the written text as revelation) by reading Islamic interpretations of writing and written texts in terms more appropriate to Christian hermeneutics. These Christian temptations (not necessities) seem to have been prompted, on the hermeneutical side, by the intrinsic complexity and frequent confusions in Christian self-understanding of the relationships established among revelation, Word, writing, and Scripture as written text. The recent rediscovery of the central role of written narrative in Christian self-understanding has provided one occasion to return to Christian interpretations of revelation, Word-as-presence, writing, and written text.

In the modern period since Hegel and Schelling, the Christian symbol of divine revelation has ordinarily been understood as the event of divine self-manifestation in the Word, Jesus Christ, as testified to or witnessed to in the written words of Scripture. Every element in this descriptive theological/philosophical definition of Christian revelation has occasioned controversy in modern Christian hermeneutics, and every element needs clarification if the intricate relationships of Word, writing, and written text in Christian hermeneutical self-understanding are to be understood.

To clarify the principal elements in this definition is to recall some of the central debates of contemporary Christian hermeneutics.

I. Event

"Event" language in contemporary Christian thought is employed to indicate what is construed as the purely gratuitous or "gracious" character of divine revelation. The very fact that God reveals Godself *is* understood as grace, an event, a happening. Hence in Christian self-understanding, revelation can never be interpreted as solely a human achievement, work, or necessity but must be understood as a divine event, a happening, a gratuity, grace. Hermeneutically, the category event *(Ereignis)* is applicable even to Word-as-Word-event *(Sprach-Ereignis)*—as a happening of language itself and, therefore, not under the control of the modern subject. The role of writing in Western cultural, philosophical, and theological-hermeneutical debates, which has been greatly influenced by Christian self-understanding of Word, is often left obscure.

II. The Event of Divine Self-Manifestation

The language of divine self-manifestation indicates that the category "revelation" is not to be construed primarily (as in many medieval and Enlightenment understandings of revelation) as uncovering "propositional truths" that would otherwise be unknown (i.e., "supernatural" or "revealed" truths). Rather, in modern Christian thought since the Romantics and Hegel, revelation has been construed primarily on some form of encounter model as an event of divine self-manifestation to humanity. This event-as-encounter model of revelation further assumes that some personlike characteristics (namely, intelligence and love) can be employed to understand the reality of God as God manifests Godself as Wisdom and Love. The dangers of anthropomorphism here are acknowledged as real, especially in Schleiermacher, who defended speech pertaining to the "living" God as more accurate than that concerning a "personal" God. For many Christian as well as Jewish and Islamic thinkers, however, some personalist language is needed to understand the covenantal God of the Hebrew Bible; the God manifested in the event and person of Jesus the Christ in the New Testament; and the gracious, compassionate, just, merciful Allah of the Qur'an. Recall, for example, Martin Buber's famous critique of Spinoza's impersonalist language and Buber's own insistence on the biblical God as Thou. Indeed, despite some strong critiques of the use of personal language for God, most modern Jewish, Christian, and Islamic thinkers who employ the category of revelation at all as divine self-manifestation appeal at some point to carefully qualified, analogical or dialectical personalist language to express "divine self-revelation."

Hermeneutically, the use of the category "manifestation" in revelation as divine self-manifestation is also indicative of the philosophical notion of truth in philosophical hermeneutics as primordially an event of manifestation or disclosure/concealment in Heidegger, Gadamer, and Ricoeur. On the side of human reception, the correlate to manifestation is "re-cognition" (Plato and the platonic strand in Western culture). In a similar manner, the category often employed as a counterpart on the side of human reception to the event/gift/grace of revelation as divine self-manifestation is the gift, grace, happening (never work) of "faith" as reorientation of trust in and loyalty to the God presencing Godself in the Logos.

III. The Event of Divine Self-Manifestation in the Word, Jesus Christ

The paradoxical and decisive event of divine self-manifestation for Christian self-understanding is, as Karl Barth insisted, not merely an event but a person, that is, the unsubstitutable person of Jesus of Nazareth, as that Jesus is understood to be present to the Christian community as the proclaimed and manifested Christ and, thereby, as the decisive Word-event of divine self-manifestation. This decisive Word-event of divine self-manifestation is understood among Christians as the divine self-presencing in the currently enacted Word and eucharistic sacrament and in the written words of Scripture. Therein lies the complexity of Christianity on presence and writing.

The dialectic of the Word in Christian self-understanding begins with the insight that Word is both Logos and Kerygma. Hermeneutically Word is, for Christian self-understanding, as Barth argued, not merely an event but a person, (that is) both disclosure/manifestation (Word-as-Logos) and proclamation/distance/disruption (Word-as-Kerygma). In history-of-religions terms, a Christian understanding of Logos can be seen as one instance of religion as manifestation, especially the manifestation of primordial correspondences obtaining throughout all reality (Eliade). The primal, meditative, and mystical traditions analyzed by many scholars of religion are the clearest examples of these Logos traditions. So too is the Christian understanding of the eucharistic sacrament as the sign that renders present what it signifies. Indeed, sacrament and proclaimed Word-as-sacrament (Luther) are the clearest Christian analogies of Word-as-Logos manifesting all reality (God/cosmos/community/self). All reality, in sum, is understood through sacrament and Word-as-Logos as a vast system of disclosive and participatory, analogical correspondences uniting God, cosmos, and humanity in and through the self-presencing Logos.

In history-of-religions terms, Word-as-Kerygma or Word-as-proclamation also becomes word as distance, difference, interruption, disruption, that is, word as a distancing from any felt sense of manifesting participation. Whereas Word-as-Logos discloses presence and thereby a vast synthesis of participatory and analogical correspondences, Word-as-proclamation distances us from such correspondence. Kerygma interrupts all senses of continuity, participation, and rootedness (all of which the Western monotheistic religions often label "paganism"). When the German Christian thinker J. B. Metz (here following Walter Benjamin) describes religion using the one word "interruption," he describes this classical kerygmatic trajectory of the distancing, disrupting, prophetic, apocalyptic, proclamatory Word in both Judaism and Christianity.

In Christian thought the dialectic between Word as disclosive Logos and Word as interruptive Kerygma can be found in the history of the classical dualities become dialectical antinomies (and, at the limit, hardened dualisms) in Christian self-understanding. For example, in early Christianity there is a strong contrast between Logos Christologies beginning with the disclosive manifestory Gospel of John and apocalyptic Christologies of distance and disruption like the Gospel of Mark with its nonclosure, self-interruptive writing or the works of Paul that use a distancing, disruptive, dialectical language for rendering in writing the presence/absence of Christ crucified. In later Christian thought there is a similar contrast in Christian theologies between the emphasis on presence in the comprehensible/incomprehensible Logos traditions' understanding of God in Thomas Aquinas and Meister Eckhart and the presence/absence orientations of the hidden/revealed proclamatory understanding of God in Martin Luther and John Calvin. In recent Christian thought, Paul Tillich's formulation of the dialectic of Protestant principle (word as disruptive, critical, distancing suspicious proclamation) and Catholic substance (word as self-presencing Logos) continues the same dialectic. Indeed, the term "Catholic substance" is best understood in the Catholic interpretations of the eucharistic sacrament as a symbol that renders present what it *materially* signifies (in material like water or bread and wine united to the materiality of words).

Catholic Christianity (with its emphasis on a Logos-centered presence) gives less importance to the distancing materiality of writing than Protestant Christianity. This Catholic emphasis on presence is made even more central for Christian self-understanding in the Christian Orthodox tradition's stress on the awareness of God's presence in icon, liturgy, cosmos, and Logos Christologies. In conceptual terms, an interpreter of Christianity should also note the differences between the analogical languages of classical Orthodox, Anglican, and Roman Catholic theologies and the negative dialectical theologies of classical Reformation theologies. Moreover, contemporary Christian theological discussions challenge both analogical and dialectical second-order languages by a new theological emphasis on narrative first-order language (Hans Frei) and by reflection on the phenomenon of writing itself (Mark Taylor). Even in terms of the central Christian symbols of the Incarnation, the cross, and the Resurrection, Word-as-

Logos instinctively appeals to a sense of presence, whereas Word-as-Kerygma instinctively appeals to difference, distance, disruption.

It would also be possible to clarify the Christian understanding of Word through a fuller exposition of one or another of the classical Christian dialectics: Incarnation/cross; sacrament/word; cosmos/history; symbol/allegory; icon/idol; analogy/dialectic; comprehensible/incomprehensible God or hidden/revealed God; Creation/Redemption; nature/grace or grace/sin; love/justice; participation/distance; continuity/discontinuity; regularity/interruption. Pervading all these dialects, however, is the originating Christian dialectic of revelation-as-Word: Jesus the Christ understood as both self-presencing Logos and self-distancing Kerygma. It also would be possible to see this same dialectic of presence and distance continued in the two classical readings of the Christian tradition: either the prophetic/apocalyptic reading of the Word-as-proclamation beginning with Mark and Paul or the meditative tradition that pervades meditative, mystical, and archaic (cosmic) readings of Word as disclosive Logos beginning with the Gospel of John, the Gospel of Christ-as-presence, spirit, Logos.

As any reader of the history of Christian thought and practice can readily observe, all these distinct dialectical formulations of the Christian dialectic of Word-as-Logos and Word-as-Kerygma have been tried and reformulated over and over again in the history of Christian reflection. Word, in this Christian scenario, seems to suggest both close proximity and distance, presence and absence, similarity and difference, participation and interruption. To ignore this dual function of Jesus as the Christ for Christian self-understanding is also to ignore the fact that the Word, Jesus Christ, is for Christians testified to and rendered present in written words, that is, in Scripture. This singular fact of writing and written text cannot be insignificant to the "present" community, even in sacrament (a sign in which signified and signifier are assumed to cohere, unlike other uses of the word "sign"). Moreover, the creed of the principal Christian churches—"We believe *in* Jesus Christ *with* the apostles"—depends on some notion of the Word's presence for the professing commuity. The professing, worshipping community understands itself as rendering present to all Christian believers the same Jesus Christ in Word and sacrament. The written texts of Scripture are for Christians the authoritative *norma normans non normata*. However, the Scripture is also constituted by writing. The written texts called Scripture are understood to assure that the Christ experienced as present in proclaimed Word and sacrament to the current Christian community is the same Christ witnessed to and testified to as present to the apostolic communities who "wrote" the texts named "the apostolic writings" or the New Testament. Earlier Reformation debates on "Scripture alone" or "Scripture and tradition" did not address this important hermeneutical role of Scripture *as writing* in Christianity.

Furthermore, the recent recovery of the import of the gospel as a genre engaged in narrative productive of meaning and not merely taxonomic of meaning can also clarify this peculiar role of written narrative scriptural texts for Christian self-understanding. For the major genre for the original Christian communities' self-interpretation is gospel: that peculiar, perhaps unique, compositional mode that unites Word-as-proclamation and disclosive Word rendered present through written narrative. Amidst the diversity of narratives in the four Gospels and elsewhere in the New Testament, moreover, the passion narratives are the principal stories by which the Christian community first rendered in written form its understanding of who this singular Jesus of Nazareth proclaimed as the Christ is. It is undoubtedly an exaggeration (but a useful one) to say with Martin Kahler that the four Gospels are four passion narratives with extended and different "introductions." The reason why this statement is an exaggeration is that the different introductions are described more accurately as different renderings of the Word in and through the writing constituting the passion narratives of the Gospels.

Indeed the recent theoretical debates on writing, initiated in the 1960s by French thinkers such as Roland Barthes and Derrida, have not only encouraged a rethinking of rabbinic and kabalistic practices on writing but also thrown a new light on the role of writing in Christian self-understanding. There are good theoretical reasons to hold that the interplay of presence (in spoken, proclaimed word and sacrament) and Scripture-as-writing in Christian self-understanding needs more attention for clarifying Christian hermeneutics of Word and Scripture.

In fact, Christian theology, with its heritage of Greek logocentrism, has characteristically obscured rather than clarified the role of writing, and thereby Scripture, in its own self-understanding. As Derrida has argued in several works and readings, in Western thought from Plato's *Phaedrus* through Saussure's *Course in General Linguistics* and Hegel and Husserl's theories of signs, writing has been interpreted as being derivative compared with speaking. In speaking, speaker and listener seem present to one another. Indeed, self-reflection can seem to suggest a form of self-presence by which my reflective and spoken words seem to be transparent representations of my thought. This theoretical model of self-presence through spoken and reflective speech constitutes most Greco-Christian models of self-communication, freed from both external forces and the seemingly derivative, material, merely technical character of writing.

This recent Derridean theoretical position on writing is, in my view, exaggerated in some cases. For example, did any thinker—even Hegel and Husserl—hold to the kind of full, simple, whole self-presence that the recent theorists of writing sometimes assume they did? Nevertheless, the new theoretical advances on presence and writing, as correctives, constitute advances for understanding Scripture. In Christian self-understanding, except for the unique status of Christ-as-Logos, there is no claim to full or simple self-presence in either manifesting Word-as-Logos or proclaimed word as rendering present the Word in distance (Bultmann) or sacrament. There is some presencing, to be sure, but mediated in and through writing/scripture. Presence is never full, simple, or whole.

The unconscious drive to repress the reality of writing in favor of some illusion of full self-presence and full presence of God and cosmos in Word or sacrament or "mystical" experience is an unconscious drive to encourage (and at times enforce) hierarchical readings of all reality. In fact, the notorious Western (especially Greco-Christian) dualisms bear striking resemblances to the hierarchization of speech and writing: spirit and letter, ideality and materiality, soul and body, reason and feeling, male and female. The newest and crucial addition to those dualisms is speech and writing. Writing can *seem* to express "undesirable," hierarchically "lower" features of language—distance, absence, materiality, mere technique, possible misunderstanding compared with speech—which can seem self-transparent and self-present. In fact, these features of language are as constitutive of speech as they are of writing. Moreover, the principal written forms of the Christian New Testament can all be seen to employ these very conditions of writing.

Much postbiblical, more conceptual and abstract Christian theological language (like the philosophical language it so obviously resembles) may claim to "clarify" and "develop" and above all "control" figurative scriptural language in the direction of fuller self-presence. But does such language (as word or sacrament or religious experience) not run the risk of repressing those very characteristics of all language best seen in (but not confined to) writing: distance, alterity, difference, materiality, lack of full or simple self-presence? Scripture as writing does not simply participate in presence but can indeed function paradoxically as the warning of the idolatrous Christian temptation to illusions of full self-presence or divine presence to the Christian. Hence the new theories of writing help Jewish and Christian (and, even more, Islamic) understandings of the central role of Scripture as not merely testimony to past presence but *as writing*. Understood as writing, Scripture exposes all pretensions to full self-presence and corrects the fatal repressions and hierarchizations that have plagued much of Western thought and existence.

A focus on writing in religious studies offers many other possibilities for scholarly critical reflection. Two developments beyond the hermeneutical and poststructuralist debates demand notice in this brief essay. First, the new theoretical emphasis on the materiality of writing has allowed for development of additional critical skills for unmasking the silences, the power conflicts, and the repressions embedded in the materiality of writing. Against a text's own drive for coherence and domination by some "master" discourses (even by the uses of such discourses in the "masters of suspicion," Freud, Marx, and Nietzsche), the materiality of writing unveils the traces of conflicts, the repressions, and the silences in any text. As a major example of this development, feminist criticism of all religious texts, but especially of those expressing patriarchal repressions and idealistic self-delusions, has freed contemporary criticism to show how these texts, in and through the material writing, conceal these traces and silences. This concealment is tied to a belief in the disclosure of an ideality allied to disparaging the capability of the "lower" materiality of writing to communicate "pure" ideas. Writing itself, of course, has also been used by colonizing powers to dominate those "others" whose "nonliterate" and nonalphabetic traditions of writing allow them to be interpreted as lower than cultures with written texts and the writing techniques of the dominant cultures. The work of such scholars as Cornel West, Henry Louis Gates, and Mary Daly have confirmed the truth of Barbara Johnson's insistence that "It may well be that it is only in a text-centered culture that one can privilege speech in a logocentric way."

Second, and finally, the recent theoretical emphasis on the materiality of writing has also provided the opportunity for scholars of religion to call into serious question the scholarly emphasis on written texts in religious traditions in favor of the far more expansive category of "materiality" or "material culture" as the more promising route for the study of religion. The central need here is to study all the physical, material objects (including but not confined to written texts) that different cultural and religious traditions employ. The historian of religion Lawrence Sullivan, for example, has shown that the capacities to conceptualize and to be reflective are deeply influenced by the particular matter given primacy by a culture. In Western cultures, that reflexivity is grounded principally in the materiality of writing. But in non-text-centered cultures, reflexivity may be rendered more authentically by such materials as performance, manual labor, pictures, and, above all, the body. Hence, representation of the principal *ideas* or *concepts* of a religious culture is more accurately described as a *presentation* or a *rendering present* of the ideas in and through a particular form of materiality. Writing, therefore, is only one form of materiality demanding interpretation in order that the principal ideas of a culture or a religion may be understood.

It seems safe to predict that in the future the former domination of written texts in the study of religion will be challenged (even in the interpretations of scriptural traditions) both by the new information technologies and by the new paths of theory and research opened by the recent scholarly emphasis on writing: the recognition of the materiality of writing, which calls into question all claims for totality; the unveiling of the traces of the silences, conflicts, and power realities in all religious and cultural traditions; the expansion of the range of reflexivity in culture to *all* material objects, not only writing. The new theories of writing call for a more finely wrought hermeneutics of suspicion with regard to all the Western hierarchical dualisms: letter and spirit, materiality and ideality, female and male, speech and writing. How strange a sea change the phenomenon of writing now discloses for all contemporary interpreters of religion and culture.

SUGGESTED READINGS

Abel, Elizabeth, ed. 1982. *Writing and Sexual Difference.*
Barthes, Roland, [1953] 1967. *Writing Degree Zero.*
Derrida, Jacques. 1974. *Of Grammatology.*
———. 1973. *Writing and Difference.*

———. 1973. *Speech and Phenomena.*

Gates, Henry Louis, Jr., ed. 1986. *Race, Writing, and Difference.*

Handelmann, Susan. 1988. *The Slayers of Moses: The Emergence of Rabbinic Interpretation in Modern Literary Theory.*

Jeanrond, Werner G. 1988. *Text and Interpretation as Categories of Theological Thinking.*

———. 1991. *Theological Hermeneutics: Development and Significance.*

Johnson, Barbara, 1995. "Writing." In *Critical Terms for Literary Study,* edited by Frank Lentricchia and Thomas McLaughlin, 2d ed.

Ricoeur, Paul, 1981. *Hermeneutics and the Human Sciences,* edited by J. B. Thompson.

Sullivan, Lawrence, 1990. "Putting an End to the Text as Primary." In *Beyond the Classics? Essays in Religious Studies and Liberal Education,* edited by Frank E. Reynolds and Sheryl L. Buurkhalter.

Taylor, Mark. 1984. *Erring: A Postmodern A/theology.*

Contributors

ANTHONY F. AVENI is the Russell B. Colgate Professor of Astronomy and Anthropology at Colgate University. He is the author of *Empires of Time: Calendars, Clocks, and Cultures; Conversing with the Planets: How Science and Myth Invented the Cosmos; Behind the Crystal Ball: Magic, Science, and the Occult from Antiquity through the New Age;* and *Stairways to the Stars: Skywatching in Three Great Ancient Cultures.* He is currently at work on a book concerning his research on the giant ground drawings of ancient Nazca, Peru.

CATHERINE BELL teaches at Santa Clara University in California. In addition to her published work on ritual—notably, *Ritual Theory, Ritual Practice* and *Ritual: Perspectives and Dimensions*—she writes on various topics in Chinese religions.

GUSTAVO BENAVIDES is associate professor of religious studies at Villanova University. His areas of research include the comparative study of mysticism, the history of the study of religion, and the relation between religion and politics. He is the coeditor of *Religion and Political Power* and has contributed articles to a number of journals and books, most recently to *Religion, Historical Reflections/Réflexions historiques* and *Social Compass.* He is currently working on a book on the study of religion during the Weimar republic.

DANIEL BOYARIN is the Taubman Professor of Talmudic Culture and a member of the Departments of Near Eastern Studies and Women's Studies at the University of California, Berkeley. He is the author, most recently, of *Unheroic Conduct: The Rise of Heterosexuality and the Invention of the Jewish Man* and *A Radical Jew: Paul and the Politics of Identity.* He is currently completing a manuscript titled *Dying for God: The Discourse of Martyrdom and the Twin Birth of Christianity and Judaism.*

FRANCIS SCHÜSSLER FIORENZA is the Charles Chauncey Stillman Professor of Roman Catholic Theological Studies at Harvard University. He is the author of *Foundational Theology: Jesus and the Church;* the editor of *Systematic Theology: Roman Catholic Perspectives* and *Handbook of Catholic Theology;* and the editor and translator of Friedrich Schleiermacher, *Open Letters.*

SAM GILL is professor of religion at the University of Colorado at Boulder. He is the author of *Mother Earth: An American Story* and *Storytracking: Texts, Stories and Histories in Central Australia.*

GORDON D. KAUFMAN is the Edward Mallinckrodt, Jr. Professor of Divinity Emeritus at Harvard University. He is the author of a number of books, including most recently *In Face of Mystery: A Constructive Theology; An Essay on Theological Method,* 3d ed.; and *God—Mystery—Diversity: Christian Theology in a Pluralistic World.*

WILLIAM R. LaFLEUR is professor of Japanese studies and of religious studies and the Joseph B. Glossberg Term Professor of Humanities at the University of Pennsylvania. His books include *The Karma of Words: Buddhism and the Literary Arts in Medieval Japan; Liquid Life: Abortion and Buddhism in Japan;* and *Freaks and Philosophers: Minding the Body in Medieval Japan* (in press).

BRUCE B. LAWRENCE is professor of Islamic studies and history of religions at Duke University. He is the author of *Defenders of God: The Fundamentalist Revolt against the Modern Age* and *Shattering the Myth: Islam Beyond Violence* as well as numerous works on premodern South Asian Muslim culture. He is currently working on two books, one exploring twentieth-century global religion, and the other immigrant Asian communities and their multiple religious formations in North America.

BRUCE LINCOLN is professor of history of religions at the University of Chicago. His writings include *Priests, Warriors, and Cattle; Discourse and the Construction of Society; Death, War, and Sacrifice;* and *Authority: Construction and Corrosion.*

DONALD S. LOPEZ, JR., is professor of Buddhist and Tibetan studies in the Department of Asian Languages and Cultures at the University of Michigan. His most recent books are *Prisoners of Shangri-La: Tibetan Buddhism and the West* and *Elaborations on Emptiness: Uses of the Heart Sutra.* He also recently edited and contributed to *Religions of Tibet in Practice* and *Curators of the Buddha: The Study of Buddhism under Colonialism.*

TOMOKO MASUZAWA teaches critical theory and religious studies at the University of North Carolina, Chapel Hill. She is the author of *In Search of Dreamtime: The Quest for the Origin of Religion,* and she is completing a book titled *The Invention of World Religions, or How the Idea of European Hegemony Came to Be Expressed in the Language of Pluralism and Diversity.*

MARGARET R. MILES is dean and vice president for academic affairs at the Graduate Theological Union, Berkeley, California. Her publications include *Image as Insight; Carnal Knowing: Female Nakedness and Religious Meaning in the Christian West; Desire and Delight: A New Reading of Augustine's "Confessions"; Seeing and Believing: Religion and Values in the Movies;* and *Reading for Life: Beauty, Pluralism, and Responsibility.*

JILL ROBBINS is associate professor of comparative literature and English at the State University of New York at Buffalo. She is the author of *Prodigal Son/Elder Brother: Interpretation and Alterity in Augustine, Petrarch, Kafka, Levinas* and *Altered Reading: Levinas and Literature.*

ROBERT H. SHARF is associate professor of Buddhist studies at the University of Michigan. He is the author of the forthcoming monograph *The "Treasure Store Treatise": Issues in the Study of Medieval Chinese Buddhism,* as well as a number of articles on Ch'an- and Zen-related subjects.

GREGORY SCHOPEN is professor of Sanskrit, Tibetan, and Buddhist studies at the University of Texas at Austin. A first volume of his collected papers has recently been published under the title *Bones, Stones, and Buddhist Monks.*

JONATHAN Z. SMITH is the Robert O. Anderson Distinguished Service Professor of the Humanities at the University of Chicago. His published works include *Map Is Not Territory: Studies in the History of Religions; Imaging Religion; To Take Place: Towards Theory in Ritual; Drudgery Divine: On the Comparison of Early Christianities and the Religions of Late Antiquity.* He is also general editor of *The Harper-Collins Dictionary of Religion.*

PAUL STOLLER is professor of anthropology at West Chester University. His books include *Sensuous Scholarship; Embodying Colonial Memories: Spirit Possession, Power, and the Hauka in West Africa; The Cinematic Griot: The Ethnography of Jean Rouch;* and *Fusion of the Worlds: An Ethnography of Possession among the Songhay of Niger.* He is currently conducting ethnographic field research among West African street vendors in New York City.

KENNETH SURIN teaches in the Literature Program at Duke University.

MICHAEL TAUSSIG teaches in the Anthropology Department of Columbia University. He has written on diverse subjects springing largely from fieldwork in Colombia since 1969—on economics, slavery, fetishism, shamanism, colonialism, state and paramilitary terror, mimesis, magic, and secrecy. His publications relevant to this volume include *Shamanism, Colonialism, and the Wild Man: A Study in Terror and Healing; The Nervous System; Mimesis and Alterity;* and *The Magic of the State.*

MARK C. TAYLOR is the Cluett Professor of Religion and Humanities and Director of the Center for Technology in the Arts and Humanities at Williams College. His many books include *Erring: A Postmodern A/theology; Deconstruction in Context; Altarity; Nots; Disfiguring: Art, Architecture, Religion;* and *Hiding.* He is co-author/producer with José Márquez of *The Réal—Las Vegas, Nevada,* a CD-ROM published by the Massachusetts Museum of Contemporary Art and the Williams College Museum of Art. Taylor is also director of the Critical Issues Forum for the Guggenheim Museum.

DAVID TRACY is Distinguished Service Professor in the Divinity School and the Committee on Social Thought, University of Chicago. His published works include *Blessed Rage for Order: The New Pluralism in Theology; The Analogical Imagination; Plurality and Ambiguity; Dialogue with the Other;* and *On Naming the Present.* He is currently completing a manuscript on the namings of God.

CHARLES E. WINQUIST is the Thomas J. Watson Professor of Religion at Syracuse University. He is the author of many books, most recently *Epiphanies of Darkness: Deconstruction in Theology* and *Desiring Theology.*

EDITH WYSCHOGROD is the J. Newton Rayzor Professor of Philosophy and Religious Thought at Rice University. Her books include *Spirit in Ashes: Hegel, Heidegger, and Man-Made Mass Death; Saints and Postmodernism: Revisioning Moral Philosophy;* and *The Ethics of Remembering: History, Heterology, and the Nameless Others.*

Index

137–40; the body as in the image of, 40, 161, 162, 163; in Christianity, 140–41, 142–45; comparative studies of, 155; as dead, 136, 147, 153, 231, 360, 375; as deity, 138–39; as disappearing from the lives of his followers, 2; feminist imagery of, 149–50; free activity of, 143, 144; Greek versus Hebraic traditions of, 140–41, 142–43, 148; high gods, 300–301; historical and sociological studies of, 154–55; in human subjectivity, 141–42, 145–50; inadequacy of human ideas regarding, 142, 150; the killing of, 360; kingdom of God, 370; linguistic background of, 137; as lord, 138; as moral agent, 138; in negative theology, 142, 150–53; Newton on, 314; *Oxford English Dictionary* definition of, 137; personalist language for, 386–87; philosophical versus popular images of, 142–45; proofs for existence of, 23, 143, 151, 368; as proper name, 137; in religious studies, 153–57; as spirit, 145–46; in theology, 136–37; three strands in meaning of term, 140–42; as ultimate authority figure, 140, 148; unity of, 142–43; uses of term, 136; value as bestowed by, 366; as Yahweh, 138. *See also* divinity; theism; theology; Trinity
Goffman, Erving, 206
Goodfield, June, 317
Goodman, Felicitas, 112, 113
Goodman, L. E., 371
Goodman, Nelson, 247
Goody, Jack, 205
Gospel of Buddha (Carus), 101–2
Gospel of John, 139, 389
Gospel of Thomas, 125
gospels, 389–90
Gospel to the Egyptians, 127–28
Gough, M., 264
Goux, Jean-Joseph, 126, 129, 130, 131
Graham, William A., 210
grand narratives, 174
Grant, Edward, 189
Great Western Transmutation, 342–45
Greece: Aristophanes, 129; Aristotle, 174; Christian theologians appropriating Greek philosophy, 142; Dionysiac elements in, 351; Empedocles, 128; Hebraic versus Greek traditions of God, 140–41, 142–43, 148; *moira*, 38; science developing

in, 189, 193; Xenophanes, 193. *See also* Hellenistic philosophy; Plato
Green, William Scott, 11–12
Gregor, Thomas, 356
Gregory of Nyssa, 150, 163
Gregory of Tours, 259, 262
Grigg, Richard, 336
Grimes, Ronald L., 207, 209, 211
Guattari, Félix, 16, 174, 367, 368
guilt, 227
Gumbrecht, Hans Ulricht, 187, 189
Gunkel, Hermann, 291
Gurevich, Aaron, 190, 197
Gusdorf, Georges, 289
Gusinde, Martin, 356
Guttierez, Gustavo, 373

Habermas, Jürgen, 341, 378
habitus, 251
Hacking, Ian, 109
Hadewijch, 196
Haitians, 337
Halbfass, Wilhelm, 99, 100
Halevi, Jacob, 294
Hall, John A., 195
Hallpike, C. R., 316
hallucinogenic images, 358
Halperin, D. M., 127
Hamas, 59
Hamilton, William, 375
Handelman, Don, 209
Handelmann, Susan, 384
Harnack, Adolf von, 264, 370
Harrell, C. Stevan, 215
Harries, Jill, 260, 261
Harrison, Carol, 164
Harrison, Verna, 126
Hart, Ray L., 12
Hartmann, Wilfried, 187
Hartshorne, Charles, 145
Hastings, James, 257–58, 263
hatta'at (sin offering), 285, 287
Haupt, Karl G., 280
Hauwerwas, Stanley, 380
Hays, Terence, 356
Hebrew Bible (Old Testament): Exodus, 138; Hosea, 287; Isaiah, 286, 287; Leviticus, 285, 286; linear model of time in, 316; New Testament's claim to supersede, 287, 288; on sacrifice, 285–87; Torah, 383–84. *See also* Genesis